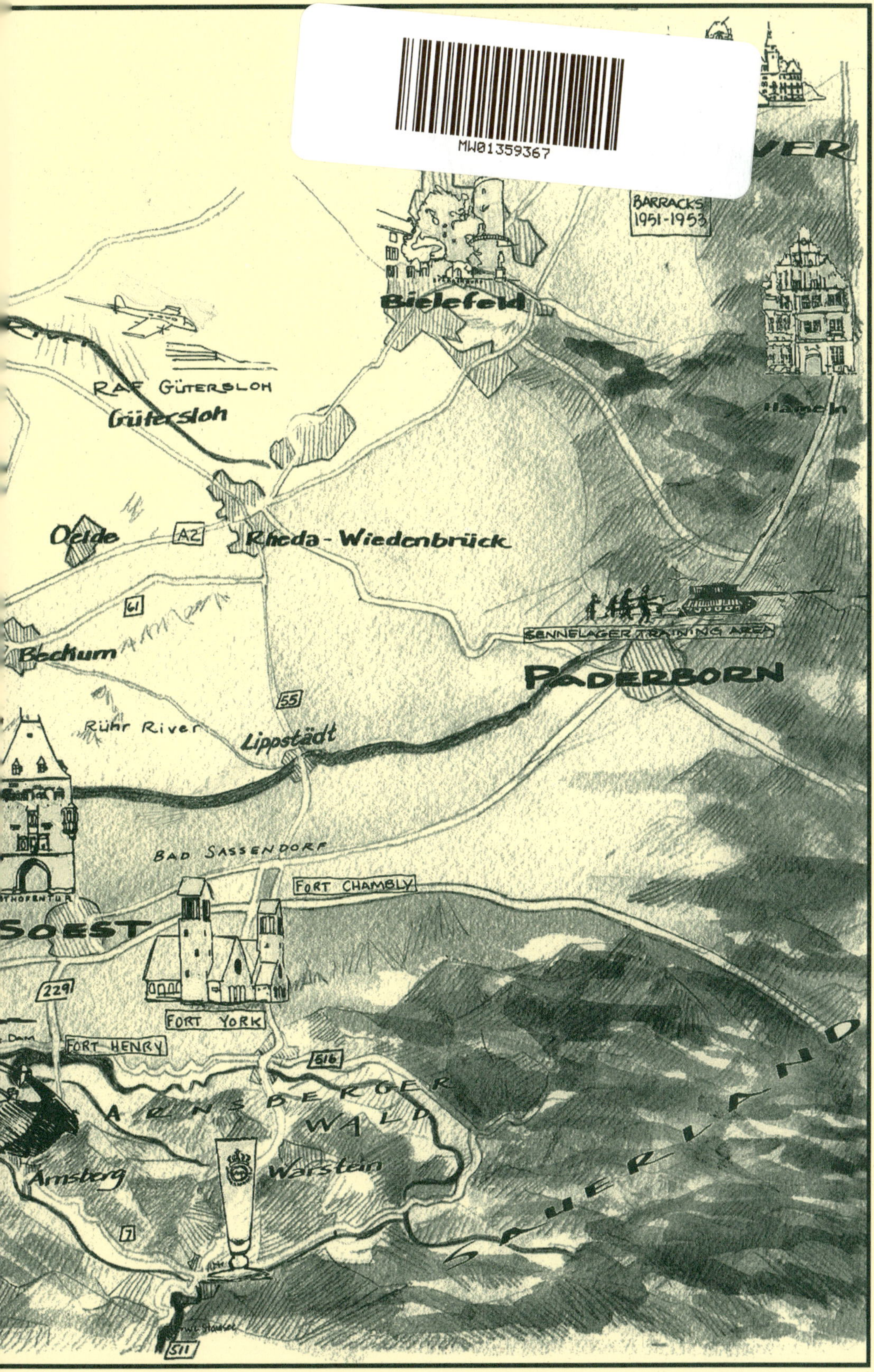

BARRACKS 1951-1953
Bielefeld
Hameln
RAF GÜTERSLOH
Gütersloh
Oelde
A2
Rheda-Wiedenbrück
61
Beckum
SENNELAGER TRAINING AREA
PADERBORN
55
Rühr River
Lippstädt
BAD SASSENDORF
FORT CHAMBLY
SOEST
229
FORT YORK
FORT HENRY
516
ARNSBERGER WALD
Arnsberg
Warstein
7
SAUERLAND
511

War Without Battles
CANADA'S NATO BRIGADE IN GERMANY
1951 - 1993

McGraw-Hill Ryerson Limited

Toronto Montréal New York Auckland Bogotá Caracas Lisbon
London Madrid Mexico Milan New Delhi San Juan
Singapore Sydney Tokyo

WAR WITHOUT BATTLES

CANADA'S NATO BRIGADE IN GERMANY

1951 – 1993

BY SEAN M. MALONEY
FOREWORD BY GENERAL SIR JOHN HACKETT

War Without Battles

Canada's NATO Brigade in Germany, 1951-1993

Copyright, 1997 by 4 Canadian Mechanized Brigade Group History Association. All rights reserved. No part of this publication may be reproduced or transmitted in any form or by any means, or stored in a database or retrieval system, without the prior written permission of McGraw-Hill Ryerson Limited.

Care has been taken to trace ownership of copyright material contained in this text. However, the publishers welcome any information that will enable them to rectify any reference or credit in subsequent editions.

McGraw-Hill Ryerson Limited
300 Water Street
Whitby, ON, L1N 9B6

Canadian Cataloguing in Publication Data

Maloney, Sean 1967

War Without Battles, Canada's NATO Brigade in Germany, 1951-1993. Includes bibliographical references and index.

ISBN 0-07-552892-4

1. North Atlantic Treaty Organization - Armed Forces - Germany History
2. Canada - Armed Forces - Germany - History.
3. Canada - Military relations - Germany.
4. Germany - Military relations - Canada.
I. 4 CMBG History Book Association. II. Title.

355'.031'09182109045

UA 646.5.C3M34 1996

C96-900033-2

Publisher: Joan Homewood
Editor: R.J. Near, Major
Production Co-ordinator: Katherine Taylor
Cover Design: Katherine Taylor
Interior Design/Composition: 71 Film Canada

Printed and bound in Canada by Gilmore Printing Ltd.

This book is dedicated to those who served.

*But the Consul's brow was sad
And the Consul's speech was low
And darkly looked he at the wall,
And darkly at the foe.*

*Then out spake brave Horatius
The Captain of the Gate:
"To every man upon this earth
Death cometh soon or late.
And how can man die better
Than facing fearful odds,
For the ashes of his fathers,
And the temples of his Gods?"*

*...When the oldest cask is opened,
And the largest lamp is lit;...
With weeping and with laughter
Still the story is told,
How well Horatius kept the bridge
In the brave days of old.*

-Lord Macaulay.

TABLE OF CONTENTS:

Author's Dedication	vii
Table of Contents	ix
List of Figures	xi
Glossary and Abbreviations	xiii
Acknowledgments	xxiii
Foreword by General Sir John Hackett	xxix
Introduction	xxxiii

PART I: UP NORTH

Ch 1: 27 Infantry Brigade: The Return to Europe, 1951-1953	5
Ch 2: Extending the Commitment, 1953-1957	63
Ch 3: Crisis and Change, 1957-1963	111
Ch 4: From Pinnacle to Nadir, 1964-1970	179

PART II: DOWN SOUTH

Ch 5: The Move South, 1970-1979	249
Ch 6: Partial Restoration, 1979-1989	331
Ch 7: 4 Brigade and The New World Disorder, 1989-1993	429
Conclusion	489
Appendix "A": Canadian NATO Brigade Group Organization for Combat, 1951-1993.	498
Appendix "B": A Note On Exercises.	505
Appendix "C": List of Brigade Commanders, 1951-1993.	507
Bibliography	508
Index	515

LIST OF FIGURES

CHAPTER 1

1-1:	27 CIB Units Deriving From the Militia	23
1-2:	Canadian Army Bases and Training Areas in Europe, 1951-53	31
1-3:	The Threat to NORTHAG, 1951-53	35
1-4:	Central Region Main Defence Line, 1950-57	38
1-5:	Exercise SPEARHEAD II	43
1-6:	Exercise HOLD FAST	47
1-7:	Exercise JAVELIN FIVE	58
1-8:	Exercise GRAND REPULSE I	60

CHAPTER 2

2-1:	Canadian Army Bases and Training Areas in Europe, 1953-70	77
2-2:	The Threat to NORTHAG, 1953-63	80
2-3:	NORTHAG Corps Dispositions, 1953-1957	82
2-4:	1 CIBG / 2 CIBG Concept of Operations 1954-57	84
2-5:	Exercise BATTLE ROYAL, September 1954	91

CHAPTER 3

3-1:	Central Region Main Defence Line 1957-63	134
3-1A:	NORTHAG Corps Dispositions, 1957-70	136
3-2:	I(BR) Corps Concept of Operations, 1957-63	138
3-3:	The Inter-Army Group Boundary Problem, 1959-61	151
3-4:	4 CIBG Reinforcement Plan 1961	155
3-5:	Exercise HOLD FAST, September 1960	157
3-6:	Exercise CANADA CUP, October 1962	168

CHAPTER 4

4-1:	The Threat to NORTHAG, 1964-1970	197
4-2:	Central Region Main Defence Line, 1963-1990	201
4-3:	I(BR) Corps Concept of Operations, 1964-70	204
4-4:	Sketch: 4 CIBG EDP Deployment, 1960s	207
4-5:	Sketch: Exercise ROB ROY (September 1967)	218
4-6:	Exercise KEYSTONE Phase II	230

CHAPTER 5

5-1:	Canadian Army Bases and Training Areas in Europe, 1970-93	267
5-2:	1970 Basing Plan: Lahr Airfield	270
5-3:	The Threat to CENTAG, 1970s	281
5-4:	CENTAG Corps Dispositions and Likely Warsaw Pact Invasion Routes, 1970-1990	283
5-5:	II German Korps Defence Plan and 4 CMBG Employment Options 1970's	290
5-6:	Exercise GUTES OMEN, September 1971	307
5-7:	Exercise GROSSE ROCHADE, October 1975	316
5-8:	Exercise LARES TEAM, September 1976	325

CHAPTER 6

6-1:	The Threat to CENTAG, 1980s	372
6-2:	Warsaw Pact Operational Level Concept to be employed against NATO Forces in Germany	374
6-3:	Probable Grouping of NATO Forces – Western Theatre of War (30-Day Variant)	375
6-4:	Probable Grouping and Intentions of [West German] Territorial Forces	376
6-5:	Early 1980s GDP planning	384
6-6:	Exercise FLINKER IGEL, September 1984	394
6-7:	Modifications to TAA SETTER	405
6-8:	4 CMBG Plan BOXER – 1986	407
6-9:	Final 4 CMBG GDP – 1988-1992	409
6-10:	Exercise CERTAIN CHALLENGE, Phase I	422
6-11:	Exercise CERTAIN CHALLENGE, Phase II	425

CHAPTER 7

7-1:	Yugoslavia, 1992	466
7-2:	1 R22eR Battle Group Deployment - UNPA Sector West	471
7-3:	Soviet Western Group of Forces, 1993	482

GLOSSARY AND ABBREVIATIONS

ACE: Allied Command, Europe; SACEUR's area of command consisting of the Northern, Central and Southern Regions of NATO, Europe.

ACR: (U.S.) Armored Cavalry Regiment; Brigade-sized formation dedicated to reconnaissance and attrition of enemy armour.

ADM: Atomic Demolition Munition; essentially a nuclear land mine.

AEV: Armoured Engineer Vehicle.

AFCENT: Allied Forces, Central Europe; NATO command subordinate to SACEUR; previously called LANDCENT.

AFNORTH: Allied Forces, Northern Europe; NATO command subordinate to SACEUR covering Denmark and Norway.

aka: also known as.

AMF(L): NATO's ACE Mobile Force, Land.

AOC: Air Officer Commanding.

AOP: Air Observation Post.

APC: Armoured Personnel Carrier.

ARV: Armoured Recovery Vehicle.

ATAF: Allied Tactical Air Force. There are two ATAF's in the Central Region; 2 ATAF with NORTHAG and 4 ATAF with CENTAG.

AVLB: Armoured Vehicle, Layer, Bridge.

AWACS: Airborne Warning and Control System.

BAOR: British Army of the Rhine.

BE: Belgian, Belgium.

BERCON: Berlin Contingency Plan.

BFOM: Black Forest Officers' Mess.

BMH: British Military Hospital.

BMP: Soviet Mechanized Infantry Combat Vehicle.

BR: British.

Brigade: A formation numbering between 3000-4000 troops and comprising a headquarters and three or four manoeuvre units such as infantry battalions or armoured regiments. Two to four Brigades are normally grouped within a Division. Combat Support (e.g. engineers and aviation) and Combat Service Support (e.g. supply and maintenance) are provided to the Brigade by the Division.

Brigade Group: Ideally, a self-contained all-arms fighting organization of between five and seven thousand men comprising three or four manoeuvre units (infantry battalions and armoured regiments), a headquarters and combat support units (e.g. engineers) and combat service support units (e.g. supply and medical units). The basic Canadian formation above the battalion/regiment level has been the Brigade Group since the late 1940s. The British adopted the Brigade Group organization between 1957 and 1967 with the introduction of tactical nuclear warfare doctrine but still retained their divisional structure. They returned to the standard divisional organization later in the 1960s.

BTDF: Bosnian Territorial Defence Force; forces belonging to the Muslim-led government of Bosnia-Hercegovina.

Bundesgrenzschutz: Federal German Republic border police; a para-military force employed in border security and at air and sea ports of entry.

Bundeswehr: The Armed Forces of the Federal Republic of Germany comprising the Heer (Army), Marine (Navy), and Luftwaffe (Air Force).

BW: Bundeswehr.

CA: Canada/Canadian.

CAG: Canadian Air Group.

CANBAT, CANENGBAT: generic designations for Canadian units serving in UNPROFOR, ie: Canadian Battalion, Canadian Engineer Battalion.

CANF(E): Canadian Army National Force (Europe).

CANEX: Canadian Forces Exchange System; Stores and shops for Canadian Forces personnel and their dependents.

CASF: Canadian Army Special Force.

CAST Bde Gp: Canadian Air-Sea Transportable Brigade Group which was tasked with the defence of northern Norway.

CAT: Canadian Army Trophy.

CATAC: Command Aerienne Tactique; French airforce organization

CB: Confined to Barracks.

CBOU: Canadian Base Ordnance Unit.

CBUE: Canadian Base Units, Europe.

CDN: Canadian.

CDS: Chief of the Defence Staff; the senior Canadian Forces officer reporting directly to the Minister of National Defence.

CENTAG: Central Army Group; NATO command in the Central Region subordinate to AFCENT or LANDCENT, encompassing Germany and the Low Countries.

Central Region: NATO area commanded by AFCENT/LANDCENT.

CER: Combat Engineer Regiment.

CF: Canadian Forces.

CFB: Canadian Forces Base.

GLOSSARY AND ABBREVIATIONS

CFE: Canadian Forces, Europe.

CFHQ: Canadian Forces Headquarters; the senior Canadian Forces headquarters prior to its amalgamation with the Department of National Defence in the early 1970s to form NDHQ.

CFX: Command Field Exercise.

CGF: Central Group of Forces (Soviet); located mostly in Czechoslovakia.

CGS: Chief of the General Staff.

CIB: Canadian Infantry Brigade.

CIBG: Canadian Infantry Brigade Group.

CIGS: Chief of the Imperial General Staff

CinC: Commander-in-Chief.

CIMIC: Civil-Military Co-operation.

CLFX: Canadian Land Forces Exchange system; MLS/CANEX in another incarnation.

CMB: Canadian Mechanized Brigade.

CMBG: Canadian Mechanized Brigade Group.

COMCENTAG: Commander Central Army Group.

CON: Contingency Plan; US term.

CPA: Czechoslovak People's Army.

CPMD: Carpathian Military District.

CPX: Command Post Exercise.

CSCE: Conference on Security and Cooperation in Europe.

CSG(C): Canadian Support Group (Centre).

CSM: Company Sergeant-Major; the senior ranking non-commissioned officer in an infantry company.

CW: Chemical Warfare.

DCDS: Deputy Chief of the Defence Staff.

DDR: Deutsche Demokratische Republic, (East Germany).

DEFCON: Defence Condition; American military readiness state.

DEW Line: Distant Early Warning Line; a chain of radar stations in the Canadian Arctic and Alaska for detection of a Soviet bomber attack over the North Pole.

DISGP: Division Support Group.

DM: Deutschmark; German money.

EC: European Community.

ECM: Electronic Countermeasures.

ECMMY: European Community Monitoring Mission, Yugoslavia.

EDP: Emergency Defence Plan; 1950s/1960s name for GDP.

8CH(PL): 8th Canadian Hussars (Princess Louise's); (Canadian armoured regiment).

EIS: Equipment Issue Scale.

ENDEX: end of exercise.

EOD: Explosive Ordnance Disposal.

EW: Electronic Warfare.

Ex: exercise.

FALLEX: Annual large scale NATO exercises held in the September-October time frame.

Fallschirmjaeger: German paratrooper.

FEBA: Forward Edge of the Battle Area; the area where friendly and enemy troops are in contact.

Feldjaeger: Bundeswehr Military Police.

FGH: The Fort Garry Horse; Canadian armoured regiment.

FIBUA: Fighting in Built Up Areas; city fighting.

FMC: Force Mobile Command; Canadian Forces functional command comprising what is essentially the Canadian army. The other principal CF functional commands are Maritime Command and Air Command.

FMSU: Forward Mobile Support Unit.

FOFA: Follow-On Forces Attack

FR: French

FRG: Federal Republic of Germany.

FSOP: Field Standard Operating Procedure.

FSS: Field Security Section.

FTX: Field Training Exercise; exercise with actual troops.

GBC: Groupment Brigade du Canada

GDP(NATO): General Defence Plan; 1970s/1980s name for EDP. The GDP/EDP was essentially NATO forces deployment positions that would be occupied in event of crisis or war with the Warsaw Pact.

GDR: German Democratic Republic.

GE: German.

Gebirgs: German term meaning 'Mountain'. Gerbirgs units and formations e.g. 1 Gebirgsdivision are troops equipped and trained for operations in mountainous terrain.

GSFG: Group of Soviet Forces, Germany.

GSO: General Staff Officer.

GLOSSARY AND ABBREVIATIONS

GTNC: German Territorial Command North; Bundeswehr command corresponding to the NORTHAG area.

GTSC: German Territorial Command South; Bundeswehr command corresponding to the CENTAG area.

HMCS: Her Majesty's Canadian Ship.

HNS: Host Nation Support.

HSB: Heimat Schutz Brigade; Bundeswehr home defence brigade made up of reserve personnel.

ICCS: International Commission for Control and Supervision (Vietnam).

IGB: Inner-German Border; the border between the Federal Republic of Germany and the German Democratic Republic prior to reunification of the two Germanies.

ILOC: (Canadian-US) Integrated Lines of Communication.

Integrated Force: Military forces allocated to SACEUR from 1951 to 1957; later replaced with the term Shield Forces in 1957.

IR: Infra Red.

IRC; International Red Cross.

Jaeger: German light infantry unit; literal translation: "hunter".

Jimmy: Signalman (Canadian Army colloquialism).

JNA: Jugoslav National Army.

JSTARS: Joint Surveillance and Target Attack Radar System

kt: kiloton, the relative yield of a nuclear weapon measured in thousands of tons of TNT. See mt.

LAD: Light Aid Detachment; RCEME (maintenance) troops responsible for repair and recovery of brigade vehicles and equipment.

LANDCENT: NATO Land Forces, Central Region; replaced by AFCENT in the 1960s. After 1993, the name and functions of CENTAG and NORTHAG were replaced with a new command called LANDCENT subordinate to AFCENT.

Land/Länder: German term for (West) German federal state/states; e.g. Bavaria, Baden-Württemberg.

LANDJUT: NATO command for the defence of the Jutland Peninsula.

LdSH(RC): The Lord Strathcona's Horse (Royal Canadians), Canadian armoured regiment.

LIB: Lorried Infantry Brigade (UK).

LO: Liaison Officer.

LRRP: Long Range Reconnaissance Patrol.

Luftlande: German term for airborne forces.

MBT: Main Battle Tank.

M-Day: NATO term initially meaning commencement of an attack on NATO; later changed to mean Mobilization Day.

MC: NATO's Military Committee.

MDAP: Mutual Defence Assistance Programme; NATO military aid programme for Western Europe begun in 1949. The US and Canada were the principal donors in the early years.

MICV: Mechanized Infantry Combat Vehicle.

MILES: Multiple Integrated Laser Engagement System; a training device consisting of laser emitters and sensors used to enhance realism in training. Laser emitters are attached to individual weapons while sensors are worn by soldiers or mounted on vehicles. When the weapons/devices were fired against targets mounting the sensors, the effectiveness/accuracy of the fire could be assessed as the sensors would "beep" when hit by the laser. At the same time the target's own laser emitter would cease to function and it would be considered a casualty.

MIR: Medical Inspection Room.

MLS: Maple Leaf Services; predecessor of CANEX.

MLVW: Medium Logistics Vehicle, Wheeled; a 6-wheeled Canadian army cargo truck introduced in the early 1980s.

MOBCOM: Mobile Command/FMC.

MSF: Mobile Striking Force; Canadian Army organization in the late 1940s and early 1950s tasked with Defence of Canada, especially in the Arctic.

mt: megaton; the relative yield of a nuclear weapon measured in millions of tons of TNT.

MTDP: Medium Term Defence Plan.

NAAFI: Navy, Army and Air Force Institute; British Forces' equivalent of CANEX.

NATO: North Atlantic Treaty Organization.

NBCD: Nuclear, Biological and Chemical Defence.

NBCW: Nuclear, Biological and Chemical Warfare.

NCF: NATO Composite Force; multi-national brigade-sized force which replaced the CAST Bde Gp when Canada terminated the CAST (defence of North Norway) mission in 1987.

NCM: Non-Commissioned Member.

NCO: Non-Commissioned Officer.

NGF: (Soviet) Northern Group of Forces; located mostly in East Germany.

Niner: Low level radio code word meaning the Commander of a unit or subunit.

NL: Netherlands.

NORAD: North American Aerospace Defence Command.

NORTHAG: Northern Army Group; NATO command in the Central Region subordinate to AFCENT or LANDCENT.

NVA: National Volkesarmee, (East German Army).

OC: Officer Commanding.

OMG: (Soviet) Operational Manoeuvre Group; OMGs were highly mobile divisional and corps size armoured and mechanized infantry forces, including self-propelled artillery, tasked with breaking into NATO's rear areas to destroy vital targets.

'on the economy': not living in military quarters; living in German civilian accomodations.

Op: operation.

OP: Observation Post

OPCON: Operational Control.

OPLAN: Operation Plan.

ORBAT: Order of Battle; units or components of a military organization.

Panzer Division: German armoured division.

Panzer Grenadier Division: German mechanized infantry division.

PGM: Precision Guided Munition.

PMQ: Private Married Quarters; military housing provided to soldiers and their families.

POL: Petroleum, Oil and Lubricants.

Polizei: (German) police.

POMCUS: Pre-positioning of Materiel Configured to Unit Sets; US equipment stockpiled in Europe to equip REFORGER troops on flyover.

PPCLI: Princess Patricia's Canadian Light Infantry.

Provost: Military Police.

PSA: Practice Survival Area.

QRA: Quick Reaction Alert.

QOR of C: The Queen's Own Rifles of Canada.

R Group: Reconnaissance Group.

R22eR: The Royal 22nd Regiment; French Canadian infantry regiment commonly known as the Van Doos .

RASC: Royal Army Service Corps.

RALC: Regiment Artillerie Légere Canadien.

RBC: Regiment Blindé du Canada.

RCA: Royal Canadian Artillery.
RCAMC: Royal Canadian Army Medical Corps.
RCAF: Royal Canadian Air Force.
RCCS: Royal Canadian Corps of Signals.
RCD: Royal Canadian Dragoons.
RCE: Royal Canadian Engineers.
RCEME: Royal Canadian Electrical and Mechanical Engineers.
RCHA: Royal Canadian Horse Artillery.
RCR: The Royal Canadian Regiment.
recce: reconnaissance.
REFORGER; Return of Forces to Germany; large scale CENTAG exercise involving the deployment of vast numbers of US-based troops to Germany.
RHA: Royal Horse Artillery.
RHC/RHR of C: The Royal Highland Regiment of Canada; The Black Watch of Canada.
RMA: Requisitioned Manoeuvre Area.
RO:RO: Roll on / Roll off (ship).
RPG: Rocket Propelled Grenade; Soviet man-portable light anti-armour weapon.
RPV: Remotely Piloted Vehicle.
RRB: Remote (radio) Re-Broadcast; for extending radio range.
RSA: Real Survival Area.
RSM: Regimental Sergeant-Major; the senior ranking non-commissioned officer in a unit, responsible for enforcing unit discipline and advising the Commanding Officer on matters of concern among the soldiers.
RTR: Royal Tank Regiment.
SA: Salvation Army.
SACEUR: Supreme Allied Commander, Europe; one of three primary NATO military commands.
SADARM: Search and Destroy Armour; high tech anti-armour munition.
SAS: (1) Special Air Service (British special forces) (2) Special Ammunition Storage site for nuclear weapons.
SGF: (Soviet) Southern Group of Forces; located mostly in Hungary.
SHAPE: Supreme Headquarters, Allied Powers, Europe; SACEUR's headquarters.
Shield Forces: military units assigned to SACEUR; replaced the term Integrated Force in 1957.
SIGEX: Signals Exercise.
SLAR: Sideways Looking Airborne Radar

SMLM: Soviet Military Liaison Mission; pronounced 'smell-em'. Soviet military office located in each of the French, US and British controlled military zones of Germany, initially established at the end of WWII. The three Western powers each had their own similar missions in the Soviet zone of East Germany such as Brixmis (British Exchange Mission). Ostensibly for the purpose of facilitating four power military issues in the divided Germany, they were primarily used to observe and report on military exercises and activities being conducted by the other side. In effect, these were legal 'spy missions' and very active throughout the Cold War as it was the only means the Western Allies and the Soviets had to actually place their people in each other's military backyard, so to speak. The existence of these military missions only ended upon German reunification and the '4 + 2' Treaty.

SOFA: Status of Forces Agreement.

SOP: Standard Operating Procedure; also Standing Operating Procedure.

SOXMIS: Soviet Occupation Exchange Mission; predecessor to SMLM (see above).

SP: Self-Propelled.

spook: Army colloquialism for intelligence and signals intelligence personnel.

SSM: Surface to surface missile.

SSO: Senior Staff Officer.

Startex: Start of exercise.

STF: Stationed Task Force.

TAA: Tactical Assembly Area.

TEWT: Tactical Exercise Without Troops.

TM: Town Major.

TOA: Transfer of Authority.

TOW: Tube launched, optically tracked, wire guided; US designed anti-tank guided missile capable of destroying tanks out to 3750 metres.

TUA: Tow Under Armour; TOW ATGM mounted under armour protection on an APC and capable of being fired without exposing the missile crew.

UK: United Kingdom.

UMS: Unit Medical Section

UN: United Nations.

UNHCR: United Nations High Commission for Refugees.

UNPA: United Nations Protected Area.

UNPROFOR: United Nations Protection Force (in the former Republic of Yugoslavia).

US or U.S.: United States.

USAF: United States Air Force.

USAREUR: United States Army, Europe.

USEUCOM: United States European Command.

VbK: Verteidigungsbezirk Kommando – Bundeswehr Territorial (Non NATO) Command corresponding to the district / regional level.

VKK: Verteidigungskreis Kommando – Bundeswehr Territorial (Non NATO) Command corresponding to the county level.

VC: Victoria Cross.

VCDS: (Canadian) Vice Chief of the Defence Staff.

VHF: Very high frequency.

WbK: Wehrbereichs Kommando: Bundeswehr Territorial (non NATO) Command corresponding to the federal state (Länder) level.

Wehrmacht: The German army during the Nazi era.

WINTEX: Winter Exercise; NATO CPX series of wargames held at the political and senior military levels every two years. These terminated with the end of the Cold War.

WVS: Women's Volunteer Service.

Zulu time: Greenwich Mean Time.

ACKNOWLEDGEMENTS

This story of Canada's NATO brigade is the result of a combined effort of a number of people, most of whom served with the brigade in its final year of existence. In 1992, it was apparent to those of us in Lahr and Baden that a remarkable era in Canadian military history was coming to an end. Our final "Fallex" the year before had been but a shadow of its former self; and most incredibly, where we once coldly eyed *National Volksarmee* border guards in their foreboding concrete towers at Hof, and grimly wondered what lay beyond the barbed wire and minefields, we could now drive to Berlin or Prague on weekend pass, unhindered except for the surfeit of smoke-belching *Trabants* and *Wartburgs* sputtering along a rather decrepit *autobahn*. Germany. An economic powerhouse, rich in history, splendidly cultured, even intimidating, and which never failed to impress us, was once again united. The Warsaw Pact, against which we prepared to fight to the death, had vanished; and the Soviet Union, in an ironic twist of Nikita Kruschev's famous quote, was itself consigned to the "dustbin of history". Living in Germany, we not only witnessed these momentous events, but in fact helped realize them. We did so as members of Canada's NATO Brigade and Air Division who, supported by our families and the Canadian civilian community, physically manifested our nation's commitment to resist tyranny and defend freedom.

This book is written to tell the Brigade's story, as well as pay tribute to those who served. It is very much a labour of love, evidenced in the detail of its telling by Sean Maloney, and by the contribution made by all those involved in its research, compiling, design, and production. We were particularly fortunate to acquire Sean as "Brigade Historian" in the final year of our existence. A Militia officer at the time, he was an ideal choice, not only in having completed post graduate studies in military history at the University of New Brunswick, but in possessing a security clearance which enabled us to open doors to him in NATO that would otherwise have remained shut. The result is a superb accounting of an incredible, even glorious era in Canadian military history, and which should bring pride to soldiers and civilians alike. To Sean, I extend gratitude for a job well done and a story well told. I would be remiss, however, if the following individuals and groups were not also thanked for their contributions and efforts:

LCol Daniel Bastien, then Senior Staff Officer Operations 4 CMB, recognized the importance of gathering and preserving the history of Canada's NATO Brigade, and launched the project back in the Fall of 1992 in Lahr, with me as his assistant. Col (now BGen) Bob Meating, the Brigade's last commander gave his authority and enthusiasm to the project and was instrumental in arranging access for the author and interview teams to various NATO and allied headquarters, including their archives. The main interviewers – Maj Alan MacLean, Capt Stu Gibson, and Capt Ron MacEachern – did sterling service; so did archival researchers Capts Steve Kiropolous, Mark Twohey, Gerry Doyle, and WO Max Rudneu who ploughed through endless volumes of *The Beaver* and *Der Kanadier* – the forces newspapers in Germany. Capt Dave Holt, a venerable artilleryman with more than two decades of service in the Brigade ran the project office in Lahr, assisted by Cpl Shaun Brown. His corporate knowledge helped fill in many gaps, and his inputs helped ensure that the common soldier's perspective on events was always present.

Other members of HQ 4 CMB helped in various ways, particularly LCol George Rousseau, Capt Luke Angiolini, Lt Emory Lalonde, Maj Terry Pollan, Capt Ben Roth, Capt Caswell, and Mrs Pat Rudneu. From HQ CFE, Ivor St Aubin D'Ancy provided useful insights into the NATO civil-military relationship in Germany, while Capt Ursula Matchett and Mrs Barbara Winters assisted with translation of German documentation. Special mention also goes to Herr Erich Reichel who served many years as 4 CIBG's interpreter, and his successor, Herr Karl-Heinz Muhlenschulte. A number of citizens from the German communities in the Soest, Lahr and Baden areas also contributed, notably Dr Koehn of Soest, Frau Dr Ruhrer – the former Lord Mayor of Werl, Herr H-J Deisling of the Werl archives, Herr Robert Schad, Herr Johann Mecher of the Rathaus Lahr archives, and Dr Philip Brucker, the former Lord Mayor of Lahr – a historian in his own right and a great friend of Canadians.

Strong support and encouragement for the project was provided by the Directorate of History at National Defence Headquarters, Ottawa. Dr Alec Douglas, Owen Cooke, Dr Steve Harris, Dr Carl Christie, Dr Bill McAndrew, Maj Bob Caldwell, Isabel Campbell, Lt(N) Rich Gimblett, Maj Jean Morin, Dr Serge Bernier, Dr Bill Rawlings and Cpl Monica Morneau provided advice, comment, and technical help. Other NDHQ assistance came from Ray York, Rena Mackey, Lise Leduc and Dave Angus who combed old files for us in the basement of the Pearke's Building. Dr Joel Sokolsky at Royal Military College, Kingston, LCol Oliviero, Maj Lelievre, Maj Nolan, Capt Kimaszouski, Capt Ward and Lt Alladay from HQ 1st Canadian Division, and Daniel German, Paul Marsden and Dr Ian McClymont of the National Archives of Canada all gave invaluable help in one way or another.

Various NATO and allied headquarters were also approached. MGen Clive Addy, Maj Kevin Mohr, LCol Bell, Maj Forsyth, Maj Brookes Chamberlain, Maj Fallon, LCol Ban Price and M/S Neurenhausen at HQ Central Army Group, Heidelberg, went to the limit to provide information, as did personnel of the CA-US ILOC at HQ USAREUR. At HQ Northern Army Group, Maj James Bond and his G-1 staff went out of their way to assist, as did Col Sperling, Maj F.H. Bach and Christa Kraehe. At HQ AFCENT, LCol Bob Guthrie, BGen Archambault, Col Tim Sparling, BGen Vollstedt, and LCol John Braby provided valuable observations and opinions on NATO planning and strategy during the Cold War. The historical section at Supreme Headquarters Allied Powers Europe, especially Dr Gregory Pedlow and Peter Cooper likewise contributed in the same vein. The assistance rendered by the Canadian National Military Representative staff at SHAPE, particularly Mrs Macdougal and Mrs Tanton, and the discussions with MGen Pierre Lalonde, were most beneficial, as was the input from Brigadier T.I.M. Waugh. Thanks also to LCol Villeneuve and LCol Grant from HQ NATO

Composite Force and to Mr Jack Wendt on the Canadian NATO staff in Brussels.

The contribution rendered by our professional colleagues in the *Bundeswehr* deserves special note. LCol Bernard Stoss and LCol Edgar Troester of HQ II (GE) Korps provided helpful insights into Warsaw Pact intentions and West German defence planning. Interviews conducted in Regensburg at HQ 4 Panzer Grenadier Division with MGen Jurgen Reichhardt and BGen Hans Jurgen Wilhelmi enlightened us on German views of the Canada's land contribution to NATO, as well as confirmed the *Bundeswehr's* esteem and respect for the Canadian army in general and 4 CMBG in particular, further convincing us that the Brigade's story merited telling to all Canadians.

Other *Bundeswehr* contributions came from LCol von Zeschau – GTSC LO at HQ CFE, Maj Winifred Heinemann, Col Norbert Wiggershaus, LCol Gero von Gerosdorff and LCol Heinz Rebhan of the *Militargeschichtliches Forschungsamt* and the *Bundesarchive/Militararchive* in Freiburg. We are grateful to all.

At HQ US Army Europe, Bruce Siemons – USAREUR historian – and Warner Stark provided valuable information, as did Millie Waters of the public information office. In Washington, Dr Goldberg at the Department of Defense history section gave access to SACEUR oral histories, and Bill Burr at the National Security Archive generously offered up NATO material on file there. Mr John Taylor and Mr Eddie Reese from the US National Archives were also helpful and supportive, as were John Peaty of the British Army Historical Branch and Dr Alastair Massie of the National Army Museum. We wish also to thank Mr Bram Oosterwiljk of the *Rotterdam Dagblad* newspaper, the staff of the Rotterdam Archives, Mr G. Snelleman of the Haarlem Archives, and Mr van Velthuizen and Mr Lex de Herder – all who provided information on 27 Brigade's arrival in 1951. We are further appreciative of David McDermott who drew the NORTHAG, AFCENT and CENTAG heraldry.

A great amount of information was also accumulated as a result of notices placed in Base newspapers across Canada and *Legion* magazine. Many "veterans" wrote wonderfully descriptive letters, and dozens were interviewed. We ended up with so much material, however, that not all of it could be used. We are nonetheless grateful to all who contributed, including:

ACKNOWLEDGEMENTS

Gen Jean Victor Allard
MGen E.A.C. Amy
Doug Barker
MGen John Barr
LGen Charles Belzile
✓ LCol Bill Bewick
✓ Maj Borchert
Col John Boyd
Maj Terry Brewster
Capt Ian Briggs
MWO Brown
R.D. Campton
LCol Peter Cameron
LCol Pierre Cantin
BGen Patrick H.C. Carew
Peter Carswell
LCol F.W. Chapman
WO Charlebois
Ian Clark
✓ John Clee
Col Gerry Coady
LCol Paul Coderre
LCol C.J. Corrigan
Capt Donna Cowan
LGen J. Chouinard
Capt Jeff Clark
✓ CWO Don Collier
Dick Coroy
BGen James Cotter
Col D. Crowe
John Cummings
LGen Jack Dangerfield
Wayne Dauphinee

Al Darche
✓ LGen Mike Dare
BGen Darryl Dean
✓ MGen Tom De Faye
Maj "Des" Des Laurier
Nick Doucet
BGen D.W. Edgecomb
LGen Richard Evraire
Marie Therese Ferguson
LGen James Fox
L/S Frye
LCol Gary Furrie
Bill Gabriel
MGen James Gardner
MGen J.M.R. Gaudreau
Col Ralph M. Gienow
Capt Tim Gorman
Bill Graham
MWO Gordon Gravelle
MGen Pat Grieve
Maj Lloyd Hackle
John Huggan
Sgt Bill Hungerford
LCol Michel Jones
Sgt Rick Kearney
✓ MGen W.C. Leonard
Therese Lessard
LCol E.G. MacArthur
MWO McNeil
WO Mike Maloney
Jack Martin
Maj Ross McLaughlin
Clive Milner

Maj Bill Mountain
John A. Parker
BGen S.V. Radley-Walters
I.M. Rettie
Maj Ray Richards
✓ Mike Ritchie
LCol David M. Robb
Richard C. Ross
LGen Roger Rowley
Royal 22e Regiment
   Museum and Archives
LCol Clay Samis
Maj Jeff Sawchuck
LCol Al Scott
BGen Wm Seamark
CWO Doug Seed
W.O. Seguin
LCol D.K. Shaver
Roy Smillie
Sgt W.E. Storey
LCol R.L. Strawbridge
Bill Stroud
Col A.J. Tattersall
✓ MGen A.J. Tedlie
LGen Jack Vance
Lyle Walker
✓ LGen Geoffrey Walsh
✓ MGen C.B. Ware
Barbara Waters
Maj Herb Weber
Capt R.E. Whelan
BGen Bill Yost
✓ Kaz Zoboski

When 4 CMB disbanded in June of 1993, its members repatriating to Canada to serve in other organizations, the book had advanced only as far as a first draft, and an incomplete one at that. So much research and effort had been invested, however, and convinced of the importance of the Brigade's story, we took the decision to continue the work in Canada. Thus on posting to NDHQ, I took with me the responsibility of bringing the project to completion. Working at long distance with Sean, who was now committed to other projects, including his PhD at Temple University in Philadelphia, progress thus continued, however, slowly. Finally, after a dozen edits, translation into French and completing publication and distribution arrangements, the work is finished. It could not have been done, however, without the help and dedication of those who assisted with "Phase II" of the project.

Bill Constable and Albert 'Durf' McJoynt, produced the maps. Working from talc overlays and pencilled sketches, the results speak for their outstanding talent and skills. In Ottawa, the Canadian Forces Photographic Unit did superb work, satisfying our photo and graphic reproduction needs, with thanks going to CWO Magden, Sgt Gallant and Cpl Sampson. Critical comments and other forms of feedback from both serving and retired service members were also an essential part of the book's development. Col (ret'd) John Marteinson edited two of the drafts, suggested amendments and, with LCol JamieArbuckle, provided critique. Jim Scott helped with technical points while Cathy Hingley and Julie Simoneau of *Esprit de Corps* did the pagination, inputted the edits and assisted with administration, as did Capt Dennis Low at HQ 1st Canadian Division. For the French version of the book I am grateful to Pierre Vallières, Jean Leveillé and Pierre Thibeault of LFCHQ translation staff. They have produced a first class work in its own right.

Meriting special praise is Katherine Taylor of 71 Film. An accomplished businesswoman and war artist (and also 4 Brigade "veteran" – having accompanied her husband to Germany with 2 PPCLI) she was a key partner in this project from the beginning, guiding and advising in all aspects of the book's design, layout and publication. Her artwork graces the book's dust jacket and end plates, vividly depicting the Brigade's story in a manner that only art can do. Katherine's enthusiasm and commitment was of great personal encouragement and instrumental in getting us to the finish line.

Finally, I wish to acknowledge the crucial financial assistance provided from non-public funds from HQ Canadian Forces Europe, HQ Land Forces Command, Commander 4 CMBG's trust account, and donations from Canadian Marconi, CAE Electronics and Bombardier Ltd. This support, combined with the efforts and contributions of everyone mentioned, is what has made this work possible.

Bob Near, Major (The RCR)
4 CMBG 1981-84, 1988-89, 1991-93
Ottawa, ON, 1 Nov 96   *Project Officer – War Without Battles*

FOREWORD

It is a privilege to be invited to write a foreword to this account of Canada's NATO Brigade, which served for 42 years in Germany from 1951 to 1993. I knew it very well, being there to help it on its arrival and working-up, and seeing a good deal of it thereafter in many different ways until I had it under my command when it was one of the outstanding elements in the Northern Army Group. Its subsequent history was not to end happily, and those in its own country responsible for this bear a heavy burden for depriving Canada of such splendid representation, seen in such high relief abroad.

My own connection with Canada is considerable. My wife and I have often been there; a grandson was born (and baptized) in CFB Borden when his officer father was there on secondment from Britain; a great-nephew of my own name passed through Royal Roads to a commission in the PPCLI. There is quite a sprinkling of close Hackett relatives settled over there.

I am not in a position to offer an authoritative estimate of the whole of Pierre Trudeau's service to his country. What I can pass judgment on is his notable disservice to Canada's position in the outside world in the treatment of the Canadian brigade in NATO, now so fully documented in Sean Maloney's book.

The Canadian Infantry Brigade Group was to become, soon after its arrival in Germany, a key element in the emergency defence planning of the Northern Army Group. This book explains most cogently how and why the development of its structure into that of a complete, small, well-balanced division admirably suited it to the task assigned to it. As a well equipped, highly trained and admirably led formation, it drew much admiring attention and ensured for Canada a position in NATO planning which had never been attained before and could not be maintained when the brigade was reduced and finally removed from a position at the sharpest end under British command in NORTHAG, to the status of reserve troops at a low level under American command further south.

It has been a saddening experience for a military professional to see something so good so mishandled, and to have to watch while its parent country threw away a prime position in NATO to became of its own volition a little considered also-ran, right down to the final withdrawal of the remnants of this fine formation in 1993.

In some 35 years service under arms, I spent eight years or so in NATO on the continent of Europe. I was a Q Staff Brigadier in HQ BAOR when 2 CIBG came into the British Army of the Rhine, and had much to do with providing accommodation for them in Westphalia. As commander of an armoured brigade and then of an armoured division in the same part of Germany, I saw much of them. As CinC BAOR and Commander Northern Army Group, I had them under my command and saw much more.

This was always a very good brigade group under very different commanders. They were active, inventive, resourceful and full of enterprise. The brigade worked hard and in harmony. It was always a pleasure to be with it. Of all the brigades I have known in my thirty-five years under arms they were more closely knit than almost any other and their equipment in supporting arms and services (particularly in artillery, both nuclear and non-nuclear) endowed them with an unusual breadth of experience. In my own esteem they ranked close to the parachute brigade I raised in the Middle East and was later to see destroyed around me in the

FOREWORD

Arnhem battle. They were, in their prime, very good indeed. I often reflected how glad I would be to have them with me in battle, perhaps commanded by someone like little Ned Amy. All their commanders were good but I probably got to know Ned best, since he took the brigade group on about the time I came in to command BAOR and the Northern Army Group and we got to know one another well.

The sad decline in the brigade's fortunes is well and clearly told here.

Reductions in British defence costs in the late fifties inevitably reduced the support given to NATO by the UK. As a small, strong and complete formation between 1964 and 1970, the position of 4 CIBG was pivotal in the forward defence of Germany against the Soviet bloc where it furnished 15 per cent of the British Corps' fighting strength with 20 per cent of its nuclear firepower. The defence policy of the Trudeau Government almost killed 4 CIBG late in the Sixties. The sad tale of decline in so many respects of a unique fighting formation is well and soberly told here, down through the move in 1970 to a miserably poor station and diminished standing in CENTAG up to the final removal from NATO of what still remained of the Canadian Brigade Group in 1993.

No one who knew this splendid formation in its prime can fail to be saddened by its decline and fall. No one who holds Canada in high regard, and finds its standing as a world power important, can fail to regret Canada's wanton withdrawal from a responsible position in the defence of western freedom. The regrets of Canada's allies at her leaving the top table and opening a gap within the alliance that was hard to fill, finds full expression in these pages. They deserve careful reading and reflection. I look back upon my own association with the Canadian Brigade Group in NATO with pride and pleasure. It was a privilege to serve with them and I am grateful for this opportunity to say so.

General Sir John Hackett,
GCB, CBE, DSO, MC

INTRODUCTION

The primary aim of this work is to chronicle the activities of Canada's NATO brigade throughout the span of its existence. Over 100,000 Canadian soldiers and their dependents served in Germany on a rotational basis in support of the North Atlantic Treaty Organization between 1951 and 1993. For a nation as small as ours in population, a nation with no territorial ambitions, deploying such a force overseas for one third of our country's existence is incredible and at times unfathomable. The impact that the Canadian Army has had in NATO is worthy of examination and thus it is important that we preserve it for the future.

There is a secondary aim. In this country it has always been fashionable among many military historians, defence policy analysts, political scientists and academics to denigrate the Canadian land force commitment to NATO, particularly our commitment to SACEUR's Central Region. This viewpoint has generally been justified either by asserting that the threat did not exist or, if it did, the numerical size of the Canadian brigade made it insignificant in the grand scheme of things. In addition to its function of providing a history of what Canada's NATO brigade did in Europe, this work will challenge these points of view.

It is tempting today to look back at the Cold War and reflect. When one does so, a question that often comes to mind is, "Was it worth all of that financial expense and ideological effort?" Some might also reflect on the now chaotic conditions in Eastern Europe and the former Soviet Union, and wonder if the threat from that quarter was always a paper tiger.

Since the Berlin Wall came down in 1989, however, the true extent of what was the threat has become clear. Now that former National Volksarmee (East German) officers are being integrated into the Bundeswehr and many formerly secret Soviet and East German documents have come to light, the reality of what was the military threat to Western Europe has been abundantly re-confirmed:

- In addition to outnumbering NATO forces, all Warsaw Pact units based in East Germany and Czechoslovakia maintained an extremely high state of operational readiness, completely unparalleled in NATO armies. Units 'lived' on their vehicles, and each had two sets of equipment, one set for training and one for wartime use. Whereas NATO units could deploy on about two hours notice and then only in a high state of alert, Warsaw Pact units could move, in most cases, on as little as 15-30 minutes notice.

- The Warsaw Pact armies had 60 days worth of logistics stocks, not in storage sites, but on vehicles and ready to go. Their storage sites had a further 90 days. NATO logistics planners had problems with maintaining 30 days of stocks in storage sites, and little of it was loaded in vehicles on a permanent basis.

- The Warsaw Pact was so confident of success that highway and directional signs in the Russian and German languages were pre-stocked for Belgian and French towns deep within NATO's Communications Zone, all the way to the English Channel.

- The true extent of Communist penetration of West German society and institutions may never be fully known, but there were large numbers of 'sleeper' agents, espionage networks, and terrorists programmed to interfere with NATO's ability to defend itself against Soviet aggression. Many of these sleepers possessed portable anti-tank and anti-aircraft weapons systems pre-positioned near important NATO installations. This was in addition to the large numbers of agents that were continually attempting to subvert West German society.

- High level East German military documents describe clearly the fictitious scenario that was to be used in the event of war to indoctrinate Warsaw Pact troops that they were resisting NATO 'aggression' into East Germany. These documents are very frank about this, and demonstrate that the Warsaw Pact leadership understood all along that NATO truly was a defensive alliance.

Many people were interviewed during the course of this project, and the experiences described by Major Ray Richards of the Royal Canadian Dragoons provide a superb summation of the situation in Europe during the Cold War. Major Richards served in Germany on a number of occasions from 1979 to 1993. On FALLEX 79, his tank troop deployed to a small town near the Czechoslovak border:

> I pulled my tank into this farmyard and the mother was very accommodating. She gave us cookies and cakes, let us stay in her living room, insisted that we come for breakfast and treated us very, very well. One night she asked, 'What are you doing here?' I thought it was the precursor to a 'Yankee go home' type speech and I started to say that we were part of NATO, defending against the Communist threat. 'I know that', she said, 'What are *you* doing here?' At this point tears started to well up in her eyes and I said, 'I'm here as part of NATO to defend you.' She said, 'What is a young man from Saskatchewan [although she didn't pronounce it quite right], half a world away – why are you here ready to die for me? What have I ever done that you would come over here and prepare to die for me?' It hit me like ton of bricks. Obviously she wasn't saying just her, but Germans in general. It really made a mark. They lived very close to the border, they knew what was going on,

they could see the fences and the wire and the minefields and towers. She lived under the shadow, under the threat, for all of her life. She knew it was real.

This experience is a typical one.
The physical manifestation of what the other side represented was readily apparent to Canadian observers. Ray Richards again:

> East Germany was definitely a country in prison. There is no way you could construe it any other way. You just had to go into the countryside between small villages. The road stops, big ditch, and that's where the border is. That's where the minefield starts, 100 metres of minefield, double wire fence bent at the top to ensure people are kept in, not kept out. You could see the automatic shotguns set alternately one at knee height one at shoulder height, the guard towers with interlocking arcs of fire, searchlights. We're not talking about the middle of Berlin here. This is the middle of the countryside, 100 miles from nowhere of any significance. Where there was a town on the border where people could see into the Western side, there was a wall that was built high enough so that nobody could see over the wall to the other side. If they lived and breathed and wandered around and stayed within the village limits and looked west, all they could see was a wall! The world ended there for them. Maybe McDonald-Douglas and Chrysler made a lot of money building weapons systems, but anybody that says that there wasn't a threat – that those people weren't in jail inside their own country – they don't know what they're talking about.

This is the system which Canada helped defend against with our Germany-based brigade for nearly 42 years.
The Brigade's operational significance was for most of its existence entirely disproportionate to its size. Time and again the Brigade was given important tasks in critical operational locations. Despite equipment and manpower limitations at some points during its existence, the Brigade earned the lasting professional respect from the armies of all of the NATO nations with which it operated. The Canadian Army undoubtedly played an important and significant role in deterring aggression by committing forces to NATO's Central Region. This is the history of

Canada's NATO brigade.

Some administrative notes are necessary as conventions used in this book require explanation. References to "the Brigade", "the brigade" "27 CIB", "1 CIBG", "2 CIBG", "4 CIBG", "4 CMBG", "4 CMB" or "4 Brigade" refer to whichever incarnation of the Canadian formation is being discussed at the time, even though the technically correct term is "Brigade Group". Some documents refer to 27 CIB as 27 Brigade Group or just 27 Brigade: I have used the terms interchangeably. For the "Battle Group" period of the early 1970s, I also refer to the organization as "the Brigade" or 4 CMBG. Please see the Glossary for the differentiation between Brigade and Brigade Group.

Canada's land forces are referred to throughout as "the Army," despite the name changes during the unification period. The standardized NATO symbols in the figures have been streamlined for clarity on the maps. Boundaries should be taken to be approximate in most cases. The designations for higher formations in NATO underwent change as the organization developed. For example, what we refer to today as I (British) Corps or I (BR) Corps used to be called I (Great Britain) Corps or I (GB) Corps. I have used the current NATO terminology and abbreviations as much as possible to avoid confusion, and a full listing can be found in the Glossary.

The sheer number of Canadians who served in Germany with Canada's NATO Brigade precluded an extensive oral history programme. Consequently, the anecdotes in this work should be considered representative, particularly those discussing social aspects.

In some cases there are two spellings for cities in Germany. I have chosen to use the German spelling in most cases.

This history primarily focuses on the operational aspects of Canada's army brigade in Germany. For those interested in pictorial souvenir albums of the Canadian presence in Europe, I direct you to Don Nick's <u>Lahr Schwarzwald: Canadian Forces Base Lahr 1967-1992</u> (Ottawa: *Esprit de Corps*, 1992); Ian McCandie's (ed) <u>Forty Years 1953-1993: 4 Wing Canadian Forces Base Baden Soellingen</u> (Ottawa: *Esprit de Corps*, 1993); and (no author) <u>Canada's NATO Brigade: A History / Brigade Canadienne Au Service De L'OTAN: Historique</u> (Lahr: Moritz

Schauenberg GmbH, 1983).

This work has received the cooperation of the Department of National Defence and is based in the main on official documents from national and international depositories and sources, supported by interviews and secondary sources. A large number of documents cannot be released at the present time but, hopefully, will be in the foreseeable future. This accounts for the lack of specific sourcing. It is my intent to place a footnoted version on file at the Directorate General, History at NDHQ for future historians re-examining Canada's land commitment to NATO. This will undoubtably be necessary given the close proximity of this work to some of the events which are described in it.

Sean M. Maloney
11 November 1993

PART ONE

UP NORTH

1951 - 1953

27 INFANTRY BRIGADE
THE RETURN TO EUROPE

CHAPTER ONE

"WE BELIEVE THAT THE MAINTENANCE OF AN OVERWHELMING SUPERIORITY OF FORCE ON THE SIDE OF PEACE IS THE BEST GUARANTEE TODAY OF THE MAINTENANCE OF PEACE."

- LESTER B. PEARSON

25 SEPTEMBER 1948

Above: Members of 27 Canadian Infantry Brigade board the MV FAIRSEA for Europe, November 1951.
Below: MV FAIRSEA, one of the three ships which transported 27 CIB from Canada to Europe during November and December 1951 (ROTTERDAM ARCHIVES).

CHAPTER ONE

Above: *General Dwight D. Eisenhower, NATO's Supreme Allied Commander Europe (SACEUR) accompanied by LCol J.E.L. Castonguay, inspects soldiers of 1st Canadian Infantry Battalion in Rotterdam after disembarkation, 21 November 1951.* (LEX DE HERDER).
Below: *General Eisenhower takes the salute in front of the Rotterdam city hall on 21 November 1951 as 27 CIB's 1st Canadian Infantry Battalion marches past. Note Canadian "Red Ensign" at centre of the flags of the 12 nations which initially made up NATO.* (ROTTERDAM ARCHIVES).

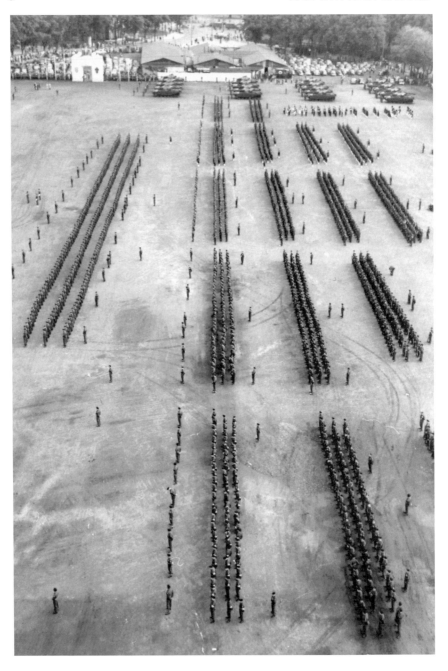

Above: *27 Canadian Infantry Brigade on parade, Waterloo Platz, Hannover, Germany, 1952.*

CHAPTER ONE

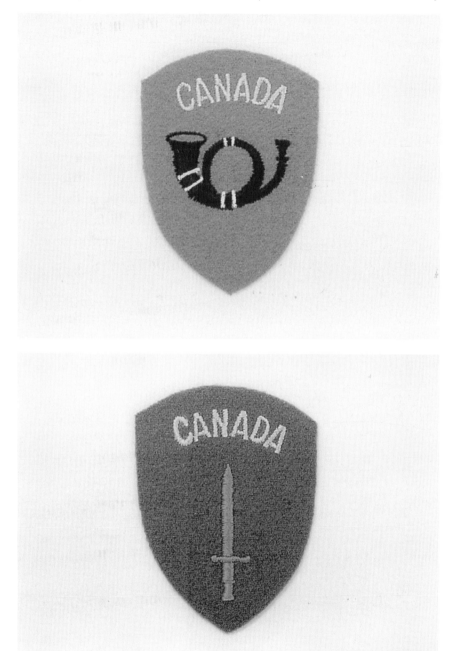

*Shoulder insignia worn by **above** – 1st Canadian Rifle Battalion; **below** – 1st Canadian Infantry Battalion,*

Above: Shoulder insignia worn by 1st Canadian Infantry Battalion. *(All patches courtesy Roy Kawamoto)*

CHAPTER ONE

Above: *27 Brigade Centurion tank is ferried across the Weser River during Exercise SPEARHEAD II, August 1952* (I.M. RETTIE).
Below: *Tanks and infantry of 27 CIB advance during Exercise SPEARHEAD II, August 1952.* (I.M. RETTIE)

Above: 27 Brigade tank-infantry cooperation exercise, Munsterlager, 1952. (DND)
Below: Soldiers of 1st Canadian Infantry Battalion receive a briefing during exercise at Bergen-Hohne, April 1952. Note the Second World War-era webbing and helmets. (DND)

CHAPTER ONE

Above: *1st Canadian Rifle Battalion on a fighting in built-up areas (FIBUA) training exercise near Hannover, June 1952. (DND)*
Below: *Elements of the 1st Canadian Rifle Battalion conduct an assault river crossing at BAOR's All Arms Training Center, Sennelager in August 1952. (DND)*

The arrival of the transport ship *Fairsea* in Rotterdam on 21 November 1951, and the unloading of the first combat elements of the 27th Canadian Infantry Brigade (27 CIB), marked the beginning of Canada's longest overseas peacetime troop deployment. By 1993, over 100,000 members of the Canadian Army had served alongside servicemen from other North Atlantic Treaty Organization members to deter Soviet aggression in Western Europe. That Canada, a nation with a population of less than 15 million in 1950, protected by the buffers of the Atlantic, Arctic and Pacific Oceans, and possessing its own incredible wealth of natural resources, should make such a commitment to assist in preserving the freedom of Western Europe, was, to borrow a phrase from Winston Churchill, "a most unsordid act". This book examines that commitment, its origins, its high points, its low points, and ultimately, its success and its ending

In 1951, Western Europe still lay prostrate from the devastation of the Second World War, a battered and burned out shell of its former grandeur. While one totalitarian enemy had been defeated another had arisen to dominate the whole of Eastern Europe. Instead of demobilizing in 1946 as had the Western Allies, the Soviet Union retained the enormous military machine that had driven the invading Germans west in 1944 and 1945. But, instead of liberating Poland, Hungary, Czechoslovakia and other victims of the Nazi yoke, freedom had been ground under the boot of the Soviet 'liberators'. Instead of withdrawing from northern Iran, these forces were reinforced, possibly for a drive on the Middle East oil fields. Instead of returning Allied prisoners of war caught in the Eastern zones, deals had to be made to exchange them for anti-Stalin Russian nationals under Allied control. Communist insurgents had destabilized Greece, while Turkey, France and Italy had to contend with internal disorder, created by local Communist agitators. Even Canada was not spared. The Gouzenko defection demonstrated that a Communist espionage network was busy collecting information on the development of nuclear weapons.

This pattern of Soviet aggression and coercion had become a routine between 1945 and 1948. In February 1948, the Czech government was overthrown by a Communist coup d'etat. Then on 24 June of that year, Stalin upped the ante: the Soviets sealed off the Western-occupied sectors of the divided city of Berlin from the Allied Occupation Zones to the west. Stalin obviously hoped to push his former allies out of Berlin and thus win a political victory that would prove to the world that the USSR was now the most powerful nation on earth. The Berlin Blockade was on. Fortunately, after a number of firm demonstrations of Western resolve, including the heroic Berlin airlift, the Soviets backed down and reopened the links between the occupation zones and West Berlin.

This retreat on the Soviets' part was, however, only temporary, as events would demonstrate. In August 1949, the USSR had tested its first atomic bomb. Then in June 1950, the Korean peninsula was engulfed in a war when the Communist North (supported materially, logistically and morally by the Soviets) invaded the Republic of South Korea. This was interpreted by the West as a feint to draw Allied forces into an inconclusive conflict on the other side of the globe, while Europe lay vulnerable. However, a response was necessary to demonstrate the resolve of the West in fighting Communism in any part of the globe. Some believed that the West was strong because of American atomic weapons. Nuclear deterrence was, however, not a reality in 1950. Only a small number of those weapons existed, so conventional warfare would remain the dominant form of potential conflict in the early 1950s.

A defence alliance called the Brussels Pact was created by the European powers in 1948 to stand up to the growing Soviet threat, but the Berlin Crisis demonstrated that such an organization lacked credibility without the military, economic and material support of North America. As a result, the North Atlantic Treaty Organization (NATO) was formed in 1949. Initially, NATO membership included Belgium, Canada, Denmark, France, Great Britain, Iceland, Italy, Luxembourg, The Netherlands, Norway, Portugal, and the United States. (Turkey and Greece joined in 1952, West Germany in 1955 and Spain in 1982). The essence of NATO as a deterrent organization was enshrined in Article 5 of the North Atlantic Treaty which states:

> The Parties agree that an armed attack against one or more of them in Europe or in North America shall be considered an attack against them all and consequently they agree that, if such an armed attack occurs, each of them will assist the Party or Parties so attacked by taking forthwith, individually or in concert with the other Parties, such action as it deems necessary including the use of armed force, to restore and maintain the security of the North Atlantic Area... .

Several regional planning organizations were formed within NATO to coordinate the defence of the NATO area; these included the Northern, Western and Southern European Regional Planning Groups, the North Atlantic Ocean Regional Planning Group and the Canada-US Regional Planning Group. Each region created two regional defence plans; these plans were then combined to form a NATO Medium Term Defence Plan (MTDP) and a Short Term Defence Plan (STDP). The STDP was constructed on the basis of the forces that existed in 1949, while the MTDP was based on the forces that should be in place some time in the near future. Both the MTDP and the STDP were 'number crunching' exercises so that the regional planners could have a rough idea of what forces might be available, allowing them to create skeleton defence plans that could be modified as necessary in the future.

NATO nations then decided in which planning groups they would participate. Canada chose to contribute to three – the Canada-US, North Atlantic, and Western Europe Regional Planning Groups. Once Canada decided to participate in the Western European group, the regional planners asked Canada in November 1949 to provide forces for the STDP and the MTDP. Canada replied that it would for planning purposes contribute a brigade group and nine squadrons of fighter aircraft.

At this point, the political pressure brought on by the Berlin Crisis and the first Soviet atom bomb test was starting to diminish. This did not mean that NATO was no longer required; continued Soviet aggression elsewhere demonstrated that this was likely to be a temporary respite. The Canadian government was in the process of re-examining its European MTDP commitment in light of the slight relaxation in tension when the Korean War broke out.

In 1949, the Canadian Army consisted of one regular force brigade group of three infantry battalions with supporting arms (The Mobile Striking Force) and two militia "divisions" in various stages of disrepair and training. The Mobile Striking Force was tasked with the land defence of the Alaskan Highway as well as provision of a training cadre for the Militia. This small force was a far cry from the days of having five divisions and three independent tank brigades in the field during the Second World War. The Canadian government under Mackenzie King had suffered problems of its own making during the Conscription Crisis in 1944, and had no intention of maintaining a large post-war Canadian Army.

By 1950, however, the Government committed itself to send a brigade group to Korea (25 CIB). The MSF could not be sent since it was essentially a training cadre and was needed for the defence of Canada. As a result, a Canadian Army "Special Force" (CASF) was created by recruiting both veterans and untrained personnel off the street. Eventually, two brigades were formed – 25 CIB and 26 CIB, with 26 CIB to act as the rotation brigade for Korea if necessary.

Because of a host of problems associated with the recruitment of personnel for 25 and 26 CIB (in one case an amputee was recruited, in another a deaf man) the government decided that this method of raising forces for special tasks was really not practical. Since conscription was, however, completely out of the question (no matter how hard Chief of the General Staff Guy Simonds tried), other methods would have to be used for any future contingency.

While the Western powers scrambled to respond to Korea, many believed that the Far Eastern operations were just a feint orchestrated by the Soviets so that scarce Western military resources would be expended in an inconclusive conflict. Once the West was distracted, planners believed, the Soviets would strike against Western Europe. In the confusion the MTDP was formally inaugurated as a force structure plan by NATO's Defence Committee without consultation with the contributing nations. In retrospect, bureaucratic problems were to blame for this; NATO decision-making structures and processes were very immature in 1950. Nonetheless, Canada found itself locked into providing land and air forces to defend Western Europe. Canada's military and political leadership met to sort out this situation in December 1950.

Prime Minister Louis St Laurent understood the problem: Canada could either withdraw the commitment, it could modify it, or it could make no changes. Withdrawing the commitment was out of the question; the likelihood of war had increased dramatically since the end of 1949 and any sign of weakness or ambivalence at this juncture could be misinterpreted by the Soviets as a fissure in the NATO alliance. As St. Laurent put it,

> With our tradition [of no conscription] it made it exceptionally difficult to bring Canada to the peak of her strength before war. Our people in the past had only achieved their maximum effort under the stress of an actual conflict. Our objective [is] to help in building up sufficient collective strength to deter an aggressor from starting such a conflict.

Since Canada was a prime mover in the creation of NATO, St Laurent concluded that a CASF similar to the Korean CASF should be raised to meet Canadian obligations in Europe. There was a special proviso, however, that the force would not be sent without parliamentary approval.

To confront the Soviet menace facing Western Europe, a special NATO command was formed to coordinate defence planning in peace and to conduct the battle in war; it was called Allied Command Europe or ACE, commanded by the Supreme Allied Commander, Europe and run from a revitalized Supreme Headquarters, Allied Powers Europe (SHAPE). The first SACEUR, General Eisenhower, noted two important factors affecting the defence of Europe. First, the occupation forces of France, Britain and the United States in Germany were not strong enough or equipped properly to ward off a Soviet attack. In addition they were configured for occupation duty and did not interact significantly. Secondly, the economies of Europe were still recovering from the effects of the Second World War and could not in the short term provide huge national forces for defence, as this would prevent the much needed economic recovery. Until Western Europe was 'back on its feet', as it were, a new form of defence organization was needed.

This new organization was called the Integrated Force. The Integrated Force, commanded by SACEUR, was to consist of specialized national contributions within the framework of integrated, as opposed to national, command and control. In other words, selected units of NATO members would be assigned to NATO command in wartime and would fight alongside other NATO formations instead of fighting in isolation.

The Integrated Force existed solely on paper in 1950. The only units that could contribute to the Integrated Force from the outset were a conglomeration of occupation divisions from the US, the UK, and France. Belgium and the Netherlands also had small militaries with some occupation tasks. Even Norway had a brigade group on occupation duty in northern Germany. For the Integrated Force to become a reality, however, NATO members had to make good on their MTDP contributions. If the Integrated Force was actually brought into existence and located in Western Europe, it could conceivably delay an enemy offensive while the mobilization and reinforcement process was set in motion in Canada, the United States and the United Kingdom. General Charles Foulkes, Chairman of the Canadian Chiefs of Staff Committee, realized that:

> Historically, our Canadian Defence Policy has been based on the premise that our role should be that of reinforcing any country under attack.... There is no doubt, however, that initially Canada may avoid an early commitment but if as it seems apparent the eleven other countries agree to the establishment of the Integrated Force and to contribute to this force, I am of the opinion that

Canada may have to make some kind of contribution to the ground forces....

Militarily, SACEUR wanted as large a formation from Canada as possible, "in being" and located in Europe in peacetime. In fact, NATO placed the requirement at two Canadian divisions during talks in the summer of 1951. However, this was not possible given Canada's other commitments and priorities. Such a commitment – that is, creating two more brigade groups in addition to the MSF, 25 CIB and 26 CIB – would have increased the Canadian Army by five times its original post-war size. Such an increase would have been prohibitively expensive in view of Canadian expenditures already committed to the air defence of Europe (nine, increased to 11 and then increased again to 12 squadrons of fighter aircraft), naval protection for the sea lanes to Europe, military equipment and aircrew training for other European armies and air forces under mutual aid agreements, and the air defence of North America.

As a result, Canada's land force commitment was changed to an infantry brigade group "in being" in Europe, with two other brigades in Canada to be shipped over in time of hostility to form a division (at this time planners hoped that the 25 and 26 CIBs would be re-tasked from Korea to Europe in an emergency, while the MSF would defend Canada). Some thought was given to sending two uncommitted armoured regiments with an infantry brigade group to form an armoured division; this was a contingency plan in case NATO insisted that Canada send a division instead of a brigade group, or if war broke out in the immediate future. Canadian planners calculated that another armoured division (an infantry brigade group and an armoured brigade) could be available as reinforcements 30 days after the start of the war. In more vague terms, Canada planned for the provision of a third division six months after the start of hostilities, followed by a fourth at 16 months; these units would be drawn from the Militia and supplemented by recruiting.

In practical terms, the provision of the initial brigade group to Europe would have to be immediately followed by the formation of another brigade group since "there is a possibility of the brigade group becoming involved in action in Europe at an early stage". Rotation was another consideration; as Lieutenant General Simonds noted, "if the Cold War continues, there must be rotation: men and units cannot stay in

Europe indefinitely...."

The St-Laurent Government concluded on 11 April 1951 that a land contribution to the Integrated Force was still necessary to demonstrate Canada's commitment to the land defence of Western Europe. On 4 May 1951, Minister of National Defence Brooke Claxton announced to the House of Commons that:

> Keeping our force in Korea up to strength will obviously continue to be the number one Army priority so long as any of our troops are engaged in actual combat. We are further expanding the Canadian Army to meet that priority and other Army tasks, including, subject to approval in Parliament and the completion of firm arrangements in that regard with our North Atlantic associates, the provision of forces for Western Europe. This expansion will include the formation of an additional Canadian Army brigade group with supporting units. The new formation, to be known as 27th Canadian Brigade Group, will be recruited around the framework of some of our famous Militia units....

Thus, Canada formally committed land forces to SACEUR's Integrated Force. In terms of time, the land commitment was indefinite but estimates suggested that the European countries could provide for their own defence some time in the late 1950s, and the Canadian land commitment would then no longer be required. Be that as it may, Canada still had to field a brigade group for service in Europe in 1951. Since a large proportion of the defence budget was already committed to Korean operations and to RCAF priorities, and since conscription was out of the question, an economical means of raising a Canadian land force had to be found. The answer, as in two previous wars, was the Militia.

General Simonds, in a written appreciation of the manpower situation, concluded that a brigade group of 5800 men and a replacement group of 4000 men was needed for the NATO commitment. Understanding that the Korean Special Force recruitment fiasco could not be repeated, Simonds noted that the Reserve Force was the primary manpower source for the Canadian Army, and that cross country regional representation in the force in Europe would be a valuable device in demonstrating Canadian unity and commitment to NATO. Additionally, rotating Militia personnel through Europe would ensure that Militia units would all contain some trained personnel, something that had been a problem before the last war and which had contributed to the Hong Kong disaster in 1941.

To ensure balanced national representation in 27 CIB and to fulfil the requirement that Militia personnel comprise the force, a compromise had to be made. The result was the decision to form composite units for 27 CIB. Since the number of units within 27 CIB was small, and because of the scattered locations of Canadian Militia units, men were recruited and formed into amalgamated units. For example, a Highland Battalion was formed with members being recruited from The Black Watch (Royal Highland Regiment) of Canada, The North Nova Scotia Highlanders, 48th Highlanders of Canada, The Seaforth Highlanders of Canada and the Canadian Scottish Regiment (Princess Mary's). The men who joined retained their parent Regiment's insignia and uniform.

The recruiting and initial training of 27 Canadian Infantry Brigade (the term "Group" was adopted, dropped and later added again) was called Operation PANDA, "PANDA" being derived from "Pacific AND Atlantic". The initial order of battle for 27 CIB included a Brigade Headquarters; 79 Field Regiment RCA; C Squadron of the Royal Canadian Dragoons; 58 Independent Field Squadron, RCE; 27th CIB Signal Squadron; 1st Canadian Highland Battalion; 1st Canadian Rifle Battalion; 1st Canadian Infantry Battalion; No 55 Transport Company, RCASC; No 27 Field Ambulance, RCAMC and a large number of support formations. Bands were also included, and each infantry battalion had either a 30 piece pipe, bugle or brass/reed band.

These units were, in the main, composed of Militia personnel recruited for Op PANDA. [See Figure 1-1] Some units like C Sqn RCD were from the regular force. Since the regular armoured regiments had only a small role to play in the MSF, provision of regular armoured sub-units to 27 CIB did not affect other Canadian defence commitments, which the provision of regular infantry battalions would have done.

The terms of service for 27 CIB and its rotation brigade was an engagement of two years for unmarried and one year for married men. They could engage for up to three years and were eligible for re-engagement after that.

CHAPTER ONE

27 CIB UNITS DERIVING FROM THE MILITIA

79TH FIELD REGIMENT RCA

209th, 258th and 284th Batteries formed from: 6th Field Regt (Levis, PQ)

11th Field Regt (Guelph, Ont)

14th Field Regt (Yarmouth, NS)

29th Field Regt (Toronto, Ont)

34th Field Regt (Montreal, PQ)

39th Field Regt (Winnipeg, Man)

1ST CANADIAN INFANTRY BATTALION

The Hastings and Prince Edward Regiment (A Coy)

Les Fusiliers Mont Royal (B Coy)

The Algonquin Regiment (C Coy)

The Carleton and York Regiment (Support Coy)

The Loyal Edmonton Regiment (D Coy)

1ST CANADIAN RIFLE BATTALION

Queen's Own Rifles of Canada (Support Coy)

Victoria Rifles of Canada (A Coy)

The Royal Hamilton Light Infantry (B Coy)

The Royal Winnipeg Rifles (C Coy)

The Regina Rifle Regiment (D Coy)

58TH INDEPENDENT FIELD SQUADRON, RCE

56th Ind Field Sqn (St John's NFLD)

6th Field Engineer Regt (Winnipeg, Man)

33rd Field Park Sqn, (Lethbridge, Alta)

1ST CANADIAN HIGHLAND BATTALION

The Black Watch (Royal Highland Regiment of Canada) (A Coy)

The North Nova Scotia Highlanders (Support Coy)

48th Highlanders of Canada (B Coy)

Seaforth Highlands of Canada (C Coy)

Canadian Scottish Regiment (Princess Mary's) (D Coy)

79TH FIELD AMBULANCE, RCAMC

7th Field Ambulance (Toronto, Ont)

9th Field Ambulance (Montreal, PQ)

FIGURE 1-1

The movement of families and household effects was not authorized at public expense and there was no provision for married quarters.

The recruiting process for Op PANDA continued in May and June 1951. General Simonds by then had selected Brigadier Geoffrey Walsh to command 27 CIB. Brigadier Walsh, who had been Chief Engineer in 1st Canadian Army during the Second World War, had just finished organizing the Northwest Highway System. Walsh, who had a reputation for being a good trainer, quickly took charge and moved his headquarters from its temporary berth at Army HQ in Ottawa to Camp Valcartier, Quebec.

Before training could get underway, however, there was a matter of extreme urgency that had to be sorted out: What equipment should 27 CIB be provided with? Up to 1950, the Canadian Army's MSF had operated with a mix of Canadian and American equipment and had even adopted (temporarily) American terminology like "Regimental Combat Team", which was 'Americanese' for "Brigade Group". In 1950-51, 25 CIB was supposed to be equipped along American lines for its employment in Korea, but this changed to British-pattern kit when 25 CIB was allocated to the Commonwealth Division alongside British troops. 27 CIB had a similar problem. Initially, 27 CIB was supposed to operate with American units in Europe and was equipped with American pattern equipment. As a result, 27 CIB infantry units training in Canada were equipped initially with Garand and Browning rifles, and 60 mm and 81 mm mortars. The artillery was equipped with 105mm howitzers, while the armour trained on M4 *Sherman* and M24 *Chaffee* tanks. All the wheeled transport, however, was of Canadian manufacture.

Captain E.C. Powell , a RCEME officer, described the uniform of the period:

> The battledress we wore in garrison was the same uniform we wore in the field. However, most of us kept one old one for just that purpose. We still used the old British-type round steel helmet. In garrison, as well as in the field, we wore a peaked cap made from the same material as the battledress. When we arrived we were issued with a new beret to be worn when 'walking out'. It was a monstrosity – dark blue with a large half moon piece of material

complete with backing sewn across the front. The RCEME beret wasn't too bad but the Service Corps had a bright yellow half moon, the Medical Corps white, while the rest of the support units had half moons of various shades of red. The Highland, Infantry and Rifle Battalions, as well as the Armoured Regiment, wore the more traditional type of headdress. It was a chargeable offence to shrink or re-shape these new berets, but most of us kept our khaki beret to wear on leave.

The move of HQ 27 CIB from Ottawa was soon followed by moving the three infantry battalions to Camp Valcartier. An additional complication was that the other arms and services were located all over Canada, in locations as diverse as Chilliwack, BC and Borden, Petawawa, and Kingston, Ontario, as well as Shilo, Manitoba. Then-Major Seamark, at the time the Brigade Major, remembered that training 27 CIB was a complex task:

> ...the Brigade Commander was like a travelling salesman, going from place to place setting his standards.... Brigadier Walsh's standards were extremely high but based on fundamental simplicity. He did not believe in giving soldiers complicated tasks to do when there was the possibility of misunderstanding. He spent that whole summer going from place to place setting these standards up because we were not involved in Brigade training; we were involved in individual training until the middle of July, and platoon and company training until the middle of August [1951].

This was necessary for a number of reasons, as Brigadier Walsh recalled:

> It was a straight slogging business of trying to get early training done because we were very short of trained officers and NCOs and had to start from scratch practically. In Valcartier two COs failed to measure up and had to be removed. Many of the NCOs were very rusty and had to be taken away from units just to get their basic training polished up just so they could act as NCOs. However, we reached a fairly good standard, good enough so that when we were inspected by Princess Elizabeth, I was very proud of them and the way they conducted themselves....

The objective of this early training was to get 27 CIB "to the level where it could undertake collective training when it got to Germany". Brigadier Walsh himself was remembered as "not only a very tough guy, but an extremely bright guy and fair". With his trademark walking stick and duffel coat, Walsh had a philosophy that emphasized leadership from the front and he was sustained by the belief that a man had to be thoroughly trained before he was tested, as one veteran remembers:

> ...there was a relay [on the range at Valcartier] lounging about a couple of hundred yards behind where the firing was taking place, and that shouldn't have been: when a relay is waiting its turn to fire it should be having some basic discussions of training. So Brigadier Walsh went to the subaltern and he said 'Is this your relay?' and the subaltern told him that it was. Brigadier Walsh said 'Well, get them to gather round here, I want to have a word with them.' The subaltern turned around and said, 'Hey, you guys, come on over here' . Those that considered that they fell into the category of 'you guys' looked over their shoulder, and if they wanted they came over... Brig Walsh asked what the number of the relay was and the subaltern replied that it was number two relay. Brig Walsh then said 'Right! Number Two Relay around me. Move now!' Zap! Everybody then faced around us. He proved to that officer on that occasion, without taking a great strip off him, the value of a formal order...

Despite equipment problems (the government was still sorting out which tank the Army would acquire), 27 CIB dutifully continued to train into the fall of 1951. After a parade on the Plains of Abraham for Princess Elizabeth, 27 CIB was warned that there was a high probability it would be under the operational command of British Army of the Rhine (BAOR) rather than under American operational command as previously envisaged.

There were a number of reasons for this; it would be too simplistic to suggest that this choice was based on any sentimental attachment to "Monty's Army" of old. Rather, high level politics played a key part in placing 27 CIB under the command of BAOR. There was great concern in the St-Laurent Government that if 27 CIB was grouped with American units and equipped with American vehicles and weapons, the

Canadian identity of 27 CIB would be submerged because of the similarity of accents. On the other hand, if the Canadians were equipped with mix of British and American pattern kit and grouped with the British, the Canadians would tend to stand out more because of the differences in equipment, accents and attitude. Additionally, if 27 CIB was located in the US Occupation Zone, opportunities to interact with the smaller NATO nations' armies like the Belgians or the Dutch would not exist. This was an important consideration for Canada, since politically she needed the support of these smaller nations to counteract the preponderance of American or British power within the NATO decision-making apparatus.

There were, of course, military benefits as well. The terrain in the British Zone was predominantly flat and not easily defended and NATO needed as many formations in the area as possible. There were better training facilities; there was a staff system and training doctrine compatibility with the British, and the supply system was already in place.

Even the timing of the arrival of 27 CIB had political overtones. Concurrent with the Canadian decision to contribute to the Integrated Force, the United States had pledged four divisions, and the British one and a half, all in addition to the occupation forces already in Germany. In order to provide maximum propaganda value, forces from North America were moved to Europe at three month intervals throughout 1951 to give the impression of unlimited support and reinforcement capability. Naturally, the movements appeared frequently in newsreels like the Movietone series. The Brigade could either arrive in August or November.

On 18 October 1951, an Order in Council was passed which stated:

> "WHEREAS the North Atlantic Treaty was entered into for the purpose of preserving peace by building up the strength necessary to deter aggression, and, to assist in this purpose, it was decided to form an integrated force in Western Europe;
>
> AND WHEREAS an Integrated Force is now being established under the Supreme Command of General Eisenhower;

AND WHEREAS, at the last session of Parliament it was announced that elements of the Canadian Army and the Royal Canadian Air Force were to form part of this Integrated Force and provision was made for the appropriate expansion of the Army and the Air Force;

AND WHEREAS, a Canadian Infantry Brigade Group has been raised and has reached the state of training where it may properly be despatched to form part of the Integrated Force, and Air Force Squadrons are being progressively formed, equipped and trained to build up an air division in the Integrated Force, but pending the provision of airfield and other accommodation some of these are to be stationed in the United Kingdom;

THEREFORE, his Excellency the Governor General in Council, on the recommendation of the Minister of National Defence, is pleased, hereby, to make the following Order:

Order

In furtherance of Canada's undertaking under the North Atlantic Treaty, authority is hereby given for the maintenance on active service of officers and men of the Canadian Army and the Royal Canadian Air Force, not exceeding 12,000 in number as part of, or in the United Kingdom in readiness to form part of, the Integrated Force under the Supreme Allied Commander, Europe."

General Simonds had very specific instructions for Brigadier Walsh regarding command and status of 27 CIB while serving under SACEUR:

Your immediate mission will be to complete the task of raising the standard of efficiency of your force to that required for operations…, [secondly] to undertake training and operations with UK forces in Europe or with such other components of the Integrated Force as may be ordered by the Supreme Allied Commander Europe…, [thirdly] The Force under your command will not undertake any occupation duties, or any tasks in aid of the civil power in Germany. In the event of riot or insurrection you may take such action as you consider necessary for the security of your own force.

and, most importantly,

> The principle of the separate entity of the Canadian force shall at all times be maintained. You will ensure that this principle is brought to the attention of commanders of formations in which you may be serving, so that your tasks and undertakings may be so allotted or arranged with due regard to operational necessity and to the size of the Canadian force, that its Canadian entity will be preserved...

At this point, SACEUR firmly decided to place 27 Brigade under command of BAOR. Brigadier Walsh also was 'doublehatted' as Senior Canadian Army Officer with NATO Forces in Europe in addition to his duties as Brigade Commander. This allowed him the ability to speak directly with Simonds, if necessary, without going through the British or SACEUR in the event of unforeseen problems.

The road was now paved for the deployment of 27 Canadian Infantry Brigade to Europe in the service of NATO. On 5 October 1951, the 'advanced' advance party flew via Trans Canada Airlines to Hannover to liaise with local British forces at London Barracks. Two days previously, the Base advance party sailed on the SS *Canberra*, followed by the Advance Party on 20 October on the SS *Columbia*. HQ 27 CIB left 5 November and by 12 November, the 1st Canadian Infantry Battalion had embarked on the MV *Fairsea*. Working in relays, the *Columbia*, *Canberra* and *Fairsea* shuttled 27 CIB across the Atlantic Ocean until 23 December 1951.

As with all deployments, the novelty of being at sea quickly wore off. Some 27 CIB personnel aboard the *Columbia* literally lost their shirts (and uniforms) to enterprising Greek crew members in a series of all night card games. As one observer noted, "the Greek crew was better dressed than the guys of the battalion". Fortunately, these individuals were not scheduled to participate in the 21 November arrival parade.

The terminus of the voyage was the port of Rotterdam in the Netherlands. An incredible array of VIPs were on hand to witness 27 Brigade disembark on 21 November 1951. Brigadier Walsh had arrived with HQ 27 Brigade on 15 November; the Minister of National Defence, Brooke Claxton and Secretary of State for External Affairs Lester B. Pearson were collected by the Canadian attaché, Pierre Dupuy, at Valkenberg Airport. Also in attendance was General Sir John Harding, commander of the British Army of the Rhine, and the senior U.S. and French occupation force commanders from Germany. Future NATO Secretary General, Dirk Stikker, who was at the time Minister of Foreign Affairs for the Netherlands, and Lt Gen BRPF Hasselman, Chief of the Dutch General Staff, along with a bevy of local dignitaries represented the Netherlands. Supreme Allied Commander, Europe, General Eisenhower himself, flew into Schiphol Airport arriving just in time to take the general salute at 'high noon' from 1st Canadian Infantry Battalion, led by Lieutenant Colonel Castonguay.

An interesting aside: Private W. Saunders of 27 Brigade was met by his Dutch mother-in-law at the dockside. Private Saunders had fought in the Netherlands during the Second World War and had married a Dutch girl, who returned to Canada with him. His mother-in-law and sister-in-law had been refused entry to the disembarkation area, but the intervention of Pierre Dupuy secured what must have been a surprise for Private Saunders!

The troops then moved to Haas Station for the train ride to Hannover, Germany. Billeting arrangements for 27 Brigade in Hannover were of a dispersed nature and provided by BAOR. The artillery and armoured units went to Chatham Barracks at Langenhagen airfield near the Bergen-Hohne training area (which was uncomfortably close to the infamous Bergen-Belsen concentration camp), while the field engineers went to Hameln. London Barracks in Hannover was home to the rest of the 27 CIB units. [See Figure 1-2.]

Hannover was still suffering the effects of the Second World War and the occupation. Jack Wendt was on the advance party in 1951:

> Most of the buildings were still bombed out...you could go on some streets that had only cellars left and people were still living in basements – they had fixed the bottom floor up and there was nothing up above the level of the basement.... however, all the rubble was cleaned away from the streets and the street cars, taxis and cars were running normally....

Even Langenhagen airfield still had crashed Luftwaffe aircraft around

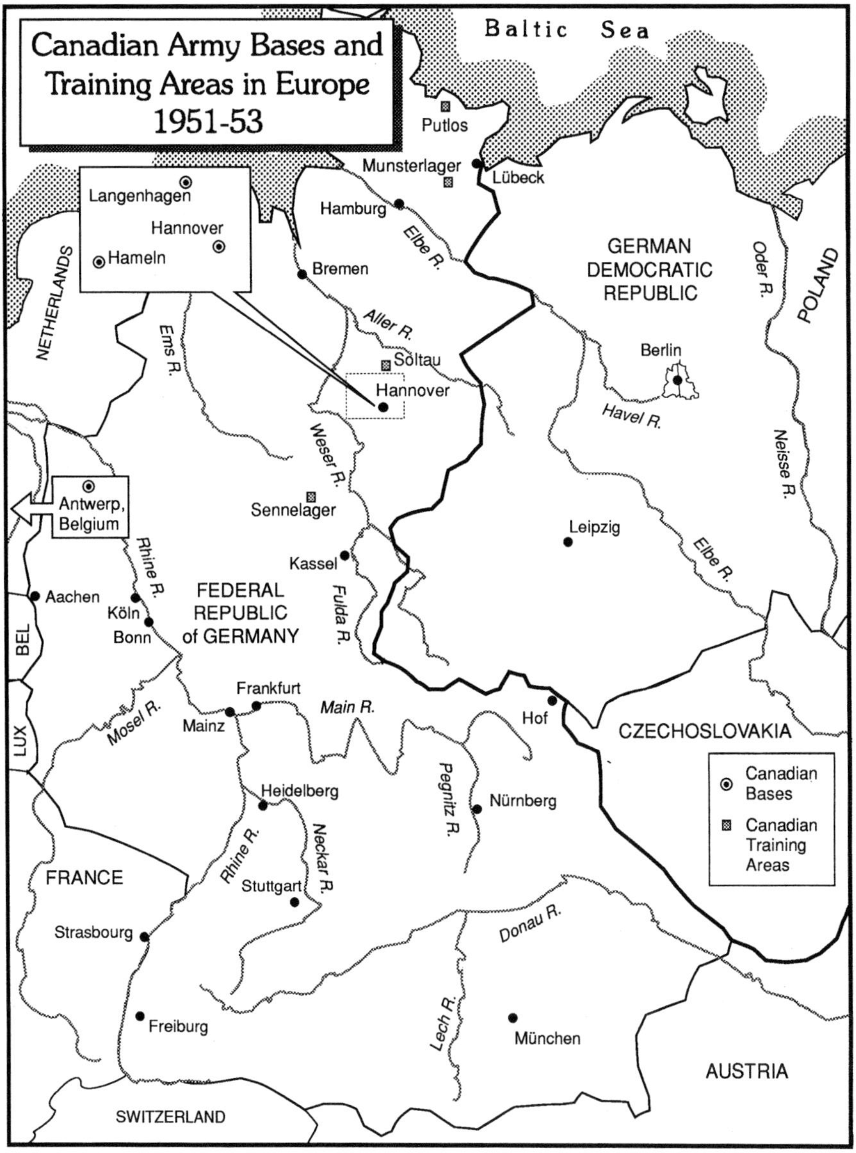
Canadian Army Bases and Training Areas in Europe 1951-53
Baltic Sea
Putlos
Munsterlager
Lübeck
Langenhagen
Hannover
Hameln
Hamburg
Elbe R.
Bremen
GERMAN DEMOCRATIC REPUBLIC
Oder R.
POLAND
NETHERLANDS
Ems R.
Aller R.
Soltau
Hannover
Berlin
Havel R.
Weser R.
Neisse R.
Antwerp, Belgium
Sennelager
Leipzig
Kassel
Elbe R.
Rhine R.
Aachen
Köln
Bonn
FEDERAL REPUBLIC of GERMANY
Fulda R.
BEL
Frankfurt
Main R.
Hof
Mosel R.
Mainz
CZECHOSLOVAKIA
LUX
Pegnitz R.
Heidelberg
Nürnberg
Canadian Bases
Canadian Training Areas
Neckar R.
Rhine R.
FRANCE
Stuttgart
Strasbourg
Donau R.
Freiburg
Lech R.
München
AUSTRIA
SWITZERLAND

FIGURE 1-2

it. John Huggins, who was with the 1st Canadian Highland Battalion, remembered that

> ...our barracks were not too far away from Continental Reifen; you know, Continental Rubber.... That place was bombed flat from one end to the other.... It was [also] around the train station where they got it. The train station and outside of the town where the big factories were – they bombed that flat....

Inevitably, there were some initial problems between some members of 27 Brigade and their British and German 'hosts':

> The Brits were leery: they thought we were all French Canadians coming [author's note: one particular Second World War regiment from Quebec, the Chaudières, had a reputation for not taking German prisoners, and not all Germans had forgotten this in the 1950s].... They were telling the Germans we were all French Canadians, and this was quite a shock.... Of course, some of our old vets, half our battalion, I would say more than half of our battalion were veterans at the time, and there was no love lost between the Germans and the Canadians. It was the same with the British Army too. They still had those bad feelings from the war and you can't blame them....

This was an example of the political 'tight rope' the Canadian soldier had to walk. He was not a member of the occupation forces yet he wore a uniform that was similar; he was still a member of a victorious army in the land which he had defeated, yet he could not allow any previous resentment to show. Germany required special handling to make NATO work, and the Canadians of 27 Brigade had a part in this, as Simonds explained to Brigadier Walsh:

> ...the attitude and behaviour of the forces under your command is of extreme importance from a political point of view, in fostering a spirit of wholehearted cooperation on the part of the German people with Allied aims and objectives. Furthermore, the German Government has made it clear that its participation in the Western defence effort would be on the principle of complete equality. It follows that any actions on the part of our troops at this stage giving the Germans the impression that they are being treated as a defeated or

subordinate people will not only be bitterly resented but will do harm to the Allied cause. At the same time, any impression that we are trying to curry favour with the Germans would also be harmful.

Even Brigadier Walsh had some problems with the local British commander. The individual in question attempted to place BAOR standard restrictions on Canadian personnel in Hannover, with regard to fraternization, with which Walsh violently disagreed. Eventually, the matter climbed the BAOR chain of command to General Hatton, where the BAOR policy was re-emphasized to Walsh. The 27 Brigade commander then informed the British general that he was here in his capacity as Senior Canadian Army Officer, noting that "you are an army of occupation. We are NATO troops." General Hatton said, "You're having trouble with so and so" to which Walsh replied, "Yes, and I had trouble with him just after Dunquerque in the south of England…." In 48 hours, the troublesome commander in Hannover was removed from his command

Despite the concerns, the population of Niedersachsen around Hannover displayed great hospitality and even invited 1500 Canadian soldiers into their homes for the 1951 Christmas season. Herr Weber, the *Oberburgermeister* of Hannover later contacted the Canadian Ambassador to West Germany and "spoke highly of the way in which the Canadians were conducting themselves and expressed approval at their coming."

Before serious collective training for 27 Brigade could commence, some materiel problems had to be sorted out. As discussed previously, the Canadian Army was in a dilemma over whether to purchase American or British pattern equipment for the Brigade. The RCA upon arriving in Germany found that acquiring 105mm howitzer ammunition was difficult: it had to be ordered from Canada. Unlike the other units of 27 Brigade, the Royal Canadian Dragoons did not arrive with their primary pieces of equipment. Prior to 27 CIB's commitment in mid 1951, an order for 400 US M-47 *Patton* tanks had been placed but teething troubles with the M-47s had delayed production. For a variety of reasons, not least the fact that it was the best tank in NATO in 1951, Canada purchased the *Centurion* Mk. 3 to equip not only 27 Brigade's armoured squadron, but the other armoured units based in Canada.

Some debate exists over when 27 Brigade got its first *Centurions*. According to a history of the RCD, the first vehicles were received in March 1952. However, I.M. Rettie, a member of 3 Troop at the time, recalls going to Moenchen-Gladbach to get the first *Centurions* on 6 January 1952. By February, most of the vehicles were having their 250 mile checks done after two months of intensive crew and troop training.

The provision of signals equipment was less of a problem. The Brigade's Signals Squadron and No. 2 Base Signals Troop were equipped with Canadian teletypes and field phone systems. Despatch riders on motorcycles were also used initially but the motorcycles were replaced with jeeps after a number of accidents on wet cobblestone roads. A rear link between 27 Brigade and the 'Rhine Army Net' was added in 1952; it used a No. 52 radio set, and allowed 27 Brigade to 'talk' to British divisions, I (BR) Corps and BAOR.

There was an urgent need to bring 27 CIB up to speed in an operational sense. With the Korean War on, there was always a suspicion that the Soviets would use it as a diversion while they conducted a surprise invasion of Western Europe. Forces in the Soviet Zone of Germany (not including occupied satellites like Czechoslovakia, Hungary and the Soviet Zone in Austria) as of 18 December 1951 included 10 mechanized divisions, eight tank divisions, four rifle divisions, eight anti-aircraft divisions and two artillery divisions, for a grand total of 303,100 personnel. [See Figure 1-3.] East German forces were still in an embryonic state and the Poles were having problems adapting to Communist indoctrination. The Soviets also possessed a 15:1 advantage in air power over NATO in Europe. Moreover, the Soviets were credited with the ability to reinforce with 60 more divisions after initial mobilization. Forces immediately available to SACEUR in the Integrated Force numbered 16 1/3 divisions, the bulk of the remaining NATO forces having to mobilize and transport across the Atlantic.

Pre-NATO thinking regarding the land battle for Western Europe if war occurred was extremely bleak, and influenced later planning. From 1946 to 1948 there were simply not enough Allied forces to conduct any form of coherent defence. As a result, pre-NATO defence planning focused on evacuating the Allied occupation forces from Germany. An appreciation conducted in 1947 indicated that the Soviets could reach

CHAPTER ONE

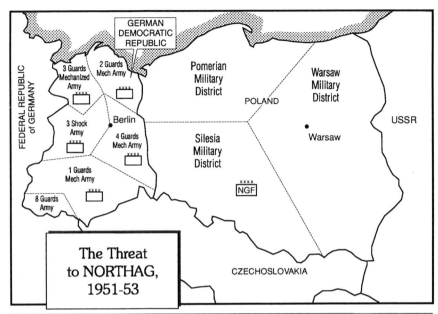

NORTHAG THREAT ORBAT 1951-53

GROUP of SOVIET OCCUPATION FORCES, GERMANY:

1st GDS MECH ARMY:
- 8 Gds Mech Div
- 9 Tk Div
- 11 Gds Tk Div

2nd GDS MECH ARMY:
- 1 Mech Div
- 9 Gds Tk Div
- 12 Gds Tk Div

3rd SHOCK ARMY:
- 18 Mech Div
- 19 Gds Mech Div
- 94 Gds Rifle Div
- 207 Rifle Div

3rd GDS MECH ARMY:
- 6 GdsTk Div
- 7 Gds Tk Div
- 9 Mtr Rifle Div
- 14 Gds Mech Div

8th GDS ARMY:
- 20 Gds Mech Div
- 21 GdsMech Div
- 39 Gds Rifle Div
- 57 Gds Rifle Div

4th GDS MECH ARMY:
- 6 Gds Mech Div
- 10 Gds Tk Div
- 11 Gds Mech Div
- 25 Tk Div

(Plus 5 Soviet Divisions in Northern Group of Forces: 2 tank, 3 infantry) (Plus 12 Polish Divisions)

FIGURE 1-3

the English Channel in eight days with little resistance.

In 1948, during the first Berlin Crisis, a number of allied contingency plans were drawn up that were more specific than the earlier plans. One of these, HALFMOON, envisaged a withdrawal to the Rhine River, followed by a fighting withdrawal to the French Mediterranean coast and the Pyrenees in Spain. No reinforcements would be available for the fighting withdrawal; the objective here was to foster "stay behind" organizations for resistance while the Allies mobilized and prepared to enter through Spain, Italy or the Middle East.

This thinking changed in principle during 1949 with the signing of the North Atlantic Treaty. It was no longer politically acceptable to abandon Western Europe and hope to retake it later. The new 1950 concept, called MC 14 or "Strategic Guidance for North Atlantic Regional Planning", noted in principle that the most desirable situation for NATO was to be able to defend on the Rhine and stop a Soviet advance there. The planners knew, however, that the forces needed to achieve this did not exist. In fact, the situation was so bleak that one appreciation noted that

> ...even if it was then possible to hold the UK, many years would elapse before we would be in a position to mount an operation on the scale of OVERLORD to liberate Europe. By that time, Russian occupation would have put an end to Western civilization.

NATO defence planning in 1951 by necessity got ahead of NATO's ability to conduct such a defence. Eisenhower's concept of operations in Western Europe revolved around the creation of two bastions, one in Denmark and one in Italy. Since the central region of Germany could not be held by existing forces, mobile Soviet divisions would rapidly fill the void and be vulnerable to counter-attacks from the north and south bastions. Some forces in the Central Region would conduct a fighting withdrawal to the best of their ability. At least that was the plan until the Integrated Force was established.

The more realistic possibility that NATO examined in 1951 included the possibility that a mobile defence of the North German Plain and Bavarian portions of Germany starting at the Elbe River could be successful, with the Rhine River and Black Forest constituting the final defensive line. [See Figure1-4.] A defence of the Ruhr was envisioned which would provide NATO with an existing bridgehead on the eastern bank of the Rhine when the counter-offensive occurred after mobilization.

These concepts were refined further in early 1952. Plan VIGILANCE reiterated the need for NATO forces to absorb the impact of the Soviet onslaught, but emphasized the extreme need to delay and deny the enemy forces mobility while a strong defence just forward of and on the Rhine was prepared. To assist in this delay effort, a portion of the still diminutive American atomic arsenal was to be deployed against the Soviets in Germany from aircraft carriers operating in the North Sea to "retard" the enemy advance.

It was against this backdrop that Brigadier Walsh developed the first emergency plans which would be implemented if a war started while the brigade was still undergoing training. The close proximity of the Soviet training areas to the border region, and the location of 27 Brigade in Hannover posed special problems. Bill Mountain, then a member of the Rifle Battalion, was in Hannover in 1952:

> So here we were, a stone's throw from the East German border and directly in the path of the main thrust of the Communist hordes should they decide to invade the West! We were front and centre of the BAOR deployment scheme and I for one slept rather uneasily for the first few nights in our new 'digs'. The Cold War suddenly took on a real life dimension that was not really discernible back home.

If the enemy chose to conduct a surprise attack, the Brigade would have less than 10 hours warning time. Therefore, 27 Brigade was placed on two hours notice to move and instructions were given to have all vehicles loaded and ready to go at all times. A Brigade Alarm Scheme was eventually established; it was based on the assumption of either a full scale attack that was unexpected or a localized East German operation which was less than full scale. On either contingency, all brigade units had to be ready to move a maximum distance of 250 miles and be able to operate without support for 48 hours.

The actual operational role for 27 Brigade within BAOR was not

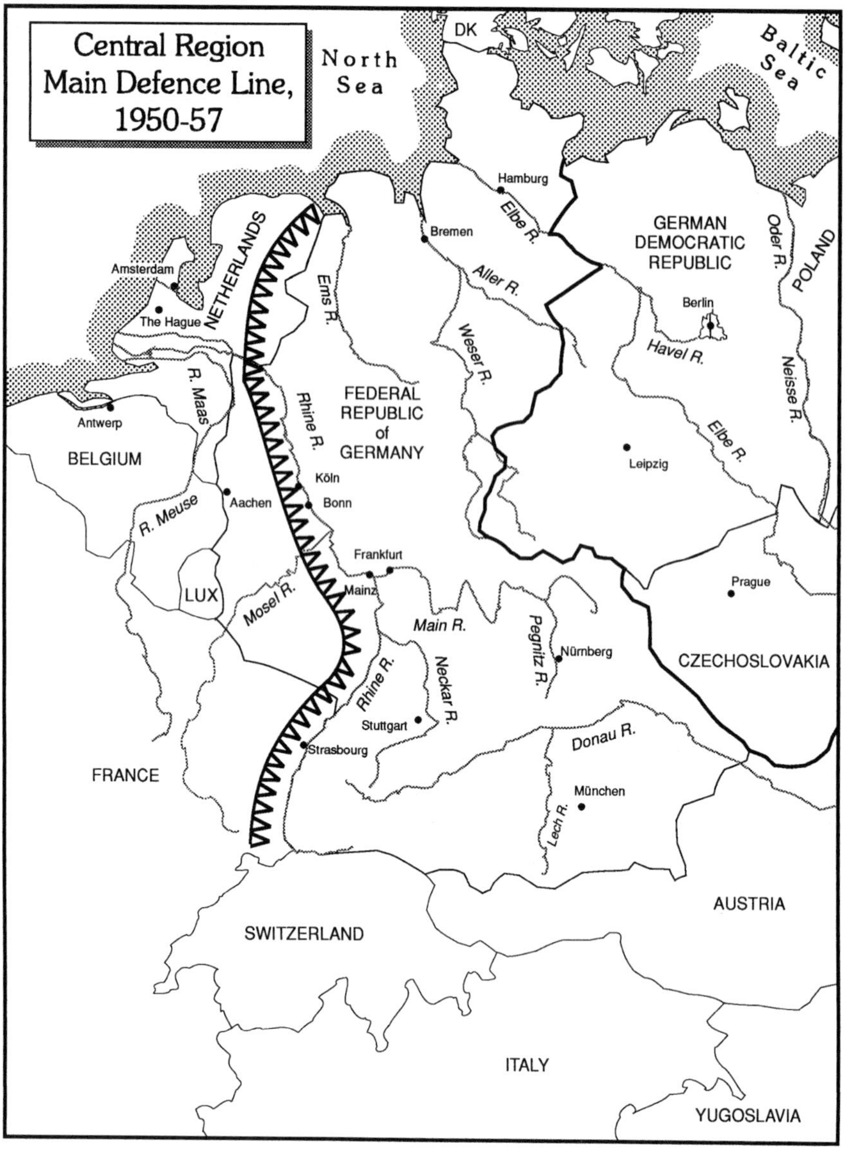
Central Region
Main Defence Line,
1950-57
North
Sea
DK
Baltic
Sea
Hamburg
Elbe R.
Bremen
GERMAN
DEMOCRATIC
REPUBLIC
Oder R.
POLAND
NETHERLANDS
Amsterdam
The Hague
Ems R.
Aller R.
Weser R.
Berlin
Havel R.
Neisse R.
R. Maas
Antwerp
Rhine R.
FEDERAL
REPUBLIC
of
GERMANY
Elbe R.
Leipzig
BELGIUM
Köln
Bonn
Aachen
R. Meuse
Frankfurt
Mainz
LUX
Mosel R.
Prague
Main R.
Pegnitz R.
Nürnberg
CZECHOSLOVAKIA
Rhine R.
Neckar R.
Stuttgart
Strasbourg
Donau R.
FRANCE
München
Lech R.
AUSTRIA
SWITZERLAND
ITALY
YUGOSLAVIA

FIGURE 1-4

CHAPTER ONE

determined until April 1952, when Brigadier Walsh attended a meeting at HQ BAOR:

> Things were ticklish at that time. There were incidents along the border. We were in Hannover and very close to East Germany; we had only the Life Guards [a British recce regiment] in front of us patrolling the border. One of their squadrons was allocated to us if there were any operations to be undertaken....
>
> General Simonds visited us shortly afterwards and by this time we had had our strategic role/tactical role given to us – which was essentially a line of defence of the Weser [river] and a final defence back on the Rhine opposite Dusseldorf...it was necessary for the commanders and myself to go back once every two months to familiarize ourselves with all the positions we might have to take up in the event of an actual emergency....

Given this broad mandate, 27 CIB had to be prepared to accept the usual wide variety of offensive and defensive options. As such, 27 CIB's training was structured to achieve proficiency in all types of operations – advance to contact, deliberate attack, deliberate defence, withdrawal, defence of a bridgehead and rearguards and the forcing of obstacles. January to March 1952 was a period of intense training at all levels; the Brigade HQ focused on Tactical Exercises Without Troops (TEWTs) and Command Post Exercises (CPXs), while the combat and support arms emphasized combined arms training to mould 27 CIB into a flexible and efficient fighting force.

It is, however, fair to say that in 1952 the defence was emphasized in 27 Brigade more than the offense. For example, the tank squadron's primary role was anti-tank defence rather than an armoured assault role, while the engineers worked at minefields and obstacle construction, with bridging becoming a secondary priority. Brigade TEWTs, sometimes conducted with I (BR) Corps, stressed defensive operations.

27 Brigade had to shape up very quickly. Lieutenant-Colonel D.K. Shaver, a Signals officer with 27 Brigade noted that:

> Training was intense in Hannover upon arrival. December and January were spent on mainly individual training in barracks; however in the next

nine months, we spent 94 days away from barracks for two or more days at a time, including six periods each of approximately two weeks on formation exercises or in concentration areas such as Sennelager, Munsterlager and Putlos, mostly under canvas....

The first Brigade training concentration was conducted from 1 April to 16 May 1952. All 27 Brigade units participated, either at Munsterlager, Soltau or Putlos training areas, the objective being to 'shoot in' all of the Brigade's weapons. The northern portion of the Munsterlager training area was declared a 'no go' area after some 27 CIB personnel discovered old German chemical munitions buried on the ranges. Putlos, on the other hand, had certain interesting benefits to Canadians training there according to John Huggins:

> We were up in Putlos, on the Baltic Sea.... The Americans put on a USO show for us, they also set up a canteen, and they were selling beer by the case. So our guys went out *buying* beer by the case, naturally, and they got out of hand. The curtain went up for the second act and the girls came on.... The Canadians got kind of rambunctious and were chasing the girls all around. We got kicked out of the show.

Bill Mountain also recalled using the Putlos training area:

> Exercises: we were constantly participating in them at various levels and it could be said from the outset that the entire country was available for this purpose. It also appeared that the weatherman was a Brigade HQ staff officer who always managed a suitable mix of rain, snow or sleet for them! The one training area I will never forget was Putlos, which was situated on the Baltic Sea adjacent to the [Inner German Border] and was large enough to accommodate full Brigade-level live firing exercises...this was possible due to the fact that the range danger area extended well out to sea. On one occasion our Battalion did a live firing night attack, including all arms supporting fire. The lines of advance were marked by MMG [Medium Machine Gun] tracer, and all supporting fire was called down by the advancing companies as per the real thing. It was a fantastic experience for those of us who had never been in combat!

All was not fun and games for many participants, however. It took the infantry battalions three days to route march the 75 miles from Hannover to Munsterlager training area, sleeping in two-man tents beside the road. C Squadron RCD worked with the 33rd Armoured Brigade from 11 (BR) Armoured Division in the Soltau area, while the remainder of 27 CIB underwent a two week period of battle group drills in delaying and defensive actions. The personnel of the Brigade HQ were not exempt either: Ex NO NAME, a CPX with 11 Armoured Division and I (BR) Corps attuned the signals people to the BAOR communications net and provided valuable insight into the workings of higher level formations, an almost lost art in the Canadian Army in the early 1950s since no allowance for any form of divisional training had been made.

After this rather gruelling work-up period, a decision came down regarding the confusing mix of weapons held by 27 Brigade. The British pattern weapons – 25 pounder guns, 2 inch and 3 inch mortars – had by now arrived in Hamburg and were issued at the end of the concentration. The 105mm howitzers and other US pattern weapons were placed in storage.

Exercise RED PATCH was conducted by 27 Brigade in conjunction with 11 Armoured Division during the first two weeks of May, with an eye towards putting into practice the lessons of the Brigade concentration. In addition to the usual defensive and offensive operations, 27 Brigade exercised its logistical system, as well as its headquarters, in an extremely realistic tactical manoeuvre. By all accounts, 27 Brigade was getting into shape, tactical decision making was falling into place and standard operating procedures were being ironed out.

27 Brigade had a brief respite in June and July 1952 before jumping off into the most demanding part of the year's training scheme. All of the 27 Brigade units participated in the Queen's Birthday Parade at Waterloo Platz in Hannover, with the commander of 11 Armoured Division and the Canadian ambassador to Germany presiding. A Brigade sports day was also held on Dominion Day, followed by a number of other social events emphasizing the Canadian identity.

By mid July, the Brigade completed initial plans for work-ups prior to the summer and fall exercise season. First off was CPX GOPHER III, in which a newly-formed '27 Canadian Recce Troop' was involved. HQ

27 CIB evidently needed more practice in HQ procedure, resulting in CPX's BADGER and RAM, while the rest of the Brigade worked-up in live firing exercises. It was at this point that the Soviet Occupation Exchange Missions in Germany or SOXMIS (pronounced 'socksmiss') were first seen covertly observing Canadian exercises.

2 Field Security Section was responsible for intelligence and counter intelligence operations as well as general security awareness within 27 Brigade. After training at the US Army Intelligence School at Fort Holabird in the United States, 2 FSS deployed to Germany and went to work. Jack Martin, a member of 2 FSS, noted that there was a problem with "I" Cards, as identity cards were called then:

> At the time of the arrival of the Brigade in Germany it must be remembered that there were hundreds of thousands of refugees with no identification to any part of the country at all. Consequently, any type of identification was extremely valuable, particularly to our friends across the border, the Russians. Tracking down the continual loss of identity cards from the infantry battalions took a bit of investigation because a lot of soldiers were young and hadn't served overseas before. We finally determined that many of the bars in Hannover and around were accepting identity cards as the value for drinks... These were not earth shattering problems [but] we know for sure that some did in actual fact make it over the border....

Exercise SPEARHEAD II kicked off on 19 August 1952. A very important exercise, SPEARHEAD II was a BAOR affair with Canadian participation designed as a work up for the first significant large scale NATO exercises scheduled for the fall and as such was a good indicator of operational planning within BAOR in 1952. [See Figure 1-5.]

27 Brigade was part of *Redland* (enemy forces) for the exercise, contrary to the emphasis placed on the defence in earlier training. As part of 11 (BR) Armoured Division, 27 Brigade's tasks were to advance and acquire crossings on the Leine river, followed by an assault crossing of the Weser river near Hoya. To achieve the objective, 11 Armoured Division was to advance on a two brigade front, with 91 Lorried Infantry Brigade to the left and 27 Brigade to the right. 33 Armoured Brigade was the Divisional reserve. The *Blueland* forces had a brigade-sized

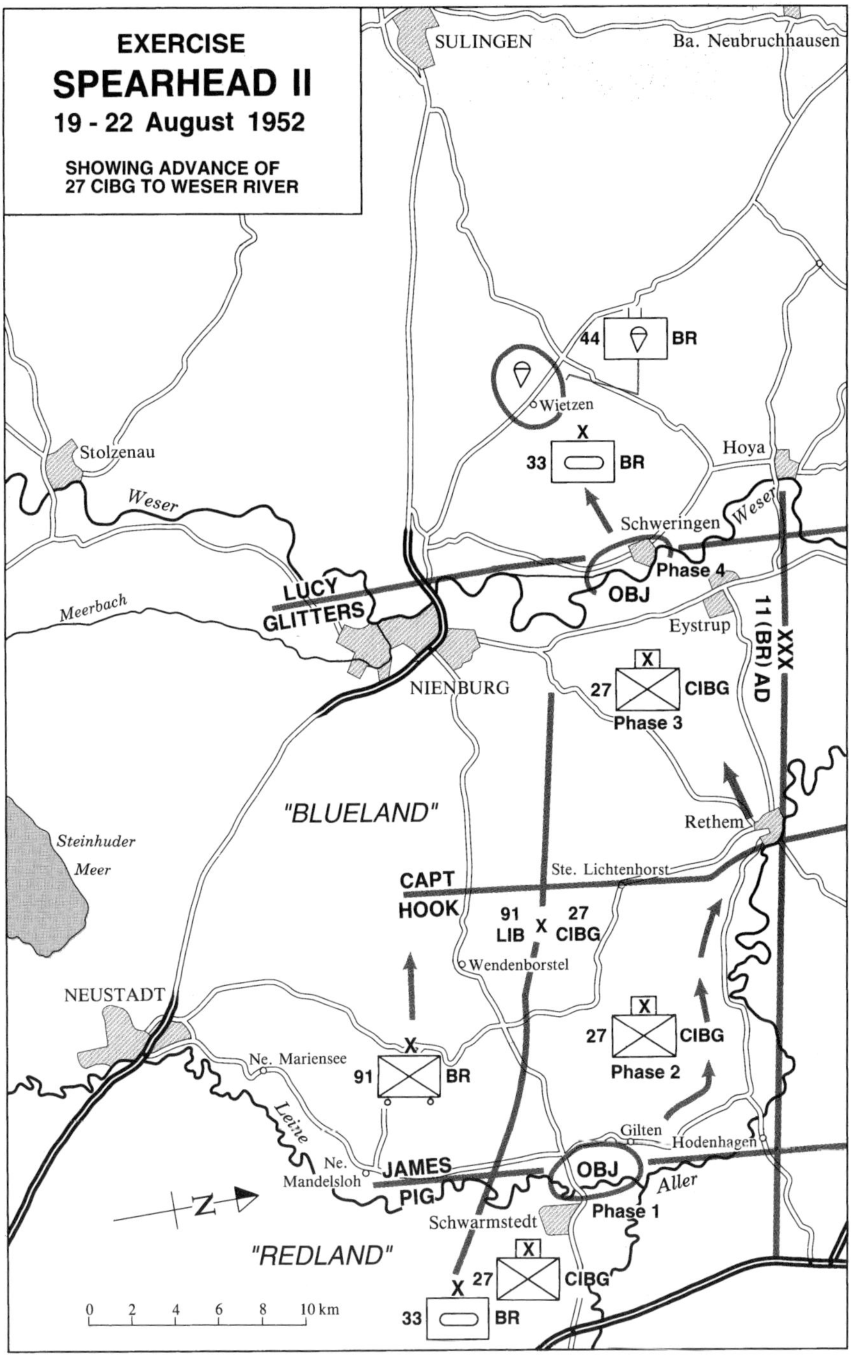
EXERCISE
SPEARHEAD II
19 - 22 August 1952
SHOWING ADVANCE OF
27 CIBG TO WESER RIVER
SULINGEN
Ba. Neubruchhausen
44 BR
Wietzen
X
33 BR
Hoya
Stolzenau
Weser
Schweringen
Weser
Phase 4
OBJ
LUCY
GLITTERS
Meerbach
Eystrup
NIENBURG
27 CIBG
Phase 3
XXX
11 (BR) AD
"BLUELAND"
Rethem
Steinhuder
Meer
Ste. Lichtenhorst
CAPT
HOOK
91
LIB
X
27
CIBG
Wendenborstel
NEUSTADT
27 CIBG
Phase 2
91 BR
Ne. Mariensee
Leine
Gilten
Hodenhagen
Ne.
Mandelsloh
JAMES
PIG
OBJ
Aller
Phase 1
Z
Schwarmstedt
"REDLAND"
27 CIBG
X
33 BR
0 2 4 6 8 10 km

FIGURE 1-5

covering force east of the Weser, with a number of observation posts along the west bank. Three brigades were positioned as a mobile reserve on the west bank to counter-attack any assault crossing.

The commander of 11 Armoured Division placed substantial British resources under 27 Brigade's command. These included an engineer squadron, an anti-aircraft regiment, an infantry transport company, three armoured vehicle launched bridges and a company of infantry. In addition, 27 Brigade also had in support 58 Independent Squadron Royal Engineers and a bailey bridge. In return, the Brigade 'lost' to 91 LIB 1st Canadian Rifle Battalion and 79 Field Squadron, RCE.

In a four phase operation, 27 Brigade was to advance to and cross the River Leine, bypass insignificant opposition, advance to the Weser River and prepare an assault crossing to the west bank. Rapidly advancing on a two battalion front in trucks provided by 111 Coy, RASC, 27 Brigade crossed the Redland/Blueland frontier of the Leine River after seizing a bridge by "coup de main". Proceeding west, light opposition around Retham was bypassed. Within 72 hours, the Canadian Highland and Infantry battalions had 'bounced' the Weser river in assault boats, allowing the engineers to emplace a bailey bridge across at Schweringin; the first *Centurions* of 33 Armoured Brigade crossed some hours afterward and penetrated deep into Blueland's rear area. Jack Martin was an intelligence officer in 27 Brigade HQ:

> The first task that was given to us was the crossing of the Weser River at various locations at night. Fortunately I'm an air photo interpreter, and with a little pull from BAOR, I was able to get really first class air photographs of all the areas we were going to cross at.... This was rather new to the forces on the ground because they hadn't used their photography in quite that close-up way; we had instant information… It became quite obvious to us in Brigade that the British forces opposite us were trying to do a major outflanking manoeuvre. We lost contact with one of their brigades. It appeared that they had left very weak defences along the part of the river which led straight down to their divisional artillery group. By using these air photographs and working at night, we were able to infiltrate a company of the Rifle Battalion across the river. We met no opposition, so the Brigade just flooded [through] the rest of the battalion and we arrived in the enemy's div artillery group in the morning

saying 'hello!', and that screwed up the exercise right there....

Brigadier Walsh:

> Believe it or not the Highland Battalion captured the First Royal Horse Artillery and their guns, and this was the first time they'd lost their guns in their history, either on an exercise or in war. All the other British gunners flopped around to see the RHA, and by god there was almost a fistfight. They weren't going to give the guns up, but eventually the umpires prevailed. They were in the bag! ...I ran into the Divisional Commander later. We were out watching the A-Bomb test at White Sands and he was still mad as hell when he heard about that exercise. In fact, he got rather rude about it....

Blueland counterattacks were repulsed by the infantry battalions' 17 pounder anti-tank guns. To assist in the exploitation of the bridgehead, the British 44 Para Battalion Group was dropped to secure an important crossroads at Wietzen to assist with the penetration. This was all quite anti-climatic in the wake of 27 Brigade's operation.

SPEARHEAD II was a considerable success for 27 Brigade. Operating in a role for which they had not trained, 27 Brigade had effected the most demanding of military tasks: an assault river crossing, with less than six months of collective training as a formation and only limited collaboration with other Allied units. This was truly a significant accomplishment.

The next important manoeuvre 27 Brigade participated in was Exercise HOLDFAST, held in September 1952. HOLDFAST was the largest western exercise to be held since 1945. Two hundred thousand troops participated from the armies of Canada, the UK, Belgium and the Netherlands; 800 aircraft also were involved from 2 Allied Tactical Air Force (2 ATAF), a new NATO command created to provide air support to NATO units working with BAOR. In general terms, HOLDFAST had many objectives. There was a distinct need to develop liaison procedures between the different armies, particularly between BAOR and the Belgians and the Dutch. Equally important, techniques had to be found so that BAOR could operate under conditions of enemy air superiority, a problem endemic to BAOR and the terrain over which it was to fight.

Thirdly, a factor critical to the morale of NATO forces in northern Germany was the need to change over rapidly from the defensive to the offensive with an eye toward keeping the enemy off balance while reinforcements poured into Europe.

Unlike SPEARHEAD II, Exercise HOLDFAST placed 27 Brigade in a defensive role [See Figure 1-6.]. BAOR was testing new defensive concepts and HOLDFAST was the testing ground, as Jack Martin recalled:

> [We created] hardened points, defensive positions, to break up the flow of an inundating Russian force, which would flow around the hardened core. [We were to be able to] attack outwardly from the core of the bastion in any direction and also had to be able to move forces back and forth across the perimeter [of the core].... Anybody knowledgeable of the town of Soest knows it was ideally located because there is a central roundabout in the centre of the city, and all the roads radiate out to the next town like spokes on a wheel...

27 Brigade occupied the central position in a series of three major bastions belonging to Blueland; the Dutch were to defend a fortified area at Beckum, 27 Brigade another (coincidentally) at Soest, while the Belgians held Ruthen. The covering force consisted of the British 6th Armoured and 11th Armoured Divisions, which would start their battle on the Weser river. Eventually, the armoured divisions would conduct a rearward passage of lines through the main defensive area and form a reserve for later counter-attacks, with 11 Armoured Division passing through the Soest area. The opposing 'Greenland' Army was armour heavy and consisted of the British 7th Armoured Division, the 4th Belgian Infantry Brigade Group, a composite airborne battalion group and elements of the British Special Air Service.

27 Brigade's orders for HOLDFAST were explicit:

> 27 Cdn Inf Bde Gp will occupy and convert SOEST into a bastion for all round defence which will be denied to the enemy at all costs and hold, even if completely surrounded, for seven days without supply or maintenance.

The town of Soest was converted into a fortified bastion, with the

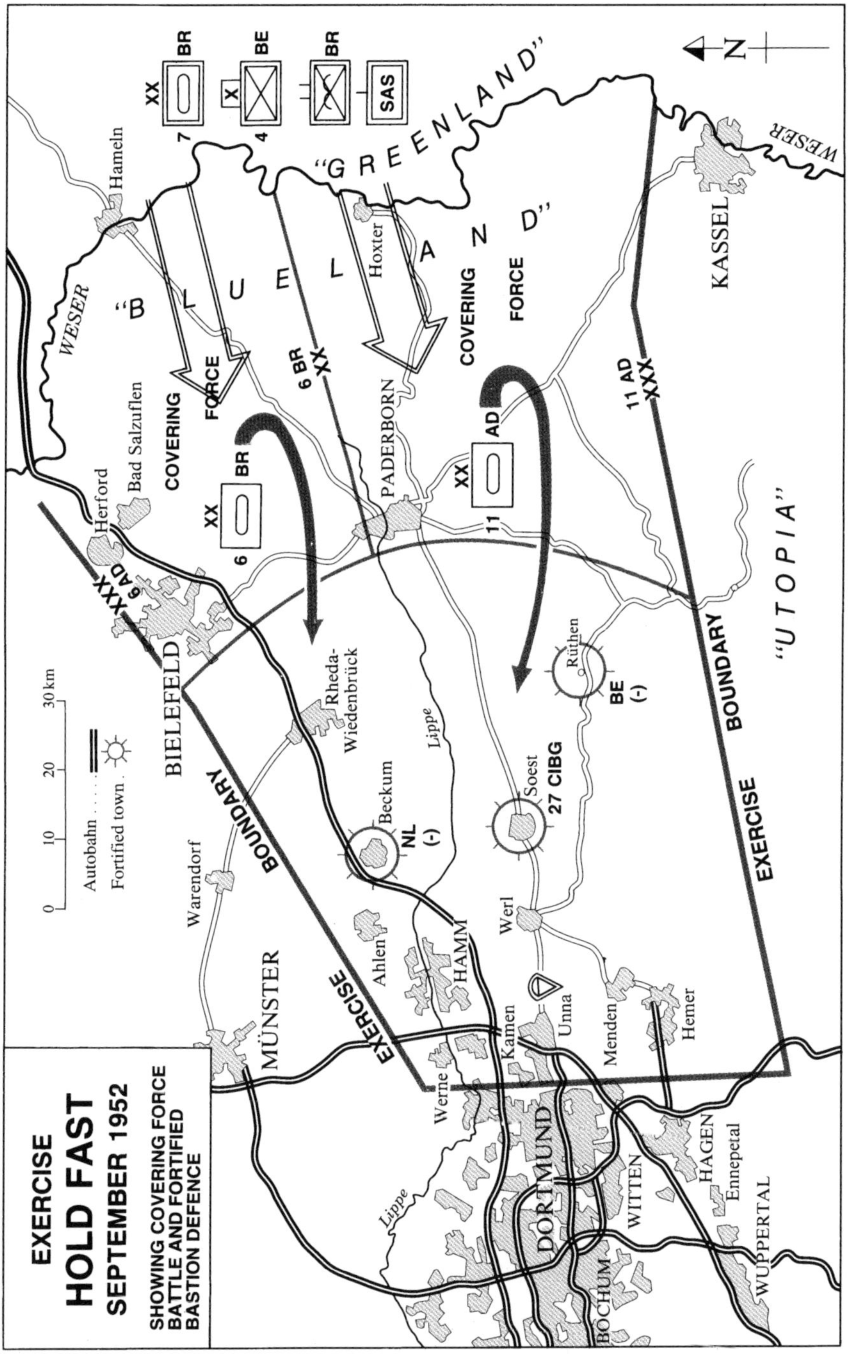
EXERCISE
HOLD FAST
SEPTEMBER 1952
SHOWING COVERING FORCE
BATTLE AND FORTIFIED
BASTION DEFENCE
Autobahn
Fortified town
0 10 20 30 km
N
"GREENLAND"
"BLUELAND"
"UTOPIA"
COVERING FORCE
COVERING FORCE
EXERCISE BOUNDARY
EXERCISE BOUNDARY
7 BR
4 BE
BR
SAS
6 BR
11 AD
6 AD
6 BR
11 AD
NL (-)
27 CIBG
BE (-)
WESER
WESER
Lippe
Lippe
Hameln
Bad Salzuflen
Herford
BIELEFELD
Hoxter
PADERBORN
KASSEL
Rheda-Wiedenbrück
Rüthen
Warendorf
Beckum
Soest
MÜNSTER
Ahlen
HAMM
Werl
Unna
Kamen
Werne
Menden
Hemer
DORTMUND
WITTEN
HAGEN
Ennepetal
WUPPERTAL
BOCHUM

FIGURE 1-6

infantry battalions deployed in a full circle, concentric minefields and demolitions. All tube artillery, be it 17 or 25 pounders, were positioned to provide 360 degrees fire support around Soest. An infantry company from 1st Canadian Rifle Battalion and C Squadron RCD formed the counter-attack force. Aggressive patrolling was the order of the day while the engineers set about developing the obstacle plan; *Greenland* had dropped an airborne battalion group near Unna with an eye towards harassing Blueland's rear area.

After fighting a 48 hour covering force battle, the weary tank crews of 11 Armoured Division in their *Centurions* passed through the Canadian checkpoints around Soest to their reconstitution areas. While the passage of lines was being conducted, the Greenland army attacked the British while 'enemy' air attacks temporarily disrupted 27 Brigade's defensive preparations. On 20 September, 27 Brigade's Recce Troop spotted two squadrons of Greenland armour advancing along the highway towards Soest; by 1115 hrs, the 'enemy' came into contact with the main defensive positions and attempted to probe through; by 1845 hrs, these probes were not successful and Greenland retreated.

This respite was only temporary. As the sun was dawning the next day, 27 Brigade was attacked with heavy shelling and rocket fire and by 1045 hrs, was under attack again by elements of two Greenland armoured divisions. This see-saw action lasted all day; 27 Brigade gave no ground and the attack fell off after dark. Brigadier Walsh took advantage of the situation and called on his battalion commanders to conduct aggressive night patrols in preparation for a brigade counter-attack from the bastion. This attack was launched the next morning on 22 September, led by the tanks of the RCD and the Highland Battalion. 27 Brigade proceeded to throw the Greenland forces off balance and by 1400 hrs Blueland forces had no contact with the enemy, who had been driven off. Greenland had succeeded elsewhere, particularly against the Belgians in Ruthen, but the Canadian bastion held.

The bastion defence concept was not adopted, however, as a more mobile defence was necessary in the face of the increasingly 'nuclearized' battlefield. Unfortunately, the exercise was not without cost; five members of the Brigade were killed in motor vehicle accidents, a lasting reminder to 27 Brigade that the price of peace was not only eternal vigilance.

After Endex, 27 Brigade was visited by British Minister of Defence and former Governor General, Lord Alexander of Tunis, accompanied by a German delegation. The British were favourably impressed with 27 Brigade's performance on Exercise HOLDFAST; the Germans were starting to rebuild their army and had wanted to observe the Canadians in action.

A summary of 27 Brigade's status as of September 1952 noted that:

> The end of this month marks the close of another phase in the training and development of 27 CIB Gp.... Much has been achieved in its nine months in Germany both from an administrative and training points of view. While most units and Brigade HQ were formed on 7 May 51 it wasn't until our arrival in Europe that we became self dependent.... The primary task was to become operational as quickly as possible for two reasons. Firstly, world tension demanded a state of readiness if disaster was to be avoided in case of war, and secondly, if the Brigade were to fully benefit from the summer training with the British and Allied nations higher formations we would have to match their soldiering skills... the operational readiness of the Brigade as a group is of much higher order than the soldiering skills of the individual. The Commander is aware of this shortcoming and the next training period is designed to raise the individual standards....

After this extremely intense period of training, the personnel of 27 Brigade could afford to relax to some degree. Hannover, contrary to belief, did have some entertainment facilities which did improve with time. There was no Maple Leaf Services organization, but the equivalent was the NAAFI which provided over fifteen canteens and grocery stores to British formations in Hannover; there was the '27 Club', and Wesley House, and that old Canadian standby, the Salvation Army's Red Shield Club. The Globe Theatre, run by the Army Kinema Corporation, had first run movies like "The African Queen" and "High Noon"; francophone personnel had access to Hoch Haus Cinema, which showed French movies. The British Forces Network radio station in Germany had Canadian content, including a morning Canadian news rebroadcast. Radio shows like "Wayne and Shuster", "The Happy Gang", "Don Messer", and the

"Maple Leaf Hour", were also brought in from a huge new Canadian Broadcasting Corporation short wave transmitter located near Sackville, New Brunswick.

Later, in 1953, a popular musical group from Canada called The Rainbow Strings visited Hannover and Hohne. This troupe, led by Marguerite Learning, quickly sold out at the box office and played to a packed house over three nights. It was not necessarily the music that drew 27 CIB personnel; as one member told the press, "Canadian girls! I don't care if they play music or not. I just want to sit and look at them!".

Not all 27 Brigade members were interested in 'Canadian Content', as one observer recalled:

> ...things were very cheap in Germany at that time, and women were a dime a dozen. As a matter of fact the main park in Hannover, the Stadt Park, or as they used to call it "two mark park", because you could have a woman there for two marks....

The military police of No. 27 Provost Detachment concurred with this assessment:

> The writer has met and corrected troops in all of their recreational habitats; there has never been a deliberate attack on Provo personnel by the troops which speaks well for good discipline...[some] unsoldierly social conduct is not, however, surprising when one considers the educational and cultural backgrounds of the average troops. This situation is aggravated by their naiveness and the amount of sinful temptations which abound in Germany today...

As a result, certain locations in Hannover were placed out of bounds by the brigade staff, and 27 Brigade members could not avail themselves of the pleasures of the house on Buebel Strasse or the seemingly innocuous Hamburger Hof restaurant or the Spanner Cafe.

Canadian soldiers will be Canadian soldiers, be they men from 27 Canadian Infantry Brigade during the Cold War, from First Canadian Army during the Second World War or the Canadian Expeditionary Force from the First World War. Captain R.M. Whelan served with 1st Canadian Rifle Battalion:

> The Battalion at that time was largely made up of very young and inexperienced soldiers. Many had never been away from home at that time and military discipline was very new to them. The result of this was that many committed minor offences, which resulted in many being tried and awarded a punishment, the majority of which resulted in a fine, confinement to barracks or pack drill (this was still an authorized punishment in those days). Pack drill was not an uncommon punishment. It was therefore not uncommon to see the Battalion Orderly Sergeant along with all the Company Orderly Corporals drilling as many as 100 or more on the Battalion parade square between 1900-2000 hrs....

Unfortunately, the media blew the Canadian soldiers' recreational habits out of proportion in a most public fashion.

Writing in *Maclean's* magazine, Lionel Shapiro referred to 27 Brigade personnel as second class soldiers and characterized them as being pre-occupied with wine and women and not with soldiering. Shapiro suggested that Canadian soldiers serving with 27 Brigade were "indifferent in military efficiency, to esprit de corps, in appearance and behaviour". Shapiro may have been expecting too much, based on the genesis of the formation, and was confusing parade ground standards with the requirement that 27 Brigade personnel be ready to fight against overwhelming odds while being stationed less than 70 kilometers from the Inner German Border. Denigrating 27 Brigade's commander, Shapiro also suggested that the Canadians were below the standards of the other NATO forces in BAOR, an assessment at odds with 27 Brigade's performance on SPEARHEAD II and HOLDFAST.

Shapiro, being a supporter of peacetime conscription, clearly had an agenda of his own. But by portraying 27 Brigade personnel in the fashion he did, he not only damaged his own case for military reform but provided fodder for the enemy's propaganda machine, which regularly spewed lies and hype from Radio Leipzig in the Soviet Zone in an attempt to cause agitation amongst and against NATO forces. In some cases, alleged 'Canadian excess' was exploited for maximum benefit in Communist newspapers and by German newspapers critical of the British occupation.

The reality of the situation was that there had been some 'bad apples' in 27 Brigade, but almost all had been sent home prior to February 1952. These individuals had been met at the dockside in Halifax by reporters who erroneously thought they were 27 Brigade personnel on normal rotation and as a result, horribly exaggerated stories about 27 Brigade abounded. To be fair, the issue was a *cause celèbre* in the Canadian press for a period and as a result Shapiro was allowed to put together an Army indoctrination pamphlet called "Off To Europe" so that future unpleasantries could be avoided.

Press problems notwithstanding, Canadians acquitted themselves quite well in Europe. Leave was available – up to two weeks per year – and Status of Forces arrangements within NATO guaranteed a wide variety of travel options on the continent. The most popular place was Britain, probably due to the minimal language barrier. Richard Ross of the RCEME:

> As we weren't allowed week-end passes, if there was enough interest we could visit places of interest near Hannover accompanied by an officer. During my two years I enjoyed my leave periods in England, Scotland, France, Belgium and Holland. I was able to visit my uncle's grave near Vimy Ridge.... When we went to England on leave we had to take a ration card as the English were still on rations from the war. Even to buy a candy bar you had to show your ration card! A German civvie mechanic said to me one day, 'Who lost the war: us or the British?' The only thing the Germans seemed to be short of was coffee.

Wives were not officially recognized, since there were not supposed to be any Canadian dependents in Europe, and there were no facilities for them. Despite this, some 27 Brigade members did have their wives ensconcd in Hannover, but did so 'on the economy'.

To forestall problems between 27 Brigade and the civil population, Brigadier Walsh reinstituted the position of "Town Major", an idea common during the First and Second World Wars. 27 Brigade's Town Major was responsible for discipline, dress and deportment of Brigade personnel 'on the town'. Liaising closely with No 27 Provost Detachment and the local *Polizei*, the TM had a number of roving patrols similar to today's Regimental Police and would assist with maintaining the peace.

By November 1952, the 1900 personnel who were married rotated back to Canada, while the unmarried members remained for another year. With this rotation, a new Brigade Commander arrived to take over from Brigadier Walsh.

Brigadier J.E.C. Pangman had commanded two infantry battalions during the Second World War, the Carleton and York Regiment in Italy and the Essex and Kent Scottish in North West Europe. Afterwards, Brigadier Pangman served with the Directorate of Military Operations and Plans, and commanded the National Defence College in Kingston.

After a breaking-in period, with Brigadier Walsh acting as guide, the formal change of command occurred at 2400 hrs 4 December 1952. Other changes were in the offing. SACEUR had recently consolidated all land forces committed to NATO's Integrated Force units in Northern and Southern Germany, and had formed two new multinational NATO headquarters in November; these were HQ Northern Army Group (NORTHAG) and HQ Central Army Group (CENTAG). Thus, NORTHAG, under command of General Sir Richard Gale, consisted of I (Belgian) Corps, I (British) Corps, I (Netherlands) Corps and 27 Canadian Infantry Brigade Group, which was part of I (BR) Corps, with BAOR acting as the British national headquarters. CENTAG remained the preserve of the Americans and the French.

The implication of this change was that 27 Brigade was no longer under command of BAOR in war *per se*; elements of BAOR were to be operationally transferred to NORTHAG on initiation of hostilities, while BAOR still handled administrative arrangements. This allowed the Canadian Army to have officers on the staff of NORTHAG HQ and participate in planning at a level higher than division, thus giving the Canadian Army a say in the operational employment of 27 Brigade.

Brigadier Pangman followed Brigadier Walsh's lead with regard to the 27 Brigade training scheme for 1953. As previously noted, there were some deficiencies with individual training, and steps were taken to get 'back to basics'. To do so, each infantry battalion rotated through Putlos on live fire exercises at the section and platoon level. In order to improve the quality of the NCOs, a 27 CIB NCO School was organized. The Brigade HQ needed refresher training and a CPX was laid on. To maintain the standard of dealing with divisions, study weeks were developed between 27 Brigade and 11 Armoured Division. Another new imperative emanating from BAOR emphasized the need to improve night operations capability; in addition, all combat arms personnel within the Brigade were to be trained in simple demolition operations.

As the training year continued into February 1953, flood waters threatened to inundate Overflakee Island in the Netherlands. To assist in combating this unexpected threat from the west, 58th Independent Field Squadron, Royal Canadian Engineers was committed in a spirit of inter-NATO cooperation.

In terms of basing, the initial locations of the 27 Brigade units in and around Hannover were considered to be temporary until BAOR could provide new bases. To do so, BAOR had initiated construction of new bases in the Soest area, with the understanding that 27 Brigade would occupy them until the Canadian commitment was no longer required, i.e. some time in the mid to late 1950s. The Canadian Government had made abundantly clear that Canada did not wish to own troop accommodations in Germany, and was prepared to rent or borrow.

One particular area that warrants examination was 27 Brigade's logistics system, a system that continually evolved throughout 1952-1953. Since 27 Brigade and its maintenance in Europe was not high on the defence priority list, the Government had a tendency to 'piggy back' logistical arrangements onto the British system, which, according to SACEUR, was incapable of taking care of itself. As one officer involved in logistical planning in 1953 noted:

> Everybody had a logistics problem.... To start, there were no war reserves. Britain had what they thought were their war reserves. The French had what they thought was theirs, the Americans had what they thought was theirs. Canada didn't have any war reserves; we had to go out and buy them from the Brits. The Canadian attitude then became, 'Oh God, lets get them for as little as we possibly can. Let's go ask the Brits to give us the war reserves, and we'll pay for them if we need them'. Wonderful Canadian deal. Let's make the British pay to establish our war reserves and we will pay them back if we use them. I was on the receiving end of the statement that said, 'Britain will not set aside one single round for which you do not pay at the start'. It was great fun sending that information back to Canada, who didn't want to

hear it at all....

The logistics end of things was not without its lighter side. An incoming telex from the Quartermaster General regarding rotation personnel arriving at a holding brigade in Canada before heading to Germany is noteworthy:

> Para One: Would appreciate more detailed information particularly re personnel who arrived at 25 CIB Replacement Group without weapons. From what units did these personnel come?
> Para Two: This information necessary if proper persons are to be scalped.

There also was the great Russian salmon fiasco. BAOR quartermaster personnel purchased canned Russian salmon from the Soviet Zone and distributed it within the BAOR area. Since 27 Brigade relied on BAOR for ration support, 27 Brigade units received the salmon as part of the ration quota. Unfortunately, the Conservative defence critic in opposition arrived for a visit in Hannover and promptly turned the issue into political caviar. Needless to say, 27 Brigade ceased to consume Russian salmon.

Britain could not, of course, provide complete logistical support to 27 Brigade. The US pattern equipment that had been replaced with British pattern equipment on the brigade's arrival remained in storage in Germany so that another brigade group could be sent over an equipped on short notice; this despite the lack of compatibility that would result between the two formations. Some commodities and equipment which were peculiarly Canadian – like uniforms, cigarettes, mail and the like – still had to be brought forward without resorting to the overtasked British system. Finally, a semi-formal stopgap arrangement was worked out between 27 Brigade, BAOR and United States European Command (USEUCOM). Equipment common between 27 Brigade and BAOR was supplied through the BAOR depots at Mönchen–Gladbach, as was petroleum, oil and lubricants. Spares for 27 Brigade's US-pattern equipment beyond the 60 days worth held by the Brigade were located on the west bank of the Rhine at a depot near Viersen. One year's worth of ammunition or US-pattern weapons was also held by the Brigade. 27

Brigade was responsible for clothing, personal kit, first and second line vehicle maintenance and for Canadian-pattern items. A special emergency deal was made with USEUCOM whereby complete vehicles, maintenance for them and ammunition could be acquired once hostilities started. These arrangements though were not 'in stone', and posed problems in the future.

Several 27 Brigade units were consolidated under the command of HQ Canadian Base Units, Europe (HQ CBUE) to facilitate the logistical path from Canada to 27 Brigade in Germany, in addition to improving its survivability if war broke out. HQ CBUE included 3 Canadian Administration Unit; 1 Canadian Base Ordnance Unit; 2 Line of Communication Postal Unit; 2 Medical Liaison Detachment; 4 Canadian Motorcycle Group, RCASC; 2 Base Signal Troop, Royal Canadian Corps of Signals, and 27 Field Detention Barracks.

Since 27 Brigade was positioned so far forward and given the operational task to defend opposite Dussldorf, it was necessary to place HQ CBUE somewhere in the rear behind the Rhine. The existing British lines of support or Communications Zone, extended back from the Rhine into Belgium and the Netherlands, where incoming men and materiel could be brought in by ship into one of the large ports.

The establishment of a Canadian Communications Zone required the participation of the Department of External Affairs, as legal agreements had to be made between Belgium and Canada to allow for the stationing of Canadian troops in Belgium in peacetime. This, of course, took time. An attempt by 27 Brigade to 'infiltrate' 1 CBUE into Belgium alongside British logistical units (Op GONDOLA) was not appreciated by the Belgians.

Eventually, Canada completed an agreement with Belgium under the auspices of NATO which allowed for the placement of HQ CBUE in the great port of Antwerp, which Canada had liberated during the last war. Located in the former convent of Notre Dame de Sion in downtown Antwerp, 1 CBUE dutifully provided rear area logistical support to Canadian Army units in Germany throughout the 1950s. Its relationship to 27 Brigade was that of a subordinate organization acting as the rear link between 27 Brigade and Canada.

27 Brigade continued its training scheme throughout the first months

of 1953. To keep the proficiency of the infantry battalions up to par, Brigadier Pangman initiated the TRAMPLE series of exercises in April. TRAMPLE I, II and III were battalion-level exercises designed to prepare 27 Brigade for work-ups with 7th Armoured Division in May.

Exercise COMMONWEALTH was the next stage in the training program. The close relationship 27 Brigade had forged with 11 Armoured Division in the past had been terminated, as 7th Armoured Division now took its place in the line. Accordingly, 27 CIB had to 're-acclimatize', with Exercise COMMONWEALTH providing the opportunity to develop new ties with this and other British formations.

This exercise was held in the Soltau training area during May, and was essentially a divisional workup for large scale NATO exercises scheduled for the fall. Unlike other larger exercises, COMMONWEALTH was a one-sided affair, that is, a live enemy force was not provided, the intention being to work on the squadron/company/combat team level of operations. Tactically, 7th Armoured Division and 27 Brigade practiced a covering force battle forward of the River Luhe north of Munster, employment which was quite different from earlier exercises.

A more ambitious exercise, JAVELIN FIVE [See Figure 1-7], was conducted on the actual terrain 27 CIB was supposed to defend in the event of a real war. JAVELIN FIVE, tactically, was similar in scale and in scope to Exercise COMMONWEALTH; 27 Brigade was again operating with its old friends, 11 Armoured Division.

In JAVELIN FIVE, 27 Brigade was tasked with securing vital bridges across the Rhine in the Dusseldorf-Neuss area from airborne assault. While this was going on, 11 Armoured Division engineers created a demolition belt extending from the Dortmund-Ems Canal to the River Lenne. A small covering force fought forward of the demolition belt, while the remainder of 11 Armoured Division established defensive positions behind it. 27 Brigade had to keep the bridges intact so that 11 Armoured Division could conduct a withdrawal across the Rhine.

It is interesting to compare Ex JAVELIN FIVE to Ex HOLDFAST. It is clear that, if these exercises are superimposed on each other, I British Corps was planning to conduct a fighting withdrawal with a covering force from the Weser River to a fortified area near Soest, where the enemy would be canalized by the road network. If the enemy was

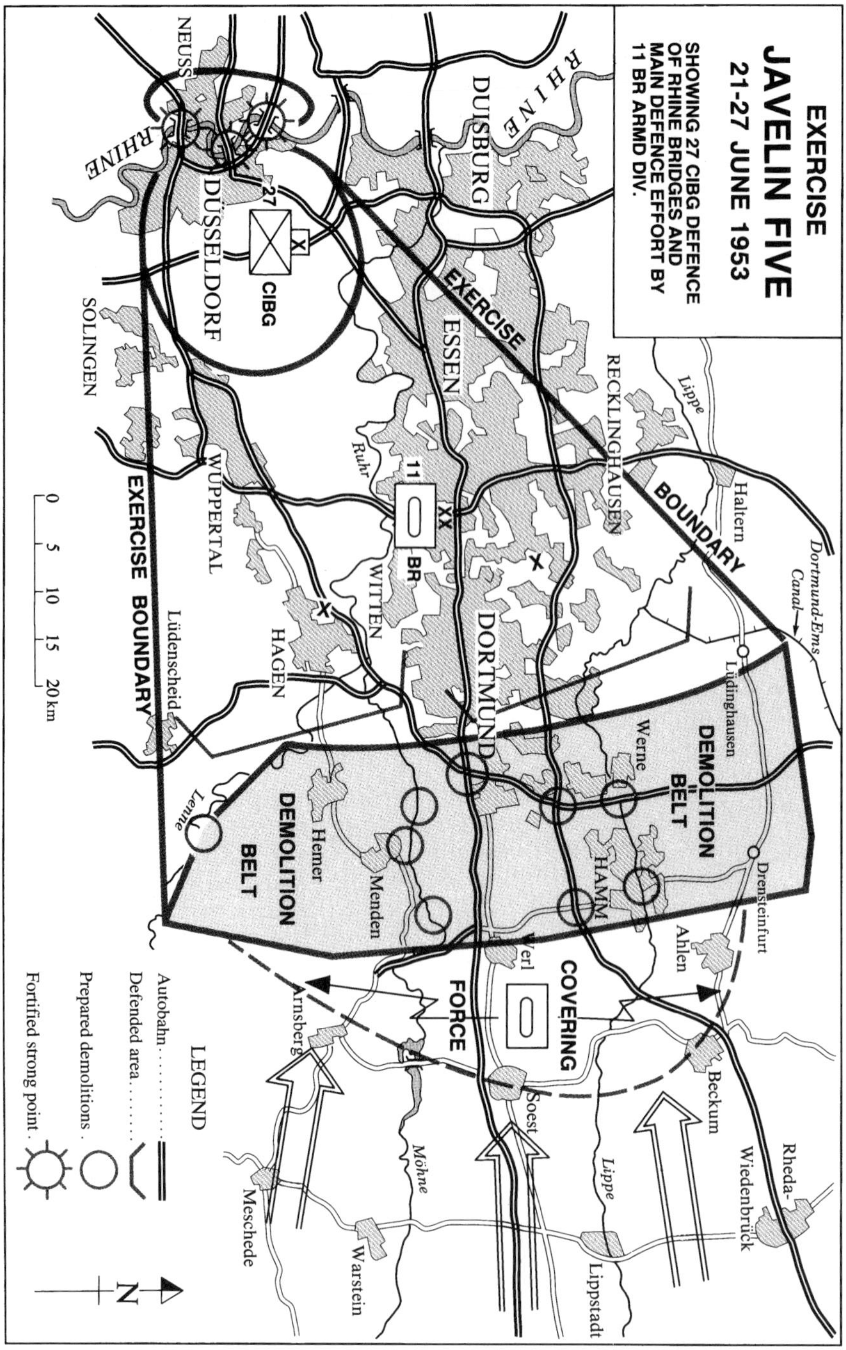
EXERCISE
JAVELIN FIVE
21-27 JUNE 1953
SHOWING 27 CIBG DEFENCE OF RHINE BRIDGES AND MAIN DEFENCE EFFORT BY 11 BR ARMD DIV.
RHINE
DUISBURG
NEUSS
RHINE
DÜSSELDORF
27
CIBG
SOLINGEN
ESSEN
EXERCISE BOUNDARY
RECKLINGHAUSEN
Lippe
Ruhr
11
XX
BR
WUPPERTAL
WITTEN
HAGEN
Lüdenscheid
EXERCISE BOUNDARY
DORTMUND
Haltern
Dortmund-Ems Canal
Lüdinghausen
Werne
DEMOLITION BELT
HAMM
Drensteinfurt
Ahlen
Lenne
Hemer
Menden
DEMOLITION BELT
Werl
COVERING FORCE
Arnsberg
Soest
Beckum
Rheda-Wiedenbrück
Möhne
Lippe
Meschede
Warstein
Lippstadt
0 5 10 15 20 km
LEGEND
Autobahn
Defended area
Prepared demolitions
Fortified strong point
N

FIGURE 1-7

not stopped here, a belt behind the fortified area was to have been prepared for denial; behind the denial area were more fortified positions with mobile formations. If the bridges over the Rhine could be kept open and protected against a parachute drop, reinforcements could be fed into the battle to counter-attack, or, the covering forces could be withdrawn and the bridges blown. The Rhine itself would have presented a formidable obstacle to the Soviets, assuming that they had not been worn down by the other defensive preparations. 27 Brigade's role in this operational planning was crucial; since it was an infantry-heavy formation, it was well suited for the defensive tasks envisioned by this planning. By holding a fortified position or ensuring that the Rhine bridge system remained in NATO hands, it is fair to suggest that 27 Brigade formed the anchor for the defensive plan within I British Corps in the 1952-1953 period.

The conduct of NORTHAG's primary fall exercise, Exercise GRAND REPULSE [See Figure 1-8], did not fall into line with the defensive thinking that I British Corps had focused on, however. SACEUR's concept of operations for 1953 was predicated on an initial contact line running roughly south of Bremen to Switzerland. By the end of the fourth day of operations, SHAPE planners believed that the forward edge of the battle area would be contracting towards the Rhine, with the enemy conducting airborne operations to seize bridges, much in line with the exercises conducted within I British Corps. Where SACEUR's concept differed from this was the prediction that the enemy would conduct an amphibious landing in the Netherlands to turn the left flank of NORTHAG and jeopardize the RAM offensive line on the Rhine.

Exercise GRAND REPULSE (19 to 25 September 1953) was structured to develop a plan to meet this amphibious threat to the left flank. An area north and northeast of Bremen [See Figure 1-8], simulated the North Sea, while 2nd (British) Infantry Division and a Danish Battle Group represented an amphibious corps from Northland which had just landed in a bridgehead between Bremen and Oldenburg. I (NL) Corps was tasked to contain Northland's offensive. I (NL) Corps for Ex GRAND REPULSE consisted of the 4th (Netherlands) Infantry Division and 11 (British) Armoured Division. The 91st Lorried Infantry Brigade was detached from 11 Armoured Division to act as the corps covering force,

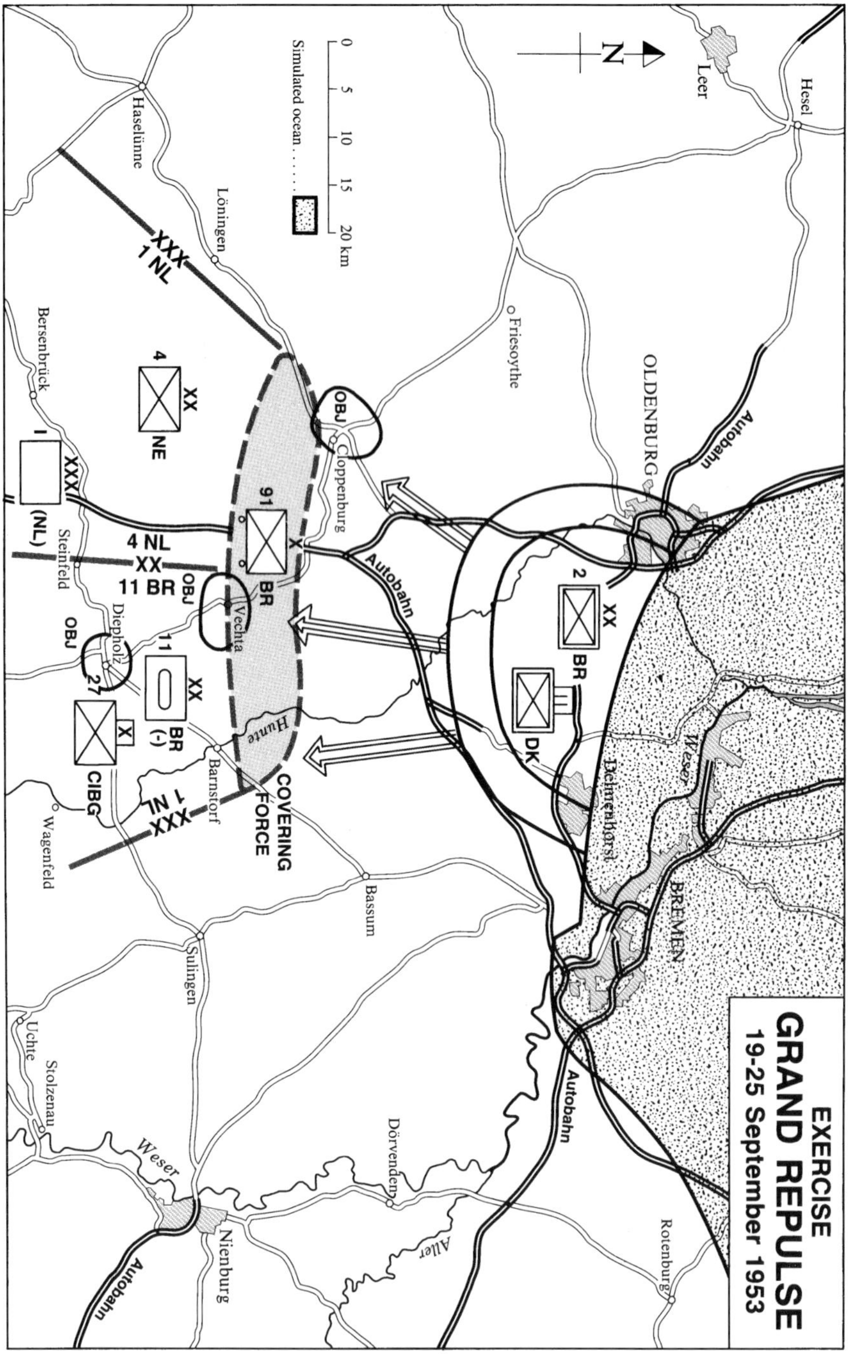
EXERCISE
GRAND REPULSE
19-25 September 1953
N
0 5 10 15 20 km
Simulated ocean . . . . .
Leer
Hesel
OLDENBURG
Autobahn
Friesoythe
Cloppenburg
Löningen
Haselünne
Bersenbrück
Steinfeld
Diepholz
Vechta
Hunte
Barnstorf
Wagenfeld
Bassum
Sulingen
Uchte
Stolzenau
Weser
Nienburg
Dörverden
Aller
Rotenburg
BREMEN
Delmenhorst
OBJ
XXX
1 NL
XX
4
NE
XXX
(NL)
91
X
BR
4 NL
XX
11 BR
XX
2
BR
DK
11
XX
BR
(-)
27
X
CIBG
COVERING
FORCE

FIGURE 1-8

while 27 Brigade was incorporated into 11 Armoured Division alongside 33rd Armoured Brigade. 7 Armoured Division acted as the directing staff for the exercise.

GRAND REPULSE was, for 27 Brigade, a return to offensive operations in the SPEARHEAD II mode. The congested terrain forced 11 Armoured Division to lead with 27 Brigade because of its preponderance of infantry. 91st LIB was spread very thin, while 33rd Armoured Brigade was in reserve in case the Northland units got the better of I (NL) Corps in an encounter battle. A key element of GRAND REPULSE was the fact that another allied corps headquarters was in command. If NORTHAG had to counter-attack an amphibious operation on its left flank, I (NL) Corps was the logical formation to do this. Given the capability deficiencies within that organization, however, it was possible that some I (BR) Corps units could be tasked to support the Dutch in such a contingency. Most importantly, exercise observers started to look for situations where atomic weapons delivered by aircraft could be employed to support the land battle. Although rudimentary at first glance, this was a portent of things to come later in the decade.

As the General Officer Commanding of I (NL) Corps noted:

> Upon the conclusion of Ex GRAND REPULSE, I sincerely wish to express my appreciation to all those who have taken part in this strenuous manoeuvre.... Soldiers and airmen from the UK, Canada and the Netherlands, working closely together in close cooperation proved themselves to be a powerful force within the framework of the Western European defence system, for the maintenance and safety of our democratic way of life.

27 Canadian Infantry Brigade proceeded back to its barracks. As usual, there was little time for rest. The new camps in the Soest area were nearing completion, despite constant surveillance from SOXMIS, local agitation from groups in Hemer/Deilinghofen and bad press. By early October 1953, 27 Brigade started to move its stores to these new camps and members began to look forward to the rotation back to Canada.

The arrival of Brigadier W.A.B. Anderson to relieve Brigadier Pangman on 15 October 1953 marked the end of 27 Canadian Infantry Brigade in the NATO line, and the establishment of 1 Canadian Infantry

Brigade Group. The men of 27 Brigade said goodbye to Germany and embarked on the SS *Samaria*, *Atlantic*, *Neptunia* and the familiar *Columbia* at the end of October 1953.

The 1951-1953 period was undoubtedly groundbreaking with regard to Canada's commitment to Europe. The symbolic need to demonstrate Canada's commitment to European defence coincided with the practical need for more land forces to defend Allied Command, Europe in the event of invasion by the Soviet Union. Other Canadian commitments such as Korea, and other Canadian defence priorities such as the defence of North America and the raising of the Air Division for ACE, limited the size of the initial Canadian Army contribution to ACE. In any event, Canadian land forces allocated to ACE and deployed in-theatre were in Europe on a temporary basis, ostensibly until the European members of NATO could become militarily viable and provide for their own defence.

27 Brigade did not live in a perfect world, of course. Problems which would plague the Brigade over the next forty years had their genesis in 1951. These problems included inadequate logistical support arrangements, the practical difficulties of working with a larger ally, the problem of finding a suitable operational role for the Brigade, and of course, the fact that the Brigade was not a priority effort in the greater scheme of Canadian foreign and defence policy. Field Marshal Montgomery of Alamein, CinC NATO land forces, was asked how good the Canadian Brigade in Germany was. Monty replied in his usual caustic fashion, "Quite tops, quite tops, but then I could have a corps of Turks for what that costs you." The raising of 27 Canadian Infantry Brigade was, however, an interesting experiment and could be considered the Army's first post-war "Total Force" organization, consisting as it did of Militia and Regular Force units. 27 Brigade trained hard and played hard under the leadership of Brigadiers Walsh and Pangman, demonstrating to NATO that, despite the size of the force allocated to ACE, Canada was prepared to take her place in the line.

1953 - 1957

EXTENDING THE COMMITMENT

CHAPTER TWO

"WE WILL BURY YOU!"

- NIKITA KHRUSCHEV

Above left: *From 1951 to 1970, Canadian Army formations in Germany served with I (British) Corps which was part of NATO's Northern Army Group. NORTHAG's symbol was the Francisca, a throwing axe used by the Franks at the battle of Chalons-sur-Marne against Attila's Mongol army.* (David McDermott)

Above right: *Northern Army Group, of which the Canadian brigade was part, was subordinate to LANDCENT (later AFCENT) the NATO headquarters responsible for the conduct of the land battle in Germany. LANDCENT's symbol was the Tower of Aix la Chapelle, the capital of Charlemagne's Empire. The motto means 'I fight against the wrong and purge all traces of evil'.* (David McDermott)

Below: *Several US 'Atomic Annie' cannons were deployed to SACEUR's Integrated Force and a number of such weapons supported 1 Canadian Infantry Brigade Group on Exercise BATTLE ROYAL in 1954. This picture shows the 280mm cannon undergoing live firing tests in Nevada, USA during Ex SHOT GRABLE.* (US NAVAL INSTITUTE)

CHAPTER TWO

***Above**: In 1953 1 Canadian Infantry Brigade Group replaced 27 Canadian Infantry Brigade. Here, infantry from 2nd Battalion, Princess Patricia's Canadian Light Infantry advance to contact in the Soltau training area, 1954. (DND)*
***Below**: The introduction of battlefield nuclear weapons by NATO in the early 1950s dictated changes in training and doctrine. Here Canadian troops undergo familiarization training with a nuclear simulator in the Sennelager training area in 1954. (DND)*

Above: *A patrol from 2nd Battalion, The Royal Canadian Regiment on Exercise COMMONWEALTH III, Soltau 1954. (DND)*
Below: *Canadian troops train with the 3.5 inch rocket launcher, Soltau 1954. (DND) Note coveralls which soldiers wore as field dress up to the mid-1960s.*

CHAPTER TWO

Above: *The Brigade's RCEME elements played an important part in ensuring equipment such as this 25 pdr gun was maintained at a high standard.*
Below: *A RCEME repair team works on a Centurion.* (DND)

Above: *2 Canadian Infantry Brigade Group on parade in April 1956. Though the location is unknown, the buildings in the background provide a good example of the garrisons constructed for the Canadian Army near Soest.* (DND)
Below: *Royal Canadian Corps of Signals personnel laying telephone wire near Soltau, 1954.* (DND)

CHAPTER TWO

As noted in Chapter One, the Canadian commitment to the NATO Integrated Force was of an indefinite nature, as far as duration was concerned. World events between 1953 to 1957, however, worked against the permanent repatriation of Canadian soldiers from Germany. The Korean conflict had bogged down into a stalemate along the 38th parallel and the Soviets tested their first hydrogen bomb in August 1953. The climate of fear that developed was further heightened by Senator Joe McCarthy in the United States who suggested that massive Communist infiltration of Western society was underway. A Soviet-suppressed revolt of East German workers had further increased the tension. By 1954, the French had lost their fight in Indo-China against the Communist Viet Minh at Dien Bien Phu. The death of Stalin in 1953 had done little to abate the tension. Laverenti Beria, the head of the Soviet secret police, was removed by a coup in 1954 and executed before he could seize control; it would be another year before Nikita Khrushchev took command after a period of severe instability in the Soviet Union.

The most important event in determining the continuing need for NATO, its military commands and forces, was the formation of the Warsaw Pact in May 1955. This move placed the armed forces of Hungary, Czechoslovakia, Poland, East Germany, Bulgaria, Romania and Albania under de facto Soviet command. The crushing of the Hungarian uprising by Soviet troops in November 1956 signalled a renewal of repression, while at the same time the Soviets threatened to intervene against Britain and France during the Suez crisis.

Throughout this period, the Red Army remained at its immediate postwar strength and, with its Warsaw Pact allies, had overwhelming conventional superiority over NATO forces in Europe. Although SACEUR's Integrated Force had gone a long way towards demonstrating NATO's resolve to counter aggression through the crucial years 1951 to 1953, Western economies could not handle the burden of maintaining a wartime economy during a time of relative peace, since this would only create the conditions necessary for Communism to flourish. Dramatically increasing the number of NATO army divisions permanently in-theatre was out of the question. Some way had to be found to ensure that any attempt by the Soviets to expand into Western Europe would be met with effective resistance. The solution to this problem had long range effects not only on the formulation of NATO plans, but on how Canada's NATO brigade was trained and equipped to fight (effects that will become apparent over the next three chapters). It is, therefore, worth some examination at this point.

The one area in which the West retained an advantage against the Soviets was in the field of nuclear weapons. Even though the Soviets did have a small nuclear capability in the early 1950s, it was comparatively primitive and they still relied heavily on conventional forces. On the other hand, a great deal of US resources had been devoted to creating a large strategic bomber force capable of laying waste to large parts of the USSR. However, the unwillingness of the Americans to employ nuclear weapons in Korea (and other places such as in aid of the French in Indo China) sent a message to the Kremlin, stating in effect that the United States probably would not engage in strategic nuclear warfare against the USSR if the Soviets used only conventional means (that is, non-nuclear) to achieve their objectives.

CHAPTER TWO

This created both a credibility and a capability gap in Europe. NATO could not afford large conventional forces to stop the Soviets and there was doubt among other NATO nations whether the US would use its strategic nuclear bombers against the Soviet Union if Western Europe was attacked by Soviet conventional land forces.

NATO planners, however, believed tactical or battlefield nuclear weapons could close this gap. The immense firepower of nuclear weapons (even small ones) was considered to be the key to righting the conventional imbalance of forces in the early 1950s. If the number of divisions assigned to SACEUR was increased with the addition of German troops and the Integrated Force was equipped with small nuclear weapons, planners believed that NATO would be more than a match for the Soviet conventional steam roller poised on the other side of the Iron Curtain.

Three things had to happen, however, before NATO could develop its nuclear capability. First, a new family of nuclear weapons had to be produced specifically for use on the battlefield. Second, techniques and doctrine had to be developed for their use, and finally, NATO forces had to have access to them. Up to this point in late 1952, NATO had approved in principle that nuclear weapons could be used in the defence of NATO members, and that planning should commence to make tactical nuclear capability a reality. Between January and March 1953, SACEUR created a Special Weapons Course at the NATO officers' school at Oberammergau Germany, and SHAPE planners started developing nuclear weapons requirements for the defence of Western Europe.

These requirements, among others proposed by what was known as the New Approach Group at SHAPE, were instrumental in the creation of a NATO strategy known as MC 48, which was approved by NATO for planning purposes in November 1954. It was widely known that the previous strategy of defending on the Rhine River (as discussed in the last chapter) was flawed from a conventional standpoint. Even if the existing units of the Integrated Force allocated to SACEUR were suddenly supplied with tactical nuclear weapons in 1954 instead of in the future, they would still be incapable of holding against a conventional Soviet attack. NATO, of course, realized that the acceptance of West Germany into NATO would provide more conventional forces to

SACEUR. However, even this would still not be enough to defeat the Soviets on the Rhine. NATO strategic planners eventually concluded that the combination of creating a West German army and the allocation of tactical nuclear weapons to units of the Integrated Force might just be enough to check an enemy attack.

The purpose behind this new strategy was to provide both a deterrent to aggression and the capability for a successful forward defence in Europe which would in turn create a climate of confidence and security at a time when Communism appeared to be triumphant around the world. In doing so, the Soviets had to be convinced that they could not overrun Europe quickly, and that if they attempted to do so they would be subjected immediately to a counter-attack that included the use of nuclear weapons. The problem here revolved around how far forward NATO could actually defend. In principle, NATO was committed to defend as far east as possible within the limits of the NATO area; that is, at the Iron Curtain. This was not feasible with only conventional forces.

To some, the mix of conventional and nuclear forces seemed confusing; why have both? Why not just have nuclear forces? The reality was that tactical nuclear weapons were seen in 1954 as being supplementary to conventional firepower, not a replacement for it. In fact, NATO planners believed that at some point in an all out war with the Soviets, one side would run out of nuclear weapons first. This side was always assumed to be the Soviets, since NATO would theoretically possess more of them. Once this occurred, NATO would cease to use nuclear weapons and finish the war with conventional means. Just obliterating the enemy with nuclear firepower was not considered enough; nuclear forces could not hold ground, they could only devastate it. Conventional forces were thus needed to counter-attack and re-take ground so that the integrity of the NATO area could be preserved.

SACEUR thus still needed conventional forces in 1954, and this need played a role in the continuation of the Canadian Army's commitment to NATO. SACEUR's forces in 1954-1955 had access only to a small number of American 280mm *Atomic Annie* cannon and some tactical aircraft which had nuclear bombs. New tactical nuclear weapons were on the drawing boards, but they would not be available for some time. Planning for their use was extremely rudimentary, and doctrine to incorporate these new weapons into ground operations was practically non-existent, primarily because of American laws prohibiting the release of important nuclear weapons information. These restrictions would loosen up to some degree in 1954, but only enough to start the development of doctrine. As a result, even though NATO had developed a new strategy, technical and political considerations delayed its full implementation until 1957. In practical terms, then, SACEUR had to make do with what he had on hand; he had conventional forces in the form of the Integrated Force, and a limited tactical nuclear capability.

The impact of the new NATO strategy on Canadian defence policy was initially marginal, since Canadian planners thought that it would take some time to fully implement the changes. Consequently, attention in Canada was focused on the small but developing Soviet bomber threat to Canada and the Government allocated a great deal of resources to continental air defence systems, including the Avro *Arrow* fighter interceptor and Distant Early Warning (DEW) Line programmes. At the same time, the 12 squadrons of No. 1 Air Division of the RCAF were fully deployed to four bases in Europe, while NATO European nations continued to receive vast amounts of military aid from Canada in the form of surplus equipment and ammunition. Previous commitments like the Mobile Striking Force, the brigade in Korea, and naval protection of sea lanes in the Atlantic continued to be supported, as did the land force commitment to SACEUR.

The Canadian Army's method of meeting its three primary tasks (defence of Canada, the Korean brigade, and the NATO brigade) before 1954 was admittedly ad hoc. There were three different types of units; Active Force, Militia and Special Force, each with different terms of employment. Since Canada was in for the long haul, some rational reorganization was necessary. In October 1953, the Government announced that all army formations would be transferred to the Active Force order of battle, and the composite units would receive new designations. Special Force or Militia personnel could choose to join the Active Force if they desired.

When all was said and done, the Regular Army was the largest it had ever been in peacetime, numbering some 49,000. It consisted of four brigade group headquarters, four artillery regiments (RCHA), two armoured regiments (The Royal Canadian Dragoons and Lord Strathcona's Horse) and 15 infantry battalions (based on six regiments: The Royal Canadian Regiment, Princess Patricia's Canadian Light Infantry, the Royal 22nd Regiment, the Royal Highland Regiment of Canada [the 'Black Watch'], the Queens Own Rifles of Canada and the Canadian Guards) in addition to numerous support units. 27 Brigade came home from Germany in 1953, and was replaced by 1 CIBG (formerly 25 CIB units), while newly formed units rotated to 25 CIB in Korea. At the same time 2 CIBG and 3 CIBG started to 'train up'. Later, in 1955, 25 CIBG was 'repatriated' and redesignated 4 CIBG.

Since SACEUR still needed conventional forces in Germany, the Canadian Army commitment to NATO in Europe continued to be one infantry division available between M-Day (start of hostilities) and M+30 days, with the 2nd Canadian Infantry Division to be raised from the Militia at some vague point beyond M+30. Now that Canada had the ability to provide enough units and equipment for it, Headquarters, 1st Canadian Infantry Division and divisional troops were activated in September 1954. However, since the Government imposed manpower ceiling for the European deployment was still in effect, only one brigade group could be stationed in Germany. This left three brigade groups in Canada – two allocated to the division and one tasked to the Mobile Striking Force role. The 2nd Canadian Infantry Division only had a small headquarters cadre and a stockpiled division set of equipment located at an airfield near Hamilton, Ontario; it never trained as an organization.

By late 1953, 27 Brigade had served its purpose. Since the NATO commitment had been extended beyond the parameters laid out in 1951, it was felt that continued reliance on the Militia to provide forces in Europe on a permanent basis was unreasonable to all concerned. Expecting Militia callouts of two years duration without implementing job protection legislation was a significant factor here. Once the Army was reorganized, the first regular formation earmarked to replace 27 Brigade was 1 Canadian Infantry Brigade Group (1 CIBG).

1 CIBG was formed on 15 October 1953 in Germany, after HQ 27 CIB was reduced to nil strength. Although it is not clear how much continuity there was between the two headquarters with regards to staff, the units that were to be placed under command of HQ 1 CIBG were com-

pletely different. Gone were the composite organizations as the Highland, Infantry and Rifle Battalions were transformed into 1st Battalion, Royal Highland Regiment of Canada, 3rd Battalion, Canadian Guards and 1st Battalion, Queens Own Rifles of Canada just before their repatriation to Canada.

Units rotating to Germany to serve as 1 CIBG included many of the units and personnel that had been in Korea. Armour support was provided by D Squadron, Lord Strathcona's Horse (Royal Canadians), and the 'guns' by 2nd Regiment, Royal Canadian Horse Artillery, while the infantry battalions were 2nd Battalion, The Royal Canadian Regiment; 2nd Battalion, the Royal 22nd Regiment; and 2nd Battalion, Princess Patricia's Canadian Light Infantry. 1 CIBG's sappers were provided by 2 Independent Field Squadron, Royal Canadian Engineers. Service support came from 54 Transport Company, Royal Canadian Army Service Corps; 25 Field Ambulance, Royal Canadian Army Medical Corps; and 195 Infantry Workshop, Royal Canadian Electrical and Mechanical Engineers.

Some 27 CIB units such as "J" Troop, Royal Canadian Corps of Signals, 27 Field Security Section, 27 Provost Detachment, 27 Field Dental Unit, 27 Ordnance Company and the overworked 27 Public Relations Unit continued to soldier on, with "1" replacing "27". HQ Canadian Base Units, Europe remained relatively unchanged at this point. Army Headquarters also decreed that, regardless of previous affiliation, "all personnel who are on strength of units of 1st Canadian Infantry Division or detailed as reinforcements for overseas units [shall wear the] distinguishing patch, a red rectangle cloth badge three inches long and two inches high in size".

The basing situation for 1 CIBG was a great improvement over the temporary arrangements in Hannover. Initially, land near the city of Soest had been set aside by the British for the construction of facilities which would then be rented by the Canadians until the 27 CIB commitment expired; then the British Army would take them over. When the Canadian commitment was extended, the decision was made to make these sites a permanent home for the Canadian Army in Europe. It should be noted here that the cost of accommodation for the British occupation forces in Germany was borne by the German population; since Canada was not an occupying power, it could not expect to receive "levy" funds for basing. However, the British were extremely anxious to move the Canadians out of Hannover as soon as possible, so they 'donated' about DM 2 million as seed money to start camp construction in 1953.

Originally known as "Camp C4 Soest, Germany", quartering for the Canadian Brigade actually consisted of several different camps spread out over a 400 square mile area east of the Ruhr industrial region. The reasons for this are obscure; either land could not be acquired in a concentrated area or the dispersion was designed to increase the survivability of the Brigade if it was attacked with nuclear weapons, a common factor in such planning in the 1950s. The layout of each camp and the type of construction of the buildings supports the case for the latter; most of the buildings only had one floor (to eliminate structures that could be knocked down), and the forts for the most part were constructed on reverse slopes. Another factor was to disperse the economic impact of the relatively wealthy Canadians in what was still a very poor country. Brigadier W.A.B. Anderson, 1 CIBG's commander, noted that the situation, geographically, was like dispersing a brigade group in Kingston, Belleville, and Gananoque, Ontario, and controlling it from Smiths Falls.

It was decided that each camp should bear the name of a famous fort from Canadian military history; it should be noted that the northern bases were forts only in name, not by function. Each unit was to become responsible for the upkeep of the fort that they occupied. There was no 'base' organization similar to what we are familiar with today; that came after unification in the 1960s. The basing plan for 1 CIBG located the brigade units to the following facilities: [See also Figure 2-1.]

Fort Prince of Wales	Hemer	2 RCHA
Fort Macleod	Hemer	2 PPCLI
Fort Chambly	Soest	Service Support units
Fort Henry	Stockum	HQ 1 CIBG
Fort York	Stockum	2 RCR
Fort St Louis	Werl	2 R22eR
Fort Victoria	Werl	2 Fd Sqn RCE
Fort Anne	Werl	"D" Sqn LdSH

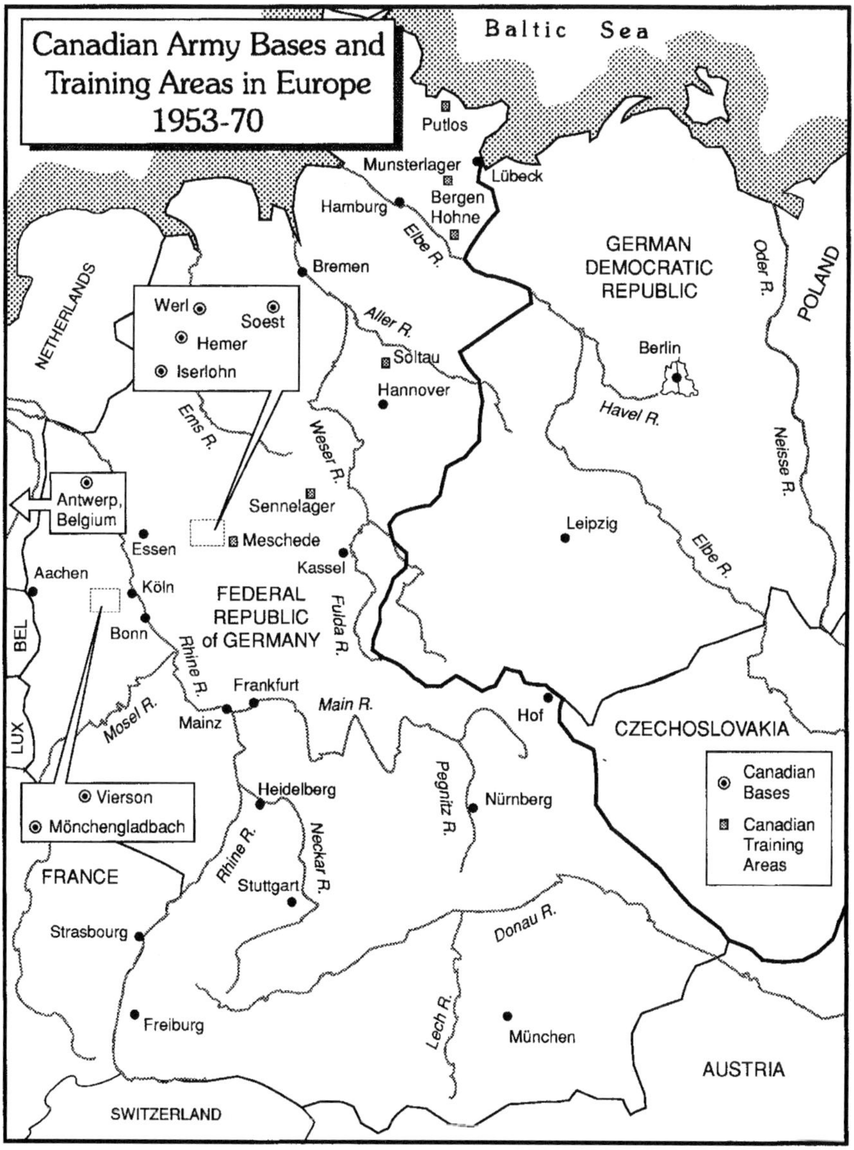
Canadian Army Bases and Training Areas in Europe 1953-70
Baltic Sea
Putlos
Munsterlager
Lübeck
Hamburg
Bergen Hohne
Elbe R.
Bremen
GERMAN DEMOCRATIC REPUBLIC
Oder R.
POLAND
NETHERLANDS
Werl
Soest
Hemer
Iserlohn
Aller R.
Soltau
Hannover
Berlin
Havel R.
Ems R.
Weser R.
Neisse R.
Antwerp, Belgium
Sennelager
Meschede
Essen
Leipzig
Kassel
Elbe R.
Aachen
Köln
FEDERAL REPUBLIC of GERMANY
Fulda R.
Bonn
BEL
Rhine R.
Frankfurt
Main R.
Mosel R.
Mainz
Hof
CZECHOSLOVAKIA
LUX
Vierson
Mönchengladbach
Heidelberg
Pegnitz R.
Nürnberg
Neckar R.
Canadian Bases
Canadian Training Areas
FRANCE
Rhine R.
Stuttgart
Donau R.
Strasbourg
Lech R.
Freiburg
München
AUSTRIA
SWITZERLAND

FIGURE 2-1:

Fort Beausejour and Fort Qu' Appelle would be added with the future expansion of the brigade.

One feature built into some of the forts were denial explosives. These were positioned to destroy key portions of the Canadian facilities once the fighting withdrawal to the Rhine was ordered. Other facilities such as married quarters (PMQs) were also constructed.

The movement of 1 CIBG to Europe was known as Operation COME AND GO. Operation COME AND GO commenced in November 1953, and essentially swapped 1 CIBG for 27 CIB via a series of sea transport lifts and commercial air flights. As Barbara Waters, the wife of PPCLI officer Stan Waters recalled, the DC-3 flight to Europe in 1953 was not exactly a picnic either:

> I went over with the two children. We flew on KLM from Montreal and the flight (it was a DC-3 I think) in those days was time consuming. We had to put down in Shannon [Ireland] overnight, off load and sleep in the hostel...I believe we then flew from Shannon, supposedly to Dusseldorf, but in fact there were only two of us getting off there so they didn't fly to Dusseldorf. They instead flew to Amsterdam and put the children, me, and some poor unfortunate man in a hot little car and drove us five hours to Dusseldorf...I think the trip took something like 17 hours in the air; it was just an absolute nightmare!

Once Op COME AND GO was completed, Brigadier Anderson and the 1 CIBG staff set about preparing the newly-arrived units for the 1954 training schedule. Before this could happen, however, some 'teething troubles' with the camps had to be sorted out. Initial problems at the new sites included a contaminated water supply at Werl, a lack of heating at Fort St Louis and a minor mumps epidemic. More disturbing was the fact that the shipment of Canadian beer destined for 1 CIBG was delayed. As for developing relations with the Germans, the brigade commander instructed that although 40 invitations for Canadian soldiers from German families had been received, unit commanders were instructed to "ensure that only such personnel that will appreciate the goodwill, are given the opportunity to accept these invitations."

While the Brigade settled in during the December 1953-January 1954 period, 1 CIBG planners had to be brought up to speed on the operational situation in the Northern Army Group area. This was necessary so that the Canadian Brigade could be trained, evaluated and positioned to support NATO operations should war occur.

The threat to the NORTHAG area in the 1954-1956 period was considered to be serious by NATO planners, and Soviet troop dispositions opposite NORTHAG forces were formidable. The Group of Soviet Forces Germany (GSFG) consisted of six "armies" (these were roughly equivalent to corps in Western terms) arranged in two operational echelons [See Figure 2-2]; the first including the 2nd Guards Mechanized Army, 3rd Shock Army, and 8th Guards Army. This first echelon included two tank divisions, five mechanized divisions and four (dismounted) rifle divisions and was tasked with pinning down and developing gaps in NATO forces' defensive lines. The second operational echelon, structured to exploit the success of the first echelon, included 1st, 2nd and 4th Guards Mechanized Armies, which disposed six tank divisions and five mechanized divisions; no rifle divisions were included since this was a mobile exploitation force. GSFG also had access to a huge support organization, including two artillery corps, two independent tank divisions, and about 2000 close support aircraft. In addition, East Germany could provide two tank, two mechanized and one motorized divisions, while the Polish Army had 11 infantry and six mechanized divisions which, it was believed, could be used alongside the Soviet forces in Poland to further exploit gains made by GSFG.

All GSFG forces were equipped and manned at near-wartime levels, and the Soviet equipment was respectable. The primary armoured fighting vehicles of the period included *Josef Stalin*-2 and -3 heavy tanks, T44 and T34/85 medium tanks and a plethora of JSU-122, JSU-152, SU 85 and SU 100 self propelled anti-tank guns. All mechanized infantry was mounted in the armoured BTR-152 wheeled APC, and the artillery possessed a staggering array (and even more staggering numbers) of tubed and rocket artillery, not only superior in numbers but in quality as well.

Prior to 1954, there had been little imagination inherent in Soviet operational art. In fact, Stalin had forbidden the development of doctrine, and as a result the Red Army still based its operational thinking on

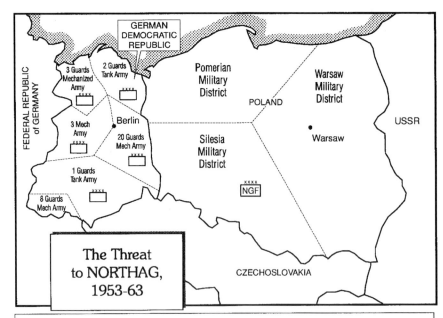

NORTHAG THREAT ORBAT 1953-63

GROUP of SOVIET FORCES, GERMANY:

1st GDS TK ARMY:
  6 Gds Tk Div
  9 Tk Div
  11 Gds Tk Div

2nd GDS TK ARMY:
  25 Tk Div
  9 Gds Tk Div
  12 Gds Tk Div

3rd MECH ARMY:
  32 Mtr Rifle Div
  19 Gds Tk Div
  94 Gds Mtr Rifle Div
  207 Mtr Rifle Div

8th GDS MECH ARMY:
  20 Gds Tk Div
  21 Mtr Rifle Div
  39 Gds Mtr Rifle Div
  57 Gds Mtr Rifle Div

20th GDS MECH ARMY:
  6 Gds Mtr Rifle Div
  10 Gds Tk Div
  11 Gds Mtr Rifle Div
  1 Mtr Rifle Div

3rd GDS MECH ARMY:
  8 Gds Mtr Rifle Div
  7 Gds Tk Div
  9 Mtr Rifle Div
  14 Gds Mtr Rifle Div

NATIONALE VOLKSARMEE (GDR):
  1 Mech Div
  4 Inf Div
  8 Inf Div
  7 Tk Div
  9 Tk Div
  11 Mtr Rifle Div
  (Plus 5 reserve NVA infantry divisions: 6, 10, 19, 27, 40)

(Plus 5 Soviet Divisions in Northern Group of Forces: 2 tank, 3 infantry)
(Plus 12 Polish Divisions)

FIGURE 2-2

the Second World War model. After Stalin's death, these constraints were loosened and allowed for much more flexibility in operational matters.

It is important to note that all Soviet land and tactical air capability in Europe in this period was conventional in scope. Tactical nuclear weapons did not enter the Soviet armoury until the 1960s while Soviet strategic nuclear forces had other tasks like attacking targets in North America. Nevertheless, Soviet attention was starting to drift towards protecting their formations against the effects of NATO's projected battlefield nuclear armoury. Chemical weapons training and equipment was also emphasized, though not to the same degree that it would be in the 1960s.

From a geographical perspective, the terrain in NORTHAG was comparatively flat and open, thereby favouring Soviet motorized and mechanized operations. Terrain in the CENTAG region south of Kassel was considerably less inviting. If the Soviets wanted to turn NATO's flank in the Central Region, it would be prudent of them to weight their attack against NORTHAG with their vast mechanized forces and hope for an early collapse of the NORTHAG front. Theoretically, this would create the conditions for a quick thrust through the Netherlands to grab NATO reinforcement port facilities, and then advance south along the Rhine into the Ruhr industrial region and into northwestern France. This would force NATO forces in the CENTAG area to retreat or be surrounded and cut off, thus destroying the integrity of NATO.

NATO dispositions in NORTHAG during this period can be seen in Figure 2-3. NORTHAG's forces included one Dutch division based in Germany on M-Day, with five more mobilizable (hopefully) by M+3 days. I (BR) Corps was the strongest element in NORTHAG, weighing in at one infantry division, three armoured divisions and 1 CIBG. The only reinforcements immediately available for three months after M-Day was the remainder of 1st Canadian Infantry Division and (hopefully) 2nd Canadian Infantry Division; after three months, two British infantry divisions would be ready. South of I (BR) Corps was I (Belgian) Corps, consisting of an infantry division and an armoured division; four other Belgian infantry divisions would be ready by M+30 days. Even though West Germany became a member of NATO in 1955, German divisions would not become available until after 1957.

As with the early days of the Integrated Force, the main defensive

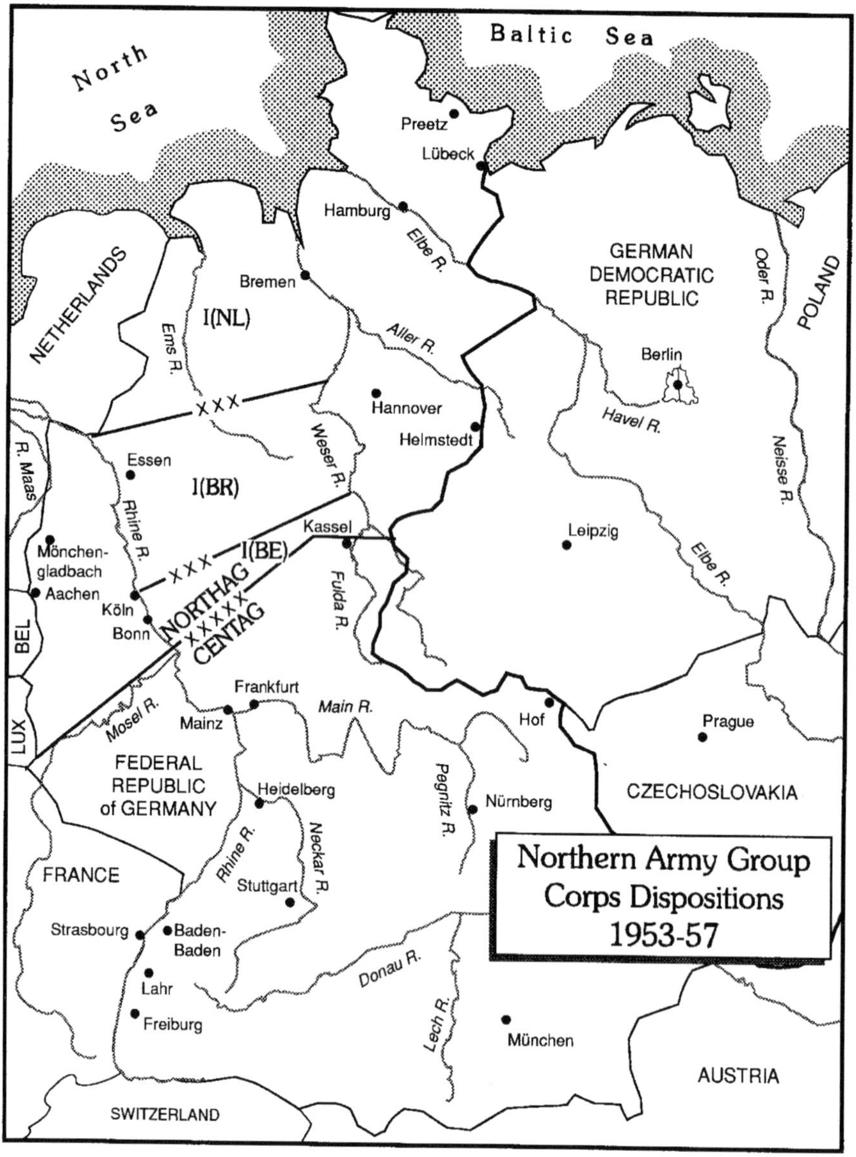

Baltic Sea
North Sea
Preetz
Lübeck
Hamburg
Elbe R.
GERMAN
DEMOCRATIC
REPUBLIC
Oder R.
POLAND
Bremen
NETHERLANDS
I(NL)
Ems R.
Aller R.
Berlin
Hannover
Havel R.
XXX
Helmstedt
Essen
Weser R.
R. Maas
I(BR)
Neisse R.
Rhine R.
Kassel
Leipzig
Mönchen-
gladbach
XXX
I(BE)
Elbe R.
Aachen
Köln
Bonn
NORTHAG
XXXXX
CENTAG
Fulda R.
BEL
Frankfurt
Main R.
Hof
Prague
Mosel R.
Mainz
LUX
FEDERAL
REPUBLIC
of GERMANY
Heidelberg
Pegnitz R.
Nürnberg
CZECHOSLOVAKIA
Neckar R.
Northern Army Group
Corps Dispositions
1953-57
FRANCE
Rhine R.
Stuttgart
Strasbourg
Baden-
Baden
Donau R.
Lahr
Freiburg
Lech R.
München
AUSTRIA
SWITZERLAND

FIGURE 2-3

line was on the Rhine River. Since the northern part of the NORTHAG area only had one Dutch division guarding it, I (BR) Corps had to spread out the 6th Armoured Division and 7th Armoured Division to the north, leaving 2nd Infantry Division, 11th Armoured Division and 1 CIBG covering the approaches to the heavily populated and industrial regions of Essen, Dusseldorf and Dortmund; the two Belgian divisions were located east of Köln (Cologne). The concept of operations here was to fight a covering force battle forward of the Rhine and then effect a withdrawal to the river's west bank; hopefully, the enemy could be delayed there until other formations could be mobilized and moved into the theatre.

It is for this reason that the Canadian contribution was significant. Since there were only a limited number of NATO divisions in NORTHAG on M-Day (seven), and two of these were occupying positions to the north of the 1 (BR) Corps area, any formation of brigade group size was important. Moreover, a typical British armoured division only had two brigades; in terms of size, firepower and staying power then, the Canadian brigade group was equivalent to about half of a British armoured division. Thus, out of six brigades available to I (BR) Corps, Canada provided one brigade group initially, or 16 per cent of I (BR) Corps forces on the Ruhr approach. More importantly, the rest of the 1st Canadian Infantry Division was the only reinforcement available to I (BR) Corps before M+90 days, when the other British divisions were supposed to arrive. The Dutch would also be severely pressed by this point in defending their portion of the Rhine Line, while the Belgians would be heavily committed forward of the Köln region.

As far as 1 CIBG (and later 2 CIBG) were concerned, the overall concept of operations differed little from that developed during 1951-1953. [See Figure 2-4.] The Brigade was to be deployed on what was referred to as the Weser River Line, on the right flank of 2nd (British) Infantry Division; 11th (British) Armoured Division was situated northeast of 2nd Infantry Division and probably would have formed a covering force if it could get into position when 1 CIBG and 2nd Infantry Division pulled back from the Weser River Line. The first fallback position behind this was the Teutobergerwald, a forested and hilly region, with the final defensive position on the Munster Line to cover the retreat

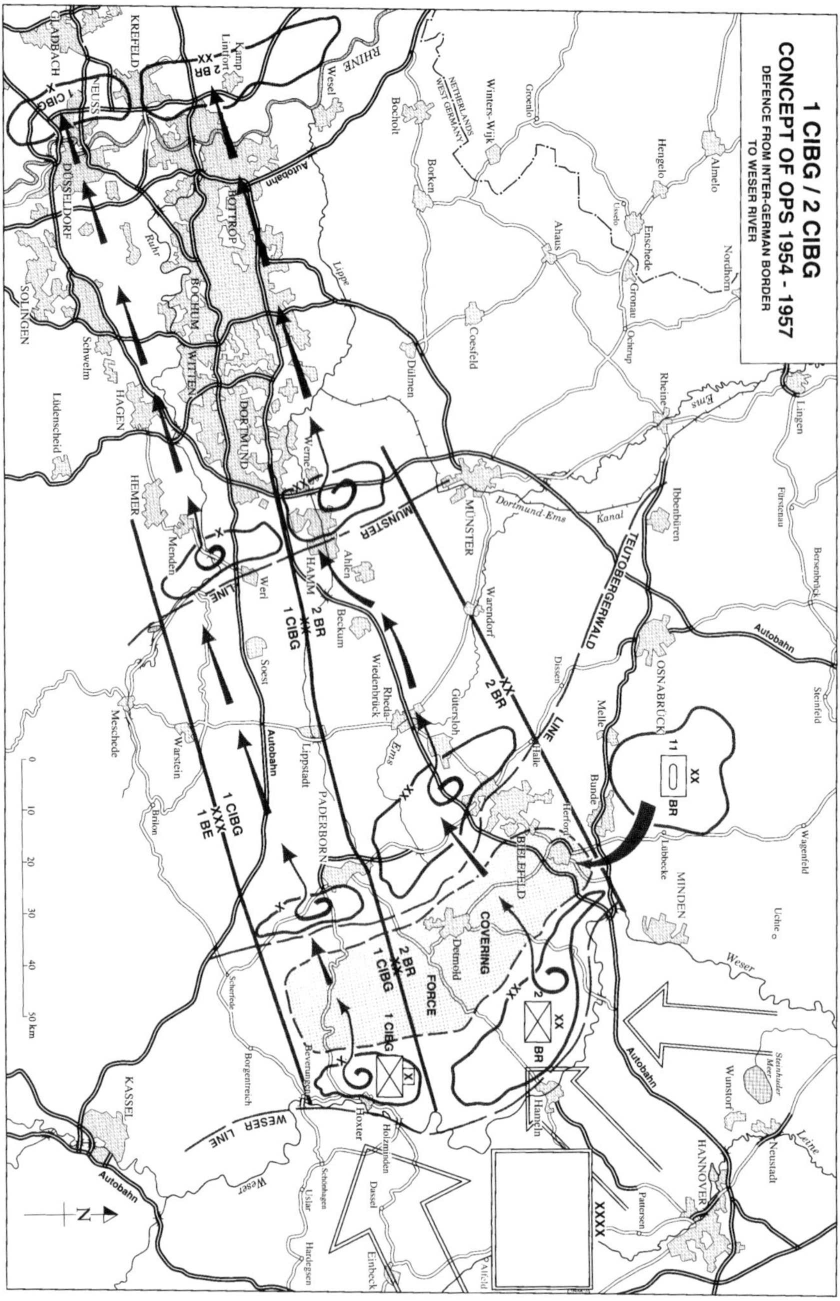
1 CIBG / 2 CIBG
CONCEPT OF OPS 1954 - 1957
DEFENCE FROM INTER-GERMAN BORDER
TO WESER RIVER

FIGURE 2-4

across the Rhine.

Defending forward of the Weser River (with the exception of some recce elements) was ruled out before 1957, despite the agreement in principle that NATO was to be defended as far east as possible. NATO formations located close to the Inner German Border were considered too vulnerable to surprise attack, since Warsaw Pact forces were deployed in strength within 30 kilometres of the border itself. Secondly, forward positioning would lengthen supply lines and exacerbate an already tenuous logistical situation. Most importantly, NATO forces in NORTHAG needed time to dig in and prepare for an enemy assault. As a result, NORTHAG was prepared to buy time with territory.

In all probability, 1 CIBG (and 2 CIBG after the 1955 rotation), 11th Armoured Division and 2nd Infantry Division would have faced the Soviets' 3rd Shock Army (four infantry or mechanized divisions), followed by either 3rd or 4th Guards Mechanized Army (two tank divisions and two mechanized divisions) in the second echelon. The prospect of these two and one-half NATO divisions holding off eight Soviet divisions for 30 days over a depth of 200 kilometres with the survivors then attempting to hold a river line 150 kilometres long was questionable, hence the urgency for developing, deploying and training for tactical nuclear warfare. Unlike today, long range anti-tank systems, surface to surface missiles and attack helicopters were in an embryonic state, and area denial weapons such as artillery-delivered mines, simply did not exist. Certainly, obstacles would have been used extensively, but I (BR) Corps always lacked significant numbers of specialized engineering units; additionally, the German *Wallmeister* (denial engineer) units were not organized yet either.

Be that as it may, 1 CIBG developed its own training plan to achieve a high level of operational readiness. Two measures were implemented: Exercise QUICK TRAIN, and the "70% Rule". QUICK TRAIN was the code word for no-warning deployment exercises. These could occur at any time of the day (usually at night), any day of the year. Some were ordered by higher NATO headquarters, some by I (BR) Corps or BAOR, and some by the Brigade Headquarters. On a QUICK TRAIN, personnel reported to their respective camps after being alerted by siren or by duty personnel banging on the door. Sometimes 2 1/2 ton trucks would enter villages in which Canadian soldiers lived, blare their horns, load up and head for the appropriate base. On arrival, soldiers picked up their weapons, clambered aboard their vehicles and then deployed to "Survival Areas" which were dispersed in the countryside around the forts. The "70 %" dictated that only 30 per cent of a given unit's strength could be away on leave or outside the Soest base area at any time. This rule persisted in the Brigade virtually up to the very end of its service in Germany.

Following the training pattern established by 27 CIB and I (BR) Corps, 1 CIBG progressed from individual to sub-unit, unit, and combined arms training over a five month period. Individual and sub-unit training was done in garrison and on local ranges, leading up to skill-at-arms competitions between 1 CIBG units. The 'bonus' for the winners involved participation in BAOR meets like the Connaught Shield competition for stretcher bearers, the Prix Leclerc skill-at-arms competition, and the Bisley small arms shoot in the UK.

These activities ended in March with the engineers conducting a bridging camp in Hameln, the infantry battalions rotating through Soltau on battalion schemes, artillery units 'shooting in' at Putlos, and the tanks conducting battle runs at Hohne. Training in Germany in 1954-55 was somewhat different from today, as Mike Ritchie remembered:

> We used to do house clearing, live fire; go in there with the Bren guns. No safety. You were your own safety. The Bren group, when they fired a section for their flankings, the Lance Corporal and two guys sat there and said 'go right, go right, go right'; and you'd be firing 20 yards ahead of him and nobody jumped up and down...you just go into these big old German buildings and you took the roofs off; nobody followed you around. You'd go into a room and throw the live grenade through the door. It would go off and you'd stand in the door and we thought it was hilarious! Fing! Fing! Ricochets going off and nobody got hurt! It was outstanding training for a young soldier.

Young officers still undergoing training at the Canadian service colleges had the opportunity to gain valuable leadership experience with the Brigade in Germany. Lieutenant General Jack Vance was an officer cadet at the time:

> The first time I went over was only for a four month summer in 1955 when I got the equivalent of my third phase infantry training. They had a wonderful scheme then, when you would walk in on a Friday, dog tired, having come from TCA [Trans Canada Airlines]...the CO would see you sometime on Saturday just casually in the mess and say things like 'What are you doing with that band-aid [a white ribbon indicating officer cadet rank] under your pip? Take it down please. We'll pretend that you're a Second Lieutenant while you're here, and by the way report to Captain Bill Hill on Monday morning because you're taking command of 2 Platoon'. The way they trained us in fact was to give us a platoon of honest to God soldiers with a relatively experienced Sergeant and go to work.

Concurrent with all of this were the Brigade HQ signals exercises and command post exercises, as well as Officers Study periods. A very important development with regard to NATO standardization also took place around this time. This was the adoption of the operation order format "SMEAC": Situation, Mission, Execution, Administration and Logistics, and Command and Signals. It is still used today in a slightly modified form.

Two CPXs illustrated 1 CIBG's tactical thinking in early 1954. The first, Exercise SHAKEDOWN 2, was designed to test 1 CIBG's rear and main headquarters in offensive operations, and was a brigade affair. The general situation being portrayed was an assault river crossing across the Rhine. Exercise FLAT OUT, however, was run in conjunction with 2nd (British) Infantry Division in the Soltau training area. FLAT OUT focused on a withdrawal operation not unlike the concept of operations within I (BR) Corps. In essence, the real defensive plan was pushed east into the Soltau training area so that the Weser River Line became the Elbe River Line, and the "Soltau Line" simulated the Munster Line. 1 CIBG operated as part of 2nd Infantry Division, which had three other infantry brigades, and was faced by '1 Fantasian Rifle Army' consisting of two rifle divisions and one mechanized division. The enemy force arrayed against 1 CIBG in this exercise ('1st Fantasian Infantry Division' with its attached '652 Medium Tank Brigade' and artillery brigade) looked suspiciously like the 19th Guards Mechanized Division from the 3rd Shock Army. The enemy was allowed air superiority.

After this experience, the entire brigade moved to the Soltau training area in May 1954 to work up for joint exercises with 7th Armoured Division. The HIGH GEAR series of manoeuvres focused on battlegroup mobile operations and were one sided affairs. Immediately at the end of HIGH GEAR III, a warning order was issued to prepare for Exercise COMMONWEALTH III. COMMONWEALTH III pitted 7th Armoured Division in an offensive role against 1 CIBG, which was defending the high ground. After withstanding at least six attacks over a 48 hour period, 1 CIBG showed 7th Armoured Division that night operations with dismounted infantry could be highly effective force multipliers; in one case an entire squadron of 'Fantasian' tanks was captured in its harbour after a gruelling six hour approach march and night raid. This capability (which would show up time and again over the next 40 years) engendered in the British "a lot of respect for the Canadians" after COMMONWEALTH III. The only casualty was the Brigade GSO 3 who, while raiding the mess tent for a late snack, fell into a six foot deep sump pit and sustained minor injuries.

There were, of course, the usual equipment problems that plague any military organization. For example, the *Centurion* tanks were approaching the third quarter of their engine life expectancy in April 1954 and there were not enough replacement gun barrels for them. The infantry's 17 pounder anti-tank guns also all had to be refitted and the state of the wheeled transport fleet was questionable. Despite these problems, 1 CIBG was rated as being able to

> ...take to the field on eight hours notice and can, if necessary, fight as a formation without further training. Its operational efficiency will however be greatly increased by the month to be spent at Soltau. On returning from Soltau, the brigade group should be regarded as a coordinated fighting team.

Equipment deficiencies notwithstanding, 1 CIBG was selected to conduct user trials for a new rifle developed by Fabrique National of Belgium. This 7.62mm weapon, rumoured at the time to be the front runner in a NATO standardization competition, was allegedly "lighter in weight than the Lee-Enfield presently in use", which as many, many

CHAPTER TWO

people now know, was not the case!

As discussed earlier, NATO forces in Europe started to receive access to nuclear weapons data in 1954 so they could develop doctrine to employ battlefield nuclear weapons. Up to June, planning and training within I (BR) Corps and thus 1 CIBG had been for conventional operations. In June 1954, JAVELIN VII, a corps-level CPX that included 1 CIBG, first introduced nuclear fire support planning during an exercise.

The troops had their first exposure to this developing doctrine at the August concentration at the Sennelager All Arms Training Centre. At Sennelager, nuclear weapons play was carefully integrated into a larger scenario that included tank/infantry cooperation with live firing, assault river crossings, patrolling, and village fighting on specially constructed ranges. The purpose of this training was to

> ...familiarize the individual soldier with the measures he must take should atomic missiles be used against him or in support of him. This training will include the digging in of one infantry platoon per battalion. This digging in will include overhead cover and the necessary stores will be provided by 2 Field Squadron. The battalion training in this subject will culminate in the demonstration of a device for simulating the explosion of an atomic missile....

To prepare the infantry defensive position for this operation, some "suggestions" had been passed down by Canadian instructors who had participated in live nuclear weapons trials in Australia and had access to test information. Eventually, Castle Range at Sennelager looked like a miniature Vimy Ridge, with revetted trenches and command bunkers. The "atomic simulator" in this case was placed 300 yards from the defensive positions, which were supposedly designed to be effective against a 20 kiloton nuclear weapon exploded nearby.

In all, three simulators were detonated and troops from 1 CIBG practiced their survival drills. It is interesting to mention here that the only nuclear weapons effects that were taught were blast, heat and immediate radiation. It appears that other critical information we are familiar with today such as the different types of radiation, the long term effects of radiation and electromagnetic pulse were not fully understood in 1954 and consequently were not part of the curriculum at Sennelager. This is not surprising since the British had exploded their first nuclear weapon only in 1952 and had just two years at this point to process the information; and the Americans were still somewhat reticent about disseminating the data which they had been collecting since 1945.

In eight months of training, 1 CIBG had participated in rudimentary tactical nuclear planning in addition to its conventional tasks; the Brigade's units could fight conventional battles and adopt a defensive stance against a tactical nuclear threat; and the soldiers themselves were well versed in personal protective measures. All of this would be put to the test in Exercise BATTLE ROYAL, the largest land force exercise since the Second World War (up to 1954).

NORTHAG's Exercise BATTLE ROYAL (like its CENTAG counterpart Ex INDIAN SUMMER) was specifically designed to practice the conduct of battles involving tactical nuclear weapons in an environment where a small conventional force equipped with nuclear weapons had the task of stopping a larger force equipped with a lesser number of nuclear weapons.

Practically all of NORTHAG's forces participated in BATTLE ROYAL. The enemy forces, Northland, consisted of I (BR) Corps and I (NL) Corps, while Southland was represented by I (BE) Corps and 1 CIBG. [See Figure 2-5.] In general terms, 1 CIBG was given a divisional frontage of 40 km by the Belgian Corps commander, Lt Gen Tromme. 1st Belgian Infantry Division was on 1 CIBG's right with 16th Belgian Armoured Division and 46 (BR) Parachute Brigade (Territorial) in reserve. The enemy facing 1 CIBG comprised 4th Netherlands Infantry Division and 6th British Armoured Division.

Since 1 CIBG had a divisional frontage in the exercise, I (BE) Corps allocated additional resources to "under command" of 1 CIBG. These included an entire recce regiment equipped with *Chaffee* and *Patton* tanks, two regiments of 155mm self-propelled guns, a transport company of 60 trucks and two air OP aircraft. HQ 1 CIBG's organization was also changed for this exercise. To reduce the possibility of destruction by enemy nuclear weapons, 1 CIBG deployed an Advanced and a Main HQ in separate locations. I(BE) Corps also had a very special form of fire support which was on call to 1 CIBG as necessary: two batteries

EXERCISE
BATTLE ROYAL
September 1954
OSNABRÜCK
Autobahn
Dortmund-Ems
Canal
Ems
Lengerich
Greven
Ladbergen
Glandorf
Bad Iburg
Melle
Bünde
Herford
TEUTOBERGERWALD
BIELEFELD
Versmold
Ostbevern
Telgte
MÜNSTER
Warendorf
Greffen
Harsewinke
GÜTERSLOH
Rheta-Wiedenbrück
Ems
Delbrück
ATOMIC STRIKE
27 SEP 54
PHASE 5 DEFENSIVE BATTLE
PLATEAU
Ennigerloh
Oelde
Ahlen
Beckum
HAMM
Werne
Lippe
Lippstadt
Autobahn
4 NL
6 BR
2 BR
7 BR
2 PPCLI
1 CIBG
2 R22eR
2 JP BE
D LDSH
2 RCR
1 BE
46 BR (-)
16 BE
0 5 10 15 20 km
N

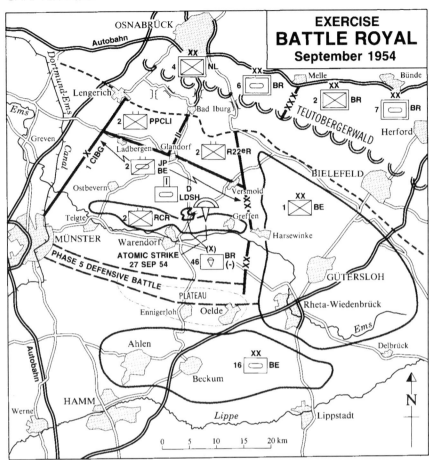

FIGURE 2-5

of the 265th (US) Artillery Battalion, equipped with the 280mm "Atomic Annie" cannon. However, Brigadier Anderson would have to be careful with his allotment of nuclear fire support since I (BE) Corps could only use a total of 16 simulated 20 kt nuclear shells for the entire exercise; four were to support counter-attacks, three to deny the Teutobergerwald passes, two against units attempting to get through the passes, leaving seven for targets of opportunity.

1 CIBG's defensive plan was elaborate. The usual deployment pattern of two battle groups up and one back was used for the first phase. 2 PPCLI and 2 R22eR had the task of destroying the passes through the Teutobergerwald region to delay the Northland forces before then passing back through the recce screen. The Belgian recce screen would delay the enemy (along with 2 RCR and the LdSH squadron) until 1 CIBG's forward units had retired through 2 RCR's reserve demolitions at Telge, Warendorf and Greffen. After the covering force had been withdrawn, the Ems river dam upstream would be 'blown', as well as the bridges and other denial demolitions. If all this failed to delay the enemy, a 'last stand' would be organized along the Enningerloh-Oelde plateau until 16th (BE) Armoured Division could conduct a counter-attack. All phases of the exercise were to include aggressive night patrolling to keep the Northland enemy off-balance. In addition to all of this, 1 CIBG's intelligence section had prepared profiles on the British and Dutch commanders as well as a detailed analysis of their likely intentions.

The 'war' started with a Northland nuclear attack on Southland's capital at 1600 hrs 22 September 1954. Almost immediately, Canadian patrols captured some Dutch documents depicting an inaccurate disposition of 1 CIBG's forces; this was exploited by shifting more Southland armour forward. By 24 September, 1 CIBG continued to delay I (NL) Corps forward of the Ems River and had beaten off an attack by Dutch *Centurion* tanks near Telgate. The personnel of the Belgian recce regiment "2JP" with their *Chaffee* and *Patton* tanks acquitted themselves well in their covering force role.

One Canadian infantry patrol, lost in the enemy rear area, stumbled upon the commanding officer of a British armoured regiment. After getting their bearings while dragging the unfortunate individual home, they spotted and reported over one hundred soft-skinned vehicles; as a result

CHAPTER TWO

Corps ordered a nuclear strike which delayed the enemy advance for five hours. To assist in the delaying operation elements of 46 (BR) Parachute Brigade were inserted north of Warendorf via 'helicopter' (simulated by using 2 1/2 ton trucks), since they were unable to get enough C-119 transport aircraft to do a proper parachute drop.

On 25 September an interesting situation developed on 1 CIBG's right flank. After some aggressive patrolling, Canadian troops gathered some very useful intelligence, and 1 CIBG was able to respond with despatch:

> From a captured document, the overall plan of attack by 6 Armd Div was gained. This plan entailed a two-phase attack. Phase I— 61 Lorried Infantry Bde was to seize a bridgehead over the Ems between Warendorf and Greffen and the engineers were to construct a bridge...Phase II—20 Armd Bde was to pass over the bridge and break out of the bridgehead and seize West Kirchen and Clarholz. With such accurate info of his plan we were able to drop an atomic missile at 2200 hrs. It so happened that the dropping of the atomic shell coincided with H-Hr for Phase I of 6 Armd Div's attack. The effect of the atomic missile was devastating, completely paralyzing the assaulting infantry and armour and halting the attack completely...

The cream of 6 (BR) Armoured Division, including The Oxford and Bucks, the Royal Sussex Regiment, the Green Howards, 5th Royal Horse Artillery, 2nd and 6th Royal Tank Regiments and the 17/24th Lancers, (90% of the division), were 'destroyed' by the simulated nuclear strike.

In sum, BATTLE ROYAL provided the Brigade with many benefits, not least training in a new doctrine involving the use of nuclear weapons. Although this was important, other favourable aspects emerged in the after action report:

> ...the Brigade Group successfully carried out two withdrawals while defending a front of 40 kilometres. The Exercise was a thorough test of the battle-worthiness of the Brigade Group and much valuable experience was gained in working with a foreign NATO army. The language difficulties and liaison problems were all successfully solved and the Brigade group worked efficiently as a component of I (BE) Corps.

Garrison developments in the Soest area continued apace with the Brigade's rather full training schedule. The decision to allow soldiers' dependents overseas had been made by Ottawa when the brigade commitment was extended past 1953. Consequently, a complete community infrastructure had to be added to the base areas to support the influx of Canadian wives and children, as well as catering to the soldiers. Unfortunately, construction of the PMQs lagged behind the construction of the forts. Some dependents had to find temporary accommodation:

> We lived in the most incredible places when we first arrived. We moved six different times in 18 months. Eventually, we moved into a very small German pension that was just awful, really awful. It was a three story building and on the top floor I think we had about five East German families; on the second floor we had one room plus a little sitting room.... We had a basin with hot and cold taps which only ran cold and of course in winter, they didn't run at all, it just froze up. There was one bathroom. [The landlord] was a big blowhard, not a nice man at all, but he was thrilled to have Canadians paying an enormous fortune (at that point 200 or so marks a month) with four marks to the dollar....

Some public relations personnel in Ottawa had erred regarding the PMQ situation in Germany, requiring public relations staff in Germany to clarify the situation:

> It is unfortunate that the Canadian press published last year that most of the married quarters would be available by April or May this year. This is, of course, not the case and it has caused a certain amount of unhappiness among those who have their families presently in Germany.... The Defence Financial Advisor came over to help speed up the German contractors....

Eventually, PMQs were completed in Hemer, Werl, and Soest. While under construction, an old German tradition called *Richtfest* was enacted. On 11 June 1954, the German builders, Canadian soldiers, politicians, bandsmen and townspeople from Soest converged on a site called *Klein Kanada* to celebrate the erection of one of the PMQ's support beams and rafters. During the *Richtfest*, a small evergreen tree was placed on the unfinished roof beam; the head constructor climbed up onto the beam to toast the good luck of the builders and the owners after which he threw the glass to the ground to signal the start of the party. Canada was now part of the Soest community.

The first complete and fully furnished PMQ was ready for occupation in November 1954, and a special handover ceremony was convened to mark the occasion. Corporal Sim and family, amid great pomp and circumstance, received the keys to House Number 146 from Brigadier Anderson and a bevy of German officials from Soest.

Schools also had to be built for the estimated 800 children that would accompany future soldiers. By December 1955, the area would boast Senior, Primary and Junior schools in Soest, both a Senior and Junior school in Hemer, and a combined school in Werl. Teachers from Canada were hired to staff the DND school system in Europe. At that time, teachers became associate members of the Officers Mess, a tradition that continued in Germany until the Canadians final withdrawal in 1993-94.

Other buildings and amenities were under construction as well. Four Roman Catholic and four Protestant chapels were constructed at several locations. There was no Canadian hospital in the Soest area, but there was British Military Hospital, Iserlohn, which was jointly manned by Canadian and British doctors and nurses. Dependents' Clinics were established at Soest, Werl, Unna, and Hemer. The British NAAFI exchange was eventually replaced with the Canadian-operated Maple Leaf Services (MLS), the forerunner of CANEX. The Hemer, Werl and Soest PMQ areas each got an MLS store where families could buy groceries, clothing and a select number of Canadian items that did not have British or German equivalents.

The importation of Canadian culture into Europe began with the construction of hockey and curling rinks at Fort York and Fort Prince of Wales; the first wave assault in this new *kulturkampf* was followed up with the establishment of Radio Canadian Army Europe in 1956 and the brigade newspaper, *The Beaver* in 1957. Bowling alleys and tennis courts were also added at Forts Henry, St. Louis and Chambly.

The Salvation Army, the venerable 'Sally Ann', was not far behind having left its facilities in Hannover for Soest. Captain (SA) and Mrs

Hopkinson, who had moved from Canada to help with the British Red Shield Club in Hannover, wanted to relocate to serve the Canadian brigade in the Soest Area. Using his own money, but having no Memorandum of Understanding with the Canadian Army, he had rented his own place in Soest :

> [Captain Hopkinson] outlined his plans for a snack bar and lounge to the Brigade Commander, Brigadier WAB Anderson, and was immediately challenged: 'What are you going to do with this building if I say I don't want a dry Salvation Army Hostel in Soest?' demanded Brigadier Anderson. 'Sir,' replied Hopkinson, 'if you don't want us, all I've lost is the $25 I paid for the first month's rent.' Well aware of the popularity of the Red Shield Centre with his men, Brigadier Anderson turned to his second in command and said, 'Tell the engineers to do all that's needed to turn this into a suitable Red Shield Centre and put it on the bus route for the last pick up at night back to camp.'

The importance of the services provided by the Salvation Army to the soldiers in the field cannot be overstated. In addition to providing reading material, snacks, souvenirs and fellowship in garrison, Red Shield Service canteen trucks accompanied the Brigade on almost every exercise over the next 35 years.

Initially, single soldiers and single officers were required to live in quarters and were not permitted to live 'on the economy'. Living conditions for the soldiers in barracks really weren't too bad, but many had a problem with the food:

> The rations were something! Brit rations. Camouflaged bully beef. Camouflaged brussel sprouts. They'd do anything to camouflage it, but it was the same old garbage…. We went to the mess to eat breakfast and they threw this crap they called 'jumbayala' all in two mess tins…so we were poking this s— around the mess tin and this big, tall lanky guy with a red sash came over and said 'How's the food today, lads?' I was pretty outspoken in those days and I pushed the plate…over and I said 'I wouldn't feed this s___ to a dog!' 'You wouldn't, huh?' and he disappears and about ten minutes later he came back with two mess tins and they were just heaping! He put them down and

started shovelling it in.... He says, 'Good food. Eat up lads, makes you big and strong.' I had no idea who he was. None of us did. The next morning we had to run everywhere we went; we came around this corner and this guy walks into the lecture room at the same time. It was the RSM of the battalion! 'Don't like the food, eh lad?' he said with a grin.

This situation persisted on training schemes as well. Usually, however, the problem could be overcome with typical soldier initiative:

[We] routinely [used] packed rations and the ones that were issued over there came through the Brit system.... It took maybe four days of hard rations for the troops to become deathly sick of them. I remember a wonderful night when one of my Corporals came to me and said 'We really need to do a little bit more patrolling'; and I said, 'Yes, but it's not really on my programme yet. We're going to do that next week'. He said, 'No sir, we'd really like to do it tonight with your permission'. What they in fact did was the famous Potato Patrol, because they went into this guy's potato field, dug up enough potatoes for the platoon, and planted cans of our pack rations in the holes and put the [soil] back on...The guy wasn't stupid. He discovered it the next day and appeared in our area that afternoon. I was expecting trouble, but he had two freshly-killed chickens. What he wanted to do was give us these for more pack rations!

Eventually, so many men got fed up with the low quality of the food that there was a mini-riot. Brigade HQ noted the problem, altered the rations to higher, more "Canadian" standards, and brought in better cooks from 'back home'.

Part of the training plan for the Canadian brigade in Germany in the 1950s involved an extensive physical training and sports programme, as well as military skills training:

The work week was 'train, train, route march'. The whole company up in full marching order and away we went all Friday morning, three or four hours in the hills. Monday and Wednesday was nothing but inter-unit sports practice...hockey and boxing were the big time ones.

Other traditional sports such as volleyball, track and field, basketball, baseball and soccer were available. Soldiers could play in inter-unit leagues, or unit leagues or they could compete against other NATO members' teams. There were BAOR leagues for basketball, swimming and boxing, in which Canadian personnel were eligible to participate, as well as regular matches against the units of 1 Canadian Air Division who were located in France and southern Germany:

> We had the Northern Army Group/BAOR boxing competition. We won a number of fights in that. There were all kinds of sporting events both within the Brigade and within Northern Army Group; believe me, we were in all of them. We got our ass kicked of course in things like soccer; we weren't too good at that, but the other things we did very well, and we had a lot of fun.

One member of the brigade even played table tennis in the Belgian league, representing the Belgian units that were also located in the Soest area.

Entertainment for Canadian personnel abounded. The ubiquitous British Army Kinema Corporation opened the Globe Theatre in Iserlohn, and Canadian troops had access to No. 6 BAOR Leave Centre, Winterberg for skiing. The Castor Club opened in Werl, and three Canadian clubs opened near the picturesque Moehnesee lake: the Yacht Club, the Old Red Patch Club and the Beaver Club.

Opportunities for soldiers to meet respectable women, contrary to popular belief, did exist. Personnel attending the first social evening at the Beaver Club were informed that "…for those men who have not a wife or girlfriend, there will be RAF girls from Dundurn present. However, their numbers are limited…" Individuals were also informed that "Lady Guests must be of a type suitable to introduce to Canadian wives", whatever that meant.

In fact, the leadership of 1 CIBG went out of their way to ensure that the men were taken care of. An advertisement was posted in Soest inviting local girls to attend a 'get acquainted' dance; two military buses were provided to pick up the girls in Soest's market square. Unfortunately, most of the population of Soest turned out to observe who got on board. Only twenty girls were brave enough to get on, amidst insults and firecracker attacks. The local press tagged along, expecting absolute drunken debauchery at the site selected for the dance. Lo and behold, girls from miles around had flocked to the gathering, and it turned out to be a marvelous evening. Both sides learned a valuable lesson according to a local newspaper:

> The Canadians, meaning it honestly, were very badly advised in giving the advertisement the form it had. There are many other ways leading to good contact....If more attempts in this form are going to be made, the Canadians could get a completely wrong impression of the behaviour of the German population (ie; the curious ones in the market place) and of the kind and intrinsic virtue of German girls.

Alternative entertainment, however, also received public scrutiny. With shades of Lionel Shapiro, the *NeuDeutscher Tagblatt* printed an 'exposé special' on "Canadian occupation troops excess" in the Soest area. Oozing with self-righteous indignation, the writer, like so many before him, failed to understand the Canadian soldier's need for a little *freundschaft*:

> ...while the Canadians were still unpacking their luggage in the new camps, heavily-painted girls knocked on the doors of honest Westphalians asking for a room.... Some citizens, up to now of good reputation, sold their conscience for this nice little extra income. The Canadian is the best paid soldier in the world, his value is accordingly high for ladies of the infamous trade. The 'soldiers fiancés' were from Grafenwohr and Baumholder, who had left their US soldiers for the better paid Canadians....

As a result of all of this outrage, the local *polizei* cracked down on a number of places like 'Brewery Baker', charging the so-called *Veronikas* with 'willful bodily injury' (that is, spreading venereal disease), and Canadian soldiers were cautioned about picking up girls while using military transport after a number of jeeps had been observed transporting civilians.

Relations with the Germans were, for the most part, quite good. The Canadians were considered to be different from the Belgians, since "they pay for everything and do not sequester anything", (the local Belgian occupation forces had a reputation for removing everything that wasn't nailed down). As in Hannover, 1 CIBG and later 2 CIBG had a Town Major and other representatives who, in addition to their other duties, sat in on town council meetings in the Soest area:

> We had regions where a battalion and a number of smaller units would be in one of our so-called forts; all the married quarters would be there for that particular group. People voted and we had an assembly hall for them....

Liaison between the *polizei* and the Provost company was necessarily close. Discipline had its ups and downs, often depending on how soon the next major exercise was to take place:

> Discipline has been, on the whole, satisfactory.... There have never been more than thirty men in the detention barracks. On the other hand, an irritating number of incidents affecting civilians has persisted. These incidents are given publicity in the local press, although the local attitude to the presence of the Brigade remains good. These offences are the work of a small minority and usually take place in conjunction with drunkenness....

As usual, Canadian soldiers played hard after working hard.

1 CIBG's tour ended on 19 October 1955 and 2 Canadian Infantry Brigade Group commanded by Brigadier Roger Rowley took on the task of being the Canadian Army's NATO contribution in Europe. As with the previous rotation, an entire brigade group performed another Operation COME AND GO over a two month period. 2 CIBG's units included:

> HQ 2 CIBG
> A Squadron, Royal Canadian Dragoons
> 4th Regiment, Royal Canadian Horse Artillery
> 1 Field Squadron, Royal Canadian Engineers
> 2 CIBG Signal Troop
> 1st Battalion, The Royal Canadian Regiment
> 1st Battalion, Princess Patricia's Canadian Light Infantry

1st Battalion, Royal 22nd Regiment
5 Transport Company, Royal Canadian Army Service Corps
4 Field Ambulance, Royal Canadian Army Medical Corps
40 Infantry Workshop, Royal Canadian Electrical and Mechanical Engineers
2 CIBG Light Aid Detachment, Royal Canadian Electrical and Mechanical Engineers

Some support units such as 1 Infantry Division Ordnance Field Park, 1 Field Dental Unit, 1 Field Security Section, 1 Provost Company and 1 Canadian Public Relations Unit, however, did not rotate and simply came under command of 2 CIBG.

The political environment in which Brigadier Rowley had to function was somewhat different from that of his predecessors. Germany had become a member of NATO in May 1955, and occupation forces in Germany like the British and the Belgians ceased to have an occupation role. As a result, the Canadian Brigade gained a higher political profile in Germany than before, and required closer liaison with the Canadian Ambassador in Bonn:

> Since the presence of the Canadian Brigade in Germany is a fact of considerable political importance, you should keep the Ambassador informed of any developments concerning the Brigade which might have an effect on political or public relations.... At no time did the Canadian Brigade in Germany have the status of an occupation force – particularly now that the Federal Republic has regained its full sovereignty, you should emphasize that Canada has contributed the Brigade to a North Atlantic Force created to deter and, if necessary, to resist aggression in Europe against the NATO allies. By helping to deter aggression, the Brigade will be protecting and defending Canada as well as its ally Germany. This is practical collective security.

In addition to the political aspects, Brigadier Rowley still had the usual task of maintaining the Brigade's operational readiness, as well as functioning as the Army's national commander in Europe.

The first problem 2 CIBG had to deal with was a virulent flu epidemic, as Brigadier Rowley recalled:

They shipped the first people out about a week before the first Asian Flu epidemic that anybody had ever heard of hit my brigade; Doc McNally said we were never going to get these people out of here. We had ships down in Rotterdam and it was a real crisis. We sent a wire to Ottawa and they flew over some serum. We had to get all these people together in community halls...some were very sick indeed and we had the hospitals full. McNally came to me and said 'we're going to have to inoculate these people en masse. I'd like you to come up just to show them there's nothing to it and raise their morale and have the first needle'. I said 'that seems reasonable – I have to take it anyway'. So I went up there and they gave me a shot of this stuff. Some of the batches weren't as good as they should have been; I came down with the flu two days later and I was on my back for nearly two weeks...

Training for 2 CIBG was not delayed long; the usual work ups, command post exercises and the like were conducted. A very intense period of officers' study occurred with 2 CIBG, BAOR, I (BR) Corps and 11th Armoured Division to discuss doctrine about tactical nuclear weapons use on the battlefield; the highlight of this activity was a visit to the 259th Field Artillery Missile Battalion (US Army) to observe the *Corporal* missile which would soon become the primary nuclear support weapon for I (BR) Corps.

2 CIBG's training plan generally followed the earlier work up scheme, except that there was no large-scale NATO exercise scheduled for the fall of 1956. Consequently, 2 CIBG did the usual deployments to Putlos, Soltau and Sennelager, including a divisional level exercise with 6th (BR) Armoured Division. Brigade exercises such as Exercise SABRE and Exercise TRAVAIL were structured to develop procedures for company/squadron and battalion advance to contact under nuclear conditions, dispersion of administrative and command units in the defence to prevent their destruction, as well as the development of medical evacuation plans in the event of mass casualties. The continuing saga of the JAVELIN CPX series was also played out with a special emphasis on corps level nuclear doctrine.

One area of particular interest for Brigadier Rowley was combat team operations:

CHAPTER TWO

> I was concerned with the standard of efficiency at the platoon and company level. I had commanded a battle school during the war (I figured I was something of an expert) and there's no substitute for teaching these fellows the drills, so I set up a series of company exercises in defence and in the attack; we ran every company in the Brigade through it.... Well, there had to be a 'carrot' at the end of the pole so I produced a trophy for each type of exercise. The first one was BATTLE AXE; I got some old weapons from antiquarians in London, had them all polished up and mounted on big boards.... That was for the attack exercises. The defensive exercise was a series of exercises called RAPIER and the final series at a lower level was PUENYARD, which is the defensive short dagger used in dueling. These were all mounted and competed for in the name of the company. They improved the standard of company and battalion tactics to a tremendous extent....

As in the early 1950s, the Soviet Occupation Exchange Mission (SOXMIS) 'spies' continued to put in appearances at Canadian exercises, and members of 2 Field Security Section, including WO Seguin, had to keep track of them:

> Whenever there was an exercise, especially at Sennelager or at Soltau, the Russian SOXMIS vehicles were around...we had to keep them out of the exercise area. There were six of these vehicles allocated to the BAOR area. We didn't have the same power as the Brits or American soldiers, so whenever this happened, the Brit field security section, either the one at Unna, Paderborn or Hereford, would send a couple of their men and they had the diplomatic authority to evacuate the SOXMIS personnel...Wherever we saw them, we were always told to take the grid reference, the time of day and report back to the Brigade Commander.

During a pause in training, 2 CIBG was tasked to conduct the 1956 Dominion Day ceremonies at the Rote Erde Stadium in Dortmund. The peculiar execution of the ceremony could put any of today's heavy metal rock band antics to shame:

> We hired the stadium at Dortmund which consisted of a grandstand on one side, a huge sort of gate at one end where all the players came in and on the

other side there was a gothic bandstand and glass-terraced viewing spots....We decided to honour our country by erecting huge screens about 20 feet high with the coat of arms of each province in the centre, about 50 feet high, attached to the bandstand. We decided that it would be great if we covered up these things with material and kept them covered during the beginning. The music would start, and a ring circuit attached to explosives was set to blow these curtains off one after another sequentially...

The song of Newfoundland was sung on a recording over the loudspeaker; the announcer was saying that this was our baby province and so on and so forth, and suddenly I noticed that there was a lot of smoke still coming from the base of this thing and suddenly the flames started. In a very short time all of the curtains were burning. The British Commander-in-Chief, Sir Richard Gale, was sitting on my left and on my right was Charles Ritchie, our Ambassador. Charlie nudged me and said 'This isn't supposed to happen, is it?' I said 'No, it certainly isn't' but it went on and there was no break in the music or anything else. Suddenly Sir Richard Gale on the other side said, 'I say, Roger, what a jolly good show!' Then the fire department came with their brass helmets; they unrolled their hoses which had all rotted, and they turned the water on full bore and the hoses started to explode. We had already deployed at one end a troop of guns to fire a 21 gun salute. The Patricias were deployed the full length of the field to fire a Feu de Joie; when we let off the first gun on the 21 gun salute, we blew out all the glass bricks at the back of the stadium, and every child in the stadium started to scream. The Feu de Joie was fired two or three more times. O Canada was played.... I'm never going to tell how much it cost to put the stadium back together again.... But it got to be a very good show.

Needless to say, this was not reported in the Brigade's Monthly Report of Activities.

Another important aspect, logistics support to the Canadian Army in Germany, continued to develop throughout 1955-1956. SHAPE had concluded in 1954 that,

...[there] are no, nor does Canada at the present plan to provide M-Day non-organic support units on the Continent. The M-Day Brigade depends on the UK for logistic and non-organic support and the UK M-Day support is inadequate for UK forces....

The Canadian Chief of the General Staff explained that this had been done for important reasons:

> [the CGS] pointed out that the Canadian Army is operating on a ceiling in manpower and money imposed by the government. In these circumstances, it is desirable to concentrate on first line troops as these are harder to train, while a large proportion of logistic support troops could be recruited from civilian life and would need less training. [Canada] favours a strong fighting element and a risk in administrative echelons. SHAPE planners agreed it would be preferable to retain front line strength at the expense of logistic support units....

Once Canada defined its divisional commitment to NATO in 1954, further planning indicated a need to find more permanent logistics and support facilities. As noted in Chapter 1, the Canadian Army maintained a logistics element in Antwerp, Belgium to liaise with British Communications Zone staff there. No. 1 Canadian Base Unit, Europe, however, was relocated to Soest so that it could handle immediate support to the Brigade. There it ceased to operate as a separate entity, and was incorporated into the Brigade.

The Canadian brigade already had 30 days worth of operational stocks and ammunition on the West bank of the Rhine near Mönchen-Gladbach under the maintenance of 1 Canadian Base Ordnance Unit (1 CBOU). These sites were considered especially vulnerable, since they were located in places from which NORTHAG units would be defending after retreating across the Rhine. As a result, these stocks were moved to a new British site called GONDOLA Base in Antwerp.

The problem now was how to ensure the safe arrival in Europe of the other two promised brigades of 1st Canadian Division and their equipment should war break out. Initially, the plans included transporting them across the Atlantic in convoys. However, the Soviet submarine threat to the sea lines of communication in the North Atlantic was massive, and thus the arrival of these formations could not be guaranteed in 30 days.

The British, on the other hand, had experimented with pre-positioning brigade and division sets of equipment in their Communications Zone and had flown over the troops to these sites during exercises. (The Americans would adopt this concept in the 1960s, and call it Return of Forces to Germany or REFORGER). Could Canada do the same thing and locate the equipment in the UK?

Talks were initiated with the British to find a suitable site. The abandoned Husband-Bosworth airfield was selected as a possible site to store two brigades' worth of equipment and supplies, a predecessor to the Theatre Base concept which appeared in the 1980s. It was anticipated that troops from Canada would fly into the airfield, pick up their equipment and move to an embarkation port in southern England for transport to Antwerp. The detonation of the first Soviet hydrogen bomb, however, changed all of this planning. SHAPE and the British concluded that in a war using H-Bombs, the movement capacity of British ports would be severely reduced, perhaps to only 25 per cent of their normal capacity. Priority of course would then be given to British movements and inward bound supplies to sustain the island nation.

The solution arrived at was to increase the size of the Canadian storage area at GONDOLA in Antwerp so to be able to accommodate the rest of the division's equipment and reserves. Because of the size of facility required, a separate Memorandum of Understanding was drawn up between Belgium and Canada; there would be no more 'piggy backing' off the British in this case. Construction was completed in November 1955 for housing 30 days worth of ammunition, stores, vehicles, POL, engineer equipment and other supplies that would be required for the division. Certain heavy equipment such as tanks would be provided by the British.

Once the logistics situation stabilized, most of 1956 was quiet for 2 CIBG. A planned exercise in which the divisional headquarters was supposed to deploy from Canada to Europe was canceled. Most of the Army's training resources in 1956 were allocated to Exercise MORNING STAR (held at the newly-acquired Camp Gagetown in New Brunswick) to train the other brigades in the Division for tactical nuclear warfare.

Things began to change, however, as the international situation grew tense in October 1956. In Hungary, after several days of anti-communist rioting, Prime Minister Imre Nagy declared martial law and ordered Soviet troops out the country on 23 October 1956. Then on 26 October, troops from the Soviet Union, Romania and Czechoslovakia invaded their hitherto ally. On 1 November Nagy withdrew Hungary from the Warsaw Pact, and appealed to the United Nations for assistance. Simultaneously, tensions in the Mediterranean regarding the future of the strategic Suez Canal prompted Britain and France on 5 November 1956 to land airborne and amphibious forces to secure the canal zone after Israel attacked Egypt. On 7 November, the Soviet Union threatened to attack Britain and France (both NATO members) with nuclear weapons, giving the implication that, if the West made moves to assist Hungary, war in Europe would result. This Soviet aggression marked a new, more dangerous phase of the Cold War.

The impact of these two events on 2 CIBG in Germany was serious. NORTHAG planners had not counted on Britain withdrawing some of her forces from BAOR to conduct the Suez operation, and this affected the operational effectiveness of I(BR) Corps:

> About the time the Suez Crisis broke, Northern Army Group was stripped of almost everything, including tank regiments.... One of the supporting tank regiments to 2 CIBG was gone, the Corps commander was gone with his headquarters...all kinds of units were gone.

Brigadier Rowley also noted that some aspects of the NORTHAG defence plan, such as contingencies for the evacuation of dependents were flawed:

> We had an evacuation plan for our civilian population, our dependents, to get them west of the Rhine, which we called TABLE TOP. It involved the British providing us with a Royal Army Service Corps transport column... [these units were not available during the Suez operation]. I pointed out to the CGS that this situation existed, and that I was not prepared to conform to the operational plan because I had no intention of withdrawing through my own married quarters. Therefore, I had an alternate plan to take the place of TABLE TOP; that was to take the vehicles that the British had left behind, man the column with my own troops and move them.... It was a touchy

situation, things were uneasy. It was a worrying time for my staff.

It was not an easy time for the dependants either, as one member noted:

> The Hungarian revolt...that kind of put a strain on the personnel and the families. We had this plan for evacuation. My car was supposed to be used to evacuate families: the car had space for six and, since my wife did not drive and I had four kids, there was this lady in the PMQs that lived across from us. She drove and they had one child...the evacuation authorities came over during the Hungarian [crisis] and asked if we consented to this arrangement and I said yes. There was Scramble One, Two and Three; those were the code words for the evacuation. Sometimes it would be more of a TEWT-like activity but sometimes on a more serious scramble, we would have to pack, go to the rendezvous as designated and, depending on the situation, wait one to seven hours to evacuate. During the Hungarian uprising, some of the ladies were a bit edgy...

The tension continued for some time afterwards; enough to prompt a review of reinforcement plans for 2 CIBG but not enough for the brigade to undertake a precautionary deployment, which would happen in later East-West confrontations. Eventually, the Suez Crisis was temporarily resolved when the Americans pressured the British and French to withdraw in the face of Soviet threats. Accompanying this was the decision by Canada's then-Minister of External Affairs, Lester B. Pearson, to deploy for the first time a United Nations peacekeeping force (UNEF I), made up of units from Canada and other non-controversial UN members, to occupy a buffer zone between Israeli and Egyptian forces. For the Hungarians, hung out to dry by the UN, there would be no such relief; Soviet subjugation was complete when 50,000 Warsaw Pact troops crushed their valiant attempt to gain freedom.

2 CIBG entered the year 1957 with the international situation still simmering. The new aggressiveness displayed by the Soviet Union prompted a review of NATO's defence planning, planning that would eventually alter the Canadian Army's commitment to ACE late in 1957. For the time being, 2 CIBG continued with routine training in

conjunction with units from I (BR) Corps until the decision was made in Canada to rotate 4 Canadian Infantry Brigade Group in place of 2 CIBG in November 1957.

Accolades for 2 CIBG came from many sources before the handover commenced on 6 November 1957. The commander of the newly-established Bundeswehr command in Westphalia, Major General Richard Schimpf, noted that "the discipline and hardiness of Canadian troops in Europe surpassed anything ever known in German military circles." Not to be outdone, BAOR commander General Sir Alfred Dudley Ward remarked to the press that the Canadian brigade was "the best fighting formation in the world." Strong praise, and not to be taken lightly. The British at the time still suffered from thinking of Canada as being a colony in many respects, while the Germans were only starting to recover from the ignominy of occupation.

In sum, 1 and 2 Canadian Infantry Brigade Groups served as important contributions to NATO from 1953 to 1957. Despite their low priority as far as overall Canadian defence commitments were concerned, the brigades were both numerically and operationally significant within the context of I (BR) Corps and of NORTHAG. The influence of new NATO strategic and operational level thinking was also important, particularly with regards to training and exercises, and the Canadians showed that they were quickly able to adapt to change. The ability to function as part of I (BE) Corps as well as I (BR) Corps was only a portent of things to come in later years, and added to the growing reputation of the Canadian Army. Finally, the construction of a permanent infrastructure in Germany to support the Canadians stationed there reinforced assertions that Canada was firmly committed to the defence of the NATO area in Europe.

1957 - 1963

CRISIS AND CHANGE

CHAPTER THREE

"WE CAN NOW SEE THAT IN WAR MANY ROADS LEAD TO SUCCESS, AND THAT THEY DO NOT ALL INVOLVE THE OPPONENT'S OUTRIGHT DEFEAT. THEY RANGE FROM THE DESTRUCTION OF THE ENEMY'S FORCES, THE CONQUEST OF HIS TERRITORY, TO A TEMPORARY OCCUPATION OR INVASION, TO PROJECTS WITH AN IMMEDIATE POLITICAL PURPOSE AND FINALLY TO PASSIVELY AWAITING THE ENEMY'S ATTACKS. ANY ONE OF THESE MAY BE USED TO OVERCOME THE ENEMY'S WILL: THE CHOICE DEPENDS ON THE CIRCUMSTANCES."

-CLAUSEWITZ, *ON WAR*

Above: *Battlefield nuclear weapons continued to influence Canadian Army doctrine and equipment; Canada's NATO Brigade was no exception. Canadian soldiers were allowed to participate in live nuclear tests in Australia and the United States. Photos of Canadians in such tests are rare; this picture shows US soldiers on such an exercise.* (US Naval Institute)

CHAPTER THREE 113

Above: Before the Wall went up Canadian soldiers were generally forbidden to visit Berlin, but an exception was made when inter-BAOR sports meets were held there. Here, two soldiers from the 8th Canadian Hussars and one from the Canadian Guards (in peaked cap) pose by the Brandenburg Gate for photos. The sign says "Attention! You are now leaving West Berlin". (DND) EF 61 922992
Below: Canadian engineer on exercise at an autobahn overpass, 1961. (DND) EF 61 9375 28

Above: Inter-allied cooperation in NATO was essential for success. US soldiers from the 24th Infantry Division get directions from an exercise umpire provided by 8th Canadian Hussars (Princess Louise's) atop a Ferret scout car. (DND) EF 61 9388 5 5 A
Below: The crew of a Centurion tank from the 8th Canadian Hussars exchange information with Bundeswehr panzer troops from an M-48 Patton tank during Exercise HOLD FAST, 1960. (DND) EF 61 9318 38

CHAPTER THREE

Above: *Some NATO planners thought that the Canadian Brigade, if equipped with small nuclear weapons like the Davy Crockett shown here, would make an excellent 'fire brigade' formation in the Central Region. This option was rejected by Canada.* (US NAVAL INSTITUTE)
Below: *Part of a successful defence is a good obstacle plan. Royal Canadian Engineers from 4 Canadian Infantry Brigade Group prepare an autobahn overpass for (simulated) demolition. Note the recently acquired FN C1 7.62mm rifle and American helmet.* EF 61 9375 7

Above: New 'eyes' for the Guns: two L-19 'Bird Dog' spotter aircraft from the RCHA Air Observation Troop conduct a fly past at Fort Prince of Wales. (DND) EF 61 9385 4
Below: On the assault: troops from 4 Canadian Infantry Brigade Group charge the cameraman during Exercise SILVER DOLLAR in September 1962. (DND) EF 62 945938

CHAPTER THREE

Above: *Two ways to kill T-55 tanks: the jeep-mounted 106mm recoiless rifle ...* (DND) EF 61 9349 46
Below: *... and the Canadian-made Heller rocket launcher.* (DND) EF 61 9282.9

Above: *A sure way to kill a lot of T-55s: The Honest John nuclear surface to surface missile.* (BGen Tedlie)
Below: *Another Honest John launch. The Canadian Brigade had four such weapons in direct support between 1961 and 1970.* (DND) EF 63 9540 2

CHAPTER THREE

Above: *In Germany, exercises frequently took place in the midst of the civilian population. Here an infantry section sets up a .30 calibre General Purpose Machine Gun.*
Below: *Canadian recce units were highly regarded in NATO. Here Nomad helicopters rendezvous with Ferret scout cars during Exercise CANADA CUP in October 1962. (DND) EF 62 9478 1*

Above: The Infrared Viewer (Medium) gave 4 Canadian Infantry Brigade Group a definite edge on Exercise *CANADA CUP*. (DND) EF 63 9563 31

CHAPTER THREE

Above: *Despite the world tension brought on by the Cuban Missile Crisis, Guardsmen from 1st Battalion, Canadian Guards advance with 8th Canadian Hussars on Exercise CANADA CUP. Troops are wearing 'bush dress' and manning jeep mounted .50 calibre Heavy Machine Gun.* (DND) EF 62 9474 41
Below: *Centurion tanks advance through some rolling countryside in Westphalia.* (DND) EF 62 9474 51

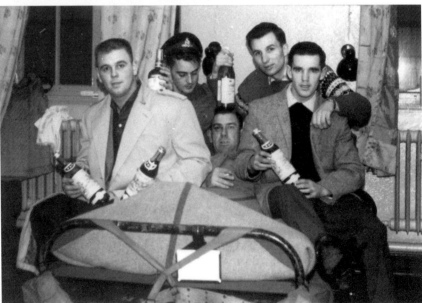

Above: *Their rotation delayed by the 1962 Cuban Missile Crisis, infantrymen from the Royal Highland Regiment of Canada, (the Black Watch) hitch a ride on a Centurion tank.* (DND) EF 62 9468 63
Below: *With only a limited amount of off time and few recreational facilities compared to today "Shack Parties" were one form of entertainment for Canadian soldiers in Germany in the 1950s and 60s. Note web gear hung at foot of bed as per kit layout regulations.* (DAVID HOLT)

CHAPTER THREE 123

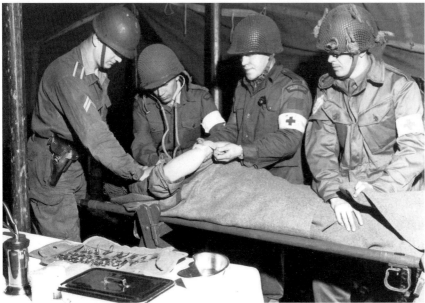

Above: *The 'enemy' on Exercise KEEN BLADE, October 1963. The combination of Bundeswehr M-48 tanks and Hotchkiss infantry combat vehicles took their toll on 4 Canadian Infantry Brigade Group.* (DND) EF 63 9563 17
Below: *Inter-allied cooperation extended to all aspects of military operations in Germany. Simulated casualties undergo treatment by a combined German-Canadian medical unit on Exercise KEEN BLADE.* (DND) EF 63 9523 5

Above: *Before the introduction of the M-113 APC, the 3/4 ton truck had to suffice for infantry transportation. Here a machine gun team deploys on Exercise KEEN BLADE.* (DND) EF 639563 1

Below: *Infantrymen from 1st Battalion, The Royal Canadian Regiment take a break. Note the red patch insignia for 1st Canadian Infantry Division on the right shoulder of the man with the helmet and machete. The rifle is the FNC1 of Belgian design but with Canadian modifications. ... And putties were still worn up to the mid 1960s.* (DND) EF 63 9532 21

CHAPTER THREE

Above: *"Air trooping" replaced sea transport in the 1960s as the primary means of getting Canadian servicemen overseas. The RCAF Yukon aircraft shown here was a common 14 hour flight 'experience' for Canadian soldiers rotating to Germany. (DND) EF 62 9421*
Below: *On Exercise HOLD FAST 1960, soldiers of the Queen's Own Rifles of Canada boarded British S-55 helicopters to seize two bridges in a surprise airmobile attack. (DND) EF 62 9474 33*

The period 1957 to 1963 was a critical time for the Canadian brigade in Europe. The new strategic direction taken by NATO in 1957 had a decisive impact on the organization, training and operational role for the Canadian Army's commitment to Allied Command Europe (ACE) over the next 14 years. This was not all; international tensions increased almost to a breaking point three times between 1961 and 1963, and the brigade had to be prepared for open conflict on each occasion. The size and disposition of the Soviet threat in Europe remained relatively constant, except for the deployment of medium-range ground attack aircraft armed with nuclear bombs. What did change was the increased willingness of the Soviet Union to push NATO to the limit.

The first indication of this was seen during the crushing of the Hungarian uprising in 1956. This action directly influenced the development of NATO strategic thinking and accelerated implementation of NATO force structure. In October 1956, NATO had tabled a 'fine tuned' version of MC 48, the 1954 strategic concept. This too was significantly

CHAPTER THREE

revised late in May 1957. Both the 1956 and 1957 versions of this strategy, known as MC 14/2, emphasized that the driving principle behind NATO was common action through self help and mutual aid to deter war, and to defend against armed attack as far forward as possible should deterrence fail. Both of these concepts reiterated the "two phase war" idea developed in 1954; that is, widespread use of nuclear weapons in the first phase, followed by employment of conventional forces in the second. The 1956 version followed the 1954 concept of the Forward Defence of Europe very closely, giving secondary priority to the strategic nuclear counter-offensive. However, Soviet threats during the Suez and Hungary affairs changed this. The May 1957 version included stronger language with regard to the use of nuclear weapons by NATO and reversed the priorities, giving first priority to the strategic nuclear counter-offensive, and second, to maintaining the integrity of the NATO area.

What did this mean in real terms? NATO forces after 1957 were categorized as belonging to one of two groups, "Shield" or "Sword". Sword forces included the US Strategic Air Command and the Royal Air Force Bomber Command; these were the strategic nuclear forces designed to attack the Soviet Union directly, if necessary. The Shield forces, previously known as the "Integrated Force", were the conventional *and* tactical nuclear forces designed to preserve the integrity of the NATO area; that is, defend NATO countries on the ground and in the air from north Norway through western Europe, down to eastern Turkey. In a war situation where deterrence had failed, the task of the Shield forces was to stop invading Warsaw Pact forces, while the Sword forces would destroy the Soviet's nuclear forces, second echelon conventional forces, and their industrial ability to continue the war. Once the Soviets were no longer able to conduct nuclear operations, NATO would reconstitute, mobilize strategic "follow on" forces other than the Sword and Shield forces, and then finish the war on conventional terms.

This strategy has often been referred to as a "trip wire" or "plate glass" strategy, whereby a Soviet invasion of NATO territory would trigger a massive US and British nuclear strike intended to destroy the Soviet Union as a functioning society. This interpretation, however, ignored the main purpose of NATO strategy which was the preservation of the NATO area, not just the wholesale destruction of the Soviet Union. NATO forces stationed in Europe served not simply as a trip wire for an American and British nuclear response as many alleged but, rather, were part of a coherent nuclear *and* conventional defence strategy for the security of Western Europe.

Ground forces were a key element in this new strategy, and they were supposed to have a dual purpose. NATO ground forces had to be able to take on and defeat larger Warsaw Pact conventional forces by using tactical nuclear weapons, as well as be able to engage them by conventional means. One element of the 1956 version of NATO strategy was the need to defend against incursions that did not warrant a nuclear response. Only conventional ground forces could do this, since it would be excessive to vapourize a 30 man infantry platoon with a 20 kiloton nuclear bomb. The May 1957 revision, however, practically eliminated purely conventional responses from consideration and focused more on nuclear operations. Nonetheless, ground forces assigned to NATO continued to develop both a nuclear and a conventional capability, even though the emphasis was clearly on the nuclear side of things.

A plan was developed by NATO in 1958 to restructure forces committed to ACE, based on the 1957 strategic concept. This plan, called MC 70, entailed integrating nuclear delivery systems into the Shield forces, thus making available to NATO members a range of nuclear-capable tube artillery, short range and medium range surface to surface missiles and nuclear-tipped anti-aircraft missiles. These weapons were only to be used in the defence of the NATO area.

A result of this was the creation in 1958 of a stockpile of US nuclear warheads available to NATO members who at the same time acquired the appropriate delivery systems; this also included an expansion of the existing NATO Atomic Information Agreement which Canada and other members had signed earlier. American owned weapons in the NATO stockpile would be provided under the joint control of both the United States and the user nation. These weapons could only be used in the defence of the NATO area, and only released on the order of SACEUR. Other NATO members, Britain and later France, created their own small nuclear weapon stockpiles so they could have a measure of independent control over these devices.

CHAPTER THREE

The impact of the 1957 strategic concept and the restructuring plan on Canadian defence policy and ultimately, on Canada's NATO brigade in Germany, was very significant. The Canadian government under newly elected Conservative Prime Minister John Diefenbaker reasoned that there was insufficient money in the defence budget to develop peacetime forces in being for both the nuclear warfighting phase and the reconstitution/conventional phase of NATO's strategic concept. Only forces that could contribute to Phase I would thus receive funding, since these forces could be justified as contributing to the overall deterrent system.

Top defence spending priority went to forces that could limit damage to Canada, that is to those capable of destroying Soviet forces that could attack Canada with nuclear weapons. Thus, first priority of expenditure went to interceptor aircraft and missiles, the northern radar system, anti-submarine ships and aircraft, and submarine detection systems. Second priority went to the re-equipping of the Air Division in Europe with CF-104 *Starfighter* nuclear strike aircraft, with third priority going to the Army's NATO brigade group. Both of these latter two formations would contribute to NATO Shield forces and demonstrate Canada's continuing commitment to Europe. The only Phase II forces that Canada was projected to have would be post-attack, national reconstitution forces. The reconstitution forces came from the Militia, which lost its kit and was reorganized into "survival columns" to enter bombed cities and restore order. The commitment of a second infantry division to ACE was dropped, and its stockpiled equipment given to other NATO members under the Mutual Defence Assistance Programme.

The Canadian brigade group in Europe was to benefit materially from this policy development, despite being last again on the defence priority totem pole. This would not take place in 1957, however, since inertia in equipment procurement programmes produced a delay that would not be resolved until 1960. As a result, the brigade that rotated to Europe in 1957 was not suitably equipped to fight under the new strategic concept. This is not surprising, nor was it an immediate problem since all of the other forces in NORTHAG were also in the process of re-equipping.

The brigade group selected for the November 1957 rotation was 4 Canadian Infantry Brigade Group (4 CIBG), under the command of

Brigadier Donald C. Cameron. Units rotating to Germany to replace those of 2 CIBG included:

HQ 4 CIBG
Royal Canadian Dragoons
Recce Squadron (drawn from the Lord Strathcona's Horse)
2nd Battalion, Canadian Guards
3rd Battalion, Royal 22nd Regiment
2nd Battalion, Queen's Own Rifles of Canada
1st Regiment, Royal Canadian Horse Artillery
4 Field Squadron, Royal Canadian Engineers
"L" Troop 1 Canadian Infantry Division Signals Regiment
1 Transport Company, Royal Canadian Army Service Corps
1 Field Ambulance, Royal Canadian Army Medical Corps
41 Infantry Workshop, Royal Canadian Electrical and Mechanical Engineers
4 CIBG Light Aid Detachment, Royal Canadian Electrical and Mechanical Engineers

Units such as No 1 Public Relations Unit, and the Intelligence, Dental, Ordnance, Provost and Postal units conducted a man-for-man rotation. Canadian Base Units, Europe continued to function, and a depot was still located in Antwerp.

4 CIBG was much stronger than the previous brigade groups. Instead of a single tank squadron, 4 CIBG possessed an entire armoured regiment of 47 *Centurion* tanks and an independent recce squadron. The reasons for these changes were numerous. First of all, the British severely cut back their forces in Germany after a 1957 defence review; the effect on BAOR was the removal of an entire division from the order of battle. As a result, the armoured and reconnaissance support that the Canadian brigade relied upon ceased to exist. It was also felt by the Army's senior leadership that the brigade should become more self-sufficient in terms of fighting capability, even if it came at the expense of some service support.

Secondly, the new Conservative government gave much more scrutiny to defence establishments and their effects on budgets than did the previous Liberal government. The combined manpower ceiling for both the Canadian Army and RCAF in Europe, which was established in 1951 at 12,000 men, had never been carefully monitored; as a result, the brigade group had reached a strength of 6230 officers and men in 1956. The Conservative government's clamp down reduced the brigade to 5500 personnel. Army Headquarters rationalized the situation and vaguely suggested that an additional 1800 personnel could be flown over in an emergency to bring the brigade group up to its required war strength. Among the actions taken to get the armoured regiment and the independent recce squadron into 4 CIBG and still remain within the manpower ceiling, the Chief of the General Staff removed one man from each infantry section and took the flame thrower section from the Pioneer platoons of each of the brigade's three infantry battalions. Other manpower changes included a reorganization of the administrative structure that supported Canadian Army representatives at the NATO headquarters.

4 CIBG's equipment now included 31 *Ferret* Mk I scout cars for Recce Squadron and the 47 *Centurion* Mk 5 tanks for the RCD. The infantry started to re-equip with the FN C1 7.62mm rifle and the *Sterling* sub-machine gun, but only after existing stocks of .303 and 9mm ammunition for the older *Lee-Enfield*, *Bren* and *Sten* weapons had been used up. The *Heller* anti-tank weapon replaced the old 3.5 inch rocket launcher, while the number of 106mm anti-armour recoilless rifles in the infantry battalions was doubled from six to 12 per battalion. The RCHA replaced its 25 pounders with 24 brand new towed 105mm guns, while Canadian-pattern 3/4 ton trucks replaced the aging bren gun carriers in the infantry battalions. According to Colonel Jerry Zypchen, 4 CIBG's engineering resources included

> ...jeeps, 3/4 ton trucks and 2 1/2 ton trucks.... We were assigned plant from Park Troop. The plant consisted of two dozers on flat bed trucks, two cranes, a grader, two front end loaders and ten dump trucks. On one exercise at Soltau, I arrived to support [1 RCR] with a dozer on a flatbed and two dump trucks. The OC Support Company was so perplexed at the sight of all this equipment that he proposed to put white mine tape around us as we went into our hide to indicate that we were some form of exercise expedient. He couldn't accept that what he saw was what we would go to war with....

The one thing that the Canadians did lack was a distinctive Canadian field uniform other than the makeshift baggy black coveralls that had been worn by a generation of post-war Canadian soldiers in training. This was a real problem in the development of a Canadian identity in NATO. David Holt, a Gunner in the early 27 CIB described this situation:

> The Canadian Army did not have a field uniform per se. The woollen battledress in winter and the cotton bush uniform for summer were the only field dress we had. Both also had to be worn on parade and for marching out. There was no waterproof footwear and there were no tents available. We slept under ponchos... .It was downright misery on exercise. In an attempt to solve this, the enterprising soldier went to Soest to Butzbach, an army surplus store and there he purchased a US-pattern combat jacket, with any luck, a liner, and, if he had enough money, he would try to get a sleeping bag since none of these were issued. The result was a rag-tag organization that looked like hell in the field, with patches and home made field uniforms of every description that soldiers had self-designed to keep themselves warm and dry....

Canadian soldiers in the field were thus often mistaken for Americans, while soldiers wearing battledress in garrison were mistaken for British troops despite Canadian insignia.

In organizational terms, 4 CIBG resembled (in terms of fighting power as opposed to supporting troops) a British armoured division that was short two armoured regiments; as a matter of course, the British took to calling 4 CIBG "The Light Division". 4 CIBG's organization also became the standard for the other two brigade groups in 1st Canadian Infantry Division. To ensure 'rotatability', two more armoured regiments would be added to the Army's order of battle in 1957 and 1958; 1/8th Canadian Hussars (Princess Louise's) and The 1st Fort Garry Horse. In terms of 'teeth' units, the 1st Canadian Infantry Division consisted of three strong brigade groups, each having three infantry battalions, an artillery regiment and an armoured regiment. The other Canadian-based brigade group was tasked with continental defence and UN operations, with the fourth armoured regiment providing reconnaissance support to the division. Logistics support and strategic mobility for all of this was, of course, another matter completely and will be discussed later.

The existing camps and infrastructure in the Soest, Hemer and Werl areas were handed over in 1957 to units of 4 CI27 CIBhome also had to be found for the RCD, and fortunately the former Wehrmacht barracks known as Seydlitz Kaserne in the town of Iserlohn was available to the armoured regiment.

The changes to the brigade's organization dovetailed with a major alteration in ACE's operational planning. As the reader will recall, the defensive concept from 1951 to 1957 was based on a deliberate withdrawal to the Rhine followed by a mobile defence behind the Rhine, using the river as a barrier. The main defensive line was moved further east in 1957 to the Weser-Lech Line. [See Figure 3-1.] A wide variety of factors prompted this change, a change which would affect the disposition of 4 CIBG in NORTHAG's operational planning.

It had been noted by SHAPE in 1954 that the one element required to strengthen the existing NATO forces defending Western Europe was a re-vitalized (West) German army. The Federal Republic of Germany was thus admitted as a member of NATO in 1955 and quickly set about building up the Bundeswehr. Once West Germany ceased to be an occupied country, however, it was no longer politically acceptable to give up 80 per cent of its territory during the early stages of a conflict and to plan to defend only that small portion of Germany which lay west of the Rhine. In this scenario, NATO's covering force battle was to be fought between the Weser and the Rhine Rivers. This plan relied heavily on the use of nuclear weapons to impose delays on the Soviet advance. This would, of course, cause so much damage to West Germany that it would be a Pyrrhic victory at best. How could the Bundeswehr be motivated to fight if most of Germany was simply to become a wasteland to protect the other European members? Exercise CARTE BLANCHE, which simulated NATO's ability to support the land battle with nuclear strikes, caused such a public outcry in Germany that pressure was placed on SACEUR to move the defensive line as far east as possible to conform with NATO's 'principle' of Forward Defence.

The increase in Shield forces and firepower between 1957 and 1960 was another factor in SACEUR's decision to shift the main defensive line eastward to the Weser-Lech line. All of SACEUR's Shield forces in

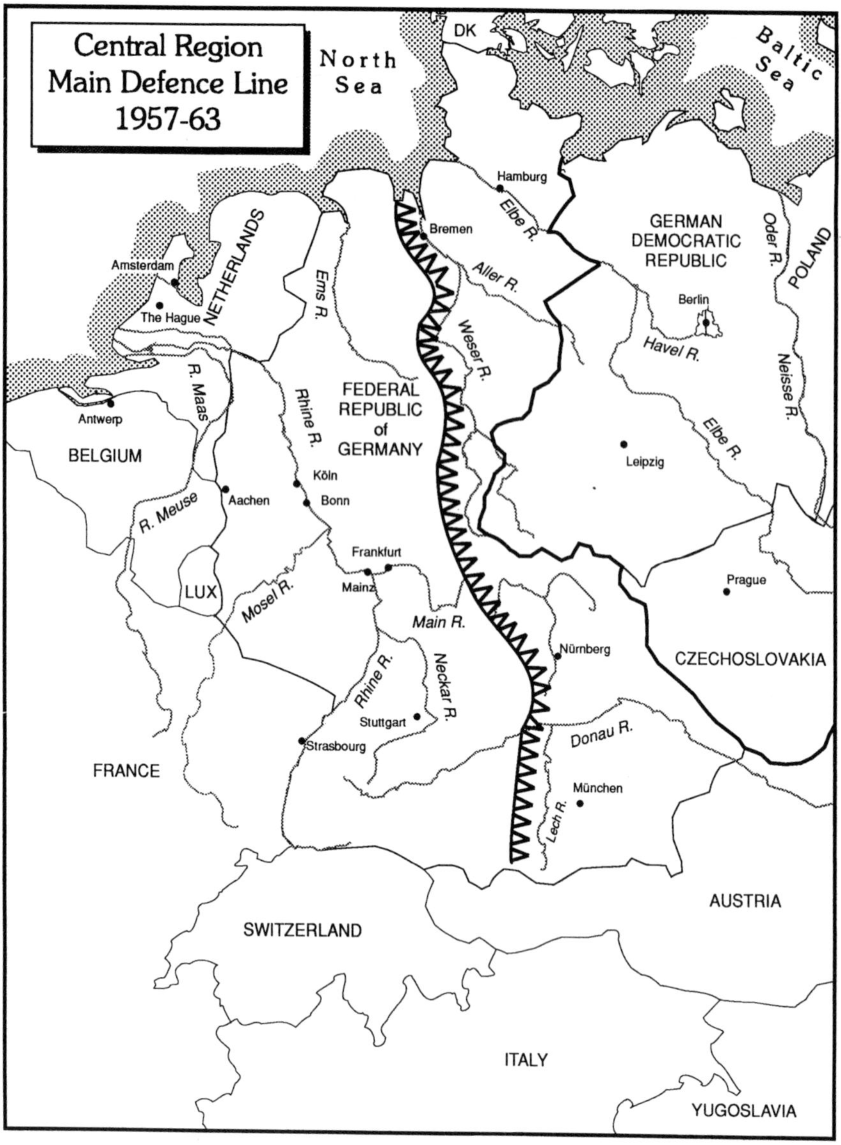
Central Region
Main Defence Line
1957-63
North Sea
DK
Baltic Sea
Hamburg
Elbe R.
Bremen
GERMAN
DEMOCRATIC
REPUBLIC
Oder R.
POLAND
Amsterdam
NETHERLANDS
Ems R.
Aller R.
Berlin
The Hague
Weser R.
Havel R.
R. Maas
Neisse R.
FEDERAL
REPUBLIC
of
GERMANY
Rhine R.
Antwerp
Elbe R.
BELGIUM
Leipzig
Köln
Aachen
Bonn
R. Meuse
Frankfurt
Prague
Mainz
LUX
Mosel R.
Main R.
Nürnberg
CZECHOSLOVAKIA
Neckar R.
Rhine R.
Stuttgart
Donau R.
Strasbourg
FRANCE
München
Lech R.
AUSTRIA
SWITZERLAND
ITALY
YUGOSLAVIA

FIGURE 3-1

CHAPTER THREE

NORTHAG and CENTAG had now been granted access to American tactical nuclear delivery systems as well as training for their use. In accordance with the MC 14/2 strategic concept and the subsequent nuclear stockpile arrangements, the Belgian, Dutch, German, British and Canadian forces in NORTHAG were encouraged to acquire nuclear delivery systems, even though the warheads remained under US custody and control (the so-called "dual-key" system). As a result, a variety of tube artillery, gravity bomb, guided and unguided missiles systems were phased into service by NATO's forces between 1957 and 1960. As an example of how much nuclear firepower SACEUR had access to, the size of the stockpile allocated for SACEUR's planning in 1959 included 2500 weapons in the kiloton range and 50 weapons in the megaton range, of which a proportion was available to NORTHAG.

SACEUR's concept of operations in the Central Region between 1957 and 1963 was based on the need to survive the initial enemy attack, destroy the Soviet's ability to use nuclear weapons, stop their land attack as far east as possible, and interdict their ability to continue offensive operations. Translation: use nuclear weapons against his airfields, delay his first echelon with conventional forces (armed with some tactical nuclear weapons), drop nuclear weapons on his follow-on, second echelon forces, communications centres and supply lines; and, make sure most of the damage is done as close to Iron Curtain as possible. Maybe the prevailing winds would blow the fallout eastwards.

For NORTHAG this meant that the absolutely final fall-back position was the Teutoburgerwald feature, not the Rhine. [See Figure 3-1A.] The main defensive line was the Weser River for I (NL) Corps, I (BR) Corps including 4 CIBG, I (BE) Corps, and the new German formation, I (GE) Korps. This line, known as the "48 Hour Line", had to be held for a minimum of two days since electronic navigation aid sites which guided aircraft conducting nuclear strikes against the enemy's second echelon were located in the vicinity of the Weser. These strike aircraft were critical to the success of the strategy; by preventing enemy second echelon forces from advancing, the air strikes reduced the numbers of enemy forces confronting NORTHAG on the Weser. Corps covering forces would be in place on the east bank of the river. The purpose of the covering forces was not so much to delay the enemy with conventional

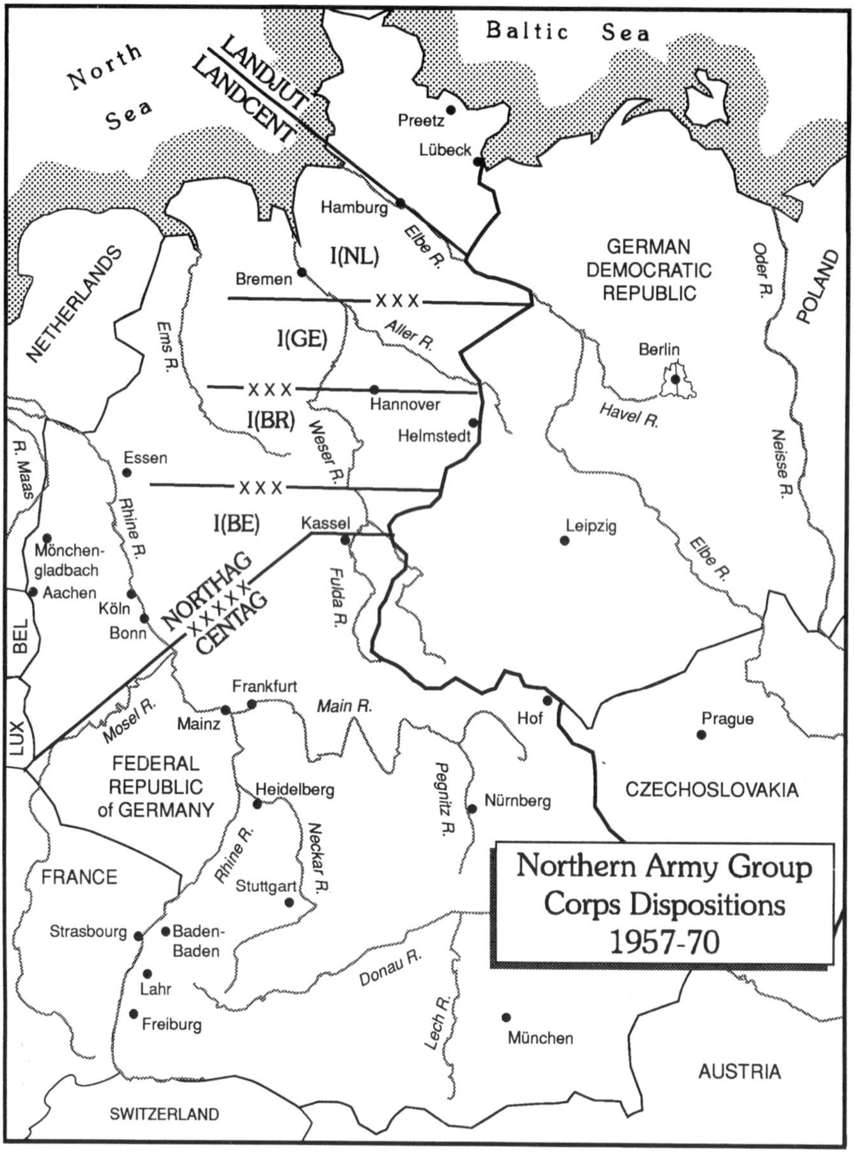
Baltic Sea
North Sea
LANDJUT
LANDCENT
Preetz
Lübeck
Hamburg
Elbe R.
I(NL)
Bremen
GERMAN
DEMOCRATIC
REPUBLIC
Oder R.
POLAND
NETHERLANDS
Ems R.
XXX
I(GE)
Aller R.
Berlin
XXX
Hannover
Havel R.
I(BR)
Weser R.
Helmstedt
R. Maas
Essen
Neisse R.
XXX
Rhine R.
I(BE)
Kassel
Leipzig
Mönchen-
gladbach
Elbe R.
Aachen
Fulda R.
Köln
NORTHAG
XXXXX
CENTAG
BEL
Bonn
Frankfurt
Main R.
Hof
Prague
Mosel R.
Mainz
LUX
FEDERAL
REPUBLIC
of GERMANY
Heidelberg
Pegnitz R.
Nürnberg
CZECHOSLOVAKIA
Neckar R.
Rhine R.
FRANCE
Stuttgart
Northern Army Group
Corps Dispositions
1957-70
Strasbourg
Baden-
Baden
Donau R.
Lahr
Lech R.
Freiburg
München
AUSTRIA
SWITZERLAND

FIGURE 3-1A

firepower as to develop targets which could then be attacked with nuclear weapons tasked from division or corps HQ.

I (BR) Corps nuclear assets included three composite artillery regiments each equipped with four *Honest John* SSMs and four 8-inch howitzers; four guns were allocated to each British division in I (BR) Corps, and the missiles were held at Corps level. In addition, two *Corporal* surface to surface missile launchers were provided to NORTHAG by the British as an Army Group resource. (Canada would eventually provide an *Honest John* unit but this will be discussed later). Weapon yields were variable, depending on the target type and mission. The *Honest John* warhead types included two, 20 or 40 kiloton yields (for comparative purposes, Nagasaki was struck with a 22 kiloton bomb) while the artillery pieces had 2 kiloton shells. *Corporal* missiles could carry a variable yield warhead ranging between two and 40 kilotons. The conventional forces deployed on the Weser would take on any forces which survived the nuclear gauntlet, while RAF *Canberra* aircraft would bomb the enemy second echelon with nuclear weapons before it got out of East Germany.

The enemy approaches to the Weser River in the I (BR) Corps area were canalized by geographic features of the Harz Mountains. [See Figure 3-2] The Soviet mechanized forces would have to move through the Gottingen Gap to the south, and along the Braunschweig approach to the north. As one soldier noted, a few people with light anti-tank weapons and chain saws in the middle of the Harz mountains could really mess up an attacker's day if they tried to advance through there.

The terrain along the Weser River was ideal for the defence, and the distance from the border provided some degree of depth. Ample opportunities, as well as time to locate and develop targets for the Corps nuclear assets, also existed. The enemy would also become hung up on artificial obstacles created by I (BR) Corps' engineer brigade. Once the enemy reached the Weser he would have to pause to conduct assault river crossings. The enemy would "pile up" on the obstacles, (much as the British had done in Exercise BATTLE ROYAL in 1954) and thereby present a worthwhile nuclear target.

The plan of battle for I (BR) Corps from 1958 to about 1963 thus envisaged three types of tactical nuclear doctrine. The "river" method

I BRITISH CORPS
CONCEPT OF OPERATIONS
1957 - 1963
SHOWING DEFENCE ON THE WESER RIVER
AND 4 CIBG "CANADA GOOSE" CONTINGENCY
0 10 20 30 km
Bassum
Twistringen
Weser
Barnstorf
I GE
XXX
I BR
Nienburg
Diepholz
Wagenfeld
Uchte
Steinhuder Meer
Neustadt
Celle
Aller
Uetze
Gifhorn
Brome
Oebisfelde
Wolfsburg
Burgdorf
X
BR
HANNOVER
Autobahn
2 BR
XX
4 BR
Minden
BRAUNSCHWEIG
Kirchlengern
BR
Herford
Hildesheim
BIELEFELD
Lemgo
Hameln
COVERING
Lage
4 BR
XX
4 CIBG
Bodenwerder
Leine
Autobahn
Detmold
Goslar
Halberstadt
Gütersloh
XX
Schwalenberg
Weser
Kreiensen
Wernigerode
1
BR
FORCE
Blankenburg
Paderborn
4 CIBG
XXX
I BE
Höxter
Osterode
HARZ
Hasselfelde
CANADA
GOOSE
Beverungen
N
Optional Reserve Area
20 ARMD BDE
WEST GERMANY
EAST GERMANY
Wünnenberg
Göttingen
Nordhausen
Warstein
Warburg
Marsberg
Brilon
Sondershausen
KASSEL
Willingen
Korbach
NORTHAG
XXXXX
CENTAG
Schlotheim
Eschwege
Hess.-Lichtenau
Mühlhausen

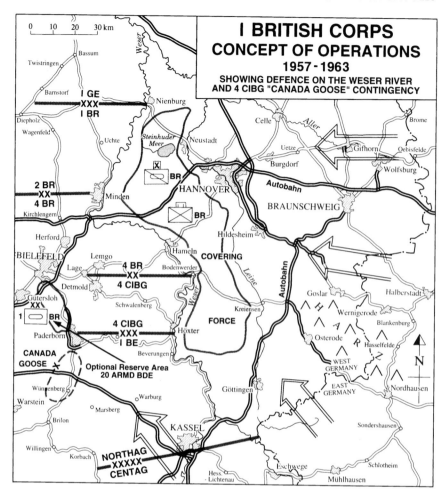

FIGURE 3-2

would be used by the covering forces, that is, these units would accept penetration, allow the enemy to bypass, and then call down nuclear fire as they went by. The "pile-up" method (described earlier), based on a major obstacle, would then be used. Finally, if all else failed, the "tag" method would be used as a last resort. Nuclear "tag" allowed units to remain in contact with the enemy while falling back; at some point, a fast, clean break had to be made before the enemy could follow up, and then a nuclear weapon dropped in the gap created by the retreating forces.

For the first part of the defensive battle in the British Corps sector, a strong covering force consisting of an armoured recce brigade group and an infantry battalion group (which could be provided by either the British brigades in 4th Infantry Division or by 4 CIBG) was deployed well forward of the Weser River. For the purposes of this Emergency Defence Plan (EDP), 4 CIBG was under command of 4th Infantry Division. The remainder of 1st Armoured Division was behind the Weser in a counter-attack role. 4 CIBG's frontage extended from south of Bodenwerder to Höxter, where the inter-corps boundary with I (BE) Corps was located (with 1st Belgian Infantry Division expected to be on the right flank).

It was around the 1959-1960 time frame that the so-called 'Belgian Problem' arose. As noted above, I (Belgian) Corps was on I (British) Corps' right flank, protecting a high speed approach heading north-west out of Kassel. [See Figure 3-2.] At this time, Belgium was involved in several military operations in her former overseas colonies and had serious problems in maintaining troop strengths in Germany. An additional problem involved the lack of barracks in Germany for Belgian troops, which forced Belgian planners to position them in Belgium proper. The result was that a distinct lack of confidence developed within NORTHAG over the ability of I (Belgian) Corps units to make it to their forward defensive positions between Kassel and Höxter. This exposed the I (BR) Corps flank to a Soviet end run into the rear area.

To deal with this contingency, a number of options were developed for the employment of 4 CIBG. If the Belgians arrived in time, the normal EDP positions between Bodenwerder and Hoxter would be manned, with an infantry battalion screen on the east side of the Weser. If the Belgians did not arrive, 4 CIBG would be grouped with 20th Armoured

Brigade from 4th Infantry Division to form a counter-attack or blocking force. This reserve formation would be located between Bielefeld and Paderborn, and 4th Infantry Division would task nuclear assets for support, while other formations within 4th Division extended their defensive line south to Hoxter.

Another option was developed strictly within 4 CIBG and not openly discussed elsewhere. Some Brigade planners were pessimistic as to whether 4 CIBG could make it to the Weser and prepare a defensive position before the enemy was able to 'bounce' the river. As a result, the operations staff developed a plan, code-named CANADA GOOSE, for a hasty defensive position. The CANADA GOOSE line was roughly half way from Soest to the Weser River, between Paderborn and Warstein. The unit survival areas were re-aligned to be within driving range of the line, or on the line itself. Thus, if 4 CIBG was deployed in a real emergency situation, it would already be in a defensible area which could be developed. If there was enough time to reach the Weser, nothing would be lost.

As in previous years, the brigade was a numerically significant contribution to the fighting strength of I (BR) Corps and crucial to the successful implementation of the EDP. I (BR) Corps had, with 4 CIBG included, six infantry brigades and two armoured brigades. The Canadians thus provided almost 15 per cent of the front line forces in the area. 4 CIBG's employment options were based on Canadian operational flexibility, the brigade's unique composition and its ability to liaise with the French-speaking Belgians. These attributes would, in twenty five years time, help CENTAG solve a critical problem similar to that facing NORTHAG in the late 1950s.

There was, of course, the question of developing a nuclear capability for 4 CIBG and this debate continued between 1958 and 1960. The MC 70 force structure plan mentioned earlier recommended that Canada provide to SACEUR a battalion of *Honest John* unguided nuclear surface-to-surface missile launchers. Canadian Army Headquarters thought that this was a rather excessive amount of firepower for one brigade group in Europe, believing the *Honest John* to be a corps support weapon because of its yield and range. Since the Canadian commitment was a division, the Army staff searched for a more 'suitable' divisional

CHAPTER THREE

support weapon. Eventually, Army attention focused on the *Lacrosse* guided missile. Paradoxically, SACEUR considered the *Lacrosse* to be a Corps-level support weapon and, therefore, unsuitable for divisional support missions!

Another weapon that was examined by Canadian planners for possible deployment by 4 CIBG was the *Davy Crockett*. *Davy Crockett* was a rather frightening weapon that was, for lack of a better term, a nuclear mortar. With a range of one mile, and a 0.4 kiloton warhead, *Davy Crockett* was jeep-mounted and air transportable. Canadian planners, being intelligent men, did not waste a lot of time on considering *Davy Crockett* for Canadian use.

In addition to all this, *Lacrosse* had developmental problems and would not be deployed in significant numbers within NATO; its primary drawback was its susceptibility to ECM jamming. An unguided missile like the *Honest John*, however, could not be jammed. Regardless, the British continued to pressure the Canadian government to acquire some form of delivery system, so that sufficient systems could be deployed to cover the whole of the I (BR) Corps area of operations. Although nuclear fire support for the Canadian brigade would be available from corps, it might not be available from division. The Canadian Army compromised by cutting the NATO recommended *Honest John* battalion requirement in half, that is, from eight launchers to four and calling it a "battery". The Canadian government concurred with the Army's proposal and committed itself to providing what it considered to be a corps support weapon on a scale of issue usually reserved for a division. This organization was then grafted on to 4 CIBG in Germany, without the rest of the division in place.

The Canadian *Honest John* nuclear delivery unit slated for Europe was called 1 Surface-to-Surface Missile Battery (1 SSM Battery) and was equipped with four launchers. It was formed on 15 September 1960 but would not be deployed to Germany until the fall of 1961. A second battery consisting of two launchers, 2 SSM (Training) Battery, was formed in Shilo, Manitoba to train personnel for 1 SSM Battery. In I (BR) Corps then, there were 12 British *Honest John* launchers and eventually, four Canadian launchers. If the tonnage of nuclear artillery fire support to I (BR) Corps is added up, Canada provided 20 per cent of the corps delivery capacity. The Canadian brigade was responsible for the administration and training of the missile unit, while targeting and control of the launchers was handled at Corps HQ.

Unfortunately, this unique Canadian contribution would not become available to the NATO Shield forces for some time. The special agreement between the US and Canada that dealt with the provision of warheads for the Canadian *Honest John* systems in Europe became entangled with other Canada-US nuclear issues and formal agreement had not yet been ratified when 1 SSM Battery arrived in Germany in 1961. This did not prevent 1 SSM Battery from training nor the I (BR) Corps planners from templating Canadian SSMs into the Corps nuclear fire support plan. According to Canadian planners,

> Warheads would probably be made available to the Canadian *Honest John* battery in the event of nuclear war. It is inconceivable that our atomic capability would not be used should the need arise.

4 CIBG was also responsible (in conjunction with the British and the Americans) for maintaining security over the warhead sites. Brigadier A.J. Tedlie, Brigade Commander from 1964-1966 explains:

> ...[this capability] required a great deal of effort being expended in constructing secure storage places for the warheads and long and complicated arrangements with the United States as to their safe custody, functioning of the "double key" system, and their movement to the Emergency Defence Position in event of imminent war. There were no additional troops given to the Brigade Group to perform these tasks. This resulted in all the regiments having to supply, on a rotation basis, the necessary troops to carry out the protection tasks. At first [this was] an exciting task, but later a rather boring way to spend your time.

This task developed after the Belgians asked the British to take over security for their sites while they diverted troops elsewhere. The British were stretched thin and asked Canada to provide, in the event of a civil emergency, a standby company group for the Special Ammunition Storage Site at Dortmund and a standby battalion for the temporary Special

Ammunition Storage Site at Lüdenscheid. The Special Ammunition Storage Support Site at Munster, where the third line maintenance was done and Atomic Demolition Munitions and reserve nuclear warheads were stored, remained a British responsibility. This security function for the Brigade was alleviated somewhat in 1964 when a Special Ammunition Storage Site was constructed at Hemer, right beside Fort Prince of Wales.

4 CIBG took all of this in stride and continued on its training programme which followed the pattern established by its predecessor formations, as one 4 CIBG member recalls:

> ...our training here was very, very much influenced by the reality of the fall exercises, and in fact it remained the theme or reality of the European soldier for many, many years, the big manoeuvres taking place in the Fall after the crops were off. Then after that major manoeuvre period one had various inspections.... Then the process of platoon, company training, battalion training would take place and the cycle would begin again.

Upon arrival in Germany, 1 RCHA had to get to know its new 105mm guns, so they deployed to the Bergen-Hohne range in April 1958 to exercise with 4th Infantry Division's artillery where the star of the show was the launch of a British *Honest John*. The RCD and the infantry battalions meanwhile deployed to the British-Canadian training area at Soltau, just to the south of Hamburg on the Lüneburg Heath. Training during this concentration focused on tank-infantry cooperation under tactical nuclear conditions. The enemy force was provided by Recce Squadron, the Queen's Own Rifles and the British 9th Lancers tank regiment. The only serious casualty was a Queen's Own 3/4 ton truck that some *Centurion* crew commander inadvertently turned into a convertible.

4 CIBG, after a period of rest and reorganization in the Soest area, proceeded back to Soltau in September for a series of battle-group level work-up exercises called SNOW FIRE. After these were completed 4 CIBG embarked on a free-manoeuvre exercise with the British. Unlike the Soltau concentration in April, this scheme was conducted across a wide swath of civilian farm land as well as in the training area proper. Known as "443 Area" exercises (from the BAOR form number), troops taking part in cross-country manoeuvres had to be careful of doing too

much damage to the German countryside and civilian property. In reality, a residue of the occupation mentality still existed in British formations. Certainly, manoeuvre damage claims were not as seriously investigated as they would be twenty years later. It was said that other armies, like the Belgians, regularly maintained their claims accounts five years in arrears.

Canadians, however, were on the whole a bit more careful than the British with regards to manoeuvre damage. The harvest season in northern Germany was late in 1958, and the umpires used it to great effect:

> As a result of the late harvest season in the area north of Hannover and the dense growth of the state tree farms in the training area, unit and brigade control maps are dotted with 'out of bounds' areas. As one of the infantry commanders expressed it, 'our regard for nature and the German farmers denies us the use of certain areas just as effectively as would contamination from a fair size nuclear strike'.

Canadian soldiers also had to be careful since other armies had been to Soltau years before:

> A terse sign, 'Prehistoric Graves–Out of Bounds' excited a great deal of interest…. In this section archeologists were still finding skeletons from the Bronze Age. A former Saxon encampment was pointed out in the manoeuvre area. Replying to a compliment on the way some of the roads were standing up to the constant tank traffic, Herr Pless said with a quiet smile, 'Yes, we're glad you like them. After all, this particular cobbled way we're driving on served adequately for Napoleon's troops too.'

The year's training plan culminated with Exercise VANITY FAIR, where the aim was to test the validity of current tactics to support nuclear weapons. 4 CIBG was pitted against 4th Division's 5 Infantry Brigade Group. Defending a line from Paderborn to Hameln, 4 CIBG made use of simulated nuclear artillery to completely disrupt the 'enemy' attack over a four day period. No other large scale exercises like BATTLE ROYAL were conducted that year, so very few opportunities existed to operate with other NATO members.

CHAPTER THREE

Only one event during VANITY FAIR proved to be somewhat shocking. After surviving mock nuclear attacks, rain, mud and bugs, nine members of 4 LAD, RCEME came under attack from a heavenly source. A bolt of lightning followed by a ball of St Elmo's Fire struck nine men in successive order, welding one into his sleeping bag after melting the zipper, striking another's identification tags, traveling into a command post vehicle shorting out all electrical equipment, and finally blowing up a naptha lamp inside a tent!

The social amenities available to the Brigade continued to develop in the late 1950s. One important source of Canadian information was Radio Canadian Army Europe. Radio CAE had five permanent staff members: two Canadians who managed the stations, two German engineers and one secretary. Members of the brigade provided the news announcers and disc jockeys. In addition to CBC network features transmitted from Canada, Radio CAE produced local shows like "Red Patch Roundup", "Club 5050", "Canadian Ramblers" and "The Down Easters". There was always extensive coverage of local sports events and 15 hours of air time out of every 110 hours were devoted to French-language broadcasts. Canadians in the Soest area could also could listen to the British Forces Network and the American Forces Network. There was of course, Radio Free Europe, though not many Canadians listened to it.

Leave policy varied but Jerry Zypchen's description of 4 CIBG's engineering organization could be considered representative of the times:

> The unit received six weeks of leave each year and it was organized that each troop went on block leave for two weeks. A large number of the soldiers went to either Amsterdam ('The Dam') or to Copenhagen ('Copie') where they spent two weeks in the company of women who made them forget about the conditions back at Fort Victoria. A large number of the soldiers married German, Danish or Dutch women. These women integrated into the Canadian way of life quickly. The one give away that a certain hockey player's wife was not Canadian was when she berated the referee in a very loud voice, calling him a "cheecken sheet bastard"!

Volunteer organizations continued to support members of the

brigade and their dependents. The Salvation Army expanded its operations, placing Red Shield Clubs in Fort Anne, Hemer, and Deilinghofen and in Werl, where they operated a francophone club. A comfort station catering to incoming dependents was also established. Also greatly deserving of mention is the Women's Volunteer Service organization, the members of which were generally British war widows who volunteered to support Commonwealth forces stationed overseas. In this era the barrack blocks were pretty spartan affairs, and other than the "wet canteen", very few had any sort of recreation areas since communal living was the norm. The WVS, however, maintained pleasant, comfortable facilities where soldiers could quietly read a book, build a model or listen to music when they weren't working, downtown or in the field. One member of the WVS who over many years loyally served the Canadian brigade, Isabel Hasluck, was decorated by Queen Elizabeth for her selfless efforts to support several generations of Canadian soldiers.

One rather explosive issue came to light in the Sorpesee, a small lake near Iserlohn/Hemer. A *Tall Boy* bomb dropped by the RAF during the Second World War was discovered when the waters behind a dam were lowered. About sixty Canadians living on the economy in the area had to be evacuated while British and German bomb disposal experts removed the weapon. The brigade laid on anti-looting patrols in the district until the operation was completed.

Once that potential disaster was averted, a record snowfall in Westphalia made things seem more 'like home' to the Canadians. The local population, however, not used to this phenomenon, required some expert Canadian assistance in snow removal.

A description of life in the Canadian area circa 1959 would not be complete without a touch of scandal. A local columnist at that time had conducted his own investigation into the "on the economy" housing situation and concluded that there were many "profiteers" renting accommodation to Canadians at "usurious" prices and he demanded a thorough investigation into local business practices. This was a common complaint for over twenty years.

Other important contacts were made between the German citizens in the region and the Canadians. Sporting activities had always been popular in both communities. The Soest Athletic Club was organized to include Canadian and German track and field at the *Spielwiese,* and the entire range of events was run. Canadian culture also was transferred to the Deilinghofen-Iserlohn area in 1959, where the first Germany hockey team, "*Eishockeyclub Deilinghofen*", was formed with the assistance and training support of the 1 RCHA hockey team. A hockey league for younger people was also set up. The team exists today in a modified form, having been split into EC Iserlohn and EC Sauerland; both teams still retain a Canadian maple leaf as the team symbol.

CWO Don Collier of the Canadian Guards remembered the close sporting relationships which were fostered during the 1950s and 1960s:

> The Germans loved track and field. All the German towns had teams [consisting of] high school kids, 17-year olds who didn't graduate and adults in the city that were very interested.... On the weekends there would be track and field competitions and the Germans would come in from the small towns all over.... There were a lot of good, close relationships that built up in the two years I was there with the German community because of track and field.... Of course in the winter time hockey was the big thing. You know, it was like the NHL on Saturday night!

Boxing was a very popular sport within 4 CIBG and BAOR as a whole, and Canadian boxers frequently trounced their opponents in the NORTHAG area. One significant event in BAOR boxing was a rare visit by the Canadian team to Berlin in March 1961, since normally Canadian soldiers and their dependents were forbidden to travel to Berlin because of diplomatic and political reasons.

Another community and cultural connection was made when the Boy Scouts of Canada set up scout troops for Canadian dependents. The German scouting movement, still recovering from the Hitler Youth period, needed all the support it could get. Canadians were more than happy to oblige and a number of joint scouting functions were conducted by the two organizations.

It is important to note here that the best (and at times no doubt the worst) of Canada was on display to people in Europe, who had little idea of what it was like to live in the New World or of the Canadian mentality. Things like Dominion Day events art shows featuring Canadian paintings, Canadian sports events, ceremonial occasions and other such things clearly demonstrated to the German population, as well as to the British and Belgian garrisons and their dependents, what Canada was all about. In addition to helping defend its NATO allies, Canada was also able to 'advertise' its way of life and its values in a way that could not be measured in dollars.

To save money, the Canadian Government announced a new rotation policy in 1959; entire brigade groups would no longer be rotated through Germany on two year tours. Instead, 4 CIBG headquarters and the smaller units would remain permanently in Germany (with man-for-man rotation), while larger units within the brigade would rotate on a unit-for-unit basis for three year tours. The incoming units for the 1959 rotation included:

1/8 Canadian Hussars (Princess Louise's)
Recce Squadron (provided by 1/8 Canadian Hussars but being an independent Brigade resource)
1st Battalion, Royal Highland Regiment of Canada (The Black Watch)
1st Battalion, Canadian Guards

Second Battalion, Queen's Own Rifles of Canada remained in Germany, while the combat service support units rotated on a man-for-man or sub-unit basis. An important addition to 4 CIBG at this time was the formation of the Air OP (Air Observation Post) Troop, 1 RCHA in March 1960. The AOP Troop initially was equipped with three L-19 *Bird Dog* light observation aircraft; their roles included artillery spotting and liaison. 1 RCHA itself rotated out in 1960 to be replaced by 3 RCHA.

Brigadier Cameron would continue on as Brigade Commander until 1960, when Brigadier C.B. Ware took over. The first personnel and dependents of the new rotation arrived on the vessel *Empress of France*, while others traveled by commercial and military air transports as the "air trooping" concept started to take over from the slower sea route.

As the new units settled into the Canadian base area around Soest, Werl and Iserlohn, the first chilly winds of one of the coldest of all Cold

War crises began to blow. The Soviets needed a propaganda victory to impress the developing third world; they did not like the arming of the Bundeswehr with tactical nuclear delivery systems and they also wanted to force the Western powers out of West Berlin. West Berlin was a potent symbol; it was an island of freedom deep inside Communist territory, it was booming economically, and it had already survived one blockade. It also contained three garrisons – French, British and American, as well as significant intelligence-gathering assets. If the Soviets could manoeuvre the West out of Berlin, two or three birds could be killed with one stone. Slowly, the temperature began to drop, barely noticeable late in 1959, but enough to prompt NATO to discretely review defence planning.

While the Berlin Crisis was in its early stages, attempts were made to change the operational role of the Brigade. It is perhaps surprising now, but 4 CIBG almost became the original ACE Mobile Force (Land) in 1960. After a visit to 4 CIBG in mid-1959, General Hans Speidel, the German commander of LANDCENT, approached Canadian generals attending a SHAPE command post exercise in Paris with a unique proposal. LANDCENT needed a mobile reserve force for use in the Central Region, particularly in areas which could not be covered continuously in peacetime. This "Speidel Proposal" however, was quickly absorbed by another requirement for a mobile reserve force.

SACEUR, General Lauris Norstad, was concerned that he had no forces available to deal with border incidents that did not warrant a general nuclear response. The 1957 MC 14/2 concept was ambiguous in that it did not recognize a requirement for such a force, but nobody could intellectually or militarily justify the use of nuclear weapons to repel a minor incursion. Paradoxically, any attempt to recognize the possibility that a situation short of all out war might occur was seen by some NATO members as weakening the deterrent value of the NATO strategic concept.

Some had suggested that such a force be multi-national, but Norstad initially believed that a one-nation force could be used. He thought Canadians were most suited to such a role because they were regular, volunteer troops. Canada also had the respect of the smaller NATO nations, and Canada was trusted by the Warsaw Pact peoples more than other, larger NATO nations. This force's mission would be to prevent a small incident from triggering off a general war, as well as deterring or stopping a small scale incursion.

Other planners' conceptions on how such a force would be used were not limited to containing Cold War border incidents. The problem with the Belgians, discussed earlier in the chapter, posed additional burdens on LANDCENT planning. [See Figure 3-3.] Since the Belgians were believed to be incapable of reaching their place in the line on time, a serious gap existed in the defence. There were two threats here. I (BR) Corps could be outflanked and there was the possibility that the boundary between NORTHAG and CENTAG could be broached. The Belgian's right flank was with CENTAG, south of Kassel. CENTAG lacked the resources to extend northward, as did I (BR) Corps to move southward to close the gap.

NATO planners figured that such a contingency force should be airmobile or airportable and be equipped with light armour and small nuclear weapons. Proposed equipment included *Vertol* helicopters and armoured personnel carriers; candidates for nuclear delivery systems included either the *Little John* or *Davy Crockett*, described earlier in the chapter. If the mobile reserve force were so equipped, it could be employed anywhere within SACEUR's area, and it would be prepared for all contingencies ranging from border patrolling to blocking operations involving tactical nuclear weapons use.

SACEUR also understood that 4 CIBG was dependent upon I (BR) Corps for logistical support. As a result, he suggested to the Canadians that 4 CIBG could be co-located with 1 Canadian Air Division on airfields in southern Germany as a "Canadian enclave" [his words], located near US lines of communications to ease supply problems. This idea was supported by General Charles Foulkes, Chairman of the Canadian Chiefs of Staff Committee. As Major General Kitching noted at the time, "Both SACEUR and Speidel were enthusiastic about getting the Brigade Group as a special reserve."

There was certainly a push from some Canadian officers that the "brigade be given a more colorful role rather than being submerged as it is at present" and there was a push to allow the brigade to be "…given a chance as a national force." Several factors militated against the Speidel

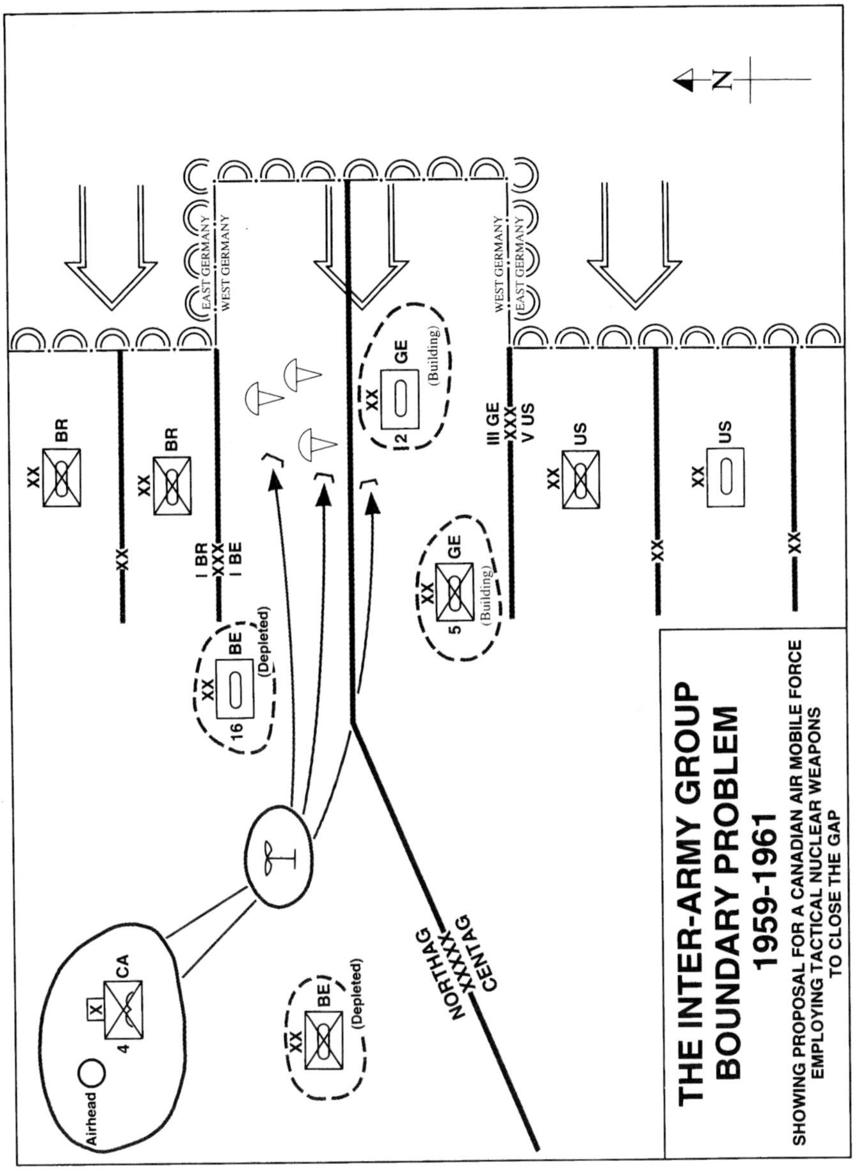
THE INTER-ARMY GROUP
BOUNDARY PROBLEM
1959-1961
SHOWING PROPOSAL FOR A CANADIAN AIR MOBILE FORCE
EMPLOYING TACTICAL NUCLEAR WEAPONS
TO CLOSE THE GAP
N
EAST GERMANY
WEST GERMANY
WEST GERMANY
EAST GERMANY
XX BR
XX BR
XX
I BR
XXX
I BE
XX 16 BE
(Depleted)
XX 2 GE
(Building)
XX 5 GE
(Building)
III GE
XXX
V US
XX US
XX US
XX
XX
Airhead
X 4 CA
XX BE
(Depleted)
NORTHAG
XXXXX
CENTAG

FIGURE 3-3

Proposal, however. The cost involved in re-equipping 4 CIBG for such a role was staggering, particularly where aircraft were concerned. The cost of developing an independent supply organization to support the brigade if it had to deploy to Norway or Italy was even more staggering and would have pushed the Canadian troop ceiling well beyond the allowable 5500.

Another factor was the debate over equipping such a force with nuclear weapons. There was a perception by some that SACEUR actually wanted a mobile nuclear force that could be rapidly deployed to NATO areas that did not want or would not allow nuclear-equipped Shield Forces deployed in peacetime. Canada was not interested in becoming involved in such a potentially divisive debate, which would be inevitable had 4 CIBG taken on that role. In any case, the contemporary domestic debate in Canada over the acquisition of nuclear delivery systems was just gathering steam, and no one wanted to rock the boat.

Not surprisingly, the British were not exactly enthusiastic about the proposal since it would weaken I (BR) Corps significantly. British politicians wanted at that time to reduce BAOR further to save money, and the removal of the Canadian brigade would force them to retain the existing forces. The British CGS, General Clark, on the other hand, was more concerned about the political ramifications if Canadian troops were involved in a border situation where too much force was used; he believed that this role was too much like a UN operation instead of a NATO one.

The decision by SHAPE in 1960 to create a multi-national AMF(L), combined with the Berlin Crisis, put the coup de grâce to the Speidel Proposal. AMF(L) would exercise regularly starting in 1965, and Canada would provide an infantry battalion group for it from one of the Canada-based brigade groups, a commitment that would end only in 1994. Discussion over the proposed change in role, however, led at the time to rumours that the Canadian brigade might be withdrawn from Europe.

Training for the new units in 4 CIBG in 1960/61 was varied. In keeping with the MC 14/2 and I (BR) Corps concepts of operations, certain aspects were stressed more than others. High on the list of training priorities were surveillance and patrolling; the siting and dispersion of headquarters; nuclear target acquisition; the creation of nuclear targets through engineering obstacle plans and camouflage and concealment. Other skills such as tank/infantry cooperation in the defence were emphasized over advance to contact.

SHAPE logisticians held Exercise FLASHBACK in September 1960 to assess 4 CIBG's ability to reinforce in a war situation. At 5500 personnel, 4 CIBG was not considered to be at full strength; to bring it up to strength and to provide 30 days reinforcements required 1712 troops. An additional 350 soldiers were needed to increase the administrative echelon required to support this influx and to support elements of 1st Canadian Infantry Division. Canadian planners relied on air trooping to bring these men over to Europe in an emergency, using RCAF *North Star* long-range transport aircraft staging out of Trenton, Ontario.

4 CIBG's plan was, however, vague regarding what happened after these personnel were received in Germany, and how 4 CIBG was to interface with BAOR for equipment and third line repair facilities. SHAPE planners noted this, and insisted that more detail be added. The problem here in fact revolved around how much support Canada could squeeze out of BAOR. Since the Berlin Crisis was accelerating through 1961, events pressured 4 CIBG logistical planners to develop more specific plans.

In doing so, 4 CIBG was shocked to find out that:

> ...The Canadian Army has always assumed on the basis of discussions with the UK, that the Canadian contribution would be less than a divisional slice because certain operational and logistical support would be provided by the UK. On this basis, 4 CIBG has been provided with the minimum non-organic support element required for providing purely Canadian administration and plans provide for this element to be augmented in war on the assignment of the balance of the division to SACEUR. In actual fact, a formal agreement for provision of logistical support in war does not exist. Planning is based on a 1955 verbal agreement between the CIGS and the CGS....

furthermore,

> BAOR logistical planing assumptions include a seven day warning period,

a first phase of 30 days in a nuclear war and no supply from or evacuation to the UK during the first 30 days. BAOR plans require the full seven days warning period for the deployment of 57,000 reservists to the continent. BAOR has no detailed plans for their own support beyond the first 30 days of war and [is] in no position to support the balance of 1 Canadian Division....

In other words, 4 CIBG was on its own logistically for the first 30 days of the war (MC 14/2's Phase I) and no Canadian planning was done to deal with the period after that (the Phase II reconstitution/conventional period). This was consistent with the Diefenbaker government's decision not to spend money on forces not contributing to Phase I. The effects of this decision were felt into the 1980s, as we will see in later chapters.

Despite this, a solution was quickly hammered out with the British regarding reinforcements arriving by air from Canada into the Central Region for the first 30 days. [See Figure 3-4.] Reinforcements arriving from Canada would arrive at RAF Gütersloh near Bielefeld, with Düsseldorf as an alternate. If either of these airbases were unusable, the *North Stars* would land at RAF Wildenrath near Mönchen-Gladbach in Germany or at Melsbroek, near Brussels in Belgium. If possible, combat reinforcements were to be flown to Langenhagen, north of Hannover. BAOR units would receive the Canadian troops, but could only guarantee transport as far as the Corps reinforcement facility at Lippstadt. From there, 4 CIBG was responsible for moving them to the Soest-Hemer bases area.

The problems with logistical support to 4 CIBG did not significantly affect the brigade's ability to participate in exercises, particularly the largest NORTHAG exercise held since BATTLE ROYAL. Exercise HOLD FAST (not to be confused with the exercise by the same name held during the tenure of 27 CIB) was conducted in September 1960 and involved 50,000 Danes, British, Germans, Canadians and Belgians. In a departure from previous exercises, 4 CIBG operated in the role of enemy force with 4th British Infantry Division against Blueland, which was represented by Denmark's Jutland Division and Germany's 6th Panzer Grenadier Division. The purpose of HOLD FAST was to test the defences of the new NATO LANDJUT command, which protected the

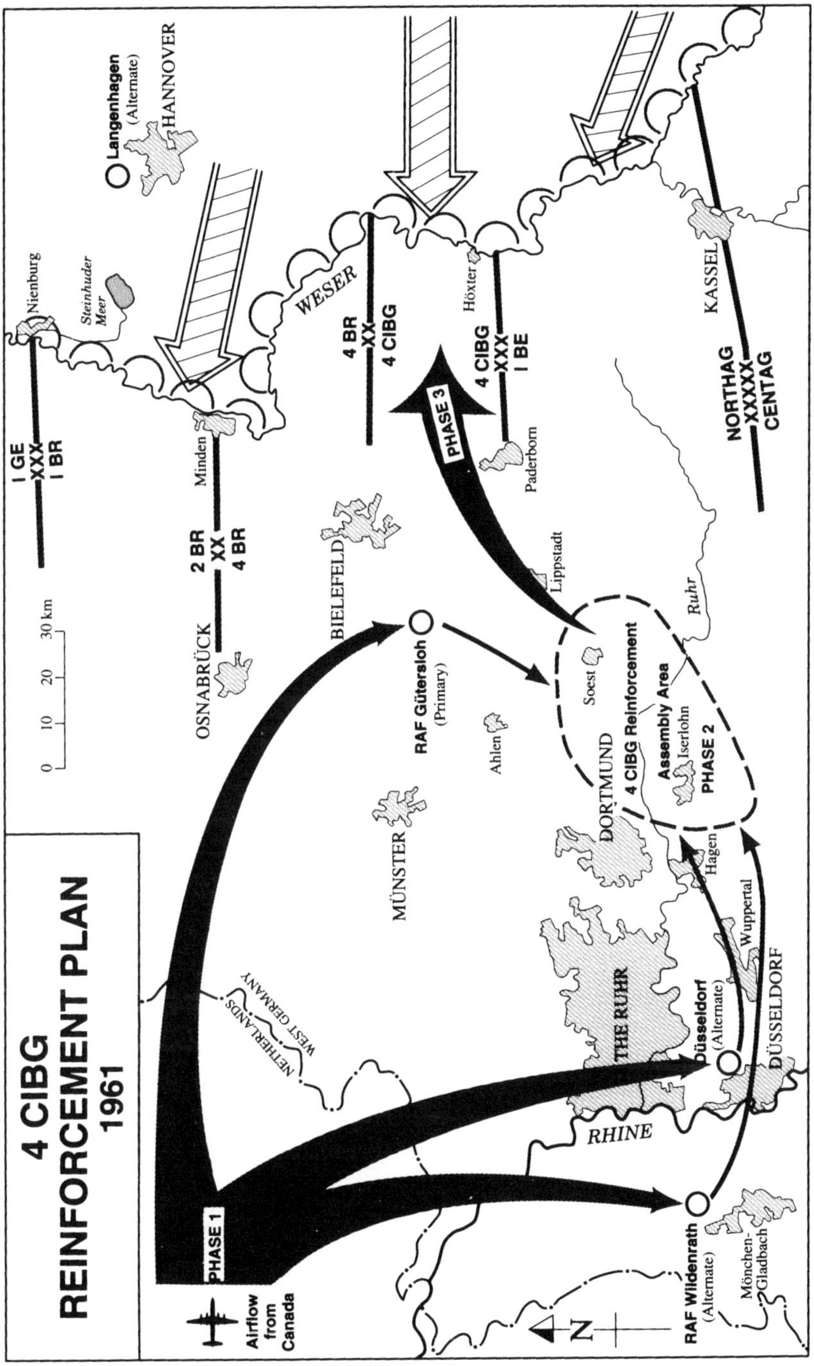
4 CIBG
REINFORCEMENT PLAN
1961
Airflow from Canada
PHASE 1
PHASE 2
PHASE 3
RAF Wildenrath (Alternate)
Düsseldorf (Alternate)
RAF Gütersloh (Primary)
Langenhagen (Alternate)
4 CIBG Reinforcement Assembly Area
NETHERLANDS
WEST GERMANY
RHINE
THE RUHR
DÜSSELDORF
Mönchen-Gladbach
Wuppertal
Hagen
DORTMUND
Iserlohn
Soest
Ruhr
Lippstadt
Paderborn
MÜNSTER
Ahlen
BIELEFELD
OSNABRÜCK
Minden
Nienburg
Steinhuder Meer
HANNOVER
WESER
Höxter
KASSEL
I GE XXX I BR
2 BR XX 4 BR
4 BR XX 4 CIBG
4 CIBG XXX I BE
NORTHAG XXXXX CENTAG
0 10 20 30 km
N

FIGURE 3-4

strategic Kiel Canal north of Hamburg. To their credit, the soldiers of the brigade trained hard for this event. The preceding Soltau concentration in August 1960, Exercise BLAZING FURY, was set up as a dry run so that troops would be familiar with ground similar to that in Jutland.

In what must be a first for 4 CIBG two combat groups, each consisting of 50 men from the Queen's Own Rifles, boarded British S-55 helicopters for airmobile attacks on 'bridge crossings' of the 'Autobahn Canal', the Lübeck-Hamburg highway which was simulating a water obstacle. [See Figure 3-5.] After successfully seizing their objectives, two British brigade groups exploited deep into Blueland territory until stopped by nuclear attacks. Despite 'nuclear play' being authorized for the defenders, 4 CIBG was able to pass through 11th Infantry Brigade Group and conduct a vicious but triumphant encounter battle against 6 Panzer Grenadier Division's M-47 tanks near Neumünster. Then-Lieutenant Colonel Radley-Walters led the 8th Canadian Hussars on that exercise:

> I had a battle group based on the Black Watch and the Hussars, and we did most of our tactical moves at night since I had experienced fair success in the war through night fighting. On this exercise we broke through the German defences just north of Neumunster and reached the Kiel Canal, which pleased our brigade commander. At the critique afterwards the German divisional commander stated that he remembered that the Canadians had done a lot of night fighting in Normandy, and since his division had been recently organized, his soldiers had not had time to practice their skills at night!

Canadian operations were assisted by "partisans" from the Belgian and British Special Air Service organizations, while British airborne and amphibious operations added to the confusion in Blueland's rear area. Despite all of this, however, LANDJUT stood firm and Redland had to withdraw in defeat.

In other training events of note, Canadians from 4 CIBG won two of the most prestigious awards in NATO during the training year 1959-1960. 1 Field Ambulance won the annual I (BR) Corps Field Ambulance Trophy, The Connaught Shield, while the guardsmen from 1 Canadian Guards out-shot NATO's best for the Prix Leclerc small arms trophy.

EXERCISE
HOLD FAST
SEPTEMBER 1960
Designed to test newly formed LANDJUT Command defence
0 10 20 30 km
Airmobile insertions ......
KIELER BUCHT
LÜBECKER BUCHT
"BLUELAND"
"REDLAND"
HAMBURG-LÜBECK "CANAL"
JUT DIV XX 6 PZ GREN
(AIRMOBILE) 21 SEP 60
CIBG
BR
DK
JUT DIV
N
Bredstedt
Süden
Husum
Eckerförde
Gettdorf
KIEL
Tönning
Erfde
Lütjenburg
Oldenburg
Preetz
Heide
Kanal
Nortorf
Büsum
Meldorf
Gokels
Neustadt
Nord-Ostsee
Neumüster
Marne
Itzehoe
Bad Bramstedt
LÜBECK
ELBE
Brunsbütel
Otterndorf
Glückstadt
Elmshorn
Quickborn
Hemmoor
Drochtersen
Pinneberg
HAMBURG
Schwarzenbek
Buxtehude
Elbe

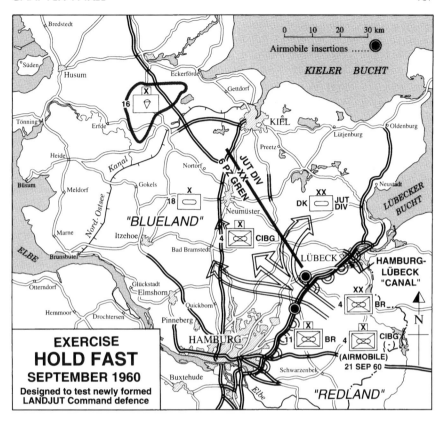

FIGURE 3-5

On 15 June 1961, Nikita Khrushchev announced that the Soviet Union would conclude a "peace treaty" with East Germany within six months. The Soviets believed that their recognition of the "true Germany" would undermine the legal right of the Western powers to occupy West Berlin; a move clearly in violation of the four power agreement set up in 1945. If the East German borders were violated, the Soviets could help their erstwhile German allies expel the squatters.

As before, Soviet objectives were to score a propaganda victory over the West and remove the showcase of freedom and strength located in the middle of their "socialist paradise". Soviet methods could take several forms. West Berlin was isolated and depended on three air and land corridors through East Germany for travel and supply. If these corridors were interfered with, the Western powers would have to respond in some fashion if they were not to lose all of Berlin to Communism. If the Western powers in Berlin decided to respond to Soviet aggression against Berlin, NATO would become involved. Did Berlin constitute part of the NATO area? If it did, NATO (including Canada) was obligated to respond against any such aggression. If it did not, three of NATO's members would have to use non-NATO forces to respond to a situation which would inevitably drag NATO (including Canada) into action anyway.

The clock started to tick on the six-month deadline as NATO debated action. Proposals to use strategic nuclear weapons were rejected outright, but tactical nuclear use was not ruled out as an option. On 7 August 1961, Allied intelligence assets detected a build up in the Group of Soviet Forces Germany. This prompted NATO to announce a comparable build up of SACEUR's forces, "visible moves to communicate unity which may give Khrushchev second thought", as one participant remarked. NATO firmly believed that the best method of dealing with the situation was a gradual one:

> The military measures have a dual purpose...to let him see our unity in pressing along with that course, we must act with cool and realistic vigour to strengthen all Alliance armed forces. The second purpose is to improve our military readiness in case the Russians, who, despite our efforts continue and conflict results.... To influence the Soviets towards reasonableness, the Alliance must promptly begin, we believe, an orderly military build up....

CHAPTER THREE

Initially, the Canadian response was to review plans to bring in 4 CIBG's reinforcements to Gutersloh or Dusseldorf. This all changed, however, on 13 August. Thousands of East Germans, grasping an opportunity to escape the totalitarian society they had lived in since 1945, fled to West Berlin seeking asylum. To prevent this drain, the East Germans and the Soviets immediately blocked off the streets between West and East and started the construction of the Berlin Wall.

The NATO build up changed gears, and this had a corresponding impact on Canadian contingency planning. In addition to 4 CIBG's reinforcements, the Army also planned for the deployment of another brigade group if things got serious enough prior to an outbreak of hostilities. At the time, 1 CIBG (at 78 per cent of its war establishment strength) in Calgary was tasked with Defence of Canada operations, while 2 CIBG in Petawawa (83 per cent) and 3 CIBG in Gagetown and Valcartier (85 per cent) comprised the rest of the division.

3 CIBG was selected to be the contingency brigade group, made up of the Lord Strathcona's Horse; 1st Battalion, The Royal Canadian Regiment; 1st Battalion, Princess Patricia's Canadian Light Infantry; and 3rd Battalion, Royal 22nd Regiment. 1 SSM Battery was nearing completion of its training and was to be included with 2 RCHA to form a composite artillery regiment. Shipping and air transport were chartered discretely on a 'just in case' basis.

The next step in the escalation of the Berlin Crisis occurred on 21 August 1961. To intimidate the West, the Soviet Union embarked on an aggressive series of atmospheric nuclear tests which would continue late into October. Fifty different megaton-yield weapons were exploded on Soviet ranges in the USSR at a rate of five a week; the final test yielded 50 megatons, one of the largest, if not the largest, nuclear explosion ever. This campaign pushed NATO countries into implementing civil defence measures.

Canada prepared for war. Civil emergency headquarters were manned, food and medical stocks were dispersed from potential target areas, possible radiation cloud paths were plotted, radiation monitoring equipment was distributed to the national survival organizations, and shipping was dispersed out of large ports. Realizing that there was not enough time to organize shipping for 3 CIBG on such short notice, 4 CIBG reinforcement continued and 1 SSM Battery was transported to join 4 CIBG in Germany on a priority basis.

The situation was so serious that Prime Minister, John Diefenbaker addressed the House of Commons and the Canadian people on 7 September:

> The international situation has deteriorated since we last met and tension has increased. The government, after consultation with allied governments in NATO, has come to the conclusion that certain measures should be taken to strengthen Canada's preparedness for defence both at home and overseas. We have decided to increase overseas forces assigned to NATO as follows.... Strengthen the 4th Canadian Infantry Brigade Group by a total of 1106 all ranks and make readily available in Canada 1515 as reinforcements.... To authorize these increases an Order in Council has been passed to increase the limit on the Regular Forces from 120,000 to 135,000.... In the interests in maintaining the present high efficiency of the Brigade overseas, it has been decided to defer until next year the return to Canada of the Black Watch battalion now with the brigade....

Naturally, Canada was not alone in this endeavour. The US raised two more divisions for service with NATO, but kept them in North America in readiness. France, heavily engaged in the Algerian War, repatriated two divisions and assigned them to SACEUR, and Germany did everything possible short of full mobilization.

For 4 CIBG, it was 'hurry up and wait'. Brigadier Ware recalled that "We went on NATO Alert at the time the 'Wall' went up and to my astonishment I got 1200 reinforcements flown over. I knew it was in the mobilization plan, but I was astounded!". The Alert did not involve the actual deployment of the entire brigade, however, as Trooper Charlebois remembered:

> At the time, I was in armoured reconnaissance. We deployed out along the border, about five kilometers out, and we worked our way back and forth all along more or less just to keep an eye on it.... [We] worked in conjunction with a British armoured regiment but [4 CIBG] did not really deploy. It went into a state of readiness. Everything was packed and ready to move....

CHAPTER THREE

Roy Smillie of 4 Field Ambulance noted that:

> We did not move out of the camp because we were confined to the area. [Personnel] away were called back off leave.... The Americans were sending over their soldiers in large numbers to Germany and I went down and visited one of their clearing hospitals which was not far from my camp.... The whole thing was brought up to strength. All the material was there....

The decision to order deployment to the EDP positions was retained at a very high level during the Berlin Crisis. NATO wanted to respond gradually and did not want to provide the Soviets with any excuse for precipitous action. Consequently, 4 CIBG did not deploy to its survival areas.

This allowed time for the 4 CIBG staff and unit commanders to review other planning details. The most contentious issue was the evacuation of Canadian dependents. NATO at the time had a 'stay put' policy regarding civilian dependents for two reasons. The first and most important was that refugees on roads could block troop movements forward to the battle area. Secondly, even though never actually stated on paper, was the 'we're all in this together' concept. The fact that North American soldiers' families were also in the rear area and not safe across the Atlantic was thought by some to improve combat motivation.

To their credit Canada's military leadership in Ottawa opposed this policy and took steps to circumvent it:

> Whether or not it would be possible to reinforce and/or build up the Canadian brigade group in Europe in the event of war depends on a number of circumstances which are at the moment not too clear.... We do not know if it will be possible to arrange a strategic airlift to Europe in the event of an emergency, nor the extent to which such aircraft could be used to evacuate dependents of our soldiers. We should have a plan to reinforce our brigade group, build it up and to evacuate our dependents.... It would, in my opinion, be militarily and morally wrong not to plan to be able to assist our soldiers and their dependents in Europe....

Within BAOR, a plan called Operation SAFE KEEP was developed to protect dependents in their PMQ areas, which were about three hours drive from the Weser River positions. British and Canadian military representatives conducted special negotiations with Belgian and Dutch authorities to move BAOR non-combatants into the Communications Zone behind the Rhine and then to the UK, a modification of the old TABLE TOP plan. In terms of numbers, there were 60,000 BAOR dependents, of which 10,000 were Canadian. Brigadier Ware felt very strongly about this and considered such a plan to be a moral obligation.

The tension brought on by the Berlin Crisis continued into late October 1961, when it reached its peak. Allied personnel stationed in Berlin were harassed on an ongoing basis and in some cases even kidnapped. One high-level American diplomat was continually harassed in the conduct of his duties, so the Americans laid on a show of force: a troop of American M-48 tanks escorting the diplomat approached the Berlin Wall at Checkpoint Charlie. Almost immediately, ten Soviet T-55s appeared on the Eastern side to block the movement. The tanks stood in a 'Mexican Standoff' posture for hours, until the Soviets ordered their vehicles to retreat. The effect of this drama was to force the Soviets' hand and break the deadlock. Once exposed, Khrushchev's options were to allow the situation to get out of control and result in war, or to back down. He backed down, and West Berlin remained free.

The Berlin Crisis never really came to an end, instead, it evolved gradually into the Cuban Missile Crisis late in 1962. During this period of evolution, NATO and 4 CIBG continued to maintain a high state of readiness:

> The short term threat has decreased since last August due to indications that the USSR is prepared to negotiate the Berlin problem and intends not to press the year end deadline.... Nevertheless, a failure in negotiations could precipitate a new crisis at any time. Long term changes in policy in light of the present lessening in tension is not justified....

There was still the problem of arming 1 SSM Battery's *Honest John* rockets with nuclear warheads. When the decision was made by the government to acquire the system, it had done so on the assumption that warheads would be made available for them from the common stockpile managed by the Americans. Beginning in 1954, Canada had signed a series of agreements allowing the transfer of nuclear weapons information for training purposes, and the crews from 1 SSM Battery were able to conduct every activity relating to the weapon's use, with the exception of arming and mounting the warhead, which was done by the US custodial detachment anyway. The specific government to government agreement authorizing further training for Canadian crews, however, remained unratified by Canada.

The reason for this was, ostensibly, a disagreement between Canadian and US diplomats over how the release of the warheads would be controlled. In reality, Canada's Secretary of State for External Affairs, Howard Green, and many on his staff were against nuclear weapons and stalled on signing the final agreement, hoping instead to convince the Prime Minister to change his mind. These individuals firmly believed that Canada was acting in a dangerous and provocative manner by acquiring nuclear delivery systems for NATO Shield forces. This attitude was wholly hypocritical. Canada had made a commitment in 1957 to provide nuclear delivery systems and had continually endorsed NATO strategic concepts with the full knowledge that they contained an important nuclear component. To renege now in the middle of a crisis situation, with the freedom of Europe hanging in the balance would make Canada look very bad indeed.

The Opposition in Canada, led by Lester Pearson, jumped on the anti-nuclear bandwagon temporarily as a political ploy to disrupt the Diefenbaker government. The government's response was to defend initially the acquisition and then, later, to come out against nuclear weapons, the net result of which was great strategic confusion. The consequence of this political manoeuvring was that the Canadian soldiers defending NATO were only partially equipped to function within NATO's strategic and operational concept.

Or were they? In reality, informal unwritten arrangements made between Canadian, British and American forces in Europe existed. These informal arrangements would have ensured that 1 SSM Battery, in a war situation, would have been able to use American warheads stored in a NORTHAG special ammunition storage facility controlled by the British. It should be strongly noted here that these weapons could not be used randomly or arbitrarily by just any commander. Brigadier Mike Dare, who took over as Brigade Commander in August 1962, had a special relationship which developed during the Cuban Missile Crisis in October:

> ...we had a [nuclear warhead custodial unit] detached to us by the Americans and they immediately put themselves (although they weren't ordered to by the central command or control) under our control. They had the independence to release the atomic weapons to us if circumstances required it. It was in their custody. We had the battery...but we didn't have the physical warheads with us. [They] weren't far away. [They] were in a US installation within two miles of where we were...it was a pretty reasonable thing, you know, because we could have demanded pretty prompt action from them....

As discussed earlier, there was a plan in I (BR) Corps for their use; it was just a question of ensuring that there was enough coverage of all potential targets. Removal of a scarce resource at the last minute could have jeopardized the defence plan for NORTHAG, and this was the nub of the matter when Ottawa was procrastinating. This situation was not understood by many officials, including Howard Green. Minister of National Defence Douglas Harkness was the exception.

At one point in July 1962, the Diefenbaker Government toyed with the idea of pulling 4 CIBG out of the Central Region and repatriating it to Canada. The Army was asked to assess the operational, administrative and financial implications of such a retreat, and its answer to the Government is worth quoting here:

> The withdrawal of all or any part of 4 CIBG from Europe would result in a repudiation to a significant degree of Canada's commitment at a time when the NATO partners are being asked to strengthen the forces in Europe.
>
> Holding the brigade group in Canada with arrangements to despatch to Europe by the fastest possible means would greatly reduce its readiness for operations during phase I. It could no longer be considered an element of the Shield Forces and would constitute a serious setback to the Forward Strategy now being considered by SACEUR in that the Canadian Brigade Group is an important element of NORTHAG's forces in the critical area of Central Europe.

CHAPTER THREE

It would be militarily unsound to assume that a formation located in Canada could return to Germany and be as effective as one permanently stationed in Germany....It would not be able to practise its operational tasks within NORTHAG plans nor would it have an intimate knowledge of the ground over which it may be required to fight....

The cost of repatriation and the lack of quarters in Canada were also factors that weighed against the proposal, which was quietly dropped.

4 CIBG's operational capability improved markedly in 1962 with the addition to it of nine CH 112 *Nomad* helicopters. This unique unit, the Royal Canadian Armoured Corps Helicopter Recce Troop, had been formed in 1961 and was deployed to Germany in the summer of 1962. This organization formed part of the Brigade recce squadron; since The Fort Garry Horse was scheduled to replace the 8th Hussars in the fall, the personnel of the helicopter troop were badged as 'Fort Garry's'. In terms of organization, it had six helicopters seven pilots, six sergeant-observers and a 12 man RCEME maintenance section. Brigade Headquarters also got two helicopters for liaison work, and one was held in a maintenance reserve.

4 CIBG put this new organization to good use in the battalion level work ups at Soltau in September. The LION CAGE series of exercises was not too different from previous work-ups with the exception of the helicopters:

> LION CAGE marked the first time in which helicopters formed part of the recce force for 4 CIBG. Recce helicopters flew over 170 hours, and one-third of this total was done at night. Valuable lessons were learned and it was found that more development and experience will be necessary to obtain full measure from this new information agency. Command-liaison flights pointed out the value of an air vehicle....

The impact on tactical thinking in 4 CIBG brought about by this enhanced recce capability was evident from the onset in some exercises:

> The enemy, ie; the attacking force which had no helicopter capacity, was reluctant in some cases, to risk detection by moving in daylight in the face of

helicopter recce. This apprehension on the part of the enemy served to the advantage of the defender....

The implications on the tactical nuclear battlefield were obvious. By increasing 4 CIBG's ability to gather information in a more timely fashion, nuclear targets could be acquired and engaged in a more efficient manner.

The Helicopter Troop also was instrumental in the development of some airmobile doctrine not only for the Canadian Army but for other NATO members as well. Some of the early helicopter pilots had been trained in the United States and had participated in the early stages of development of "nap of the earth" flying, that is, flying a few feet off of the ground and using terrain features for concealment. These techniques were refined and perfected in Germany. As John Marteinson, a Fort Garry Horse pilot, recalled:

> ...[the helicopters] were hard to conceal because of their distinctive engine noise and the inevitable reflective glint off the spinning rotor. The tactics developed attempted to take all of these factors into account...We would go to great lengths to avoid silhouetting the helicopter against the sky and we would almost always fly under telephone and power lines. In fact, wires of this sort were the greatest danger when flying 'nap'; they were very hard to spot in many light conditions and the obsessively tidy Germans would often put poles inside woods or tall hedgerows....It was a very demanding and indeed very dangerous type of flying. While Bell Helicopter had developed some of the initial techniques involved, (such as sideways flares to slow down without exposing the helicopter, or 'pop ups') the helicopter troop pilots refined and improved upon the concept and the manoeuvres, and in fact we taught the techniques to the Americans in the early days of the Vietnam War....

Exercise CANADA CUP and its work up, Exercise SILVER DOLLAR, were interesting because they highlighted new tactics and equipment. Held in October 1962 as the Cuban Missile Crisis was brewing, CANADA CUP was played out on 4 CIBG's actual EDP positions on the Weser River. The only difference was that the direction of the enemy and the defence were reversed. In case actual hostilities broke out, however, ammunition had been pre-positioned nearby.

4 CIBG was the defending force in CANADA CUP, protecting the Weser River against a mixed British-US force based on 4 Guards Brigade Group augmented with an American battalion group equipped with brand new M-113 Armoured Personnel Carriers (APCs). 'Enemy' armoured support was provided by the very heavy and experimental Conqueror tanks of the 5th Iniskilling Dragoon Guards. 4 CIBG had only one extra squadron of tanks attached to it, provided by 15/19 Hussars.

4 CIBG's defence plan was innovative. The usual brigade recce screen of *Ferrets* and helicopters were first deployed behind the Emmer River. [See Figure 3-6.] The Brigade covering force was then deployed behind the recce elements but its composition was different. In this case 1st Battalion, Queen's Own Rifles of Canada was the covering force but it included a composite anti-armour group created from the 106mm recoilless rifle sections of all three infantry battalions. These recoilless rifles, which were jeep mounted, were grouped with the machine gun platoon from the Queen's Own to form several "snipe teams". The mission of "Snipe Force" was to remain forward of the main obstacles on the Weser and create as much havoc as possible in the enemy's rear as he advanced.

The main obstacle was the Weser and behind it were two battalion groups based on the Black Watch and 1 Canadian Guards; the *Centurions* of the 8th Hussars were attached to the battalion groups.

Immediately after the start of 'hostilities' on 8 October, an American unit equipped with the new M113 APC managed to quickly pass through the covering force and hit the Weser river, forcing 4 Field Squadron to prematurely blow up reserve demolitions at Höxter and Holzminden. This in turn forced the covering force to withdraw over the bridge at Bodenwerder. Not all of the covering force made it; a detached battery of 105mm guns from 3 RCHA (supporting the screen) was caught in its gun positions by the enemy advance. Nuclear weapons could not be used because of the speed of the enemy advance and the long delays in getting release authority.

As night fell, the Queen's Own withdrew and reconstituted behind the main defensive line to act as the counter-attack force. "Snipe Force" then came out of its hides behind enemy lines and started to make life

EXERCISE
CANADA CUP
OCTOBER 1962
HAMELN
4 GDS
Ex. Bösingfeld
1 LAN R
5 IDG
Weser
Salzhemmendorf
DO. HUMFELD
1 I GDS
OBSTACLE BELT
N
BARNTRUP
BAD PYRMONT
Halle
US
BODEN-WERDER
FORCE
LÜGDE
BLOMBERG
ESCHERS-HAUSEN
Schieder
1 QOR (-)
1 CDN GDS
Polle
Emmer
SNIPE
STADT-OLDENDORF
Langengrud
Deensen
Bevern
SAS
STEINHEIM
HOLZMINDEN
1 QOR
(Division reserve on withdrawl)
M. Vörden
Hö. - Albaxen
2 RHC
NIEHEIM
Bridges blown
HÖXTER
Da. Sieversshausen
Hö. - Neuhaus
Special Air Service drops
BAD DRIBURG
BRAKEL
Weser
BEVERUNGEN
USLAR
Bad Karls-Hafen
WILLEBADESSEN
0 2 4 6 8 km
WL. PECKELSHEIM

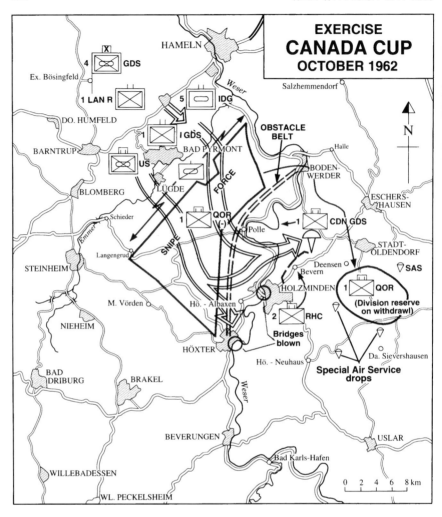

FIGURE 3-6

interesting for 4 Guards Brigade Group, eventually knocking out 44 armoured vehicles, 26 soft skinned vehicles, two helicopters and a radar site. The Black Watch and the Canadian Guards then unveiled another secret weapon, the Infrared (Medium) Viewer. This unwieldy instrument allowed the infantry battalions to capture not just one, but several Special Air Service patrols that had infiltrated into the main defensive position.

Three crossing sites were detected in the morning light of 9 October, at Polle and Albaxen, but all were disrupted by spoiling attacks from the Black Watch and Canadian Guards battle groups. These actions took all day; nuclear release still had not been received. At dusk on the 9th, frogmen from 4 Field Squadron conducted a very successful attack against the bridges and ferries at Polle.

On the 10th, the enemy was finally able to cross in strength at Heinsen and thrust towards Bevern. Unable to stop them, the Black Watch canalized them along the road towards Deensen into a killing zone where, finally, a simulated 20kt 'nuclear strike' eliminated the Irish Guards as a fighting formation. While this attack was in progress, SAS teams attacked 4 CIBG's headquarters and an enemy nuclear strike took out Recce Squadron. Even though the entire staff of the Brigade Headquarters was fighting off SAS paratroopers with pistols, 4 CIBG's response was to drop a 'nuclear weapon' on 4 Guards Brigade Group HQ, in revenge.

In the after action report, 4 CIBG's staff was impressed with the performance of the American APC battalion:

> The M113 equipped US battalion brought the tremendous flexibility of cross-country performance into sharp focus. This battalion was able to bypass with great speed the covering force, which was essentially road bound. Failure to realize the full extent of enemy mobility led to weaknesses in the demolition belt.... In one case, the US battalion successfully used a stream as a means of overcoming the demolition belt.

Canadian assessors also noted a flaw in the 'river' method of nuclear target planning:

> The enemy must not be allowed to penetrate; he must be defeated in his

most vulnerable hour, on the obstacle.... In the current EDP philosophy, the defender cannot count on nucs for the initial actions of this phase. Therefore, conventional fire systems must be strong and, in particular, armour must be available for the task, and demolitions must augment the extent of the obstacle.

Everyone involved was enthusiastic about introducing the APC into 4 CIBG's infantry battalions but this would have to wait another two years. A Canadian APC, the *Bobcat*, was under development at the time, but like so many other Canadian defence projects, it collapsed under its own weight.

International tension, just simmering beneath the surface, was visible again late in September 1962. The Soviets were extremely concerned about certain elements of NATO's Sword Forces, particularly medium range ballistic missiles located in Italy and Turkey. Khrushchev believed that this gave the West an 'unfair' advantage in the balance of power game since they were located in close proximity to the Soviet Union proper and were deterring him from expanding Communism. To compensate, the Soviets decided to place some of their own missiles in Cuba and up the ante again.

This precipitated the Cuban Missile Crisis. Even though the events were happening several thousand miles away, NATO was intimately involved. Consequently, a large NATO-wide command post exercise that was evaluating command and control procedures was shifted into 'real time'.

The Americans imposed a blockade on Soviet shipping headed for Cuba to put pressure on Khruschev to remove the missiles being set up there. Would Khrushchev retaliate by blockading Berlin in return? Would he go even further and attack NATO on a wide front? Moves by the West to relieve Berlin would have ramifications for NATO Shield Forces stationed in the Central Region. If push came to shove, NATO was in a situation similar to the 1961 crisis.

Unlike the 1961 crisis, NATO was better prepared to deal with a Berlin situation this time. Unfortunately, the measures taken to do this altered NORTHAG's carefully constructed EDP during the crisis and contributed to a permanent change in EDP planning for 4 CIBG later in 1963-64. NATO had approved what was referred to as a "catalogue" of contingency plans to respond to any possible Soviet move. The plans in this catalogue were called BERCONS (Berlin Contingencies) and were intended to supplement other plans for the defence of Berlin. The three occupying powers (France, Britain and the US) had formed a special planning group called LIVE OAK to develop non-NATO plans in this capacity prior to the 1961 crisis, but it was felt by NATO that other more comprehensive plans were needed.

The BERCONS included a variety of NATO responses, including an airlift and an air battle for control of the air corridors to Berlin. Four ground plans existed, BERCON CHARLIE 1 through 4. The first called for a one division attack down the Helmstedt-Berlin autobahn from the NORTHAG area. The second and fourth involved a two or four division attack in the Kassel area designed to extend the front into East Germany before the Soviets could put in an attack. (This would allow NATO to have more space to trade for time. Forces from both NORTHAG and CENTAG were earmarked to participate in these operations). The third option involved a four division attack down the Helmstedt route with twice the depth as the first option. The purpose behind the BERCON CHARLIE plans was to demonstrate resolve and force an access route to Berlin under conditions short of general war in the Central Region.

The most extreme contingency included the selective use of five nuclear weapons against five military targets away from populated areas. The objective here was to demonstrate NATO resolve if necessary, without resorting to general nuclear war. Although many NATO members including Canada initially objected to the inclusion of this option, they were quietly informed that the BERCON information would surely make its way back to Moscow. If this contingency was not included, Khrushchev might think the West lacked resolve and attack Berlin, the Central region, or both. By throwing an element of uncertainty into the mix, the enemy might be deterred.

The effect of the implementation of these plans directly affected the NORTHAG EDP, and thus 4 CIBG. Although Brigadier Dare was not made fully aware of these developments, the commander of 4th British Division was. By a twist of fate, the commander of 4th Division happened to be Canadian Major General Jean Victor Allard. (The reason behind MGen Allard's unique position was that Canada wanted to maintain some experience with divisional command, and wanted to ensure that a Canadian would have control over Canadian troops at a level higher than Brigade. This had been under discussion with the British since the mid-1950s; Allard was the first and only Canadian to occupy such a position in BAOR.) 4th British Division was the British contingency formation for BERCON tasks. Allard was pressured by British higher authorities to include 4 CIBG in 4th Division's BERCON planning. This, of course, was a political problem since Canada was not part of the post-war Berlin arrangements and the Department of External Affairs was adamant that Canada should not be involved in any Berlin relief operation.

In any event, once the storm clouds started to gather, a composite division was formed under General Allard consisting of a French brigade, an American brigade, two British brigades and some German logistics units; the British brigades were from 4th Division. The composition of the division was conventional since the only nuclear delivery unit that was attached was a single *Honest John* launcher. These units moved to the Helmstadt border area in early October and prepared to implement their part of the BERCON plans if called to do so.

The problem for NORTHAG was that the composite division was deployed more than fifty miles forward of the main Weser River obstacle. The two British brigades from 4th Division were removed from the left of 4 CIBG's EDP positions, leaving 4 CIBG all by itself. If the composite division moved into East Germany down the autobahn, and, if the situation escalated into a general war, there was no other formation that could fill the gap in the EDP positions on the Weser except 4 CIBG. This made sense, given the fact that 4 CIBG was the strongest brigade group in I (BR) Corps; why use a valuable resource like 4 CIBG for a high risk mission into East Germany when other formations were available? Thus, 4 CIBG participation in one of the larger BERCON options like the four division attack in the Kassel region or down the Helmstadt approach, was unlikely.

SACEUR's forces assumed an alert posture on 23 October 1962 after US forces world-wide moved up to DEFCON 3, two levels away from war. The Soviets continued to move ships and submarines in the Atlantic towards Cuba in defiance of the US blockade, and they

CHAPTER THREE

continued to build up forces in Germany. Two days later, DEFCON 2 was ordered, and the NATO alert system responded accordingly. SACEUR's nuclear strike aircraft 'bombed up' and prepared to execute their missions.

NORTHAG's forces were alerted for possible action. To avoid panic and to avoid provocation, 4 CIBG and the other forces in I (BR) Corps did not deploy outside of their camps. Brigadier Dare was 4 CIBG's commander during the crisis:

> …there was a NATO-wide alert put out and the Canadian Ambassador to NATO, George Ignatieff, came out after the crisis was over…he said 'boy, it's a lonely world isn't it?' It didn't really hit me as a military person the same way it hit him as a diplomat…the diplomatic world is really guided almost hourly by Ottawa, External Affairs or some form of consultation. We were using a means of communications back to Ottawa, the Commonwealth Communications Systems Wireless and the thing got so plugged that operational immediate messages were taking two days to get through. Flash messages certainly were not flagged. He was just shaken to the bottom about that. I had to sit down with him and say, that's the way it is…. The AOC of the Air Division phoned me up and he said 'are you evacuating all of your dependents?' I said no. He said, 'Well, I heard a rumour the brigade people are being put through Dusseldorf and filling up the airplanes'. I said, 'No, I'm not. I'm trying to play this as quietly as possible'…. The whole of Northern Army Group [was on alert and the American custodial detachment attached to us] immediately did so, although they were not ordered by their central command. They had independent release for atomic warheads if circumstances required it… The young man in charge of the American detachment moved his men to the storage area, ready to respond…. The ambassadors to NATO were in constant session about this in Brussels because they had a political responsibility but the military responded to the military assessment and the politicians fiddled around….

David Edgecomb was serving with 4 Field Squadron at the time:

> There was an urgent requirement to review demolition dossiers and war stocks of explosives held on wheels in the Corps Ammunition Depots. It was

a very tense time and, in spite of Government statements to the contrary, 4 CIBG went on standby, officers were recalled from leave and all ranks were confined to the brigade area.... For a time the 'pucker' factor was high in the brigade.... It was most interesting to follow the crisis on Voice of America and Radio Moscow. By taking the story as presented by these two propaganda mills and dividing by two we thought we were getting something close to the truth...

Mike Maloney and the other armoured soldiers from the 8th Canadian Hussars were rather busy:

We had upgraded the *Centurions*' guns from 20 pounder to 105mm just before the Cuban Missile Crisis broke....Unfortunately, there was not enough 105mm ammo available yet. There was lots of 20 pounder ammo, and we still had the barrels. The British refitting facilities were a ways away in Viersen, but there was a British tank transporter unit located nearby. These tank transporters were driven by Free Poles who were serving with BAOR and by an American unit....With their help, we re-barreled the tanks in record time.... We eventually deployed to our survival area and then to a river crossing site. We were told to take out anything crossing the bridge. A lot of people thought this was it....

At the height of the crisis, 4 CIBG deployed out to its survival areas. Gordie Gravelle was with the Black Watch serving with the Brigade Defence and Employment Platoon:

We bugged out to an area outside of the Möhnesee Dam. It was the usual spot that the Brigade HQ moved to on an alert. We were mobilized for five days and live ammunition was handy in our vehicles....All the [German Nike] missile bases nearby were ready, our SSM battery was ready. You had to play it by ear in case someone pushed the wrong button....

The high alert levels within NATO continued into late October. Eventually, US President John F. Kennedy came to an accommodation with Khrushchev by trading removal of the Soviet missiles in Cuba for the removal of American missiles in Turkey. Kennedy did this without consulting NATO. This created a row with the French over control of nuclear weapons and led to France withdrawing from NATO's integrated military structure. In a convoluted process of events, this also in turn resulted in the expulsion of the RCAF from its bases in France and the acquisition of the base in Lahr, Germany.

Personnel in 4 CIBG breathed a collective sigh of relief. For the second time in one year NATO had been pushed to the brink, but thanks to Western resolve the Russians had backed down from leading everyone over the edge. Troop rotations commenced after NATO alert forces stood down, bringing the following units to the Brigade in November and December 1962:

The Fort Garry Horse (replacing 8 CH); and
1st Battalion, The Royal Canadian Regiment (replacing 1 Cdn Gds)

Drama in Germany in the early 1960s was not limited to international tension. As members of the Westphalian community, 4 CIBG personnel had their opportunity to do the odd good deed or two. The Möhnesee, south of Soest, attracted its share of people who could not swim. In August 1963, three Germans disappeared near the British Yacht Club south of Soest and could not be located. In a multi-national operation, divers from the Brigade Free Diving Club, the German Life Savers and the Royal Engineers' 25th Field Squadron combed the murky depths of the lake. Tragically, all three victims had drowned; their bodies, however, were recovered by the team for burial.

In two other cases, Canadian soldiers were responsible for saving a farm and a factory from destruction by fire. Two troopers from The Fort Garry Horse, Hans Klene and Bill Hintze, assisted by a Dental Corps NCO Bill Fiddler, roused the sleeping family and formed a bucket brigade from the residents of Lunzen to save the farm and its animals. In a second incident, riflemen from the Queens Own Rifles noticed that a steel factory near Hemer was ablaze. Led by Sergeant 'Buck' Pacholzuk, drivers from Transport Platoon were organized into firefighting teams, driven to the site and commenced firefighting. The factory, valued at three million Deutschmarks, sustained less that DM 200,000 damage due to the timely intervention by Canadian soldiers. Two kegs of beer were provided by the factory management as a gesture of thanks.

Canadian soldiers apparently liked hot stuff. Signaller W.J. Tramble was in a *gasthof* one evening and, in an effort to be polite, apparently said "Ja!" once too often. Tramble accidentally joined the Delecke Volunteer Fire Department. After acquiring his International Driver's License, he was soon driving Delecke's only fire truck and was on call from his duties at Fort Henry.

One extremely significant problem in 4 CIBG was a very high rate of motor vehicle accidents that progressed to alarming levels in the early 1960s. The weekly brigade newspaper, *The Beaver*, had a special space on the front page reserved for pictures of car accidents. From 1959 to 1961, there was almost one major accident a week in the brigade area, many of them fatal since seat belts were not yet mandatory. The Provost Marshal swung into action, supported by a media awareness campaign on Radio CAE and the paper, which included a special address from the brigade commander. Thankfully, the rate dropped to much lower levels.

Training in 1963 followed the generally well established patterns once again. The Fall exercises in 1963 were not of a large scale, deliberately so since NATO did not want to provide the Soviets with any excuse to precipitate more extreme action. The work up for 4 CIBG in September 1963, Exercise IRON MAIDEN, was held in the Soltau training area and featured Eastland (4 CIBG) against Westland (the British) in conventional and nuclear operations. As with the other exercises in the early 1960s, extensive use was made of helicopters in all roles. 4 CIBG, of course, maintained its reputation for rear area and night patrol work.

The October exercise was a departure from other training schemes. Instead of a multi-Corps NORTHAG exercise, 4 CIBG conducted Exercise KEEN BLADE which pitted 4 CIBG against the Bundeswehr's Panzer Brigade 3 in the Hildesheim area. The Germans, in the role of attacker, inflicted a disproportionate number of casualties on 4 CIBG as German *Hotchkiss* mechanized infantry combat vehicles and M-48 tanks constantly outpaced the dismounted Canadian defenders. KEEN BLADE, in conjunction with the experience with M-113s during Exercise CANADA CUP, hammered home the need to equip 4 CIBG with an armoured personnel carrier.

While undoubtedly out-manoeuvred, Canadians used their initiative in creative ways to disrupt the enemy. A stay-behind party from 1 RCR was left in the 'enemy' area around the town of Irgen once 4 CIBG had retreated across the primary defensive obstacle, the Leine River. Dodging German recce parties, a hidden forward observation team was able to call down accurate artillery fire on the Germans as they advanced on the obstacle. Before the stay-behind team could make their way back, some 'enemy partisans' (German children) informed the German recce troops that there were Canadians holed-up in the town. A frantic search started; inadvertently, a German M-48 moved right on to the Canadian hide. Fortunately, the German locals whose land the stay behind team was using did not give the game away and the team was not caught. In addition to stay-behind teams, 4 CIBG utilized a special group made up of eight German-born soldiers serving with 4 CIBG to conduct surreptitious recce and sabotage operations in the 'enemy' rear area.

Just as 4 CIBG units were settling back into garrison after the Fall exercises, a lone gunman shot US President John F. Kennedy in Dallas, Texas. Was this a 'decapitation' operation in preparation for a Soviet first strike? No one could be sure. In Soest, patrons of the *gasthofs* and the rest of the citizenry were clustered around radios attempting to glean the facts of the situation. Staff officers contacted the Brigade Duty Officer, who informed them that the only information available was emanating from media sources. Ottawa was then contacted; Ottawa was at a low stage of alert in anticipation of an attack but no other indicators existed. The Americans in Europe were on alert; I (BR) Corps decided to freeze leaves but not to recall anybody. SAFEKEEP plans were dusted off once again. Gordie Gravelle of the Black Watch recalls this second alert during his tenure in Germany:

> We were at home and I heard it over the news. It was ten or fifteen minutes later we got a HIGHLAND LADDIE [the Black Watch equivalent to a QUICK TRAIN] and buses were ready to move to take the families out.... Alerts were going in North America. We grabbed out kit and away we went. We drove to Fort St Louis, got our equipment and weapons and ammunition and we went to Wickede. Charlie Company had high ground there and that's where we went. We didn't dig in; we got into a defensive position and sat there for a day and half, carrying out our defensive position routine. We had our ammunition

shadowing us nearby, about 10 minutes away. There were no other code words passed, though, and we came home.

As the facts on the assassination emerged, 4 CIBG was able to relax its alert posture.

In overview, the six years between 1957 and 1963 can be characterized as a period of excitement and change for Canada's NATO brigade. The Berlin Crisis in 1961 injected a dose of reality into Canadian logistical and sustainability planning in NORTHAG, while the Cuban Missile Crisis confirmed that the instituted improvements worked. The organizational changes and additions to 4 CIBG's structure enhanced its combat capabilities and made it the most potent brigade-sized formation in NATO. Large scale NATO exercises confirmed time and again how aggressive and innovative the Canadian soldier was. The addition of *Honest John* Canadian nuclear delivery units ensured that the place of the Canadian Army in I (BR) Corps was one of great influence. The quality of Canadian troops was extremely high, given the fact that they were all regulars and not conscripts. Higher NATO headquarters were sufficiently impressed with 4 CIBG to consider it for other missions, including possibly as a LANDCENT reserve force in the Central Region and as a Mobile Force for SACEUR. Though these possibilities were discarded, 4 CIBG played a key role in the defence of NORTHAG, especially with regard to resolution of the 'Belgian Problem'. No other formation was available for, or capable of this role. On the negative side, however, the first ideas of either withdrawing the Brigade from Europe or consolidating it with the RCAF units in southern Germany were starting to germinate.

1964-1970

FROM PINNACLE TO NADIR

CHAPTER FOUR

"IT IS TYPICAL OF STRATEGIC THREATS
THAT THE PUNITIVE ACTION (IF THE THREAT FAILS AND
HAS TO BE CARRIED OUT) IS PAINFUL AND COSTLY TO BOTH SIDES.
THE PURPOSE IS DETERRENCE *EX ANTE*, NOT REVENGE *EX POST*.
MAKING A CREDIBLE THREAT INVOLVES PROVING THAT ONE
WOULD HAVE TO CARRY OUT THE THREAT, OR CREATING
INCENTIVES FOR ONESELF OR INCURRING PENALTIES THAT
WOULD MAKE ONE EVIDENTLY WANT TO."

-THOMAS SCHELLING, *THE STRATEGY OF CONFLICT*

Both: *The French ENTAC, a 1st generation anti-tank guided missile, when mounted on a jeep, provided 4 Canadian Infantry Brigade Group with additional mobile tank killing power. In the Fall of 1964 "B" Company, 3 R22ᵉR was given 15 of these weapons plus a number of 106mm recoiless rifles to form the Brigade Anti-Tank Company.* (DND) EF 64 9737 3, EF 64 9775 1

CHAPTER FOUR

Exercise TREBLE CHANCE in 1964 was instrumental in altering I(BR) Corps concept of operations. 4 Canadian Infantry Brigade Group dedicated the entire 1964 training year working up for the event. **Above**, *Centurion tank manoeuvring in a training area.* **Below**, *infantry pass by a farm house, typical of the style found on the Luneburg Heath, where many exercises were held.* (DND) EF 63 9532 56, EF 64 9683 8

Above: A Canadian 'stand by'. Throughout the Brigade's existence, the Salvation Army provided an invaluable service to Canadian soldiers in Germany both in garrison, and in the field as shown here. (DND) EF 64 9644 3

Below: Local intelligence was often very useful on NATO exercises. Here a 106mm recoilless rifle detachment confers over a map with local boys. (DND) EF 66 9846 7

CHAPTER FOUR

Above: *Equipment upgrades dramatically increased the Brigade's effectiveness. Acquisition of the M113 APC in 1964 prompted a name change to 4 Canadian Mechanized Brigade Group. (DND) EF 64 9730 4*
Below: *The M-109 self-propelled gun was acquired by 4 CMBG in 1968. Numbers fielded varied between 18 and 24 depending on how many batteries of the RCHA were manned in accordance with government policy of the day. (DND) ILC 75 393*

Above: *Ceremonial occasions played a major part in the Canadian brigade's activities in Germany. On 26 May 1965 Queen Elizabeth II and HRH Prince Philip visited the Brigade and the new Canadian maple leaf flag was marched passed her for the first time. The troops pictured here are from 1 R22^{e}R. The Brigade Commander, Brigadier Tedlie is at the left of the podium.*
Below: *Ex TREBLE CHANCE: Canadian L-19 spotter aircraft prepare for a mission against 'Blueland'.* (DND) EF 64 9642 8

CHAPTER FOUR

Above: *Centurion tanks mounting Infra Red viewing kit. (DND)*
Below: *The M-113 APC mounted with the ENTAC Anti-Tank Guided Missile, introduced into service in 1966.*

The middle years of the 1960s were no doubt the 'golden era' for the Canadian brigade in Germany. After 12 years in Europe, brigade personnel had settled into a routine; not a comfortable routine given the ongoing potential for war, but a stable pattern nonetheless. The strength and composition of the Brigade made it a formidable formation. Peaking at just over 6700 men, 4 CIBG was often referred to as a "light division" by the British, possessing as it did a full armoured regiment, three mechanized infantry battalions of four rifle companies each, an artillery regiment, an independent recce squadron with armoured vehicles and helicopters, nuclear firepower suitable for a division, and extensive second line logistical support. By 1970, however, this powerful, respected force had been reduced to a shadow of its former self after the Trudeau government embarked on a defence policy to match its own benign view of the world.

The pinnacle period from 1963 to 1968 was rife with controversy and excitement. The Liberals under Lester Pearson had defeated the Diefenbaker government in 1963 over the nuclear weapons issue and

CHAPTER FOUR

Paul Hellyer, the new Minister of National Defence, set about implementing his vision of a unified force on the Canadian Army, Royal Canadian Air Force and the Royal Canadian Navy. In this same period, Canadian overseas commitments proliferated.

This changed emphasis in Canadian defence policy was enshrined in the 1964 White Paper on Defence, which established new priorities for Canada's defence programme. First priority was given to Collective Security, manifested by UN operations, followed by Collective Defence NATO operations, with third priority being given to the continental defence of North America.

The fact that the number one priority was allocated to UN operations was not unexpected since Pearson was the architect of the UN peacekeeping mission in 1956 to resolve the Suez affair. The objective here was to prevent Third World conflicts from breaking out into superpower confrontations that could result in nuclear war. The government believed that Canada could play an important and useful role here, in part because we had no 'baggage' as a former colonial power, in part because Canada was perceived in some quarters as being relatively impartial.

Second priority remained the defence of the NATO area. The Air Division still was the largest consumer of the budget allocated for NATO operations, with four bases and eight squadrons of CF-104 aircraft dedicated to the nuclear strike role. But the Brigade/Division commitment also remained important, as Paul Hellyer reasoned:

> It has been suggested that Canada might withdraw from this commitment, at which time the brigade could be assigned a role as a mobile reserve. After the most careful consideration it has been decided that this would not be in the best interests of Canada and the Alliance for several reasons.
>
> The Canadian brigade group holds a pivotal position in Northern Army Group. With the desire to increase the conventional strength available to the Alliance in order to reduce reliance on nuclear weapons, it would be a move in the opposite direction if the brigade was withdrawn....

Unfortunately, Prime Minister Pearson had other ideas which were revealed later, as Hellyer remarked:

> I finally met informally with the PM [Prime Minister] [who was also] the defence committee chairman, at his home. I was shocked at the nature of the discussion. The PM was most sympathetic but he too took the attitude that we didn't have to set an example in NATO. He didn't want NATO to break up but was unwilling to accept the concept of an 'effective' Canadian contribution.

The impact of the 1964 reorientation of defence priorities was important from the standpoint of the continued visibility of a divisional commitment to NATO. Keeping in mind that the regular Canadian Army consisted of only four brigade groups and that the Militia had been decimated during the Diefenbaker years, the Army's capability of fulfilling the divisional commitment was in serious jeopardy. The new primary focus on UN operations also dictated that a proportion of the Army had to be prepared for UN duty anywhere around the world in multiple locations on a moment's notice. The Army attempted to resolve that problem by reducing the emphasis on the brigade group commitment for the defence of North America. Two brigade groups were thus in theory still available to round out the NATO division, however, they were not adequately equipped to form a complete division, nor was there enough dedicated sealift to get them there in time. Canada had also committed two infantry battalions to SACEUR's new ACE Mobile Force (Land), reducing the number of battalions available to the division even further.

A decision was made at that time to revive the pre-positioned stock concept, and to plan to fly the brigades to Europe as necessary. Money, however, was never allocated for this project, and in any case the old stocks of weapons had been given away under the Mutual Defence Assistance Programme to other NATO allies during Diefenbaker's tenure. As a result, the divisional commitment existed only on paper in the late 1960s before Trudeau gave it the coup de grâce in 1969.

In the 1964-70 period the Canadian Army had a brigade group in Europe and two battalions committed to AMF(L) as its in-place NATO commitment. Peacekeeping operations involving the Canadian Army included Cyprus, Lebanon, the Belgian Congo, Yemen, India-Pakistan, Laos, New Guinea and Egypt, as well as the ill-fated ISCS/ICCS missions in Vietnam. There were even troops conducting military assistance programmes in Ghana, Nigeria and Tanzania. The end result was that in real terms Canada's primary land commitment to NATO continued to be a brigade group instead of a division.

The means by which the existing Canadian military forces were to be commanded and controlled was through a completely re-vamped defence structure called "The Canadian Armed Forces". Minister of National Defence Paul Hellyer unified the existing three military services into what he thought was one whole. One of the early events in the process of trying to make a reality of unification was the creation of functional commands. The field army in Canada, along with a tactical air group of CF-5 fighters, light transport aircraft and helicopters, became Mobile Command in 1965. From the outset, Mobile Command's emphasis was on the creation of a rapidly-deployable force for use anywhere in the world, principally to carry out peacekeeping or peace-restoring tasks, but as well, to be able to engage in limited conventional war. 3 CIBG in Gagetown remained tasked to back up 4 CIBG and was equipped and trained to conduct mechanized warfare; 1 CIBG in Calgary and 2 CIBG in Petawawa, since they were not fully equipped for European operations, were retasked as light air-portable brigades intended for use in a low intensity environment.

The creation of Mobile Command was initially thought to pose problems for the Germany-based brigade group. Was 4 CIBG part of Mobile Command or not? Could training for high intensity operations in Europe be reconciled with training for low intensity UN operations? What about equipment differences? How about command?

4 CIBG could not come under wartime command of Mobile Command since it was part of NORTHAG and I (BR) Corps, and its training requirements and equipment scales were quite different from the Canadian-based brigades. By 1965, 4 CIBG and Canadian Base Units Europe (CBUE), were placed under a single headquarters called Canadian Army National Force Europe (CANF(E)). In reality, the Commander 4 CIBG was simply double hatted as the national commander of all Canadian Army units in Europe, including the Army personnel at various NATO headquarters. He did not, however, have a completely separate staff. CBUE had been created in 1963 to streamline Army logistics and administrative support and to provide clear lines of communication with

the British logistical system. It commanded 1 Canadian Base Ordnance Unit located in Antwerp, its depots in Mönchen-Gladbach, Wetter and Vierson, and Canadian logistical liaison personnel attached to the British units. Brigadier A.J. Tedlie, 4 Brigade commander from 1964-1966, noted that

> It cannot be stressed too strongly how important the contribution made by CBUE was to the welfare and efficiency of the Brigade Group. Although the Brigade Commander wore two hats (one as Commander CIBG and the other as CANF(E), the commander of CBUE carried out all the burdensome tasks connected with the CANF(E) appointment.... The base units performed Herculean feats of running all the matters connected with housing, schools, grocery stores and the myriad of other tasks necessary to allow the Brigade to function effectively.... All the duties attendant to running a Canadian formation on a British lines of communication were coordinated by the CBUE. This day to day supervision of the Canadian units outside the Brigade area allowed the Brigade Commander great flexibility in carrying out his operational duties.

Unification did not alter this arrangement and, as a result, CANF(E) existed in limbo before coming under de facto control of Mobile Command later in the 1960s. Because of its isolation, the only tangible impact of unification on 4 CIBG before 1970 was the replacement of the Divisional red patch with the Mobile Command badge on the walking out uniforms in October 1966.

One notable development happened in 1965: the first-ever post-war Canadian combat clothing was issued to replace the mechanics coveralls which were worn for field clothing up to that point. Even though Canadian soldiers wore an American helmet, the addition of distinctive Canadian field uniforms went a long way towards furthering the brigade's Canadian identity in I (BR) Corps.

In a 1965 appreciation on manpower, 4 CIBG was recorded as having reached a peak strength of 6719 personnel. But Mobile Command at that time was searching for ways to cut back in all areas and, understandably, focused its attention on 4 CIBG. Within the brigade, the manpower limitations being imposed by the government produced a 'number

CHAPTER FOUR

crunching' exercise to determine where best and how personnel cuts could be made. Part of this included a debate over artillery support. Was it more economical in manpower to have four batteries of six guns or three batteries of eight guns? Could manpower be 'saved' and applied elsewhere?

To protect the combat effectiveness of 4 CIBG, a descending list of priorities was created to determine what combat functions could and could not be cut. This list placed nuclear firepower at the top to preserve, followed by obstacle development capability, mobile conventional firepower, static tank-killing firepower, anti-personnel artillery fire and, finally, conventional infantry firepower. The infantry battalions of the time had strengths of 900 to 1000 men, something virtually unheard of in the Canadian army today.

The end result of this review was no change. 4 CIBG successfully resisted attempts to whittle away its component parts and reduce its ability to fight. One area in which it did require more people was for equipment maintenance. With the increase in mechanization came the need for more 'maintainers' and logistical support. Although this would not adversely affect the Brigade in the mid-60s, it was a portent of things to come.

There were also more sophisticated weapons systems coming 'on line'. The increased armour threat in NORTHAG prompted the addition of more anti-tank systems to 4 CIBG. Existing systems like the 106mm recoilless rifle and the *Heller* were adequate for some tasks, but new technology started to surpass these weapons. Two first-generation anti-tank guided missiles, the SS-11 and the smaller and shorter-ranged ENTAC were acquired (15 of each system) for use in 4 CIBG. Both were carried on vehicles, the ENTAC on a jeep or a *Ferret*, and the SS-11 on a 3/4 ton truck.

The Brigade's anti-tank resources were eventually grouped together in an anti-tank company formed on B Coy 3 R22eR. 3 R22eR as a whole was converted to an anti-tank battalion, with two companies in Canada and one with the brigade in Europe. (This was in addition to 2 R22eR, which was already serving with 4 CIBG.) The 106mm recoilless rifles from 2 R22eR were grafted on to the anti-tank company's table of equipment, in addition to the ATGMs. The other new addition in the anti-tank field was the Swedish-made *Carl Gustav* man-portable recoilless rifle, which replaced the *Heller* weapon in the infantry battalions. With this variety of weapon systems, 4 CIBG was able to provide a multi-layered anti-tank defence designed to absorb the shock of an enemy armoured attack.

In a similar vein, the armoured regiment's *Centurions*, now 56 in number, were also upgraded to mount an infra-red viewing system for night operations. Once the large IR spot lights had been added to the tanks, proposals were examined for finding a replacement for the Brigade's 34 *Ferret* scout cars. Candidates for the recce vehicle role included a mixture of American *Sheridan* light tanks and the M-114 recce vehicle. This did not come to pass, however, since another vehicle was available that was more compatible with a new and very important acquisition – the M-113 APC.

After 4 CIBG had been repeatedly 'victimized' on exercises by mechanized infantry mounted in the American M-113 and the German *Hotchkiss,* the lack of mobility in the infantry battalions was finally seriously examined. An additional factor of course, was the lack of any form of protection offered by the Brigade's 3/4 ton trucks; the M-113 provided a quantum leap in protection against shrapnel and the elements, although the extent of protection from direct fire was always suspect. The requirement for an armoured personnel carrier for the Canadian Army had been developed during a series of exercises in Canada in the late 1950s, and this brought about the *Bobcat* project described in the last chapter. After the *Bobcat* project failed, the search began for an off-the-shelf vehicle. The Americans were well ahead of everybody in this field and in fact were testing the M-113 family in Vietnam when Canada took an active interest in the machine.

The M-113 family acquired by Canada over the 1965-1968 period included the basic M-113 APC, the M-577 command post, the M-548 tracked cargo carrier, engineer 'kits' for the basic M-113 vehicle, and the *Lynx* recce vehicle. Other variants were created in the 1960s, most notably by the addition of the ENTAC ATGM system to M-113 carriers. All in all, 316 of the 961 M-113s ordered by Canada were allocated to 4 CIBG. Some of the more worn out 3/4 ton Dodge trucks were sold to the Belgians. 4 CIBG wasn't the first formation in I (BR) Corps to deploy a tracked APC however; the British started to replace the *Saracen* wheeled APC with the FV 432 (similar to the M-113) while the Belgians had a number of American M-75 APCs, an obsolete predecessor to the M-113. The Germans retained improved versions of the *Hotchkiss* vehicle.

The introduction of the M-113 posed some problems for 4 Brigade. American trials with a gasoline-engined M-113 in southern Germany had resulted in a few deaths when the vehicle caught fire. Consequently, the Canadian version was provided with a diesel engine, which reduced the possibility of 'brewing up'. Another feature was power pivot steering which allowed the vehicle to pivot rapidly with little or no delay. After a number of fatal accidents resulting from the vehicle flipping over, this device was disconnected.

Yet another advance in operational capability was the introduction of the M-109 155 mm self-propelled gun which entered service with the artillery regiment in Germany in 1968. The original 105mm towed howitzers had been given away to Greece under MDAP and replaced with an upgraded model around 1962. (Eight 155mm towed howitzers were also added in 1965 to augment the 24 towed 105s) Once the infantry and other elements of 4 CIBG were mechanized, it took no great leap of the imagination to envision the replacement of the RCHA's towed artillery with self propelled. The increased mobility of the guns and their higher rate of fire were definite assets and greatly added to the Brigade's combat power. As with the M-113s, the gun crews now had some modicum of overhead protection and shelter.

Apart from the introduction of the APCs and the M-109s, other equipment holdings in 4 CIBG included 158 1/4 ton jeeps, 662 2 1/2 ton trucks, 27 five-ton recovery vehicles, four tank recovery vehicles, two tank transporters, three POL tanker trucks, and four bulldozers. The RCHA retained all of its organic L-19 aircraft, and an airfield was built near Fort Chambly to house Recce Squadron's helicopters. This supplemented the L-19 airfield at Fort Prince of Wales.

The state of signals communications within 4 Brigade during the latter half of the 1960s also improved significantly. The adoption of the M-113 APC accelerated the acquisition of the "46 Set" as the basic vehicle radio, though there were some problems with track noise in the early days. Another important acquisition was the BRUIN secure teletype system. BRUIN linked the Brigade main and rear headquarters and also provided a secure link with whichever divisional headquarters 4 Brigade happened to be operating with; a liaison detachment was formed and a number of BRUIN nodes were mounted in M-113s thus giving 4 Brigade defensible and mobile secure communications with higher headquarters.

The usual changes in commanders and units took place between 1964 and 1968. Brigadier A. James Tedlie assumed command from Brigadier Michael Dare in December of 1964, with Brigadier E.A.C. (Ned) Amy replacing Tedlie in September of 1966. Troop rotations for the 1964-1967 period altered the composition of 4 CIBG. In 1965, The Fort Garry Horse and the FGH Recce Squadron were replaced by Lord Strathcona's Horse (Royal Canadians) and the recce squadron from the 8th Canadian Hussars (Princess Louise's). Despite the risk of confusing the reader with a combination of alphabet soup and musical chairs, the rotations were thus: 2 RCR and 2 R22eR rotated with 1 RCR and 2 RHC. In 1966, 2 PPCLI relieved 1 PPCLI, and in 1967, 2 R22eR replaced 1 R22eR. 2 RCHA, which had been stationed in Germany since 1963 was relieved by 1 RCHA.

After the rotations there was always some reshuffling of quarters in the Canadian base area. Between 1964 and 1966, in the area of Soest, Fort Henry was home to HQ 4 CIBG, HQ CBUE, 4 Signals Squadron, 4 Field Dental Coy, 4 Provost Platoon and 1 Field Detention Barracks. Fort York usually held the infantry battalion originating from central Canada (whether Guards or RCR). 4 CIBG's independent Recce Squadron, along with the RCASC Transport Company, the Field Ambulance, the Ordnance Field Park and the RCEME Workshop occupied Fort Chambly.

In Werl, Fort St. Louis held the eastern Canada-based infantry battalion (Black Watch or Van Doos), and Fort Anne was home to the Anti-Tank Company and the 4 CIBG Battle School. 4 Field Squadron and Radio CAE occupied Fort Victoria. In the Hemer area, Fort Prince of Wales had the Artillery regiment and 1 SSM Battery, as well as the L-19s of the Air OP Troop. Fort Macleod hosted the western Canada-based infantry battalions (QOR of C or PPCLI), and last but not least, the armoured regiment resided in Fort Beausejour.

4 CIBG's increased firepower and mobility would have been much needed if war had broken out in the mid to late 1960s. The immediate threat to the Central Region in general and NORTHAG in particular had changed since the late 1950s. Although enemy approach routes into the NORTHAG sector remained the same as before, what was new and more worrying was the composition and capabilities of the Warsaw Pact forces, only a few hours drive to the East.

The most important development was improvements in the Pact's nuclear and conventional equipment as well as doctrine for their use. Soviet doctrine in the 1960s emphasized tactical nuclear war fighting with little real emphasis on conventional operations except advancing to occupy captured ground. If the Warsaw Pact had decided to initiate hostilities against NATO on the ground, nuclear and probably chemical weapons would have been used from the outset. This shift was manifested by the proliferation of several tactical and theatre-level nuclear weapons within GSFG from 1961 onwards. In terms of missiles, GSFG fielded the short-range Free Rocket Over Ground (FROG) in three versions, the *Scud* 1A (the early version of the weapon used by Iraq in the 1991 Gulf War), the SS-4 *Sandal* theatre support missile and, in the late 1960s, the SS-12 *Scaleboard*. With the exception of the SS-4, these missiles were mounted on self-propelled tracked or wheeled chassis and had variable warhead yields up to 100 kt. The Soviets placed less emphasis on nuclear-capable artillery but did field a nuclear shell for the D-20 towed 152mm howitzer and for some large calibre self-propelled mortars. Tactical support aircraft, of course, continued to have a nuclear free-fall bomb capability.

Warsaw Pact conventional re-equipment programmes continued throughout the 1960s. The primary main battle tanks fielded by the Soviets in the 1960s were the T-55 (1961) and the T-62 (1965), which were significant improvements over tanks of Second World War vintage (which continued to serve in other Warsaw Pact armies). The BTR-152 open-topped, wheeled APC gave way to the closed-topped BTR-60PB eight wheeled amphibious APC. The first BMP-1s, tracked infantry fighting vehicles carrying eight infanteers and mounting a 76mm gun as well as an anti-tank guided missile (the *Sagger*), made their first appearance in 1967. In real terms, the Soviets and their allies built up a completely mechanized force that emphasized mobility, protection against conventional fire and protection against nuclear fallout. The tanks and BMPs employed a sealing system and the APCs provided overhead cover against fallout.

The second change was in the composition of Group of Soviet Forces, Germany. [See Figure 4-1.] The 18th Guards Army was deactivated and its units distributed among the other Armies. The infantry divisions in GSFG were converted to motorized formations so that every division in GSFG was either a Tank Division or, in new Soviet terminology, a Motor Rifle Division. As deployed in East Germany, it is likely that 2nd Guards Army and 3rd Shock Army would have been deployed against NORTHAG, with 8th Guards Army and 1st Guards Tank Army employed either against CENTAG in conjunction with forces based in Czechoslovakia or against the inter-army group boundary. Three mechanized divisions and two tank divisions from the East German National Volkesarmee would have accompanied GSFG in the first wave into the West. Of course, some forces would have been tied up in a siege operation against West Berlin.

Depending how the battle progressed, 20th Guards Army could have followed 2nd Guards Army into LANDJUT or the Netherlands, hoping to move south along the Rhine into NATO's rear area. Follow up forces from Poland (9 mechanized and 5 tank divisions) would have been used to exploit any gains. Other forces available to GSFG included two independent tank divisions and a substantial number of airborne troops, probably the equivalent of two airborne divisions.

NATO strategy to confront this was undergoing significant change in the 1963-1968 period, and this once again directly affected the milieu in which 4 CIBG was expected to fight if deterrence failed. There were a number of political problems posed by the MC 14/2 strategy and this also had an impact on operational thinking. As was discussed in the last chapter, MC 14/2 tended towards immediate use of nuclear weapons, with little political consultation over the decision to utilize these weapons. This was considered dangerous by a number of political planners and military analysts. The 1961 Berlin Crisis highlighted these concerns; that is, that nuclear weapons should not be used against small scale incursions or in situations short of general war.

CHAPTER FOUR

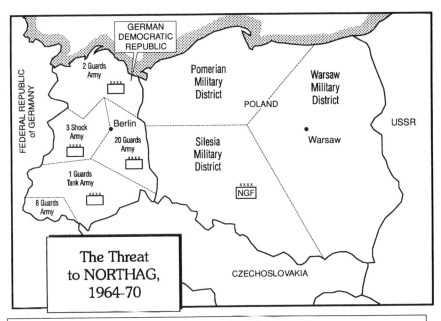

NORTHAG THREAT ORBAT 1964-70

GROUP of SOVIET FORCES, GERMANY:

1st GDS TK ARMY:
  6 Gds Tk Div
  7 Gds Tk Div
  9 Tk Div
  11 Gds Tk Div
  27 Gds Mtr Rifle Div

2nd GDS ARMY:
  32 Mtr Rifle Div
  9 Gds Tk Div
  94 Gds Mtr Rifle Div

3rd SHOCK ARMY:
  26 Gds Tk Div
  10 Gds Tk Div
  12 Gds Tk Div
  25 Tk Div
  207 Mtr Rifle Div

8th GDS ARMY:
  20 Gds Tk Div
  20 Gds Mtr Rifle Div
  39 Gds Mtr Rifle Div
  57 Gds Mtr Rifle Div

20th GDS ARMY:
  6 Gds Mtr Rifle Div
  1 9 Gds Mtr Rifle Div
  14 Gds Mtr Rifle Div

NATIONALE VOLKSARMEE (GDR):
  1 Mech Div
  4 Inf Div
  8 Inf Div
  7 Tk Div
  9 Tk Div
  11 Mtr Rifle Div
  (Plus 5 reserve NVA infantry divisions: 6, 10, 19, 27, 40)

(Plus 5 Soviet Divisions in Northern Group of Forces: 2 tank, 3 infantry)
(Plus 12 Polish Divisions)

FIGURE 4-1

The solution to this problem was proposed by the then-SACEUR, General Lauris Norstad, in a strategic concept known as MC 100/1. MC 100/1, among other things, suggested that conventional forces employing conventional means instead of tactical nuclear weapons should attempt to create a "pause" or a "firebreak" in the action. In real terms, this meant convincing the attacking enemy that his attack could not succeed quickly but that if he continued his aggressive action nuclear weapons would then be employed. This firebreak would allow time for consultation and debate within NATO (and the Warsaw Pact) to occur and prevent precipitous action on the part of any one NATO member.

There were of course a number of problems with the MC 100/1 concept. One of the reasons for deploying tactical nuclear weapons in the first place was to make NATO's existing smaller military forces more effective so that Western Europe could recover economically, leading to Europeans eventually being able to provide for their own conventional defence. But now that Western Europe had recovered, the desire to save money prompted NATO members to continue to rely on the nuclear equalizer and avoid spending funds on large conventional forces. If MC 100/1 were adopted, the emphasis would shift back to expensive conventional forces, mobilization and transportation. Secondly, the French believed that MC 100/1 would weaken the deterrent value of MC 14/2 and prompt a Soviet attack before the shift back to conventional forces could take place. A more important consideration from the French point of view was the fact that France wanted more control over the NATO-tasked nuclear weapons based on French soil, since there was a public perception that American weapons under the dual-key system was an affront to French sovereignty.

Consequently, MC 100/1 was not adopted by NATO. The situation regarding nuclear weapons use remained ambiguous, and the MC 14/2 tendency towards early nuclear use remained in place until 1963. In the wake of the Cuban Missile Crisis, the NATO Military Committee met in Athens to debate political control over nuclear weapons. The result of this meeting was the so-called Athens Guidelines. The Athens Guidelines laid out the specific situations in which tactical nuclear weapons could be used. In effect nuclear weapons could be used if the Soviets used nuclear weapons in the NATO area, but only on a scale proportional to that employed by the Soviets. If the Soviets attacked with conventional forces, NATO could use tactical nuclear weapons if necessary, and then only on a scale appropriate to the circumstances. Any other situation requiring nuclear weapons use would be considered on a case-by-case basis. The implications of the Athens meeting were clear: NATO's conventional forces needed to be improved in quality and in quantity in order to reduce dependency on nuclear use and provide greater response options.

This was the basis for an important but later NATO strategic concept, MC 14/3, known as Flexible Response. However, the reality in 1964 was quite different. There were never enough conventional forces in the 1960s to create a pause or a firebreak to enable consultation regarding a nuclear response to occur. Additionally, there simply would not be enough time for consultation. More importantly, since the late 1950s SACEUR (always an American commander) had pre-delegated nuclear release authority from the US President for the use of nuclear weapons if he felt a delay would endanger NATO or non-NATO tasked American forces in the Central Region. This distinction was left deliberately vague. As a result, the forces in NORTHAG and CENTAG continued to function with a nuclear-centred strategy throughout the 1960s.

The official, ideal concept of operations in the Central Region throughout the 1960s differed significantly from the previous 1957-63 concept. If the enemy used conventional forces, NATO ground forces would (ideally) fight back on conventional terms until the enemy either decided to withdraw or until he broke through. If the enemy broke through, Shield forces would be authorized to use tactical nuclear weapons to stop them. At that point, the air element of the Shield, along with the intermediate-range nuclear missile forces, would attack enemy follow-on forces and logistical nodes in the enemy rear area with nuclear weapons. The Shield land forces would fight to retain and regain the integrity of the NATO area. While these actions were in progress, a decision would be made whether to employ strategic nuclear forces against the Soviet Union. This was no longer an automatic event if NATO Europe was attacked with conventional and/or tactical nuclear forces, but this was never clearly stated in order that the credibility of the deterrent could be maintained. If, however, the Soviets initiated strategic nuclear use on day one of the conflict, some NATO members would in turn use strategic nuclear weapons against the USSR. NATO countries would ride out the attack, reconstitute, and end the war on conventional terms. It should be noted that a "no first use" policy was never adopted or even seriously considered by NATO planners.

These changes did have some effect on ground force operational planning. As discussed in the last chapter the general plan in the Central Region was to defend on the Weser-Lech line. After the Athens Conference in 1963, the main defensive line was pushed eastward all the way to the inner-German border, finally achieving (on paper at least) the forward defence envisioned by MC 14/1 in 1951. [See Figure 4-2.]

Several factors influenced this change in the LANDCENT Emergency Defence Plan. The West Germans once again recognized that the continued reliance on tactical nuclear weapons posed dangers to the Federal Republic and lobbied with even more fervor to push the forward edge of the battle area even further east. This they succeeded in doing, but this was not the primary motivation for the change.

A very significant factor in extending the line to the inner-German border was the continuing need for NATO forces to be able to implement Berlin Contingency plans and support the LIVE OAK organization in Berlin. The deployment of the tri-partite composite division to Helmstadt during the Cuban Missile Crisis highlighted this problem, as SACEUR noted:

> As you know, the present NATO land strategy in the center is to fall back on the line of the Weser in the North and to align roughly through Würtzburg/Ulm....It would be almost impossible to carry out any of the minor operations in connection with the Berlin Contingency Planning with any measure of success since these minor operations would be taking place in a vacuum....These operations would be taking place many miles in advance of our main battle positions and would therefore be vulnerable to quick destruction and quick exploitation by the enemy....

Another problem from the West German perspective was the makeup of the Bundeswehr. As a conscript organization, the Bundeswehr posted personnel to units mainly in the region where the conscripts came from.

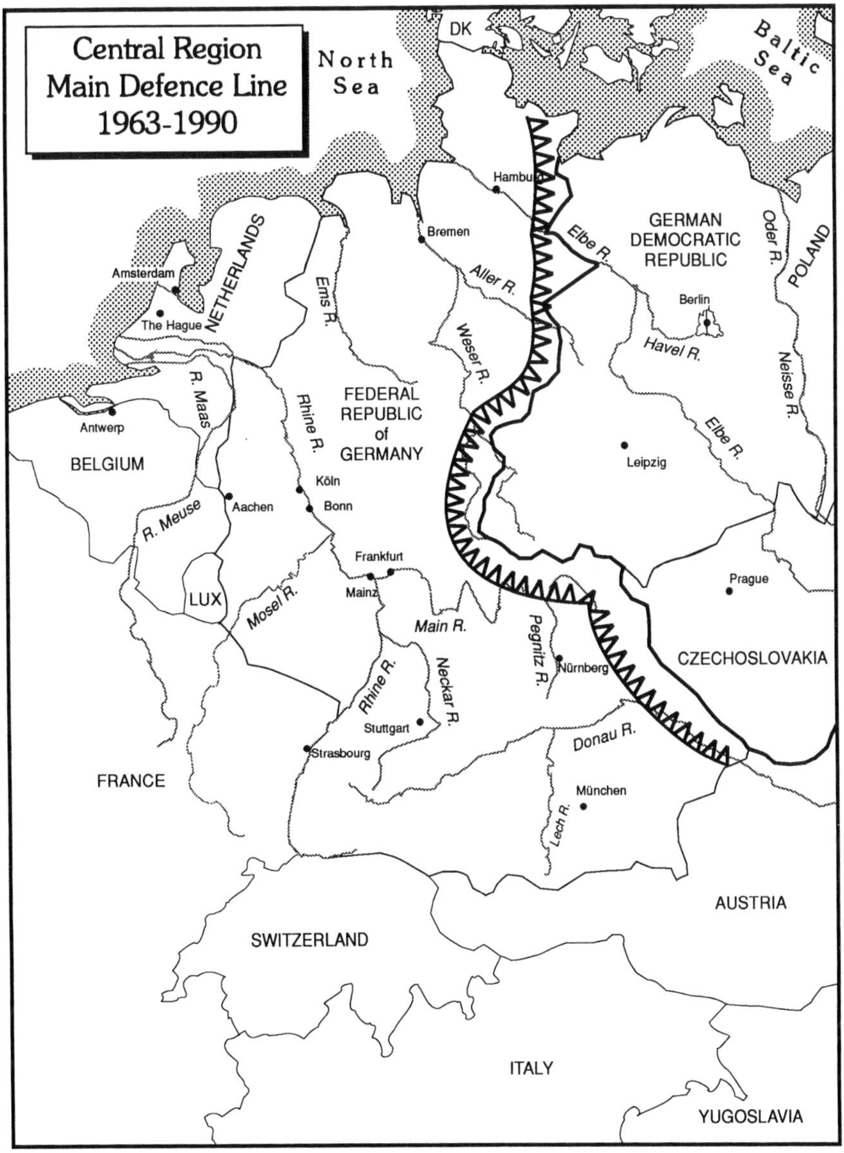
Central Region
Main Defence Line
1963-1990
North Sea
Baltic Sea
DK
Hambu
Bremen
Amsterdam
The Hague
NETHERLANDS
Ems R.
Elbe R.
Aller R.
GERMAN
DEMOCRATIC
REPUBLIC
Oder R.
POLAND
Berlin
Havel R.
Weser R.
Neisse R.
R. Maas
Antwerp
Rhine R.
FEDERAL
REPUBLIC
of
GERMANY
Elbe R.
Leipzig
BELGIUM
Köln
Bonn
Aachen
R. Meuse
Frankfurt
Mainz
Prague
LUX
Mosel R.
Main R.
Pegnitz R.
Nürnberg
CZECHOSLOVAKIA
Rhine R.
Neckar R.
Stuttgart
Strasbourg
Donau R.
FRANCE
München
Lech R.
AUSTRIA
SWITZERLAND
ITALY
YUGOSLAVIA

FIGURE 4-2

For units based in the westernmost part of the Federal Republic, there was no direct threat to the families or dependents of the soldiers. Soldiers who had families in cities located in close proximity to the forward areas, however, had an additional burden placed on them. If NATO fought a depth battle all the way back to the Weser, elements from I (GE) Korps near Hamburg and III (GE) Korps south of the Belgian Corps would be left with open flanks since the probability was high that the soldiers would not withdraw to positions behind their homes and leave their loved ones open to Soviet occupation. If large population areas were not protected and instead abandoned to the enemy advance from the outset, what was the point of West Germany being in NATO?

It is worth noting here the West German concept of *Wiedervereinigungskrieg* and its potential effects on EDP planning in NORTHAG. This term, roughly translated, means "war of reunification". The West German concern over Forward Defence apparently prompted some contingency planning within the Bundeswehr. If war appeared inevitable and the Soviets were going to attack, it would be prudent to fight as much of it as possible inside East Germany. To cater to such a contingency, plans may have existed within the Bundeswehr to push I (GE) Korps forward into East Germany north of Magdeberg and then conduct a fighting withdrawal back to the inner-German border in order to reduce enemy forces before they reached the main NATO defence line. A similar plan possibly existed for III (GE) Korps south of Kassel. Another possible contingency was armed support for an East German revolt against the Soviets. If the East German Army and the people had become engaged in a Hungarian-like or Czech-like revolt, it is conceivable that West Germany would not have stood by idly. Although these potentialities were never formally coordinated within the NATO command organizations, some Canadian officers were convinced of their existence and were concerned about the truncating effects of this on the NORTHAG defensive line and thus on the positioning of 4 CIBG.

British commanders in NORTHAG were extremely pessimistic about their ability to defend forward of the Weser, and they informed SACEUR that an additional four divisions were needed in NORTHAG to implement such a plan. These formations were not forthcoming from any of the other nations assigned to NORTHAG. The original 1950s basing plan for I (BR) Corps forces, including 4 CIBG, had been based on the Rhine defence scenario and was modified for the Weser scenario. Now that the line had been pushed even further east, the logistical tail grew even longer and posed problems related to forward stocking of supplies. Eventually, however, I (BR) Corps accepted the political and operational imperatives and took steps to modify the situation accordingly.

I (BR) Corps 'soldiered on' to produce the best plan they could under the circumstances. Problems with the Belgian and Dutch deployments continued to plague the development of the NORTHAG EDP. As noted in the last chapter, the Belgian ability to deploy to the Weser positions, let alone to forward positions on the border was suspect. The Dutch only had one brigade deployed in Germany, with the remainder of I (NL) Corps based in the Netherlands. Having to deploy two divisions 300 kilometers to the inner-German border in an emergency did not enhance the credibility of Forward Defence in NORTHAG. As a result, the only forward deployed units in NORTHAG were I (GE) Korps, I (BR) Corps and 4 CIBG, leaving great gaps on the inter-Army Group boundary with CENTAG and with LANDJUT in the north.

By way of contrast, the previous EDP based on the Weser River was basically an obstacle plan, while the concept adopted in I (BR) Corps after 1963 was more of a mobile defence plan. Planners in I (BR) Corps determined that there was no equivalent operational level, Weser-like obstacle forward of the Weser, nor was there any good defensive terrain comparable to the Teutobergerwald backing it up. Another more critical factor was the increase in Soviet tactical nuclear delivery systems. A positional defence based on a natural obstacle simply increased the vulnerability of the defenders to nuclear attack and, therefore, was out.

There was one advantage in adopting a forward posture. If the enemy used tactical nuclear weapons first, a mobile defence concept would assist in the survivability of the formations and allow them the flexibility to respond at a conventional or tactical nuclear level.

The terrain forward of the Weser was relatively open and the only significant water obstacle was the Leine River. [See Figure 4-3.] The Leine, however, was only of tactical significance because of its depth and width. The Harz Mountains did canalize enemy movement and an attacking force would have to manoeuvre around the built-up areas of

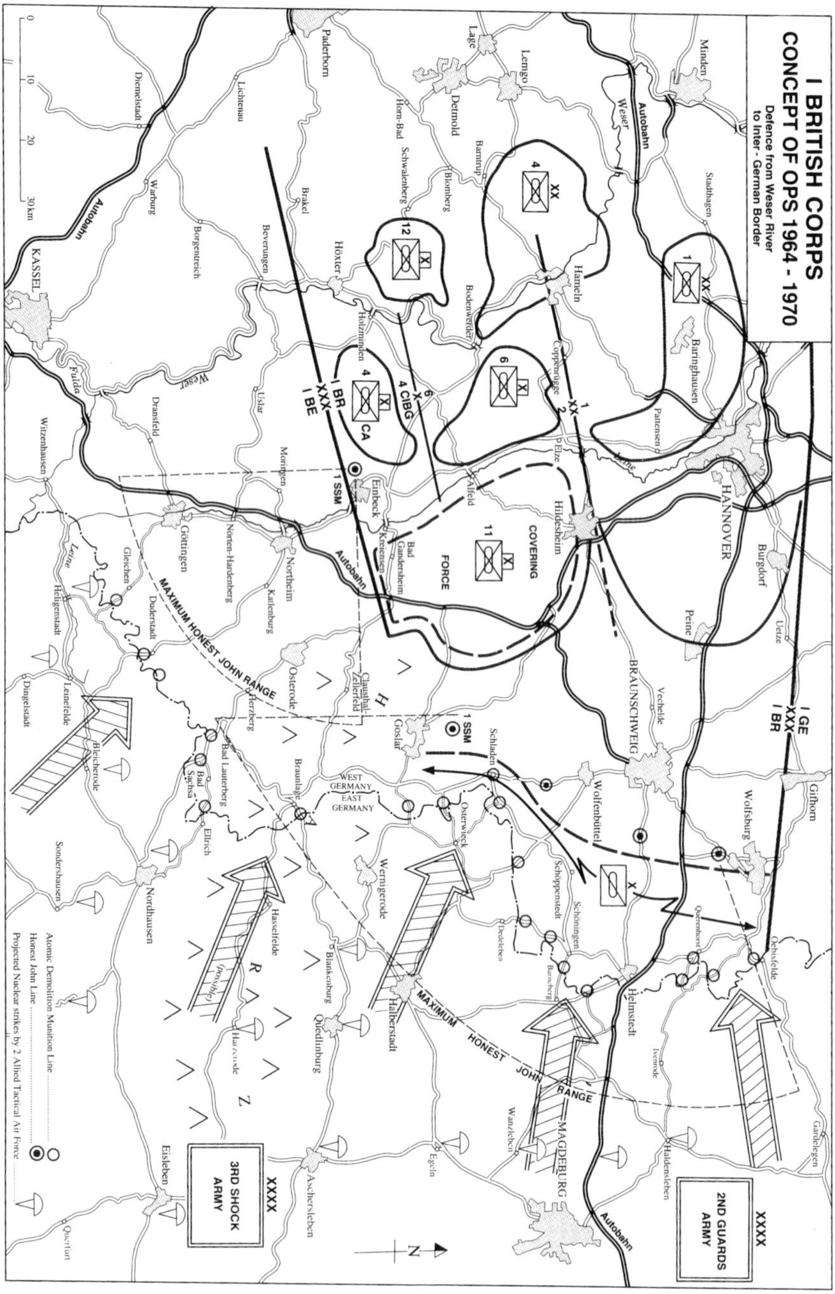
I BRITISH CORPS
CONCEPT OF OPS 1964 - 1970
Defence from Weser River to Inter - German Border
COVERING FORCE
MAXIMUM HONEST JOHN RANGE
WEST GERMANY
EAST GERMANY
3RD SHOCK ARMY
2ND GUARDS ARMY
I GE XXX I BR
I BR XXX I BE
Atomic Demolition Munition Line
Honest John Line
Projected Nuclear strikes by 2 Allied Tactical Air Force
HANNOVER
BRAUNSCHWEIG
MAGDEBURG
KASSEL
Autobahn
Weser

FIGURE 4-3

Braunschweig and Hannover to get crossing points on the Weser. In real terms, I (BR) Corps would have to fight a huge covering force battle with the Weser as a back drop. Unlike previous operational thinking, all of the I (BR) Corps forces would be engaged in the covering force battle east of the Weser, with no one left defending the Weser positions. The battle had to be won between the inner-German border and the Weser.

Despite the raging debate over high-level control of nuclear weapons on the battlefield, a new type of weapon was deployed and incorporated into I (BR) Corps' EDP. The Atomic Demolition Munition (ADM) was essentially a nuclear land mine. Its role in the EDP was to destroy significant defiles - like bridges or mountain passes - in an efficient manner, hopefully while the enemy was traversing it, and to create an irradiated crater to prevent the enemy from using the area afterward.

The ADMs were under joint control with American custodial detachments, like the *Honest Johns*, but this control was exercised at Corps level. There were twelve ADM teams in NORTHAG. Once use of the weapons was authorized, these engineer teams would move them by helicopter to the detonation sites and place them in pre-positioned concrete silos, where they would be remotely detonated later. The ADMs could have a yield between one and 15 kilotons.

The "pile up" tactics referred to in the last chapter were thus no longer dependent on having a convenient river obstacle. If the enemy moved through any significant defile he could be delayed and/or destroyed there; his follow up units would pile up and a nuclear target would present itself, even if it was right on the border. *Honest Johns* and nuclear artillery could then be brought to bear right into East Germany. In fact, if ADMs were buried along the border region and the enemy was halted right on the border, Forward Defence would be preserved from a political standpoint. Canadian, Dutch and German F-104 strike aircraft and the *Vulcan* and *Canberra* bombers from UK Bomber Command could finish off the follow on forces with nuclear weapons before they even left East Germany.

This was, however, at variance with the "firebreak" concept that some NATO members were pushing for. There were even some West Germans who objected to nuclear use on East German soil, since they considered it to be an occupied part of Germany as opposed to enemy territory in any sense. Be that as it may, nuclear weapons were targeted on military targets in Warsaw Pact territory, including East Germany.

It should be emphasized that the conventional forces in I (BR) Corps were still vitally necessary as part of these operational concepts. If the enemy broke through the ADM line, he had to be stopped. If nuclear release did not occur immediately, the enemy would have to be delayed until it could be passed on. Again, as discussed in the last chapter, only conventional forces could conduct BERCON and LIVE OAK type operations.

The deployment of I (BR) Corps forces and 4 CIBG was altered to accommodate these changes. [See Figure 4-4.] The 4th British Division, with which 4 CIBG had worked closely with over the past few years, was tasked with providing the Corps reserve astride the Weser. I (BR) Corps deployed 1st British Division left between the Weser and the Leine, with 2nd British Division right. 4 CIBG became part of 2nd British Division and once again was tasked with protecting the flank of I (BR) Corps. Note that this deployment was similar to that developed in 1957, except that it was displaced eastward to the Leine. The EDP envisioned a recce screen just behind the border area, with the West German *Bundesgrenzschutze* (Border Police) forces between them and the inner-German border. I (BR) Corps planners placed the 11th Infantry Brigade Group from the 2nd Division forward of the Leine as a covering force.

4 CIBG's EDP positions had more of a south-eastern orientation rather than an eastern one. The most probable enemy course of action was to attempt to outflank I (BR) Corps after passing through the Belgian sector in the Gottingen Gap. The British 6th Infantry Brigade Group from 2nd Division was on 4 CIBG's left flank facing east, with 12th Infantry Brigade Group to the west acting as the divisional reserve. The impact of mechanization on 4 CIBG's planning was considerable, according to Brigadier Tedlie, who commanded 4 CIBG from 1964 to 1966:

> ...Our positions had been essentially defensive, but became slightly more offensive as a result of the up-gunning of the tanks and the mechanization....I emphasized cutting down on the brigade administrative tail. I found over the years that more and more vehicles had been added to the Brigade HQ in the field; it looked like a Barnum and Baily Circus. I cut out things like the

CHAPTER FOUR

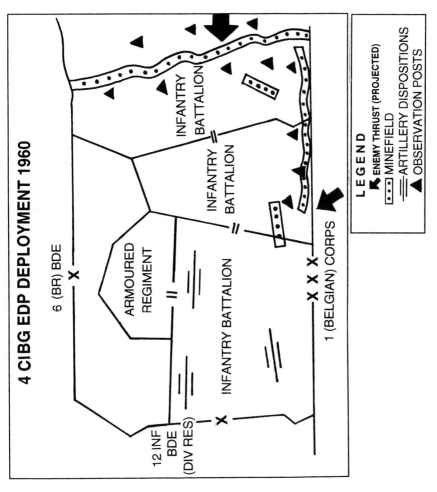

FIGURE 4-4: THIS SKETCH, REPRODUCED FROM THE ORIGINAL, PORTRAYS THE BRIGADE IN ITS PROJECTED EMERGENCY DEFENCE PLAN POSITIONS DURING THE 1960S.

caravans and trucks that were not really needed....The [EDP positions] now were overladen with all of these vehicles, causing problems with respect to vehicle hides....

This ability to rapidly redeploy the infantry certainly influenced the decision to retain 4 CIBG on the right flank of I (BR) Corps. In its EDP position, 4 CIBG deployed one infantry battalion along with the brigade anti-tank elements facing east behind an obstacle belt, but forward of the Leine River. The second infantry battalion with some attached armour, covered the south-east approaches, while the third battalion was in a depth position. The brigade reserve included the remainder of the armoured regiment and an infantry company. Nuclear fire support was provided by eight-inch howitzers from 2nd (BR) Division. If the Belgians could not make the Leine River in time, some method had to be found to protect the gap that would develop. As the Belgians possessed the *Honest John,* proper coordination between 4 CIBG and I (BE) Corps allowed nuclear firepower to fill the gap if necessary.

4 Brigade's own *Honest John* launchers were not in direct support of the Brigade and were located elsewhere. This was a point of contention within the Canadian command structure and there was still confusion over whether the *Honest John* was a Corps, Divisional or Brigade resource. The *Honest John,* as will be recalled, was a SACEUR requirement and four of them were acquired by Canada from the Americans as a compromise system in lieu of a divisional or brigade nuclear support weapon. The policy within NORTHAG was to hold nuclear weapons release authority at Corps level, a command level that Canada did not have in NORTHAG. However, the service-to-service agreement signed between the Canadians and the Americans on acquisition of the system made it perfectly clear that Canadian command authority, not British, was required before the Canadian weapons could be used. These arrangements and schools of thought worked at cross purposes and added to the confusion. Some partisans even suggested that the *Honest Johns* should be considered a brigade resource, with independent targeting and release procedures!

Despite these problems, 1 SSM Battery remained operationally tasked to I (BR) Corps as a Corps resource Administration training and non-nuclear logistics remained the responsibility of 4 CIBG. Once Canada signed the general agreement on nuclear weapons in 1964, the service-to-service agreement between 4 CIBG and USAREUR was signed. This gave 4 CIBG 'legal' access to the *Honest John* warhead stockpiles in NORTHAG. On 14 October 1964, 1 SSM Battery passed the USAREUR Nuclear Safety Inspection; this allowed 1 SSM Battery to continue nuclear weapons training and planning, something that it had been doing unofficially since its arrival in 1961.

Operationally, the four *Honest John* SSM launchers generally worked in pairs, with one launcher moving and one firing. The first pair was to be deployed far forward in concealed positions behind the recce screen in the covering force area around Goslar; the other two were deployed further west to cover the south-east approaches out of the Harz Mountains and the Gottingen Gap. Goslar is less than 10 km from the inner-German border and the average maximum range of the *Honest John* was a little more than 30 km (minimum range: 6 km). This allowed 1 (BR) Corps to project nuclear firepower at least 20 km into East Germany to take out elements of 3rd Shock Army as they piled up on the ADM line along the border, or as they were moving into their assembly areas around Halberstadt. The terrain here is very open and was conducive to nuclear targeting.

In light of all of the discussion surrounding alternatives to nuclear weapons, SACEUR's CPX HOSTAGE JAUNE, held in 1964, demonstrated that the new NORTHAG positions could not be defended without the use of tactical nuclear weapons. The new restrictions enshrined in the Athens Guidelines, coupled with the vulnerability of the now forward deployed forces, in all probability would have resulted in the use of nuclear weapons from the outset. The firebreak concept was a noble attempt but was not realistic yet given the significant numerical disadvantages in NORTHAG vis à vis GSFG.

One important and often neglected operational problem that would have affected 4 CIBG's ability to fight was communications. Although Canadian signals equipment was as good as or better than any other in NORTHAG, factors beyond the control of money or technology limited the Brigade's ability to communicate. Colonel D. Crowe, then of 1 SSM Battery:

> We used to try and get as much distance as we could out of our radios. The big problem as you well know with the radios in Germany was the spectrum. The spectrum is a definite amount of VHF space on the radio band, and we had so much of it and the divisions had so much of it; this was repeated every 20 or 25 miles because that was the range...the spectrum was divided without taking into account that the Russians had a need for radios. So it was quite crowded.

Brigadier E.A.C. Amy:

> The strength of 4 CIBG was the equivalent of the other two brigades in our division and consequently the size of our operational areas and frontages were larger than normal. This imposed a severe strain on our communications since exercise settings were based on a nuclear battlefield. The British brigades had the "black box" which permitted them to warn troops of a planned nuclear strike or the cancellation of one without overloading their command net. We had to resort to slidex [a long drawn out code system] on an already overloaded and stretched out command net. It was frustrating, in the middle of a mobile battle, with the net tied up for such long periods with 'say again' and 'I spell'.

Canadian signalers worked around the problem with the resources they had:

> What I would do – and we used to do a lot of radio re-broadcast work – [was to try] to get a reasonable frequency, which we had to change quite frequently, and then put out an RRB [remote re-broadcast] on the top of the highest hill. I could get about forty miles out of my radios that way, instead of fifteen.

Training in 1964 was just as intense as it had ever been. One important 'first' was the addition of flyover augmentees for 4 CIBG. In this test, 77 men were selected from units in Canada to see how quickly specialists could be found, equipped and flown over to take positions in the Germany-based units. For Exercise ESPERANTO ONE, 48 men were allocated to the armoured regiment, and 29 to the helicopter troop in

CHAPTER FOUR

Recce Squadron and the RCHA Air Observation Post flight. CPXs like Exercise MAPLE LEAF X kept 4 CIBG HQ and the signals people occupied. Exercise NEW HARPOON VII ensured that 4 CIBG could operate doctrinally with higher formation headquarters in I (BR) Corps and in NORTHAG.

One unique exercise was Exercise COLD STEEL, a series of company exercises laid on by the 1st Battalion, Royal Highland Regiment of Canada. The Black Watch had developed an informal relationship with the Bundeswehr's Panzer Grenadier Battalion 192 from Panzer Grenadier Brigade 19 and this relationship was carried on with 2 RHC. COLD STEEL involved company sized advance to contact and assault river crossing operations on the Lippe River. One platoon from Panzer Grenadier Battalion 192 was incorporated into each of the Black Watch's four companies for the exercises. Other 4 CIBG units developed *partnerschafts* (partnerships) with German units. Although all examples are too numerous to mention here, Canadian personnel were attached to Panzer Grenadier Brigade 19 on many occasions, and The Fort Garry Horse exchanged tankers with Panzer Battalion 194.

Another example of inter-NATO cooperation in NORTHAG was Exercise PRINTEMPS held in March 1965. PRINTEMPS was a joint Canadian-Belgian CPX involving 4 CIBG and the 1st Belgian Division. This exercise was extremely important in the development of liaison procedures between the two organizations, as they shared the boundary between I (BR) Corps and I (BE) Corps. 4 CIBG was placed under command of the Belgian division. Brigadier Tedlie attended the first orders group, and found that Canada was not the only country with bilingual problems:

> The orders group convinced me of the need for a lingua franca in NATO if we were to be successful in the event of war. [Major General De Schmidt] first gave his orders in Flemish, which took forty five minutes. He then repeated the orders in French, which took fifty minutes. When these French orders were completed, he then said 'Because we have the honour of having a Canadian Brigade under our command, today I will now give my orders in English.' At this point I turned to the General and said, 'Please don't bother sir. I understood the orders in French, and if we have the orders in a third

language I'm afraid that the war will be over before we get into it.'

The importance of these interallied relationships cannot be overstated. By breaking through the prejudice that had developed between the former occupiers and the Germans, and by searching for solutions to the truncated inter-Corps boundary situation with I (BE) Corps, Canadians facilitated better relations within the NATO armies in NORTHAG which also had the added benefit of forging stronger links in the chain. These relationships would bear fruit in the next two decades.

After acting as umpires on the joint Danish-British-German Exercise LOWLAND FLING, preparations for the 1964 Fall exercises started before the Brigade deployed to Soltau for them. A disagreement between the Canadians and the British over how long a covering force battle could defend against a determined enemy brought a competitive edge to these workups. The British asserted that a covering force from I (BR) Corps should and could be able to delay an enemy attack for 36 hours so that a depth obstacle could be defended. The Canadians were skeptical about this and suggested that the covering force could be routed in less than 12 hours. The gauntlet was thrown down!

The scheduled exercise was named TREBLE CHANCE, and 4 CIBG was designated the enemy force from Redland. Blueland, for the purposes of TREBLE CHANCE, consisted of the 6th Infantry Brigade Group provided by 2nd British Infantry Division and Panzer Grenadier Battalion 323. Other Redland forces included 2nd Battalion, The Parachute Regiment and 7th Para Light Regiment, Royal Horse Artillery, if the weather proved adequate.

TREBLE CHANCE was a unique exercise for 4 CIBG. Brigadier Dare re-organized the Brigade into 16 "troop-platoon groups" each consisting of one tank troop, one infantry platoon, one "sub-FOO", a field engineer section and two *Ferret* scout cars. These "Ploops", as they were called, operated independently so that the Brigade could infiltrate the Blueland covering force and not present a concentrated target. The other infantry battalion and two armoured squadrons formed into two combat teams to follow the Ploops through weak areas in the covering force area. Training for this once-off organization continued for many months leading up to the exercise.

4 CIBG also took part in testing the flyover concept again. Unfortunately, there were technical problems which grounded Recce Squadron's helicopters. Brigadier Dare improvised:

> The reinforcements flown over from Canada for the fall training arrived on schedule and were quickly integrated into their units. In particular, the tank crews from the LdSH(RC) were quick to fit into the FGH, thus permitting us to operate a full armoured regiment of 56 tanks. Due to the grounding of the aircraft, I am afraid the fly-over flight crews did not get the training we planned for them. To partially overcome this problem I organized the helicopter troop of the Recce Squadron as a long range infiltration patrol force, which gave them a good opportunity to practice infiltration, ground patrolling and observation...

4 CIBG moved into position at 2200 hours on 4 October 1964, prepared to jump off at midnight. Over the next five and a half hours 'General Confusion' was in command as 4 CIBG's Ploops overran startled and half asleep Bluelanders. John Marteinson, author of The Fort Garry Horse regimental history and a participant in TREBLE CHANCE, recalled that:

> Some of the battle groups got lost, others hit minefields and had to find ways around them. A German Panzer Grenadier Battalion headquarters was captured intact and a half squadron of British armoured cars were taken, their crews still in their sleeping bags....

Redland's objective was to close on the Warburg River and establish crossing sites. 4 CIBG's recce elements were on the river by 0530 hours, six and one half hours before the 12 hour deadline set by the Canadians. Blueland put in a counter-attack in the afternoon of 6 October; Redland picked off an entire regiment of Blueland *Centurions*, including some 'allied' M-48s thrown in. The engineers from 4 Field Squadron also gained some experience in close range anti-tank work as one sapper, then-Lieutenant David Edgecomb, recounted:

> During the 5 Brigade counter-attack, my troop sergeant discovered some

> Guards Armoured tanks stopped in a village with their hatches open. He came back to the troop lines, gathered up [some other sappers] and some flour bag grenades and went tank hunting. Their score for the night was four *Centurions* and a collection of surprised, flour-covered armoured corps crews who bailed out with some alacrity. Later on in their enthusiasm and out of grenades, they threw an artillery simulator into an armoured command vehicle. Fortunately the crew escaped injury but the radios were badly damaged. In war it probably would have been VC's all around!

After the failed counter-attack, Blueland decided to put in a nuclear strike. Before this could happen, Redland forces withdrew across the river to safety, leaving behind a light recce screen. The nuclear strike came to naught as 4 CIBG was gone, but this didn't prevent Blueland from putting in another attack to exploit the effects of the blast. This attack just punched into empty space; as it ran out of steam, 4 CIBG counter-attacked with the objective of pushing Blueland forces back over the river. Conceding that the point had been made, the British stopped the exercise.

Not all training in 4 CIBG was directly related to large scale exercises. 4 CIBG ran its own battle school to ensure that its incoming personnel had more than just the minimal skills needed to fight on the modern battlefield. One interesting training scheme, FLY CATCHER, involved the use of tracking dogs to find enemy long-range recce parties. The Brigade retained its edge in recce skills by holding an annual patrolling competition. For Canadian tankers, the newly-instituted Canadian Army Trophy provided the opportunity to rub elbows with other NATO armoured units by way of a gunnery competition.

A particularly important non-training event was the lowering of the Red Ensign and the raising of the new Canadian flag in February 1965. Brigadier Tedlie was Commander of 4 CIBG:

> Although the first official unfurling of the national flag of Canada took place on Parliament Hill on 15th February 1965, it was some time later before our troops in Germany received the new flags. When they arrived, the various Canadian forts had compelling ceremonies as the old Red Ensign was lowered and the new Maple Leaf raised. One such occasion had a lone

CHAPTER FOUR

piper from the Black Watch play the Scottish lament, *The Flowers of the Forest* as the old flag came down and the whole band played *Oh Canada* as the new one was raised. There was hardly a dry eye amongst the participating Canadians.

The occasion was used to entertain various local dignitaries. Whether as a result of our hospitality or because Germans understand national pride, I noticed thereafter a marked acceptance by the natives that we were indeed a Canadian national army and not just part of the BAOR wearing Canada badges.

4 CIBG's training remained top notch in the 1960s, constantly building on previous experience. The introduction of the M-113 APC into the infantry battalions dictated significant changes to doctrine. Some infantry leaders had foreseen the introduction of the APC, and had used their existing 3/4 ton Dodge trucks as simulators to develop standard operating procedures (SOPs) for M-113 employment. Innovation was not restricted to the infantry units; the key to any mechanized operation is the ability of armoured and infantry units to operate in harmony. Tank-infantry cooperation, already emphasized in 4 CIBG, continued to be the focus of training once the M-113s arrived in quantity. The British, who were starting to develop similar SOPs, constantly visited 4 CIBG to observe Canadian doctrine in action.

One extremely important M-113 attribute was that it was amphibious, that is, it had the ability to swim across water obstacles by propelling itself through the water by its tracks. This required special training, and a watermanship site was established on the Weser River so that crews could gain experience in this area. The first memorable test of the M-113's aquatic ability was on Exercise CHECK MATE in October 1966, when the three infantry battalions mounted in 300 or so M-113s crossed the Weser in quick succession.

Many individuals in the battalions got carried away with their new mobility. Lieutenant-General Jack Vance was a Major and a company commander at the time:

> One of the most hilarious and embarrassing things for me personally was an event during one of these RMA [Requisitioned Manoeuvre Area] exercises in which I reached a stage at long last where I could do some company

level work. I've always been a good map reader and I'll swear to this day that the map was not marked to show this airfield sort of in the woods on this hilly feature which I chose to be the place where the mounted mechanized assault of my company would take place. Here I was lord of the manor, emperor of the hill sort of thing, standing up in my M-113, waving my arms, talking on the radio, moving a platoon in this glorious attack, when my driver came up on the intercom and said, 'Sir, you'd better look over your right shoulder.' I did and here was this guy thundering across the field firing his Very pistol straight at my APC.... What I was in fact doing was an attack down the length of this airfield for which he was responsible....

Another break in training occurred in 1967. Centennial year brought forth an outpouring of Canadian pride and the Canadians based in Germany were no exception. As the Canadian showcase in Europe, the Soest-Hemer area became the focal point for much curiosity. Those Europeans unable to afford a trip to Expo 67 in Montreal could travel to Soest and visit several exhibits, demonstrations and events depicting Canadiana. Naturally, "centennial projects" proliferated in the Canadian community. There was a parade and a tattoo of course, but nothing quite rivaling the 1956 Rote Erde stadium barbecue.

Once more to the field again! And, once again, 4 CIBG was playing the enemy force against the "Lionians". Exercise ROB ROY was another multi-national NORTHAG extravaganza; 4 CIBG was augmented by the 101st (Netherlands) Tank Battalion, 1st Falsterke Fod Infantry Regiment (another Dutch unit), elements of the Queen's Royal Irish Hussars, and a variety of British engineer odds and sods. That was not all. Operation ORION SPECIAL 67 commenced 19 August 1967 and by the start of ROB ROY, 300 Militia and 160 Regular soldiers had been flown in from Canada to provide 4 CIBG with even more punch. This brought 4 CIBG almost to division strength (British armoured division equivalent). The 'Lionians' were provided by 4th Infantry Division and The Brigade of Guards, including the Grenadier Guards and the Scots Guards. A number of Danish units also participated. Truly formidable competition!

The first phase of ROB ROY got underway on the night of 27 September 1967. The '4 CIBG Division' jumped off the start line near

Barsinghausen (southwest of Hannover), rapidly closed on the Weser at locations north and south of Hameln and then stopped! The scheduled night assault crossing using M-113s had to be delayed until daylight so that river traffic would not bump into the APCs. Heavy fog delayed the operation again until noon on the 28th. The umpires initially did not want a full scale crossing and allowed only 81 APCs to cross south of Hameln; the others used bridges instead.

The situation got tense for 2 PPCLI as they exploited a weak point in the Lionian defence and got around an enemy defended bridge:

> As it turned out, we had selected a boundary line between two enemy units; this boundary line was a road. We were moving along (this was during daylight) and the enemy wasn't active.... We were under British umpires and they wanted to know what we were doing in this here area, how did we get there, how did we get across the start line, how long did we take getting the APCs ready to swim.... We swam across and got into their rear area and that's how the enemy found out; when the umpires started querying where we were going....
>
> [We found out] from our long range patrol person that this road was a retreat MSR [Main Supply Route] for the British forces and we waited until a convoy came down. We opened fire on them which caused great confusion and great dodging into ditches. I went back to my niner and told him 'I have a problem here. I'm across the MSR. I have two SS11B batteries firing down range at their tanks protecting the bridge'. He told me to block the MSR and I had to explain to him that if I did this it would cause physical violence to take place.... We had to go back half a day and start over; we weren't sure if it was because of our screwing around in the rear area or not.

Making up for lost time, 4 CIBG advanced on several axes to seize the city of Kassel from Lionia. [See Figure 4-5.] The Lionians reacted with vigour, forcing 4 CIBG onto the defensive. With their back against the mythical Gulf of Lionia, a strong covering force was positioned near Warburg, with a recce screen and an obstacle belt behind it. Three battle group defensive positions and a battle group in mobile reserve completed the plan.

After a two day 'truce' on the weekend to permit the local

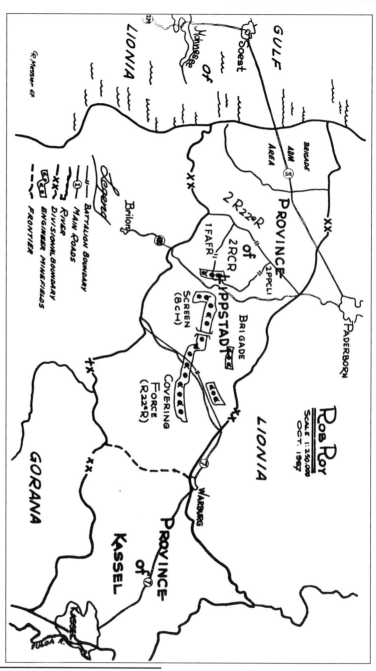

FIGURE 4-5: EXERCISE ROB ROY (SEPTEMBER 1967). THIS MAP APPEARED IN THE BRIGADE NEWSPAPER *THE BEAVER*. IT PORTRAYS THE DEFENSIVE BATTLE DURING THE EXERCISE.

CHAPTER FOUR

Westphalians to get some sleep, the Lionians counterattacked. The covering force gave good account of itself but had to withdraw as nuclear strikes were put in. Again, RCE combat divers put in an appearance to harass the enemy while making river crossings. The Lionian attack ground to a halt and 4 CIBG put in their final counter-attack with M-113 mounted infantry and Dutch *Centurion* tanks. International mediation saved the Lionians from embarrassment as 4 CIBG's recce organization got into their rear area.

As an aside, the navy's HMCS *Provider* transported two CH113A Voyageur transport helicopters to Germany for participation in ROB ROY. 1 Transport Helicopter Platoon performed resupply operations in all phases of the exercise in conjunction with other 4 CIBG logistics units. In the end, the brigade staff assessed that helicopters, though useful in many ways, could not fully replace wheeled vehicles as a method of resupply for a Canadian brigade group operating in a European environment. The machines were maintenance intensive and possessed no capability for night operations.

It would be remiss not to mention the continuing social development of the Brigade as it spent the 1960s in Westphalia. As we have seen, there was a paradoxical relationship between the Canadians, their Belgian and British comrades in arms, and their German hosts. At one level, there was the extensive community contacts, sports events and goodwill activities. At another level, there was friction between the four communities.

But innumerable cases of *freundschaft* abounded. One example was when flood waters struck the Paderborn area in July 1965. The town of Lippestadt was inundated, and Neuhaus village was completely cut off. Many minor bridges were washed away, while power and telephone service was totally disrupted. The damage was on par with any hurricane in Florida. It is not a cliché to say that the entire community pulled together to limit the damage, rescue the people and rebuild. 4 CIBG provided manpower from the troops, women and child power from the dependents as well as helicopters, assault boats, ambulances and fresh water supplies. Working in concert with the Bundeswehr, Belgian and British units, 4 CIBG played a major role in helping the civilian population overcome this disaster; there was no Memorandum of Understanding, no bureaucracy and no requirement for compensation.

Another interesting aspect to the Canadian presence in northern Germany was support provided to Schloss Varler, as Brigadier Ned Amy recalled:

> Our officers' wives continued the tradition started by the British to make periodic visits to Schloss Varler where a small group of Yugoslav high ranking officers and their wives were billeted. They had been exiled after World War II and while the Germans provided them with housing they were elderly, in poor health and virtually penniless. The Canadian wives brought them food comforts which they would not otherwise have been able to afford and provided them with a modest amount of spending money. Equally important to them was the opportunity to socialize….

On the other side of the coin, there was friction with some of the German population, as Wayne Dauphinee from 1 Field Ambulance experienced:

> It was difficult. I at one point had a German girlfriend who was engaged by the Canadian schools to teach German. Her father…was a Colonel in the Bundeswehr who had wartime service, and was still very much the Prussian officer. He viewed me as part of this occupying force that was only there to rape and pillage. It wasn't the same comfortable times as you have now…there was a standoffishness, whereas [during] my second tour, there was a real effort [on our part] to speak German. [On] my first tour there wasn't.

Canadian troops were comparatively well-paid and this caused some problems with the British troops. Donna Cowan worked as a Canadian nurse at British Military Hospital, Iserlohn:

> BMH Iserlohn had a combined British/Canadian staff. Whereas the British had a more military background, we were more casual. They had the usual British parochialism and rank consciousness, and they thought Canadians were spoiled. Their pay was one third of what we were getting, and they were still on wartime rates for rations and amenities in some cases.

This resentment regularly spilled over into the *gasthofs* in the Soest-Hemer area. These places were informally marked off as 'turf' belonging to various British, Belgian or Canadian units. Dick Coroy was in the Canadian Provost Corps serving in Soest:

> The Canadian troops at that time seemed to have a rivalry, and [many] times a unit would take over a *gasthaus* and only [members of] that unit [were] allowed in. If you weren't a member of that unit and you walked in, you got severely beaten and thrown out the door. On numerous occasions, the [evicted] troops would go back to their unit and [a] whole platoon would go down and they'd bust up the whole *gasthaus* and all the Brits that were in the place…. I remember in one case 18 people were in the hospital [with] fractured skulls and broken arms, broken noses…. Of course there was [also] the 50,000 marks damage, which was a lot of money in those days. There would be no furniture left, no bar left, no windows left. The units used to get together, at that time the Green Jackets and the Queen's Own, and they would divvy up for the damages. It used to be common.

No. 1 Field Detention Barracks, otherwise known as the "Crowbar Hotel", was a very busy place in the 1960s. One of the most celebrated incidents was the Great Iserlohn Punchup:

> The *gasthofs* were 'owned' by different regiments, and the clientele inside were owned by the regiments, that is, the female clientele, and when I say owned, I don't mean that in a literal sense…. This particular bar had been owned by the Green Jackets, and this young lad from the Strathconas went into the bar to pick up his girlfriend. [The British] took offense at this and threw him out a window after bouncing him around the floor a bit. Not to be outdone, the [Strathconas] Judo Team with their buddy in hand headed down to said bar, where upon the entire bar was destroyed. They put the run to the Green Jackets and then the German riot police arrived on the scene. The fray came to an end but not before a riot policeman had been stripped naked and sent running off up the street….

This did not deter one individual from borrowing from a contemporary American fad from Vietnam:

[The fight] didn't save them from 14 days CB [confinement to barracks]..., Right between Iserlohn and Deilinghofen was an old bar called the Kamikaze or the Saddle Bar. It was owned by the Patricias, and the same kind of rules applied. There was a similar type ruckus, except the young lad came back not wanting to do 14 days CB. Fearing to tell his buddies in the Judo Team, he decided to launch a couple of hand grenades in the front door, which went off and readjusted the front door of the Kamikaze....

If this were not enough, the Brigade continued to make the German news in other ways:

> **'Canadian Amok Pilot Cuts through VEW Circuit lines: Questionable Clever Trick Cuts Out Power Supply.'**
> He, who is stationed in one of the Deilinghofen Camps, used the spring-like afternoon to visit the south and east areas. With a single engined military plane, his first victim was the 30,000 volt high-tension line near Haarweg.... With his landing gear he detached two of the three copper wires which fell sparkling to the ground.... The next target of the wanton pilot was the low tension wire (only 380 volts) in Buecke. That was not enough. The Canadian dared again at the Lohner Flur to pass in a terrible vertical dive between two poles of 10,000 volts each. Countless witnesses observed this amok flight and also later observed a second Canadian plane leisurely circling the places of action. The pilot, after his return, evidently reported about his heroic deed, and sent his successor out for examination....

Who said the RCAF had to have the monopoly on aerial acrobatics?

In terms of sports and entertainment, the Brigade Hockey League continued to be very important in promoting Canadian culture in Europe. Basketball, track and field and boxing still reigned supreme. Other sports such as judo, competitive swimming, and even free-fall parachuting were becoming available. A golf course was constructed to satisfy addicts of that Scottish vice. Travel to exotic European locales expanded in the mid-1960s and Canadian personnel and their families were allowed to partake in the benefits of the American Forces Recreation Centres in Bavaria such as at Garmisch, Berchtesgaden, and Chiemsee. Even visits to Berlin were possible, though Canadian politicians still quaked in their boots at the thought of an 'incident' involving Canadian personnel. The rules for Berlin were simple: no uniform, no travel by train or car, (plane only), and no entry into East Berlin for any reason. Perhaps there was good reason for this caution. British and American personnel had been kidnapped by the Soviets on a number of occasions. These men were declared missing and never heard from again.

This potentially sinister backdrop did not exist only on the other side of the Iron Curtain. Iserlohn had its share of 'comrades' working for the cause of international socialism. One officer from the Strathconas noted:

> [Across] from Fort Beausejour was a chocolate factory…. The interesting thing about it was that no one had ever seen any trucks go in or out. I don't think anybody really had an idea what the purpose of it was until our IO [intelligence officer] saw one of our intelligence summaries [on agent activities]. It came out with a series of pictures. One picture showed one of our tanks obviously moving out to load at a railhead somewhere. When you looked closely at where the picture had been taken, it was obvious that it came from the window of the chocolate factory!

As in earlier years, Radio CAE continued to be important to morale of the soldiers and dependents. Apart from *The Beaver*, Radio CAE was the only source of Canadian news available. Once in a while, the Canadian Broadcasting Corporation would send a variety show to visit Canadian troops stationed overseas in Europe and the Middle East. Big names of the period included Tommy Hunter, Gordie Tapp, The Hanes Sisters, and Claudette. Other than these, the primary source of entertainment was visiting with friends and neighbours.

By the end of 1967, 4 CIBG began entering the nadir stage of its existence. A decreased defence budget for 1968 forced several changes in the structure and strength of 4 CIBG, and the Army struggled to adapt to this situation. While this was going on, Lester Pearson retired and in 1968 Pierre Elliot Trudeau became Prime Minister of Canada.

The 1968 changes in the organization of the Brigade were stimulated by pressures from the Pearson government to reduce the number of personnel in the Armed Forces as a whole. Once Pearson had stood down, the Trudeau government accelerated this reduction programme not once but twice, the second time in 1969. 4 CIBG's share of the 1968 cuts amounted to a reduction in authorized strength from 6606 to 6000. In the final measure, after months of discussion with Mobile Command, the structure of the Brigade was radically altered. As of 1 May 1968, 4 CIBG changed its designation to 4 Canadian Mechanized Brigade Group; another variant, 4 Canadian Mechanical Brigade Group, was rejected.

The infantry battalions were each reduced from four to three rifle companies. The Artillery had just converted to M-109 self-propelled guns, which theoretically 'saved' artillery manpower, but in fact increased the logistics tail needed to maintain the vehicles. 1 SSM Battery was reduced from four launchers to two, and NATO was informed that two launchers were more suitable support for a brigade group than four. The brigade anti-tank company was disbanded; the SS11B1s were given to the recce squadron and mounted on M-113s, while the ENTACs and 106mm recoilless rifles were returned to the infantry battalions. Recce Squadron replaced its wheeled *Ferrets* with *Lynx* tracked recce vehicles, while the infantry battalion recce platoons also received one platoon of *Lynx* each. The brigade Signal Squadron was combined with the brigade Headquarters Company to form a composite Headquarters and Signal Squadron for HQ 4 CMBG.

In a major change to the service support structure, the Ordnance Field Park was disbanded while the RCEME Workshops and RCASC Transport Company were grouped into a new organization known as 4 Service and Transport Company, later changed to 4 CMBG Service Battalion. The sub-units within this organization included a service and transport company, and a maintenance company. (This process was not completed until May 1969.) The unit establishments were in some cases less than a fifth of those that existed under the old system. In effect, the Brigade's service and support organizations were gutted.

4 Provost Platoon became 4 MP Platoon, also joining 4 CMBG Service Battalion. The medical and dental units narrowly missed becoming 1 Canadian Base Medical Unit but at the last minute retained their identities in the form of 4 Canadian Medical Support Unit. Some standardization in unit names was required, since some units added "mechanized" to their titles on an unauthorized basis. Some variations included

4 Field Squadron RCE (Mechanized) or 4 Mechanized MP Platoon. In the end, the old designations were retained.

In terms of location, 4 CMBG units played musical chairs again. 1 SSM Battery and 4 CMBG Service Battalion took up residence in the newly acquired Fort Qu'Appelle, a former British barracks located near Fort Beausejour in Iserlohn.

Other changes affected the logistics and support infrastructure. CANF(E) changed its name to Canadian Land Forces, Europe but this did not alter its function. CBUE, on the other hand, was scheduled to be replaced with an organization called Canadian Forces Base Northern Germany which was to control 1 Canadian Base Ordnance Unit, 1 Field Detention Barracks and the chimeric 1 Canadian Base Medical Unit. By December 1967, this reorganization had stabilized into Canadian Land Forces, Europe; 4 CMBG; and Canadian Forces Base Soest. CFB Soest eventually became responsible for the welfare of the garrisons at Soest, Werl, and Hemer from a service support point of view. These garrisons incorporated the existing forts, married quarters and the Canadian Land Forces Exchange System (CLFEX), the successor to Maple Leaf Services.

The overall impact of the 1968 cuts was not hard to assess. The loss of the three infantry companies, that is, one quarter of the available infantry strength in the brigade, affected how the brigade could fight. As to the changes in the anti-tank resources, this was just a change of hands and did not alter the number of weapons to be aimed at enemy tanks. The mobility of the M-109 SP guns was an improvement over the towed mounts, but it reduced the number of available tubes from 24 to 18.

Unlike the early 1960s, the anticipated battlefield was tending towards even greater conventional engagements and away from tactical nuclear use. The force structure that 4 CMBG had in 1968 was designed to cover the wide, dispersed frontage believed to be essential in nuclear operations. As the swing back to emphasis on conventional operations occurred, the frontage that could be held by 4 CMBG decreased, and as 4 CMBG itself shrunk in size, it became less and less operationally significant, since it could occupy progressively less space in the overall Corps area. The incremental loss of the Canadian nuclear delivery capability further reduced Canadian operational influence at Corps level where nuclear targeting and command decisions were made. Arrangements, of course, were made for flyover augmentation in the event of war, but in reality, Canada's relative importance in NORTHAG could not be based only on potential strength. It could only rest in actual capability, since the EDP positions were so close to the border.

There were other cuts to Canadian units based in Europe, especially in 1 Canadian Air Division, which reshuffled its aircraft amongst three airfields in Germany and carried on as before. Taken as a whole, NATO reaction to Canadian reductions was quite negative, since these cuts coincided with another dangerous international situation: the 'fraternal' invasion of Czechoslovakia.

On 20 June 1968, the Warsaw Pact initiated Exercise SUMAVA. An apparently innocuous exercise, SUMAVA would grow in size until 500,000 troops, including 22 Soviet, two East German, two Polish and one Hungarian divisions were to manoeuvre on Czechoslovakian soil. This exercise was actually a scheduled one, but had been heavily modified after Czech President Alexander Dubcek introduced reforms so that Socialism in his country could have a "human face". This was known as the "Prague Spring". On the night of 21 August, a Soviet airborne division seized Prague International Airport in a *coup de main* and Soviet strategic nuclear forces were put on alert. After five days of operations, control of Czechoslovakia passed from the Dubcek government to "suitable" individuals loyal to Moscow.

Reacting instinctively, NATO called for a QUICK TRAIN. 4 CMBG was, for the most part, well prepared as then-Captain Daryll Dean recalled:

> The Alert was called on a Friday evening. It was actually called about 8:30 PM by that time in the evening if memory serves me correctly. I lived in a small village. It was 10:30 PM when I got a phone call; I was one of the only houses in the area that had a phone. We went around and alerted people and the trucks came out from Iserlohn. Well you can imagine a Friday evening TGIF [Thank God Its Friday] on and the entire brigade on a QUICK TRAIN! When I arrived about 11:30 there were a large number of people who should not have been in vehicles and driving them around. Fortunately, once we got everybody in, the Kaserne gates were locked and nobody was permitted to

leave. I suppose that's the closest we had come in Germany for some period of time to a real threat situation where we loaded all the EIS [Equipment Issue Scale] onto the tanks. The ammunition was stacked so that the bulk could be broken down quickly and the tanks could be loaded onto the rail cars.... Watching the brigade crank itself up operationally was something....

An infantry soldier from 4 CMBG thought this was it:

It was during this time period that the Czechoslovak crisis occurred and we thought we would be all marching off to the Czech border in order to defend and protect the Czech people. However, what actually happened was we were bugged out to our PSA [practice survival area] and we spent approximately four hours there before returning to camp....There was no upload of ammunition. It was not broken down to the companies or the soldiers [unlike in the Armoured Regiment]. All we did was go to our deployment areas and dig in to await further orders. We were quite surprised to be ordered back into camp....By four in the afternoon we were allowed to go home and no further action was taken.

On 4 September, seven Soviet divisions were mobilized and moved from the Soviet Union to East Germany. NATO's leadership, already in session to determine an appropriate response to the situation, grew more and more alarmed:

There are larger Soviet forces now present in Central Europe than at any other time since the early postwar period. The changed East-West military situation in Europe is of significance for the security of [NATO]. In the light of these events we are reviewing with our allies what the implications may be for existing arrangements to provide for our common security....

Exercise SCHWARZE LOEWE, a joint US-German affair near the Czech border in CENTAG, was moved westward so that it would not be seen as being provocative or used as an excuse for action by the Soviets. It barely needs mentioning that SACEUR's nuclear forces were placed at a higher state of readiness; in some cases nuclear strike aircraft 'bombed up' and prepared to launch. General Lyman L. Lemnitzer, SACEUR at the time, "put into effect all of the clandestine military arrangements and plans that [NATO] had, but we [in SHAPE] couldn't get any guidance from the Secretary General. The American attitude was to stand back and see what positions its NATO allies took."

Canadian response to the Czech crisis, from the standpoint of 4 CMBG, was to re-examine the cuts that had been made earlier in the year, just in case 4 CMBG had to brought back to that level in the event of war. NATO firmly believed that

> The events of the past six weeks have shown that the Soviets have not changed their basic ruthlessness and that a situation of danger still exists, particularly in Europe....

Canada concurred with this assessment. There was some talk about reactivating the 1st Canadian Division, but CFHQ recognized that there was not enough sealift to transport it to Europe. Other NATO members, notably the United States, canceled some troop rotations and even flew over some troops to augment those already in the Central Region. Eventually, as in 1961 and 1962, the crisis atmosphere waned once the Soviet Union consolidated its grip on Czechoslovakia and pulled back the bulk of its forces.

The Czech situation gave added impetus to 4 CMBG's fall training in 1968. Exercise KEYSTONE (21-30 October 68) became important not only from a military point of view but a political one as well. Ex SCHWARZE LOEWE had been altered to accommodate the political situation but NATO still needed to demonstrate its capability as an alliance. Since the NORTHAG area was relatively far removed from the immediate Czech border region, a large scale exercise there would not be so provocative.

The exercise instructions for KEYSTONE reflected the tension in 1968:

> The threat to 2 Div security and in particular 4 CMBG will be strong during this exercise. Units will ensure that all personnel are aware of this threat and personnel are conversant with appropriate measures.

CHAPTER FOUR

In fact, for this exercise, provisions had been made if fighting broke out over the Czech situation:

> The codeword RAMPART will be issued by Con[trol] HQ through 4 CMBG in the event of emergency cancellation of Ex. This may be the prelude to a switch to real ops. If this codeword is issued units will cease ex activity and await further orders. On order, GSO3 Ops and GSO3 Int HQ 4 CMBG under escort will proceed to Fort Henry ASP [As Soon as Possible] to be prepared to issue all documents and instructions pertaining to real ops.....If necessary, units will draw ammo from its normal locations directly from exercise locations on order Commander, 4 CMBG.

Exercise KEYSTONE involved 2nd (British) Infantry Division, 4 CMBG and 20th (British) Armoured Brigade. The exercise area [See Figure 4-6] was divided into Redland, Keystonia, Blueland and Ruritania. Redland and its nominal ally, Ruritania, were represented by 20th Armoured Brigade and the Special Air Service. Blueland forces occupying Keystonia included 4 CMBG, 12th Infantry Brigade and 6th Infantry Brigade; 6th Infantry Brigade was flown over from the UK, married up with its prepositioned kit and moved into position in Keystonia. As with previous exercises, an ORION SPECIAL was done to add Militia flyover personnel into 4 CMBG's units.

Exercise KEYSTONE exemplified the shift to NATO's new strategic concept; nuclear weapons were placed on a short leash for the duration of the exercise. Phase I of the exercise involved low intensity operations against Redland sympathizers, agents and agitators in Keystonia. This action was stepped up when the "Keystone Frontier Police", (otherwise known as the Keystone Kops by some wags), were attacked by Redland special purpose forces. 4 CMBG's task was to back up the Keystone Kops with dismounted operations, prevent border incursions, contain demonstrations and disrupt guerrilla attacks.

The simulated low intensity problem in Phase I caused some Canadian units consternation:

> During the first phase, the battle narrative for all battalions called for 'political unrest' in the mythical country the Canadians were occupying. While

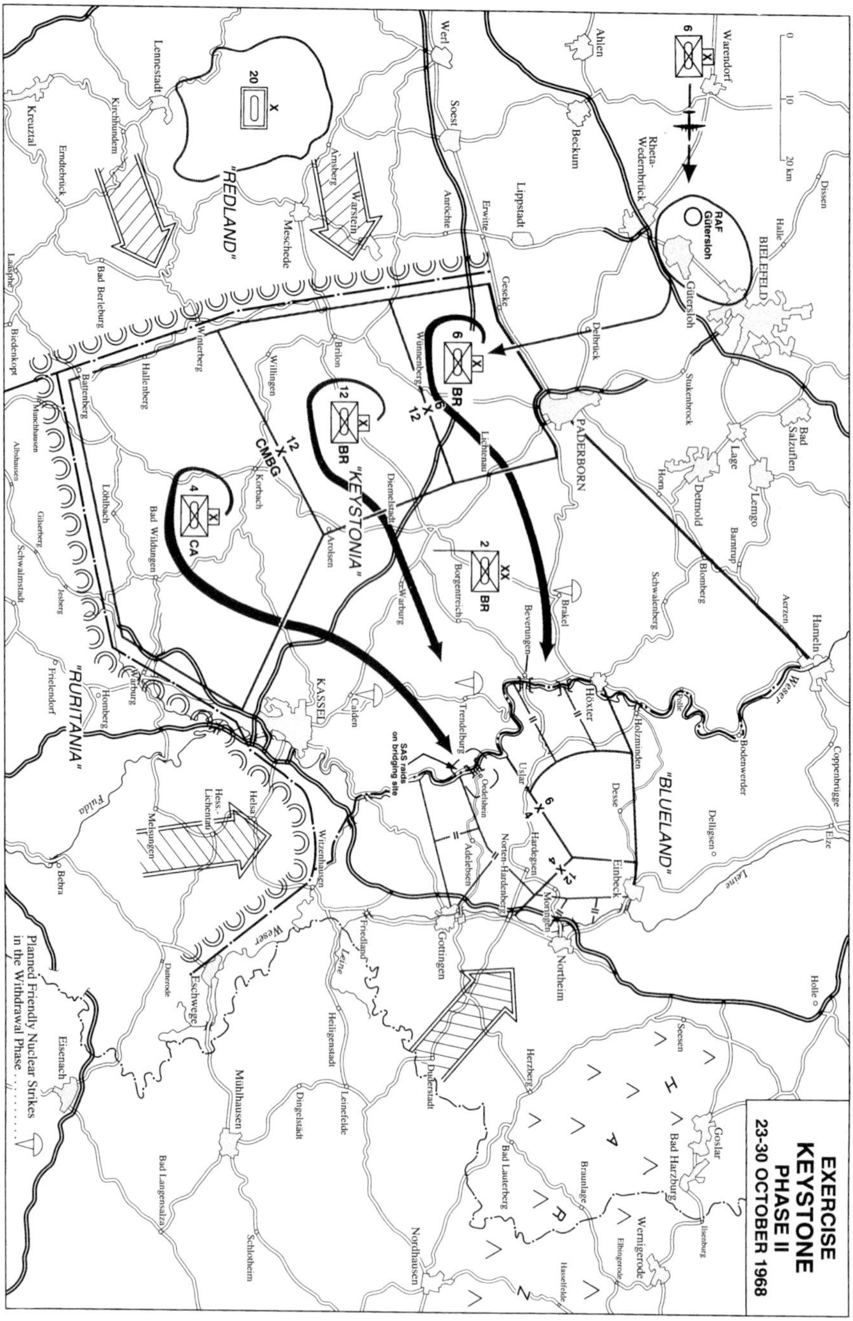
EXERCISE
KEYSTONE
PHASE II
23-30 OCTOBER 1968
"REDLAND"
"KEYSTONIA"
"BLUELAND"
"RURITANIA"
RAF Gütersloh
SAS raids on bridging site
Planned Friendly Nuclear Strikes in the Withdrawal Phase
PADERBORN
KASSEL
BIELEFELD
12 X CMBG
0 10 20 km

FIGURE 4-6

the troops were not called to actually deal with the 'demonstrators', they were warned to expect harassment during vehicular movements.... In the town of Erndtebruck the [demonstrator] contingent from 1 Bn R22eR caused a real hubbub. As APCs roared through the town to take up positions on commanding hills, the 'demonstrators' threw sticks at drivers, shouted slogans, blocked streets and effectively re-routed some vehicles out of their intended path.

...The streets were crowded with interested civilians who were shocked and dismayed that demonstrators had turned out to jeer the Canadian troops. Little groups formed to discuss the incident. They were quick to point out to Canadian observers that the demonstrators were not German and in fact spoke a language that they had not heard before....

Phase II kicked off on 23 October, when Redland battle groups crossed the border. The Blueland High Command informed 4 CMBG that the enemy should be delayed as long as possible so that the Keystonia-Blueland frontier (the Weser River) could be prepared for defence. Keystonia was to be abandoned to the enemy. 4 CMBG withdrew under pressure through its sector, harried by enemy saboteurs and sympathizers. Nuclear weapons were initially not used during this phase. Ignoring Redland's protestations regarding nuclear first use, Blueland remained in a dispersed disposition in case the guarantee was rescinded. To affect a clean break with Redland forces, some very limited and controlled nuclear strikes were prepared, but not required. By the end of Phase II, 4 CMBG had successfully broken contact and conducted an amphibious withdrawal across the Weser.

Redland's ally, Ruritania, entered the conflict after Redland forces had been halted by stubborn Blueland actions. To meet this new threat from the south, 4 CMBG occupied a defensive position that was oriented against a western or southern threat. Ruritanian forces penetrated into 4 CMBG's positions on the east bank of the Weser but were quickly driven back by a Strathcona/PPCLI counter-attack force. This action realistically paralleled 4 CMBG's EDP mission, albeit in a different direction.

Post-exercise reports were laudatory and complimented Canadian professionalism. Besides serving as a message to the opposition,

Exercise KEYSTONE was a good test of Canadian initiative and skill.

Before discussing the 1969 defence review and its effects on 4 CMBG, it is important to examine the new NATO strategic concept adopted in 1967. Only by understanding what NATO was doing at this time can the real impact of the Canadian government's thinking be assessed or the damage it caused be fully understood.

As the reader will recall, for some time NATO had experienced problems in reconciling a strategic concept, a force structure and an operational strategy that had a tendency towards the use of tactical nuclear weapons, with the need to conduct operations like BERCONS, support to the LIVE OAK organization or repelling small-scale incursions. The concern here was that the lines between conventional, tactical nuclear, and strategic nuclear warfare had been blurred for so long that an event at the non-nuclear end of the spectrum would start a chain reaction that might lead to strategic nuclear war.

Attempts to change this situation formally were consistently blocked by the French. Unable to accept anything short of complete nuclear reliance, (which they equated with strong deterrence of any war) France withdrew from the integrated military structure of NATO in 1966-1967. Once France no longer had a veto, however, a new strategic concept was formally adopted by the Alliance on 22 September 1967.

This new concept, contained in document MC 14/3, was called Flexible Response. Unlike the previous strategic concept MC 14/2, Flexible Response recognized that there was a whole spectrum of aggressive action that the enemy could use against the Alliance, and that NATO had to have the ability to respond appropriately to each of these so that potential enemy actions would be deterred. These included everything from covert actions, to limited attacks, to major aggression and strategic nuclear war.

MC 14/3's defensive principles consisted of three elements: Direct Defence, Deliberate Escalation, and General Nuclear Response. NATO had to have the ability to defeat aggression at the level that the enemy chose to fight. If, for example, the enemy attacked with conventional forces only, NATO had to have the ability of defending effectively with only conventional forces. The threat of escalating to tactical nuclear use would provide a deterrent to the enemy's escalatory use of tactical nuclear weapons. If the enemy used tactical nuclear weapons or chemical warfare, NATO had to have the ability to protect itself from the effects of such an attack and to respond in kind.

Deliberate Escalation was linked to this. If it looked like NATO might lose at the level that the enemy had chosen to fight, NATO reserved the right to escalate the conflict either by intensity or by weapon type. Thus, if NATO was going to lose a conventional fight for the NATO area, NATO could respond with tactical nuclear weapons, but only in a deliberate, planned and controlled manner so that tactical nuclear use would not be mistaken for strategic nuclear attack and thus force the enemy's strategic nuclear hand. Deliberate Escalation measures could include progressively selective nuclear strikes (intended to "dominate" the process), expanded conventional activity in a non-active theatre, or other appropriate measures.

General Nuclear Response was the ultimate level of response in MC 14/3. Unlike MC 14/2 in which strategic nuclear forces were integrated into a strategy to destroy the enemy's ability to wage war at the onset of a conflict, MC 14/3 made allowance for the fact that the ability of strategic nuclear forces to inflict catastrophic damage to Soviet society was the final option of last resort. The fact that NATO planned for and had the capability to conduct general nuclear war was what was supposed to deter such a war in the first place. At the same time, the General Nuclear Response strategy was to serve to end hostilities on terms favourable to the Alliance.

The place of conventional forces in MC 14/3 was critical. Conventional forces now were more important than ever since they would have to ensure that the 'firebreak' held, and that resort to nuclear use was not immediate or inevitable. At the same time, nuclear weapons were still available to ensure that damage to NATO conventional forces would be limited if the Soviets decided to escalate beyond conventional weapons use at the theatre level. If NATO conventional forces in-being were reduced, and the conventional and tactical nuclear forces were unable to stop the enemy, the danger existed that the "threshold" between conventional fighting and nuclear fighting would be lowered, thus precipitating a general nuclear response. Hence, the need for strong NATO conventional forces.

This begs the question: how could the Canadian Army in Europe be a significant contribution since it was "only" a brigade? How would its removal from Europe in the 1960s affect NATO's operational capability? So far, it has been demonstrated that the Brigade was numerically and qualitatively significant in NORTHAG. It possessed 20 per cent of I (BR) Corps' nuclear firepower and made up 15 per cent of I (BR) Corps fighting strength. I (BR) Corps was the strongest corps in NORTHAG, and as such it occupied the key terrain in the NORTHAG area. The Brigade itself occupied vital ground within the NORTHAG EDP, and would have been essential to the success of the plan in the event of war. Certainly, any pullout of the Canadian brigade would greatly destabilize NORTHAG's EDP and, for a time at least, jeopardize the integrity of the defence of the Central Region. It is far more difficult to judge the effect of the removal of the Canadian tactical nuclear capability. Such removal would clearly limit NATO's ability to respond against a Soviet attack on NORTHAG. However, since success in the NORTHAG sector under MC 14/3 was not supposed to rest on tactical nuclear use, the importance of these weapons waned to some degree.

The manner by which the Brigade was cut a second time in two years bears examination here, because it is similar in some ways to the events which would lead to the Brigade's withdrawal and disbandment in 1993. There was a push within the Trudeau cabinet (and more importantly, from some of his unelected personal advisors) for Canada to become less "aligned" in world affairs. This view was also tainted with an anti-nuclear weapons bias. These ideas were not foreign to Trudeau, who heartily endorsed them, and Lester Pearson's earlier initiatives gave the project momentum. Canada, it was felt, should cater to the Third World and act as a mediator between the two superpowers. Such an outlook logically should result in Canada ceasing to be part of NATO, and this view, was endorsed by some of Trudeau's advisors. (Trudeau himself was only partially persuaded by their arguments at the time.) Trudeau believed that the Cold War was atrophying into place and that the existing bi-polar arrangement needed alteration. Unfortunately, the target for change this time was Canada's NATO commitment.

Trudeau set up a situation whereby his advisors produced one view on NATO commitments, and the 'establishment' at the Departments of External Affairs and National Defence produced theirs. In his memoirs, External Affairs minister Mitchell Sharp described what happened:

> The Prime Minister gave notice that the cabinet would meet over the weekend of 26 March [1969] and reach a decision. Defence Minister Leo Cadieux and I...met in my office to prepare for the discussion. We recognized that it would be virtually impossible to convince our colleagues to increase defence expenditures.... We were reconciled to a substantial reduction. We also shared the views of many of our colleagues that the revival and prosperity of European members of the Alliance justified reconsidering the size of the Canadian contingent.
>
> In the midst of our discussion in my office, the agenda for the forthcoming meeting was delivered and included an item unfamiliar to either the Minister of National Defence or myself. We were puzzled and curious. Our curiosity was satisfied by the delivery of a document accompanied by a covering note that it was being distributed at the Prime Minister's request. I glanced at it to discover that it was a paper on defence policy. [Author's note: a paper which probably recommended a complete Canadian pull out from Europe.] I turned it over to my cabinet colleague Cadieux and asked him not to resign immediately....Did the distribution by the Prime Minister of this paper on defence mean that he had lost confidence in his Minister of National Defence? Trudeau protested that this was not his intention...he would withdraw it.

Eventually a compromise was reached. Canada would leave forces in Europe, but the numbers would be reduced. As Mitchell Sharp noted:

> I was happy and so I think were most Canadians, that we stayed in NATO with troops in Europe as part of the containment of the Soviet threat until the cold war came to an end. In my opinion it would have been extremely damaging to Canada's interests and international reputation if we had withdrawn all of our troops from Europe, or worse still had withdrawn from NATO. I was confident that this wouldn't occur, so I didn't at the time consider what actions I would take if either withdrawal happened. I felt so strongly that I probably would have offered my resignation as foreign secretary.

By completely arbitrary methods, the authorized strength of the Brigade was chopped from 6000 to 2800 officers and men.

General Andrew Goodpaster was SACEUR in 1969. His reaction is worth quoting at length:

> Further reductions in our combat capability in Central Europe could only result in earlier use of tactical nuclear weapons which is the antithesis of the objective of the MC 14/3 strategy.... [4 CMBG] with a peacetime strength of 5385 and a war authorized strength of 6239 is one of the most effective army formations in ACE. The M-Day formation is assigned important defensive missions in the 1st British Corps zone of NORTHAG....
>
> SHAPE strongly supports the retention of the present Canadian contribution in Europe. Current forces are very thin in the Central Region resulting in a marginal capability. Canadian land and air components play an important part in the defence of NATO and consequently of North America and Canada. There is no military justification for further reduction....
>
> The withdrawal of 4 CMBG will open a serious gap in the main defensive position of NORTHAG.... With little or no warning, Warsaw Pact forces have the capability to attack in I (BR) Corps zone with a minimum force of one mechanized and four armoured divisions. By moving Warsaw Pact forces forward, this capability would be increased to 11 or 12 divisions....
>
> The British Corps, charged with the defence of the most direct and accessible invasion routes to the Ruhr has forward forces consisting of a covering forces and two divisions. Should these forward forces not be capable of containing such an attack, a withdrawal to more favourable main defensive positions would be mandatory. 4 CMBG is tasked with organizing this main defensive position. Without this force in prepared defensive positions, the forward units in contact would not be capable of being reinforced to allow orderly transition to the main defensive battle. This could increase the likelihood of the early use of nuclear weapons....

The Trudeau reductions achieved a number of things. First, and most importantly, they conveyed a message that one of the founding and primary members of NATO was reconsidering its involvement, a point which could be (and was) exploited later by the Soviets. Secondly, it heightened European fears that the United States might make severe reductions or even pull out based on the precedent of the Canadian decision. Finally, a reduction in conventional forces at that time generally called into question MC 14/3 as a viable strategic concept.

The immediate effect of the reductions on 4 CMBG was substantial. Planners in Mobile Command had to find some structure that 2800 people could 'fit' into. A proposal to create an armoured brigade was rejected, since this would involve replacing the aging *Centurion* with a new tank, something nobody wanted to bring up lest further reductions were made. Converting 4 CMBG into an airmobile formation akin to the 1960 proposal, discussed in Chapter 3, was ruled out on similar grounds, as helicopters and strategic transports were extremely expensive items. The search for a new structure continued throughout 1969, but it did not actually affect 4 CMBG until 1970.

4 CMBG as a proper brigade group went out with a bang in the 1969 fall exercises. Exercise WAR AXE involved battalion workups in preparation for brigade level Exercise TOMAHAWK (17-26 September) and divisional level Exercise MARSHMALLOW (13-24 October). It was unusual to have two large scale exercises back to back, but it was a good way to end 4 CMBG's association with NORTHAG.

TOMAHAWK was conducted in an area that ranged from the city of Munster, Germany to the Netherlands. 5th Royal Tank Regiment and 5th Lorried Infantry Battalion acted as the enemy force, while 4 CMBG conducted a series of delays, hasty defences, withdrawals and counterattacks. Interoperability was also emphasized as a Belgian infantry battalion and a British armoured recce squadron augmented 4 CMBG.

Exercise MARSHMALLOW was 4 CMBG's last large manoeuvre as part of NORTHAG, and while this was no doubt a period of difficulty for the Brigade, exercise documents show clearly that it had not lost its sense of humour. 4 CMBG played the starring role as the Orangeland enemy force fighting the Bluelanders. In what has to have been one of the most creative uses of the Brigade's newspaper, *The Beaver*, a special exercise edition was published called "The Liberators's Tongue: Cheek by Jowl with the Glorious Over-Estimated Soldiers of Orangeland". Since 4 CMBG was the enemy force for the exercise, it was only appropriate that the order of the day be written by Major General J.C. Gardnerov, commander of 4 Orange Mechanized Rifle Division, aka "The Cobra Division".

4 OMRD included some strange formations and even more interesting personalities leading them. There was the Recce Company, led by Major Ivan Dangerflag (Jack Dangerfield), 404th Medium Tank Regiment with Comrade Colonel Gutnecktovich (René Guteknecht), and 402nd Motor Rifle Regiment under Colonel Igor 'Curley' Snidinniov (Curley Snider). Other Orangefolk undoubtedly existed, but 4 OMRD was supported by Orangeland allies from the 194th (German) Medium Tank Regiment equipped with brand new *Leopard* tanks.

According to the exercise script, the UN was unwilling to suppress the capitalist movement in Blueland, so Orangeland was preparing for war. Blueland belonged to an alliance called NATO or "Nations Against The Orangeland"; negotiations had broken down, forcing Orangeland to invade the Blueland occupied state of Westphalia. Formations from the Blueland Armed Forces included 5 Royal Tank Regiment, 3rd Regiment, Dragoon Guards, The Gordon Highlanders, the Sherwood Foresters, 2nd Battalion, Scots Guards, 16/5 Lancers and 14/20 Hussars. 5 RTR was assessed by the Orangelanders as being of low quality after "completing a rather unsuccessful campaign against the insurgent Canadian forces in the Munster area. As a result of their disgraceful activities in the TOMAHAWK Wars, this unit was due to be disbanded."

Boasting that Orangeland was superior, "The Liberators' Tongue" displayed a 1942 picture of Stalingrad, noting that "the last time BLUELAND tangled with our forces we smashed them with a gigantic blow from our peaceloving fist." 4 OMRD personnel were exhorted to protect what they had created:

> Orangelanders unite! Remember you are defending all the greatness of your homeland. Remember the CLFEX? The Holiday Shop? The Chinook Club? The Curling Club? Your hockey team and all the patriots who have volunteered to stay on rear party while you have been given the glorious opportunity of defending our Motherloving leaders. Remember all these things as you proceed to battle brothers and you will surely be victorious.

Despite the light-hearted preliminaries, MARSHMALLOW was a

very rigorous exercise. 4 CMBG had under command a Bundeswehr panzer grenadier battalion and a British parachute battalion; an entire squadron of the new UH-1 light transport helicopters and a squadron of Buffalo transport aircraft were brought in from Canada, and Exercise ORION SPECIAL deposited more Militia soldiers onto German soil. MARSHMALLOW was held from Braunschweig (only 15 miles from the inner-German border region) to Munster. 4 CMBG practiced all phases of war and airmobile forces were used extensively. As with previous exercises, 4 CMBG revelled in the role of enemy force and the whole variety of the usual Canadian 'improvisations' (opponents tended to call them dirty tricks) were used.

Widespread reductions were made to the Canadian Armed Forces in 1970, with the land forces being hit heavily. One armoured regiment, The Fort Garry Horse, was disbanded, and the 8th Canadian Hussars narrowly missed extinction. 4 RCHA was also reduced. Six infantry battalions were reduced to nil strength and their personnel redistributed. Proud regiments – the Black Watch, the Canadian Guards and the Queen's Own Rifles of Canada – were removed from the order of battle. Personnel from these six battalions were consolidated into third battalions for The RCR and the PPCLI. (The Van Doos retained three battalions).

No secret had been made about Trudeau's aversion to nuclear weapons. The reductions of Canadian forces in Europe provided the excuse to strip the Air Division and 4 CMBG of their nuclear support units. 1 SSM Battery was duly disbanded, as was 2 SSM (Training) Battery. The MC 14/3 concept and its tendency away from tactical nuclear use was used as justification for the elimination of these units, even though MC 14/3 demanded stronger conventional forces to make up the shortfall. Obviously, stronger conventional forces were not forthcoming. Plans to replace *Honest John* with the *Lance* missile system were quietly dropped, even though the airforce and navy continued to possess nuclear-capable systems and have access to nuclear weapons. At one point, SACEUR queried Canadian military authorities as to whether the M109 self-propelled guns could be certified as a nuclear delivery unit in lieu of the *Honest Johns*. The M-109 was capable of firing the M-454 AFAP nuclear shell (yield: around 1 kt) and Canadian gunners certainly knew how to employ such a munition, but the lack of the requisite firing tables, permissive action links and US custodians, as well as the political problems made such a move undesirable.

By July 1970, the Trudeau reductions were complete. 4 CMBG was reduced from three to two infantry battalions of three infantry companies each, one tank regiment consisting of two armoured squadrons and a recce squadron, one artillery regiment with 18 M-109s, an engineer squadron and the Service Battalion. 1 SSM Battery was disbanded, and with it the Canadian Army's nuclear capability. 4 CMBG was renamed yet again as 4 Combat Mechanized Battle Group and then finally, 4 Canadian Mechanized Battle Group. The units that made up 4 Canadian Mechanized Battle Group included 1 RCHA, the RCD, 4 Fd Sqn RCE, 1 R22eR, 4 Service Bn, and a strange new unit called 3 Mechanized Commando.

3 Mechanized Commando was the offspring of two parents, and not a bastard child as alleged by some detractors. The 'father' was a 1969 FMC requirement to have two airborne battalions in the order of battle. The 'mother' was the Trudeau cuts. The Van Doos could not be removed from 4 CMBG since the francophone identity was considered to be a crucial part of the Canadian identity in NATO. The RCR and the PPCLI battalions in 4 CMBG were both due to be rotated anyway when the cuts were announced. 3 Mechanized Commando was thus created with personnel drawn from both Anglophone organizations (2RCR and 2 PPCLI). Since the FMC requirement for two airborne battalions still existed, and the fact that another unit could not be found in the re-organization to form the second airborne unit, 3 Mechanized Commando personnel wore a maroon beret and paraded Canadian Airborne Regiment colours while mounted in M-113s and *Lynxs*! Truly a unique unit, 3 Mechanized Commando was formed in 1970 at Sennelager during a rain squall, prompting the motto, "Born in a Storm".

The associated decision to move 4 CMBG from the Soest area to Lahr and Baden in southern Germany was the result of a variety of factors. The first, and most important, was the problem of operational role. The reduction of the Brigade to a Battle Group and the removal of its nuclear missiles meant that 4 CMBG could not defend the vital EDP sector on the right flank of I (BR) Corps in NORTHAG. 4 CMBG, in essential terms, was no longer capable of fulfilling the task for which it had trained for since 1957.

There were attempts to resurrect the 1959-60 airmobile brigade group concept so that 4 CMBG could still fulfil some worthwhile high profile role. As before, the cost of re-equipping the Brigade with helicopters, light transport aircraft and airportable armoured vehicles (as well as maintaining them) far exceeded the financial resources that the government was willing to spend on a land force commitment in Europe. Additionally, from an operational standpoint, the notion of light airmobile forces operating in a high intensity environment was a new concept and had yet to be proven.

The ability of BAOR to provide logistical support to 4 CMBG was also reduced substantially between 1968 and 1969. The progressive introduction of more and more American pattern equipment into the Canadian force structure forced 4 CMBG to negotiate agreements with the Americans in CENTAG for the provision of spare parts. Other BAOR support facilities were closed down, resulting from economic problems between the British and the Germans. This complicated the Canadian logistic arrangements, since Canadian policy had been to piggy back the Brigade's logistics needs with the British system.

The cost of maintaining separate army and air force commitments in Europe at widely separated locations was also considered by some Canadian financial people to be excessive. The RCAF's Air Division already had a close relationship with the Americans, and it was felt that with CF unification and an allegedly unified logistic system, arrangements might be modified to accommodate 4 CMBG with the Air Division organization. Thus, SACEUR's 1959 concept of co-locating the Air Division and the Brigade was rejuvenated.

The Air Division had done some consolidation of its own after they suffered damage in the Pearson and then the Trudeau cuts. Prior to 1966, the RCAF operated nuclear strike aircraft at airfields at Marville and Grostenquin in France, and Zweibrucken and Baden-Soellingen in Germany. As the reader will recall, De Gaulle did not agree with NATO's strategic concept and forced NATO-tasked forces armed with nuclear weapons located in France to either leave or subject themselves to French control. As a result, Canada chose to leave France. There was, however, not enough room at the other air bases. In a feat of 'liquid diplomacy', Canada's Chief of the Defence Staff, General Jean V. Allard made a deal with French General Jacques Massu. In the basement dining room of what would eventually become the Black Forest Officers Mess, Allard and Massu swapped the Canadian base at Marville for the French airfield Base Aerienne 139 and the facilities of HQ 1st Commandement Aerien Tactiques located at Menard Caserne in Lahr, Germany. The RCAF base at Zweibrucken was closed in 1969 when the Air Division was reduced from six squadrons to three, leaving Baden-Soellingen and Lahr as the final Canadian air bases in Southern Germany.

Thus it was a combination of changing logistic requirements and problems, the incompatibility of 4 CMBG's reduced structure with defensive requirements in NORTHAG, and the availability of a new base area that all pointed towards re-locating 4 CMBG from Soest to southern Germany. A 1969 study on the possible co-location of the brigade and air elements concluded that the only factors militating against such a move were the lack of married quarters in Lahr, the lack of funds to construct additional buildings to house 4 CMBG, and restrictions placed on manpower for the new base structure.

In the final measure, the reduction of 4 Brigade's capability and its removal from NORTHAG was, in the words of Commander, Northern Army Group, General Sir John Hackett, a national disaster:

> I said to the campaign in the Canadian press at that time [which was] suggesting that it was a waste of money and effort to participate in NATO or anything that attracted attention outside of the North American continent, that this was Canada's opportunity to emerge out of the nursery....There was an acceptance among some supportive people that it was incumbent upon Canada to accept the invitation to the top table and bloody well stay there. This didn't go over well. But still, one of the sadnesses within my *Weltanshauung* was that Canada has never yet taken the place it deserves in the councils of the world.
>
> This is one reason why I so much welcomed the association I had with the Canadian Brigade. I spent a lot of time with that Brigade. They were very, very good men, good soldiers, well trained, well motivated; the sort of people you'd love to have with you in a war. For administrative reasons which

CHAPTER FOUR

seemed to be not wholly compelling, they were moved out from where we treated them as some of the best front line troops, [and] they were moved down into a third line, as it were, reserve capability in Lahr. This is disastrous and I never agreed with it. I regarded the Canadian Brigade as one of the best elements in our front line defence. In the shop window of the world the Canadian Brigade in NORTHAG was one of the star items. To take it out of there and put it somewhere where its value wasn't realized was really very difficult to accept.... What wasn't in the plans and was always a probability is that the Brigade was capable of application in so many roles and areas not as yet identified. This is what happens with really good first line troops.

But the stage had been set for the move South.

With that move, 4 CMBG fell from the pinnacle to the nadir of its existence. During its time in NORTHAG, the Brigade's operational capability had been greatly enhanced beyond what had been possible in 1957-1963 period through widespread mechanization. The infantry was now mounted in APCs and the artillery had self-propelled guns. Reconnaissance units changed over to the *Lynx* recce vehicle and night vision equipment was used in increasing numbers for greater efficiency in surveillance tasks. The creation of an independent anti-tank unit equipped with a variety of anti-tank systems also added to the brigade's ability to counter the heavily mechanized Warsaw Pact forces, which had greatly increased its capabilities since the 1950s. These enhancements left the brigade by 1968 in superb shape to cope with the advent of the MC 14/3 Flexible Response strategy and the push for more and better conventional forces. 4 CMBG retained the ability to function with or without nuclear weapons; this in turn enhanced the flexibility of the Canadian contribution in Europe. The RCAF had claimed for years that its CF-104s could only handle nuclear operations; yet this clearly limited Canada when the new calculus demanded by MC 14/3 became NATO's new strategy. With a versatile, respected land formation, however Canada was still a reliable and valued partner.

Unfortunately, all of this capability – the combination of excellent equipment in large numbers, of superbly trained officers and men, of finely honed operational and tactical skills – was destroyed by the cumulative effects of the Pearson and Trudeau governments' reductions.

The elimination of the tactical nuclear weapons capability was bad enough from an alliance standpoint, but the gutting of one of the most effective conventional formations in the Central Region severely damaged Canada's credibility within the Alliance, weakened NATO's ability to conduct a successful conventional defence of the Central region and would have contributed to the early use of nuclear weapons if the Warsaw Pact had attacked.

PART TWO

DOWN SOUTH

1970 - 1979

THE MOVE SOUTH

CHAPTER FIVE

"LEARNING TO COOPERATE/SYSTEM BARGAINING:
ANY CRISIS WHICH REACHES THE UPPER RUNGS OF THE
ESCALATION LADDER IS LIKELY TO BE REGARDED BY BOTH
PARTICIPANTS AS A DISASTER. POSSIBLY EVEN REGARDLESS OF THE
POLITICAL GAINS ACHIEVED....AS EACH SIDE LEARNS THAT THE
GAINS OF THESE CONFLICTS ARE SMALL COMPARED TO THE COSTS,
THEY ARE LIKELY TO BE CAUTIOUS ABOUT EITHER
STARTING OR INTENSIFYING SUCH CONFLICTS..."

-HERMAN KAHN, *ON ESCALATION*

Top left: *From 1970 to 1993, 4 Canadian Mechanized Brigade Group served as a reserve formation in NATO's Central Army Group. CENTAG's insignia was the Rampant Lion (a symbol of the city of Heidelberg) superimposed on a NATO compass rose. The Rampant Lion is in a defensive posture symbolizing power and courage.* (DAVID MCDERMOTT)
Top right: *4 CMBG acquired its own shoulder patch insignia as well, which was worn on the right shoulder.*
Below: *HQ 4 Canadian Mechanized Brigade Group was located in building K-1 at the Kaserne in Lahr from 1971 to 1993.* (AUTHOR)

CHAPTER FIVE

Above: Exercise GUTES OMEN in 1971 was 4 CMBG's first big exercise in CENTAG after the move south. Here a Centurion of the Royal Canadian Dragoons enters the fray against 4 Jaeger Division (Note the "wildlife" in the background). (DND) IL 71 18 8
Below: Meanwhile 1st Battalion, Royal 22nd Regiment moves into the suburbs of Neu Ulm in their M-113 APCs. (DND) IL 71 18 6

Above*: After some problems with minor water obstacles .... (DND) IL 71 18 2*
Below*: ... 3 Mechanized Commando continues the advance. Note the 106mm recoiless rifle mounted on the M-113 APC and the two Lynx recce vehicles. (DND) IL 71 18 4*

CHAPTER FIVE

Above: *Exercises like GROSSE ROCHADE held in September 1975 required close German-Canadian cooperation and enhanced considerably Canadian-German interoperability.* (DND) ILC 75 438
Below: *An M-577 command post vehicle of 3 Mechanized Commando crosses the Donau River on Ex GROSSE ROCHADE, utilizing a Bundeswehr ferry. The number 2A indicates a company command post.* (DND) ILC 75 387

Above: Careful camouflage and concealment was a must against 'Blueland's' air force. Here 4 CMBG HQ "tucks in" next to farm machinery. (DND) ILC 75 398

Below: The Bavarian countryside proved to be just as scenic as Westphalia. A 106mm recoilless rifle antitank detachment of 1 R22^{e}R on the move during Exercise GROSSE ROCHADE. (DND) ILC 75 496

CHAPTER FIVE

Above: *Tanks and infantry of 3 Mechanized Commando and the Royal Canadian Dragoons in a German farmyard.* (DND) ILC 75 428
Below: *One armoured vehicle is the same as another to this Bavarian.* (DND) ILC 75 493

Above: During Ex GROSSE ROCHADE held in Sept 1975, 4 CMBG in a surprise move, crossed the Donau (Danube) river near Vilshofen. This is a Lynx recce vehicle being driven aboard a Bundeswehr ferry. (DND) ILC 75 412

Below: An M-548 cargo carrier and an M-577 armoured command post vehicle get the same treatment. (DND) ILC 75 389

CHAPTER FIVE

Both: *After crossing the river on Ex GROSSE ROCHADE, 4 CMBG encountered and defeated a French armoured recce regiment which was deployed in a screen behind the river. This combat team 'bumped' a group of French EBR armoured cars on the road to Vilsbiburg.* (DND) ILC 75 426

Above: *With 'Blueland' on the run, the Canadians exploited every weak spot they could find in the 'enemy's' defences not withstanding civilian traffic.* (DND) ILC 75 425
Below: *Having self-propelled artillery such as the M-109 155mm SP Gun greatly increased 4 Canadian Mechanized Brigade's mobility in the rapid advances encountered on exercises like GROSSE ROCHADE in 1975.* (DND) ILC 75 392

CHAPTER FIVE

Above: *Carl Gustav anti-tank team from 3 Mechanized Commando on REFORGER V, October 1973.* (DND) IL 73 128 6
Below: *Host Nation Support was a critical factor for any successful defence plan in Germany. These measures also were incorporated into large scale NATO exercises.* (DND) IL 76 189

Above: *The Bundesbahn railway system in Germany was even more critical to the Brigade in CENTAG given the distance between Lahr, Baden and the deployment areas in Bavaria. (DND) Here, Centurion tanks are loaded for transport.*
Below: *Over the course of the forty-two year Canadian presence in Europe, Canadian Army units in Germany assisted in disaster relief operations when requested by other NATO allies. One such occasion was Operation DOLOMITE after earthquakes hit northern Italy in October 1976.*

Above: US 'C-rations' being crossloaded at a 4 Svc Bn Ration Point. In Germany 4 CMBG received its rations, while in the field, through the US supply system. (DND)
Below: The movement of thousands of vehicles on NATO Fall exercises necessitated close liaison between Canadian, American and German traffic control units. Here MPs of 4 CMBG discuss road movement details with US MPs. (DND) DLR 82 580 8

Above: *The lack of adequate air defence resources within 4 CMBG prior to the mid 1980s necessitated a high standard of camouflage and concealment among all brigade units. Here 4 CMBG HQ and Sigs Sqn sets up in a church-yard orchard.* (DND) ILC 75 499
Below: *As the brigade operated for long periods of time on radio silence to avoid being detected by 'enemy' electronic warfare units, communications were effected by the laying of land lines. This photo shows Brigade linesmen at work.* ILC 75 498

CHAPTER FIVE

Both: *One of the best training areas in West Germany available to 4 CMBG was the Hammelburg "Fighting in Built-Up Areas" (FIBUA) training facility of "Bonnland". Here Infantry from 1 R22ᵉR and tanks from the RCD advance through the 'village'.* (1 R22ᵉR)

The move to southern Germany in 1970 was a traumatic experience for 4 CMBG. Every aspect of it's existence, be it wartime role, logistics, or community services, was completely altered. Adaptation to these changes was done remarkably quickly and everyone serving in the newly titled 4 Canadian Mechanized Battle Group worked hard to establish a reputation within the new environment of Central Army Group (CENTAG).

Overseeing the close-out and move from NORTHAG was Brigadier General W.C. Leonard, who had taken over from Brigadier General Gardner in July 1970. The close out of CFB Soest was done with complete professionalism on the part of 4 CMBG. The schedule was, as usual, tight. 4 CMBG dropped all operational commitments in NORTHAG on 1 June 1970 and deployed unit advance parties to Lahr in July. CFB Soest, with a skeleton crew, was scheduled to close in April 1971. All of the buildings in the forts in the Soest-Iserlohn area had to be repaired, cleaned and preserved. Before locking up, all facilities had to inspected and their commanders marched out. Canadians were not going to leave the garrison area in a shambles as other NATO allies had done elsewhere!

BAOR units from the 6th Armoured brigade were scheduled to take over some of the Canadian forts. To preserve the facilities from damage, some units resorted to unusual measures. Then-Major R.L. Strawbridge was with 1 RCHA:

> Soldiers had to remain in the Northern garrisons for a few months until our operational role in NORTHAG expired. Simultaneously, a small advance party was deployed to Lahr to take over meager accommodation on the airfield. The impact of this was that for a few months we in effect had a Regiment of single soldiers, men without their wives and families, living in garrison. Mess life became very active with all units trying to run down their bar stocks….
>
> A final Mess Dinner prior to handing over our Mess to 2nd Field Regiment Royal Artillery [was held] where the Mess piano was totally destroyed…. Prior to the Mess Dinner the CO wisely suggested that a car hulk be positioned in front of the mess, to allow officers to work off steam with a view to saving the Mess from party damage. The car became a mass of twisted metal over the course of the evening. The Mess was handed over to 2 Fd Regt in first class condition….

The mayor of the town of Deilinghofen paid tribute to 4 CMBG and a portion of his speech is worth quoting here:

> All political parties in the Bundestag of the Federal Republic of Germany, regional governments and all the representatives of our people down to the smallest communities are well aware, without reservations, of the importance of NATO for the liberty of the German Nation. NATO is the strong alliance which is to this very day and tomorrow as well the only lasting guarantee for democratic liberty of the western world and the form of life of our nations, together with everything which makes life worth living….
>
> From 1953 until 1970, Canadian troops, as members of NATO, have served on German soil in constant readiness, on duty for liberty. Loyal to their command, they have performed their military affairs here in Westphalia for nearly two decades as partners and friends without making any financial claim for

that service against the Federal Republic of Germany. Many times, I am certain, they made personal sacrifices of many kinds, of which we Germans were not aware....

We all know that Canada is a partner upon whom every Nation with whom she is allied can depend in times of crisis. We have repeatedly witnessed the standard of training and of the superb discipline of the Canadian soldiers since they have been stationed in Germany....

In my capacity as Mayor of Deilinghofen, I wish to express in this parting hour, to all officers and all ranks as well as their families, a hope for good fortune in the future, which may present us with peace, happiness and God's blessing. My wish accompanies those who are returning to their homeland and also those who will continue to serve in NATO when going South.

Finally one more request: Please do not forget Europe!

Unofficially called Operation EXODUS, the actual movement of 4 CMBG units to its two new bases in southern Germany was accomplished with few problems. [See Figure 5-1.] Rail, road, and even foot was used. Leading the way was C Squadron, RCD, the Brigade's new recce element. Lead by Captain Bob Meating, 16 members of C Squadron conducted a grueling 50-hour, 300-mile run from Fort Henry to Lahr. The runners carried a scroll of greeting from the Brigade Commander to the *Oberburgermeister* (Lord Mayor) of Lahr.

Mike Ritchie of 3 Mechanized Commando was there for the corresponding move to the air base at Baden-Soellingen where part of 4 CMBG was to be stationed:

> We loaded all the tracks [APCs] in Iserlohn, shipped them by train to Baden and parked them in a French Army camp there for a day.... We all put on our nice shiny new maroon berets and clean combat clothing and about three o'clock on a Sunday afternoon we off loaded everything nose to tail and rumbled through this little town of Hügelsheim. We roared through the front gates of the Air Force base.... They were awed and we were hooting it, and it was intentional. I mean, the whole battalion was on tracks then, 113s, 548s, 577s and *Lynx*s. My wife was in the PMQ and she said it sounded like thunder. It got louder and louder. We just roared right through the gate and made a right into the marguerite on the button and parked them. The Air Force, the

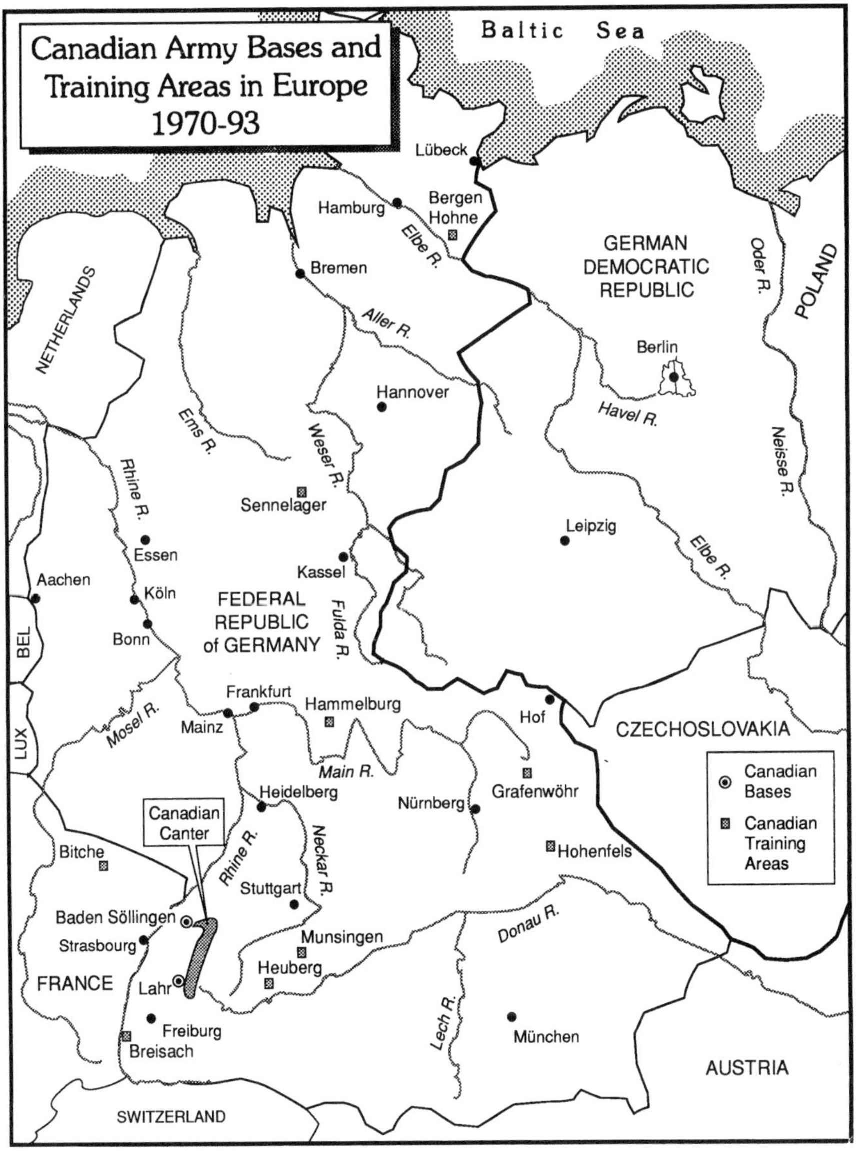
Canadian Army Bases and Training Areas in Europe 1970-93
Baltic Sea
Lübeck
Hamburg
Bergen Hohne
Elbe R.
Bremen
GERMAN DEMOCRATIC REPUBLIC
Oder R.
POLAND
NETHERLANDS
Aller R.
Berlin
Hannover
Havel R.
Ems R.
Weser R.
Neisse R.
Rhine R.
Sennelager
Leipzig
Elbe R.
Essen
Kassel
Aachen
Köln
FEDERAL REPUBLIC of GERMANY
Fulda R.
BEL
Bonn
Frankfurt
Hammelburg
Hof
Mosel R.
Mainz
CZECHOSLOVAKIA
LUX
Main R.
Heidelberg
Nürnberg
Grafenwöhr
Canadian Bases
Canadian Training Areas
Canadian Canter
Rhine R.
Neckar R.
Bitche
Hohenfels
Stuttgart
Baden Söllingen
Donau R.
Strasbourg
Munsingen
Heuberg
FRANCE
Lahr
Freiburg
Lech R.
München
Breisach
AUSTRIA
SWITZERLAND

FIGURE 5-1

Germans, everybody was awestruck....

The Dragoons moved onto the other Canadian airbase located some 70 km further south in Lahr. Then-Lieutenant Colonel P.H.C. Carew was Commanding Officer of the RCD at the time:

> We absorbed a squadron of 8th Hussars and re-badged two squadrons of Strathconas to Dragoons.... The move from North to South was already in train and families had already begun to move into the Lahr area. We had an advance party in Lahr consisting of officers and senior NCOs; people were being pulled out of Sennelager to go down south and settle their families....
>
> The Lahr airfield where the Dragoons were to be based, was not a suitable spot, particularly from the point of view of men's accommodations. In fact we took over existing air force hangers and below standard single mens' quarters. By October 1970, the Regiment complete was established on the north and centre marguerites of the Lahr airfield. Dependents were living in, I think, 20 or 30 villages and towns in the Lahr area. There were still some of our families living up north because accommodation had not been found for those people. The last wife, a mother with children, had moved on three different occasions up north until she finally joined her husband in Lahr six months after the Regiment had been established there....

Finding space for 4 CMBG in Lahr and Baden-Soellingen posed a large number of problems. Funds did not exist to build new accommodations for 4 CMBG, and there was no 'big brother' ally or occupation levy to borrow from. The existing facilities in Lahr included the airfield, the former Menard Kaserne, and PMQ areas built by the French. Baden had an airfield and a limited number of PMQs which had been built to handle only the families of the air force personnel from the two squadrons based there.

Baden-Soellingen had been an RCAF base since 1953, and as such was already well established as a Canadian enclave in southern Germany. Lahr, on the other hand, had been occupied by the French from 1946 to 1967. The Lahr Kaserne, which had been bombed during the Second World War, had been rebuilt by the French and used as the headquarters for 1 CATAC, a French Air Force nuclear-strike formation assigned to SACEUR in the 1960s. The French had constructed married quarters, but these were in abominable shape when the RCAF took possession of Lahr in 1967. Detailed horror stories of chicken excrement, deceased pigs, and of concrete having been poured into the few toilets that existed abounded on the 'rumour net'. It cost the Canadian taxpayer several million dollars to make the Lahr facilities habitable, while the French took over pristine accommodation at the former RCAF Stations, Marville, Metz and Grostenquin.

The Brigade's initial basing plan placed one infantry battalion in Baden-Soellingen, one battalion in the Lahr Kaserne, and the armoured regiment, artillery regiment and the service support units going onto the Lahr airfield itself. HQ 4 CMBG, HQ 1 Canadian Air Group, Canadian Forces Base Europe and the new command HQ for Canadian Forces Europe were to be located in the Kaserne as well. As space was at a premium, the infantry battalion slated for the Kaserne was later shifted to the airfield. [See Figure 5-2.]

The units located on the airfields had to jostle for room with their air force counterparts. The airfields at Baden and Lahr were both laid out in 'Marguerites' (French for "daisy") and 'Buttons'. Buttons were revetted circular spaces which aircraft could be parked on, while Marguerites or 'Margs' (like the shape of the flower) were collections of buttons. This configuration was designed to disperse aircraft and thus limit the damage that an enemy air attack could do. At Baden, 3 Mechanized Commando occupied the north marg and some converted H-huts next door. In Lahr, the RCD had the north marg, while the center marg held 4 Field Ambulance, and the aviation units. The south marg became the Artillery Park, occupied by 1 RCHA. The Van Doos, the Engineer Squadron, and 4 CMBG's service support units were located in the airfield base area to the southeast on the other side of the runway.

Facilities in the margs were rudimentary at best. The lucky ones had access to the facilities formerly occupied by the US nuclear weapons custodial detachment; the Americans at least had had flush toilets and showers installed. Then-Captain Bob Meating, after his long run down to Lahr, noted that:

> It was just like somebody had lived in it and walked away and closed the

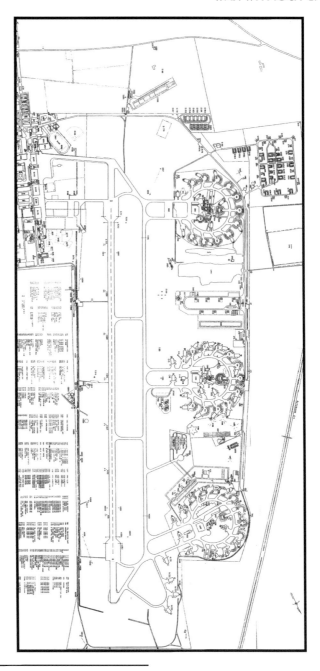

FIGURE 5-2: THE BULK OF 4 CMBG'S UNITS WERE STATIONED ON THE FORMER FRENCH AIRFIELD NEAR LAHR. NOTE THE LOCATIONS OF THE NORTH, CENTRE AND SOUTH MARGUERITES.

CHAPTER FIVE

door; we opened the door and found dirt...we didn't find things ripped off the wall [as we had heard]. We put tanks in aircraft facilities. We put more people per room than normal, so there were a lot of cramped quarters. We didn't have the shower facilities in the north marguerite to take care of the soldiers.... We had two stalls for 150 men; we had 16 men jammed into a small room the size of an office.

As a result of the barracks and PMQ shortage, a far greater percentage of personnel, both single and married, lived on the civilian economy in the Lahr and Baden areas than had been the case up north. Around Baden many soldiers from 3 Mechanized Commando and its successors lived in the surrounding towns and villages. This sudden proliferation of Canadians was a key factor in developing very close relationships with the local Germans as rooms, apartments and houses were passed on from Canadian soldier to Canadian soldier, and from Canadian family to Canadian family. Not surprisingly, this had a significant impact on the local German economy. It also served to directly immerse Canadians into German culture and mores, and to some extent vice versa.

The environment in southern Germany produced a double culture shock for 4 CMBG. Soldiers not only had to adapt to an air force mentality (especially in Baden-Soellingen) but to a southern Germany mentality as well. On the other hand, the air force was quite upset to see hundreds of "Foreign Object Damage" producing pieces of equipment sitting on their two airfields. The brigade newspaper *The Beaver* had closed, and the air-force dominated *Der Kanadier* in Lahr seemed to have a different cartoon every week to comment on some army idiosyncrasy. (Many were actually quite funny and frequently targeted 3 Mechanized Commando).

The Black Forest Officers' Mess (BFOM) and the Centennial Club (built in 1973) were the primary messes in Lahr for the commissioned officers and junior ranks respectively. Baden had similar arrangements. 'Brown' and 'light blue' had to learn to get along. It was a situation quite different from up north where each brigade unit had its own mess. Punch-ups were not uncommon in Lahr and Baden, and duty officers generally had very busy Friday nights.

Although combined service messing was in vogue during the

unification period, there were exceptions in Germany. As Wayne Dauphinee recalled, units did create their own informal messes:

> When the Brigade got down to Lahr, none of the army units had officers' messes. They fell into the air force base concept, where there was a single base mess in Lahr and a single base mess in Baden. There was an attempt in some cases to recognize that the army was there, but it was very, very token. Then the development of the 'Rest Easy' sort of evolved because of a need to re-kindle esprit de corps....

In the era of Canadian Forces Unification, the importance of regimental messes on morale and esprit de corps cannot be underestimated. The fact that the base messes were a long distance away from most soldiers' place of daily work, particularly for units on the Lahr airfield, contributed to this development. Unit 'Rest Easys' became de facto regimental messes and, for many years, functioned as the social centres of the Brigade's units; the base messes, by comparison, were sterile, colourless environments.

The Brigade's new neighbours, the southern Germans, had a different outlook on life in the 1970s and 1980s than did the northern Germans from the earlier period. The north, of course, was heavily industrialized and as such had been heavily damaged during the war. The pace of life was faster there. Canadians had assisted with the reconstruction of Soest, and the vestiges of the occupation period were still apparent. It is not out of line to suggest that relations between Germans and Canadians up north were closer than they ever came to be down south. The south was different. It had not suffered in the same way as the north during the war, although post-war occupation by the French was, to be sure, no picnic. The picturesque *Schwarzwald* (Black Forest) was tourist country, and to the delight of many, white wine country. The pace of life was more pastoral. Not being on the front line of the Cold War, there was less to be grateful for. (It should be noted that the closer to the Iron Curtain a German town was, the more appreciative the inhabitants were of NATO military activity.) Although Lahr had been a garrison town since a Roman Legion had occupied it before the birth of Christ, a military presence was considered to be somewhat of a nuisance.

CHAPTER FIVE

Dr. Philip Brucker, *Oberburgermeister* of Lahr when the Brigade moved south, recalled:

> As the Lord Mayor I have always had a good relationship with the members of the brigade, you know. There were problems when the Canadian Army stationed tanks and armoured carriers in Lahr, however. We had been promised two years before the brigade moved to Lahr that no tanks would operate in the [small] Langenhard [training area near Lahr]. Now the tanks were here! The intention was to drive the *Centurions* from the airbase, downtown and up to the Langenhard for training exercises on a regular basis. I could not allow this [because of the noise and the potential for damage]. I went to Bonn and the German government gave us money for the construction of a road around the hill through Sulz and up to the Langenhard [training area]. All was OK. I always said that we must discuss problems and we will always find a solution....

An important social link in the German-Canadian relationship occurred in October 1972 with the twinning of Lahr with Belleville, Ontario and which encompassed student and community exchanges. This was facilitated by Dr. Brucker:

> I was invited for a dinner in the General's residence because your Minister of Defence was in Lahr to visit the troops with General Dextraze [the CDS]....At this dinner I was sitting at the side of Mrs. Dextraze and I said, 'we have a very interesting city partnership with a French city, Dole, and we have a student exchange and an orchestra exchange.' Suddenly she told her husband about this partnership. Can we arrange a partnership between Lahr and a Canadian city?...We discussed this with Minister Cadieux. He said, 'Good Idea! What city?' Mrs. Dextraze said to her husband, 'Look, you served in Belleville as a young officer and we have relatives there. Why not Belleville? It's near the airbase where the planes that go to Lahr are based.' Some weeks later I got a letter from the Mayor of Belleville accepting the proposal.

The supporting infrastructure in Lahr and Baden was an improvement in many ways over that up north. The MLS exchange system underwent another name change that paralleled Unification, stabilizing as CANEX. CANEX developed extensive facilities in Lahr and Baden, stores that even the Americans from Heidelberg and Frankfurt came down to use. French personnel stationed around Baden-Baden also had access to CANEX, even though they tended to hoard butter. A Canadian Forces Network (CFN) radio station was established in 1968, adopting a new type of sound called "stereo" in 1969. CFN eventually developed a Francophone counterpart, Radio Forces Canadien – RFC. The Astra movie house in Baden and The Globe in Lahr provided current films for the Canadian population. Television for the Canadians in Lahr and Baden was still something of a rarity in 1970, as there were only two German channels and no English or French language broadcasting.

Other infrastructure items of note were the Rod and Gun Club located at the Lahr airfield, the golf course located on the Baden airfield, and the Arrowhead Arena at the Lahr Kaserne. Canadians could transact their financial affairs at the Bank of Montreal branch in Lahr or Baden, send their children to the Canadian Youth Centre, relax at the Community Centre or grab a sandwich at the Salvation Army's Red Shield Club.

CFB Soest closed its doors in June of 1971 in a small ceremony near a commemorative stone emplaced near the Möhnesee. Fort York became Graf Yorcke Kaserne and was occupied by the 21st Anti-aircraft Missile Battalion of the Bundeswehr. The British 6th Armoured Brigade took possession of the other facilities. Fort Henry was retitled to Saint Sebastien Barracks; Fort Chambly became Salamanca Barracks; Fort St Louis and Fort Anne became Albuhera Barracks. Fort Victoria changed its spelling to become Vittoria Barracks, while Fort Macleod was changed to Barrosa Barracks. Fort Prince of Wales still remained home to artillery as Peninsula Barracks. The Germans took over Fort Qu' Appelle and stationed *Luftlande* (Airborne) Battalion 271 there, while Fort Beausejour became Corunna Barracks, housing a British engineer regiment. The German official in charge of NATO properties in Germany commented that he had never seen a turn over of facilities in such good shape, a tribute to those who replaced the last broken window, scrubbed the last bathroom floor, turned out the last light and locked the last gate.

The strategic environment that affected 4 CMBG also changed in the 1970s. The early '70s have been described by some observers as a period of détente between the Soviet Union and the West. There were, of course, two differing views on what détente actually meant. One perception held that détente was a permanent relaxation of tension between the two adversaries, and took a positive outlook towards improved relations in the future. The other point of view was that détente was a tactic to allow the Soviets some breathing space so that they could prepare for future expansion.

NATO itself was experiencing problems at this same time. If détente was real, was NATO still necessary? Although there were many adherents to this viewpoint, one had only to look at the extraordinary military advances made by the Soviets between 1968 and 1972. In addition to maintaining the full strength and constantly ready forces of GSFG, the Soviets had embarked on a huge naval construction programme which posed a threat not only to the NATO area but to other Western interests outside of it. In the strategic nuclear weapons field, the Soviets were well on the way to overcoming the numerical imbalance and moving towards parity with the West throughout the 1970s.

In theoretical terms then, once the Soviets had achieved parity with the West in strategic nuclear forces and parity in tactical nuclear forces, the nuclear arsenals would tend to cancel each other out if a conflict came about. Both sides would be afraid to escalate to tactical nuclear use, fearing that it would escalate to strategic nuclear use: the Armageddon scenario. This situation was very different from that of the 1950s and 1960s, when the West possessed unquestioned superiority in tactical and strategic nuclear weapons. Boiled down, if the Soviets were to initiate conventional operations against NATO, the Alliance might not be able to escalate to tactical nuclear use as that might escalate in turn into a catastrophic strategic nuclear exchange. As noted in previous chapters, NATO's conventional forces were thin on the ground, and the Alliance relied heavily upon tactical nuclear weapons to augment their conventional firepower.

The solution, as before, was for the members of NATO to provide more and better conventional forces. Weapons technology had improved in the late 1960s and early 1970s but not enough to replace tactical nuclear weapons as a force multiplier. In an era of détente, however, NATO members could not be convinced to spend a lot more money on conventional force improvements.

NATO military commands had to carry on with what they had. Since the effects of Soviet nuclear parity was still uncertain before 1977, MC 14/3, or "Flexible Response", remained NATO's dominant strategic concept. There was some re-examination of MC 14/3 in the form of a working group on the study of Alliance defence problems, but their report entitled "AD 70" concluded that MC 14/3 remained a sound basis for NATO strategy. Unlike the 1960s, NATO shifted from a Phase I, 30 day war/Phase II reconstitution period concept (as in MC 14/2) to a 90 day war concept in 1974, which anticipated protracted conventional and possible nuclear phases of variable lengths.

With the ever-growing Soviet naval threat and expanding conventional capabilities in other areas, NATO shifted its focus away from the Central Region starting in the late 1960s. This did not mean that the Central Region and its forces was less important or received fewer resources; it only signified that some resources might be retasked to cover new dangers.

These circumstances had an effect on Canadian defence planning in the Trudeau government. The formal expression of this new defence policy came in the 1971 White Paper which reoriented defence priorities away from those that had been set in 1964. Priority number one was the protection of Canadian sovereignty, followed by the defence of North America. NATO collective defence commitments were third place, with peacekeeping taking the back seat, as it were.

This new orientation, however, proved to be thinly disguised defence on the cheap. If protection of Canadian sovereignty really was the number one priority, why did the number of ships and aircraft dedicated to this role decrease? Defence of North America in the era of the intercontinental ballistic missile was not really a serious possibility. Although some anti-ballistic missile systems existed, Canada did not own, plan to own, or contribute to any nation possessing them. Peacekeeping commitments remained in place, particularly the Cyprus UN operation. NATO commitments were, as we have seen, cut to the bone with the Germany based Brigade reduced to a strength of 2800, and the eight CF-104 squadrons reduced to three. The commitment of two battalions to the ACE Mobile Force (Land) was reduced to a single battalion.

Canada also had committed, on paper, a Canadian Air-Sea Transportable (CAST) brigade group for the defence of NATO's northern flank in 1968; this commitment was retained in the 1970s. The supposed rationale for this new commitment was the increased Soviet threat to Norway, which was a direct result of the huge increase in the size of the Soviet fleet operating from ports on the Kola peninsula next to Norway and in the Baltic Sea opposite Denmark. (A similar situation prevailed in the Southern Region at the Bosporous straits in Turkey.) If NATO was to stop these forces from threatening North American-European sea lines of communications in the Atlantic, Norway and Denmark had to be retained as a base from which to launch attacks against Soviet naval forces, not to mention the fact that the principle of Forward Defence of NATO territory in Norway was as valid as it was in the Central Region.

The northern flank was a legitimate security problem for NATO and a serious threat did exist. This was played to advantage by the Trudeau government which now wanted to end the Canadian divisional commitment to the Central Region. Allocating a Canadian-based brigade group to AFNORTH now allowed the Trudeau government to extract itself from the divisional commitment while keeping Canada's NATO allies placated. A number of conditions, however, seemed to have been built into the CAST commitment to ensure that a Canadian brigade group would never actually deploy to Norway in wartime. For one thing the CAST Brigade Group was not equipped for a combat landing in-theatre; it needed to have secure ports and airfields. It would also take time to assemble and transport the Brigade Group to Norway. As a kind of 'Catch 22', the Norwegians also had to first request the CAST deployment before the outbreak of hostilities, something Canadian planners were certain Norway would not do for fear of aggravating the Soviets. Initially, Norway would not even allow equipment to be pre-positioned so that CAST could arrive in a timely fashion. Essentially, as originally envisioned, the deployment of the CAST Brigade Group was unlikely. SACEUR was not ignorant of this situation. Indeed, he capitalized on it.

The uncertainty with regards to the arrival of the formation in Norway during a conflict or crisis situation, coupled with the ambiguity of its role, served to confuse the Soviets as much as NATO planners. In this sense, the overall CAST commitment could have functioned as a part of a larger deception plan. In addition, the CAST Brigade Group could serve the same deterrent function as the AMF(L) in a protracted crisis situation in keeping with the escalatory principles of MC 14/3. In any case, 2 Combat Group in Petawawa, (and later 5^e Groupment de combat in Valcartier), was re-roled as the CAST Brigade Group and set about planning for deployment in the event of war. Canada would not actually exercise the CAST brigade in-theatre until 1986, long after the true origins of this unreal commitment were forgotten. In sum, Canada continued to maintain a brigade commitment in the Central Region, albeit in a reduced state, and a brigade plus a battalion (the AMF(L)) commitment to the northern flank. This state of affairs resulted in confusion over sustainment and reinforcement policies for 4 CMBG.

Another change that affected 4 CMBG was the creation of a new command, Canadian Forces Europe (CFE). CFE was a direct result of Unification, which as we will recall, created Mobile Command and also created considerable ambiguity in Mobile Command's control over 4 Brigade. There were many views regarding what CFE was supposed to do. Some viewed CFE as an attempt by the air force to impose an air force-dominated mechanism over all of the Canadian forces stationed in Europe. Others saw it as a logical step towards developing a Canadian national commander for Canadian units committed to ACE on par with BAOR or US European Command (USEUCOM).

CFE itself had no command function over 4 CMBG in wartime, although it would develop a logistics support function in the 1980s. In peacetime, it was supposed to serve as an administrative "node" between Canadian forces deployed in Europe and National Defence Headquarters in Ottawa. As with CANF(E) in northern Germany, CFE also became administratively responsible for Canadians posted to NATO headquarters at AFCENT, AFNORTH, and CENTAG. As a result, 4 CMBG found itself administratively subordinated to a unified command that included 1 Canadian Air Group, CFB Lahr, and CFB Baden-Soellingen. In wartime, 4 CMBG would be operationally 'chopped' under the Transfer of Authority (TOA) agreement from HQ CFE to HQ Central Army Group (CENTAG).

There was inevitably some friction since CFE had to balance the needs of very different types of formations which had different operational and logistical requirements. If 4 CMBG wanted to conduct an exercise, it had to be cleared through CFE. If logistical arrangements between 4 CMBG and an allied formation needed alteration, it had to be done through CFE. If war plans needed modification, it had to be done through CFE. This was quite different from the arrangement up north where the Brigade Commander had been 'double hatted' as the Canadian national commander and was able to conduct his business with more autonomy. The lack of understanding and/or sympathy between the air and land elements in Europe with regard to procedures, needs and conduct of everyday business was a fact of life in the initial development of CFE in the 1970s and at times caused many problems.

There were continued attempts to alter the composition and role of 4 CMBG in the early 1970s. The old idea of an airmobile reserve was trotted out once again and, once again, was sent packing. The Army was caught in a dilemma. The *Centurion* tanks were in decrepit shape and maintenance costs were soaring. Few wanted to propose a main battle tank replacement programme for fear that the need to have heavy armour would be reviewed and discarded by the Trudeau government. One proposal to purchase the British *Scorpion* family of light armoured vehicles was hotly debated and initially approved, but then abandoned. Mobile Command informed the Government that:

> ...a Canadian land force presence cannot continue usefully to be manifested in Europe beyond 1976 unless either (i) the armoured capability provided by the *Centurion* medium tank is in some way replaced or (ii) the force undergoes a major reconfiguration to a force highly specialized in anti-tank and air defence capabilities and designed to support and be integrated at the divisional, corps or army group level into formations of other allied countries such as those of the USA or Germany....

A study was conducted to examine the feasibility of turning 4 CMBG into an airmobile brigade that would be compatible in terms of equipment, organization and doctrine with an American concept called the TRICAP division. This was the predecessor to the airmobile-mechanized formations deployed by the Americans in the 1980s, which included armoured and mechanized infantry brigades, as well as a brigade of anti-tank and transport helicopters. 4 CMBG would be made completely integral to the US TRICAP-pattern division. Although in some ways appealing, this was rejected on the grounds that:

> The concept of organizing our field forces specifically so as to facilitate the incorporation of its primary elements into a US Army Division is challenged. Historically, Canadian political leadership has gone to great lengths to maintain a separate and distinctive Canadian identity. The current political attitude in respect of US economic domination of Canada leads one to conclude that future governments are certain to insist that a Canadian Forces contribution to any joint undertaking be organized in such a way as to leave the Canadian military element separate.

It is interesting to compare this situation to that of 1951 when the Government was deciding where to place 27 Brigade. In 1951, Canada could rely on the UK to provide support in certain areas. Canada's military leadership was still fresh from the Second World War, had extensive contacts with the British Army, as well as operational experience with them. This was coupled to the belief that a Canadian identity could be maintained in I (BR) Corps, an idea that was not fully realized until the 1960s but was eventually achieved even though the Brigade had to rely on a British logistics system. The Brigade also had a measure of relative autonomy including a formidable role in NORTHAG, nuclear firepower and a say on how it was employed.

In the 1970s, the decision to maintain the Brigade on the cheap resulted, paradoxically, in a situation whereby Canada wanted to maintain its autonomy within CENTAG but was unwilling to pay for the tools necessary to maintain that autonomy, that is, to have a formation that was self-contained and could be supported through purely national means without resort to a larger ally. Nor did it any longer have a critical role in the front line or have specialist equipment. Having an independent brigade group not part of a higher formation such as a division, or corps, and at the same time, not really being capable of fulfilling a critical function or task, was a contradiction which would not be overcome until the mid-1980s.

This is not to say that 4 CMBG commanders or their staffs in Europe

CHAPTER FIVE

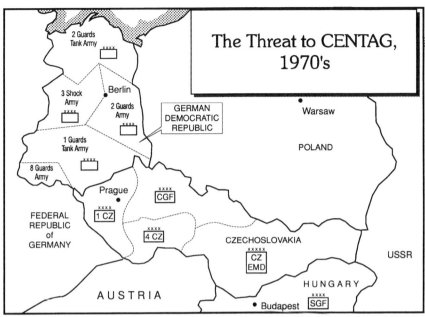

CENTAG THREAT ORBAT 1970's

GROUP of SOVIET FORCES, GERMANY:

1st GDS TK ARMY:
- 6 Gds Tk Div
- 7 Gds Tk Div
- 9 Tk Div
- 11 Gds Tk Div
- 27 Gds Mtr Rifle Div

8th GDS ARMY:
- 79 Gds Tk Div
- 39 Gds Mtr Rifle Div
- 57 Gds Mtr Rifle Div
- 27 Gds Mtr Rifle Div

SOUTHERN GROUP of FORCES (Soviet, Hungary):
- 2 Tk and
- 3 Mtr Rifle Divs

NATIONALE VOLKSARMEE (GDR):
- 1 Mech Div
- 4 Inf Div
- 8 Inf Div
- 7 Tk Div
- 9 Tk Div
- 11 Mtr Rifle Div

(Plus 5 reserve NVA infantry divisions: 6, 10, 19, 27, 40)

CZECH EASTERN MILITARY DISTRICT:
- 14 Tk Div
- 13 Tk Div
- 3 Mtr Rifle Div

CENTRAL GROUP of FORCES (SOVIET):
- 18 Mtr Rifle Div
- 15 Tk Div
- 48 Mtr Rifle Div
- 31 Tk Div
- 30 Mtr Rifle Div

CZECH WESTERN MILITARY DISTRICT

1st CZECH ARMY:
- 1 Tk Div
- 20 Mtr Rifle Div
- 19 Mtr Rifle Div
- 2 Mtr Rifle Div

4th CZECH ARMY:
- 15 Mtr Rifle Div
- 9 Tk Div
- 4 Tk Div

FIGURE 5-3

were sitting idle throughout the 1970s. There was no shortage of creative ideas, role considerations, plans and employment options, and it is to the credit of those commanders and staffs that the Brigade was kept as operationally capable as possible and in one piece. Overcoming the limitations placed on the Brigade in the 1970s through circumstances beyond its control was a necessary step to the partial restoration of the Brigade in the 1980s.

To understand the employment and training of 4 CMBG in the 1970s and 1980s, it is once again necessary to delve into the operational planning environment. The situation in CENTAG was quite different from that in NORTHAG. The threat facing CENTAG came not only from Group of Soviet Forces Germany and the East German Army (NVA), but from the Soviets' Central Group of Forces (CGF), the Soviet Southern Group of Forces (SGF) and the Czechoslovakian Peoples Army (CPA). [See Figure 5-3.] The forces from GSFG arrayed against the northern part of CENTAG included 8 Guards Army (one tank, three motor rifle divisions), with 2 Guards Tank Army (two tank, two motor rifle divisions) in the second operational echelon.

Soviet CGF units in Czechoslovakia had two tank and three motor rifle divisions and an independent artillery brigade, while the CPA consisted of five tank, five motor rifle, and one artillery division. 1 CPA – one tank and three motor rifle divisions – had a fairly high readiness level, while 4 CPA (two tank, one motor rifle divisions) had a significantly lesser rating. Two tank and one motor rifle divisions assigned to the Eastern Military District had an even lower rating. That said, the CPA was able to mobilize one tank and two motor rifle divisions in addition to these other forces. The Soviet SGF, located in Hungary, was structured along the lines of CGF.

The echeloning of forces in CGF and CPA was the subject of some debate. One school of thought believed that the CPA would be used in the first echelon as cannon fodder and the CGF would be used as the exploitation force. The other school believed that the CGF and elements of the CPA would be in the first echelon, with the remainder of the CPA as the second echelon. This appears to have been more likely. Once hostilities were initiated by Soviet forces against NATO, the already indoctrinated Czechs would have been led to believe that they were par-

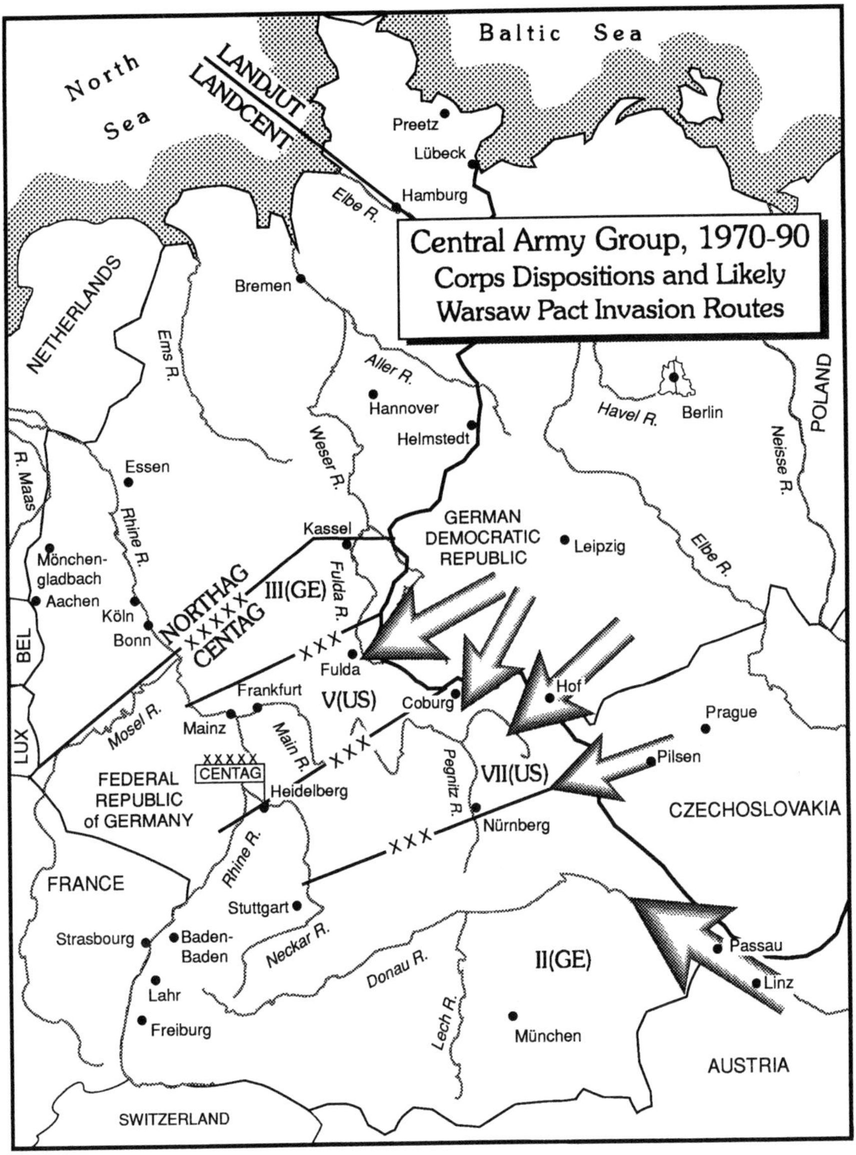
Central Army Group, 1970-90
Corps Dispositions and Likely
Warsaw Pact Invasion Routes
Baltic Sea
North Sea
LANDJUT
LANDCENT
Preetz
Lübeck
Hamburg
Elbe R.
Bremen
NETHERLANDS
Ems R.
Aller R.
Hannover
Helmstedt
Havel R.
Berlin
POLAND
Neisse R.
Weser R.
R. Maas
Essen
Rhine R.
Kassel
GERMAN
DEMOCRATIC
REPUBLIC
Leipzig
Elbe R.
Mönchen-
gladbach
Aachen
Köln
Bonn
NORTHAG
XXXXX
CENTAG
III(GE)
Fulda R.
XXX
Fulda
BEL
Frankfurt
V(US)
Coburg
Hof
Prague
LUX
Mosel R.
Mainz
Main R.
XXX
Pegnitz R.
Pilsen
XXXXX
CENTAG
FEDERAL
REPUBLIC
of GERMANY
Heidelberg
VII(US)
CZECHOSLOVAKIA
Nürnberg
Rhine R.
XXX
FRANCE
Stuttgart
Strasbourg
Baden-
Baden
Neckar R.
Donau R.
II(GE)
Passau
Linz
Lahr
Freiburg
Lech R.
München
AUSTRIA
SWITZERLAND

FIGURE 5-4

ticipating in a defensive action and any 'counterattack' into NATO would not be questioned by the Czech military leadership.

Other formations available for operations against CENTAG included some of the existing eight Soviet airborne divisions, probably two divisions assigned to GSFG. CGF itself had its own organic airborne regiment. Second strategic echelon forces for CGF were to come from the Carpathian Military District (CPMD). CPMD consisted of nine motor rifle divisions and four tank divisions at varying states of readiness, two artillery divisions and an airborne brigade. If the Soviets chose to do so, they could move the four divisions of Southern Group of Forces in Hungary and/or some of the eight Hungarian divisions to act as a second echelon through Czechoslovakia, or employ them directly against and through Austria and then southern Germany. In a simple 'bean count', twenty divisions were Category A, meaning available for immediate use against CENTAG, with an additional eighteen to twenty-two divisions of other readiness categories in the second strategic echelon.

Soviet doctrine in the 1970-1978 period had not changed significantly since the late 1960s. Exercise DVINA held in 1970 indicated that tactical and theatre nuclear operations were still integral to all levels of operations and simulated nuclear use was used extensively in the manoeuvre. In terms of equipment, self propelled artillery was deployed in large numbers in 1974, and most of the T-62 and T-55 tanks underwent upgrades. More mechanized infantry in BMPs was added into the tank divisions.

The terrain in CENTAG was much more defensible than in NORTHAG in terms of hills and forests, but the frontage which CENTAG had to defend was more than three times that of NORTHAG. [See Figure 5-4.] The most vulnerable area from NATO's point of view was the front extending from the inter-Army Group boundary south of Kassel to the Hof Gap area. The distance here from the inner-German border to the Rhine was less than 150 kilometers; consequently, CENTAG's strongest forces were deployed to stop an enemy attack as close to the border as possible. III German Korps (two panzer and one panzer grenadier division) took up where the Belgians left off, with V (US) Corps (one and a half armoured and one mechanized infantry divisions) on their right flank, followed by VII (US) Corps (one and half armoured and one and a half mechanized infantry divisions) extending down to Nürnberg.

Once this critical area was covered, southern Germany still remained open, however. With the withdrawal of the French from NATO's military structure in the 1960s, II German Korps (one infantry, one airborne, one mountain and one armoured division) was left to handle most of the sector facing the Czechoslovak front, as well as covering southwards from the Austrian border to Switzerland, a situation which we will come back to later.

In very general terms, the physical make up of the CENTAG area consisted of a hilly and heavily forested belt 10 to 30 kilometers wide extending all the way from III German Korps down to Passau on the Austrian border. This range of features was flush up against the Iron Curtain. Since the best defensible terrain in CENTAG was close in along the border, enemy routes of advance would have to be along corridors through the rough, wooded countryside. These corridors were well-known terrain features and came to be widely known, even by civilians, by their code names [See Figure 5-4]. The most well known to the public was the Fulda Gap in the V (US) Corps sector, but others like the Coburg Entry, the Hof Corridor, the Pilsen/Highway 14 group of approaches, the Fürth Gap and the Böhmerwald (Bohemian Forest) were also critical sectors.

The lack of depth in the III (GE) Korps and V (US) Corps sectors notwithstanding, what really made the defence of the CENTAG area a tricky prospect was the Donau (Danube) Approach. If the Soviets chose to violate the neutrality of Austria, the good defensive terrain along the East German-Czech border could be outflanked south of Passau. This of course was dependent on how the Austrians would react in the face of Soviet nuclear weapons and overwhelming forces operating from the Central and Southern Groups of Forces. If the Soviets violated Austrian neutrality and got to Linz, they would have access to a fast-approach highway system leading into southern Bavaria to Munich, Ulm, Stuttgart and the Rhine. CENTAG's forces there would be encircled, while III Korps and V Corps further to the north would be pinned down under heavy pressure by GSFG.

This situation would have stretched the CENTAG defences very thin, making the dispositions of II (GE) Korps almost as important as those on the more direct routes further north. If Munich and Nürnberg were lost, it would be very difficult for West Germany to continue to fight, particularly if other large population areas like Hamburg in NORTHAG were lost. These political realities continued to make Forward Defence the guiding principle in the development of CENTAG planning. Yet CENTAG did not appear to have enough forces to guarantee a successful forward defence.

Other factors affected planning in CENTAG (and 4 CMBG's role within it) as NATO planners sought to create a coherent defence of the CENTAG area. There were problems with the quality of forces assigned to key sectors, and there were problems with the use of tactical nuclear weapons. CENTAG needed a mobile reserve, and it also needed a massive reinforcement concept.

CENTAG planning between 1970 to 1973 was in the doldrums until the 1973 Yom Kippur War in the Middle East demonstrated the effectiveness of conventional firepower and portable anti-tank missile systems. This 'doldrum period' was the result of several things. The United States Army, which provided 50-60 per cent of the forces in CENTAG, was experiencing the traumatic 'end-game' in Vietnam. Drug use in the US Army was rampant, as was disrespect for military authority. The Bundeswehr at the same time was going through its 'hairnet' period. Both armies were composed of conscripts, not regular soldiers. The French had just withdrawn two armoured and two infantry divisions and had left a gaping hole in the front line. If this was not enough, a residue of MC 14/2 thinking, that is, immediate and large scale tactical nuclear use, still existed.

This situation was compounded by the 'French Problem'. France, it will be recalled, had withdrawn from NATO's integrated military structure as a result of a dispute over NATO strategy. Still adhering to 1950s thinking, France developed a strategy called the *Manoeuvre nationale de dissuasion* in which the French Army based in Germany near the Rhine planned to utilize tactical nuclear weapons and conventional firepower to keep the Warsaw Pact away from French territory. If this failed, France's independent *Force de frappe* would use strategic nuclear weapons against the USSR proper. The Germans, on whose territory the tactical nuclear weapons would detonate, were not amused, even though they fervently believed that deterrence of any war had to work, and had convinced everybody else in the Central Region to ratify and implement conventional Forward Defence. Little of this French operational concept was coordinated with CENTAG's defence planning in the early 1970s.

CENTAG's developing concept of operations in the 1970s took all of this into account. Large scale, immediate tactical nuclear weapons use was not anticipated as it would violate the very spirit of MC 14/3. In fact, nuclear first use by NATO would have been announced to the Soviets and did not necessarily involve battlefield use in the Central Region. Demonstrative first use probably would have been at sea. Subsequent use of NATO nuclear forces was at the discretion of SACEUR and would likely have involved limited strikes against fixed targets in eastern Europe like logistics nodes or airbases. Ultimately, battlefield use was projected in four to five days, and only after the Soviets indicated they would continue their conventional assault.

CENTAG did, of course, still retain substantial nuclear forces of several kinds, but they were essentially corps and army group resources. Corps commanders were permitted to conduct contingency planning which included nuclear weapons use. These Corps 'packages', once approved, were supposed to speed up the employment process if the existing battlefield conditions were the same as in the plans. (For example, in VII (US) Corps there were four or five 'packages' consisting of roughly 200 weapons each, while II (GE) Korps had three 'packages' of six or seven weapons.)

Every nuclear weapon request prior to General Nuclear Response was a "Selective Release", that is, every target had to be requested and justified by Corps. Approval had to be given at each higher level, or the request was denied. This included Army Group, AFCENT, SHAPE/SACEUR and the North Atlantic Council, and finally the US President. There was no short-cutting the chain of command unless the US National Command Authority had been destroyed, in which case SACEUR did have some release authority still subject to the North Atlantic Council.

The process, which was practised regularly, was very slow, probably a minimum of 48 hours at first, then only 36 hours after the first 20 or so strikes. It was understood that if General Nuclear Release ever came, the war had already been lost. Corps commanders then would have had some leeway in using their nuclear resources if there were any left. Army Group still retained control. Nuclear planning, thus, was quite different in the 1970s from the 1960s.

With respect to the Canadians, having nuclear-capable delivery systems like the M-109 self propelled gun did not provide a 'seat at the table' at Corps-level when nuclear fire planning was being set up. This reflected the diminution of 4 CMBG's influence since coming down to CENTAG.

As in the past, NATO forces-in-being had to be able to delay the Soviets until reinforcements could arrive. The whole effort in the Central Region was designed to stabilize the enemy as far forward as possible until reinforcements arriving from the United States could pick up their equipment from the POMCUS sites and deploy forward, and for the European members of NATO to mobilize. The questions were, what was the best method of imposing a delay with existing forces, and could the reinforcement process become more efficient? The Germans had very little time in the event of conflict to mobilize, but had plans to mobilize some 700,000 troops (all conscripts) to flesh out their existing twelve front-line divisions and their extensive Territorial Army. The Bundeswehr maintained six (later twelve) Territorial Home Defence Brigades which in the 1970s had a light infantry rear-area defence role. These units were spread throughout Germany, with approximately two assigned in wartime to CENTAG.

The Americans, on the other hand, developed a system called POMCUS (Pre-positioning of Materiel Configured to Unit Sets). POMCUS sites were enormous storage depots west of the Rhine near the large American airbases. Enough equipment for reinforcement divisions was pre-stocked in these sites, and in time of war, the troops were to be flown by commercial air from the United States, married up with their equipment, and sent off to fight.

This concept, similar to the Canadian concept developed in NORTHAG in the 1950s, was first tested in 1968. The US, under budgetary pressure as a result of the war in Vietnam, had withdrawn the personnel from two mechanized brigades to the continental United States in order to save money. It was planned that these brigades would be returned to Germany every year for large scale training exercises, usually in the Fall. This gave birth to REFORGER, or "Return of Forces to Germany", an event which culminated in large scale CENTAG exercises in which 4 CMBG frequently participated. The POMCUS and REFORGER programmes were expanded throughout the 1970s so that a number of US reinforcement divisions had their equipment pre-positioned in Germany.

The results of the 1973 Yom Kippur War forced a re-appraisal of the value and effectiveness of conventional firepower within NATO armies, and particularly the dramatic success that had been demonstrated with new anti-tank guided missiles. At the same time, the Americans had become very enthusiastic over their 'brainchild', air-mobility. The widespread use of helicopters in Vietnam left a lasting imprint on the US Army, which set about developing doctrine for their use in Europe. These two types of equipment were melded into a proposal to provide an airmobile brigade each to CENTAG, NORTHAG and AFCENT (LANDCENT changed its name in the early 1970s) to function as mobile reserves and block any penetration past the forward defence. As we will see, 4 CMBG assisted in pointing out some of the limitations of the airmobile concept in a high intensity European battlefield environment.

Overall, the operational situation in CENTAG during the early 1970s was uncertain. There was a reinforcement concept, but the ability of forces-in-being to resist penetration until the reinforcements arrived was always uncertain. There were plans to develop a counter-penetration capability, but they were untried. The utility of tactical nuclear weapons was suspect, and their immediate use contravened the existing NATO strategic concept. Be this as it may, Brigadier-General Pat Grieve, who commanded 4 CMBG from 1972 to 1974, noted that

> ...Delay operations could only have lasted about three days. After that, it was clearly NATO policy to employ nuclear weapons to halt the Warsaw Pact forces. This was the script in all CENTAG formation exercises and the WINTEX exercises. I used to wonder what the Canadian people and [Prime Minister] Trudeau in particular, would have thought had they been aware of the script....

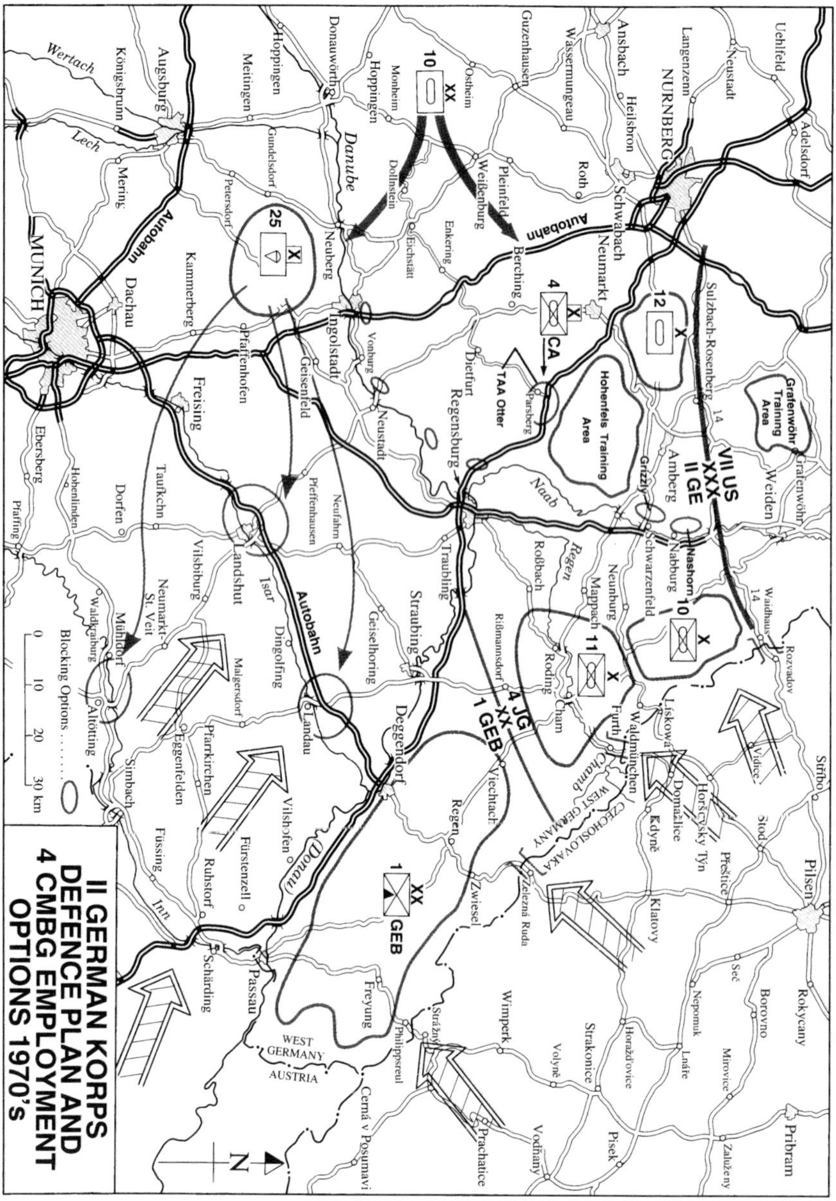
II GERMAN KORPS DEFENCE PLAN AND 4 CMBG EMPLOYMENT OPTIONS 1970's
Blocking Options
0 10 20 30 km
Grafenwöhr Training Area
Hohenfels Training Area
VII US XX II GE
4 JG XX 1 GEB
TAA Otter
Autobahn
Danube
Donau
Wertach
Lech
Isar
Inn
Naab
Regen
Chamb
NURNBERG
MUNICH
Augsburg
Ingolstadt
Regensburg
Straubing
Deggendorf
Landshut
Passau
Pilsen
WEST GERMANY
AUSTRIA
CZECHOSLOVAKIA

FIGURE 5-5

CHAPTER FIVE

Because of its reduced size and the fact that plans were still under development for its wartime augmentation, 4 CMBG had no real role in CENTAG from the time of its arrival in Lahr in October 1970 to July 1971. Brigadier-General Jacques Chouinard, who took over from Brigadier-General Leonard in July 1971, discovered that 4 CMBG only had a rather vague role in CENTAG's General Defence Plan (GDP):

> There was one thing, however, which was somewhat disturbing when I arrived.... The role of the brigade in July 1971 was something like [having] responsibility for the rear areas in V(US) Corps with an emphasis on refugee control.... That wasn't the reason 4 CMBG was in Germany. (Even though the Brigade was somewhat deficient by one infantry battalion, and was not in any manner or means a full brigade), it was nevertheless, in my mind, able to take on other responsibilities than the one that seemed to be on the books for us.
>
> Representations were made then to CENTAG, and the Commander gave me an occasion to meet with him for a rather long period of time.... He wanted to know what it was that we wanted to do, because we didn't seem to be satisfied with what he had in mind. I told him that as far as we were concerned, what we wanted was a role in the front line, and not one behind the logistics system in the V(US) Corps organization or for that matter in II (GE) Korps. He agreed, and gave us at the time a definite role which was to be a brigade in Corps reserve either in V(US)Corps or with II (GE) Korps....

This initial role was altered once again in 1971 so that 4 CMBG became a reserve force for either VII (US) Corps or II (GE) Korps, with priority to II (GE) Korps because of its overextended deployment. [See Figure 5-5.] II (GE) Korps consisted of 4 Jaeger Division (1 armoured and three light infantry brigades); 10 Panzer Division (2 armoured and one mechanized infantry brigades); 1 Mountain Division (one mountain, one armoured and one mechanized infantry brigade) and Airborne Brigade 25, for a total of 11 brigades. With 4 CMBG added, Canadian content in a II (GE) Korps deployment amounted to nine per cent of the forces in the II (GE) Korps area, compared to 15 per cent in the I (BR) Corps area in the 1960s.

VII (US) Corps consisted of 1st US Armored Division (three brigades); 3rd Infantry Division (three brigades); one independent infantry brigade (3rd Brigade, 1st Infantry Division); and 2nd Armored Cavalry Regiment which was a brigade-sized formation. For a VII (US) Corps deployment, 4 CMBG was one of nine brigades, amounting to 13 per cent.

This planning, of course, depended on a full brigade group rather than on the existing battle group, and 4 CMBG was operationally deficient in many areas because of the Trudeau cuts. Most notably, an entire infantry battalion was missing, as were a tank squadron and an artillery battery, not to mention the large number of service support troops. In numerical terms, the Brigade's 1969 war establishment was 6606 men, of which 5517 were deployed in Germany. By 1970, the Brigade had 3220 men deployed, with no augmentation plans. After the re-introduction of war establishments in 1973, and after a concerted effort on the part of the CDS, General Dextraze, 4 CMBG's war establishment in 1976 was raised to 5343, of which 3212 were in Germany. Incremental increases gradually occurred throughout the 1970s. In 1977, the figures were 5517 war establishment, 3220 peacetime. By 1979, the war establishment was at 5615 and the peace establishment was 3268.

To be able to carry out its GDP responsibilities, plans had to made to increase 4 CMBG's strength in time of crisis or war. The plan to bring 4 CMBG up to its war establishment strength was called Operation PENDANT. OPLAN PENDANT called for the use of civilian airlift to bring Canadian-based personnel to Europe in the event of a NATO alert. In 1973, the plan only handled an immediate augmentation of 211 men; by 1979, PENDANT was supposed to be capable of providing 2347 augmentees. Op PENDANT was supposed to fill out the two infantry battalions by adding another infantry company to each, and providing personnel for the third armoured squadron in the armoured regiment and the fourth battery for the artillery. Dependents in Lahr and Baden were to be flown back to Canada on the aircraft that brought in the augmentees, under a separate evacuation plan called MAYFLOWER.

To add the third infantry battalion to the brigade (as called for in Canadian doctrine), some thought was given to airlifting the Canadian UN infantry battalion in Cyprus to Germany in the event of war, but there were no pre-positioned APCs or equipment for it, and the unit would still have to be augmented with a fourth rifle company from Canada. Where the aircraft were going to be found for such an operation was never clear, nor were any reception plans laid on by CFE or CFB Lahr for such a contingency. The UN was certainly not brought in on this thinking. Also, SHAPE apparently included NATO-member UN forces in Cyprus into its contingency planning to secure the island in war, and did not want Canada to use the Canadian battalion there as an augmentation force for 4 CMBG.

In order to provide 30 days of sustainment personnel for the Brigade, NDHQ planners created Operation Plan BARBET. Theoretically, OPLAN BARBET was supposed to provide 938 casualty replacements over a 30 day period, but little thought was given to the equipping of these personnel once they arrived in Germany or where they were going to come from. Apart from OPLANs PENDANT and BARBET then, there were no plans in the event of war to reinforce the Canadian army in Germany beyond the existing Brigade Group. Moreover, the planning focus at NDHQ and FMCHQ had now switched to the CAST Brigade Group and the Northern Flank, despite the unrealities of that commitment.

NATO's transition away from a strategic concept emphasizing nuclear use resulted in the need to restructure national forces in the Central Region so that they could fight a protracted conventional war. While other NATO allies struggled to adjust, the Trudeau government chose not to. In a war, 4 CMBG would have to fight unsustained and undermanned. Some planners even referred to the CAST and 4 CMBG commitments as 'Hong Kong North' and 'Hong Kong Centre', in reference to Canada's ill-fated Hong Kong deployment in 1941. Lieutenant General Charles Belzile, who commanded 4 CMBG from 1974 to 1976, assessed the Brigade's combat capability in retrospect:

> I think we could have accounted for ourselves reasonably well in a short battle, a blocking battle. I don't think our durability would have been that great unless there was a massive infusion of fly-over troops from Canada, [and] as long as we kept the commitment to the CAST Brigade. You tried to build up the Brigade as best as you could given the circumstances….

In addition to the sustainability situation, there were many difficulties with the OPLANs which continued to plague 4 CMBG into the mid-1980s. There was little interface between CFE and 4 CMBG on implementation. Neither had the details been worked out or even exercised at any point to determine where the flaws were. There was no mechanism in place to bring the PENDANT personnel forward to the battle area, let alone the BARBET replacements. There was no plan for CFB Lahr to equip, feed or house BARBET personnel either. PENDANT and BARBET in reality were, in the 1970s, only intentions of action and not detailed plans.

If these were not problems enough, the ability to sustain 4 CMBG logistically in a conflict was virtually non-existent prior to 1978. The decision to move South severed the close service support relationship 4 CMBG had with BAOR and for some time 4 CMBG was not provided with the funding to develop an independent logistical system. As a result, Canada once again developed logistics arrangements 'on the cheap' as it had in the 1950s. When Canadian planners reassessed the logistic situation in 1974, they discovered that no arrangements existed at all beyond the provision of M-113 spare parts from the Americans. Here was 4 CMBG in southern Germany with British tanks, American APCs, Canadian trucks, a mixed family of small arms and no wartime system to maintain them!

Certainly, 4 CMBG needed a great number of items so that it could operate effectively in wartime. Rations, fuel, ammunition, and third line maintenance were only some of the requirements. In NORTHAG, these had come from BAOR. In CENTAG, 4 CMBG turned to the Americans for support. The US Army was at first reluctant to take 4 CMBG into its logistics structure and some of the leadership in Ottawa was wary as well. The pre-1974 uncertainty as to the duration of 4 CMBG's stay in Europe played a role, but there was also a streak of anti-Americanism in the Canadian political environment. Trudeau's concept of an independent Canada, with more free wheeling foreign and defence policies was theoretically endangered if Canada went hat in hand to the Americans for logistical support in Europe. Although brigade and CFE planners made what in-theatre arrangements they could, the wartime support problems for 4 CMBG remained acute. One planner summed up the situation succinctly in 1976:

> Due to the conditions under which the [support] agreements were developed, they eventually proved to be neither consistent with any one overall concept of support, nor consistent internally with one another. In fact, the Command line-of-communications plans consisted of a series of unrelated solutions which had been created as individual requirements were recognized. Thinking of the war plan as a tire, as leaks developed, patches were slapped on to cover them. The patches were of different material, of different colours, used different glue, and eventually were so numerous that it was impossible to discern whether or not there was still a tire underneath the patches.

Even with signed support agreements with the allies, the planners also noted that

> In discussing at both NATO and CENTAG HQ, statements have been made to the Commander CFE indicating grave doubts that the countries involved will have excess capacity available to fulfil the terms of international agreements. At the working level, it quickly becomes apparent that agreements can be signed and supported by higher levels for political reasons, and yet cannot be honoured by working levels which are already overcommitted to their own support.... It is clear at this point that support from other nations which is not guaranteed is not professionally acceptable....

This impasse continued until 1978.

Despite these problems Brigade planners soldiered on in an attempt to develop a role which 4 CMBG could fulfil, hoping that the situation would improve in the future. Once 4 CMBG was moved forward, CENTAG had to decide which corps to release it to. In the 1970s, II (GE) Korps was the priority commitment. As a result, a number of 4 CMBG employment options were developed in conjunction with the staff planners of II (GE) Korps.

The situation from the point of view of II (GE) Korps was dependent on the nature of the threat from the Donau (Danube) Approach through Austria. As noted earlier, the probable enemy objectives in the southern part of CENTAG included the cities of Nürnberg and Munich before the enemy's second echelon pushed on to the Rhine. There was also a strong possibility that the Cheb / Highway 14 Approaches would be used, supported strongly by enemy units moving through the Fürth Approach. Any attack along Highway 14 would also be along the inter-corps boundary between VII (US) Corps and II (GE) Korps. (This violated several tactical principles; apparently, the boundary was 'movable' in the plans, depending upon the situation at the time.) If the enemy attacked on the US side of the boundary, CENTAG had to be able to shift 4 CMBG to support 1st US Armored Division. If the weight of the attack was on the II (GE) Korps side, 4 CMBG had to be able to support 4 Jaeger Division or 1 Mountain Division. [See Figure 5-5.]

II (GE) Korps deployed 4 Jaeger Division to cover the Highway 14 and Fürth approaches, with two Jaeger Brigades forward and Panzer Brigade 12 as a counter-attack force. 1 Mountain Division was deployed to the south down to the tri-border area, while Airborne Brigade 25 was prepared to cover vital crossing areas on the Isar river. 4 CMBG was to deploy to Tactical Assembly Area (TAA) OTTER, located near Parsberg, south of the Hohenfels training area. 4 CMBG's employment depended on a number of situations. If 4 Jaeger Division had to withdraw from its forward positions, 4 CMBG had two options, nicknamed NASHORN and GRIZZLY. These were blocking positions on the Naab River. The retreating Jaeger Brigades would pass through 4 CMBG and consolidate behind, perhaps near Amberg. If the pressure was too great, Panzer Brigade 12 would counter-attack through 4 CMBG. If this move failed, the II (GE) Korps reserve, 10 Panzer Division, would counter-attack.

If, however, the 4 Jaeger Division sector was relatively stable and the enemy exercised the Donau option, 4 CMBG would be used to back up Airborne Brigade 25, and to develop blocking positions on the Donau River to delay the advance of the Soviets' Southern Group of Forces. Panzer Brigade 12 remained in its counter-attack role behind the two Jaeger Brigades. This would assist in the extrication of 1 Mountain Division if it was in danger of being cut off. 10 Panzer Division, again as the Corps reserve, and if not employed elsewhere, would counter-attack in order to stabilize the front along the Regensburg-Landshut-Munich axis.

Though numerically small, 4 CMBG provided the Commander

II (GE) Korps with a formation which would allow him to buy time and consolidate his hard pressed forward-deployed forces after the initial enemy assault. This also increased his reserve counter-attack force in the sense that he did not have to split 10 Panzer Division to handle both the blocking role and the counter-attack role, thus maintaining the integrity of the formation.

There were many problems with this arrangement as it affected 4 CMBG. Lahr and Baden were more than 350 kilometers from the TAA and GDP area. Depending on the type of movement, it could take between one and three days before 4 CMBG could be brought into action. To get forward, 4 CMBG would have to run the gauntlet of enemy air strikes, ambushes, sabotage by agents against rail lines, and German civilians fleeing westward on the autobahns. Supplying a formation this far forward of the logistical airhead in Lahr was next to impossible unless some means were developed to either move 4 CMBG forward in peacetime or to pre-position some of its supplies and equipment near the expected battle area. The solution to this problem would have to wait until the 1980s.

One very positive benefit for 4 CMBG in the CENTAG area was increased access to Host Nation Support (HNS). An agreement was signed under NATO auspices in 1960 to guarantee HNS to SACEUR's forces operating in Germany. Since any war in the Central Region would be fought on German soil, the West Germans had made elaborate defence plans that sequestered everything from civilian trucks to hospitals for the defence effort. Even roads and bridges were not spared; highways were strengthened to support armoured vehicles and bridges were constructed with demolition chambers integral to their design.

Several aspects of HNS are worth noting here, since 4 CMBG could not fight effectively without it. The Bundeswehr divided Germany into two territorial or home defence type commands: Territorial Command North (GTNC) and Territorial Command South (GTSC). 4 CMBG fell into the GTSC area. GTSC had three Defence District Commands or WbKs (*Wehrbereichs-Kommando*). These WbKs corresponded to the German *Länder* or provinces. 4 CMBG had dealings with WbK V in Stuttgart and WbK VI in Munich. Each WbK was divided into Defence Region Commands (VbK) and each VbK was divided into Defence

County Commands or VKKs (*Verteidigungskreis Kommandos*), which corresponded to counties.

The mission of GTSC was to provide HNS to NATO formations so that the effectiveness of the defence of Germany could be increased. In broad terms, GTSC and its subordinate commands provided rail transport coordination, road and bridge repair, maintained the civilian phone system for military use and, requisitioned public utilities and civilian motor transport. This was not all. In addition to maintaining the civilian infrastructure to support military operations, GTSC was responsible for rear area security, refugee movement control, NBCD recce, engineer support of all kinds, the holding of prisoners of war, and the maintenance of hospitals.

GTSC also provided valuable support in the forward areas where the importance of engineer resources cannot be overstated. To ensure the success of CENTAG's obstacle plan, several special denial engineer units called *Wallmeisters* were located in the forward areas. The personnel for these units were all reservists who lived in the forward area itself; they were responsible for maintaining target folders and for setting explosive charges on bridges and other features which could canalize enemy forces invading West Germany. In the rear combat zone, other reserve engineer units manned bridging equipment to support NATO forces in the withdrawal and counter-attack phases of the battle. Other GTSC units handled chemical reconnaissance. In any war the effect of these units as "force multipliers" would have been considerable and were vital to CENTAG's defence plan.

Medical support to supplement that of the national forces also existed under the HNS agreements. Every German hospital was designed to support battle casualties, and medical supplies were pre-stocked. Lists of civilian medical personnel were maintained for call up, and conscientious objectors to military service were assigned ambulance and paramedic tasks. The German Civil Defence organization in each VbK could provide Medical, Repair, NBCD, Welfare, Rescue and Salvage platoons composed of civilian personnel, in addition to the reserve units called up under the WbKs.

Since the rear area security threat became more and more critical in the 1970s, the GTSC also provided special units to support NATO forces.

The effect of enemy guerrilla and terrorist attacks on the rear area support network would have been considerable, and HNS planning took this into account as well. Each VKK was responsible for the defence of vital points in their particular area. For example, VKK 5334 provided a Security Company to protect the Lahr airfield, while area security for Offenburg-Lahr was handled by a Rifle Battalion from the VbK. Bundeswehr *Feldjaeger* (Military Police) units ensured that main supply routes were patrolled and that military traffic was controlled. German security and intelligence units cooperated with CFE HQ preparatory to protecting dependents before and during any evacuation.

In the event of a Warsaw Pact attack on NATO, 4 CMBG was reliant upon GTSC for assistance in controlling its movement forward to the GDP area, security of its units while moving forward, protection of the logistics base area and dependents from sabotage and terrorist attack, and, to some degree, on engineering resources for mobility and counter-mobility planning. GTSC medical resources would have been badly needed in the 1970s given the decrepit state of CFE medical support for 4 CMBG. Since 4 CMBG lacked an NBCD recce capability, it would have had to rely on GTSC for support here as well. It should be emphasized, however that German HNS resources were limited and would have had to divide their energies between all formations in CENTAG, in addition to supporting the civilian population. The bottom line, however, was that any help provided by GTSC would have significantly added to the operational capability of 4 CMBG at a time when it was needed the most.

With the move south, the Brigade had to develop new training relationships with the Germans and the Americans, since training areas were in high demand. Because 4 CMBG was not organic to a higher formation, as it had been with I (BR) Corps, special arrangements had to be made to allow for gun camps, small arms shoots and the like. This was not easy as the existing training areas in CENTAG were jealously protected 'turf'.

Fortunately, CFE was able to sign an agreement with the Americans so that 4 CMBG could have access, albeit at some financial cost, to the Hohenfels and Grafenwöhr training areas near the Czech border. Other reciprocal arrangements were made with the Germans for the use of the

Münsingen training area south east of Stuttgart. This was very different from the situation up north in the 1950s and 1960s. There, when the Brigade was part of BAOR, it was automatically incorporated into the BAOR training plan so that special arrangements did not have to be made every time the Brigade wanted to train. But, even after moving to Lahr, by judicious use of the 'old boy net', 4 CMBG was still able to send units up to the British training areas in Sennelager, Bergen-Hohne and Soltau.

A short term agreement with the French was made so that 1 R22eR could train at Mourmelon near Reims in France. Later in the 1970s, the Fighting in Built Up Areas (FIBUA) training site of Bonnland, constructed by the Germans at their infantry school in Hammelburg, also became available to 4 CMBG. For local unit training less than squadron/company level, the Brigade had the use of Stollhofen near Baden-Soellingen, Langenwinkel, beside the Lahr airfield, and the Langenhard, just behind the Kaserne in the Black Forest. Squadron and company level tactical training could be conducted in the "Canadian Canter", a semi-permanent Requisitioned Manoeuvre Area running north-south in the Black Forest behind Lahr and Baden.

Training opportunities with allied units and organizations at the unit and sub-unit level abounded. These relationships were extremely important from many points of view. First, they engendered a professional respect for the Canadian soldier on the part of other NATO allies. Secondly, training techniques, ideas and equipment capabilities could be 'cross-pollinated' and all contributors could benefit from this. Thirdly, the increased emphasis on interoperability in CENTAG demanded it.

Two notable items of allied training opportunities deserve mention – the French Commando Course and parachute jumping with German airborne troops. Regarding the former, 4 Brigade soldiers were regularly given the opportunity to participate in the *Entrâinment de commando* course in Neuf-Briesach (just south of Freiburg and across the Rhine) and be awarded the qualification. One willing participant, Major Jeff Sawchuck, recalled:

> ...the facilities were fantastic. The obstacle course was incredible. It was a really demanding course...good fun, probably the best training you could get outside the brigade. All the instructors were Legionnaires and they were sons

of bitches. The instructors were mostly fifty year old Legionnaires, pretty fit. Few of them were married, and many of them had been at Dien Bien Phu, in Algeria and in Chad, so there were a lot of skilled soldiers…

Part of the exercise was held in an old fort which was part of the Maginot Line…. [During WWII] it had been a German concentration camp where they brought people to experiment on and exterminate. It was full of ghosts, that old fort.

For the airborne-inclined, Canadian soldiers could earn the Bundeswehr's *Fallschirmjaeger* jump wings. This was facilitated by a *partnerschaft* between 3 Mechanized Commando and Airborne Battalion 252; 1 R22eR also had a *partnerschaft* with Airborne Battalion 251. Canadian soldiers who passed the French Commando Course or who parachuted with the Germans were permitted to wear the appropriate insignia on their uniform.

Training relationships between Canadian units and their German, French and American counterparts often developed into these formal *partnerschafts*. Examples are too numerous to mention here, but all units in 4 CMBG eventually had some form of partnership activity, be it exercises, mess dinners, sports meets or soldier exchanges. The Brigade even hosted the Portuguese Army and assisted in training some of their troops after Portugal acquired the M-113 vehicle series.

Inter-NATO competitions continued to flourish in the 1970s. The already familiar Canadian Army Trophy (CAT) and Prix LeClerc continued as before, with 2 RCR winning the Prix LeClerc in 1970 and the RCD winning CAT in 1977. One addition was the Boeselager Cup, a Bundeswehr sponsored armoured recce competition named after Colonel Georg Freiherr von Boeselager – a German cavalry officer involved in the plot against Hitler, and who was killed in action on the Russian front. Other training events included the grueling Nijmegen Marches, and the BAOR sailing course and yachting competition. There was, of course, the annual Brigade Sports Day, which through dedicated effort the Van Doos won consistently over a 16 year period.

One particularly interesting training highlight in CENTAG was the Iron Curtain border tour provided by the Americans or the *Bundesgrenzschutz* (Federal German Border Police). Major Jeff

Sawchuck participated in one such tour during a REFORGER exercise:

> Everybody was conscious of the fact that there was a legitimate threat and to put things in perspective, I had the good fortune of deploying with two units [to the border area]. I went with the *Bundesgrenzschutz* unit which was responsible for border security and with an American Cavalry unit who invited me to patrol the border with them. If you didn't think there was a threat, this tour changed your mind....
>
> I came back and I said that every Canadian serviceman who got posted to Europe and every dependent should have a tour of the border and see the three-meter concrete or brick wall or the three-meter barbed wire fence. The fences were the best ones to see because you could see the whole development of the defence plan – double fence, mine fields, control towers, patrols, dogs on long cables.... Sitting there in a jeep with binoculars looking at border guards, it puts everything in perspective. There was a threat, and we were looking at it. Whether the wall was there to keep people in or out was irrelevant. There on the other side of that wall was a gigantic military machine that, once somebody pushed the right buttons, was ready to steamroll her way across Western Europe....

Alert recall practice down south differed from the Brigade's experience in NORTHAG. The SNOWBALL replaced QUICK TRAIN as the code word for the 'bug out' and a variety of means of alerting the troops were used. The dispersion of the individual soldiers in the areas surrounding Lahr and Baden and the lack of a phone system produced much confusion in the 1970s, leading to the use of air-raid sirens in the communities. Eventually, this method lost its appeal as the local population resented being awakened at three o'clock in the morning by sirens followed by the movement of soldiers' cars and motorcycles, followed by the movement of armoured vehicles through the narrow cobblestoned streets for the next two hours. Later, sound trucks with loudspeakers were used. On average, there were ten or more Snowballs a year, usually once a month.

Brigade actions on a Snowball could take a number of forms. A typical Snowball could originate from Brigade, CFE or a higher NATO headquarters like SHAPE or CENTAG. Upon receipt of the message by

CHAPTER FIVE

Brigade duty personnel, the sirens would be activated, the sound trucks would go out, and Brigade members would start pouring in to their vehicle compounds and unit stores. CFN Radio would also come on the air with a "This is a Snowball!" broadcast. Standing Orders dictated that all personnel were to have their combat kit and fighting order packed 24 hours a day; this could be stored either at the place of work or at home. Upon arrival at the margs or place of duty, weapons and ammunition were issued. All sub-units also picked up sealed containers which held maps of the Real Survival Areas and Tactical Assembly Areas. These could only be opened on a special order. Trucks and cargo carriers proceeded to the ammunition storage site to up-load all of the Brigade's ammunition holdings, while the soldiers mounted their APCs, tanks and self-propelled guns and deployed to the Practice Survival Areas (PSAs). All of the Brigade's units were to be clear of the margs within two hours after the initial alert had been given.

The PSAs were pre-selected field sites scattered around Lahr and Baden so that the Brigade could practise a dispersed posture and limit any damage from enemy air attack. The Real Survival Areas were some distance further out, but these were not used for security reasons. Unit officers, however, normally conducted familiarization visits to these sites once a year, in some cases in civilian clothes. In NORTHAG, dispersion was necessary to limit exposure to a nuclear attack. Down south, the primary threat in times of crisis was an air or missile attack against the airfields at Lahr and Baden. The co-location of the Brigade on the airfields with the fighter aircraft was a dangerous proposition dictated by political considerations. Planners in 4 CMBG developed the survival area concept to enable a quick getaway from these targets, and give the Brigade a fighting chance.

In a real war situation, NATO planning was based on having upwards of 48 hours tactical warning prior to the attack. The Snowball exercises were based on a no-warning situation, which was prudent since enemy aircraft and missile flight time from behind the Iron Curtain was about 20 minutes, barring interception. If a crisis developed more gradually, the NATO Alert System provided for a phased deployment to protect ACE forces as much as possible against surprise. The levels of alert included the State of Military Vigilance, Simple Alert, Reinforced Alert and finally, General Alert at the outbreak of war. The Counter Surprise System included State Orange and State Scarlet and was intended for use in an unexpected crisis. For example, State Orange would require units to deploy to survival areas but not to move forward to the Tactical Assembly or GDP areas. Once the Brigade had cleared the airfields, they would be used to receive three US Air Force reinforcement fighter squadrons flown over from the United States.

Another purpose for the Snowballs, besides ensuring physical survival, was to maintain mental preparedness. It would be stretching things to suggest that everybody in the Brigade believed that every Snowball called could mean the Brigade was going to war; but nobody could ever be 100 per cent certain that war was not about to start. By practising the procedures necessary to deploy, and with great urgency, it became ingrained in 4 Brigade personnel that Snowball meant "Move quickly! Your lives depend on it!" If a crisis situation developed and a Snowball was called, only the Brigade's leadership would know for sure what the real context of the situation was. It was imperative that the attitude "Not another Snowball!" did not develop into operational complacency.

4 CMBG's need to conduct combat operations in conjunction with US and German formations led to the development of a high degree of interoperability during the 1970s. In a NATO context, interoperability was "the ability of systems, units or forces to provide services to and accept services from other systems, units or forces, and to use the services so exchanged to enable them to operate effectively together." The Brigade had been practicing interoperability with the British throughout its service in NORTHAG but these skills and procedures now had to be much further developed in CENTAG so that 4 CMBG could function in its new operational environment.

The Brigade's first formal moves towards interoperability with the US Army started in 1975. The Americans had withdrawn two brigades of the 1st (US) Infantry Division from Europe, leaving only one brigade in place. It appears that the VII (US) Corps commander, General George Blanchard, had developed a contingency plan to 'mate' 4 CMBG and this US brigade if the rest of the 1st (US) Infantry Division were prevented from arriving in theatre in the event of war. 4 CMBG was approached by VII (US) Corps prior to REFORGER 75 about using the exercise to develop information which could be used to create joint Canadian-US Standing Operating Procedures (SOPs).

The essence of interoperability (which became increasingly important throughout the 1970s and into the 1980s) was communications. This was not limited to radio communication, although this was an important part of interoperability. The objective was to develop an understanding with the Americans so that 4 CMBG could be employed properly if it was 'chopped' to VII (US) Corps. The American headquarters under whom 4 CMBG would serve, would have to be well versed in Canadian doctrine, battle procedure and capabilities. On the other hand, 4 CMBG would have to learn how to call in American fire support (artillery, and aircraft) and 'plug in' to the American logistical system. Comparing and comprehending simple things like military language and map symbols were critical to this endeavour. If the Canadian Brigade Group was "grouping" its forces during battle procedure, the Americans had to understand that this was the same as their "task organizing". Similarly, a Canadian Forward Observation Officer was the same as an American Forward Observer, and a US "retrograde action" meant a "withdrawal" to Canadians.

Joint SOPs were only part of interoperability. That ephemeral, non-quantifiable quality called "personality" was the key to creating successful relationships in CENTAG. And, like a piece of equipment, interoperability required regular maintenance. Another important element was the exchange of liaison officers between the formations, either on a full-time or exercise basis. Since 4 CMBG could be tasked to operate with II (GE) Korps as well as VII (US) Corps, permanent Senior Canadian Liaison Officers were established at the headquarters of these two formations in 1974 in Ulm and Stuttgart respectively.

A similar need for better interoperability existed between II (GE) Korps and 4 CMBG but in this case the process of creating joint SOPs was somewhat easier because of the fact that Canadian doctrine and German doctrine had more similarities than Canadian and American doctrine. Additionally, Canadians and Germans tended to adhere more closely to NATO standardization agreements. By 1979, formal documentation on a final Joint SOP was signed between II (GE) Korps and 4 CMBG.

The first German exercise in which 4 CMBG participated in CENTAG was Exercise GUTES OMEN (Good Omen), held from 19 to 24 September 1971; not only was it the first, but GUTES OMEN established 4 CMBG's reputation with the Bundeswehr in CENTAG. [See Figure 5-6.] After working up in the Hohenfels training area on Ex ROCKY MOUNTAIN, 4 CMBG joined II (GE) Korps for their first corps-level exercise since the ill-fated Ex SCHWARZE LOEWE in 1968.

The purpose of Ex GUTES OMEN was to test the newly-implemented Bundeswehr *Jaeger* concept, using 4 Jaeger Division as the 'guinea pig'. The *Jaeger* concept emphasized the use of light mobile forces, (some of them mechanized in M-113s), close up to the border, rather than more heavily mechanized forces used elsewhere by the Bundeswehr. 4 Jaeger Division (consisting of two light infantry brigades and an armoured brigade) and Panzer Regiment 200 (three tank battalions) defended the prosperous 'Blauland' against the standard 'Roteland' invaders. For the purposes of GUTES OMEN, Roteland forces were represented by the troops of 1 Mountain Division (Mountain Brigade 23 and Panzer Grenadier Brigade 24) with 4 CMBG filling in as the third brigade. 4 CMBG also had limited access to a battalion of German *Leopards*.

GUTES OMEN was held in a region which was completely unknown to 4 CMBG units and thus the exercise provided a rigorous test for the Brigade's capabilities in CENTAG. Forming up in the Black Forest around Lahr, 4 CMBG was sandwiched between Mountain Brigade 23 on the left flank, and Panzer Grenadier Brigade 24 on the right. The Blaulanders had an armoured covering force on the FEBA, with the two *Jaeger* brigades in the hilly area of the Schwäbischer Wald behind it. Interestingly, the exercise area was close to being the reverse of the actual II (GE) Korps defensive area, with the mythical Grünland (Switzerland) simulating Austria. Blauland had to plan for a possible "violation" of Grunland neutrality, neatly simulating the real life situation.

Roteland implemented its exercise OPLAN HAGELSCHLAG (Heavy Hail) on 19 September 1971. The enemy objective was a bridgehead on the Donau River north east of Ulm, which was to be reached in four days. To accomplish this, 4 CMBG crossed the Alb River (the exercise FEBA) at night and move through the Blauland border defences,

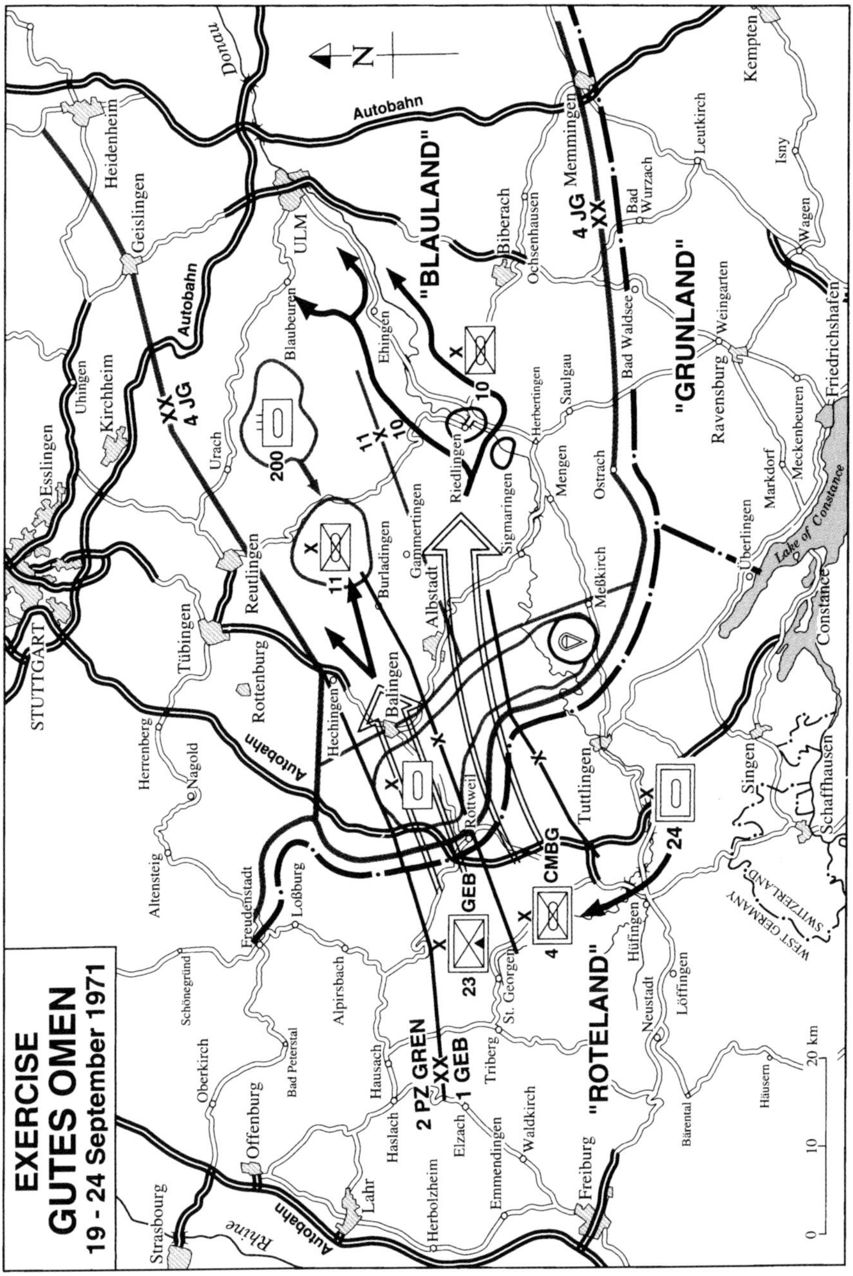
EXERCISE
GUTES OMEN
19 - 24 September 1971
"BLAULAND"
"GRUNLAND"
"ROTELAND"
4 JG
2 PZ GREN
1 GEB
GEB
CMBG
Autobahn
Donau
Rhine
Lake of Constance
STUTTGART
ULM
SWITZERLAND
WEST GERMANY
0 10 20 km

FIGURE 5-6

supported by the other two brigades operating on parallel axes. Diverted by a Roteland airborne drop, Blau forces did not notice that Panzer Grenadier Brigade 24 had moved behind 4 CMBG so that it could exploit any success made by the Canadians. 4 CMBG's initial objectives, crossing sites on the Donau south of Riedlingen, were seized quickly after 4 CMBG cleaved its way through the sparse Blauland covering force, and engineers from Mountain Pioneer Battalion 8 put 4 CMBG's *Centurions* and M-113s across the Donau River.

Blauland had been anticipating that the Roteland point of main effort would be against Jaeger Brigade 11 and had placed its reserve force, Panzer Regiment 200, in position to counter-attack into the area Jaeger Brigade 11 occupied. While Blauland Command was distracted with the efforts of Mountain Brigade 23, 4 CMBG stole the march on Panzer Grenadier Brigade 24 and continued the advance along both sides of the Donau River. The axis of advance on the north bank nearly succeeded in getting in behind Jaeger Brigade 11 while Panzer Regiment 200 was dealing with Mountain Brigade 23. Beating off counterattacks from Jaeger Brigade 10, 4 CMBG was almost into the outskirts of Ulm when endex was called.

GUTES OMEN was by all accounts a successful exercise for 4 CMBG. One report of the action noted that, despite the reductions to 4 CMBG, initiative was still a significant Canadian attribute:

> By late Wednesday the Canadians, in an unstoppable mood, smashed through the last of the opposing defences and were the first Redland forces to reach the Danube River and secure a crossing, one of the main objectives of the exercise…. The battle group's advance was often so fast and effective that time and time again it threw the exercise scenario for a loop. Then, much to the annoyance of the Canadians, umpires would get into the act and impose temporary restrictions on their movement so as to allow the planned plot to catch up with the action.

4 CMBG did not have time to rest on its laurels, and was immediately inserted into Exercise CERTAIN FORGE from 8-15 October 1971, the field portion of the American exercise REFORGER III. This time 4 CMBG operated with the 1st (US) Infantry Division, which had only

one brigade deployed in Germany on a permanent basis. The other brigade was flown over from the United States, married up with its pre-positioned equipment, and set out to fight Redland. For the purposes of CERTAIN FORGE, Redland was represented by two brigades of the 2nd (US) Armoured Division and Panzer Brigade 35 from the Bundeswehr's 12 Panzer Division. CERTAIN FORGE took place between Munich and the Grafenwöhr training area, with Blueland conducting a series of withdrawals across the Isar, Amper, and Donau rivers.

Compared to GUTES OMEN, CERTAIN FORGE was considered by the 4 CMBG staff to be of only limited training value. The reasons for this were numerous. The lack of interoperability with 1st (US) Infantry Division resulted in a great deal of confusion, particularly when 4 CMBG had to call down nuclear fire and did not have the proper codes and communications. The lack of umpire control resulted in 'instantaneous' minefields, 'blown' bridges still capable of supporting the movement of armoured brigades, and other assorted anomalies. The exercise did, however, serve to identify many areas which could be improved by inter-operability arrangements.

After two straight months in the field, 4 CMBG had demonstrated to both the Americans and the Germans that Canadians could operationally fit into CENTAG. Thee was, however, still a lot of work to be done and this continued throughout the 1970s.

Joint exercises in autumn continued to be the centrepiece of 4 CMBG's training in CENTAG, as Major-General Tom de Faye recounts:

> It was a very exciting time for us. The thing that consumed us I think and inspired us and directed most of our efforts were the fall exercises. No doubt about it. The Fallex's had to be the real highlight, and I think that tested us, tested our abilities, in some ways frustrated us – and of course there was a lot of artificiality in it. These were major free play exercises, and I think that we saw them as a visible test against our NATO allies. Its wrong to say anybody won or lost on a REFORGER, but one certainly went through them and assessed oneself quite stringently against what happened....

There was no REFORGER in 1972 because of US budgetary constraints, and II (GE) Korps did not have a corps-level exercise that year either. Fall training activities for 4 CMBG in 1972 included combat team/battle group workups (Exercise CLEAN CUT) in the Grafenwöhr and Hohenfels training areas. Once CLEAN CUT was finished, Airborne Battalion 261 acted as the enemy force for 4 CMBG in Ex CANADIAN CLUB. This training was limited to the area in and around Hohenfels, after which 4 CMBG participated in a VII (US) Corps Command Post Exercise LARGO PASSAGE.

The training pace picked up early in 1973 and 4 CMBG took every exercise opportunity that came available. During a biennial NATO CPX, WINTEX 73, 4 CMBG worked with II (GE) Korps. For the purposes of the exercise, the Brigade had Panzer Regiment 200 under command. Panzer Regiment 200 was a large organization and it was heady stuff to have over one hundred *Leopards* supporting 4 CMBG. It was on WINTEX 73 that 4 CMBG's leadership encountered one of the Bundeswehr's more colourful individuals, as Captain Dave Holt observed:

> It was 1973, the brigade was on an exercise of the command post type....Panzer Regiment 200, a unit of three battalions of tanks from the II (GE) Korps reserve was placed under command for a counter-attack task. Brigadier-General Pat Grieve had just given his orders for the mission and had attached 3 Mech Commando to the Panzer Regiment for support. The CO of 3 Mech Commando was Lieutenant-Colonel Mike Barr. At the end of orders the commander of the Panzer Regiment, Colonel von Rodde, a man who actually looked like and really was a survivor of the Eastern Front, complete with missing hand and a patch over the right eye, moved over to the map to sort of review his plan. All eyes were on him as he stood before the great chart, breathlessly awaiting for something magic from this venerable old soldier....
>
> 'Well Colonel', said Barr, 'How do you see this going down?' 'Ach, Ja!' said the Colonel. 'I will send der zwei hundert and zehn hier, und der zwei hundert dreizig hier,' he said, gesticulating the routes out on the map with his good hand. 'Ah, Colonel', said Mike, 'What can I do for you with my battalion?' The Colonel fixed Mike with his good eye and snorted, 'Nussink!' As if infantry could do anything useful for him!

CHAPTER FIVE

The 'missing' REFORGER exercise, REFORGER IV, was run in January. As in the previous REFORGER, the field training portion (Exercise CERTAIN SHIELD) tested the flyover elements of 1st (US) Infantry Division and the 2nd (US) Armoured Division. The Orange forces were 4 CMBG and their *alte Kamaraden*, Panzer Regiment 200. Militia augmentation from Canada continued to add to 4 CMBG's numbers and 200 gunners, drivers, and signallers flew over to Lahr to join the Brigade. To provide more weight to the Orangelanders, elements of the 1st (US) Armoured Division were added. Again, as in REFORGER III, the exercise was pre-scripted and 4 CMBG was supposed to lose in the face of valiant Blueland resistance. In an orders group, Brigadier-General Pat Grieve told his commanders: "We're not programmed to win, but we can make it damned uncomfortable for them and we don't intend to lose gracefully!"

CERTAIN SHIELD continued the early 1970s tradition of exercise unreality, which frustrated Canadian troops who were accustomed to what they considered to be more professional exercises in NORTHAG.

One such example was a US mechanized infantry attack near the town of Bernsfeld. An error on the part of the US commander sent the American APCs into the attack first, where they were confronted by the *Centurion* tanks of the RCD. Umpires ruled that the Americans suffered heavy casualties and must withdraw. The practicalities of the situation were such that it was physically impossible for the US commander to get his huge number of tracked and wheeled vehicles through the village. After consultation, the Canadians withdrew. They had won the battle but were denied the ground.

Other problems with CERTAIN SHIELD included the unrealistic starting dispositions of the two sides in the exercise. There was no covering force battle play. Both sides were simply positioned nose to nose and the orders came down to "go at it".

REFORGER IV was memorable for Corporal Robert Neilson and Captain Barry Hamilton of 4 CMBG Headquarters and Signal Squadron. A US liaison detachment co-located with HQ 4 CMBG became trapped inside their APC which had caught fire. Seeing that the hatch was blocked by a camouflage net, Corporal Neilson cut the net away and pulled out two Americans. Captain Hamilton saw that the APC was parked beside a barn which contained explosive material. He then opened the rear hatch, forced his way through the smoke, started the machine and drove it away from the barn. Both received praise from General Grieve and the lasting gratitude from the American liaison detachment.

Exercises in the fall of 1973 were modeled on the 1971 exercise year. Exercise POWER PLAY in Hohenfels was only a warm up. After a river-crossing exercise, DONAU DASH, 4 CMBG was asked by the Bundeswehr to assist in training one of the new home defence brigades in the Munich area. Before proceeding onto Exercise RAUB VOGEL, militia flyover once again augmented 4 CMBG. While simulating a Soviet motor rifle division, the Brigade continued to demonstrate the sort of initiative Canadians had a reputation for. According to Terry O'Connor of the RCD:

> The fighting in RAUB VOGEL moved so quickly that many of the enemy were bypassed by the advancing *Lynx* and tanks and they posed a very real rear area threat to the rest of the regiment, [Headquarters Squadron and the Regimental Headquarters....] We were driving along when suddenly I saw three German soldiers standing beside a *Gasthaus*. After a bit of confusion, we captured them, sticking them into the back of the ambulance. We had just started off when a truck with four German engineers came over the hill. I cut them off though, the same way Steve McQueen did in the movie 'Bullitt'. I always knew that technique would come in handy...

The busy training year climaxed with REFORGER V (Exercise CERTAIN CHARGE) which was held from 10 to 16 October 1973. Once again operating with 1st (US) Infantry Division, 4 CMBG deployed against 3rd (US) Infantry Division and Panzer Brigade 29 in an area west of Nürnberg

CERTAIN CHARGE was a considerably better exercise for 4 CMBG than previous REFORGERS. At various times, 4 CMBG had under command either an American infantry or armoured battalion, as well as AH-1G *Cobra* attack helicopters and close support aircraft. At one point, the entire Panzer Brigade was destroyed by 4 CMBG in a furious defensive battle and in several cases, successful passage of lines with brigades from 1st Infantry Division were conducted at night. Significantly,

4 CMBG was able to "interface" effectively with the American supply system.

A special US unit was employed by 4 CMBG during CERTAIN CHARGE: the 337th Army Security Agency Company, an electronic warfare unit. With the assistance of the 337th, 4 CMBG was able to capture enemy recce teams in the 4 CMBG area and thus deprive the enemy of valuable movements information. Two messages emanating from the recce teams described *Centurion* tanks. A quick check on which Canadian units were moving at the time indicated the most likely location of the teams and the enemy was 'put in the bag' in just under one hour after the intercept had taken place! Thanks to the signals 'spooks', 4 CMBG was able to react in a more timely manner to some enemy actions during the exercise, most notably enemy nuclear fire operations. With this information, 4 CMBG was able to avoid at least one nuclear strike. This EW capability would become standard for 4 CMBG on future REFORGERS.

Despite these positive points, major command and control problems continued to exist between 4 CMBG and 1st (US) Infantry Division. For example, the use of ZULU time confused 1st Division planners who had just stepped off their C-141 aircraft. Codes and frequencies were not passed on to 4 CMBG and, more importantly, two friendly nuclear strikes took place in 4 CMBG's defensive area without 4 CMBG being informed of the event, resulting in the loss of an entire infantry battalion. In sum, CERTAIN CHARGE continued to emphasize the need for better interoperability.

The next instalment in the REFORGER series was the main focus of 4 CMBG's training efforts in 1974. Ex CERTAIN PLEDGE, the FTX portion of REFORGER 74, paired 4 CMBG with the 1st (US) Armored Division against their former allies, 1st (US) Infantry Division and Panzer Brigade 30. Now under the command of Brigadier-General Charles Belzile, 4 CMBG took the offensive as part of the Orange forces in the Stuttgart-Ulm-Munich-Nürnberg area. Once again, C-141 transports disgorged soldiers of 1st (US) Infantry Division for the longest REFORGER yet – 11 days. True to form, 4 CMBG confounded the enemy in a series of night operations culminating in a deep penetration of the Blueland defensive positions.

Interestingly, there was some French Army participation in CERTAIN PLEDGE, to the surprise of the Canadian staff:

> [there] was the capture of two French LRRP [long range reconnaissance patrol] teams who had been captured and held by Blue forces for two days and were recaptured by 4 CMBG. These people seemed pleased to be able to talk to someone in French and in fact talked at great length. They were eventually turned over to the umpires who seemed reluctant to take them....

Despite the horrible weather, CERTAIN PLEDGE was rated by 4 CMBG as an improvement over previous REFORGERS. This time there was a realistic covering force battle and interoperability, though by no means perfect, was improving. US units attached to 4 CMBG included an armoured battalion, an 8-inch artillery battalion, an engineer company and some air defence assets. All worked well under Canadian command.

It would appear at first glance that 4 CMBG was often used by the Americans as a training tool on these large exercises, and in fact this criticism was constantly levelled by some Canadians regarding 4 CMBG's participation. The situation, however, was different in CENTAG from that in NORTHAG. Since 4 CMBG was no longer guaranteed training areas and time, every opportunity had to be exploited so that 4 CMBG could maintain its operational effectiveness. This last point was critical. The quality of the US forces in CENTAG (which provided a good 50 per cent of the forces deployed there) was not especially high in the 1970s. Drugs and racism were rampant and the divisive effects of the Vietnam war were causing a lot of damage. In fact, V (US) Corps and VII (US) Corps were generally viewed by the US Army as a vast replacement depot for Vietnam, with troops in Europe being 'levied' for service in Southeast Asia. Consequently, anything that could be done to assist the Americans in maintaining their edge in Europe would benefit CENTAG's ability to resist enemy attack, and thus contribute to deterrence. This included the rigorous training that 4 CMBG contributed during the fall exercises.

It is also important to note why 4 CMBG was able to be so successful in these exercises. Given that 4 CMBG was a formation smaller than a true brigade group, and given that the exercises had a finite duration, 4 CMBG appeared more effective in the exercises than would have been the case in real life. 4 CMBG could, on the REFORGER exercises, conduct sustained operations without fear of logistical disruption. The need to provide reinforcement and sustainment forces never entered into the equation in the 1970s REFORGERS. Thus, 4 CMBG could 'reconstitute' quickly after 'taking casualties', never having to worry about replacing 'killed' soldiers with replacements. Trained tank and gun crews and infantry sections (understrength as they were in real life: on some exercises tanks had only two crewmen in them) remained intact after 'destruction'. These observations should, however, be balanced with other factors. Canadian initiative was rarely in short supply, and the willingness of the well-trained commanders at all levels to improvise with understrength units and obsolete equipment in the pressure cooker of the exercises, also in part accounts for Canadian success.

It was with great satisfaction that 4 CMBG was invited to work with II (GE) Korps on Exercise GROSSE ROCHADE in 1975. GROSSE ROCHADE demonstrated how well the Germans understood 4 CMBG's capabilities and how to employ it properly in a corps-level battle. [See Figure 5-7.] 4 CMBG once again was cast in the role as the Red Force aggressor, along with the three brigades (10, 11 and 12) of 4 Jaeger Division; 7 Panzer Division was 'CPX'd' while the other units conducted real manoeuvre. Blue forces were multinational in composition but based for the most part on II (GE) Korps. Airborne Brigade 25 and Home Defence Brigade 18 represented an airborne division, and a notional 4 Jaeger Division was placed opposite 7 Panzer Division. A US mechanized brigade and 10 Panzer Division were the counter-attack force, while a French armoured regiment acted as a covering force on the right flank.

The Red force task was daunting. Blue forces held the west bank of the Donau River, so any attack would have to be an assault river crossing. Red put in a frontal assault against the Airborne Division using Jaeger Brigades, 10 and 11. After a day of vicious fighting, Red secured crossing sites and had pushed the paratroopers back ten kilometers from the river. Blue reacted immediately. Noting that the notional 4 Jaeger division was successfully holding off Red's 7 Panzer Division in the CPX, the American brigade and two armoured brigades from 10 Panzer

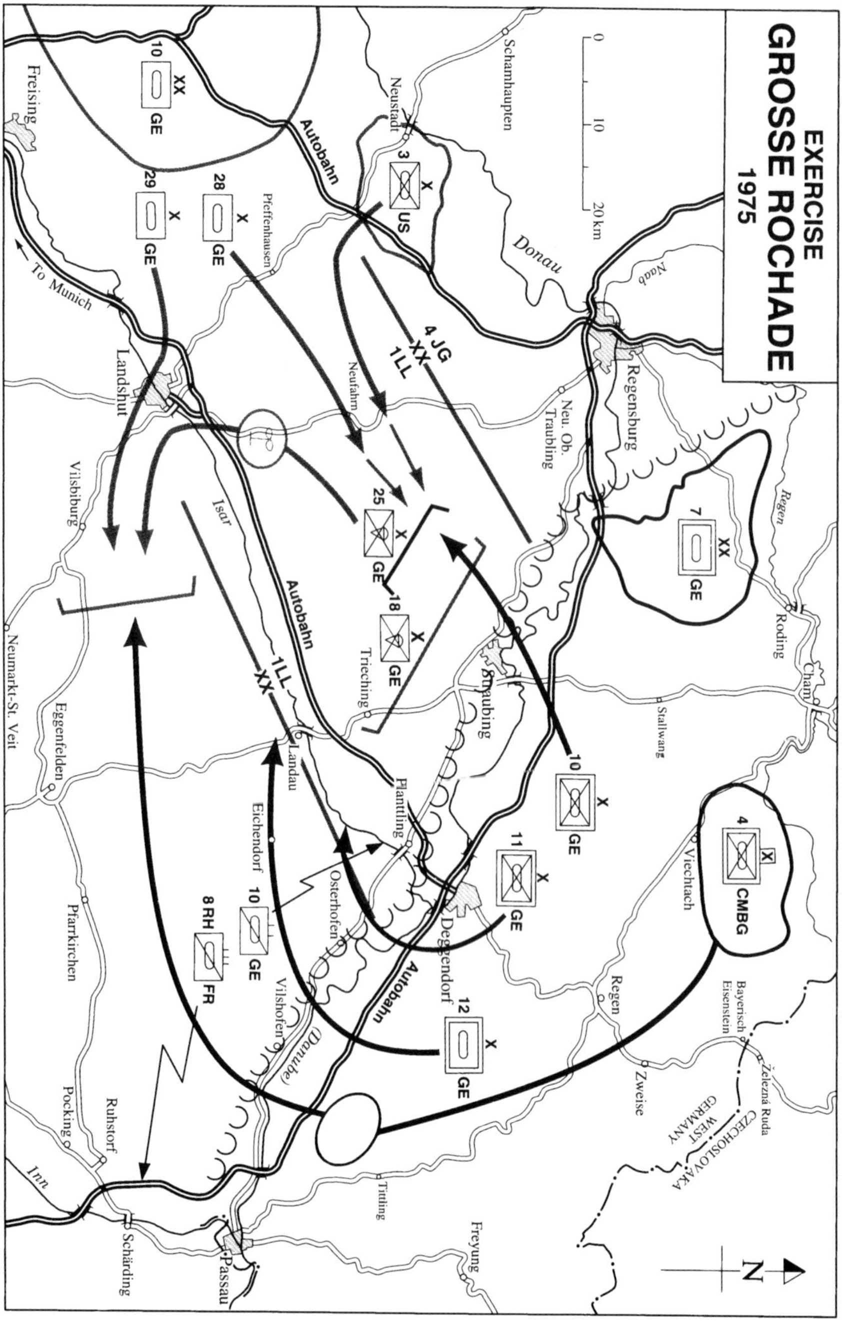
EXERCISE
GROSSE ROCHADE
1975
0
10
20 km
Schamhaupten
Neustadt
Donau
Naab
Regensburg
Regen
Roding
Cham
Stallwang
Viechtach
Bayerisch Eisenstein
Železná Ruda
CZECHOSLOVAKIA
WEST GERMANY
Zweise
Regen
Freyung
Titling
Passau
Schärding
Inn
Ruhstorf
Pocking
Pfarrkirchen
Eggenfelden
Neumarkt-St. Veit
Vilsbiburg
Landshut
To Munich
Freising
Pfeffenhausen
Neufahrn
Neu. Ob. Traubing
Straubing
Triefching
Landau
Eichendorf
Osterhofen
Vilshofen
(Danube)
Plattling
Deggendorf
Isar
Autobahn
Autobahn
Autobahn
4 JG
XX
1LL
1LL
XX
10 XX GE
29 X GE
28 X GE
3 X US
25 X GE
18 X GE
7 XX GE
10 X GE
11 X GE
12 X GE
4 X CMBG
10 GE
8 RH FR

FIGURE 5-7

Division were committed to push the Jaegers back into the Donau River.

4 CMBG's location had been carefully concealed from Blue's view, while Blue was deceived into believing that Panzer Brigade 12 had been committed against Blue's counter-attack force in the Airborne Division sector. This deception was complete. In a long road march, 4 CMBG swung down to the south and was employed with Panzer Brigade 12 against the thinly stretched French recce regiment northwest of Passau. After gaining virtually unopposed lodgments in an assault crossing over the Donau, 4 CMBG turned the flank of the hard-pressed airborne force and its reinforcing armour from 10 Panzer Division. Even after reconstituting 10 kilometers back and being reinforced by helicopter-borne forces, Blue was barely able to halt 4 CMBG's advance as endex was called.

GROSSE ROCHADE was not a 'scripted' exercise, and allowed for a great deal of free play, a condition sought after in exercises of that scale. This allowed exceptional leeway in the employment of forces, and was a situation that 4 Brigade always favoured. After GROSSE ROCHADE, it was said that the Germans added a new step to their battle procedure: locate the Canadians before doing anything else. If they are part of the enemy force, they will be used creatively. If they are part of the friendly force, they must be used very carefully!

4 CMBG deployed from GROSSE ROCHADE to REFORGER 75 (Exercise CERTAIN TREK) in October 1975. Held from 14 to 23 October 1975 in the Würzburg area north of Nürnberg, CERTAIN TREK pitted the 3rd (US) Infantry Division and Panzer Brigade 36 against the Blue Forces, represented by 4 CMBG, a US armoured brigade, 2nd Armoured Cavalry Regiment (a brigade-sized recce formation) and 1st (US) Infantry Division.

REFORGER 75 served a dual purpose. In addition to acting as a demonstration of US reinforcement capability and as an annual NATO training event, REFORGER 75 tested some concepts that were part of a new US operational doctrine called "Active Defense". By 1975 with the war in Vietnam over, the Americans had perceived the need to improve the effectiveness of their army contribution to the Central Region. NATO's shift away from tactical nuclear use also had occurred (on paper in 1968) but, as we have seen, it took some time for the forces on the ground to shift their operational thinking to more conventional defence. Active

Defense was the US Army's response to this changed strategic thinking; it was seen as a new way of harnessing substantially increased battlefield mobility with the new and far more effective conventional weapons that had recently been developed, such as the TOW ATGM and the attack helicopter.

Active Defense had several attributes, among which were the increased use of airmobile forces, and their integration into the land based forces at the brigade and divisional level. More emphasis was placed on the covering force battle, and the Armored Cavalry Regiments that were part of V (US) and VII (US) Corps were converted from pure recce into armour-attrition formations. There were no more static defensive positions neatly lined-up. Instead there were a myriad of "defended localities", often unsupported and unconnected. A fluid battle with no defined front was envisaged.

4 CMBG would eventually play an important role in the test of Active Defense during REFORGER 76, but in the course of REFORGER 75 Canadians detected no real change in US doctrine short of the addition of a covering force battle. Ex CERTAIN TREK employed 4 CMBG as part of the defending Blue forces, which provided them with a grandstand view of 2nd Armored Cavalry Regiment's operations, but "it [was] not possible to assess the effectiveness of forward flexible defence, [and] its application on the ground was not evident to 4 CMBG umpires".

Not surprisingly, 4 CMBG operations were quite effective in the counter-attack portion of CERTAIN TREK. Actions by the recce squadron were "particularly effective", as was a dismounted infantry night attack supported by tanks: "One counter-attack on a particularly dark night was very skilfully executed and would have been successful despite umpires!".

The evolution of 4 CMBG's organization continued throughout the 1970s. The L-19 spotting aircraft and the CH-112 helicopters continued to provide service in 4 CMBG until 1972. On 1 October of that year, in line with overall CF restructuring, the Air OP Troop of the RCHA, the Air Recce Troop of the RCD, the Command and Liaison Flight of Headquarters and Signals Squadron, and the Aircraft Servicing Platoon of 4 Service Battalion were consolidated into the newly resurrected 444 Tactical Helicopter Squadron of the CF "air element". The L-19s and CH 112s were retired and replaced by Bell CH 136 *Kiowa* helicopters which had arrived in Lahr earlier that May. "Triple Four" Squadron now joined 4 CMBG as its integral light helicopter capability. In addition to retaining the traditional roles of its predecessor elements, 444 Squadron assumed the important task of co-ordinating all tactical aviation resources assigned to the 4 CMBG area of responsibility, particularly the integration of attack helicopters of other Allied armies.

One very important change was implemented by Brigadier-General Grieve after he took command of 4 CMBG in July 1972. 4 Canadian Mechanized Battle Group once again became 4 Canadian Mechanized Brigade Group:

> In 1972, none of our allies knew what a 'battle group' was. Most assumed it was a reinforced battalion rather than a Brigade Group. I sought the support of [Chief of Defence Staff, General] Dextraze, to revert to the former title of 4 Canadian Mechanized Brigade Group, which he supported. This may seem a minor point but it had a great positive reaction from our US and German allies.

Other changes were in the offing. In the fall of 1974, more cuts to the Canadian Forces were announced. Disturbed by the continual chipping away at the operational capability of the army, General Dextraze informed the Minister of National Defence, James Richardson, that

> [the Armed Forces] could not reduce below that assigned level without running a grave risk of being unable to carry out all of our assigned tasks as well as denuding the Canadian military profession to an unacceptable point....Any further loss of basic combat capability should be in response to basic defence policies, and not just current budgetary objectives....

In May 1975 Pierre Trudeau was persuaded that the situation was serious enough to establish a Defence Structure Review. This review was conducted by the Cabinet with consultation from the Department of National Defence. With firm support from General Dextraze, the Deputy Minister, Sylvain Cloutier and Mr. Richardson, the ongoing erosion of the Army was arrested. The conclusions of the review, announced in

November 1975, recommended that more money should be spent on equipment programmes to maintain the existing capability, but not to increase it. This conclusion was accepted by Trudeau after significant pressure was brought to bear by Germany and other NATO nations.

The impact of the review on 4 CMBG was very significant. Up to 1975-76, 4 CMBG was equipped with essentially the same equipment it had when it left NORTHAG, and some of this equipment was showing its age. Stories are legion about the state of the *Centurion* tanks in the early 1970s. By this time, the *Centurion* was well behind the curve in main battle tank development, having been replaced by the *Chieftain* in the British Army in the late 1960s. Spare parts were scarce, particularly for the transmission, and this sometimes gave rise to a situation called 'Mexican Overdrive' as reported by journalist Gerald Porter:

> While mechanics strained and invented new ways to keep the *Centurions* alive, tank drivers practiced the infamous 'Mexican shift' to keep them under control. This tricky procedure (trying to get back into gear after the tank went into neutral) compensated for worn transmission linkages that could no longer be replaced because of age. On Exercise CERTAIN TREK in October 1975, a driver lost control of his tank when he missed the shift, which had to be made before the tank was rolling too fast. The *Centurion* careened wildly down a steep hill, injuring three crewman who jumped from the runaway monster. One suffered paralysis from a spinal injury.

Incidents like these prompted the implementation of a *Centurion* rebuild programme, a service provided to Canada by the Netherlands. The Dutch also used the *Centurion* and had developed a respectable plan to extend the life of their vehicles. From 1974 to 1976, 4 CMBG's *Centurions* were rotated through 574 Tank Workshop in the Netherlands.

The decision to replace he *Centurion* tank with the German *Leopard* series was complicated by a number of political factors, notably the belief by some of Trudeau's advisors that tanks were "offensive" weapons and a potentially destabilizing factor in East-West relations. Pressure from Germany in the form of threatened trade restrictions as well as some behind the scenes manoeuvring by the CDS, General Dextraze, forced the issue and the decision to acquire the *Leopards* was implemented.

This lead to the 'rent-a-tank' agreement whereby 4 CMBG borrowed two squadrons of Bundeswehr *Leopard* A2 tanks. These tanks served from March 1977 to October 1978. Once the production *Leopard* A3's were ready for Canada in November 1978, the rentals were returned (Canada redesignated the A3 as the C1). One hundred twenty-six *Leopard* C-1s and other *Leopard* family vehicles were acquired, including armoured recovery vehicles (ARV), bridge layers (AVLB) and armoured engineer vehicles (AEV). Of the main battle tanks (MBT), three squadrons worth (59) were assigned to the RCD (only two squadrons were manned; the third squadron's tanks went into storage for the flyover troops) and the rest were sent to Canada. Two AEVs and two AVLBs went to the brigade engineers, and 4 Service Battalion received the ARVs.

The M-113 family was still able to serve in its capacity as 'battlefield taxi' but the Brigade's wheeled vehicles were showing their age. In 1976, the first Chevrolet one-and-a-quarter-ton trucks, the civilian pattern 'five quad', were introduced into 4 CMBG. The five quads replaced the remaining 3/4 ton trucks and the ambulances and would continue to serve 4 CMBG through the rest of its existence, despite their lack of ruggedness and considerable maintenance burden.

Other equipment problems remained, however. Since 4 CMBG was supposed to operate as a semi-independent formation, it could not always draw on a higher formation all the time for air defence resources. There were no air defence units in the Canadian army, leaving 4 CMBG vulnerable to enemy air attack once it left Lahr and Baden. This had to be remedied.

In January 1976, two airfield defence batteries were formed, 128 Air Defence Battery at Baden and 129 Air Defence Battery at Lahr. These units were equipped with 40mm *Boffin* anti-aircraft guns removed from HMCS *Bonaventure* when she was scrapped in 1970. Although not brigade resources, the air defence batteries provided some personnel for the first Air Defence Troop formed in September 1977. This Air Defence Troop was equipped with the man-portable *Blowpipe* very low level, surface-to-air missile. Eventually called 127 Air Defence Battery, 4 CMBG finally received some modicum of protection from the vast enemy air threat.

The Brigade artillery, 1 RCHA, saw other areas of improvement. By 1977, the M-109 self-propelled guns were upgraded to M-109A1 standard. Late in 1977 a decision was made to increase the number of artillery batteries from three to four, and in August 1978, Z Battery was added to 1 RCHA for a total of 24 guns. Z Battery was a flyover organization like C Squadron RCD with its equipment maintained in Germany and the soldiers based in Canada.

There were also several important changes in the infantry. 3 Mechanized Commando officially became 3rd Battalion, The Royal Canadian Regiment in July of 1977. Prior to that, 3 Mechanized Commando and 1R22eR took delivery of the Tube-launched, Optically-tracked, Wire-guided (TOW) anti-tank guided missile system. Mounted on a pedestal on M-113 APCs, TOW had proven itself during the 1973 Yom Kippur War. The 36 launchers dramatically increased the anti-tank capability of the Brigade. The aging SS-11B1 systems were given to Portugal.

Other Brigade combat support and service support units changed their designations. 4 Combat Medical Support Unit was re-named 4 Field Ambulance and given a wider responsibility for battlefield medical support. The engineer organization, at one point called 4 Field Squadron, was changed to 4 Field Engineer Squadron in 1976, and in 1977 it was finally changed to 4 Combat Engineer Regiment, although the strength remained virtually unchanged. 4 Military Police Platoon was also formed as a separate unit in 1976, separating from the 4 Service Battalion organization.

The move to CENTAG dictated a number of changes to 4 CMBG's signals and communications system. In NORTHAG, 4 CMBG had operated a mix of British and American systems. By 1971, the BRUIN secure trunk system was discarded and the Brigade acquired US equipment that gave 4 CMBG a secure trunk line capability between Brigade Headquarters and the divisional level. A secure trunk line also existed between the Service Battalion and 4 CMBG HQ. New radio relay equipment and the US-made NESTOR secure voice device was acquired for the vehicle radios, thus giving 4 CMBG a secure Brigade command net.

Canadian signallers had to be flexible when operating in the new CENTAG environment. Though the problems with a crowded electromagnetic spectrum and 'dirty' radios were no different than the problems in NORTHAG, operating with new and unfamiliar formations sometimes taxed the 4 CMBG communicators. At one point during WINTEX 73, 4 CMBG saved the day. Lieutenant-Colonel Paul Coderre of 4 CMBG Headquarters and Signals Squadron explained:

> When the Brigade deployed to the field, normally the higher formation we were working with was supposed to provide a communications liaison detachment to the lower formations, like 4 CMBG. In CENTAG, we usually provided to the higher formation, that is, we sent a communications van and liaison people to Division to send down information emanating from there.... [During WINTEX 73] we were connected to CENTAG and the probability was high that we would be chopped to VII (US) Corps, so we sent equipment to connect with their telex through the *Deutches Bundespost* [the German Post Office which also handles telephones in Germany]. We were in contact with CENTAG and we were going to drop CENTAG and pick up VII Corps, which we did. We were now holding both headquarters with our equipment, and then we got chopped to II (GE) Korps! Then CENTAG's communications failed! For 48 hours, 4 CMBG was the only means of communication between CENTAG, VII (US) Corps and II (GE) Korps! The heat from our equipment was so great that the snow around us was melting....

As in previous years, elements of the Brigade were called upon to assist in disaster relief of a NATO ally. In May 1976 earthquakes ravaged northern Italy and the Italian government appealed for help. A force of 300 officers and men was despatched from 4 CMBG units in an operation dubbed DOLOMITE. Personnel and equipment from 4 Combat Medical Support Unit, 4 Combat Engineer Regiment and 444 Tactical Helicopter Squadron were rushed by C-130 Hercules to Rivolto Airbase near Venice. From there, the DOLOMITE team headed to the villages of Venzone, Gemona, Sante Daniele and Maiano, which were almost leveled. Water was purified, roads were cleared, power was restored and lives were saved. Tragically, 'Triple Four' Squadron lost a *Kiowa* in the operation and the pilot, Captain Buck McBride was posthumously awarded an Italian bravery decoration. Although Canadian Forces Europe received the credit from the Italians for mounting the relief effort, the officers and soldiers who performed hard work under primitive conditions for the better part of a month were justifiably proud of their part in assisting in the operation.

Exercises and training continued to be 4 CMBG's focus in the latter half of the 1970s, and one of the more important was REFORGER 76. REFORGER 76 was somewhat different from the earlier REFORGERs in that the aim and scope of the exercise was far greater:

> Prior exercises had as their central theme a US national effort to demonstrate a firm resolve to honour the reinforcement commitment. In REFORGER 76, SACEUR wanted a multi-national series of exercises to take place concurrently in areas ranging from NATO's southern to its northern flank....The REFORGER series, by the completion of the 1976 exercise, had grown to encompass political and operational considerations which transcended the original theme of return of forces to Germany. REFORGER units participated in four major FTXs, two of which were in the NORTHAG area of operations, clearly establishing that REFORGER had become an integral part of the overall defence of Europe.

This expanded NATO-wide exercise concept was called AUTUMN FORGE and included Exercise GORDIAN SHIELD (V (US) Corps), Exercise LARES TEAM (VII (US) CORPS), Exercise GROSSER BAER (I (GE) Korps), Exercise COOL GIN and Exercise SPEAR POINT (BAOR), and Exercise BLAUWE DIEMEL (I (BE) Corps). The finale was a nuclear CPX called ABLE ARCHER. Thus, 4 CMBG found itself participating in an annual show of force and commitment, as well as gaining valuable training and increased cooperation from its allies. The Autumn Forge series of exercises undoubtedly contributed to deterrence, given the scale and the widespread publicity of the Fallexs.

As noted earlier, REFORGER 76 also served to exercise the Americans' new Active Defense doctrine, and this was rigorously tested in Exercise LARES TEAM, held 10-20 September 1976. In addition to 1st (US) Infantry Division, the 101st Airborne Division (Airmobile) was also brought to Germany as part of REFORGER. The 101st was equipped with two light infantry brigades, light artillery, transport and attack helicopters. The objective of LARES TEAM was to determine how well

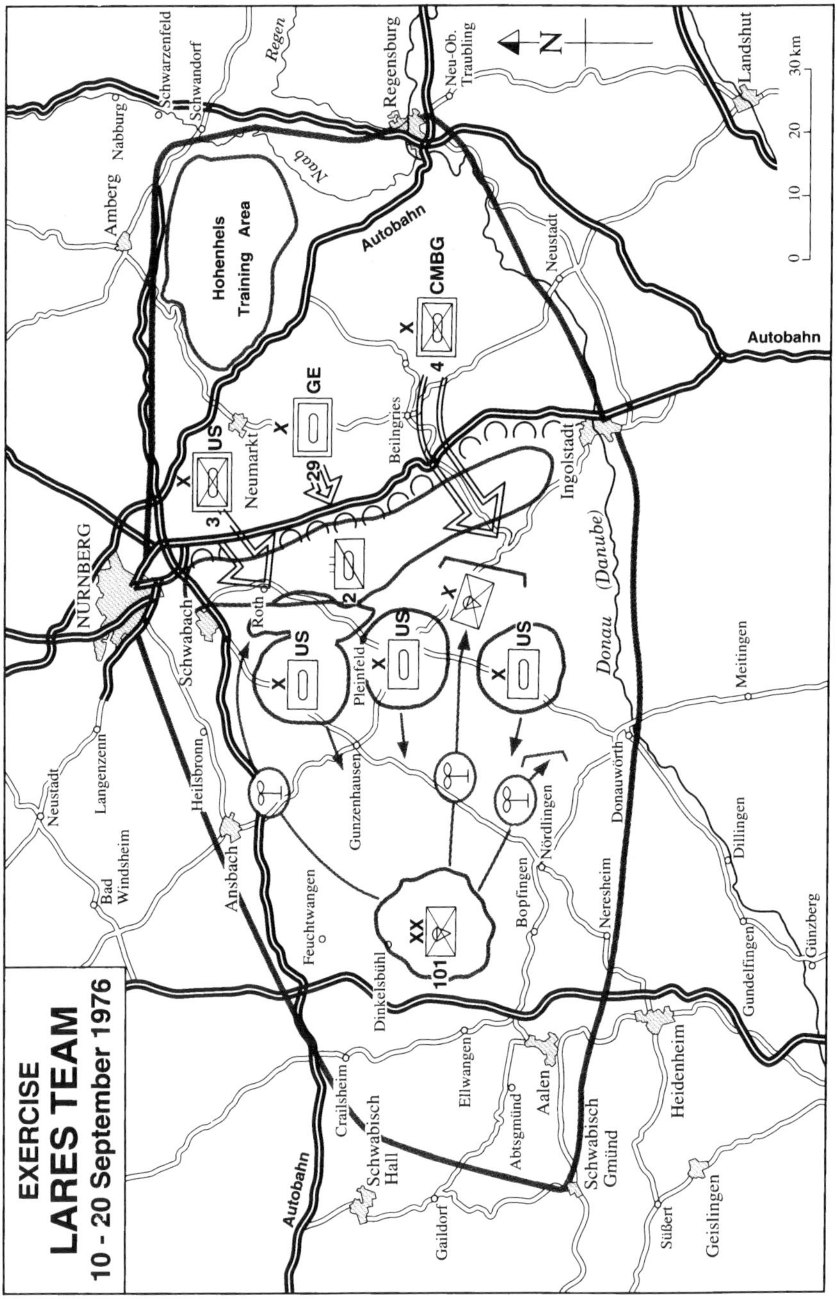
EXERCISE
LARES TEAM
10 - 20 September 1976
Hohenhels Training Area
Autobahn
Autobahn
Autobahn
CMBG
GE
US
US
US
US
XX
101
Regen
Naab
Donau
(Danube)
NÜRNBERG
Schwarzenfeld
Schwandorf
Nabburg
Amberg
Regensburg
Neu-Ob. Traubling
Landshut
Neustadt
Beilngries
Neumarkt
Ingolstadt
Roth
Schwabach
Pleinfeld
Gunzenhausen
Heilsbronn
Langenzenn
Neustadt
Bad Windsheim
Ansbach
Feuchtwangen
Dinkelsbühl
Crailsheim
Schwäbisch Hall
Gaildorf
Ellwangen
Abtsgmünd
Aalen
Schwäbisch Gmünd
Bopfingen
Nördlingen
Neresheim
Donauwörth
Meitingen
Dillingen
Gundelfingen
Günzberg
Heidenheim
Süßert
Geislingen
0 10 20 30 km

FIGURE 5-8

light infantry formations armed with tripod-mounted TOW anti-tank missiles and transported about by helicopter could function on the armour and mechanized-heavy battlefield of the Central Region.

An experienced enemy force was needed so that the exercise could be as valid as possible. 4 CMBG and Panzer Brigade 29 were selected, and they operated with the 1st (US) Infantry Division as the Orange Army. Blue consisted of 2nd Armored Cavalry Regiment, 1st (US) Armored Division, with the 101st Airborne Division acting as the Corps reserve. [See Figure 5-8.]

Blue's plan was for 2nd ACR to absorb as much of Orange's assault as possible and then conduct a rearward passage of lines with the brigades from 1st (US) Armored Division, which were right behind the covering force. After the enemy had come into contact with the 1st (US) Armored Division and perhaps had broken through in some places, the two brigades from the 101st were to be inserted by helicopter to form defensive positions through which the 1st (US) Armored Division would pass, re-group and then counter-attack. The enemy would then come into contact with the 101st Airborne Division's brigades. The six infantry battalions from these brigades were each equipped with 18 TOW anti-tank missile launchers in addition to their light infantry companies, and it was hoped that these would severely damage the Orangelanders' armour-heavy force.

What actually happened bore close resemblance to the plan, except for the last part. Panzer Brigade 29 and the US mechanized brigade moved against 2 ACR, while 4 CMBG punched through in the south. To plug the gap, a brigade from the 101st was inserted to stop 4 CMBG. 4 CMBG immediately engaged one battalion from the airmobile brigade while it was unloading from it helicopters. Before the second battalion could set up its TOW launchers, it too was overrun. The 101st's artillery unit had just landed and was unloading when it was caught flatfooted not once, but twice. Only the timely intervention by *Cobra* helicopter gunships halted 4 CMBG in its tracks, as it had out-run its anti-air defences.

To increase the pressure on Orangeland, two battalions of US Army Rangers were inserted into Orange's rear area, to little effect: Brigadier-General Jack Vance, who was commanding 4 CMBG felt that this constituted no real threat and took no action except to bypass where necessary:

CHAPTER FIVE

They were trying to see how well an airmobile force would work in a high intensity battleground.... By the end of it it was quite clear that the world of the high-intensity battlefield was not a safe place for the air assault division. They were not able to hold ground. They were not able to stop heavy forces, assaults, and advances. Their lack of experience in amalgamating with and integrating with mechanized forces was not advanced at all, and the result was that they were being deeply penetrated. The last phase of the exercise was supposed to have been an enemy airborne battalion group landing, but it was eventually called off because my recce squadron had already captured the US divisional headquarters. It was a fairly painful affair. I thought it was a good exercise....

It was clear that mechanized forces mounted in APCs could avoid the light infantry forces who never had enough helicopter lift or organic mobility to move them all at once; mechanized forces could keep moving and keep out of range while continuing to penetrate into the rear area. The effectiveness of the *Cobra* attack helicopters was never in question, however.

After LARES TEAM, the Americans modified their doctrine for the employment of airmobile forces, and this ultimately became part of their new AirLand Battle doctrine in the 1980s. Henceforth, large airmobile light infantry formations would never be used again in the Central Region, although the use of attack helicopters in the anti-tank role was proven as a valid concept and implemented. 4 CMBG can justifiably take some credit in pointing out some of the deficiencies in Active Defense and in helping refine US Army doctrine.

In 1977, the citizens of Lahr and Rastatt were disturbed to wake up one morning and see Canadian soldiers pour out of trucks and jeeps, knock down doors and drag off apparently normal citizens. Later, M-113 APCs and *Centurion* tanks rolled through the streets with unfamiliar tactical markings painted on, headed for the Rastatt museum. What was going on? A FIBUA exercise run amok?

Things were eventually clarified for the alarmed populace. If one looked closely, the familiar faces of actors Peter O'Toole, David Hemmings and Donald Pleasence could be seem amongst the deployed troops. The Department of National Defence had allowed the film crew of the movie *Power Play* to have access to DND units and facilities. Rastatt and Lahr acted as the 'capital city' of an unnamed country subjected to a military coup d'état, with Peter O'Toole riding a *Centurion* tank in a successful effort to seize control from the 'civil authorities'. This movie was based on Edward Luttwak's *Coup d etat: A Practical Handbook*. Despite the outstanding support provided to the film makers by 4 Brigade, the movie bombed at the box office.

Once again to the field! After the usual work-ups in Hohenfels, 4 CMBG deployed south of Stuttgart for REFORGER 77. This exercise demonstrated the ever-growing importance of large-scale fall exercises in NATO. As with the previous year's exercises, REFORGER 77 was NATO-wide and included operations in the northern and southern regions in addition to the Central Region. After six years of interoperability development at the unit level, SACEUR formally declared that all of the sub-exercises in REFORGER 77 would incorporate interoperability as much as possible with a focus on HNS, artillery fire support, intelligence operations, target acquisition and attack coordination between allied formations.

4 CMBG was involved in Exercise CARBON EDGE which was a multi-national extravaganza. The Blue forces, of which 4 CMBG was a part, also included the Belgian 1st Lancers, the Dutch 43rd Mechanized Infantry Battalion, the British 23rd SAS Regiment, all under the command of 1st (US) Infantry Division. Orange was structured around the 3rd (US) Infantry Division, Panzer Brigade 29, the French 13th Dragoons, and the 100th LRRP from the Bundeswehr. 4 CMBG had under command the US 223rd Aviation Battalion's *Cobra* attack helicopters, as well as some other allied units. Brigadier-General Jack Vance commanded 4 CMBG for CARBON EDGE:

> I started off that exercises on the right flank which gave me a front of 70 km but I had seven manoeuvre units under command for it including two thirds of one of the Armoured Cavalry Regiments.... I had a Belgian tank battalion; the 1st Belgian Lancers played in that exercise. Very good unit. I had an American mechanized infantry battalion under command for the whole damn thing. My engineer was just in heaven. He had about a division and

CHAPTER FIVE

half's worth of engineers under command for the whole exercise. [CARBON EDGE] was along one too. This was almost ten days, and we retired in good order against some very solid pushes by the American Red Force...

This time, 1 Canadian Signal Regiment from Kingston, Ontario deployed its Electronic Warfare Squadron to support 4 CMBG. As before, EW support proved invaluable.

The training schedule in the fall of 1978 was somewhat different from in previous years. REFORGER 78 had a variety of NATO corps-level exercises in the Central Region, but the US focus in CENTAG was on V (US) Corps rather than VII (US) Corps. As a result, Ex CERTAIN SHIELD was an all-American affair. Fortunately, 4 CMBG was invited by II (GE) Korps to play in Exercise BLAUE DONAU, a command post exercise held in the same area that GROSSE ROCHADE had been. Brigadier-General J.A. Fox, who took over 4 CMBG from Brigadier-General Vance in July 1978, ensured, however, that 4 CMBG would participate in the Winter REFORGER planned for January 1979.

To summarize, the move South had posed new challenges for 4 CMBG. Severe problems in the logistical system, coupled with the practical unreality of sustaining 4 CMBG in wartime during the 1970s, posed severe limitations on how long a Canadian force could fight. The reduction of the Brigade's fighting capability to two three-company infantry battalions and a two squadron armoured regiment dramatically reduced the operational effectiveness of Canada's land force commitment to the Central Region. Despite all of this, there was still a lot of potential in 4 CMBG in the 1970s and plans were made to remedy the situation. Canadian soldiers were aggressive and extremely capable. The brigade commanders knew this and, in the absence of any political interest or direction, kept 4 CMBG in the game, hoping for a better day. The development of new relationships with the German and American formations in CENTAG were beyond doubt useful to all concerned. 4 CMBG was a valuable asset to the Americans in the areas of doctrinal development and assistance in maintaining the US Army's professionalism through a period of trying times. The German-Canadian exercises were extremely valuable experiences, as they exposed 4 CMBG to German military concepts and, more importantly, to tough and realistic training. All of these attributes would have been critical factors if war had broken out. Interoperability would perhaps have saved the day in addition to the Brigade's fighting spirit and material contributions to the main defensive battle. The political realities in Canada vis à vis defence issues, however, made the restoration of 4 CMBG's operational capability an impossibility in the 1970s. 4 CMBG had to bide its time and wait for improved fortunes.

1979 - 1989

PARTIAL RESTORATION

CHAPTER SIX

"WE HAD TO AVOID THE EXTINCTION OF OUR OPEN SOCIETY AND THE SUBJUGATION OF ITS MEMBERS TO THE GRIM TOTALITARIAN SYSTEM WHOSE EXTENSION WORLDWIDE WAS THE OPENLY AVOWED INTENTION OF ITS CREATORS. WE HAD AT THE SAME TIME TO AVOID NUCLEAR WAR IF WE POSSIBLY COULD. WE COULD BEST DO SO BY BEING FULLY PREPARED FOR A CONVENTIONAL ONE. WE WERE NOT WILLING IN THE SEVENTIES AND EARLY EIGHTIES, TO MEET THE FULL COST OF BUILDING UP AN ADEQUATE LEVEL OF NON-NUCLEAR DEFENCE AND CUT IT FINE. IN THE EVENT, WE JUST GOT BY. SOME WOULD SAY THIS WAS MORE BY GOOD LUCK THAN BY GOOD MANAGEMENT, THAT WE DID TOO LITTLE TOO LATE AND HARDLY DESERVED TO SURVIVE AT ALL. THOSE WHO SAY THIS COULD WELL HAVE BEEN RIGHT."

- GENERAL SIR JOHN HACKETT,
THE THIRD WORLD WAR: THE UNTOLD STORY

Above: *There was a greater emphasis on chemical warfare defence in the 1980s within 4 CMBG. This 1 RCHA Forward Observation Officer is wearing an NBCD 'bunny suit' and respirator on exercise. Individuals were identifiable by marking name and rank on a piece of chemical agent detector paper, such as this Captain has done. The difficulties with communicating while wearing such equipment are obvious.* (DND)
Below: *There are varying states of NBCD protective measures. These infantrymen from O Company, 3 RCR are at "State Two" protection level – without respirators but wearing NBCD suits – on Exercise CERTAIN RAMPART in 1980.* (DND) ISC 80 750

CHAPTER SIX

Above: The Polish Crisis in 1980 elevated NATO-Warsaw Pact tensions. The sentiments of some are clear in 3rd Battalion, The Royal Canadian Regiment as they conduct another Fallex.
Below: A mechanized rifle company of 3 RCR on the move. Each rifle company possessed 16 tracked vehicles plus fuel, cargo and kitchen trucks. The number 51 is for exercise identification purposes, necessary when thousands of troops were on the same manoeuvre.

Above: *4 Canadian Mechanized Brigade Group's 'eyes in the sky': Kiowa helicopters from 444 Tactical Helicopter Squadron on Exercise CERTAIN RAMPART.* (DND) ISC 80 733
Below: *M-109 155mm self-propelled guns from 1st Regiment, Royal Canadian Horse Artillery giving fire support on Exercise CERTAIN RAMPART.* (DND) ISC 80 734

CHAPTER SIX

Above: *The Leopard C-1 replaced the Centurion as Canada's main battle tank in 1978. Its Low Level Television Viewing System, seen forward on the turret, was a considerable improvement over earlier infrared night fighting equipment.* (DND) ISC 80 739
Below: *A troop of Leopards of the RCD advances to contact in Bavaria during Exercise CERTAIN RAMPART, September 1980.* (DND) ISC 80 754

Top left: *A 'Blueland' A-10 "Thunderbolt" close air support aircraft about to make a strafing run on German "Marders" on Exercise CERTAIN RAMPART, Sep 1980. (DND) ISC 80 751*
Top right: *4 CMBG soldiers not only had to contend with fatigue on the FALLEX manoeuvres, but had to be wary of rabid animals as the "Tollwut" sign warns. (DND) IL 82 216 1*
Below: *1 R22^{e}R defensive position with 50 calibre Heavy Machine Gun (HMG), dismounted from the APC; Exercise CARBINE FORTRESS (REFORGER 82). (DND)*

CHAPTER SIX

The heightened international tensions of the early 1980s saw Fallex conducted with seriousness and heightened vigour. **Above**: *A mechanized platoon on a country road in eastern Bavaria.* **Below**: *Infantry and armour commanders coordinate a defence layout during Fallex 1981.*

Infantry and armour combat teams were the teeth of 4 CMBG. **Above**: *A mechanized infantry company in "leaguer" in the Hohenfels training area, Fallex 1981.* **Below**: *RCD tanks and infantry from 3 RCR take up a reverse slope position in the Bavarian countryside, Fallex 1981.*

CHAPTER SIX

In 1981 Mobile Command Headquarters commissioned British author and military historian Kenneth Macksey to write a training manual on combat team tactics, but in the form of a military novel. The result was the book <u>First Clash</u> which portrayed how 4 CMBG would conduct operations in war against the Warsaw Pact. **Above**: *Kenneth Macksey conferring with troopers of the Royal Canadian Dragoons.* **Below**: *Some things in the infantry never change...like "digging-in", which these soldiers are doing in the Hohenfels training area.*

Throughout the 1980s, weapons training was heavily emphasized in 4 CMBG and every opportunity taken to conduct "live firing". **Above**: .50 cal Heavy Machine Gun team at Hohenfels. **Below**: The British Army's training centre at Sennelager remained 4 CMBG's principal facility for conduct of live fire exercises. Here a rifle company from 3 RCR in June 1981 conducts a live fire assault. (The soldiers wearing berets are exercise safety staff.)

CHAPTER SIX

Fuel, rations and ammunition were what 4 CMBG consumed in huge quantities during training. **Above**: *A company kitchen truck set up in a village square.* **Below**: *A mechanized rifle company from 3 RCR is refueled from the company "bowser".*

Because of the huge numbers of troops involved on Fallex, and the requirement for weekend "stand fasts", there were frequent periods of "just waiting". **Above**: *A mechanized company marks time in 3 RCR's battalion "leaguer".* **Below**: *Maps were vital, but because of the great distances covered on an exercise, the glued together map sheets sometimes became the size and thickness of blankets. Here they are being marked.*

CHAPTER SIX

Bavarian farmyards or "hofs" were routinely utilized by 4 CMBG troops during Fallex, indeed as they would be during war. **Above**: *M113 APC, always an attraction to the local children.* **Below**: *Taking up positions amongst manure piles was one of the "hazards" of Fallex.*

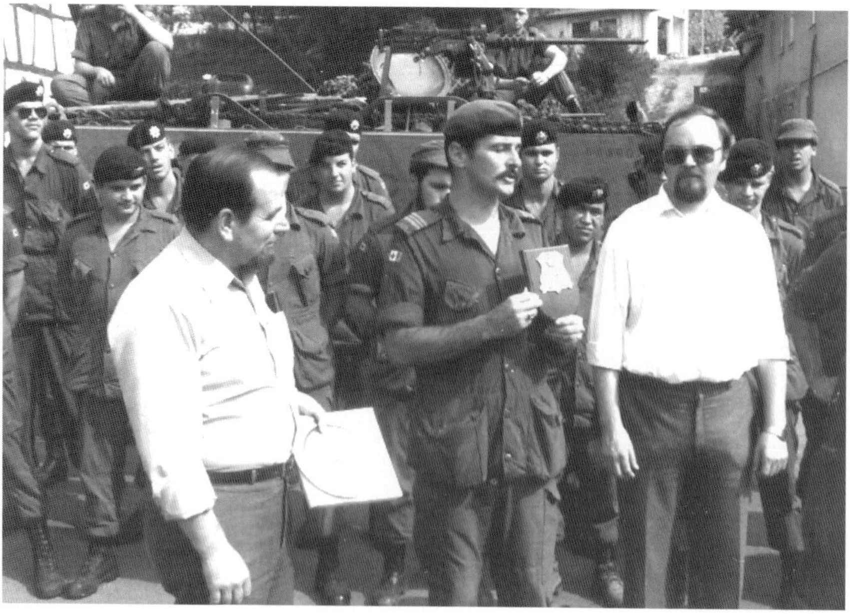

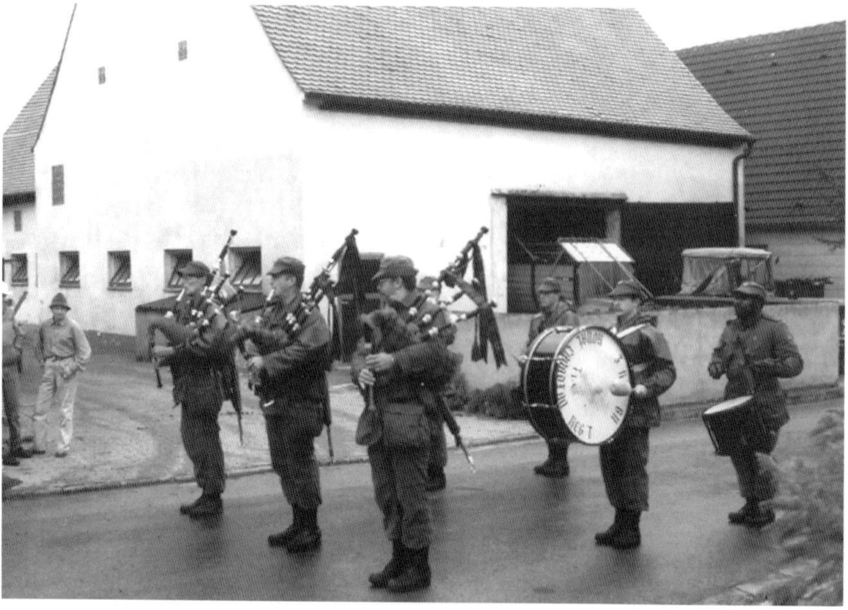

Maintaining good relations with the local German population during exercises was always viewed as important by 4 CMBG. ***Above****: Major Don MacInnis, Officer Commanding N Coy, 3 RCR, presents a regimental plaque to the Burgermeister of Zell during a weekend "standfast" during Fallex 82.* ***Below****: The Pipes and Drums of 3 RCR were always a big hit with the local Germans, and helped build the Canadian reputation.*

CHAPTER SIX

The great victory at Vimy Ridge in April 1917 is seminal in Canadian history. For Remembrance Day, 4 CMBG was frequently tasked to provide the Guard of Honour at Vimy and to organize the appropriate ceremonies. **Above**: *The Vimy Memorial atop the still shell-pocked ridge.* **Below**: *The 4 CMBG Guard on the left (in this case from 3 RCR) opposite the host French Army Guard, at the Moroccan memorial at Vimy during the 1981 commemorative ceremonies.*

Throughout the 1980s FIBUA training at the Bundeswehr's infantry school in Hammelburg was a highlight for the infantry soldiers in 4 CMBG. **Top Left:** *A thunderflash is tossed into an upper window.* **Top right:** *Rope work and grappling hooks were essential.* **Bottom:** *Various means were taught on how to enter the upper floors of buildings.*

CHAPTER SIX

The Hammelburg village of Bonnland, in addition to providing house clearing training, was ideal for street fighting and learning how best to employ armour and APCs in the village. **Above**: *An infantry platoon "fighting through" the village.* **Below**: *German Marder and Canadian troops on the village main street.*

Above: The "Last Gallop": Exercise CERTAIN CHALLENGE 1988 was the largest NATO exercise ever staged in Germany. Lynx recce vehicles from 8th Canadian Hussars (Princess Louise's) push hard, looking for 'Goldland' forces. (DND) ILC 87 111 1
Below: American "Goldland" soldiers captured during Ex CERTAIN CHALLENGE by the echelon of 3 RCR.

CHAPTER SIX

349

Above: SACEUR, US General James Galvin, *"descended from the clouds"* to visit 4 Canadian Mechanized Brigade during Exercise CERTAIN CHALLENGE. Here he is talking to a Canadian reporter with Brigade Commander BGen Tom de Faye at background left. (DND) ILB 88 18 8
Below: The real enemy kept close tabs on Canadian movements. This is an officer from the Soviet Military Liaison Mission (SMLM) caught by Canadian counter-intelligence taking pictures of Canadian forces exercising in the field. (DND)

Above: *Warsaw Pact agents tailed Canadian units on road moves and kept track of equipment types and breakdown rates. This is a Polish 'tourist' checking out 4 Combat Engineer Regiment's vehicles at a rest area off the autobahn.* (DND)
Below: *In some cases, Canadian soldiers trapped SMLM personnel. Under the terms of the 1950s agreements, SMLM were forbidden to leave the autobahns to observe NATO military activity. These two Soviet officers were blocked in by a Canadian 5/4 ton truck. They clearly did not like having their picture taken.* (DND)

CHAPTER SIX

Above: *Not all FALLEXs were without casualties and 4 Field Ambulance was on hand to handle this one.* (DND) IL 82 208 5
Below: *4 Combat Engineer Regiment sappers in 'Dozer' APC during Exercise CARBINE FORTRESS. The number 1 in the circle was to facilitate recognition of units by umpires and was not otherwise on the vehicle.* (DND) IL 82 211 5

Top left: Sentries, Exercise CARBINE FORTRESS, 1982. The man on the left carries a 9mm Sterling submachine gun. (DND) IL 82 208 4

Top right: Militia flyover troops such as these Highlanders regularly augmented 4 Canadian Mechanized Brigade Group on FALLEX. (DND) IL 82 210 1

Below: The heart of the matter: radios, maps and umpire (identified by white armband). Exercise CARBINE FORTRESS, 1982. (DND) IL 82 211 1

CHAPTER SIX

Above: *RCHA officer updates American soldier, probably a liaison officer. Exercise CARBINE FORTRESS 1982.* (DND) IL 82 211 2
Below: *Bundeswehr umpire with Sergeant Marsh of 4 Combat Engineer Regiment - Exercise CARBINE FORTRESS 1982.* (DND) IL 82 207 3

In 1988 4 CMBG continued to be well represented in the gruelling 100 mile four day Nijmegen March through Holland. **Above**: Part of the Brigade contingent marches past in Nijmegen. **Below**: The 4 Service Battalion team at a rest halt.

CHAPTER SIX

Unlike service in Canada, the "enemy" for 4 CMBG was for real and could even be seen, such as at the inner-German border town of Hof.

All of East Germany was, literally, walled in, not just East Berlin. During Fallex, regular tours to the inner-German and the Czech border were conducted to show 4 CMBG soldiers exactly the nature of the "socialist paradise" they were defending against.

CHAPTER SIX

The events of the 1980s have barely entered the realm of history as this book is published. This examination of 4 CMBG and its place in NATO in the 1980s must thus be viewed as provisional at best. That need not, however, deter us from making the attempt. For 4 CMBG, the 1980s can be characterized as a restorative period. Although 4 CMBG would never see the equipment and manning levels that it enjoyed in the 1950s and 1960s, the 1980s proved to be significantly better than the 1970s in almost all respects. Much had been improved, including equipment, manning, GDP planning, logistics support and finally the re-forming of 1st Canadian Division; but some aspects were only partially implemented before the Berlin Wall tumbled in 1989. Thus, Canada's intentions to improve the state of its conventional land forces in the Central Region was never completed. Yet, there was a restoration of sorts, not only in materiel but also in a spirit of optimism that permeated the Army after a very difficult decade of neglect.

The early 1980s were a dangerous time, almost as dangerous as the 1960s. The Soviet Union, its leadership and its institutions were decaying, though the full extent of this would not be apparent until after 1989. Decay produces instability, and instability produces the inclination toward rash action.

The event that was the catalyst for change in NATO was the Soviet invasion of Afghanistan in 1979. Though motives for such a move were complex, it was a clear message to NATO that the Soviet Union could and would initiate conventional operations regardless of international opinion or sanction. In this very dirty conflict, all Soviet weapon systems short of nuclear weapons were used.

Some felt that this provocative move was the result of a number of factors besides the Soviets' need for power projection into the Persian Gulf. The Soviets had earlier made several moves in Africa and the Caribbean, that were interpreted as attempts to outflank the NATO area. The USSR had succeeded in modernizing its nuclear forces in the late 1970s, and in fact was considered to have achieved strategic and theatre nuclear parity in every respect. They were also making great strides in improving the quality of their conventional forces, which had not been significantly reduced since 1946.

The implications of this were alarming to those who were knowledgeable. The West had never kept pace with the Warsaw Pact in improvements to conventional forces, and had not significantly improved theatre and strategic nuclear forces since the late 1960s. For all intents and purposes both sides' strategic and theatre nuclear forces cancelled out each other, with the result that this increased the chances of conventional conflict in Europe and elsewhere. If the Soviets had chosen to attack NATO with conventional forces, NATO's will to escalate the conflict by using theatre and especially strategic nuclear weapons would have been seriously impaired by the number and quality of the Soviet nuclear forces. In the 1950s and 1960s, the West had held a clear lead in both theatre and strategic nuclear forces and was confident that this superiority would deter the Soviets from escalating a conventional and/or tactical nuclear conflict into a theatre and strategic conflict. Now things had changed.

If Afghanistan was an indicator or a test case of this new state of affairs, was there a possibility that conventional war could be unleashed against NATO? NATO's leadership still could not be sure. Alliance

CHAPTER SIX

planners believed that the Soviets were still hesitant about using their increased freedom of action. They also believed that the Soviets credited NATO and the West with having a much greater defence capability than was actually in place. NATO had to use this borrowed time wisely.

As a result, in late 1979, NATO defence ministers decided to modernize NATO's theatre nuclear forces as the first step in restoring the balance and thus also strengthening deterrence. At about the same time, it became apparent that new technology now existed to increase the effectiveness of NATO's conventional forces significantly, hence the actual emphasis on tactical nuclear warfare could be lessened. This stimulated the development of new doctrine for the conventional defence of the Central Region based on "deep battle" and "Follow-On Forces Attack" (FOFA). These steps were announced to the public, but NATO's leadership knew that implementation would take considerable time.

NATO's endeavours were assisted by a new mood in the West. It was apparent to the public in the NATO countries that the West had been weak and impotent in the early part of the 1970s. This was blamed on a combination of Soviet gains in Africa, the Middle East and elsewhere, the humiliation of the United States in Vietnam and Iran, and by the exponential increase of revolutionary terrorism in Germany, Italy, the Netherlands and France. The election of Margaret Thatcher in the United Kingdom in 1979 and Ronald Reagan in the United States at the end of 1980, however, reflected a fundamental shift in public mood and provided the renewed leadership the West needed. This leadership, practical as well as moral, helped facilitate the flow of money into defence programs so that conventional, theatre, and strategic forces could be revitalized. On another plane, the accession of the charismatic Pope John Paul II to head of the Catholic Church added a spiritual and moral dimension to the effort, particularly during the Polish Crisis in 1980.

Canada's early part in this general effort at renewal was confused at best. The election of Joe Clark as Prime Minister in 1979 was a promising development as Canada's allies "expected Clark to reinforce Canada's ties with NATO." They were to be sorely disappointed. Clark was quickly unseated in 1980 after only nine months in office, and Pierre Trudeau once again assumed the mantle of power. The Canadian defence efforts in support of NATO would subsequently be stalled for the next three critical years as Trudeau focused on schemes to "mediate" between the superpowers, his 1983 international peace initiative being but one example of this. Other NATO members, however, were not impressed, and Canadian representatives in Brussels were told that if Canada did not increase its defence expenditures as it had agreed to earlier, there could be problems:

> ...it would be bound to tarnish the image of a mature, responsible and reliable partner which we need for our own self respect and for the establishment of mutually beneficial relations with the rest of the world. It would introduce a weak spot where now there is a modest but high quality contribution into NATO's stretched resources on the crucial Central Front, and on the Northern Flank of Europe and on the Atlantic Sea lanes....

The run-down of the Canadian Armed Forces in the 1970s affected all three services, and the defence priorities established by the Trudeau Government would not change significantly until 1985. It was against this backdrop that 4 CMBG continued to participate in the conventional defence of the Central Region.

The state of 4 CMBG from 1979 to 1983 was little changed from the 1970s. The Brigade's combat elements still consisted of an armoured regiment with three tank squadrons and one recce squadron (only two tank squadrons were manned), two mechanized infantry battalions of three rifle companies each, and the artillery regiment (three M-109 batteries). But when all the deficiencies in combat service support were added, 4 CMBG only reached 58 per cent of the equipment and manpower it required to fight as a full-strength brigade group. It may be worth noting that, according to the annual Defence Planning Questionaire information provided to NATO by Canada, the CAST Brigade Group was reported at 100 per cent, (even though this was significantly inflated and cut into Op PENDANT reinforcements for 4 Brigade) with the two other brigades in Canada rated at 53 per cent and 64 per cent of war establishment.

The training programme for 4 CMBG was highlighted by its participation in two large scale exercises in 1979. The first, Ex CERTAIN SENTINEL, was the first REFORGER to be held in winter since 1973.

4 CMBG operated under the command of 1st (US) Armored Division, (which acted as the enemy force against 1st (US) Infantry Division), which had a German panzer brigade in support. Both sides also had the services of special operations forces from the UK, Germany, France and Belgium. The specific purpose of CERTAIN SENTINEL, besides the usual inter-allied cooperation and unit training, was to test NATO's reinforcement and logistics system in winter conditions, something that had not yet been tried on a large scale.

Held in the Frankfurt-Stuttgart-Nürnberg triangle, 4 CMBG quickly adapted to its enemy force role once flyover troops for 1 RCHA were incorporated into the regiment. Brigadier-General Ian Douglas, who was a Lieutenant Colonel at the time and 4 CMBG's SSO Operations, recalled:

> The exercise scenario saw 4 CMBG coming under command of the 1st(US) Armored Division commanded by Major General Glen Otis, which was then tasked as aggressor force against the remainder of VII (US) Corps. The exercise plot saw the Division driving across the Main River in an attempt to dislodge Blue forces.... As per normal Reforgers, we would remain on the offense for about four or five days after which, through attrition and normal brilliant Blue tactics, we would be worn down to the point where Blue would switch to the offensive and drive us back...
>
> We prepared options for [Brigade Commander] General Jim [Fox]'s approval, including a plan to do the operation on radio silence. 'Impossible!' was Major Percy Tappin's [the Brigade's signals officer] reply, 'There is not enough WD-1 [telephone wire] in the world!' After some discussion it was decided that if we supplemented our own meager WD-1 resources with rented and strategically located 'Bundespost phone' drops, we might just make this work. The other controversial decision was the camouflage policy. We decided to camouflage all of our vehicles German-style, using a thick slurry of whitewash which, although not colour fast, was cheap and easy to patch up...
>
> H Hour was at 0200 hours as the Division Task Force drove forward on a front of some 30-40 kilometres. 1 R22eR and 3 RCR both did conventional dismounted assaults and quickly gained the far bank and pressed on. Happy was the battalion signals officer who found his phone drops at the correct location, and the recce units with their 50 pfennig coins who used village

phone boxes to send in reports....By 0900 hours the next morning intercept told us that all aggressor forces had been identified except the Canadians!

The snow fell steadily as 4 CMBG moved into its staging areas on the night of 30 January in preparation for a night attack. With surprise, daring and more than a little bit of luck, 4 CMBG conducted a night assault river crossing (with the help of the 16th US Engineer Battalion) and moved into defensive positions as the weather worsened. The Blue forces counter-attacked at first light, but Canadian infantry held off the Blueland M-60 tanks with small anti-tank teams armed with *Carl Gustav* and M-72 anti-tank weapons. Moving in the forests, the Canadians picked off enemy vehicles with alacrity.

The newly acquired *Leopards*, with their state of the art night viewing equipment, also had their share of success, as Major Ray Richards of the RCD attests:

> We were working with a Vandoo company, and they were leading that night, as per doctrine. We were doing a move, and [using our low light television viewers] we started calling out contacts 1500 to 2000 metres away. But the infantry section out front could only see 100 metres in front of them, depending on what ambient light conditions there were. [The company commander] came over and said, 'What are you talking about?' I said, 'Over there in that woodline I count four M-60s and six APCs. He then came over and got into the tank, and saw on the viewer himself all of the targets we were calling out. 'OK,' he said, 'you guys lead at night'. It was outstanding. It was like a shooting gallery along that woodline. We hammered away at what we could see but there was no return fire and you could see these guys diving and jumping around, wondering what was going on.
>
> Then an umpire jumped up and said 'You're all dead'. We replied, 'What do you mean? They haven't even returned fire yet!' He said, 'That was a reinforced tank battalion, and you've only got four tanks'. I told him it didn't matter how many vehicles they had if they didn't pull their triggers. I showed him the scope, and he thought it was a painted picture! He just couldn't believe it. He then said ' OK, I'll go see how many casualties I can assess'. He came back and said, 'I hate to tell you this but you really are all dead. There were fifteen TOWs with thermal imaging three kilometers over there on your

CHAPTER SIX

right. But I've given you credit for all the damage you did back there.'

Fortunately for the 1st (US) Infantry Division and their Blue allies, SACEUR called off CERTAIN SENTINEL three days before its scheduled end. The weather once again demonstrated its fickleness; temperatures soared to well above freezing. The German fields turned into muddy quagmires, manoeuvre became impossible without causing massive manoeuvre damage, so everyone was told to go home.

In addition to the bizarre weather, two other notable things happened during CERTAIN SENTINEL. Soldiers from 1 R22eR came across a member of a Dusseldorf Hiking Companions group who had suffered a heart attack. Although the soldiers were unable to prevent his death, many letters of appreciation flowed into Lahr from the organization. On a happier note, the Mayor of Grossenseebach sent a congratulatory note to 4 CMBG:

> My fellow citizens still talk with appreciation of the exercise period and in conversations everyone remarks on the discipline and friendliness of your troops…. It is pleasant when a mayor doesn't receive complaints from the local population after an exercise ends. Officers and other ranks left a good impression in Grossenseebach. Perhaps there will be an opportunity for you to visit Grossenseebach again? You are extended a hearty invitation!

This was quite a change from the usual manoeuvre damage complaints and demonstrations!

The second NATO exercise in 1979 was Ex CONSTANT ENFORCER. Held while the Polish situation was coming to a slow boil, CONSTANT ENFORCER was the first-ever Army Group-level FTX, involving the bulk of V(US) and VII(US) Corps, 4 CMBG, a British armoured regiment, a Belgian battalion and French special recce patrols. This time, a third tank squadron drawn from the 8th Canadian Hussars (Princess Louise's) was flown over instead of the artillery to augment 4 CMBG.

According to one CONSTANT ENFORCER exercise control officer:

> On a couple of occasions we had to make major adjustments to the exercise

scenario because the Americans could not cope with the relentless Canadian night offensives. We then had 4 CMBG change sides and come in as a Blue reinforcement formation. They were just as good in the offense!

General Frederick Kroesen, COMCENTAG, arrived at the first Exercise Control Conference on Day 1. We needed his blessing on action for the next 24 hours. He looked around the makeshift conference table where the exercise planners from the various divisions of the CENTAG staff were seated. Of the thirteen officers present, nine were Canadians. General Kroesen turned to Brigadier General Cowan and said, 'I thought this was a multi-national headquarters. You never told me that the Canadians had taken over!'

Brigadier General A.J.G.D. de Chastelain (later to become CDS) assumed command of 4 CMBG in July 1980. That September, 4 CMBG deployed south of Nürnberg to participate in Exercise CERTAIN RAMPART. CERTAIN RAMPART was part of the NATO AUTUMN FORGE exercise series, which was the largest exercise series since 1970 and included Exercise SPEARPOINT (I (BR) Corps) in NORTHAG and Exercise ST. GEORGE in (III (GE) Korps) in CENTAG, in addition to CERTAIN RAMPART. As such, the exercises that comprised AUTUMN FORGE were increasingly seen by NATO as demonstrations of resolve, in addition to the training benefits afforded to NATO armies through collective training.

CERTAIN RAMPART was specifically constructed to test the GDP in the VII (US) Corps area, even though the actual exercise was not held on the ground itself. 4 CMBG operated with the 1st (US) Armored Division on the Blue side against the 3rd (US) Infantry Division. There were many problems with interoperability on CERTAIN RAMPART, particularly with communications between 4 CMBG and its adjacent American formations. The Americans were still working with their Active Defense concept which placed little emphasis on obstacle and barrier plans. This was very alien to Canadian doctrine, but 4 CMBG 'played American' for the duration of the exercise.

The Polish Crisis of 1980 was, in retrospect, very similar to the 1968 Czech Crisis as regards NATO's reaction. The Solidarity trade union movement, supported by the Church, was attempting to reform the system in Poland and had garnered widespread support. This was viewed by Moscow as a crack in the Warsaw Pact dam that had to be patched before the whole structure collapsed. As a result, a period of tension existed from August 1980 to late 1981. On 22 December 1980, NATO roundly condemned Soviet actions in the region and sent a clear message to Moscow: if the Soviets continued to escalate military activity in the East Bloc, NATO would be forced to do the same in the West to ensure that NATO would not be caught by surprise if the situation got out of control.

Even though Soviet and other Warsaw Pact forces were directed inward and prepared for action against Poland, NATO could not sit idly by given the possibility that the situation would get out of hand. Soviet forces were at a high level of alert, and some second strategic echelon forces were mobilized. Soviet propaganda became more strident, blaming "Western interference" and "German revanchism" for the increased support for the Solidarity Movement. If this were not enough, elements of the Soviet nuclear forces were put on even higher alert status.

It was feared that anything could happen given the volatile situation. Even if the Polish Army was unreliable from the Soviet standpoint (which it wasn't) the mobilization of Soviet second echelon forces added further to the NATO-Warsaw Pact force imbalance in Europe. Moreover, the Soviets had a record for carrying out aggression under the guise of exercises or other limited operations (Czechoslovakia, Hungary and Afghanistan): Could the Polish Crisis be used as a pretext for war against NATO? Could accusations of Western interference in Warsaw Pact affairs be used as an excuse to attack NATO forces in Germany?

In accordance with the precedent established during the 1968 Czech Crisis, NATO chose not to declare its alert measures, though some units, including 4 CMBG, deployed on readiness exercises. Warrant Officer Max Rudneu recalls:

> The jukebox was going and the noise level was fairly high. Our course officer was an air force captain and he was trying to get our attention. Someone turned down the music and quieted the crowd so he could be heard. His announcement was just what a roomful of partyers wanted to hear: 'Gentlemen, SNOWBALL.' Someone said: 'Good one Sir!'. We all laughed and the

music came back on. He tried to convince us he was not joking and he eventually pulled the plug on the jukebox and put a radio on top of it. The radio was tuned to CFN and playing the overly familiar SNOWBALL announcement in English, French and German. The place emptied as if by magic.

I had to go home for my kit and [my wife] Pat expressed surprise because her employment [in the headquarters] put her in a good position to know if a practice SNOWBALL was going to be held. The fact that she was not aware of any SNOWBALL and it was a Thursday night, not a Monday morning, gave me a sinking feeling that this was for real. I was so convinced that I figured OP MAYFLOWER was the next logical step. I left for work and on arrival at the troop discovered that I was not alone in figuring the balloon had gone up. When we were ordered to draw the small arms ammo from the compound, that settled it. The ammo was never broken down from the cases. The fact that we drew it confirmed that this was a different SNOWBALL. We rolled from the marg to our survival area and we stayed out two days before returning to base. I think we all expected to load trains for points east!

NATO's political leadership had at this point publicly condemned the Soviet Union on the Polish matter; it was feared, however, that any move at increasing alert levels would be interpreted by the Soviets that NATO was planning action against the Warsaw Pact to take advantage of the internal division of the Pact. This did not, however, prevent NATO military forces from continuing their annual training, unlike in 1968 when Ex SCHWARZE LOEWE was toned down.

After a year of individual and collective training, 4 CMBG was invited by II (GE) Korps to participate in Ex SCHARFE KLINGE ("Sharp Sword") held in the fall of 1981. II (GE) Korps once again was testing the ability of 4 Panzer Grenadier Division (formerly 4 Jaeger Division), with support from WBK [Home Defence District] VI, to operate in the defence. An American mechanized brigade and the Germans' Airborne Brigade 25 completed the Blue forces. The enemy force for SCHARFE KLINGE consisted of 10 Panzer Division, including 4 CMBG, Panzer Brigade 28 and Panzer Grenadier Brigade 30. Since 10 Panzer Division was the II (GE) Korps reserve, SCHARFE KLINGE was also used to exercise this formation in the attack/counter-attack role. Although

CHAPTER SIX

4 CMBG was, once again, a training tool for a larger ally, on another level it was viewed by the Germans as a good opportunity to exercise interoperability.

Exercise SCHARFE KLINGE took place in the same area as GUTES OMEN, with the enemy force start line on the eastern edge of the Schwarzwald. The Blue defenders, facing west, were arrayed, north to south, starting with Panzer Brigade 12, Panzer Grenadier Brigade 10 and the 1st(US) Mechanized Infantry Brigade. Airborne Brigade 25 and a French recce regiment covered the southern flank of 4 Panzer Grenadier Division, dispositions which mirrored the actual dispositions in II (GE) Korps.

The Red assault also mirrored the projected threat to II (GE) Korps. The weight of 10 Panzer Division's attack, that is, Brigades 28 and 30, was directed against the Airborne Brigade and then into the US Brigade. 4 CMBG's role was inauspicious. After conducting an unsuccessful attack against Panzer Brigade 12, 4 CMBG moved into defensive positions just inside the Blue border and pinned down Panzer Grenadier Brigade 10 while the remainder of 10 Panzer Division rolled up the enemy.

Unit training in the 1980s was not vastly different from the 1970s. 4 CMBG units still deployed to Hohenfels, Münsingen, Bergen-Hohne and Grafenwöhr for training schemes. The Bonnland FIBUA training site at Hammelburg was always a favourite, as Major Bob Near, then of 3 RCR, recalls:

> The FIBUA training we conducted at Hammelburg was really superb, probably the best training the battalion did in Germany. The Bundeswehr had taken this typical German village, Bonnland, complete with church, gasthof, castle, houses, barns, streets, alleys – the works, and used it to practise troops in both attacking and defending. No doubt they based a lot of it on what they had experienced during the war.
>
> The training covered everything – how to get into second story windows by running a soldier on a pole up a wall, preparing rooms for defence, booby traps, room-clearing, mouseholing, street crossing, etc. On the last day we practiced a full battalion dismounted attack at dawn on Bonnland – three rifle companies against the Administrative Support Company, who were defending.

> We had MILES equipment...borrowed from our American *partnerschaft* battalion, so that you were able to tell when someone was hit as their laser receivers would beep. Everybody in the rifle companies thought this attack would be a piece of cake, over in an hour, but instead the battle raged all day. The Adm Company guys were really well sited, and hard as hell to dig out of their defended buildings. Our own MILES receivers were sounding off all the time, indicating we were taking a lot of casualties. Some really good lessons were learned, especially about fire and movement and use of cover....

In other areas, Canadian medical units were involved with the German-run GRUNER LAUBFROSCH multi-national medical exercises each year, and the Headquarters and Signal Squadron was constantly exercised in a multitude of national and NATO CPXs. Parachuting with German partnership units and the French commando course were still popular. The other annual or bi-annual events, like the Nijmegen marches, the CAT shoot and the Boeselager competition also continued to help focus the Canadian training year.

Brigadier General R.J. Evraire took over command of 4 CMBG in July 1982 in time to prepare for Ex CARBINE FORTRESS. As part of REFORGER 82, CARBINE FORTRESS had many objectives. In addition to the usual training activities, CARBINE FORTRESS was specifically set up to test interoperability in the VII (US) Corps area. The Orange forces for the exercise included 1st (US) Armored Division and 4 CMBG with a Belgian infantry battalion attached. These were pitted against Blueland forces consisting of 3rd (US) Infantry Division, 12 Panzer Division, 1st (US) Infantry Division ('reforging' in from the US) and the 8th (US) Infantry Division attached in from V(US) Corps. There was even an entire airborne brigade parachuted into the area on a non-stop deployment from the continental United States.

CENTAG Headquarters was quite concerned about VII (US) Corps' ability to employ and control allied formations. As a result, 12 Panzer Division was placed under command of VII (US) Corps, and 4 CMBG worked closely with 1st (US) Armored Division. This training reflected proposed changes to the CENTAG GDP, where 12 Panzer Division might become part of VII (US) Corps. The poor state of interoperability between 4 CMBG and 1st (US) Armored Division dictated that improved

CHAPTER SIX

FSOPs be developed during CARBINE FORTRESS. Given the advanced state of 4 CMBG's GDP development, especially regarding its options in VII (US) Corps, this was considered to be a priority task.

The exercise was held in the VII (US) Corps area. As with other exercises, the forces were aligned in a mirror image of the actual GDP positions, but on a north-south axis. The operational focus of the exercise was the Blueland counter-attack. Since 4 CMBG and 1st (US) Armored Division were on the Orange side, both formations practiced counter-penetration and blocking missions against Blue, also in accordance with the existing GDP. CARBINE FORTRESS was a considerable improvement over CERTAIN RAMPART and SCHARFE KLINGE from a Canadian point of view, and the lessons learned from the entire experience were valuable ones.

Although examples are too numerous to catalogue here, there was a marked change in the attitude of the civilian population regarding manoeuvre damage in the 1980s. The old days of the occupation were fading away in memory. The rather careless attitude towards manoeuvre damage taken by the British in NORTHAG and by the French in CENTAG back in the 1950s and 1960s was becoming, politically, no longer acceptable. Damage was still tolerated in the 1970s, but troops were cautioned that if damage to fields occurred, it had to be justified by the need for tactical realism. All NATO land formations, including the Bundeswehr, were perpetrators of manoeuvre damage, both justified and unjustified.

The advent of the Green Party, coupled with the rising environmental movement in Germany, served notice to NATO formations that damage would be examined and reported on by local authorities. In many cases, manoeuvre damage was used as a domestic political tool by some politicians to gain local support, and in other cases some localities attempted to restrict NATO units from exercising in their vicinity. HQ CFE decided at the time that any damage caused by Canadian units would be compensated by Canada. Manoeuvre Damage Control teams thus followed in the wake of 4 CMBG units, did repairs where possible, investigated claims, and doled out cash on the spot if the situation was justified.

The effect of this new attitude was to greatly decrease tactical realism in a general sense. Holding major manoeuvres in the Fall after the harvest, an idea dating back to the 1700s and one that had been in effect since NATO started having large scale exercises in the 1950s, went a long way towards limiting damage. However, the carping criticism of Canadian exercise activities because an APC broke off a single tree limb was a bit much; tanks did not smash down fences on a systematic basis like they had in the 1950s and 1960s. Manoeuvre damage got to be a game, and an expensive one at that, as it came to be seen as a source of easy money for some "victims". Damage also took on an international dimension as complaints frequently were forwarded through the German Interior Ministry to the Canadian Embassy in Bonn.

4 CMBG had to do without a corps-level exercise in the Fall of 1983. Exercise CONFIDENT ENTERPRISE, part of REFORGER 83 was strictly a V (US) Corps show; and VII (US) Corps was involved in its own CPX. As for II (GE) Korps, it was preparing for its own large exercise in 1984, and also was unavailable. This was coincidental to the increased international tension in 1983. (Only years later did NATO learn that the Soviet Union actually contemplated attacking NATO in November 1983 after they misinterpreted SACEUR's ABLE ARCHER 83 CPX as preparation for a NATO attack on the Warsaw Pact. Rampant paranoia brought on by the Soviet mentality and their decaying economic system interpreted the West's new willingness to defend itself as a threat to be countered.)

Left to their own devices, 4 CMBG planners conceived Exercise SWIFT THRUST III. This was held in TAA SETTER, with the exercise main defensive line less than ten kilometers away from what eventually became 4 CMBG's General Defence Plan position (GDP) between Vilseck and Amberg. The enemy force was provided by the Bundeswehr, who attacked straight down Highway 14, the axis which CENTAG anticipated the Warsaw Pact would use in a real attack. Besides providing 4 CMBG with an opportunity to operate near the actual deployment area, SWIFT THRUST III placed a great deal of emphasis on NBCD training, and 4 CMBG was pleased to have under command the US 11th Chemical Company for decontamination and NBCD recce tasks.

The Americans were impressed with 4 CMBG's training standards during SWIFT THRUST III, as reported by 11 Chemical Company:

CHAPTER SIX

The outstanding support received from the Canadians, coupled with their energetic cooperation (as well as participation in realistic NBC play and tactical utilization of a chemical company) was made possible by [4 CMBG]. The Canadians were anxious to experience progressing through a chemical company for two reasons; they have no organic decontamination of their own and [if] during some future conflict they were attached to VII Corps, they would utilize decontamination assets of VII Corps, probably the 11th Chemical Company.... The Canadians also placed in their scenario an impressive demonstration of integrated training.

It is common knowledge that major unit training is both limited and expensive. Therefore, many major commanders cannot rationalize 'wasting' valuable training time on NBC defence tasks. Not only did [Brigadier] General Evraire [Comd 4 CMBG] emphasize use of chemical defence themes throughout the exercise but he also integrated activation of an alternate command post with a tactical decontamination of the Brigade Headquarters!

The threat to CENTAG altered in a number of ways in the 1980s. [See Figure 6-1.] The scope of employment for the 8th Guards Army (redesignated 8th Guards Combined Arms Army in 1987) had increased, and the disposition of 1st Guards Tank Army had altered so that it could be used to support either CGF against CENTAG, 3rd Shock Army against NORTHAG, or 8th Guards Army. Several divisions were re-subordinated in 1983 and 3rd Shock Army lost its mechanized divisions completely and gained a tank division. Organizationally and numerically, first and second echelon forces followed deployments similar to those described in the previous chapter with some modification. CGF consisted of two tank and three mechanized divisions, while the Czech forces retained the same organization as before. The Czechs also had undertaken a number of qualitative improvements, particularly in self-propelled artillery.

Likely invasion routes against CENTAG were not remarkably different from those in the 1970s. The only exception was the threat from the Donau Approach, which appeared in some planning to receive less emphasis after 1986. Apparently, the Austrians believed that NATO planning based on the fragility of Austrian sovereignty could become a self-fulfilling prophecy in the event of hostilities, and they expressed this

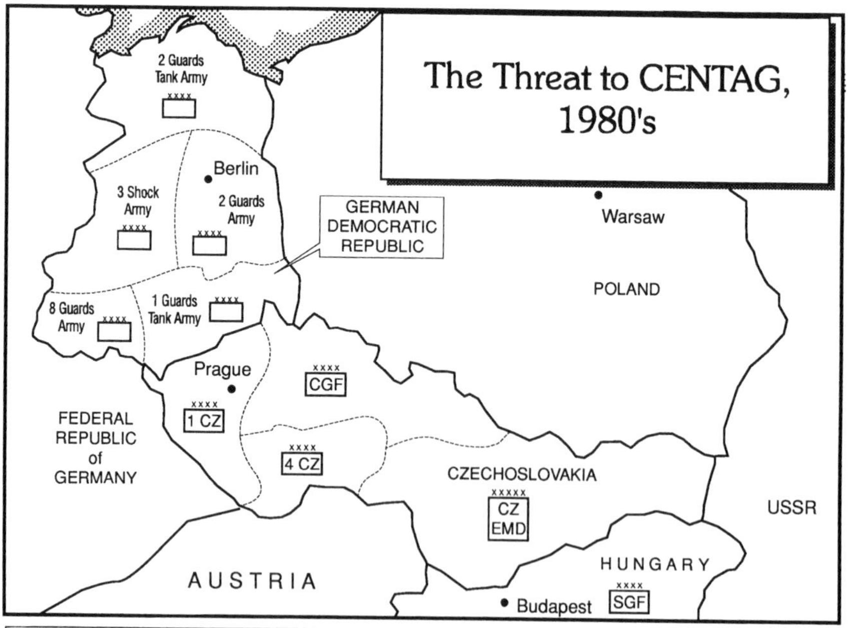
The Threat to CENTAG, 1980's
2 Guards Tank Army
Berlin
3 Shock Army
2 Guards Army
GERMAN DEMOCRATIC REPUBLIC
Warsaw
POLAND
8 Guards Army
1 Guards Tank Army
Prague
CGF
1 CZ
FEDERAL REPUBLIC of GERMANY
4 CZ
CZECHOSLOVAKIA
CZ EMD
USSR
HUNGARY
AUSTRIA
Budapest
SGF

CENTAG THREAT ORBAT 1980's

GROUP of SOVIET FORCES, GERMANY:

1st GDS TK ARMY:
- 9 Tk Div
- 11 Gds Tk Div
- 20 Gds Mtr Rifle Div

8th GDS ARMY:
- 79 Gds Tk Div
- 39 Gds Mtr Rifle Div
- 57 Gds Mtr Rifle Div
- 27 Gds Mtr Rifle Div

SOUTHERN GROUP of FORCES (Soviet, Hungary):
- 2 Tk and
- 3 Mtr Rifle Divs

NATIONALE VOLKSARMEE (GDR):
- 1 Mech Div
- 4 Inf Div
- 8 Inf Div
- 7 Tk Div
- 9 Tk Div
- 11 Mtr Rifle Div

(Plus 5 reserve NVA infantry divisions: 6, 10, 19, 27, 40)

CZECH EASTERN MILITARY DISTRICT:
- 14 Tk Div
- 13 Tk Div
- 3 Mtr Rifle Div

CENTRAL GROUP of FORCES (SOVIET):
- 18 Mtr Rifle Div
- 15 Tk Div
- 48 Mtr Rifle Div
- 31 Tk Div
- 30 Mtr Rifle Div

CZECH WESTERN MILITARY DISTRICT

1st CZECH ARMY:
- 1 Tk Div
- 20 Mtr Rifle Div
- 19 Mtr Rifle Div
- 2 Mtr Rifle Div

4th CZECH ARMY:
- 15 Mtr Rifle Div
- 9 Tk Div
- 4 Tk Div

FIGURE 6-1

CHAPTER SIX

concern to NATO. The subsequent shift away from the Donau Approach at some levels of NATO planning was not reflected at other levels, and it continued to be an area of concern. Informal discussions between those other levels and the Austrians clarified many problems. Be that as it may, the projected axes of a Warsaw Pact main effort against CENTAG were the Fulda Gap and the Highway 14 approaches, with all other approaches expected to support these two. [See Figure 6-2.]

The Warsaw Pact had deliberately over-estimated the number of NATO forces available in the Central Region to satisfy their own indoctrination and propaganda requirements. [See Figures 6-3 and 6-4.] In Figure 6-3, the forward deployed NATO forces are seen in their approximate GDP positions with the exception of a formation called the 1(KA)MD, clearly 1st Canadian Division, which was located behind Nürnberg instead of in front of it. Other formations like the IV (GE) Korps, V (GE) Korps, and II (BR) Corps do not and did not exist. Clearly, the arrows showing NATO formations moving into Poland were exaggerations. Similarly, Figure 6-4 shows units which did not exist, like the 46th and 66th Infantry Divisions in II (GE) Korps. Some Warsaw Pact plans even showed Portuguese and Spanish divisions employed as NATO's 'Second Echelon' to attack Poland!

The Warsaw Pact forces opposing CENTAG had been increasing since the mid-1970s in quality, if not in quantity. A new generation of armoured fighting vehicles was progressively introduced. These included T-72 and T-64 main battle tanks, BMP-2 MICVs, as well as 2S1 and 2S3 self-propelled guns. All of these vehicles were designed to operate in nuclear and chemical environments. More and more artillery was made available to GSFG, including one artillery brigade per Army and an Artillery Division under GSFG. There were, of course, vast numbers of *Scud* and *Scaleboard* missile systems with conventional, chemical or nuclear warheads. Large numbers of the feared Mi-24 *Hind* attack helicopter were also deployed in the early 1980s, vastly increasing NATO's already massive low-level air defence problem.

Airborne formations had already figured significantly in NATO's threat estimates in previous years but the increased Soviet emphasis on airmobile operations posed new problems. Throughout the 1970s, the Soviets had deployed more and more helicopters of all types,

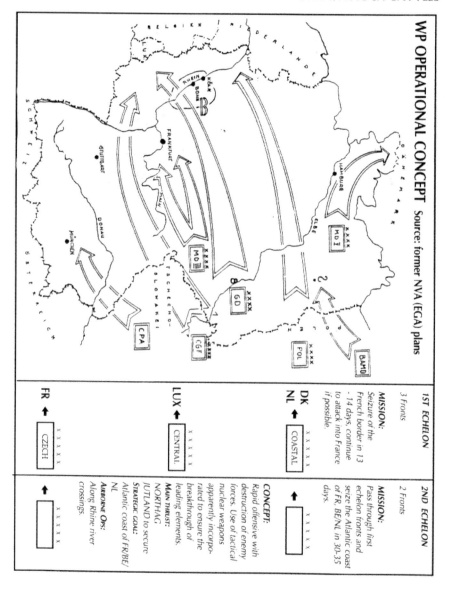

FIGURE 6-2: WARSAW PACT OPERATIONAL CONCEPT FOR OPERATIONS AGAINST NATO FORCES IN GERMANY

This information was extracted from 1980s NVA planning documents acquired by the Bundeswehr after German reunification. Note that the Donau Approach option does not seem to have been passed on to the East German planners, probably because of a desire not to show the Soviet intention of violating Austrian neutrality.

CHAPTER SIX

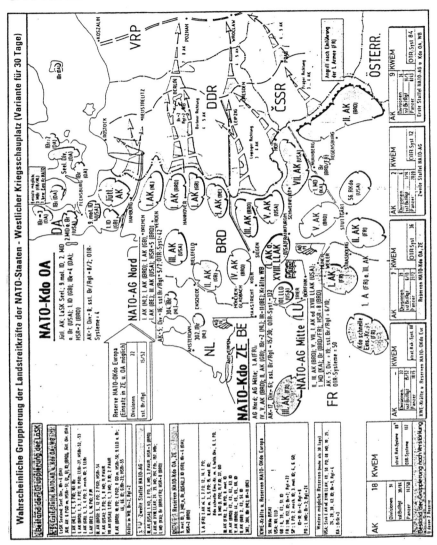

FIGURE 6-3: PROBABLE GROUPING OF NATO FORCES - WESTERN THEATRE OF WAR (30 DAY VARIANT)

This is an extract from NVA documents provided to the lower planning levels in the Warsaw Pact organization. Note the location of '1 MD(KA)' behind, instead of in front of Nürnberg. Note also the locations of non-existent NATO formations like II(BR) Corps, IV(GE) Corps and V(GE) Corps as well as NATO 'attack routes' into the East Bloc.

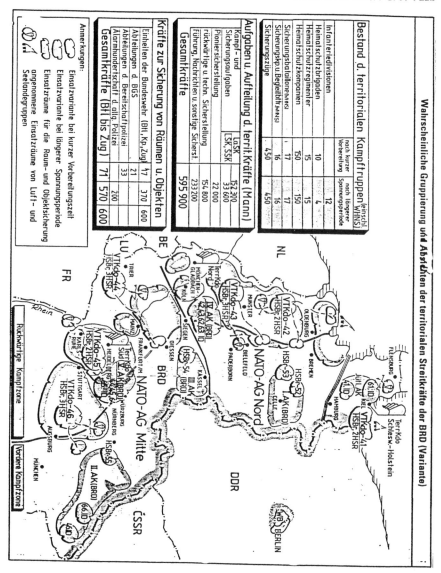

FIGURE 6-4: PROBABLE GROUPING AND INTENTIONS OF [WEST GERMAN] TERRITORIAL FORCES

This is another NVA document 'demonstrating' the offensive nature of NATO planning and the alleged strong array of West German forces posed against them.

capabilities and sizes. In Germany, this included five Mi-24 regiments (total 210 *Hinds* and 100 *Hips*), as well as four airmobile battalions (one per Army) and an Airmobile Brigade under GSFG's direct control. The airmobile battalions and the Brigade were actually 'air mechanized' brigades, as they were equipped with the parachute-droppable BMD infantry combat vehicle. In all, three Soviet airmobile brigades were available for operations in Germany, as well as two airborne brigades.

Doctrinally, the Soviets had been experimenting with more combined arms formations, and had increased the proportion of armour to mechanized infantry in the motor rifle divisions. The Operational Manoeuvre Group (OMG) concept that Western observers noted in the early 1980s was the subject of great debate and concern. Regardless of whether it was a brand new concept or an old one in new clothing, OMGs were considered by some to be an example of new and more flexible Soviet thinking and a move away from the rigid, doctrinaire approach that many observers had characterized the Soviets with. The prospect of an OMG of division or corps size breaking into and running loose in NATO's rear combat zone, destroying communications centres and the fragile logistical system was an alarming scenario. Additionally, the advent of the Reconnaissance-Fire Complex, that is, the linking of Army-level artillery resources to reconnaissance forces, was another indicator of new Soviet flexibility.

One area that was emphasized more and more within NATO in the early 1980s was the Soviet chemical weapons threat. Confirmed use of nerve and blister agents in Afghanistan really brought to the fore NATO's lack of preparedness in this area. There were a large number of fully equipped chemical decontamination units in GSFG, and much of the Soviet artillery was chemical-capable. Although this threat had always existed, NATO in the past had an adequate retaliatory capability. This capability had deteriorated since 1970, and the situation was believed by some to encourage early Soviet chemical use in any Warsaw Pact attack on NATO.

The increased threat to NATO's rear area was another significant area of Soviet development. In addition to the confusion that would be created by irregular terrorist forces operating in NATO countries, the Soviets had their own special forces, commonly referred to as *Spetsnaz*, although there were in fact several different types of these forces. *Spetsnaz* targets included NATO's nuclear and chemical forces, its military and political leadership, command facilities, as well as fixed logistics systems like the NATO pipeline. Other *Spetsnaz* functions included long range reconnaissance, airfield attack and delay/disruption operations against NATO reinforcement formations. About three brigades worth of Soviet special purpose forces were directed against the Central Region, including 200 ten-man teams against CENTAG's rear area alone.

Another Warsaw Pact formation, the East German Army's *Willi Sanger* Brigade, deserves mention. This organization possessed M-113 APCs and M-48 tanks obtained from communist captured South Vietnamese stocks. Its role was to mimic a Bundeswehr brigade in order to sow confusion in NATO's rear area. All of its personnel wore Bundeswehr uniforms.

The Soviet ability to conduct operational/theatre level nuclear warfare against NATO had existed for two decades. The main question that puzzled NATO planners was, when, in the course of a conflict, would the Soviets resort to nuclear use? The assessment in 1983 was that

> ...the Soviets consider that any conflict with NATO will quickly expand into nuclear warfare at the theatre level. If not initiated by NATO, the Soviets themselves may initiate nuclear exchange if they deem it necessary to achieve their stated objective, or if their intelligence indicates that NATO is preparing to employ such weapons. In any event, the initial strike is expected to be theatre wide and may involve the employment of hundreds of weapons per front.

Information that has come to light since the end of the Cold War confirms that NATO planners were not wrong. The Soviets' 1983 nuclear strike plan against the Central Region included the use of 840 nuclear weapons, delivered by *Frog* or *Scud* missiles or by tactical aircraft. Primary targets were NATO's theatre and tactical nuclear delivery systems (right down to divisional weapons including the M-109 SP guns), all airfields (including Lahr and Baden), command and control bunkers and troop assembly areas, particularly the Tactical Assembly Areas behind the main battle positions in the forward area. Nuclear use was

CHAPTER SIX

incorporated into all Warsaw Pact exercises in the 1980s. The existence of separate Warsaw Pact conventional war plans and nuclear war plans is not clear. It appears that the Warsaw Pact was prepared to go nuclear on any indication that NATO was *preparing* to use nuclear weapons at any level.

In sum, the Warsaw Pact had developed a number of new capabilities, the most significant being (in addition to the qualitative improvements), its ability to massively threaten NATO's vital rear area. NATO would have been hard pressed to deal with this problem and, arguably, never developed an adequate defence against it.

As we have seen in earlier chapters, NATO was continually seeking ways to develop a credible response to any Soviet attack on the Central Region. General Bernard Rogers, SACEUR in the early 1980s, was worried about the overall military balance which was unfavourable to NATO: if trends were not reversed, NATO would soon reach a point where deterrence would no longer be credible.

Significantly, Rogers believed that the present imbalance already precluded NATO from conducting effective forward defence. As the aim of forward defence was to blunt the initial Warsaw Pact attack, NATO's forces were capable of this. However, the whole of NATO's defence concept was based on a short war. The key question was, how short? In order to apply a successful forward defence, he believed that NATO needed to be capable of blunting not only the first echelon forces of a Warsaw Pact thrust, but the second echelon as well. Existing NATO forces could not do that without resorting to the use of nuclear weapons. Prior to 1970, NATO forces were permitted to do so. With the implementation of Flexible Response, they could not. The onus on nuclear use at this level of warfare, Rogers believed, should rest on the Soviets, not NATO. Thus, the doctrine of Follow-on Forces Attack or FOFA was born.

The development of FOFA as a concept prior to 1982 need not concern us here in detail, except that it was a response to the inadequacies inherent in the US concept of Active Defense in the 1970s, and was an important aspect of the new 1982 US AirLand Battle doctrine. As a general concept, FOFA was not radically different from the operational planning in the 1960s which used nuclear-capable aircraft and land-based missiles to attack the enemy second echelon in East Germany, Poland

and Czechoslovakia. The difference now was that such a second echelon attack would be conducted with conventional weapons. The fact that weapons technology had advanced sufficiently to greatly increase the accuracy and lethality of conventional weapons systems, enabled NATO to develop a defence that did not require immediate or near-immediate tactical nuclear use.

If war came, NATO forces already deployed in Germany would be responsible for conducting a successful forward defence along and behind the border region. At the same time NATO deep strike forces based on aircraft missiles, long range artillery, and Multiple Launch Rocket Systems (MLRS) and Precision Guided Munitions (PGMs) would then be employed against the Warsaw Pact's second echelon forces (the follow-on forces). Concurrently, US reinforcements would be pouring in from North America to man the POMCUS equipment. These units would take up positions behind the forward defence forces – which were already delaying the Warsaw Pact invasion – and prepare to counter-attack. As an aside, the 'French Problem' discussed previously was starting to change in the 1980s. The French concept of fighting on the Rhine and using tactical nuclear weapons was still in effect, but contingency plans had been drawn up to move divisions from II (FR) Corps d'armée forward to TAAs behind VII (US) Corps, II (GE) Korps and 4 CMBG. In this sense, the French forces contributed to the reinforcement of NATO's forward deployed forces in contact.

As envisioned, FOFA had three types of forces: forward defence forces, target acquisition forces and deep battle (also called deep strike) forces. The existing conventional forces defending the Central Region, including 4 CMBG in CENTAG, were to bear the brunt of the enemy first echelon attack and deny the enemy deep penetration into the rear area. Simultaneously, NATO's target acquisition forces which included photo recce aircraft, JSTARS, AWACS, satellites, special forces teams and remotely piloted vehicles, would search for the Warsaw Pact's second strategic echelon in an area extending from the Iron Curtain back to the Soviet Union. These targets would include concentrations of enemy forces, logistics nodes, command and communications facilities and storage sites. Once the second echelon had been identified, deep battle forces would be deployed to attack them before they could pass through the first echelon and engage NATO's main defences. NATO deep battle forces could include, depending on the distance away from the FEBA, strike aircraft from 4 ATAF, long range attack helicopters (AH-64s), the MLRS or a new weapon called SADARM, a missile-launched dispenser containing a large number of "smart" sub-munitions which individually home in on enemy armoured vehicles.

Of course, the development of FOFA capability would take time. While FOFA was shifting from concept to reality, the US and German forces in CENTAG were upgrading their conventional forces. The US Army received the M-1 *Abrams* tank and the M-2 *Bradley* infantry combat vehicle, providing a quantum leap in capability over the M-60A1 and the M-113 APC. The Germans started to replace the *Leopard I* with the *Leopard II*; they already possessed a MICV in the form of the *Marder* and deployed a multiple launch rocket system as well. Eventually the first FOFA systems came on line. The US deployed the MLRS in 1983, and the AH-64 helicopter in 1986. SADARM would have to wait till 1991, as would the JSTARS target acquisition aircraft.

It should be emphasized here that there was still a significant battlefield nuclear threat in the Central Region in the early 1980s. NATO planners believed that the Soviets considered that any conflict with NATO would quickly escalate into nuclear warfare at the theatre level. If NATO was being successful at the conventional level using FOFA, it was unlikely that the Soviets would restrain themselves. Indeed, as noted earlier, Warsaw Pact plans included options for the immediate use of battlefield and theatre nuclear weapons from the outset of a conflict.

Canada's role in the FOFA concept was constrained both by the size of its NATO contribution and a lack of appropriate weaponry. Certainly, 1 Canadian Air Group's strike aircraft could have operated in a FOFA role, but 4 CMBG did not possess either MLRS or attack helicopters, which were really divisional or corps-level weapons systems in any case.

As noted earlier, the assessment of the Warsaw Pact threat to CENTAG in the 1980s emphasized the Fulda, Cheb and Highway 14/Nürnberg approaches. As the Fulda Gap was the exclusive domain of V(US) Corps, where 4 CMBG had no role, the primary focus of the Brigade was on the latter two enemy thrust lines. 4 CMBG's employment priority also changed from II (GE) Korps to VII (US) Corps, which corresponded with the altered CENTAG assessment regarding the Donau Approach.

Nürnberg, one of the largest and most famous cities in Germany, lay 100 kilometers from the Czech border; if Nürnberg were to fall, the loss of Munich would not be far behind, resulting in a severe blow to the morale of the German people as well as a major loss of NATO territory. Fortunately, the terrain between Nürnberg and Czechoslovakia favoured the defence. The forested and hilly areas of the Bayerischerwald (Bavarian Forest) and the Fränkische Alb, and the large number of minor water obstacles, were ideal for the type of defensive battle envisioned by CENTAG.

The Warsaw Pact was rated as being able to attack with two divisions along the Cheb, Highway 14 and Fürth approaches (possibly the 2nd Czech Motor Rifle Division and the 9th Czech Tank Division) in the first operational echelon, with three divisions following in the next. CENTAG had only seven brigades to cover these three approaches. The addition of 4 CMBG would have been important to any defence on these threat lines, and this factor figured prominently in the development of 1980s GDP planning.

Before 4 CMBG could focus on the Nürnberg approaches problem, overtures were made in 1982 at a higher level to alter the employment of 4 CMBG even more radically. CENTAG planners were still concerned with the defence of the critical V(US) Corps and III (GE) Korps area, the Fulda Gap and the approaches to Frankfurt. (The assignment of a third German airborne brigade from III (GE) Korps to II (GE) Korps to cover the Donau Approach probably influenced this). 4 CMBG was quizzed on such employment options; what did Canada think about being made priority call to V(US) Corps?

In principle, 4 CMBG was not against deployment to the V(US) Corps area, but several factors militated against the proposal. Although this area was in fact closer to Lahr/Baden than the II (GE) Korps sector, the intimate familiarity that 4 CMBG clearly had with the II (GE) Korps sector as well as the decade-long relationships with German and American formations in Bavaria were things to be considered. A no less important factor was training costs. Normally, 4 CMBG travelled to Hohenfels and Grafenwöhr to work up for Fallexs, and then deployed immediately into Bavarian countryside for the large scale manoeuvres. The VII (US) Corps or II (GE) Korps exercises were always held adjacent to these training areas. If 4 CMBG was going to operate with V(US) Corps on a REFORGER, it would cost money to move it three times instead of two – once to the training areas, once again to wherever V(US) Corps was exercising, and then home. No, 4 CMBG would not be committed to V(US) Corps.

4 CMBG's GDP did, however, change in 1982-1983. In line with CENTAG's reassessment of the threat on the Nürnberg approaches, the priority employment of 4 CMBG changed from II (GE) Corps to VII (US) Corps. [See Figure 6-5.] In the late 1970s, 4 CMBG was to deploy to TAA PUMA and await orders for one of several employment options near the Fürth approach or to back up 4 Jaeger Division. The northern edge of PUMA rested on the inter-corps boundary between II (GE) Korps and VII(US) Corps. The 1970s inter-corps boundary was a key enemy route of advance, that is Highway 14. Having a corps boundary on such a route was dangerous from the standpoint of coordination between the two corps. As a result, the boundary was moved north so that Highway 14 became the responsibility of II (GE) Korps.

The movement of the boundary as well as the priority change to VII (US) Corps dictated that PUMA be altered, which was implemented immediately. PUMA was extended north to the new inter-corps boundary and was re-named TAA SETTER. This allowed 4 CMBG the ability to deploy into the VII (US) Corps area as well as to II (GE) Korps, which was second priority. VII (US) Corps had 1st (US) Armored Division in place prepared to fight from behind the Naab River to counter enemy forces moving through the Cheb gap. North of 1st (US) Armored Division was 4th (US) Infantry Division. 4 CMBG's role (after some discussion) was to provide a blocking or counter-penetration force if the enemy broke through the lead elements of these divisions. 4 CMBG thus had a blocking or counter-penetration mission as opposed to a counter-attack mission. Given the fact that 4 CMBG was infantry-heavy, was short on tanks, and had a large number (36) of TOW systems, it was felt that the counter-attack mission should be left to other allied formations which were tank-heavy.

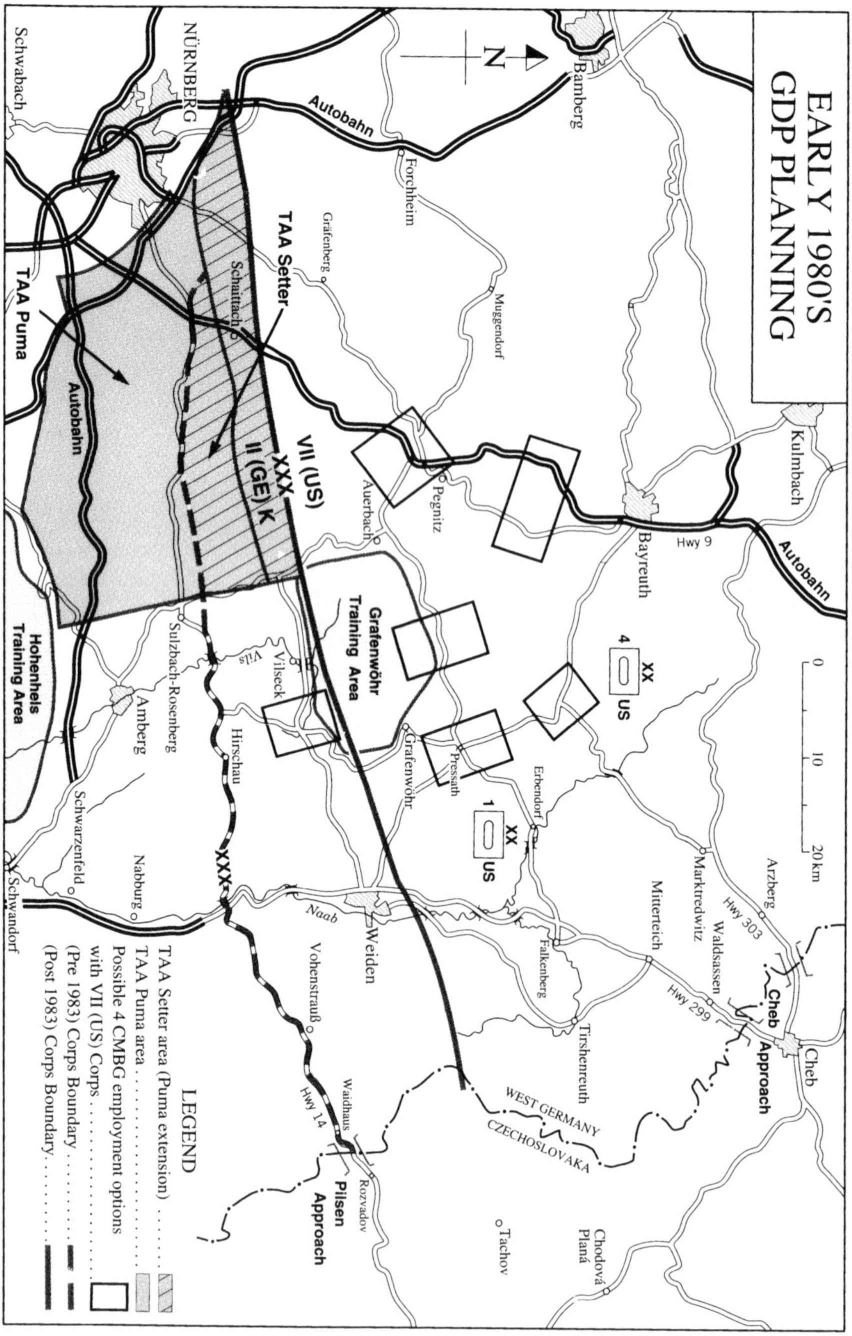
EARLY 1980'S
GDP PLANNING
N
Bamberg
Kulmbach
Bayreuth
Hwy 9
Autobahn
Forchheim
Gräfenberg
Muggendorf
Pegnitz
Auerbach
NÜRNBERG
Schwabach
Schnaittach
TAA Setter
TAA Puma
Autobahn
VII (US)
XXX
II (GE) K
Grafenwöhr
Training Area
Hohenfels
Training Area
Sulzbach-Rosenberg
Vils
Vilseck
Amberg
Hirschau
Grafenwöhr
Pressath
Erbendorf
4 XX US
1 XX US
0 10 20 km
Arzberg
Hwy 303
Marktredwitz
Waldsassen
Mitterteich
Hwy 299
Cheb
Cheb
Approach
Falkenberg
Tirshenreuth
Schwarzenfeld
Nabburg
Schwandorf
XXX
Naab
Weiden
Vohenstrauß
Waidhaus
Hwy 14
Rozvadov
Pilsen
Approach
WEST GERMANY
CZECHOSLOVAKIA
Tachov
Chodová Planá
LEGEND
TAA Setter area (Puma extension)
TAA Puma area
Possible 4 CMBG employment options with VII (US) Corps
(Pre 1983) Corps Boundary
(Post 1983) Corps Boundary

FIGURE 6-5

CHAPTER SIX

Consequently, a number of employment options for 4 CMBG were created. Options PLUTO, MERCURY, SATURN, JUPITER and MARS would have provided crucial support to the Americans, who would have their own resources in VII (US) Corps spread thin. Brigadier General Rick Evraire was 4 CMBG's commander from 1982-1984:

> General Galvin's whole approach to soldiering was different, and among other things he undertook when he arrived was a complete review of the GDP....We were initiating the AirLand Battle concept and there were quite a number of changes at the operational level....One of the plans prepared by General Galvin's staff required 4 Brigade to go from its GDP positions east of Nürnberg south of the inter-corps boundary, into tremendous sweeps all over the place, two, three, or four options that were more developed later on depending on what stage the battle was in or how II(GE) Korps, [12] Panzer Division or 4 Jaeger Division were doing, etc.
>
> We had these options of zapping all over the place, and I remember making the report to General Galvin one day after the initial set of briefings. That was fine except that, as far as I was concerned, 4 Brigade was not equipped [properly] and not capable of undertaking that sort of tasking....We were essentially defensive in nature, and the best use he could make of 4 Brigade was to make sure that it was in a fairly static defensive position with the possibility of counterattacking here and there, but not as an offensive weapon....I know this did not please too many people, but it was hardly the place to be untruthful about this....

The GRIZZLY and NASHORN blocking options in II (GE) Korps were retained as contingency plans in case 4 CMBG had to swing south.

In 1984 the Chief of the Defence Staff, General Gerard Thériault, was exploring areas to save money, and re-raised the possibility of allocating 4 CMBG permanently to either II (GE) Korps or VII (US) Corps instead of having 4 CMBG remain as CENTAG's reserve. Over the next year or so, this idea was bandied about but eventually rejected on a number of grounds. As in the 1950s, 'visibility' issues were critical. If 4 CMBG was assigned to any one national force, there was a risk that the Canadian identity would be submerged. As one observer noted:

Dual assignment highlights the fact that 4 CMBG is a COMCENTAG formation. If the Brigade were assigned to a corps, it would become 'just another brigade', one of a dozen assigned to each of the corps commanders within their divisional structures. This would clearly reduce the visibility of the Canadian formation within NATO.

In a more selfish sense, 4 CMBG had much to gain by playing both sides of the fence:

> In our present deployment area we are wanted by both Corps. Each considers us a valuable operational asset. This works to our obvious advantage and we derive the benefit of excellent support in all areas from both the German and American commanders and staff....

When Brigadier General Jack Dangerfield took over 4 CMBG in 1984, he was asked many times about this issue:

> There were tremendous advantages to being the Army Group reserve. First of all, this brought you to the Army Group 'table', rather than some Corps 'table'. The Canadian Brigade Commander attended Army Group conferences where there were four corps commanders and one brigade commander. That was a significant advantage, and we also got advantages that allowed us to train. We could train with either [Corps] at our choosing, and we were a very popular selection for the major exercises. So, for example, II (GE) Korps trained on an exercise every two years, [VII (US) Corps and V(US) Corps trained on alternate years], this meant that we could train every year with either an American corps or II (GE) Korps....

Besides having the possibility of participating in a major corps-level exercise every year, the logistics implications were obvious. 4 CMBG used German tanks, American APCs and anti-tank missile systems, while all three nations used the M-109 SP guns. By remaining 'on the fence', 4 CMBG could benefit from all sides. 4 CMBG thus remained dual-tasked in wartime, with priority to VII (US) Corps.

Operational support plans for 4 CMBG augmentation and reinforcement prior to 1986 were not radically different from those described in

CHAPTER SIX

the last chapter. Operations PENDANT, MAYFLOWER and BARBET still existed on paper but were never fully exercised; their usefulness in a crisis situation was as suspect in the early 1980s, as the 1970s. PENDANT was modified in September 1979 and again in September 1980, probably in response to the heightened international tension. The revised PENDANT added one armoured squadron, an engineer troop, two infantry companies and an unspecified number of combat service support troops. This, on paper, would bring the units in 4 CMBG back up to normal establishment levels, ie: four infantry companies, three armoured squadrons, four artillery batteries. The revised plan, however, did not restore the third infantry battalion or other service functions.

Although the Americans in CENTAG were starting to rise out of their Vietnam malaise by the late 1970s, humorous FALLEX incidents involving US soldiers and the Canadians continued to be part of 4 CMBG lore into the 1980s, as Corporal Shaun Brown explains:

> On FALLEX 84, for a change, we were set up in a woods instead of a village. It had been raining all day and was getting fairly late. The nearest other force was about five kilometers from us (another part of the squadron). All of a sudden our guard showed up at the CP with this American (the enemy at the time) who was wearing [nothing but] a T-shirt, combat pants and combat boots, holding a shovel and a roll of toilet paper. It seems he had gone into the woods to attend to his bodily functions and got lost. For about five hours he had been wandering around trying to find somebody. One of the first things [that he said] was 'Jees, now I'm in s—. I've lost my rifle for the third time this month!' After feeding him and finding where he belonged, we drove him back to his unit and never heard anything else from him.

Warrant Officer Max Rudneu's experiences are also representative of the contacts between Canadians and Americans in Germany:

> During the Grafenwöhr gun camp we had the privilege of going to the PX [post exchange] and we always had a chance to talk to the US soldiers relaxing there. Rick Ostashower made friends with an American tank crew and was sitting with them when I walked in. I joined them and the conversation turned to Canadians and their way of doing things. One of the examples we

hit on was the fact that we were allowed to carry knives in uniform (a policy which has since been changed). Rick carried a K-Bar (the USMC fighting knife) and one of the Americans noticed it. He asked to see it and Rick obliged by sticking it into the table top. This impressed the Yanks and one of them jokingly said: 'Oh Oh, we got Canadian trouble!' It was just loud enough that everyone in the place stopped and looked. Rick and I were alone. Sizing up the situation, Rick says, 'OK Max you take this half and I'll take the other half'. Sensing that bravado was the word of the day (and I figured we were dead meat anyway) I answered, 'Sure, give me the big guys again!' Everyone laughed and I started breathing again. The Americans went on to comment on the toughness of the Canadian soldiers and we asked why he was so interested because we were really not too different from them in certain respects. This led to the comment that the Yanks had a briefing prior to our arrival at the base, and the Base Commander was quoted as saying that the Yanks were to leave all Canadian soldiers alone because he did not want his base flattened...

Canadian discipline was handled in a different manner:

During our deployments to Grafenwöhr we were accompanied by a detachment of Canadian military police. In some cases it was a good thing they did, since the US MPs had a reputation for preferring more forceful methods of settling a fray before getting to the root of the problem. They would break a few heads, throw everyone in cells and then let the innocents go....Some of our boys got into a 'discussion' with some of our allies and someone called the MPs. Our MPs were riding in a US patrol car and went along because Canadians were involved. Arriving at the scene, the Americans bailed out of the car with batons, flashlights and sidearms. Our MPs only carry sidearms: I suppose the US MPs were surprised that they did not draw them, and commented on the fact. Our MPs told them they would not be needed and proceeded inside. Apparently when the Americans waded in to stop the action, the Canadian MPs yelled at our guys to stop, pointed at the guilty parties, and told them to follow them out to the waiting patrol car. Our guys did not resist, and the Americans were amazed at the cooperation. One said to the Canadian MPs 'You have to teach me how you do that!'

No account of 4 CMBG's activities during this time would be complete without mentioning British military historian and author Kenneth Macksey's book, *First Clash*. In 1984, Macksey was commissioned by Mobile Command to write a training manual that portrayed tactics at the combat team and battle group level. To research the 'battlefield' and 'players', Macksey spent time with 4 Brigade units during FALLEX observing training exercises and familiarizing himself with Canadian thinking and operating procedures. The resulting book showed 4 CMBG (without its flyover infantry companies and armoured squadron) conducting a three-day blocking action in the face of an assault by elements of the Soviet First Guards Tank Division. An interesting and thought provoking work, *First Clash* graphically described what a conflict in the Central Region at 4 CMBG's level would have been like and provided a useful discussion of factors influencing this type of battle. The work later hit the bookstands as a commercial product.

4 CMBG also assumed the mantle of social test-bed. In response to the Human Rights Act (1 March 1978), the Canadian Forces were ordered to evaluate the possible placement of women in combat or near-combat roles. Between 1980 and 1984, the Servicewomen In Non-Traditional Roles and Environments (SWINTER) trials assessed the female soldier's ability to function in 'near combat' units. 4 Service Battalion and 4 Field Ambulance were selected for this task. The results were not encouraging, with one report going as far to state that, "should women be placed in combat situations, more Canadians will likely die." Be that as it may, political considerations overruled and women were given the opportunity to join CF combat units by the late 1980s, though none served in such units in 4 CMBG. Women, however, did serve in service support roles in the Brigade, and made up about 15 per cent of 4 Service Battalion and 4 Field Ambulance by the time of the Brigade's disbandment in 1993.

European terrorism formed part of the milieu which 4 CMBG soldiers and families had to live in the late 1970s and 1980s. These terrorist groups had many names and just as many objectives. Some were self-contained and revolutionary in nature while others received direct aid from Warsaw Pact countries. In some cases it is difficult to distinguish purely anti-American acts from anti-NATO acts. The results of the activities of Germany's Revolutionary Cells, Red Army Faction, its predecessor – the Baader-Meinhof Gang, the Belgian Communist Combattant Cells and the Italian Red Brigades as well as their far right counterparts, was to create an air of danger and risk in everyday life in Europe.

Some incidents struck close to home. In one case, SACEUR himself, General Alexander Haig, was the target of a bomb attack, while the CENTAG commander, General Kroesen, was subjected to a rocket propelled grenade attack in downtown Heidelberg. Many attempts were made against NATO's Central European Pipeline System, and in another case terrorists used Bundeswehr uniforms to infiltrate an arms dump. A car bomb was used against the important reinforcement airfield at Frankfurt, while the headquarters of NATO's Central Region Air Forces was also bombed. Even the SHAPE School at Oberammergau was the target of a bomb attempt. If one were looking for a pattern, there appeared to be more than enough evidence to show that terrorist groups were conducting some not so dry runs against live targets and preparing for the day Warsaw Pact forces poured across the border.

In retrospect, Canadian forces were fairly safe. Canadian commanders were not high-profile enough to provide media fodder for the terrorists' propaganda campaign, and there were too many American and NATO targets that were less well protected. There were only two occasions before the 1991 Gulf War that brought CFE up to a heightened level of internal security. In 1980, after the successful rescue of Americans in Iran by the Canadian embassy there was some concern that a German terrorist group could be used to pinch hit for the Iranians. New precautions were taken to discourage easy targeting of the CFE leadership, and Canadians were instructed to be more observant. An explosion at a POL dump on the Lahr airfield in 1987 was initially believed to be a terrorist attack. In reality, it was an inside job, done by a couple of individuals who did not want to go out on exercise. Security was heightened for a number of days while the matter was investigated.

Other threats existed besides terrorism. Troops operating in the CENTAG area had to contend with the Soviet Military Liaison Missions (SMLM) in the same way that their predecessors had with SOXMIS in Northern Germany. Warrant Officer Wayne Ivey of the Brigade Intelligence Section was in a good position to observe Warsaw Pact

CHAPTER SIX

intelligence activity in West Germany:

> Down here we had SMLM, one group located in Frankfurt to monitor the Americans and one located in Baden-Baden to monitor the French. When we or other NATO partners went on exercise, they were out having a look at us, looking for new equipment, how long it would take you to move from point A to point B, how you refueled, what your logistics were. Logistics to these people appeared to be one of the most important things they were after. The rules were that they were not allowed off the Autobahn. If they got off the Autobahn into a restricted area during exercises or into a permanent restricted area, our job was to find them and 'neutralize' them. To neutralize, all we had to do was let them know we were there and follow them. That in fact is what did the trick. They could not do anything once they knew we were there. If we felt that they were up to something, then we went a little more in depth....

Besides SMLM, the Soviets employed other methods of intelligence gathering against 4 CMBG. A favoured method was the *Transport International Routier* (TIR) trucks – roughly 50 000 East Bloc commercial vehicles per year – moving goods around Europe. Not all could be watched or followed. Some of them carried concealed electronic intelligence collection equipment, some had concealed cameras, and many could be seen parked near important NATO installations. Drivers would routinely measure highway underpasses, bridges and other parts of the transportation infrastructure, obviously compiling data that would be of use to Warsaw Pact forces invading West Germany. East Bloc barge traffic moving along the Rhine or other rivers also carried intelligence gathering apparatus.

In addition to being subject to a vast amount of intelligence gathering, 4 CMBG and other NATO formations were targeted by a low intensity harassment campaign which, if not under the complete control of the Soviets, was strongly encouraged and morally supported by them. This campaign took many forms, some of them lethal. NATO's decision to improve its nuclear and conventional forces was clearly an obstacle to Soviet aims of hegemony in Europe. If public support in the West for this modernization could be undermined and a pacifist mindset developed in the population, Soviet aims in Europe and elsewhere might be achieved without firing a shot.

This campaign used every means in the Soviet's low intensity arsenal. Terrorism, discussed earlier, and infiltration and control of peace groups was part of this. Sabotage against NATO units on exercise was another important element. Such sabotage took many forms, some of them occasionally lethal for NATO troops. Bridge load capacity and height signs were painted over or altered, resulting in accidents which killed soldiers and civilians. Debris was piled on the Bundesbahn railway lines to block or derail military trains; elements of the Bundespost telephone system were tampered with or destroyed, preventing emergency communication. Tires were punctured, military telephone land lines were cut, and convoys were hindered by demonstrations.

Nuclear weapons had been an emotional issue for many years. Once NATO announced its force modernization, a vast number of violent demonstrations occurred. The Soviet infiltrated anti-nuclear movement in Europe did not focus exclusively on NATO's nuclear facilities. Practically every national installation supporting NATO was targeted for demonstrations, intrusion and harassment. Starting in 1982, demonstrators picketed and harassed Canadian personnel entering CFB Lahr at least one day every week. The base commander was deluged with demands by the peace movement to allow demonstrators access to the ammunition storage sites to ensure that Lahr was a "nuclear free zone".

One group even created leaflets which were allegedly from the Commander, CFE to the people of Lahr thanking them for their support and saying that Canada was pulling out. These were very professionally done and looked official. This, needless to say, caused some consternation.

The effect of this campaign was to drive a wedge deeper between Canadians and some of the Germans in Lahr and Baden. As noted in the previous chapter, the relations between the Canadians and the Germans 'down south' differed from those 'up north'. Germany in the 1980s was not 1950s Germany. The environmental movement had gained widespread support in the population and many citizens in the area were tired of jet aircraft noise, helicopter overflights, SNOWBALL alert measures, and armoured vehicles moving through cobbled streets late at night.

By portraying Canadians as a nuisance and a danger rather than a necessity, the enemy could and did exploit this situation. One propaganda theme suggested that if there were no Canadian forces in Lahr or Baden, these towns would not be a nuclear target. The nuclear target theme was quite prevalent in the 1980s and held strong appeal to those who had been duped into believing that the Soviets only had a huge standing army and vast numbers of missiles simply because NATO existed. In reality it was the decay on the other side of the Iron Curtain which was more of a threat to peace than any NATO force modernization. In any event, the considerable monetary benefits to the Lahr and Baden areas because of the Canadian presence was always appreciated, and Germans at large understood the need for a strong NATO presence.

As a postscript to this issue, it is also gratifying to note that, in response to the POL dump explosion in 1987, Dr. Olaf Feldmann of Lahr wrote to the senior Canadian commanders:

> I am deeply distressed over the violent attack on the Lahr airfield. Terrorism is a mental and political entanglement against which politics and police are helpless to some extent. It is my concern at this point to express my gratitude for the important contribution which the Canadian Forces in the Federal Republic of Germany contribute to the joint defence of peace and freedom. Terrorism cannot and must not affect the political understanding between Canada and the Federal Republic of Germany, especially between [the German population] and the Canadian soldiers and their families staying here with us as our guests....

Although the real reason for the explosion was not known to Dr. Feldmann, this sincere appreciation of the situation was perhaps more indicative of the local population's attitude than that of the vocal minority.

The Brigade's normal pattern of training continued in 1984. Even though the priority for employment of 4 CMBG had been changed from II (GE)Korps to VII (US) Corps, 4 CMBG was still invited to act as part of the enemy force in Ex FLINKER IGEL (Speedy Hedgehog) in September 1984. FLINKER IGEL was a very large exercise designed to test both Bundeswehr mobilization procedures and II (GE) Korps' ability to defend the Donau Approach based on the use of the actual ground. [See

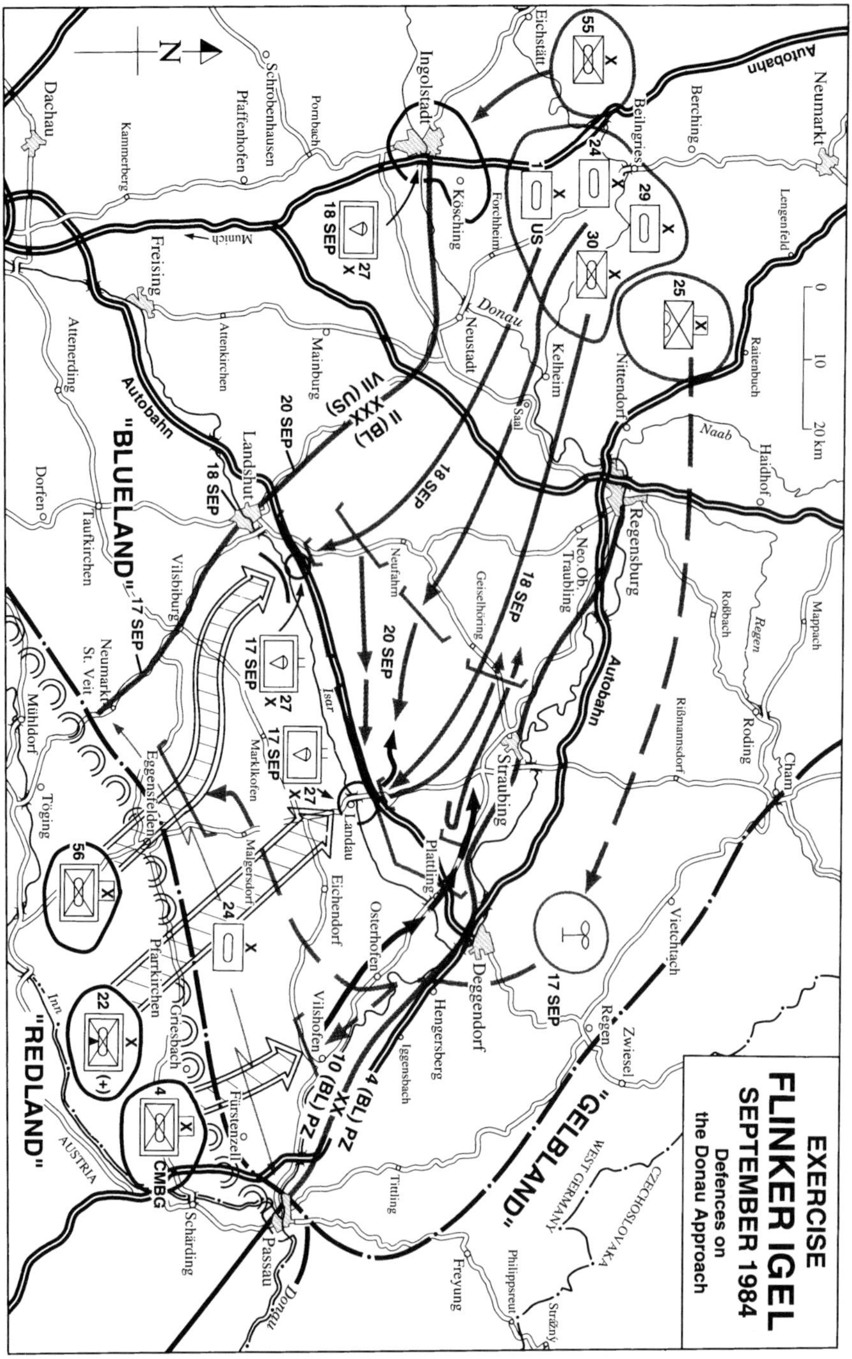
EXERCISE
FLINKER IGEL
SEPTEMBER 1984
Defences on
the Donau Approach
"BLUELAND"
"REDLAND"
"GELBLAND"
VII (US)
XXX
II (BL)
10 (BL) PZ
XX
4 (BL) PZ
CMBG
17 SEP
18 SEP
20 SEP
Autobahn
Munich
0
10
20 km
WEST GERMANY
CZECHOSLOVAKIA
AUSTRIA
Donau
Isar
Inn
Naab
Regen
Neumarkt
Berching
Beilngries
Eichstätt
Ingolstadt
Kösching
Forchheim
Neustadt
Kelheim
Saal
Nittendorf
Regensburg
Landshut
Neufahrn
Geiselhöring
Straubing
Landau
Plattling
Deggendorf
Osterhofen
Vilshofen
Passau
Dachau
Freising
Schrobenhausen
Pfaffenhofen
Mainburg
Attenkirchen
Erding
Dorfen
Taufkirchen
Vilsbiburg
Neumarkt St. Veit
Mühldorf
Töging
Eggenfelden
Pfarrkirchen
Griesbach
Fürstenzell
Schärding
Markikofen
Eichendorf
Hengersberg
Iggensbach
Tittling
Freyung
Philippsreut
Regen
Zwiesel
Viechtach
Cham
Roding
Rißmannsdorf
Roßbach
Mappach
Haidhof
Raitenbuch
Lengenfeld

FIGURE 6-6

Figure 6-6.]

The defending force, II (Blauland) Korps, included 1 Airborne Division (Airborne Brigade 25 with Panzer Brigade 24), 10 Panzer Division (including Panzer Brigade 29, Panzer Grenadier Brigade 30 and a US armoured brigade) and Heimat Schutz Brigade (HSB: Home Defence brigade) 55. The Blauland Forces, including the territorial forces, were alerted from peacetime locations with little or no warning before deployment. The Roteland Division was under the command of 1 Mountain Division and included 4 CMBG, Panzer Grenadier Brigade 22, Heimat Schutz Brigade 56, and a brigade-equivalent made up of units from 1 Mountain Division. Roteland also had under command Airborne Brigade 27.

Blauland deployed Panzer Brigade 24 along the exercise 'border' (which conformed to the Austrian border but was 10 kilometers inside Germany) in a covering force operation. On 17 September, Airborne Brigade 27 conducted two airmobile assaults on the bridges over the Isar River at Landshut and Landau. 4 CMBG on the right flank, and HSB 56 on the left flank engaged the Blau covering force, while Blau took advantage of the delay to move Airborne Brigade 25 by helicopter into two blocking positions well forward of the Isar. Before 4 CMBG and HSB 56 could reach the Isar River, the US armoured brigade reached Landshut and wiped out the Rote airmobile force. Panzer Grenadier Brigade 30 was slower off the mark and was unable to prevent 4 CMBG from crossing the Isar; it was more successful at blocking the Rote Panzer Grenadier Brigade 22 (which was committed to destroy the withdrawing Blau Panzer Brigade 24) at Landau.

The Isar Line stabilized on 18 September, with HSB 56 conducting a failed attack against the Americans. Panzer Grenadier Brigade 22 was able to cross the river and drive back the enemy but they were not decisively engaged. Only 4 CMBG was able to continue its drive forward. The surviving elements of Rote Airborne Brigade 27 conducted an airborne assault against the Donau River crossings at Ingolstadt but were wiped out by the hastily mobilized Blau HSB 55.

The last brigade in 10 Panzer Division, Panzer Brigade 29, was brought in on the left flank of the US brigade and initiated a counterattack against 4 CMBG and Panzer Grenadier Brigade 22 on 20

September. While 4 CMBG was withdrawing in good order the Blau counterattacks were not fully played out and the exercise ended the next day.

4 CMBG's participation was of considerable value to the Germans in assessing the Donau Approach. Exercising 10 Panzer Division and the Home Defence Brigades in such a situation certainly demonstrated to the Bundeswehr areas which needed improvement if II (GE) Korps was to be flexible enough to handle an attack on the Donau as well as through the Highway 14 and Fürth gaps.

FLINKER IGEL also gave further weight to the well-known argument that Canadian mechanized doctrine utilizing M113 APCs was obsolete in the face of new developments in allied equipment:

> The operation of 4 CMBG battle groups with *Marder* equipped German units reflects the obvious view that Canadian units are not ideally equipped for such operations. Our mobility remains a means of delivering the infantry to a protected dismount area for foot operations while our allies, using [Infantry Fighting Vehicles] attempt to fight an all armoured battle. The major successes of 2 PPCLI against such an enemy force were primarily when dismounted....

It was gratifying to 4 CMBG to note that by 1984 a high level of interoperability between the Canadians and the Germans had been reached. For example, on FLINKER IGEL, the RCD recce squadron operated very closely with the Reconnaissance Battalion of the Mountain Division, and 1 RCHA had no problem coordinating artillery fire support from 1 Mountain Division's artillery resources. Other interoperability opportunities were exploited, particularly the use of heavy lift helicopters to resupply brigade units.

In addition to the usual Militia flyover augmentees, 4 CMBG was also augmented on this exercise with 2 Electronic Warfare Squadron from Kingston, Ontario. Although this was not the first deployment of the unit to 4 CMBG, its new role was specifically to support 4 CMBG in war. In a number of cases, this Squadron was able to disrupt Blauland counter-attacks against 4 CMBG during the Isar river crossing and to disrupt the main counter-attack in the final day of the exercise.

CHAPTER SIX

The Canadian tradition of aggressive and innovative recce was carried into the 1980s and it can be said that the flexibility of the Brigade on operations was due to its ability to collect and process information rapidly and efficiently. RSM Doug Seed was part of Recce Squadron on FLINKER IGEL:

> I can recall an exercise where we were deployed well forward. Our soldiers would stay out there for three and four days at a time, sometimes up to one week, without re-supply. I can remember being forward of the battalions and tucked away [in an observation post]. We had a whole division of German tanks against us and some Americans as well...[We] were sitting in living rooms looking out windows, overlooking valleys and so on, anywhere we could establish an OP....

Sergeant Bill Hungerford also had recce experience with 8th Canadian Hussars:

> Sometimes it got very hairy. You were surrounded but not detected and you had to be careful about what type of information that you radioed back. If you started asking for fire missions to come in on an enemy location, that tells the enemy that somebody's out there, and they'd do a detailed search....I found that when you're by yourself the only restriction you had was your own lack of imagination or initiative. If you were able to get into somebody's living room, if you... walked downtown scoping out enemy positions, well and good....If you used your imagination, you got all kinds of information.

Sergeant Rick Kearny, also with 8th Hussars:

> One of the big things we had to do was identify the enemy. We identified the enemy by going down and reading the numbers on their vehicles. Now you can't do this with a pair of binoculars, the numbers are black on green and very difficult to read. The only way you can do this is to go up to the vehicle and get as close to it as possible.... I got up to a vehicle and I had my flashlight shined on it when the door opened and they started chasing me. I was just as scared as if the Russians were chasing me, with the adrenaline flowing and all. I don't remember getting caught, so they must have trained

me well....

On the whole, FLINKER IGEL was indicative of the state of 4 CMBG in the early 1980s. The Brigade had excellent relations with its NATO allies and could operate effectively with them in a wartime situation. The Brigade was aggressive in its operations. The only problem was equipment. The Canadian government's unwillingness to provide the funds necessary for qualitative upgrades would have posed problems if 4 CMBG had had to fight BMPs and T-64s.

The most profound changes to 4 CMBG in this period occurred in the wake of Brian Mulroney's election as prime minister in 1984. After the resignation of Minister of Defence Robert Coates, resulting from a round of drinks at Tiffany's strip club in Lahr, Erik Neilson took the reins at Defence and initiated a review of Canada's land force commitments.

This review was almost as critical as the Trudeau review in 1968. Could Canada afford to maintain the CAST Brigade Group commitment as well as 4 CMBG? Certainly both commitments had their problems. Was it possible to sustain both forces simultaneously from a logistics standpoint? Could Canada reinforce 4 CMBG and deploy the CAST Brigade Group, as well as provide replacements for both formations?

4 CMBG once again came within an ace of being withdrawn from Germany. NATO allies pressured Canada to keep both commitments; if the other NATO members were increasing their defence budgets to meet the "three per cent challenge" (later called the "four per cent challenge") was there any reason why Canada could not? Partisans for one commitment or the other fought out the issue in the halls of National Defence Headquarters.

The issue was ostensibly solved by Exercise BRAVE LION in 1986. BRAVE LION was a full-scale CAST Brigade Group deployment to Norway, the first such exercise during the 14-year existence of the CAST commitment. The results were not encouraging, and many flaws with the CAST concept were revealed. Despite accusations by some that BRAVE LION was rigged, the exercise clearly demonstrated that Canada could not logistically sustain both the CAST Brigade Group and 4 CMBG in a war situation. In the end, 4 CMBG survived to fight another day.

CHAPTER SIX

The new defence climate created by the election of the Mulroney government facilitated a number of personnel and equipment improvements which benefited 4 CMBG. Prior to the election, 4 CMBG took delivery of 384 MLVW 2 1/2 ton trucks in 1982 and 193 Iltis jeeps in 1984 to replace the aging 'deuce and a halfs' and 1960s-era jeeps. Forty-two 10-ton German MAN trucks were also purchased to move ammunition. After the election, the Canadian Army shifted from the FN C1 and FN C2 7.62 mm rifles and the *Sterling* 9mm submachine gun to the C7 5.56 mm rifle (based on the US M-16), the Belgian C9 5.56 mm *minimi* light machine gun and the C8 5.56 mm carbine. By 1986, 4 Field Ambulance had also received a number of new Mercedes-Benz *Unimog* ambulances. Although the RCD and 1 RCHA retained their previous numbers of armoured vehicles (*Leopard* C-1 MBTs, M-109A3 SP Guns) the two infantry battalions acquired the lethal TOW II missile and each replaced their 18 open pedestal mounts with the TOW Under Armour (TUA) anti-tank missile system, which came equipped with a thermal imaging sight. This increased 4 CMBG's anti-tank capability exponentially.

Another change was the adoption of the Distinctive Environmental Uniform or DEU. Even though CF 'de-unification' had been under study since 1980, the money was not available to implement the recommendation for a return to three distinctive service uniforms. By 1987, 4 CMBG (army) personnel received tan uniforms for summer wear and a heavier green uniform for winter. Combat clothing remained the same, except that a new improved webbing harness was fielded. A Garrison Dress was also introduced, which included a disruptive pattern smock (not for use in the field!) for base wear. A 4 Brigade shoulder patch was also authorized, which incorporated the NATO compass rose superimposed over a red maple leaf. There certainly would be no mistaking Canadians for British or US troops.

The only significant organizational changes in unit stationing were the rotation Operations PRINCESS ROYAL I and II, and Operation SPRINGBOK-CORONET. Even though the army had shifted to a man-for-man rotation in the 1970s, steps were taken to allow other Canadian-based units to serve in Germany. In 1984, Operation PRINCESS ROYAL I replaced 3 RCR in Baden with 2 PPCLI from Winnipeg. With SPRINGBOK CORONET in 1986, the 8th Canadian Hussars replaced the RCD as the brigade's armoured regiment. Then in 1988, 2 PPCLI rotated home, and 3 RCR returned to Germany on OP PRINCESS ROYAL II. These were the only unit rotations conducted by the brigade while in southern Germany.

In November 1987 all air defence elements in Europe, including 128 and 129 Air Defence Batteries and the Air Defence Troop of 1 RCHA were combined to form 4 Air Defence Regiment, RCA. 128 and 129 batteries remained in the airfield defence role, while the newly-formed 127 Battery supported 4 CMBG. By 1988, 4 AD Regiment replaced its static 40mm *Boffins* with sixteen 35mm Oerlikon anti-aircraft guns towed by new Steyr heavy trucks (HLVW). Steps were also begun to replace the *Blowpipe* shoulder-launched anti-aircraft missile with the *Javelin* system. The first ADATS (a self-propelled Air Defence and Anti-Tank System) were also deployed in 1988, giving 4 CMBG state-of-the-art air defence capability.

4 CMBG personnel levels also increased at this time. In the 1970s, 4 CMBG's peacetime strength (garrisoned in Germany) increased from the originally imposed 2800 ceiling to 3200 men. The wartime authorized strength of 4 CMBG in 1984 was 5618 all ranks. Augmentee lists were maintained for specialist personnel; these lists, known initially as the "Top 100" and later as it increased, the "Top 400", were part of the OP PENDANT augmentation.

Eventually, the Top 400 list became the basis for an actual increase in 4 CMBG's peacetime strength. This list grew to 1200 men, of which 935 were designated as part of 4 CMBG and the rest given over to CFB Lahr. Starting in 1987, 335 of these troops arrived in Lahr, followed by 600 more in 1988. (A third batch of 400 more personnel was planned but never implemented) These increases brought individual 4 CMBG units in Germany up to 70 and 80 per cent of war establishment or to 4215 in total number. OPLAN PENDANT was modified for flyover of the additional 1403 troops required to bring the entire brigade group to 100 per cent of its war establishment strength of 5618.

In real terms the Brigade's armoured regiment was now able to man its third tank squadron instead of relying on flyover personnel from CFB Gagetown, and the RCHA also got to man its fourth gun battery which it lost in 1979 to flyover status. The two infantry battalions were each now provided with their fourth rifle companies plus headquarters for a combat support company. The remaining brigade support units also received some strength increases. In a crisis the third infantry battalion probably would have been brought from Cyprus, but detailed plans were not made to receive it in Lahr, nor was enough equipment pre-positioned for it.

As before, Operation BARBET was designed to provide 938 battle casualty replacements for a thirty-day period, based on the assumption that 4 CMBG would sustain a five per cent casualty rate. This was, however, a 1970s model. By the 1980s, DND had developed more sophisticated casualty models in response to a SACEUR initiative, and a new casualty rate of 14 per cent was derived. This change made BARBET dangerously obsolete, a problem which was never corrected. Even after the implementation of BARBET, there was still no plan for wartime sustainment after 30 days, at least prior to 985.

The essential elements of Operation MAYFLOWER did not change much in the 1980s. Civilian and military transport aircraft bringing in Operation PENDANT augmentees were to remove DND dependents from Lahr and Baden. An old version of Operation SAFEKEEP was revised so that dependents could be protected if the Soviets attacked with less than five hours notice. SAFEKEEP was designed to ensure that DND dependents were protected from the effects of an air strike on the two airfields.

It is important to note that the protection of Canadian families serving with CFE were completely integrated into war planning. Adherence to the 'Stay Put' policy had been completely discarded by the 1980s. If DND civilians and dependents could not be evacuated, however, everybody, be they a teacher or a dentist, had a role to play in maintaining the morale and physical well-being of the CFE civilian population.

With the arrival of Brigadier General Jack Dangerfield as Brigade Commander in 1984 came a complete overhaul of 4 CMBG planning and training. General Dangerfield was determined to inject reality into what he perceived was an unrealistic planning environment.

The resulting 4 CMBG Operational Review was a no holds barred appreciation of 4 CMBG's situation. The primary culprits were not just uninterested politicians, but a lack of corporate memory and superficial thinking in operational matters not just by 4 CMBG but at all levels of the Canadian Forces. This Operational Review took two years, and by 1986, General Dangerfield reported that:

> ...We have made progress, but not nearly enough in planning for the eventuality of going to war tomorrow....War requirements have not been identified, matched to resources and, where there is a shortage, a plan to minimize the impact of that shortfall produced. Instead, we have cloaked these problems behind a mask of idealistic and quite probably unrealistic plans such as war-task assigned personnel, the CSG(C) and so on. The main purpose of our review was to try and identify how we should go about solving our problems with today's resources and in today's circumstances.

There were equipment shortfalls, particularly in logistics vehicles (214) and APCs (58). To give 4 CMBG the ability to fight on the 1980s battlefield, other areas needed improvement. Brigadier General Dangerfield advocated the return of 4 CMBG to its pre-1968 establishment and strength, that is bring back a third infantry battalion and a fourth tank squadron, or else a second four-squadron armoured regiment. 4 CMBG needed an air defence battery organic to the Brigade (which it eventually got); it also needed an independent anti-tank company, an electronic warfare unit and remotely piloted vehicles for surveillance and security tasks; ammunition types needed to be upgraded; the APCs needed replacement with a mechanized infantry combat vehicle like the *Marder* or *Bradley*; 4 CMBG was too dependent on a higher formation for NBCD decontamination support; most important, 4 CMBG had to alter thinking at NDHQ, since "there is a perception in NDHQ that 4 CMBG is fully equipped, [a perception] which must continue to be countered".

As part of the 4 CMBG "Get Well" programme, more rigorous alert exercises were inaugurated. The Operational Review noted that 4 CMBG was too complacent about alerts, with too many personnel recalls and not enough PSA deployments and practice ammunition uploads. Alert frequency was another problem. CFE guidance indicated that ten alert exercises be undertaken per year, of which two were always called by AFCENT (called ACTIVE EDGE exercises). Was this too many, resulting in a 'cry wolf' syndrome? Or was it not enough?

CHAPTER SIX

To restore a sense of urgency, a series of exercises called RIGID RUNABOUTs were run twice annually, in addition to normal SNOWBALLs. The RIGID RUNABOUTs were 'piggy backed' with a SNOWBALL. Unlike the SNOWBALL, after the brigade units had deployed to the PSAs, one or two units were secretly selected for further deployment.

In the first RIGID RUNABOUT, the RCD was chosen to deploy. After uploading its ammunition, the entire regiment was deployed by rail from their PSA to a defensive position near Stuttgart. They were not told what was happening, and many Dragoons were sure that war had broken out. As it turned out, some troops did not have their proper kit or their weapons and the tie down chains for the rail cars were left back in Lahr. After spending a day or two in the positions, the RCD went home. They had learned a lesson that nobody forgot and the next time the RCD was picked for a RIGID RUNABOUT, it was ready.

The inquiry into 4 CMBG's operational effectiveness was carried on by Brigadier General Pierre Lalonde when he took over 4 CMBG in 1986. In addition to identifying other deficiencies, the Lalonde inquiry noted that ammo stocks were malpositioned and needed to be moved forward. There were not enough defensive stores, and only enough mines for a single brigade defensive position. It took 4 CMBG 40 hours to move to its GDP position, but there was not enough time to make it defendable, given only the 48 hours NATO strategic warning time. Throughout 4 CMBG's deployment forward, it was vulnerable to air attack, sabotage and ambushes by enemy special purpose forces.

In accordance with the 4 CMBG survival plan, units were to deploy to survival areas in and around Lahr and Baden. By the 1980s, there was a real paucity of unoccupied dispersal sites in the Rhine Valley. The French II Corps d'Armee was situated in Baden-Baden and its divisions were positioned all around 4 CMBG's areas. There were inevitable conflicts with coordinating survival areas with the French. In some cases, Canadian and French units shared the same ground, a situation that was not conducive to the survival of either formation. One proposal was to move 4 CMBG's survival areas in the vicinity of Crailsheim, a town north east of Stuttgart.

One possible solution to the problem of deployment time and distance, and to logistics support, was to move 4 CMBG off the airfields and closer to its GDP positions near Nürnberg. For years, commanders had complained about co-location on the airfields vis à vis enemy air attack, the vulnerability of logistics, supply routes, etc. One idea beyond moving the survival areas, was to trade CFB Baden for a US Army facility somewhere near Crailsheim, or for another site near Neu Ulm. The third line logistics problems was to be solved later by moving the third line FMSU to Ansbach (10 kilometers west of Nürnberg). The financial implications of such moves were, however, considered to be prohibitive by the political leadership in Ottawa.

In addition to the malpositioning problem, Brigade staff officers such as then Lieutenant Colonel George Oehring, grew tired of the CFE staff and base organizations misusing the brigade's soldiers.

> 4 CMBG is regarded as an inexhaustible pool of unskilled labour. My staff have argued for relief but are usually forced to capitulate because 'the Brigade has the most people so it should do the most work'....4 CMBG is not organized, manned or equipped to do Base tasks....

The point was clear. Even though soldiers were perceived by some base units as 'grunts', many had jobs that were just as essential and just as sophisticated as aircraft maintenance. Every soldier tasked with base security, kitchen or other menial work took away from training needed to build up unit esprit de corps and teamwork, not to mention the technical skill needed to operate sophisticated systems like TOW, air defence or *Leopard* gunnery.

By 1987, the ability of 4 CMBG to fight had improved significantly in many areas. Brigadier General Lalonde could happily report that 4 CMBG was self-sufficient for four days of combat operations, with enough material stockpiled for 26 more days. Even though operational support plans like PENDANT and BARBET still had problems, the arrival of TOW thermal imaging sights (and other night observation equipment), mine rollers for the tanks, new secure communications systems (VINSON) and forty more APCs were positive developments. Out of the 5618 personnel authorized in wartime, 4203 were in Germany and ready to go. Although the situation was far from the standard established

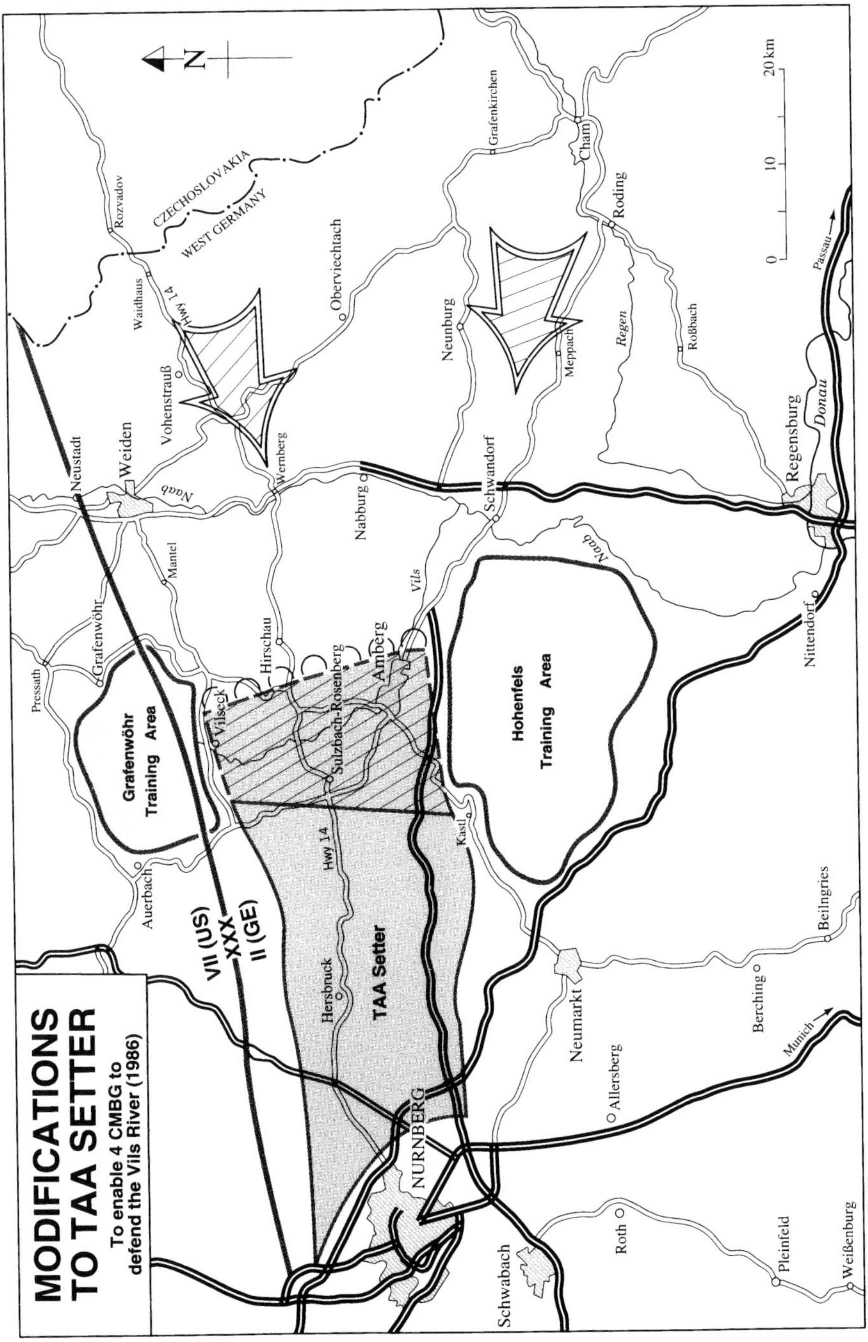
MODIFICATIONS TO TAA SETTER
To enable 4 CMBG to defend the Vils River (1986)
N
0
10
20 km
CZECHOSLOVAKIA
WEST GERMANY
VII (US)
XXX
II (GE)
TAA Setter
Grafenwöhr Training Area
Hohenfels Training Area
Hwy 14
Rozvadov
Waidhaus
Vohenstrauß
Oberviechtach
Grafenkirchen
Cham
Roding
Neunburg
Meppach
Regen
Roßbach
Wernberg
Neustadt
Weiden
Naab
Nabburg
Schwandorf
Regensburg
Donau
Passau
Mantel
Grafenwöhr
Pressath
Hirschau
Vilseck
Sulzbach-Rosenberg
Amberg
Vils
Kastl
Nittendorf
Auerbach
Hersbruck
Beilngries
Berching
Neumarkt
Allersberg
Munich
NURNBERG
Schwabach
Roth
Pleinfeld
Weißenburg

FIGURE 6-7

in the 1960s, it was far superior to that of the 1970s.

4 CMBG's General Defence Plan changed again in response to the Dangerfield and Lalonde initiatives. General Dangerfield was concerned about the location of TAA SETTER. [See Figure 6-7.] In the GDP, 4 CMBG moved from its survival areas to TAA SETTER and awaited orders. It then just sat in the TAA, dispersed, waiting for orders to move. If the enemy broke through the West German division defending in front of TAA SETTER, 4 CMBG was there on the ground but not prepared to do anything about it other than to conduct a hasty defence. As a result, a proposal was made by 4 CMBG to extend the dimensions of TAA SETTER by a number of kilometers, right up to the Vils River. Instead of just sitting and waiting, 4 CMBG would develop defensive positions along the river while awaiting orders to be deployed, if necessary, across the inter-corps boundary into the VII (US) Corps area. Thus, if the situation in II (GE) Korps were to get out of hand early on, 4 CMBG would be able to support II (GE) Korps operations without delay. The SETTER extension was approved by CENTAG and incorporated into 4 CMBG's planning.

At this point, 4 CMBG had a variety of taskings depending on which of the allied Corps it was 'chopped' to. As noted earlier, there were a number of employment options in VII (US) Corps, many which drew 4 CMBG away from its logistics dumps in TAA SETTER. Missions within VII (US) Corps now included Canadian assistance in defending the Kemnath Bowl, an area northeast of the Grafenwöhr training area, behind an American brigade from the 1st (US) Armored Division. In II (GE) Korps' area, 4 CMBG had to be prepared to relieve Panzer Brigade 12 from 4 Panzer Grenadier Division, which was deployed in positions in front of 4 CMBG. CENTAG wanted 4 CMBG to have the ability to defend the Vils River behind the Kemnath Bowl.

Brigadier General Lalonde consolidated all of 4 CMBG's potential missions both in the VII (US) Corps and II (GE) Korps areas astride the inter corps boundary into an innovative plan called BOXER. Plan BOXER [see Figure 6-8] pre-selected the most likely areas that 4 CMBG would be tasked to defend. BOXER consisted of eight (later ten) pre-surveyed battalion-sized defensive positions configured in an inverted "Y"; 4 CMBG had the ability (in terms of numbers) to occupy, and set up

4 CMBG
PLAN BOXER - 1986
SHOWING PREPLANNED DEFENSIVE POSITIONS
TO SUPPORT VII (US) CORPS AND II (GE) KORPS
N
F
E/F
E
E/G
D/E
D
G
C/D
Grafenwöhr
Auerbach
C
H
VII US
XXX
II GE
WEIDEN
J
B/C
Vilseck
H/J
K
B
K
TAA
A/B
SETTER
A
Hirschu
AMBERG

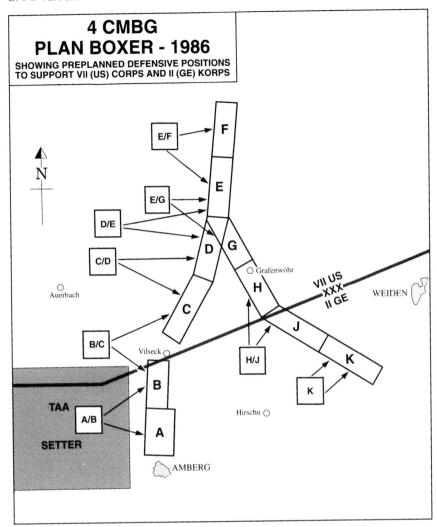

FIGURE 6-8

defensive positions in any two adjacent boxes. The terrain in the VII (US) Corps areas covered by BOXER was, however, not as defensible as it was in the II (GE) Korps area.

Once international tension increased, 4 CMBG was to occupy TAA SETTER, which included the A and B boxes. On occupation, these boxes would be developed as defensive positions. Positions C and D would be developed immediately afterwards to assist in a possible deception operation if this were deemed necessary, or for future taskings.

If 4 CMBG were 'chopped' to II (GE) Korps to back up 4 Panzer Grenadier Division fighting in front of 4 CMBG, 4 CMBG was already in positions to do so in boxes A and B and could occupy boxes G, H, J, and K. If chopped to VII (US) Corps, boxes C and D were ready to be occupied, and E, F, G and H could be developed on order. Each box would contain one infantry battalion, with the armoured counter-attack force occupying one of the area boxes behind the main defensive positions, for example, B/C. If the situation warranted, 4 CMBG could be deployed to any adjacent pair of boxes within the plan, and the plan could accommodate another brigade if necessary. 4 CMBG was then ready to defend in prepared positions or unprepared areas, or to act as a blocking or counter-penetration force against any threat developing along the inter-corps boundary.

A portion of BOXER became part of a special contingency plan called COP VILS RIVER or just COP VILS. 4 Panzer Grenadier Division, deployed in front of TAA SETTER, had all three of its brigades (one panzer and two panzer grenadier) deployed up on the Czech border with no reserve brigade for a counter-attack operation. The German division commander wanted the option to withdraw Panzer Brigade 12 from the line through 4 CMBG to form his divisional counter-attack force. If he did so, the gap left by the removal of Panzer Brigade 12 needed to be covered. Thus, the VILS RIVER contingency plan allowed for 4 CMBG's occupation of boxes A and B or J and K in support of this manoeuvre.

The SETTER extension and Contingency Plan VILS RIVER became the basis for the finalized 4 CMBG GDP which was in effect right up to 1992. [See Figure 6-9.] The increased US conventional capability in the mid-1980s increased VII (US) Corps' ability to perform the counter-

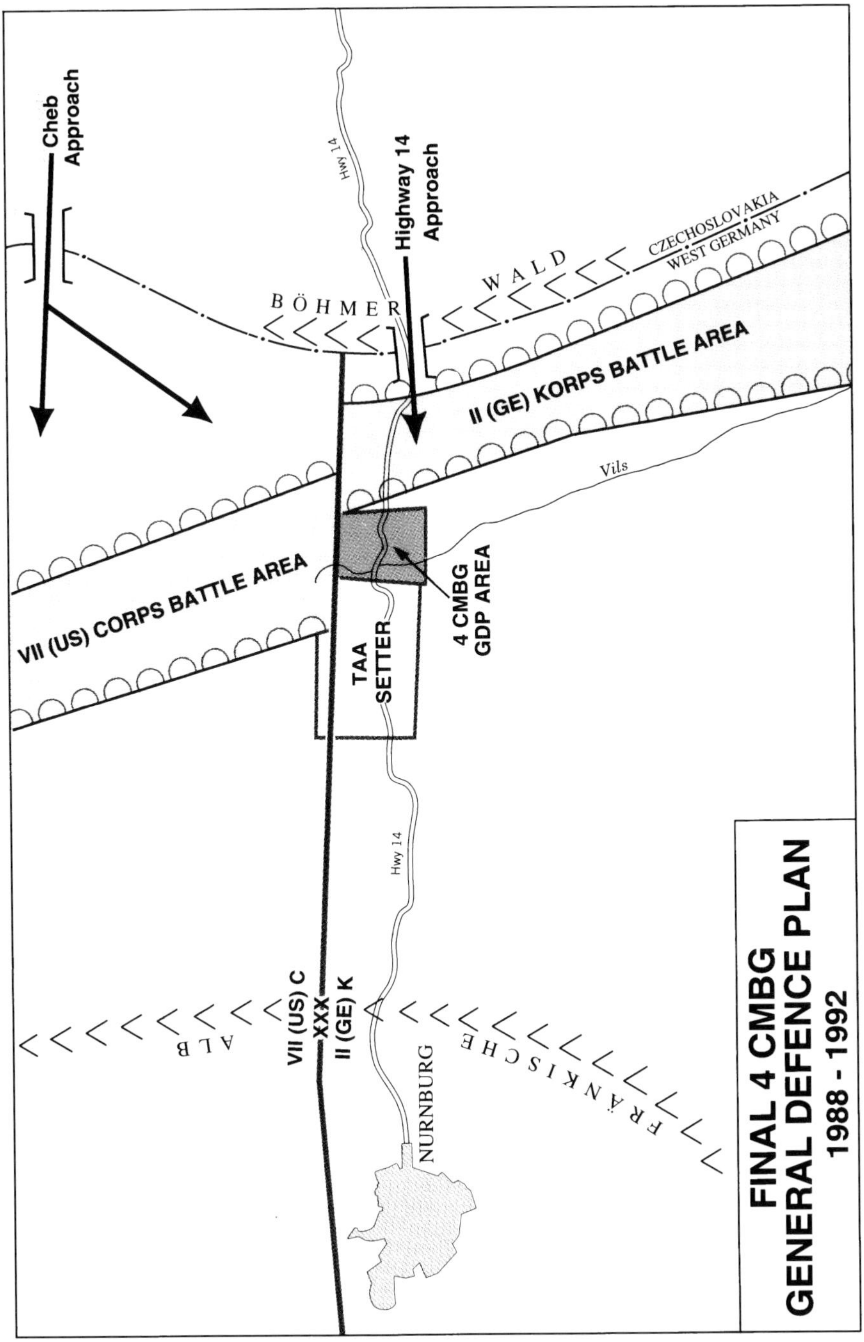

Cheb Approach
Highway 14 Approach
Hwy 14
BÖHMER WALD
CZECHOSLOVAKIA
WEST GERMANY
II (GE) KORPS BATTLE AREA
Vils
VII (US) CORPS BATTLE AREA
4 CMBG GDP AREA
TAA SETTER
Hwy 14
VII (US) C
XXX
II (GE) K
ALB
FRäNKISCHE
NURNBURG
FINAL 4 CMBG
GENERAL DEFENCE PLAN
1988 - 1992

FIGURE 6-9

penetration mission, particularly with the introduction of an airmobile brigade with A-64 attack helicopters into their order of battle. The older 4 CMBG employment options near Bayreuth were no longer necessary. Paradoxically, the changing concept of operations in VII (US) Corps increased the importance of 4 CMBG's defensive positions in the eastern part of TAA SETTER, that is, Contingency Plan VILS RIVER.

The nature of the geography in the VII (US) Corps area as well as American tactical doctrine dictated, in general terms, that the US defensive lines would not conform to the shape of the border. Consequently, their main battle area was at an acute angle to the inter-corps boundary. The Germans, with their religious adherence to Forward Defence, were, however, deployed right up to the border. Despite all the rhetoric about FOFA, the US defensive positions were still away from the border to a significant degree. The staff of II (GE) Korps were skeptical, believing that the Americans planned to fight a depth battle instead of defending on the border. In any battle, massed mechanized forces follow the path of least resistance, much like water does running down a hill.

If the enemy attacked through the Cheb approach, he would come into contact with the US forces, which would be strong in firepower. The enemy would then attempt to find and exploit weak portions of the defensive line. The weakest point was the connection between VII (US) Corps and II (GE) Korps where they met on the inter-corps boundary. The positioning of 4 CMBG in TAA SETTER and the Vils River extension filled this gap, in the same way that 4 CIBG provided the interface between I (BR) Corps and I (BE) Corps back in the 1960s. The ability of 4 CMBG to work closely and well with either the Germans or the Americans was an added bonus to this arrangement.

The finalized GDP positions were located between the towns of Vilseck and Amberg, with 3 RCR left and 1 R22eR right. Brigade recce forces were deployed forward of the town of Hirschau, with 8 CH as the Brigade reserve. 4 CMBG would be positioned astride Highway 14 in a blocking role to hold the Nürnberg approach from an attack from the north east or from the east. In a two phase operation, 4 CMBG would have conducted a covering force battle followed by a main defensive battle. Once Panzer Brigade 12 (from 4 Panzer Grenadier Division in front of 4 CMBG) had effected its rearward passage of lines through

4 CMBG, a Canadian guard consisting of recce elements, two tank squadrons and one infantry company was to fight at the handover line and then delay and inflict the maximum number of casualties on the enemy without being decisively engaged. The guard would then withdraw into reserve.

Meanwhile the Brigade's obstacle plan would have been implemented with help from the German *Wallmeisters* from GTSC. Using TOW Under Armour and recce units in an economy-of-force role, the enemy would be cut down further before being channelled into the killing zone of the main defensive position. 1 R22eR on the right near Amberg, and 3 RCR on the left, held the Brigade's vital ground astride Highway 14, with the 8 CH priority tasked to counter-attack to help hold it. The whole of 4 Brigade then would have to hold on until a further counter-attack could be put in by either the withdrawn Panzer Brigade 12 or by 10 Panzer Division, the II (GE) Korps reserve.

4 CMBG's mission was *not* to counter-attack and drive the enemy back to the Czechoslovak border. It was understood in CENTAG that the Brigade was not equipped to do so. That mission belonged to the armoured forces which formed the reserves of VII (US) Corps and II (GE) Korps. The Brigade's mission was to act as a blocking force to prevent enemy penetration and force him to deploy. By employing well dug in infantry with TOW under armour and by employing the *Leopard* tanks in local counter-attack operations, the enemy would suffer casualties and be "fixed" for a counter-attack from one of the German or American armoured formations. If the enemy followed his doctrine and did not reinforce failure, he would try elsewhere, leaving those forces in the 4 CMBG sector weak and vulnerable for counter-attack. There was no other formation in the VII (US) Corps or II (GE) Korps areas that was capable or structured for the role assigned to the Canadians; both the Germans and Americans were already thinly spread, and the presence of 4 CMBG was critical in the early stages of a war. Later, once French forces arrived and the Americans flew in their people to the POMCUS sites, the situation would turn to NATO's favour in CENTAG, but this was only possible if the situation was stabilized at the front as quickly and as far forward as possible. The ability of 4 CMBG to operate effectively with either II (GE) Korps or VII (US) Corps made it an extremely

valuable link in this context and gave it a critical role to play in NATO's Forward Defence strategy.

A German assessment of 4 CMBG's situation in CENTAG is described here by Major General Jurgen Reichardt, who commanded 4 Panzer Grenadier Division;

> [Clearly] your brigade is only a small contribution in the overall dimension of CENTAG forces. But it is a large part of the military power of your country, [and] it was a high percentage of the defensive forces close to the [Czech] border. No other country had this high a percentage of their forces for the purposes of [forward] defence.... CENTAG always tried to hold reserves back for later use, while the discussions between the Canadians and the German division here in Regensburg was to get the Canadians engaged very early. I knew the political problems. One Brigade in the front at the strong point sector could take heavy losses very early and be out of the conflict. [And if] Canada lost its contribution very early, it would not have as much weight in the Alliance in future operations....
>
> We have over the years discussed the question of the limitation of the extension of the Canadians. I remember one of our brigade commanders (who didn't speak very good English) made a short speech. He said: 'You Canadians have one mistake, you are not enough!' So, we do not consider just the numbers, but the quality of the engagement.

Great strides were made in improving logistic support to 4 CMBG in the 1980s. A War Structure Study in 1983 and a NATO logistics review provided the basis for increasing the third-line capability. Exercise BOLD STEP, a CFE logistics exercise, demonstrated conclusively that support plans for CFE were illusory. These studies, coupled with the BRAVE LION after action report, were a catalyst for change. Prior to 1984, third line logistics support to 4 CMBG, that is, the logistics link between Lahr-Baden and the forward deployed brigade group, was limited to a four-man detachment operating under the auspices of CFB Lahr. This unit was called the Forward Mobile Support Unit or FMSU ('Fum soo'). In wartime, FMSU was to be augmented with 30 drivers and a number of local commercial vehicles. Clearly, there were serious problems with this concept, and logistics planners worked to resolve

CHAPTER SIX 413

them.

At the operational level, it was proposed that a Theatre Base be constructed in Scotland or Wales to support the CAST Brigade Group, 4 CMBG and the Air Group. At the time, the Soviet submarine threat to the sea lines of communications in the Atlantic was immense, and Canadian planners believed that the probability of being able to provide support to Canadian forces on the continent was greater if the resources were located in the UK, the same conclusion that their predecessors had come to in the 1950s. From the Theatre Base, supplies were to be moved through the Canadian Communications Zone in Belgium (this was based on the 1953 agreements) and then through the Canada/US Integrated Lines Of Communication (ILOC) to Lahr, Baden or 4 CMBG.

The CA/US ILOC had been proposed as early as 1977 and was formally agreed to in 1979. The ILOC allowed CFE and 4 CMBG to share US transport facilities (ports, airheads, trucks and trains), as well as depot and maintenance facilities, and incorporated Canadian requirements into US logistic plans.

A re-vamped FMSU, eventually consisting of 50 permanently stationed personnel, was established in 1985 and removed from base Lahr control. FMSU became a CFE resource and was equipped with a fleet of tractor-trailer trucks, as well as the forty two 10-ton MAN trucks mentioned earlier, which were dedicated ammunition transporters. After the 1987 Defence White Paper was published, FMSU also became responsible for a number of dispersed forward storage sites. The vulnerability problems with the co-location of 4 CMBG on the airfield were understood but the money did not exist in the 1970s to provide an alternative. Once the money was available, a number of dispersal sites for equipment and supplies were created, some in the Schwarzwald, and some near Nürnberg in TAA SETTER.

Medical support to 4 CMBG was also reviewed in the 1980s. As with the logistics side of the house, there was no third line medical support for 4 CMBG, that is, there were no resources to move Canadian battle casualties from the second line 4 Field Ambulance to Canadian rear area facilities. Canadian casualties would have to be looked after by a German or American hospital but no detailed medical arrangements like the ILOC existed. 313 Field Hospital in Lahr was not adequately equipped to handle large numbers of battle casualties until new facilities were constructed in 1990.

New medical support plans which paralleled the logistics developments, were being drawn up. Along with the Theatre Base concept, plans were made to construct or borrow a 1000 bed general hospital in the UK, in addition to two field hospitals (one 300 bed and one 500 bed) in Germany. The cadre for the field hospitals was supposed to be 313 Field Hospital and the Canadian Forces Medical Depot in Lahr but the end of the Cold War put an end to this planning.

To streamline support functions in Germany, the CFE postal unit, 35 Dental Unit and FMSU were combined to form 3 Canadian Support Group (Centre) (3 CSG(C)) in 1989, and an augmentation plan, HATLESS, was created to increase its strength in wartime. Plans also called for the formation of a Canadian Medical Group (Centre) which would have placed all CFE medical resources under one command but again, this was not fully implemented prior to the end of the Cold War. The Theatre Base concept was never fully implemented either; only the CSG(C), FMSU and ILOC elements were in place by the end of the 1980s.

4 CMBG's fall training in 1985 for the first time in many years was not integrated into the larger framework of REFORGER, it being V (US) Corps' turn for this. Under the command of Brigadier General Dangerfield, 4 CMBG embarked upon what amounted to a three part work up for FALLEX 86. First, 4 CMBG deployed to the Hohenfels training area in August to work up as a brigade in Exercise RAPID THRUST. After all the problems were identified, a series of combat team exercises called REBEL SADDLE and using MILES equipment honed the armoured and infantry units into effective tactical teams. The climax was Exercise SOLO SABRE which pitted 4 CMBG against Panzer Battalion 293 in terrain near the actual GDP north of Amberg.

General Dangerfield had a reputation for placing great emphasis on training realism. The REBEL SADDLE exercises contained a sequence whereby the combat teams would encounter a dug-in enemy position which included actual Soviet vehicles and 'enemy' soldiers equipped with Soviet-bloc weapons. One participant believes that this was some of the most effective training done by 4 Brigade in the 1980s:

We rolled up to this position to recce it....It had an anti-tank ditch in front of it, wire, minefields, the works. Our plan was to have the artillery smoke off the fighting positions, which we estimated to contain a company of enemy, plus dug in (real!) BMP's and tanks. Our AVLB [bridge laying tank] and the mine roller tanks would then breach the obstacle, the tanks and APCs would cross, and we'd rush the position. Everybody had their adrenaline pumping when the smoke came in and the AVLB rushed across the field through the smoke. Across went the ramp, the AVLB detached and bugged out. By this time, the smoke has drifted over the ramp as the first tanks reached it. The ramp had been emplaced properly, but the banks of the ditch were soft, so that every time a tank crossed, the bridge was out of kilter. Never mind! Everybody was so intent on getting across that safety went to the wind. Anyway, we got across the ramp and into the position, the tank guns were roaring (no Hoffman devices here!) and the infantry piled out of the APCs screaming their heads off, clearing out bunkers trenches and dug outs, all the while smoke was drifting and swirling all around us. By the time the smoke had cleared, we were all ready for the counter-attack. It's incredibly fortunate that nobody got hurt! It was awesome training!

The 1986 training year was even more active but it started out badly. Another CERTAIN SENTINEL winter REFORGER was laid on in January 1986, with 4 CMBG participating on the Blue side. The Americans 'reforged' a division's worth of troops but by the time the forces had been deployed to Bavaria, the ground was too sodden for mechanized movement. To prevent unacceptable damage to the terrain, CERTAIN SENTINEL 86 was called off after four days and the troops were relegated to unit and sub-unit training.

While the other units in 4 CMBG were concentrating on individual and sub-unit training in the spring, the HQ and Signal Squadron was busy on all manner of CPXs. CENTAG completely overhauled its communications system in 1986 and Exercise CARBON EDGE tested it out. In another CPX, Ex CARBINE SIGHT, VII (US) Corps tested their GDP. Since 4 CMBG formed part of the plan, 4 CMBG participated.

One unexpected training event occurred on 5 May 1986. A serious accident at a Soviet nuclear reactor near Chernobyl in the Ukraine spewed radioactive material into the atmosphere. The extent of this contamination was unknown for a number of days and as a result, extensive precautions against radioactive fallout were taken in Western Europe. Dependents were advised only to consume food that had been tested. Food purchased locally was to be washed and CFE authorities cautioned that personnel "having prolonged contact with the ground" should shower immediately after such activity. By 28 May, radiation levels dropped to normal levels and the precautionary measures were no longer required.

Brigadier General J.E.P. Lalonde took command of 4 CMBG in August 1986, just prior to work ups for the fall. His response to media questions during one FALLEX is worth noting here. Lieutenant Colonel Daniel Bastien, then with 1 R22eR, recalled:

> One reporter, whose intent was to embarrass the General vis à vis the small proportion of Canadian troops to American, British and German troops, asked how many Canadian soldiers were serving with NATO. General Lalonde answered, 'There are 102 653 Canadians serving in NATO'. With puzzled looks, the media representatives tried to figure this out. Over one hundred thousand Canadians serving in NATO? Was this man crazy? 'As I stated before, there are 102 653 Canadians serving over here. 5 000 in Germany and 97 653 in France, Belgium and The Netherlands.'

Lalonde was, of course, referring to Canada's war dead buried in Europe.

RAPID THRUST 86 prepared 4 CMBG for REBEL SADDLE II, a two-sided battle group exercise using Recce Squadron as the enemy in the Hohenfels training area. MILES equipment was used once again. A joint Canadian-German divisional level exercise was scheduled for the end of October, so 4 CMBG worked up for this in Ex RADIANT SABRE. This exercise was held in roughly the same are as FLINKER IGEL, between Ingolstadt on the Donau, Regensburg and Straubing. 4 CMBG was on the offensive for the first week, pursuing Panzer Grenadier Battalion 102, which acted as an enemy Motor Rifle Regiment. After this phase, 4 CMBG went into defensive positions to repel an all out enemy assault. 4 CMBG employed somewhat exotic information-gathering resources on RADIANT SABRE. 2 EW Squadron provided electronic support measures and the Americans gave 4 CMBG access to OV-1D

Mohawk recce aircraft equipped with Sideways-Looking Airborne Radar (SLAR). RADIANT SABRE was characterized by very fluid situations, with numerous assault river crossings, a non-stop tempo and very mobile action.

The finale for the fall training season was Exercise BUNTES FAHNLEIN (Coloured Flag) held north of Regensburg in 4 Panzer Grenadier Division's area of operations. Working in conjunction with Panzer Grenadier Brigade 11, 4 CMBG defended against a US armoured battalion equipped with M-1 tanks, Panzer Brigade 12 and 4 Panzer Grenadier's divisional recce battalion. Although the exercise was shifted slightly away from the actual GDP positions, BUNTES FAHNLEIN confirmed the high level of interoperability between 4 CMBG and the Bundeswehr. Brigadier General Hans Jurgen Wilhelmi, who became Deputy Commander of 4 Panzer Grenadier Division was an umpire on BUNTES FAHNLEIN:

> ...I participated in Ex BUNTES FAHNLEIN in 1986 as an umpire at the brigade level. It was a divisional exercise. I think it was characteristic of Canadians [and particularly] 4 CMBG that you have a highly professional team on the defence. And I must say, the professionalism in how to defend a battalion is higher than it was at that time in the brigade I commanded....I had to admit that the Canadian infantry battalion[s] were for more than three days in a position which could not be overrun! This was a professional demonstration from which German tactics could learn. At that time we were more oriented towards the Second World War German experience of mobile warfare [which] is different from your tactics.

The manoeuvring in BUNTES FAHNLEIN corresponded to changes in the GDP; passage of line phases were emphasized between 4 CMBG and Panzer Grenadier Brigade 11; the high percentage of armour in the Red forces also provided 4 CMBG another high tempo battle.

The state of the world situation from 1986 to 1988 was, in retrospect, quite different from the early 1980s. Mikhail Gorbachev came to power in the Soviet Union, committed to reform, although few in the West and fewer in his own country understood this at first. The changes that were occurring in the Soviet Union and within the Warsaw Pact were not recognized as long term changes and NATO continued to view the Warsaw Pact as its primary adversary in the event of conflict. Gorbachev's hold over the Soviet Union was not absolute and, in any case, he was still committed to communism as a system. Despite the Soviets' restructuring and openness, there was still a legitimate fear within NATO that this détente-like situation could change for the worse at any time. Prior to 1990, troop levels in Group of Soviet Forces Germany and their state of readiness did not change to any significant degree, although there were notable breakthroughs on the arms limitation front. Thus, when viewing the events of 1986 to 1990, one should recall that the events of 1989 and 1990 were not pre-ordained or even anticipated. Consequently, NATO was still committed to deterring any threat to its members' territory and still continued to plan to resist any attempt to infringe upon it.

1986 and 1987 were also important years for Canadian defence policy, particularly with the unveiling of the 1987 White Paper on Defence, *Challenge and Commitment*. Although these events did have an interesting impact on 4 CMBG, they will be examined in detail in Chapter 7.

Brigadier General Tom de Faye replaced Brigadier General Lalonde as Commander 4 CMBG in 1987. The 1987 training plan had 4 CMBG proceeding to Hohenfels for its annual work ups. The training pattern that had been established in the 1980s regarding Corps-level exercises dictated that V (US) Corps would be 'reforging' in the fall of 1987. Thus, 4 CMBG's staff created Ex ROYAL SWORD. This exercise was held on the Main River in the northern part of VII (US) Corps area between Bamberg and Schweinfurt. It was a controlled exercise designed to place 4 CMBG in a variety of situations that might not develop in a free play exercise.

The enemy force provided by Panzer Grenadier Battalion 102, with its *Marder* MICV's and a complement of *Leopard* tanks, was prepared to give 4 CMBG a run for its money. 4 CMBG was fortunate to acquire the services of an M-1 tank squadron from the 3rd (US) Armored Division, a recce squadron from 1 Troop, 3/11 Armored Cavalry Regiment and elements of the 501st Attack Helicopter Battalion. Bridging support was provided by a French engineer unit. This interallied support to the

CHAPTER SIX

Brigade was indicative of the good relationship and level of interoperability Canadians had achieved with their German, American and French comrades in arms.

All phases of offensive and defensive operations were conducted during ROYAL SWORD. After moving to its assembly area, 4 CMBG crossed the Main River, lead by elements of 1 R22eR mounted in UH-60 *Blackhawk* helicopters. After a series of aggressive delay operations, Panzer Grenadier Battalion 102 broke contact. 4 CMBG then threw out a recce screen consisting of Canadian *Lynx*s and American M-2 *Bradley*s. The infantry battalions dug in for a free-play defensive battle, as dismounted German recce patrols probed 4 Service Battalion and 4 Field Ambulance at night in the Brigade's rear area. On the last day of the eight-day exercise, a furious defensive battle took place, with 4 CMBG not giving away any real estate (except vertically, given the sodden state of the ground).

As an example of how sensitive the manoeuvre damage issue was becoming in the late 1980s, ROYAL SWORD became a political issue not only within the exercise area but within the state of Bavaria itself. During the exercise, an American civilian employed with 3rd (US) Infantry Division, a unit which regularly used the area that ROYAL SWORD was currently being executed in, angrily called HQ CFE demanding that 4 CMBG cease the exercise. Without giving specific information, he yelled at the duty officer, telling him that "4 CMBG are behaving like Huns". When pressed for specifics, this individual only replied that the Bonn Government would make sure that 4 CMBG never exercised in the region again. He alleged that massive and unacceptable manoeuvre damage had occurred and that the Bavarian Chancellery had been informed. The Bavarian Chancellery elevated the issue to Bonn.

Fortunately, the efforts of the Canadian Civil-Military Affairs liaison officer at CFE HQ, Ivor St Aubin d'Ancey, and the GTSC liaison officer, Lieutenant Colonel Dieter Egelseer, set things right. Apparently, the local population had been 'warned' by an American from 3rd Infantry Division that the Canadians were coming and that 4 CMBG had a reputation for being 'cowboys'. After consultation with the Senior Canadian Liaison Officer at VII (US) Corps on the 'QT', it turned out that 3rd (US) Infantry Division was unhappy with what they saw as preferential treatment of 4 CMBG regarding training areas. The Canadian LO had been told by staff from this unit beforehand that ROYAL SWORD was doomed to fail. There was some manoeuvre damage but it was quite obvious to any experienced observer that it was by no means excessive; certainly, it was far below the level of damage caused on other exercises. Ironically though, it turned out that the damage in question had been caused by other US units that were not part of 4 CMBG's exercise, and who had conducted a 'bugout' in the area.

All of this was temporarily sorted out just in time for the largest FALLEX/ REFORGER ever – Exercise CERTAIN CHALLENGE 88. Known by some as "The Last Gallop", CERTAIN CHALLENGE was held in an area which encompassed approximately one tenth of West Germany's land mass. According to CENTAG press releases, over 125 000 NATO troops, 7000 tracked vehicles, 15 000 wheeled vehicles, 400 guns and MLRS, and 630 helicopters simulated a corps versus corps battle. Twenty thousand Americans were 'reforged' and 4 CMBG tested parts of Operation PENDANT for the first time.

Major Peter Devlin of 3 RCR recalled the scope of the exercise:

> My most memorable FALLEX was the first one that I participated in in 1988. It was a Corps exercise, and it was huge! The number of troops and equipment that were involved was unbelievable....To be able to exercise in the German countryside after having recently arrived and exercising alongside our NATO allies was tremendously rewarding. We talk about [exercising] a division on the RVs [RENDEZ-VOUS exercises in Canada] but here we are talking about Corps.... I was 2IC Administration Company at the time and I was supposed to do a hide recce for the echelon. The sun was just coming up and I was blasting off about two hours before the echelon to conduct my recce. I came upon the red route on the map, but there were tanks as far as I could see in both directions and they were nose to tail.

Compared to previous exercises, which were usually division against division, CERTAIN CHALLENGE pitted three US and one German division (Goldland Forces) against Blueland Forces consisting of two US divisions, one US armoured cavalry regiment, one German panzer division and 4 CMBG. The Goldland "Army Group North" was represented by V(US) Corps, and Blueland's "Army Group South" by VII (US) Corps. The exercise was completely free-play, that is, not scripted, and played out on a north-south axis.

The training goals for 4 CMBG were diverse. It was time to test out Operation PENDANT and see how well flyover troops could be integrated in large numbers. The usual objectives of testing 4 CMBG's deployment from Lahr and Baden to the area of operations were also included, as well as practising the usual offensive and defensive operations. On the larger scale, CERTAIN CHALLENGE was to test German-Canadian-American interoperability. This was extremely important in VII (US) Corps as we have seen earlier. In addition to the inter-corps boundary problem involving 4 CMBG and II (GE) Korps, VII (US) Corps also wanted to test wartime operational control over 12 Panzer Division in a larger context.

Operation PENDANT brought over 653 augmentee personnel to 4 CMBG, including 240 Militiamen. (Most of the regular soldiers came from 1 Canadian Brigade Group). In addition to this increment, 147 Canadian umpires were flown over to Germany and 20 additional logisticians for FMSU. 427 Tactical Helicopter Squadron from Petawawa was also deployed with its Twin Huey and *Kiowa* helicopters. 2 (EW) Squadron from Kingston also deployed but due to the lack of airlift, had to be brought in by sea, which neatly exercised the ILOC.

4 CMBG participated in both phases of the two-week exercise. Phase I [see Figure 6-10] put Blueland on the attack. The Gold Forces had, prior to startex, attacked Blueland and been forced to stop by a mythical covering force. Goldland had just resumed the offensive moving south when CERTAIN CHALLENGE started. Blueland had, by the night of 10 September deployed into its TAAs south of Highway 6. Blue's objective in Phase I was to destroy the 3rd Goldland Armored Division, which occupied an area south of Würzburg and was steadily advancing south. Army Group South formed what was referred to as an interoperability division under the command of 12 Panzer Division. This division included Panzer Grenadier Brigade 35, 3rd Mechanized Infantry Brigade from the 1st US Infantry Division, and 4 CMBG. 4 CMBG received command of a US 203mm long range artillery battalion, a US engineer company, two *Patriot* anti-aircraft missile batteries and the US 4-27

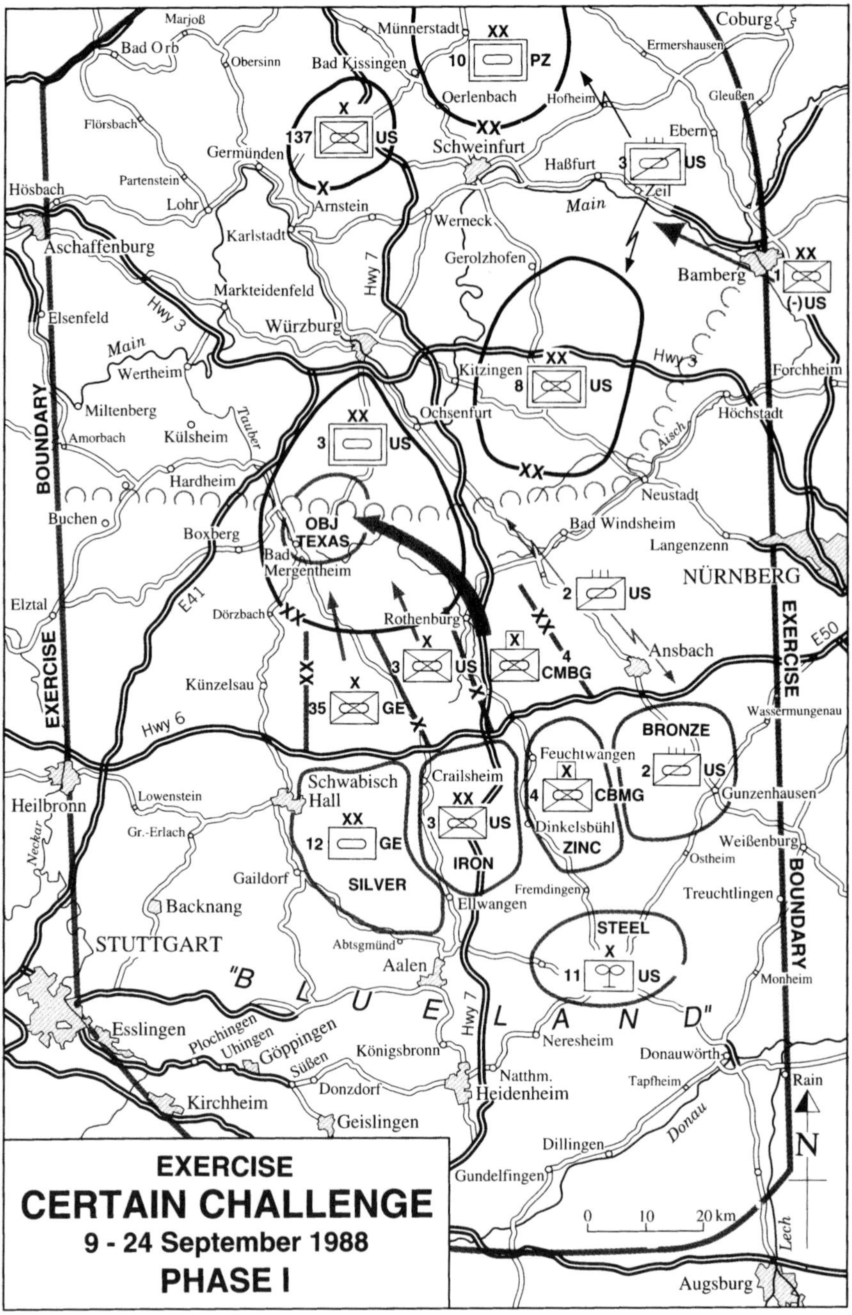
EXERCISE
CERTAIN CHALLENGE
9 - 24 September 1988
PHASE I
Marjoß
Bad Orb
Obersinn
Bad Kissingen
Münnerstadt
10 PZ
Oerlenbach
Hofheim
Coburg
Ermershausen
Gleußen
Ebern
Flörsbach
137 US
Germünden
Schweinfurt
Haßfurt
3 US
Zeil
Main
Hösbach
Partenstein
Lohr
Arnstein
Werneck
Aschaffenburg
Karlstadt
Gerolzhofen
Bamberg
1 (-)US
Hwy 7
Markteidenfeld
Hwy 3
Elsenfeld
Würzburg
Main
Wertheim
Kitzingen
8 US
Forchheim
Miltenberg
Ochsenfurt
Höchstadt
Amorbach
Külsheim
Tauber
3 US
Aisch
BOUNDARY
Hardheim
Neustadt
Buchen
OBJ TEXAS
Bad Windsheim
Boxberg
Bad Mergentheim
Langenzenn
NÜRNBERG
E41
2 US
Elztal
Dörzbach
Rothenburg
4 CMBG
EXERCISE
Ansbach
E50
Künzelsau
3 US
35 GE
Hwy 6
Wassermungenau
BRONZE
Feuchtwangen
Schwabisch Hall
Crailsheim
2 US
Heilbronn
Lowenstein
4 CBMG
Gunzenhausen
12 GE
3 US
Dinkelsbühl
Neckar
Gr.-Erlach
Weißenburg
Ostheim
ZINC
IRON
Gaildorf
SILVER
Treuchtlingen
Fremdingen
Ellwangen
Backnang
STEEL
STUTTGART
Abtsgmünd
Aalen
11 US
Monheim
"B L U E L A N D"
Esslingen
Plochingen
Uhingen
Göppingen
Neresheim
Donauwörth
Königsbronn
Süßen
Natthm.
Heidenheim
Tapfheim
Rain
Donzdorf
Kirchheim
Donau
Geislingen
Dillingen
N
Gundelfingen
0 10 20 km
Lech
Augsburg

FIGURE 6-10

MLRS Battalion. While the remainder of 1st (US) Infantry Division attacked Gold's two divisions to the north, the 3rd (US) Armored Cavalry Regiment would screen the interoperability division's right flank. With 4 CMBG to the right of the line, Panzer Grenadier Brigade 35 to the left and the US brigade sandwiched in between, the interoperability division conducted an advance to contact. The 3rd (US) Infantry Division was held back as the exploitation force or counter-attack force if necessary.

12 Panzer Division's plan was to use 4 CMBG as the point of main effort. This role was awarded to 4 CMBG by the German divisional commander, Major General Verstl, who understood what the Canadians were capable of. To destroy the enemy division, the Blue Army Group Commander selected an objective, code-named TEXAS. Objective TEXAS was essentially a piece of ground to drive for and hold in a hasty defence after enemy formations along the way had been neutralized.

With the Recce Squadron from 8 CH leading the way, 4 CMBG swung into action. Army Group South's 203mm gun support and the attached MLRS battalion supplemented the M-109s of 1 RCHA as 4 CMBG cleaved its way through the incoherent enemy recce screen. The key to Objective TEXAS was crossing the Tauber River; Brigadier General de Faye selected sites around Rothenberg, which would allow 4 CMBG to move along the north side of the Tauber and west towards TEXAS. These sites were seized in rapid succession on 12 September, and the infantry battalions in their APCs quickly exploited the situation, crossing bridges constructed by 4 CER and protected by the *Blowpipe* gunners from 4 Air Defence Regiment. The other brigades in the division were tasked with fixing enemy formations so they would not interfere with 4 CMBG while the Canadians got in behind them and knocked out their support. The enemy was pressed back against the Tauber River by the US and German brigades, and the presence of 4 CMBG on the north side prohibited the enemy from withdrawing. By 14 September, 8CH's *Leopards*, and the 1 R22eR and 3 RCR Battle Groups succeeded in smashing through to Objective TEXAS. Service support from 4 Service Battalion and 4 Field Ambulance was unceasing, even when enemy forces attempted to break out across the Tauber River into what had become 4 CMBG's rear area.

The only glitch came in the hasty defence portion of Phase I. The

3rd (US) Infantry Division had moved up to TEXAS, and 4 CMBG was temporarily placed under its operational control. Procedural matters relating to interoperability, however, caused a delay in the passage of lines by 4 CMBG. This division had not developed joint FSOPs with 4 CMBG like other US and German divisions, and this was the root of the problem. Tactically, some ground was lost to the 3rd Goldland Armored Division during the confusion, and 4 CMBG was mauled by the enemy forces.

4 CMBG's role in Phase II was no less important. [See Figure 6-11.] Blue forces pulled back from TEXAS into defensive positions and 4 CMBG was placed under the operational control of their old friends, 1st (US) Infantry Division, while a US Armored Cavalry Regiment in front provided a screen. 12 Panzer Division was on the left flank.

4 CMBG took the brunt of the Goldland attack. The enemy was desperate to re-take the crossing sites at Rothenberg and assaulted from the more open ground northeast of the town. They made no headway against 4 CMBG. Once the enemy was committed against the four defending Blue brigades, the Army Group commander unleashed a double envelopment using the 3rd (US) Infantry and 1st (US) Infantry Divisions. The objectives were IOWA and UTAH, where the Goldland armoured divisions were located. While the enemy was still attempting to reduce the Rothenberg salient with small probes, 4 CMBG and the US infantry brigade on its right flank launched an attack to support 1st (US) Infantry Division's envelopment. These attacks were successful and all three formations converged on UTAH to destroy the Goldland armoured division. Subsequent objectives IKE and OHIO remained notional for exercise purposes, and CERTAIN CHALLENGE ended with Blue's Army Group South continuing the advance into history.

In addition to the other training aspects of CERTAIN CHALLENGE, it is pertinent to mention here the levels of Canadian-US and Canadian-German interoperability attained by 1988. As discussed in the last chapter, the key elements of interoperability included the development of Joint Field Standing Operating Procedures, joint planning and training, liaison officers and personal contacts. By 1988, JFSOPs and the liaison system between 4 CMBG and 1st (US) Armored Division, and between 4 CMBG and 4 Panzer Grenadier Division, had been in effect and

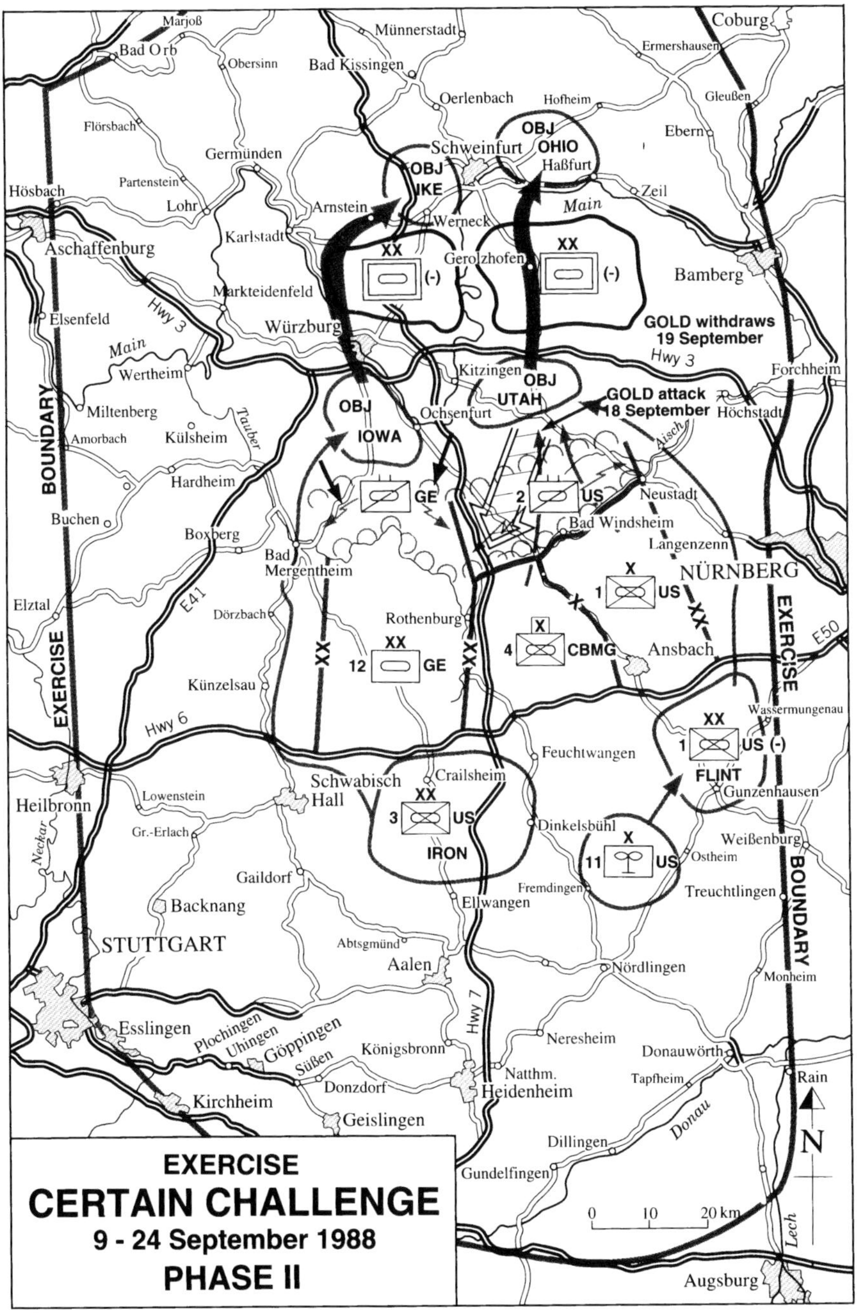
Coburg
Marjoß
Bad Orb
Münnerstadt
Obersinn
Bad Kissingen
Ermershausen
Oerlenbach
Hofheim
Gleußen
Flörsbach
OBJ
OHIO
Ebern
Germünden
Schweinfurt
Haßfurt
OBJ
IKE
Partenstein
Zeil
Hösbach
Lohr
Arnstein
Main
Werneck
Karlstadt
Aschaffenburg
XX
(-)
Gerolzhofen
XX
(-)
Bamberg
Markteidenfeld
Elsenfeld
Hwy 3
Würzburg
GOLD withdraws
19 September
Main
Hwy 3
Wertheim
Kitzingen
OBJ
UTAH
Forchheim
Miltenberg
OBJ
IOWA
Ochsenfurt
GOLD attack
18 September
Höchstadt
Amorbach
Külsheim
Tauber
Aisch
BOUNDARY
Hardheim
GE
2
US
Neustadt
Buchen
Bad Windsheim
Boxberg
Langenzenn
Bad
Mergentheim
X
NÜRNBERG
1
US
Elztal
E41
Dörzbach
Rothenburg
EXERCISE
X
4
CBMG
Ansbach
XX
XX
12
GE
XX
E50
Künzelsau
Wassermungenau
EXERCISE
Hwy 6
XX
1
US (-)
Feuchtwangen
FLINT
Crailsheim
Schwabisch
Hall
Gunzenhausen
XX
Heilbronn
Lowenstein
3
US
Dinkelsbühl
Neckar
Gr.-Erlach
IRON
X
Weißenburg
11
US
Ostheim
Gaildorf
Fremdingen
Treuchtlingen
Backnang
Ellwangen
BOUNDARY
STUTTGART
Abtsgmünd
Aalen
Nördlingen
Monheim
Esslingen
Plochingen
Uhingen
Göppingen
Hwy 7
Neresheim
Königsbronn
Süßen
Donauwörth
Natthm.
Tapfheim
Rain
Kirchheim
Donzdorf
Heidenheim
Donau
Geislingen
N
Dillingen
Gundelfingen
0
10
20 km
Lech
Augsburg

EXERCISE
CERTAIN CHALLENGE
9 - 24 September 1988
PHASE II

FIGURE 6-11

continually tested. The degree of interoperability was so finely tuned that 4 CMBG was regarded quite differently from other NATO formations by the Germans. Major General Jurgen Reichardt, Commander of 4 Panzer Grenadier Division:

> Our role in the multi-national alliance brought lots of possibilities, and the necessity to compare the doctrines of each single country. We had been in discussion with the British on doctrine, with the Americans and with the French and always with the intention to adapt as far as possible. We have not had these discussions with the Canadians. Not at all. The reason for this was that the understanding of the Canadian land forces [of tactical operations and command and control] is so close to our understanding, and the understanding between German and Canadian commanders is so close, that there was absolutely no need for theoretical seminars of doctrine comparison. We could resolve any problems, attach any battalion to 4 CMBG or accept a Canadian battalion. It worked the same way, only in another language. This did not happen with any other nation of the NATO Alliance.

4 CMBG never did completely regain the numbers and capability that it had enjoyed in the 1960s, so the 1980s was a period of only partial restoration. The changing threat environment in the 1980s prompted NATO to re-assess its conventional forces in order to provide a more viable deterrent. 4 CMBG benefited from these changes in a number of ways. The Brigade's numerical strength increased significantly, and new equipment enhanced its fighting capability beyond the level attained in the 1970s. After a period of 'catch up' between 1980 and 1985, attempts were made to rationalize the logistics and sustainment situations, but these had not been completed by the end of the decade. The increased capability of the Brigade resulted in a more focused role in the defence of the VII (US) Corps and II (GE) Korps sectors. This role was no less important in some ways than the role played by 4 CIBG in NORTHAG in the 1960s. Canada now provided CENTAG with a high quality formation to close a critical gap in NATO's Forward Defence Area. This high level of quality was demonstrated time and again on the large scale NATO exercises, while the Germans, Americans and Canadians all benefited from the close inter-army relationships which developed in

CENTAG. Though the Brigade did not return to the halcyon days of the 1960s, it could no longer be considered a "Hong Kong" like commitment in the way that it had been throughout the 1970s.

1989 - 1993

4 BRIGADE AND THE NEW WORLD DISORDER

CHAPTER SEVEN

"WE CANNOT REVIVE OLD FACTIONS
WE CANNOT RESTORE OLD POLICIES
OR FOLLOW AN ANTIQUE DRUM...
WHAT WE CALL THE BEGINNING IS OFTEN THE END
AND TO MAKE AN END IS TO MAKE A BEGINNING
THE END IS WHERE WE START FROM...."

- T.S. ELIOT, *GERONTION*

Both: *The Multiple Integrated Laser Engagement System (MILES) was a training device which enabled casualty assessments to be made without resorting to umpires during exercises. This equipment was borrowed from the Americans and used in the training area at Hohenfels to increase training realism. It could be mounted on rifles as with these 1 R22ᵉR soldiers (above), or on the heavy (.50 calibre) machine guns of the APCs (below). (DND) ILC 91 019 027, ILC 91 019 024*

CHAPTER SEVEN 431

Above: *Even though large scale exercises in the German countryside were a thing of the past by 1990, gun camps and small scale exercises were still held in military training areas such as here in Hohenfels. (DND) ILC 01 019 008*
Below: *Parsberg was the rail terminus for 4 CMBG troop trains travelling to Hohenfels for the annual FALLEX workups. (DND) ILC 91 019 163*

When Canada despatched a squadron of CF-18 Fighters to participate in the Gulf War in 1991 the security for the Canadian air base in Qatar, known as Canada Dry 1, was provided by an infantry company from 4 CMBG, first from M Coy, 3 RCR, then C Coy, 1 R22eR.
Above: One of the CF-18s at Canada Dry 1 under guard. **Below:** Associate Defence Minister, Mary Collins, visiting C Coy, 1 R22eR machine gun post at Canada Dry 1.

CHAPTER SEVEN

Above: *The re-activation of 1st Canadian Infantry Division in 1989 prompted a number of changes to the Canadian army's structure in Germany. (DND) ILC 91 019 015*
Below: *4 CMBG's relationship with the Bundeswehr remained close and important right to the end, thanks in large measure to German speaking Canadian Liaison Officers. The last Brigade LO to 4 Panzer Grenadier Division, Maj J.R. Near (The RCR) is here flanked by the Division Chief of Staff, LCol Skodowski and the Division Commander, MGen Jurgen Reichardt. The dog, naturally, is the General's.*

Above: *1992: Yugoslavia explodes and 4 CMBG is called upon to provide units for the United Nations Protection Force (UNPROFOR). In Sector West, a Canadian observer surveys the damage.* (DND) ISC 93 5104 24
Below: *1 R22ᵉR Battle Group, after a series of perilous encounters, reached the Sarajevo Airport and secured it in July 1992. Note the Night Observation Device mounted on the APC's Heavy Machine Gun.* (DND) ISC 92 4019 1

CHAPTER SEVEN

Both: *4 Combat Engineer Regiment was responsible for mine clearance and unexploded ordnance disposal in the UN Protected Areas.* (DND) ISC 93 5104 4, ISC 93 5104 14

Both: Convoy escort, for the United Nations High Commission for Refugees (UNHCR) was only one of many humanitarian tasks performed by the 1 R22ᵉR Battle Group during its seven month deployment to the wartorn former Republic of Yugoslavia. (DND) ISC 92 5369, ISC 92 5368

CHAPTER SEVEN

The Brigade knew the Cold War was really over when reciprocal visits took place between 4 CMBG senior officers and a Polish military delegation. The 15 Polish officers spent two days in Lahr as guests of the Brigade during 5 - 6 May 1992. **Above**: BGen Clive Addy (Comd 4 CMBG) accepts a badge from LCol Bogdan Kaminski, head of the Polish delegation. **Below**: Polish officers observe 4 Service Battalion EME soldiers change the engine of a Leopard tank.

*One of 4 Brigade's final farewell ceremonies took place, fittingly, in Soest - the very place Canadian troops in Germany first developed their professionalism and reputation. The "Boerdetag" weekend of 14 - 16 May 1993 saw thousands of Soesters (**above**) turn out for band concerts, historical displays, receptions and a final marchpast of 4 CMBG soldiers (**bottom**) through the historic streets of the old Hanseatic League city.*

CHAPTER SEVEN   439

The final years of 4 CMBG's existence were characterized by uncertainty and rapid change. No sooner had 1st Canadian Division been formed than the first signs of cracks in the Iron Curtain appeared. The implications of these events in 1989 were not apparent at the time, and business continued as usual in the Central Region. Only when it was clear that the Soviets really were dismantling their military apparatus in East Germany and Czechoslovakia did Canada give serious consideration to repatriating 4 CMBG. This consideration was put on hold temporarily when Saddam Hussein of Iraq invaded Kuwait in August of 1990. Canada, as part of the UN response, dispatched small naval and air contingents to participate in the international blockade of Iraq, while military planners assessed the viability of contributing ground forces, 4 CMBG being the prime candidate for such a deployment.

The vicious internal conflict in Yugoslavia erupted soon afterward in the summer of 1991, and once again the United Nations asked Canada to contribute to a multi-national peace effort. The proximity of 4 CMBG to Yugoslavia dictated that any Canadian contribution to a United Nations force there would initially come from 4 CMBG, even though the order already had come for it to pack up and go home. 4 CMBG's officers and non-commissioned members accomplished this task with great professionalism and dedication. When they finally did depart Europe in 1993, they did so with heads held high, proud of having served in the cause of peace right to the very end, in NATO and even under the Blue Beret.

All this, of course, was unforeseen when viewed from the perspective of 1989. At that time – a period that now seems like decades ago – the threat was still formidable in NATO's Central Region. But by then the inherent contradictions of the Communist system were becoming increasingly evident. Throughout 1989, popular mass demonstrations and protests erupted in Czechoslovakia and the East German cities of Dresden and Leipzig which the authorities, seemingly, were unable or unwilling to contain. In quick order East German refugees flooded westward through Czechoslovakia into Austria and West Germany. On 9 November 1989 a massive crowd partied on top of the Berlin Wall beside the historic Brandenburg Gate. Within days, the whole of the Wall had been peacefully breached in the East and another flood of people headed West, the East German state teetering on the brink of collapse. The situation was still in flux, however, since no one could be certain how the Soviet Union would react.

It was not without some irony then, when, on 30 November 1989, the ceremonial drums from the units that comprised 4 Canadian Mechanized Brigade Group were solemnly stacked on the tarmac of the Lahr airfield and a red flag emblazoned with a gold maple leaf was draped over them by Major General Jack Dangerfield. In the presence of SACEUR, the Canadian CDS and the Deputy Commander of CENTAG, chaplains intoned a prayer for those who would serve with the historic formation now being re-consecrated. The bands played and the flags waved as the 300-strong guard, its members wearing the 'Old Red Patch' of the 1st Canadian Division, marched off. The 1st Canadian Division, almost 30 years after its disbandment, had been re-born.

This re-birth was a long time in the making. By 1986, it had become clear to the Canadian government that planned increases in defence spending would not be enough to complete the modernization of the Army in order for it to meet its NATO force goals. Out of thirty NATO force goals agreed to by Canada, only six were met; out of the thirteen priority force goals from the thirty, only two were met. Unmet force goals included adding the third mechanized battalion to 4 Brigade, a main battle tank replacement programme, a replacement for the *Blowpipe* air defence missile, and the acquisition of more TOW anti-tank missiles. Another unfulfilled project was the replacement of the *Kiowa* helicopter with a new light helicopter capable of engaging enemy armour.

By SACEUR's criteria, Canada's contribution to the defence of the Central Region in 1986 had its high and low points. In terms of Canada's military contribution to crisis management, Canada was applauded; unit manning levels and personnel training matched or exceeded ACE forces standards. The decreased reliance on augmentation by increasing the stationed strength of 4 CMBG was considered a substantial improvement. Canada's contribution to ACE's ability to defeat the Warsaw Pact's first echelon was considered to be adequate, but still in need of enhancement. In terms of the FOFA concept, only the CF-18s of the newly formed Air Division provided any Canadian capability.

The 1987 White Paper on Defence was a somewhat belated attempt by the Mulroney government to live up to commitments made to make substantial improvements to Canadian defence capabilities. Although there was some freeing up of monies to give impetus to re-equipment programmes, many of these programmes had been in the proposal and early implementation stages for some years. Other attributes of the White Paper regarding force improvements and re-deployments also had their genesis prior to 1987. Most significantly, earlier recommendations stemming from problems with the CAST commitment came into play.

Canada thus started formal consultations with NATO about consolidating the CAST Brigade Group and 4 CMBG commitments. Although SHAPE rated the CAST mission as the more important because of its role in pre-war crisis stability, SHAPE could not ignore possible improvements to forces in the Central Region confronting the Warsaw Pact first echelon. These consultations, combined with the severe problems encountered on Exercise BRAVE LION in North Norway in 1986, resulted in the Canadian government's decision to end the CAST Brigade

Group commitment in Norway and to consolidate all NATO European land deployments in the Central Region as part of a new Divisional commitment. In the words of the 1987 White Paper, *Challenge and Commitment*,

> The Government has concluded that consolidation in southern Germany is the best way to achieve a more credible, effective and sustainable contribution to the common defence in Europe. Consolidation will reduce, although not eliminate, the critical logistical and medical support problems posed by our current commitments....The task of the Canada-based CAST Brigade Group will, therefore, be shifted from Norway to the Central Front, thus enabling the Canadian army to field a division-sized force in a crisis. The resulting combat power will be enhanced and made more effective than what could have been achieved by two separately deployed brigades. Consolidation will thus be of significant value to NATO's Central Army Group as the size of its operational reserve will be doubled.

In effect, the Canadian Government had now come full circle from 1968.

The hole in the northern flank left by the removal of the CAST Brigade Group was filled to some degree, and after considerable arm-twisting in the Alliance, with a new organization – the NATO Composite Force (NCF). Canada committed itself to providing a battalion group (which was to be separate from the AMF(L) commitment) to the NCF, and the CAST Brigade faded into history.

In the reorganization, 5^e Groupe-brigade du Canada (5GBC) in Valcartier and 4 CMBG in Germany constituted the manoeuvre brigades in the new Canadian division. Along with its changed status, 4 Brigade received a new title; "Group" was dropped from the 4 CMBG designation which became 4 Canadian Mechanized Brigade, while 5e GBC became 5e Brigade mechanisée du Canada (5e BMC).

Brigadier General J.M.R. Gaudreau took command of 4 CMB in 1989, while former 4 CMBG commander Jack Dangerfield – now promoted Major General – took command of 1st Canadian Division. Headquarters 1st Canadian Division was established in Kingston, Ontario, with 4 CMB and 5 BMC under command. A detachment of the new headquarters, 1st Canadian Division HQ (Forward), was established in

CHAPTER SEVEN

the Kaserne in Lahr. This concept was based on American experience with the 1st (US) Infantry Division (Forward), with which 4 Brigade had worked with in the past. 1st (US) Infantry Division had a deployed forward headquarters in Germany with one brigade, with the rest of the division available in the US to return to Germany. In Canada's case, having a forward divisional headquarters detachment in Germany allowed the Division Commander in Kingston to maintain contact with both CENTAG and 4 CMB to co-ordinate planning and training. The original intent was to start up the forward headquarters in 1989 with about 40 personnel, and then move the main headquarters from Kingston to Lahr gradually over a period of time. As with many other aspects of planning, this was never implemented because of the great changes in the European situation.

The Divisional structure blended the assets of 4 CMB and 5^e BMC, and included some forces from other units based in Canada. 4 CMB remained essentially unchanged from the 4 CMBG structure in 1987. 5^e BMC however, had only three-quarters of 4 CMB's establishment in men and equipment. The divisional planners thus had to find a way to form a rational and militarily-sound divisional structure. This was intended to be a proper division that exercised regularly in Germany, not just a paper entity that simply re-badged and re-roled some forces based in Canada.

In its final form, 1st Canadian Division had two 'basic' brigades as its fighting formations, with the support organizations centralized at the divisional level. Each brigade had (once the forces had been married up in Germany in a crisis) one small armoured regiment (two tank squadrons each of 20 tanks) and two four-company infantry battalions. The 8th Canadian Hussars in Germany were to give up some of its tanks to 12e Régiment Blindé du Canada, the division's second armoured regiment. The Canada-based infantry battalions were supposed to have their equipment pre-positioned in Germany in the same manner as the US REFORGER forces. Thus, 4CMB had 8 CH, 1 R22eR, and 3 RCR, while 5e BMC consisted of 12e RBC, 2 RCR, and 3 R22eR. It was further assumed that in a war time situation, either a German or an American brigade would be attached to the Division to give it its necessary third manoeuvre element, and training and exercises were conducted with this in mind.

Divisional troops were essentially amalgamations of former 4 CMBG and 5ᵉ GBC units, along with some 1 CMB units. The Artillery Brigade included 1 RCHA in Lahr (4 batteries of M-109A2 SP guns), 5e Régiment d'artillerie légère du Canada in Valcartier (3 batteries of M-109s) and 3 RCHA from Shilo, Manitoba which was intended to be re-armed with the Multiple Launch Rocket System. 4 Air Defence Regiment rounded out the Artillery Brigade.

Once the division was constituted in Germany, the recce squadrons from both 8 CH and 12e RBC were to be withdrawn from their parent units to form, along with the recce squadron and regimental headquarters of the Lord Strathcona's Horse, the divisional recce regiment. The recce regiment's designation was to be The Fort Garry Horse, but while the CO and RSM were named and posted, the unit was never officially re-formed. Similarly, the 36 TOW under armour systems were to be taken away from the infantry battalions and grouped to form a divisional anti-tank battalion. The infantry battalions themselves were to be re-equipped with a new medium range anti-armour weapon of the *Milan* type, then on the Army's order books.

Engineer organization followed the artillery model. 5e Régiment du génie du Canada, 4 CER and an unformed 6 CER formed the Engineer Group, while the Division Aviation Wing included 444 Tactical Helicopter Squadron and 430 Escadron tactique d'hélicoptères. Other divisional troops included an Intelligence Company, a Military Police Company, and a Headquarters and Signal Regiment, which was based on 1 CSR in Kingston. 4 Service Battalion and 5 Service Battalion were to combine to form the Divisional Service Group (DISGP). Medical support, in the same fashion, was to come from 4 Field Ambulance and 5 Field Ambulance, which would combine to handle third line medical support and act as a link between the Canadian Medical Group in Lahr and the Division at the front.

Geographically, 4 CMB and the forward detachment of Division Headquarters were in Germany, with the main Division Headquarters and some divisional troops in Kingston, Ontario, and 5ᵉ BMC in Valcartier, Quebec. Other divisional troops were drawn from 1 Canadian Mechanized Brigade Group in western Canada. This situation was similar to the one of 1st Canadian Infantry Division in the 1950s. Unlike the 1950s, however, the plans to marry up the division's component elements were much more concrete.

GDP employment options for 1st Canadian Division did not, however, progress beyond those already developed for 4 CMBG in the 1980s. The division's planners, though, had to be flexible. If there was a "no warning" crisis, COMCENTAG had to be able to employ 4 CMB in the same manner that he would have done before the creation of 1st (CA) Division. That is, 4 CMB would have to hasten to TAA SETTER, deploy into its GDP positions and await further orders. In a longer warning scenario involving a build up of tension between NATO and the Warsaw Pact, plans had to be made for the rapid augmentation of 4 CMB by means of Operation PENDANT, followed immediately by the deployment of the remainder of the Division – Operation BUGLE. The problems of getting the Canadian based elements of the Division to Europe mirrored those of the 1950s. Canada still did not possess enough strategic lift for such an operation. Fortunately, Canada had access to the ILOC. Although it was never developed in planning documents, Brigadier General Gaudreau believed that the deployment of the Division would not have been a problem:

> Bringing the Division over was not different from a REFORGER; we could do it in the same time frame as the Americans could have been able to do it....If you were SACEUR, [and] you have a Canadian division…I think you would say, 'I'd like that Canadian flag planted on the ground.' If you're controlling transit across the Atlantic, [SACEUR] would make sure the Canadians would have a fairly high priority in deployment; more flags. Although there were a lot of people who never believed in our capability to deploy early to reinforce, I was quite positive that it would have happened for political reasons....

Other details – such as finding room for the balance of the Division in TAA SETTER were never sorted out by the time the word came to draw down in late 1991.

In terms of positioning, concepts were considered for moving 4 CMB to a barracks near Munich; this never happened for the same reasons discussed in the last chapter. Moving 5ᵉ BMC to Germany in the Lahr/Baden area, after moving 4 CMB forward, was another possibility, but this thinking was never examined seriously at any level.

1st Canadian Division missed FALLEX 89, though some recce elements from 12e RBC were flown over. 4 CMBG (as it was still called) moved north to Frankfurt to work with the 8th (US) Infantry Division against 3rd (US) Armored Division on Exercise CARAVAN GUARD. This exercise was very different from its predecessors; it utilized the Joint Exercise Simulation System (JESS) a computer wargaming tool. CARAVAN GUARD was a "Command Field Exercise" or CFX, where smaller units or forces represented larger ones, while most of the exercise was conducted like a Command Post Exercise. The ever increasing demand to limit manoeuvre damage was an important factor in this type of training. On the whole, CFXs were unsatisfying for the soldier in the field: operations were carefully scripted and tactical situations were generally unrealistic on the ground. As Brigadier General Gaudreau put it:

> This was the first year they were playing with computer-assisted exercises…. We had live battalions facing phantom battalions, where an APC represents a company. We had a real company on the ground, and they're facing one APC. You're really stretching the soldier's mind!…. This thing was controlled through [Fort] Leavenworth in the American context. It was frustrating for us. We were in the field, and normally we would have live forces against live forces. In this case we didn't. People sneak across boundaries [because there is nothing there]. In theory there is a battalion/brigade/division/corps over there, but in reality there is nothing on the ground.

Other highlights of FALLEX 89 included the use of a new communications system, LTARS, the destruction of 'enemy' M-1 tanks by Headquarters and Signal Squadron, and the ignominy of getting 'Lanced' twice by enemy surface-to-surface missiles.

The first test of 1st Canadian Division in Germany was conducted the following year on Exercise ROYAL SWORD, otherwise known as FALLEX 90. While 4 CMB deployed to the Hohenfels training area for battle group work ups, the Main Headquarters of 1st Canadian Division married up with its forward component and moved to Kammersbruch, near Amberg. Part of Headquarters 5ᵉ BMC also deployed. ROYAL SWORD was a CFX; 4 CMB was exercised in a requisitioned manoeuvre area, while 5ᵉ BMC and the Division headquarters operated in Command Post Exercise mode. In the final measure, ROYAL SWORD demonstrated that the divisional concept was workable from command and control as well as Field SOP standpoints. As for 4 CMB, it got a good workout operating against elements of 4 Panzer Grenadier Division.

How should the re-activation of 1st Canadian Division be assessed? Was it merely the re-badging of formations in Canada and Germany with a red shoulder patch? Certainly the Division never got to the stage of development that its creators wanted. From a NATO standpoint, however, having another high quality Canadian brigade in CENTAG plus additional divisional troops, increased NATO's ability to defend West Germany in a conflict. Certainly, the strengthened defences in front of Nürnberg would have enabled II (GE) Korps to release additional forces to handle the vulnerable Donau Approach. (After examining Warsaw Pact planning following German unification, it has become quite clear that the Warsaw Pact would have attacked along the Donau Approach in the event of war.) In the end, the full potential of the Division was never realized given the geo-political changes in the early 1990s.

Following the breach of the Berlin Wall in November 1989, the speed with which subsequent events in East Germany and the rest of the Warsaw pact happened was breathtaking. It was only a matter of time before the two Germanies were politically unified, and this was the aim of the "4+2 Agreement", as the Soviets, tried to exercise what dignity and control remained to them in their rapidly crashing empire. Finally, on 3 October 1990, after 45 years, Germany was reunited, the event marked by an uncharacteristic outpouring of national euphoria across the whole of the Federal German Republic. The situation was still far from certain however; the Group of Soviet Forces Germany still remained in the eastern part of the country, and maintained high troop levels well into late 1990.

It became obvious to all, however, that the chances of a NATO-Warsaw Pact confrontation were rapidly diminishing. Once German reunification was a *fait accompli*, it was next to impossible for Moscow to block free elections and the spread of democracy within other Warsaw Pact member nations. Soviet President Mikhail Gorbachev also no longer resisted the Conference of Security and Cooperation in Europe's long standing push for a conventional arms treaty to reduce Soviet conventional superiority. The Conventional Forces in Europe Treaty (CFE Treaty) was signed on 19 November 1990. It set ceilings on the numbers of NATO and Warsaw Pact weapons systems and military vehicles within defined areas, and developed a verification and inspection regime. Canada could now expect to send observers on Warsaw Pact exercises and to examine their bases. 4 CMB could also expect to be inspected in return. Inspectors from Czechoslovakia promptly did so during FALLEX 90.

On 2 August 1990, Iraq overran and occupied its smaller, oil-rich neighbour Kuwait. This act not only threatened the delicate balance of power in the Middle East but posed a direct threat to the economic well-being of the Western world, of which Canada was a part. If Saudi Arabia and other Gulf states were invaded in turn by Iraq, the flow of Persian Gulf oil could be shut off, precipitating a world-wide economic crisis. Additionally, the brutal occupation of Kuwait, coupled with the Iraqi seizure of Western embassies and citizens (including Canadians) were indications that Saddam Hussein could not be negotiated with. The United Nations, with unprecedented haste, passed Resolutions 660 and 661, demanding that Iraq vacate Kuwait immediately or face imposition of economic sanctions.

In the wake of the Gulf War a great deal of debate, even criticism, was generated within the Canadian Forces regarding the apparent inability of the Army to deploy and sustain a brigade-sized force in a regional conflict. Much of this criticism resulted from inter-service disputes and defence budgetary matters. This could be ignored in this work, except that the alleged inability of the Army to carry out such a deployment was used by some to question the viability of Canada's land force commitment to NATO's Central Region since 1951. It thus deserves examination.

Responding to the UN's request for forces to enforce economic sanctions against Iraq, Prime Minister Mulroney announced on 10 August 1992 the deployment of a Canadian Naval Task Group to the Persian

CHAPTER SEVEN

Gulf, consisting of two destroyers and a supply ship. Operation FRICTION had started. Other commands within the Canadian Forces were anticipating further action on the part of the Canadian Government and used their initiative to prepare a number of contingency plans in case the military was called upon to provide options to the political leadership. By 13 August, seven contingency plans were proposed, even though no detailed staff work on them had been done. In order of priority these plans included:

1. Evacuation of Canadian nationals from the Gulf Region;
2. The deployment of CF-18 fighter aircraft to Turkey;
3. Resupply and sustain the Operation FRICTION Naval Task Group;
4. Replace vessels involved in Operation FRICTION;
5. Provide in-theatre airlift support to Pan-Arab forces;
6. Provide logistical support to multi-national forces in the Gulf region;
7. Deploy ground combat forces.

As the Canadian Naval Task Group departed on 24 August for its 'Persian Excursion', the first US pre-positioning ships from Diego Garcia arrived in Saudi Arabia, disgorging enough equipment for two US Marine divisions. By 25 August, the UN passed Resolution 665, which permitted the use of military force to back up the economic sanctions against Iraq.

Around this time, Canadian Forces Europe had prepared a contingency plan to deploy a CF-18 squadron and an airfield protection element from 4 CMBG to an unspecified location in the Persian Gulf. This was a logical contingency to the planners who felt Canadian ships would require air cover, and, in turn, the aircraft would require protection from hostile ground forces. This contingency was quickly adopted by the Government, and Operation SCIMITAR was announced on 14 September. The first CF-18s from CFB Baden deployed on 6 October for their new base in Qatar, which by then had been secured by M Company 3 RCR from Baden. 3 RCR also provided a Defence and Security Platoon commanded by Lt Ken Hill for the Canadian Joint Force Headquarters Middle East, set up on 27 October in Bahrain to co-ordinate support for

CF units in the Gulf.

Although the air force planners at first had to be convinced to take an airfield security company with them, the infanteers rapidly proved their worth. Later on, C Company, 1 R22eR took over from M Company the job of securing the Op SCIMITAR bases CANADA DRY 1 and CANADA DRY 2. The security threat was rated as "high" in theatre; Saddam Hussein also publicly announced that terrorist groups sympathetic to Iraq would wreak havoc within those nations arrayed against him.

The Americans had already committed a Marine division, an airborne division, an airmobile division and a mechanized division to Saudi Arabia for Operation DESERT SHIELD. In addition to this, the United Kingdom announced Operation GRANBY on 14 September and set about deploying the 7th Armoured Brigade from BAOR to the Gulf. At the same time, France implemented Operation DAGUET which deposited the 6th Light Armoured Division into the desert sands of Saudi Arabia. The British wanted to commit an entire three-brigade division to Saudi Arabia, but could only provide 7th Armoured Brigade initially, followed by 4th Armoured Brigade on 22 November. Sometime around 14 September, Canadian officers at higher-level NATO headquarters were informally contacted by British officers from BAOR: could Canada provide a brigade under British control to form a Commonwealth Division along the same lines as was done in Korea in 1951?

This was a tempting request. It was, however, fraught with problems. The political dimensions went well beyond command and control on the battlefield. Some Canadian officers believed that the British wanted "more flags" on the battlefield to balance out American influence; in the British mind a Commonwealth partner might be easier to influence than say, the French. This would be important in the post-war resolution of the conflict. In Canada, however, there were the issues of national pride and the old colonial relationship. For this and other reasons, the British proposal was put on hold. (Eventually, what Canada did provide was a fully equipped field hospital with an attached infantry company from 1 RCR for local defence, to 1st British Armoured Division, and which served with distinction, being the only Canadian ground unit to partake in the coalition ground war.)

CHAPTER SEVEN

Canadian military staff planners at all levels knew that force would ultimately be needed to evict Iraqi forces from Kuwait. They also knew from the list of planning priorities generated in August that the last Canadian option was to deploy ground troops to Saudi Arabia. Nothwithstanding this, Mobile Command HQ, with input from 1st Canadian Division HQ, conducted a quick staff check on 26 October on the feasibility of deploying a brigade-sized formation to Saudi Arabia. The assumptions in this staff check formed the basis for what would eventually be called Operation BROADSWORD.

Mobile Command HQ determined that any Canadian formation sent to Saudi Arabia would have to fight in a high-intensity battlefield environment, and one that might include the use of chemical and biological weapons. The headquarters also assumed that Canadian units in Europe could be released by SACEUR for this operation. Furthermore, the planners knew that such a formation would have to work within the framework of a higher formation – an Allied division or corps. More importantly, any Canadian contribution of less than a brigade group was unacceptable for "visibility reasons".

After surveying the existing formations in the Army, Mobile Command HQ logically determined that the formation best suited for operations in the Middle East was 4 CMB. It was at 75 per cent of war establishment strength, while the other brigades in Canada ranged from a high of 70 per cent to only 45 per cent strength. Moreover, only 4 CMB had main battle tanks. Notably, the FMC planners did not think that enough lift could be acquired to move a brigade group to Saudi Arabia immediately; they judged it would take eight to 10 weeks to fully deploy the formation.

These assumptions were critical in the creation of the more detailed contingency plan, OPLAN BROADSWORD. The Chief of the Defence Staff, General de Chastelain, ordered a staff check with the aim of analyzing the factors influencing the deployment and employment of a viable brigade group to support UN coalition action against Iraq. This CDS' staff check was prepared by 13 November, and added more detail to the FMC HQ staff check. The CDS check assumed that a Middle East deployment would receive first priority over existing Army operations, and that resources could be drawn from anywhere. Again, it was assumed that the force would be integrated into a higher formation (division or corps). Most importantly, this check assumed that the force would be based on 4 CMBG after augmentation by Operation PENDANT and including adding a third infantry battalion with APCs and a fourth tank squadron. 4 CMBG (renamed from 4CMB for this operation) also had to have enough supplies for 30 days of operations, and it had to have time to acclimatize. It further assumed that 2 PPCLI from Winnipeg would be the third infantry battalion.

The timings for the deployment of 4 CMBG to Saudi Arabia in the CDS staff check assumed that it would take seven days to produce the plan, 45 days to assemble the force, 55 days to move the force and 35 days of training and acclimatization in-theatre (a time similar to that for the mobilization and dispatch overseas of 1st Canadian Division in 1939). Some general shortfalls needed to be made up, however. The long standing problems in 4 CMBG's logistics and medical structures, problems which had been identified in the 1970s, had not been corrected even though major attempts at overhaul had taken place in the mid-1980s. The other critical area was combat sustainment. The problems inherent in Operation BARBET had never been solved either, even though attempts had been made to improve the state of Canada's reserve forces. If Canada wanted to sustain a brigade group in-theatre for a period longer than six months, reserve forces would have to be employed, and there was no job protection legislation to guarantee Militia soldiers their livelihood once they returned from the Gulf.

While the CDS staff check was undergoing review, External Affairs Minister Joe Clark met with his American counterpart, James Baker, in Bermuda on 13 November. The effect of this meeting on the CDS tasking instruction of 14 November is unclear, but the media speculated that the Americans sounded out Clark on sending land forces to Saudi Arabia. Whatever the impact, 1st Canadian Division HQ was tasked to prepare a plan to deploy a mechanized brigade group to Saudi Arabia, and this plan was called Operation BROADSWORD. For all intents, this tasking instruction used the same assumptions as the CDS staff check. It should be noted here that no decision had been made by the Canadian Government in November 1990 to deploy ground forces to Saudi Arabia; this was strictly a military contingency plan in case the Canadian

CHAPTER SEVEN

Government was asked to do so and agreed to such a course of action.

Over the next 15 days, the Division and Mobile Command HQ planning staffs in Lahr, Kingston and St. Hubert laboured to produce a concrete concept that would keep the Canadian Government's options open. As a result, the BROADSWORD plan was an amalgamation of several elements that included a concept of operations, a risk assessment, a movement estimate, and a casualty estimate.

The concept of operations for BROADSWORD, as in the earlier estimates, postulated that 4 CMBG would operate as part of a division within the framework of an Allied corps. The threat environment in which 4 CMBG would be operating was a heavily armoured one, with the enemy in prepared defensive positions in the desert. Iraqi chemical capability was as diverse as it is was prolific; known Iraqi chemical weapons stocks included mustard blistering agents, phosgene choking agents as well as Sarin and Tabun nerve agents. The Iraqis were also credited with producing BZ, a psychochemical similar to LSD. Finally, the Iraqis had combat experience from the long Iran-Iraq war; Canadian troops had not been in combat since Korea.

As to tactical employment, 4 CMBG was incapable of participating in an advance to contact or deliberate attack based on the generally inferior and obsolete equipment that it possessed in Germany. *Leopard I* tanks and M-113s advancing in the open desert were especially vulnerable to direct fire from superior Iraqi tanks and guns. The planners reasoned that 4 CMBG could, however, participate as the reserve formation within an armoured division. Once the other armoured brigades bypassed strongpoints and took on the enemy's armoured reserve, 4 CMBG could be used to assault bypassed Iraqi units. If the situation worsened, and allied forces were forced onto the defensive, 4 CMBG was already attuned and equipped for defensive operations in an armoured heavy environment. Other potential 4 CMBG missions could include flank or screen operations, or corps rear area security.

With regards to assigning 4 CMBG to a division or corps, there were a number of possibilities. 4 CMBG could go as part of the multi-national Gulf Cooperation Council Corps; but this option was rejected immediately. The choice then came down to placing 4 CMBG under the British division or under a US division operating within a US Corps. As noted earlier, a bias had developed against placing 4 CMBG under British command. This emotional bias was, however, backed up with undeniable facts. 4 CMBG had not served with the British since 1970, but had operated effectively with the Americans since 1971. When the list of advantages and disadvantages was compiled, the situation favoured placing 4 CMBG with VII (US) Corps, preferably with 1st (US) Armored Division. Interoperability means, including liaison officers, training and equipment compatibility simply no longer existed between the British and the Canadians. Standardization did exist in the form of the usual NATO agreements, but Britain no longer had anything comparable to the Canada-US ILOC which would be vital in a protracted conflict. As a result, placing 4 CMBG with the British armoured division was just not a sound option.

The organization of 4 CMBG for a Middle East deployment was not radically different from having 4 CMBG augmented in Europe by Operation PENDANT. 4 CMBG would have had a four-squadron tank regiment (8 CH) plus a recce squadron, while the infantry battalions (3 RCR, 2 PPCLI, 1 R22eR) would have been augmented to include four-company battalion structures. 444 Tactical Helicopter Squadron would be re-organized as a composite squadron with *Kiowa's* and *Twin Hueys*. The other arms and services required little modification, at least initially. Some planners called for the deployment of a complete Canadian Support Group and a Canadian Medical Group, along the lines of those proposed for CFE in the 1980s. This would have increased the number of troops in theatre to 12 000 from the 7000 to 9000 originally envisioned.

Once the planning process was underway, units were solicited to provide material and organizational improvements that they deemed necessary for a Middle East deployment. Planners at the several headquarters involved in BROADSWORD also added changes and suggestions. An 'attitude' appeared to develop in many places simultaneously, best described as the "We can't go without" syndrome. This was understandable since some equipment programmes which had been put off in 1989 could now be put on the fast track. Some (but not all) of these organizational 'grafts' included the deployment of the new ADATS anti-aircraft system, an artillery target acquisition battery, an entire intelligence company, a forward personnel replacement holding unit, all of 2 (EW)

Squadron, a decontamination unit, a medical evacuation company, and a 400-bed field hospital. Personal equipment for fighting in a desert environment was needed, as well as improved NBCD detection and protective gear. The latter was not a problem, since Canada led NATO in the development of NBCD protective equipment. Procurement of other additional armaments and equipments would, however, delay the deployment and would increase costs.

It would be easy to call this situation 'gold plating' and to blame inter-branch rivalry. The real problem was that the Canadian army was still playing catch up from the 1970s era deficiencies and the heightened expectations of the 1980s. Many of these essential equipment improvements had been identified back in 1985, but had not yet been provided by 1990.

The movement estimate for BROADSWORD was not encouraging. There was no sealift capability organic to the Canadian Forces, and this forced the logistics planners to look to commercial shipping. But the Americans had already hired much of Canada's commercial sea and air lift to support their own deployment operations. Even the United Kingdom was chartering Eastern Bloc shipping to move the bulk of their division to Saudi Arabia! The use of the large Newfoundland RO/RO ferries was looked at, but this was not feasible for political reasons. Moving manpower was less of a problem. Standing agreements between the Canadian Government and commercial air carriers in Canada ensured Canada's ability to move troops and some light equipment. But the apparent lack of a heavy lift capability would probably have imposed a significant time delay on the deployment of 4 CMBG had BROADSWORD been implemented.

Another problem that the BROADSWORD planners had to deal with was conflicting casualty estimates which were driven by extremely pessimistic threat assessments emanating from American sources who appeared to expect a protracted and bitter war against a battle-hardened Iraqi army. Medical specialists involved in BROADSWORD planning calculated that, after 30 days of combat, the entire brigade group would need replacement: they estimated that out of a 9000 man force, there would be 1971 killed and 7434 wounded. Other BROADSWORD planners developed a smaller estimate, which calculated only 3000 killed and wounded needing replacement after thirty days. Another DND agency put the anticipated casualty rate at 1000 killed and 3472 wounded. They all appear to have failed to take into account that the allied coalition being formed was in every way a vastly superior military machine than anything Iraq could muster.

By 20 November the window for deployment was closing fast. The BROADSWORD planners established early on that 1 December was the go/no go date in their planning – again allowing for 45 days to assemble, 55 days to move, and 35 days to train and acclimatize. This would put the BROADSWORD force in theatre and ready to fight by April 1991. Events, however, conspired against this timetable. On 29 November, the UN Security Council passed Resolution 678, which set a 15 January 1991 deadline for Saddam Hussein to withdraw his forces out of Kuwait. When asked on 7 December, 1990 about the feasibility of BROADSWORD in light of this development, 1st Canadian Division planners replied: "There are no show stoppers per se but one issue, the composition and availability of battle casualty replacements could impose limitations on the employment of 4 CMB(G) plus."

BROADSWORD hung in limbo for the next month. On 12 January 1991, an "anonymous military source", recently returned from Germany, leaked significant aspects of the BROADSWORD plan to the media, including the size, composition and the possibility that the brigade might come under British command. That source was evidently motivated by a belief that BROADSWORD planning was being done behind the backs of the Canadian people, and that Canadians were not being given a say in the deployment of their troops into a war zone. The source was, however, mistaken: BROADSWORD planning was simply prudent anticipation on the part of the military for the possibility the Government might decide for a ground force option. It was never intended to circumvent the democratic process, but parliamentary critics of the Government's handling of the Gulf situation pounced on the issue without having the facts. On 14 January 1991, Minister of National Defence Bill McKnight told the media that the Government had no intention of sending a brigade to the Gulf. Two days later the allied air campaign started, and by 28 February the lightning five-day land attack portion of the campaign was complete. The Iraqi forces were completely routed.

After the fact, it was easy to say that 4 CMBG was not needed in the Gulf War, that it could not have arrived in time to do anything, and that it was not sustainable. Comments such as this can only be made in hindsight, however, since no one knew how long the war would go on. Many planners believed that the ground war would last between several weeks to many months. There was no thought that it would last only 100 hours. Had it had been the long war many expected, Canadian land forces undoubtedly would have been a valuable contribution.

What really doomed BROADSWORD was a combination of factors. Cost was one of these. There have been arguments made that too many 'bells and whistles' were added to the existing 4 CMBG structure, that this drove up the cost of deployment, and that the refitting increased the deployment time. This argument does have some merit, but there were many cases where BROADSWORD planners just said no to the wish lists. On the other hand, if 4 CMBG was to have deployed as part of VII (US) Corps, why did it need its own decontamination capability, target acquisition battery, an EW squadron, its own field hospital and the brand new ADATS system? Could these resources not have been provided by Division or Corps? Exercises in Germany demonstrated time and again that 4 CMBG was capable of assimilating non-Canadian units into its organization and planning structure, or utilizing support provided by a higher headquarters. Canada had a 'free ride' with many such resources in Germany since the 1970s; why change now?

Though many shortcomings (primarily equipment and lift) could have been overcome if the effort and initiative had been made in November, the casualty estimates and the sustainability problem gave the military and political leadership a serious case of cold feet. One BROADSWORD planner thought that this was the primary reason for not deploying to the Gulf:

> I honestly believe the reason that it got turned off was that people realized there would be casualties. There was DEATH involved! It was pretty easy to continue to sit offshore, embargo shipping, fly some airplanes, come back to a relatively secure environment....The government could see that we were talking 30 casualties a day, half of them being deaths. That was startling to the politicians....

Another planner had a similar point of view:

> We may have been too pessimistic. The casualty estimates were up there and the shopping lists too big. That was the straw that broke the camel's back. When all was accumulated, with the high risk assessment and a long shopping list, the thing became intolerable and it was cancelled. I wonder what would have happened if we had gone with a less grandiose shopping list....The Chief of Defence Staff [ultimately] did not recommend it to the political level.

The operational commanders for BROADSWORD certainly believed that the deployment plan was a good one, and that it was capable of being executed. Many logisticians also believed that the movement problem could have been overcome, and that the equipment could have been acquired quickly. What was lacking was the will to do it.

The important question here is, does the failure to implement BROADSWORD show in any way that the NATO brigade commitment was not a viable one? (Certainly the VCDS at the time, Vice Admiral Thomas, implied this.) Most well informed people, however, believe that the answer is no. To have to redeploy 4 CMBG to an entirely new and unfamiliar theatre of operations against a new enemy cannot be compared to having that brigade in theatre for decades, where almost every soldier had an intimate knowledge of the ground, the allies and the opposing forces. There is no doubt that the sustainment and logistical problems of 4 CMBG were significant for operations in NATO's Central Region. But this ignores that fact that Canadian planners knew what the problems were and could have fixed them given the political support. Additionally, the Canadian soldier's ability to improvise should never be underestimated. A war in Europe involving NATO also would have been more important than a Gulf deployment, and the entire national effort would have been directed to supporting the Central Region and the Canadian Forces engaged there.

Despite the high-level haggling, the troops in Lahr and Baden were pumped up and ready to go. Many believed that Ex ROYAL SWORD would be cancelled, and the rumour net was overloaded. Once Saddam Hussein announced that he would employ terrorism against countries opposing him, 4 CMB had work to do. Operation READINESS was implemented to provide security to the Canadian bases, dependent areas and schools in the Lahr and Baden areas. Intelligence flowing into CFE indicated that there was a strong possibility that a Canadian facility would be targeted, a fear which was realized soon afterwards when a bomb threat was made against the schools in Baden.

Even though 4 CMBG could not participate directly in Operation DESERT STORM, considerable indirect support was given to the Americans and the British. Most of 4 CMBG's heavy transport lift went to Ramstein and Rhine-Main USAF bases to assist the Americans with their logistic effort. And all of 4 CMBG's war stocks of 155mm ammunition were given to the British.

Tension continued to be high in CFE. Another bomb threat was made, this time against the Kaserne in Lahr. It was quite a sight: APCs blocked the gates at the Kaserne, and armed guards escorted the school buses and patrolled the PMQ areas. Corporal Shaun Brown assigned to bus guard duty at the time:

> Our job was to ride the school buses and provide security against any terrorist attack. We were to be the first off the bus at every stop and the last on. Magazines were to stay in our pockets unless we believed that there was a definite threat to us or the children.... [Private] Jeff [Boynton] and I had decided that to do the job properly we had to make ourselves easy targets....At every stop I would get out and move to the front of the bus and slightly away from it. Jeff got out the back and moved away from it. We not only called attention to the fact that the bus was guarded, but made it easier for the terrorist to take a shot at us, and it gave the one that wasn't shot a few seconds to react...

Major Peter Devlin, of 3 RCR:

> There was a heightened threat here in Europe for Canadians. The task came down to 3 RCR to look after all of CFB Baden including the PMQs on base here and in Weitnung. We also looked after the schools and the school bus runs. It was a demanding task to look after the base. We had a number of observation posts, we had people that reinforced the gates, we had people in

their vehicles ready to go. We also had rovers that roamed around at night, and we had a platoon quick-reaction force that was also available. We were at this level for about four weeks.

The small coterie of peaceniks in the Lahr area reacted to this new level of alertness:

> [There was a complaint in the letters to the editor in the local German paper. The man that wrote it was, as he put it, 'physically sick to see all those foreigners wandering around Lahr with guns'. The next day there were letters in the paper defending and thanking the Canadians, and pointing out that there had never been an act of terrorism in Lahr, that the Canadians were not foreigners and had been nothing but polite and so forth.

Unit training in the Brigade was curtailed for the duration of the security alert after word had been passed down that there would be no Gulf deployment. (If BROADSWORD had been implemented, security forces from Canada would have been flown in to do the job; it is possible that the local VKK also would have helped under the Host Nation Support agreements.) The *polizei* in Lahr got a strength increase from the nearby police training academy and stepped up patrols. Fortunately there were no attacks against Canadian installations or personnel.

The completion of the Coalition ground campaign against Iraq at the end of February 1991 did not end Canadian involvement in the region. Saddam Hussein for some time had been conducting a brutal campaign against the Kurdish people who populated northern Iraq. He had even used chemical weapons on Kurdish villages in the 1980s, and refugees had flooded into the border region between Turkey and Iraq. To bring an end to the campaign against the Kurds, a Coalition humanitarian relief effort was mounted. Dubbed Operation PROVIDE COMFORT, British Royal Marines, French rapid reaction forces and US Special Forces moved in to secure the area and to deter Iraqi forces from continuing their inhumane persecution of the Kurds.

The Coalition medical effort drew medical resources from the Netherlands, Germany, France, the US, Britain and Canada. Canada's commitment, Operation ASSIST, included 4 Field Ambulance from 4 CMB.

4 Field Ambulance, fresh from assisting the 7th (US) Medical Command at Ramstein AFB during DESERT STORM, was deployed to Incirlik, Turkey on 18 April 1991. Operating in conditions reminiscent of those in Operation DOLOMITE in the 1970s, 4 Field Ambulance was instrumental in relieving the suffering of thousands of Kurds. It was by no means an easy or enviable task. At one point, 12 Turkish commandos drew weapons on Canadian medical personnel who caught the Turks pilfering Canadian military supplies. In another incident Turk soldiers continually cocked their weapons and pointed them at Canadian troops. In a tense standoff, some Royal Marines and US Special Forces personnel backed up the Canadians, and the Turks dispersed.

Other events in 1991 included 4 CMB's final FALLEX, held that September. Brigadier General Clive Addy had just taken command of 4 CMB before it moved for the last time to the Hohenfels Training Area. Exercise ROCHET SABOT was a series of Battle Group work-ups preparatory to Exercise RASOIRE SALAIRE, the final brigade group FTX. RASOIRE SALAIRE was conducted entirely within the confines of Hohenfels and, unlike past exercises, there was no outside force brought in to act as enemy. This much reduced Fallex was symptomatic of the training rundown that had begun in 4 CMB. An era of Canadian soldiering in Germany was drawing to an end.

In September 1991, 1st Canadian Division's exercise, ROYAL ALLIANCE, was held. ROYAL ALLIANCE was a CFX in which 1st Canadian Division Headquarters and most of 1 Canadian Signal Regiment from Kingston deployed to Germany, taking to the field south east of Regensburg to practise operating under the operational command of HQ II German Korps, which also deployed. Apart from giving administrative support, 4 CMB's part in the exercise was to provide a lower control brigade HQ organization. HQ 5^e BMC flown over from Valcartier, performed the same function. The third brigade needed to round out 1st Canadian Division was 4 CMB's old friends, 10 Panzer Grenadier Brigade. Thus, for the first time since World War II, a fully manned Canadian division headquarters operated with three brigade headquarters under its command. Likewise, for the first time since 1945 1st Canadian Division was under the direct control of an Army Corps, only this time the Corps was German; true evidence one might say of the changing tides of history.

Apart from these final exercises, the only other activity of significance was the tasking received by 4 Combat Engineer Regiment in June of 1991 to undertake Operation SPIRAL, a UN mine-clearing operation in Cyprus. After four months of training and preparation for this task, including dispatch of a 12 man recce party to the island, the operation was called off because of lack of Turkish concurrence in the plan. The training in mines and demolitions undertaken by 4 CER during this period was, however, not in vain and would shortly be put to good use in another troublespot, the former Republic of Yugoslavia.

4 Brigade was fast approaching the twilight of its existence when Yugoslavia spiraled into a bloody civil war. The causes of this conflict are rooted in history and will not be examined here in detail save to say that Yugoslavia was an ethnically-fragmented state cobbled together after the First World War. Ethnic hatred going back many centuries was unleashed during the Second World War, but was brought to heel by the Yugoslav partisan leader Josef Broz Tito who became the "President" of a Communist dictatorship at the end of the war. Tito imposed order on chaos through a complex power sharing agreement, backed up with force. The death of Tito in 1980, coupled with the later collapse of Soviet Communism after 1989, resulted in the weakening of all of the mechanisms and forces that held the country together.

Politically, Yugoslavia consisted of eight "republics" within a dictatorial confederation. The republics which concern us here are Croatia, Serbia, Slovenia and Bosnia-Hercegovina, none of which was ethnically homogeneous. The first republic to break away and declare independence was Slovenia. Following a half-hearted military campaign during June and July 1991 against irregular Slovenian forces, the Yugoslavian National Army (JNA) was forced to withdraw from Slovenia.

Following on the heels of Slovenia in jettisoning the Yugoslav federation was Croatia. Unlike the relatively homogeneous Slovenia, Croatia contained two large Serbian enclaves called the Krajinas. With Croatia's declaration of independence, long standing hatreds came bubbling to the surface. Additionally, Croatians had allied themselves with the Germans in the Second World War and had conducted extremely vicious operations against the Serb dominated and Soviet supported resistance movement led by Tito, which also had utilized extremely bloody methods. Tens of thousands of Krajina Serbs were killed or disappeared and there were bloody reprisals by all sides. Now in 1991 with the breakup of Yugoslavia, the Krajina Serbs were not willing to become minority members in an independent Croatia.

The stage was set for a bloodbath. Croats fought Serbs all along the border between Serbia and Croatia, which included a long siege of the city of Osijek. Serbs purged their enclaves of ethnic Croats. Irregular operations by both sides were also conducted in the Krajinas and Slavonia, with no-holds-barred fighting. The objectives were brutally simple. The Serbs wanted to maintain their enclaves and to have corridors from them to Serbia proper. The Croats, on the other hand, wanted the Serbs out by any means necessary in order to secure Croatian territory.

The JNA, meanwhile, was fragmented and could not have interposed itself between the belligerents even if it had wanted to. Croats serving in the JNA left with their equipment and headed west, while Serb-dominated units of the JNA operated either in defence of the Krajinas or in operations to relieve Osijek. Some JNA units did nothing, and opted out. Journalist Misha Glenny provides us with an example of the insanity gripping the Krajinas:

> [two commanders, one Croat and one Serb, spoke on the telephone]...'Is that you Mladic?'
> 'Yes it is, you old devil. What do you want?'
> 'Three of my boys went missing and I want to find out what happened to them.'
> 'I think they're all dead.'
> 'I've got one of their parents on to me about it...so can I tell them for certain that they're all gone?'
> 'Yep, certain. You have my word. By the way, how's the family?'
> 'Oh, not so bad, thanks. How about yours?'
> 'They're doing just fine, we're managing pretty well.'
> 'Glad to hear it. By the way, now I've got you on the line, we've got about twenty bodies of yours near the front and they've been stripped bare. We slung them into a mass grave and they're stinking to high heaven. Any chance of you coming to pick them up because they really are becoming unbearable?'

The European Community (EC), gravely concerned by unfolding events, decided to try its hand at resolution of the conflict, much like the United Nations had done in Cyprus, Egypt and elsewhere. The EC, however, did not have any kind of military organization to execute a peacekeeping operation. Consequently, the European Community Monitoring Mission, Yugoslavia (ECMMY) was created, with the twelve EC member nations and three EC applicant nations providing a mix of civilian and military monitors. Canada's extensive experience in peacekeeping operations was considered to be a valuable asset by the EC, so a Canadian offer to assist, made through the Conference on Security and Cooperation in Europe was accepted. Fifteen Canadians, most of them from 4 Brigade and CFE, joined the ECMMY for this operation, termed Operation BOLSTER by the Canadian Forces.

The ECMMY's role was to place neutral monitoring personnel between the Croat and Serb forces on the existing demarcation lines in Croatia (and later in Bosnia-Hercegovina) with an eye towards disengaging belligerent forces and establishing cease-fire lines. The first teams arrived on the ground in September 1991 and immediately deployed to the disputed areas. The monitor teams themselves were unarmed, wore white uniforms, and traveled in unarmoured vehicles.

It was abundantly clear after two and half months of monitoring operations that ECMMY was simply not able to function effectively as a peacekeeping force. It was too small (150 people), and its communications left much to be desired. It simply could not be everywhere at once. Most importantly, the impartiality of ECMMY was called into question and effective propaganda campaigns orchestrated by both the Serbs and the Croats detracted from its effectiveness. Though individual monitors performed feats of valour in a highly dangerous environment, ECMMY was really a forlorn hope, attempting a mission far beyond its capabilities. A very different kind of peacekeeping force was required for Yugoslavia.

The only possible solution seemed to be the UN, especially when the Secretary General's special mediator for the conflict, Cyrus Vance, achieved a breakthrough of sorts in November 1991. Agreement was reached that civilians occupying the areas that were roughly delineated by the ECMMY ceasefire lines and some municipal boundaries were to fall under UN protection. Under the "Vance Plan", three United Nations Protected Areas (UNPAs) divided into four sectors, were to be de-militarized and occupied by a United Nations Protection Force (UNPROFOR). UNPROFOR's mandate was to protect the civilian populations of the sectors, while the JNA withdrew from the UNPAs to Bosnia-Hercegovina and Serbia. The inhabitants of the UNPAs were to be disarmed and their local irregular defence forces demobilized. Only after these steps had been taken would UN humanitarian aid be allowed into the UNPAs.

The three UNPAs were divided into four Sectors; Krajina North, Krajina South, Slavonia East and Slavonia West. Each sector was commanded by a Brigadier General. Formally established on 21 February 1992 after the UN Security Council passed Resolution 743, UNPROFOR's commander was Indian (Lieutenant General Nambiar), the Deputy Commander was French (Major General Morillon) and the Chief of Staff was Canadian (Brigadier General Lewis Mackenzie). Again, Canada's expertise in peacekeeping operations was a major factor in the UN decision to ask Canada for an infantry battalion and an engineer regiment.

UNPROFOR was a multi-national peacekeeping force, initially consisting of twelve infantry battalions drawn from twelve different countries (Canada, Argentina, Belgium, Czechoslovakia, Denmark, France, Jordan, Kenya, Nepal, Nigeria, Poland and Russia). Additionally, the Netherlands offered up a signal battalion, Canada a combat engineer regiment, the British a medical battalion, the Finns construction engineers and the Norwegians a movement control unit. (Other nationalities rotated in and out later on in both infantry and support roles.) UNPROFOR's logistic base was originally to be Banja Luka, but this was found not to be practical so Zagreb, along with a site near Belgrade (for the appearance of neutrality), was selected. UNPROFOR HQ was, after much controversy and deliberation, located in Sarajevo, as the Bosnian situation had not yet flared up.

The Canadian code name for the Yugoslavian peacekeeping mission was Operation HARMONY. [See Figure 7-1.] Anticipatory planning for Operation HARMONY began in Lahr in December 1991 after the External Affairs minister, Barbara MacDougal, announced that Canada

OPERATION HARMONY
March - August 1992
UN PROTECTED AREAS
1 Sector South
2 Sector North
3 Sector West
4 Sector East
Adriatic Sea
ITALY
SLOVENIA
Trieste
Sava
THE KRAJINAS
CROATIA
Zagreb
Knin
Bihać
Banja Luka
Split
Daruvar
Pakrac
Nova Gradiška
SLAVONIA
HUNGARY
Vukovar
BOSNIA & HERCEGOVINA
Travnik
Vitez
Visoko
Sarajevo
Pale
Goražde
Srebrenica
Tuzla
Mostar
Drina
Dubrovnik
MONTENEGRO
ALBANIA
SERBIA
VOJVODINA
Danube
Belgrade
Battalion boundaries
0 50 100 km

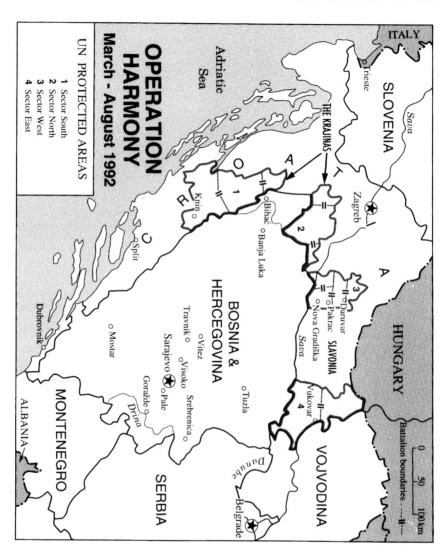

FIGURE 7-1

would send forces to be part of UNPROFOR. Thanks to a 'bootleg' copy of the Vance party's military estimate for the UN operation obtained by the Division HQ Forward staff, the rough outlines of the task were known to the planners in Lahr. A division of labour was established between HQ 1st Canadian Division (Forward), which worked on the larger assumptions for the operation, while 4 Brigade staff worked out the details for a potential Battle Group deployment from 4 CMBG.

The November UN estimate of the situation, now in Canadian hands, developed in detail what the UN planners thought they might need from Canada and other contributing countries to secure the designated UNPAs. By January 1992 the staffs of the Division HQ detachment and 4 Brigade were well into developing a coherent organization and deployment plan for Op HARMONY. The UN estimate required contributing nations to provide four light infantry companies and an APC company totaling 900 men, as well as 200 to 250 combat engineers. This gave the planners in Lahr their basis for establishing an Operation HARMONY force drawn from 4 CMB units.

By early February, the Canadian planning assumptions being made by the brigade and division staffs were more concrete. The principal assumption was that any Op HARMONY force would likely be drawn from 4 CMB because of European basing and close proximity to Yugoslavia, though a second rotation in six months time would have to come from Canada, since 4 Brigade was closing out. HQ CFE would also have to provide logistic support and movement to the area of operations. The ideal organization for the mission was an infantry battalion augmented with other combat support and service support elements to form a self-contained battle group. Most significantly, the planners rejected the light force concept that the UN wanted. The UN thinking was along the lines of previous peacekeeping operations; minimum force, few heavy weapons or armoured vehicles, primarily soft-skinned vehicles, and light weapons for personal protection only. Noting the amount of firepower in the region and the fact that the belligerents' command and control was shaky at best, the Division and Brigade planners assumed that "the contingent must be able to protect itself from artillery and tank fire" and "the contingent must be prepared to defend itself against ground assault including tanks".

Three options for a peacekeeping force were developed in Lahr. There was the Armoured Vehicle General Purpose (AVGP) option, which was an infantry battalion group mounted in *Grizzly* wheeled APCs, including an armoured recce squadron equipped with *Cougar* armoured cars. This was discarded early on since 4 Brigade did not possess AVGPs. This option would also delay reaction time for the operation if vehicles had to be shipped in from Canada. Another option was deploying with MLVW, 1 1/4 ton trucks and *Iltis* jeeps. This wheeled option was considered too light, and did not fit with the assumption that the force would be operating in a high risk environment. The final option, which was selected, was the APC option. The units in Germany had them, and were trained to use them; they were tracked, which increased their mobility off road, and they did give some protection against small arms fire and shell fragments.

One problem that cropped up revolved around providing heavy weapons to the Operation HARMONY battle group. Brigadier General Clive Addy was Commander, 4 CMB during Operation HARMONY:

> When we started this, I wanted to send fire support for the troops…[the VCDS] said, 'No way, there's no intention to do that.' So I talked about TOW missiles and he supported me there. So did Mobile Command. When it got to NDHQ, they said, 'Oh no, we're going into peacekeeping. This is a very fraternal organization and TOWs would be too offensive' and they were in fact deleted from the order of battle…. I had by that time phoned Lew Mackenzie and said, 'What would you like there?' and he said 'I'd like to go for TOW'. So I pushed it up and banged my feet until I finally got a firm 'No' from the DCDS level in Ottawa, so we went on and did what we did without TOW [at least initially]….

The Operation HARMONY Battle Group organization developed by 4 CMB originally conformed to the UN estimate, though there was some trouble determining which battalion (3 RCR or 1 R22eR) would command the operation. Neither battalion had five companies, so one would have to augment the other. According to Brigadier General Addy, 1 R22eR was selected as the lead battalion since it was in Lahr, closer to the planners and the logistical base. An 8 CH squadron was designated as the armoured recce component, and re-equipped with M-113 APCs, while 3 RCR prepared to augment 1 R22eR.

The 900 man limit imposed by the UN (later reduced to 860) constrained the Canadian Op HARMONY organization in some respects. Canadian planners felt that the battle group had to be self-contained for maintenance and logistics, and it had to have communications means back to Canada. 1 R22eR was also short 350 personnel because of the drawdown of 4 CMB that had begun and the fact that the difference between the Van Doos' peacetime strength and war establishment was 200 men. Consequently, the need to augment 1 R22eR with soldiers mainly from 3 RCR, but also from other brigade units. Once the CO's "R" Group under LCol Michel Jones completed its recce to Yugoslavia, however, it was decided that the Battle Group's structure should be changed from four rifle companies, each of 117 men, to two large companies of 250-300 men each. Thus, 1 R22eR Battle Group consisted of Headquarters Company, A Company and Administration Company from 1 R22eR, and from 3 RCR, N Company and Recce Platoon. The armoured recce squadron was deleted on the recommendation of LCol Jones, much to the chagrin of the Hussars. (BGen Addy, in retrospect, believed that this was a mistake and subsequent Canadian rotations to Bosnia included an armoured recce squadron. Units in Croatia, however, remained solely infantry.)

The Operation HARMONY Engineer unit for UNPROFOR, based on 4 Combat Engineer Regiment, was not part of the 1 R22eR Battle Group, but a separate organization under "Canadian Contingent Commander UNPROFOR" assigned to the operational control of UNPROFOR HQ. For this task, 4 CER was augmented by the Pioneer Platoon from 3 RCR and by personnel from 22 Field Engineer Squadron from CFB Gagetown. 4 CER's organization for Yugoslavia included 17 Armoured Engineer Squadron (equipped with *Badger* AEVs and *Beaver* AVLBs), and 41 Field Squadron which possessed limited construction capability. In practice, the two squadrons were shuffled to form two composite squadrons so that 4 CER could work in more than one UNPA at a time.

After weeks of preparation, the Minister of National Defence on 10 March 1992 announced Operation HARMONY to the Canadian public. The soldiers from 4 CER and the 1 R22eR Battle Group had been training non-stop; vehicles which had been slated for return to Canada had to be 'de-mothballed' and painted white with large black "UN" insignia. Brigadier General Lewis Mackenzie, in his "double-hatted" capacity as Chief of Staff, UNPROFOR and the overall commander of the Canadian contingent, approved the final organization of the Op HARMONY force on 24 March. Deployment of 4 CER's advance party commenced the same day. Canada was the first country to get its UNPROFOR designated forces into Yugoslavia.

The movement from Lahr of 4 CER and 1 R22eR Battle Group was done by rail, first directly to Zagreb, and then by a circuitous route due to destroyed track, to Daruvar in UN Protected Area Sector West. Each train chalk took about 40 hours to cover the distance, the last elements arriving on 13 April 1992.

There was a "warm" reception for the soldiers of N Company, who had just arrived and were settling into a schoolyard in Sirac when ten mortar rounds hit. The troops did a "crash action", but four men were wounded. Corporal Tony Carew noted in his journal:

> We are now close to the Daruvar sector in Croatia, and the train is driving very slow because of broken track.... The destruction I can't even begin to explain; its very sad... everything's just leveled. We arrived in the city of Daruvar and we moved on to Sirac where we will set up camp. 2120: It sounded like thunder off in the distance; then seconds later we were being bombed with mortar shells. As the rounds hit, we all scrambled from the UMS to our ambulances and our APCs. All hell was breaking loose. I couldn't believe this was happening to us. As Tony, my driver, and I took off in our ambulance, a piece of shrapnel hit the back of it. All I could think was 'God don't let me die now, I have a family back home.' As we RV'd [rendezvoused] in our safe area I heard, 'Starlight!' (which is, 'Medic get here fast!') We had a man hit in the buttocks. I took care of him and he was later released. As we returned to our bivouac area, the boys were digging in....

Sector West encompassed the Slavonian towns of Daruvar and Pakrac, and its ethnic composition was a 40/60 per cent mix of Serbs and Croats. In the UNPROFOR plan for Sector West, four UN battalions were allocated to occupy the area. The Canadians held the central area, with the

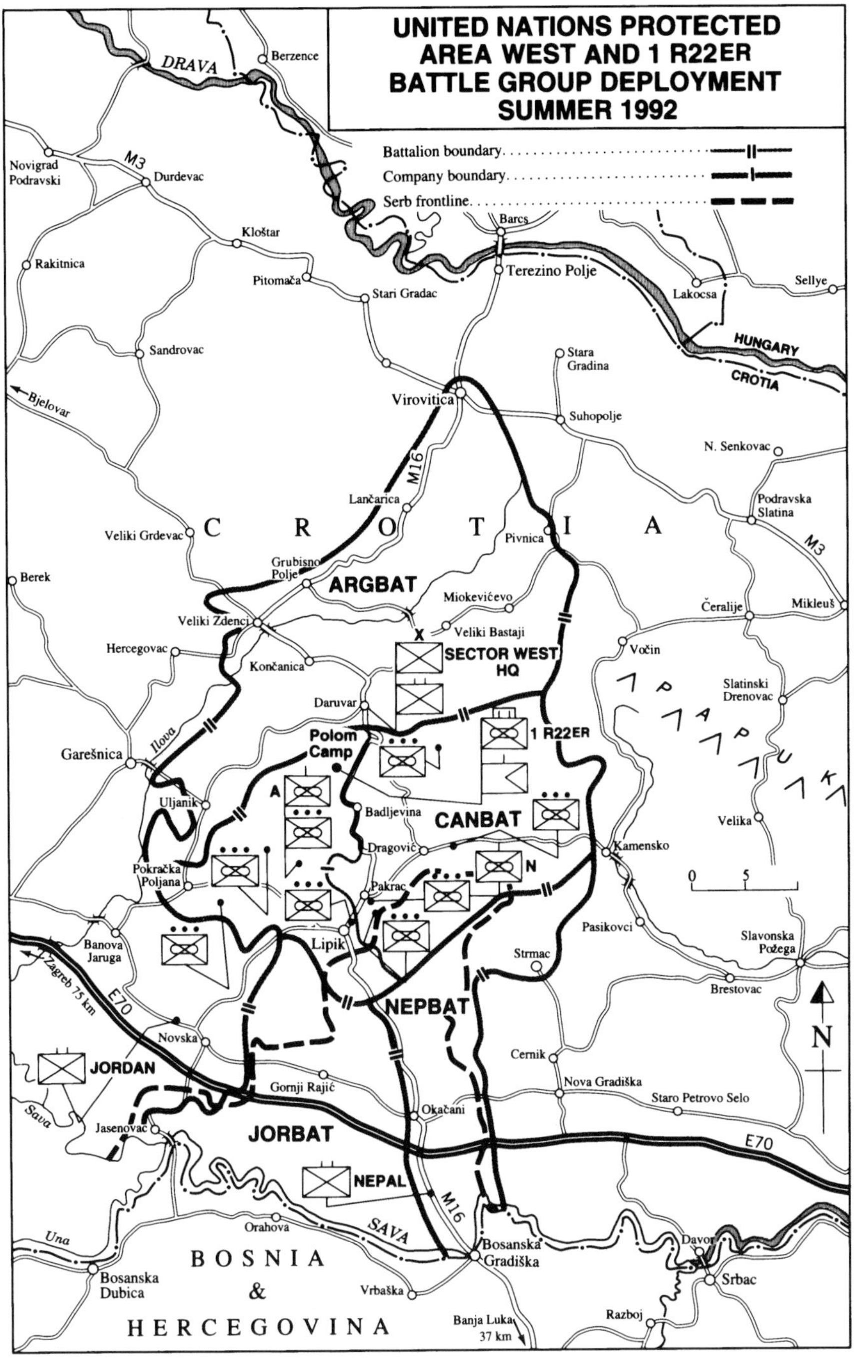
UNITED NATIONS PROTECTED AREA WEST AND 1 R22ER BATTLE GROUP DEPLOYMENT SUMMER 1992
Battalion boundary
Company boundary
Serb frontline
DRAVA
Berzence
Novigrad Podravski
M3
Durdevac
Kloštar
Barcs
Rakitnica
Pitomača
Stari Gradac
Terezino Polje
Lakocsa
Sellye
HUNGARY
CROTIA
Sandrovac
Stara Gradina
Bjelovar
Virovitica
Suhopolje
M16
N. Senkovac
Lančarica
Podravska Slatina
C R O A T I A
Veliki Grdevac
Pivnica
Berek
Grubisno Polje
ARGBAT
Miokevićevo
Čeralije
Mikleuš
Veliki Zdenci
X
Veliki Bastaji
SECTOR WEST HQ
Hercegovac
Končanica
Vočin
Daruvar
Slatinski Drenovac
Polom Camp
1 R22ER
P A P U K
Garešnica
Ilova
Uljanik
A
Badljevina
CANBAT
Velika
Dragović
Kamensko
Pokračka Poljana
N
Pakrac
Lipik
Pasikovci
Slavonska Požega
Banova Jaruga
Zagreb 75 km
Strmac
E70
NEPBAT
Brestovac
Novska
N
JORDAN
Cernik
Gornji Rajić
Nova Gradiška
Staro Petrovo Selo
Sava
Jasenovac
Okučani
JORBAT
E70
NEPAL
M16
SAVA
Orahova
Una
Bosanska Gradiška
Davor
BOSNIA & HERCEGOVINA
Bosanska Dubica
Srbac
Vrbaška
Banja Luka 37 km
Razboj

FIGURE 7-2

Argentine battalion to the north and the Nepalese and Jordanians to the south. [See Figure 7-2.] 1 R22eR, being the first unit into the sector, controlled the entire UN Protected Area until the other battalions arrived. The UNPROFOR operation at this point had now expanded from the Vance Plan's generalities. 1 R22eR was to dominate the Canadian battalion area within the Vance Plan boundaries. Checkpoints were set up between the UN battalions; a proper survey was conducted in the UN Protected Area to facilitate control, while mounted and dismounted patrolling established the UN presence in the sector. There were perimeter surveillance tasks to monitor the belligerent forces, and a Quick Reaction Force to respond if incursions were detected. Meanwhile, 4 CER was given mine clearance tasks in Sector West and later to the other sectors as needed. The sappers also conducted some limited route maintenance and minor construction tasks in support of 1 R22eR Battle Group and the other UNPROFOR contingents.

The Vance Plan was fine in theory. In practice, the Yugoslav Army was reluctant to withdraw from the UNPAs, indicating that the Serbs lacked confidence in UNPROFOR's ability to protect the Serb majority in these regions from outside Croatian attack. On the Croatian side, the Croat military forces did not really believe that the JNA would withdraw and certainly did not seriously entertain the notion that the Serb irregular forces would disarm. Moreover, virtually all men in the area were armed. These factors posed many problems for UNPROFOR.

Canadians deploying into Sector West were appalled at what they found. Warrant Officer Wayne Ivey operated in a liaison capacity:

> Several things shocked me. First of all was the amount of destruction that we saw.... I had the opportunity on a daily basis to get out of the camp area, pass through the front lines and across the ceasefire lines, as I dealt on a daily basis with both sides.... The other thing I think that bothered me most were the children standing, looking at you with just a hollow stare, a glaze in their eyes and you wonder sometimes if they're even seeing anything at all. I can remember going through Pakrac [which had been] a very nice town but was now totally destroyed. It had been fought over three or four times. Then, all of a sudden, out of the ruins runs this little boy, in filthy, dirty clothes, jumping up and down and waving.... Once we got the crossing route open, we

would pack sandwiches, an apple, an orange or something in ziploc bags and drop them off to him as we went by every morning.... Its not like a war that we might expect to see....

The belligerents were still conducting operations in the vicinity of Sector West, sometimes through the UN Protected Area. Lieutenant Colonel Michel Jones:

> There were two main factions, the Croats and the Serbs. There were extremists within each of these two ethnic groups, that were called the Ustashi and the Chetniks.... The Ustashi, on the Croat side, were not liked very much by their own people, but there were [lots] of them because this was a special mission for them (reducing the Serb enclaves).... On the Serb side, the Chetniks were a small group; they were respected by the Serbs but we didn't see too many of them. There were maybe about forty of them..... The actual number was hard to determine....
>
> [Larger formations] on the Croat side included three Operational Groups, each about the size of a brigade, about 15 000 men total. On the Serb side, there was the 5th Corps of the JNA, say about 15000 men. The Croats didn't have much heavy equipment, but they had a few tanks like the T54/55, a few mortars, and they had anti-aircraft guns; the rest was small arms. The Serbs were well equipped with combat helicopters, guns, heavy mortars, and M-84 tanks.... The fighting was a mix of conventional and unconventional, because there were specialist groups blowing up houses every night.

The arrival of the Canadians did improve the state of affairs in some parts of Sector West. Leading Seaman Frye, a cook who was part of 1 R22eR, noticed a change:

> When we first got to Daruvar, everywhere you walked around or in bars, guys were in military uniforms with AK 47s, or packing pistols or whatever. One guy I remember had a holster that had a double barreled shotgun on the side.... Everybody was packing weapons. A month or so after we got there, you didn't see them as much any more; everything was put away. You still would see guys in uniforms, but you didn't see the weapons. That was a big change.

The biggest threat to UNPROFOR troops probably came from mines and unexploded munitions. 4 CER deployed into Daruvar and prepared for the dangerous task of clearing the area. Maj "Des" Des Laurier was the Deputy Commanding Officer of 4 CER:

> [Prior to the move to Yugoslavia] the brigade commander, [Brigadier] General Addy, talked to some very high-level people on the German side of the house and almost the next day we were given authority to use a lot of ranges and vehicles to support our training....[We got] permission to do a lot of things that we weren't allowed to do in the past, such as live mine training....I was amazed at the lack of knowledge of the mines in the area. We went through a lot of sources trying to get an update on what mines we could expect in theatre, but we didn't get much....
>
> What really helped us was that on about day three after we arrived in Daruvar one of the sections found an abandoned ordnance facility, complete with bunkers.... Our EOD [explosive ordnance disposal] teams [found] pallets and pallets of mines there literally piled up and thrown helter-skelter.... These bunkers contained examples of just about every type of mine, anti-tank round, artillery shell, etc, that the Yugoslav Army had used, and subsequently the Croatian Army, because the Croats used whatever they could capture from the JNA. That saved our bacon because we could get in there, x-ray them, pick them up very carefully, take them apart and see how they operated, and then develop a lesson package to teach everybody else....We were tasked right from the start to conduct mine awareness training for every single person, from any country and even civilian UN personnel....

Croat and Serb reactions to 4 CER's minelifting task were mixed; in some cases local commanders provided maps and diagrams of defensive minefields while others refused information. Irregular groups even placed their own minefields surreptitiously at night.

The types of situations that 1 R22eR Battle Group and 4 CER encountered in the UN Protected Areas varied. Canadian peacekeepers were subjected to sporadic mortar and machine-gun fire. Canadian vehicles were held up at impromptu roadblocks by irregular forces and in one case an APC hit a mine; fortunately there were no casualties. Irregulars from one side or another even blew up an unmanned November

Company observation post. Despite all of these negative things, it was gratifying for the Canadians when the local civilians turned to UNPROFOR for assistance instead of to the local authorities. Indeed, the Battle Group's success was considerable. It opened six official and 30 non-official crossing sites along the front line, and the Zagreb-Belgrade highway was also re-opened after the first week on the ground. Shooting incidents reduced drastically, and in fact Sector West was the only UNPA to be completely de-militarized. By the end of Summer 1992, life for the people in the sector had returned to a quasi-normal level.

Just as 1 R22eR was settling into Sector West, the war in Yugoslavia was about to take another turn. On 5 April 1992, fighting broke out in the city of Sarajevo, the capital of Bosnia-Hercegovina. Sarajevo, as noted earlier, was at that time the location of UNPROFOR Headquarters. The next day, the JNA occupied the airport when the European Community formally recognized the independence of the Bosnian Presidency, which was mostly Muslim. Once this happened, Bosnian Serbs from Sarajevo moved to the town of Pale and proclaimed a separate Bosnian Serb republic.

A state of anarchy now reigned. The Bosnian Serbs formed irregular forces and started to fight against the Bosnian government's newly-formed Bosnian Territorial Defence Force (BTDF). The JNA was split, with Serbian elements supporting the Bosnian Serbs and the Croat troops remaining more or less neutral for the time being. By 20 April, the BTDF attempted to blockade the JNA in the same manner as the Slovenians had the previous year. The JNA retaliated by bombarding Sarajevo, prompting the Croats to invade Bosnia-Hercegovina in the north and in the southwest.

UNPROFOR had just completed moving its headquarters to Belgrade when, on 5 June 1992, the Bosnian Presidency and the Bosnian Serbs agreed to re-open the Sarajevo airport for humanitarian reasons. Anti-aircraft weapons were to be removed, while tanks, artillery and other heavy weapons were supposed to withdraw to areas subject to UNPROFOR observation. Both sides agreed that UNPROFOR should secure the airport, and a plan was drawn up to deploy a UN battalion to Sarajevo. 1 R22eR Battle Group was equipped with APCs, and it was well armed. Since no other UNPROFOR unit was so equipped at that time, the decision was made to deploy 1 R22eR for this task.

After the Warning Order was received by 1 R22eR on 6 June, Lieutenant Colonel Jones sought to augment his organization with mortars and TOW Under Armour (TUA). In the Canadians' initial planning, eight TUAs and a number of 81 mm mortars and ammunition were supposed to have accompanied the Battle Group to Yugoslavia, but the UN in New York forbade this in its concern of UNPROFOR appearing too warlike. TUA were, in the end, allowed, but without their missiles, and solely for use in a surveillance role using its superior thermal imaging equipment. A similar situation existed with the mortars; according to New York, 1 R22eR was permitted to have only illumination rounds for any mortars it brought, and no high explosive rounds. It was easy for decision makers to rule on these issues from their comfortable offices, without having any real understanding of the situation in Yugoslavia. But if the situation for Canadians in UNPROFOR was to become untenable, they would possibly have to conduct a fighting withdrawal over 300 kilometers to the Adriatic coast. Brigade planners had considered this in their plans back in March, so there was no problem accommodating these requests for additional firepower. The requisite Tow Under Armour missiles and 81mm mortars and ammunition were sent from Lahr, and would accompany 1 R22eR to Sarajevo.

1 R22eR's mission was twofold; first, Sarajevo airport had to be secured before humanitarian relief flights could land to bring in aid to the population of the besieged city. Second, corridors between the airport and the downtown part of Sarajevo had to be opened up so that the aid could be distributed and to allow freedom of movement for UNPROFOR and relief workers in the divided city.

At 0400 hours 30 June 1992, 1 R22eR left Daruvar for the dangerous 250-mile journey south to Sarajevo. Seventy-four miles north of the city at a place called Donja Vakuf, northeast of Vitez, 1 R22eR encountered a roadblock manned by drunken Serb irregulars who would not let the Canadians pass. Lieutenant Colonel Jones:

> ...I met the 'warlord'. He was unhappy and he was [drunk]. And there was the political advisor with him, cranking him up against the Canadians. The situation was very, very tense. I negotiated two hours with him but to no

avail, I mean he was so intransigent there was no way. So, we turned around for 15 kilometers and we spent the night there…. The following morning there was another Serbian commander, and he was surprised to see us there. He said there was no reason [for us to be there]; he had received orders to let me go through. So he went to the command post. When he came back two hours later however, he said there's no way, he wouldn't let us through….

Finally [a Serb] liaison officer arrived from the headquarters to see the warlord, but he still wouldn't let us through. So I said, 'That's enough; I'm going through.' They said, 'If you force your way through, we will open fire.' I said, 'If you open fire, I'm going to respond and that's it. Two o'clock: if the warlord doesn't show up, we're going through.' [We had] a few elements deployed for security, and I moved my APC up front. At that point some Serbian reinforcements moved up to the check point. I told the captain in charge that if he didn't send back the reinforcements, I would open fire without provocation. So he did, and the warlord then appeared. I sat with him [while] our snipers deployed. The TOW and every machine gun had their target and the fire orders were given….

…After half an hour of negotiations, I wrote in his book that I was discharging him of all responsibilities…He said, 'OK, I'm going back to my command post to give orders to my people and I'll come back in 20 minutes to give you some information about minefields you're going to encounter.' He did so and we went through.

Meanwhile, in Sarajevo, the local Serb commander who was occupying the airport was defying the Bosnian Serb pledge to turn the airport over to the UN. Knowing that 1 R22eR was en route, the commander made a public statement that said "[BGen] Mackenzie won't take the airport from us. We will kill you all if you try."

His threats became irrelevant; On 1 July, 130 French Marine Commando's disembarked from two aircraft despatched by the French Government (following President Mitterand's surprise visit to Sarajevo) to secure the terminal, but they were too thin on the ground to enforce the Serb withdrawal. Once 1 R22eR got to the airport on 2 July, they immediately dug in. The TUA vehicles were deployed to observe all belligerent parties around the airport, while the engineers from 4 CER developed shelters and trenches so that M-113 APCs and their passengers could get some protection from mortar rounds and snipers. Canadian snipers also deployed to watch and if necessary, retaliate, against any belligerent taking pot shots at UNPROFOR personnel. It was later learned that the most effective Bosnian sniper was a woman who had been on the Yugoslav Olympic team in 1988. Many belligerent forces pretended to comply with the agreement clause, which stipulated that heavy weapons be removed from the area around the airport. These weapons, particularly anti-aircraft guns, were a significant hazard to the humanitarian airlift operation. Satellite imagery was provided to 1 R22eR to help the battalion in its efforts to negotiate the weapons out of the area.

Sarajevo airport itself was situated southwest of the city and surrounded by all of the factions in the conflict. It was also key terrain for the southwest approaches into the city. Belligerent forces were arrayed in a circle around the runway in a clockwise direction; at the one o'clock position was the city of Sarajevo; then there was Dobrinja which was between the airport and Sarajevo, under Bosnian Muslim control. The Serbs held the JNA barracks at Lukavica at four o'clock, while the Bosnian Muslims occupied Butmir at seven o'clock. Finally, there was Ilidza at eleven o'clock, which was controlled by the Serbs. Later on, the Croats closed the circle from the north.

Activity around the airport was intense from the time the Canadians arrived on 2 July until 31 July, when they were relieved by French, Egyptian and Ukrainian troops. Given the airport's tactical importance to the belligerent forces, it was not unusual for tanks and machine guns to fire across the runway. The heaviest fighting was in Dobrinja. Serb and Bosnian artillery and mortar rounds flew over the airport, and many times rounds landed short. Errant rounds in a tank battle in Ilidza also landed in the Canadian area. Not all fire was directed between the Serbs and the Bosnians; many times snipers shot at UNPROFOR troops and UN workers. In one case, an RPG was fired at a Canadian APC, but the round missed and killed three civilians. Canadian soldiers were extremely lucky; most wounds were superficial and, miraculously, there were no Canadian fatalities. In one incident the RSM of 1 R22eR was hit by a ricochet, which fortunately struck his pistol worn on the belt, but caused him no injury. The situation was, however, so serious at the airport during this time that plans were made to evacuate all UNPROFOR personnel if it looked as if the airport would be overrun by one side or the other. An American aircraft carrier stationed in the Adriatic stood by to offer air cover if this option had to be chosen.

The Canadian contingent had entered a totally chaotic situation and attempted to provide an island of tranquillity in the entropy which was Sarajevo. C-130 *Hercules* transport aircraft from several nations formed the bulk of the relief effort, and supplies had to be delivered from the airport to Sarajevo by road. These routes had to be secured and patrolled on a regular basis so that the cargo would arrive in a timely fashion and get to the right agencies. All of the belligerents had become adept at hijacking civilian UN trucks and stealing their cargoes. Even ambulances were not immune; these vehicles, loaded down with wounded, were sometimes stopped, the wounded removed to the roadside or killed, and then loaded up with the wounded of the side who took the vehicle. Initially, UNHCR workers refused UNPROFOR escort because they believed somehow that this would damage their own neutrality (as if UNPROFOR was simply another belligerent!). After a number of firing incidents, however, this attitude changed.

UNPROFOR troops were not immune from impromptu roadblocks either. In one case a November Company relief convoy was stopped by a group demanding to search the APCs. They apparently believed that the Canadian APCs were being used to smuggle ammunition to the opposing side. A 'Mexican standoff' then developed for several hours, which was only resolved through the intervention of the Sarajevo UN Sector commander, MGen Mackenzie. According to Mackenzie, these sorts of actions were stimulated by an aggressive propaganda campaign orchestrated by the Bosnian Presidency. UNPROFOR was now a threat, in a manner of speaking, to all sides. The Bosnian Serb objective was to establish a Cyprus-style "Green Line" demarcation between the Bosnians and themselves in the region. The Presidency, on the other hand, wanted the separatist Bosnia Serb government put down and the territory they controlled restored to Bosnian government authority. This, they believed, could only be accomplished through a massive international intervention into Bosnia. Thus, it seemed that the Bosnian Presidency wanted to establish itself as a victim of separatist Bosnian Serb aggression to prompt this intervention.

UNPROFOR, and more specifically, the Canadians, refused to play this game and remained completely impartial. The Bosnian Serbs didn't like this either; they too wanted a monopoly on victim status, and the Canadians' impartiality worked against their agenda. 1 R22eR became subjected to increased propaganda and physical harassment. Major General Mackenzie himself was the object of a number of assassination plots from both sides. It was at this time that the Battle Group's first serious casualty occurred, despite many earlier close calls. On 9 July, Cpl Dennis Reid of N Coy stepped on a land mine, losing a foot, and had to be medically evacuated back to Lahr. Finally, on 31 July, after more than a month of protecting and conducting humanitarian relief operations in Sarajevo, 1 R22eR was relieved by replacement troops from France, Egypt and Ukraine, and returned to Sector West.

By September 1992, the UNPROFOR mandate, because of the worsening situation, had been extended to Bosnia-Hercegovina for purposes of getting international humanitarian aid to the populace there. Operation DAGGER (later Op CAVALIER) saw deployment to the former Yugoslavia of a second Canadian battle group (CANBAT 2) based on 2 RCR from CFB Gagetown, and tasked with convoy escort and other humanitarian aid protection duties. At about the same time, 1 R22eR Battle Group's and 4 CER's own seven month tour with UNPROFOR had come to an end, and they returned home to Lahr after first turning the bulk of their equipment over to their relief – 2 PPCLI and 1CER from western Canada. The only fatality suffered during 1 R22eR's and 4 CER's deployment in former Yugoslavia was, unfortunately, that of Sergeant Mike Ralph from 22 Field Engineer Squadron in Gagetown. Sergeant Ralph, who was attached to 1 R22eR Battle Group, was killed when his 1 1/4 ton truck hit three buried anti-tank mines stacked on top of each other during a clearing operation near Novska. His body was received with full military honours in Lahr prior to his last flight home, serving to remind all of the dangers and sacrifice this new form of "peacekeeping" entailed.

While the Yugoslav situation was deteriorating, bureaucrats within the Department of National Defence and the Ministry of Finance decided that the time was ripe for Canada to greatly reduce its military presence in Europe. It is clear that the changed threat situation and the reality of the Warsaw Pact collapse in 1991 were the two major considerations leading to this decision. For example, the Soviet military presence in Germany had been reduced to 10 divisions by 1992/3. [See Figure 7-3.] By the beginning of 1993, there were six divisions left in the former East Germany, and these were in the process of packing up and leaving for an uncertain future in the Soviet Union. Other NATO nations in the Central Region were also drawing down. There were other factors, though, in the decision to end the stationing of Canadian Forces in Germany.

According to a number of sources in the Canadian government, an ad hoc group consisting of representatives from DND, External Affairs, Treasury Board, Finance and the Privy Council Office met in the fall of 1990 to examine the future parameters of Canada's commitment to NATO's Central Region. This was in response to information received from the Privy Council office that the defence budget would be subjected to severe cuts in the pending federal budget. Obviously, the changing political situation in Europe made a cut in Canadian Forces Europe an attractive option, but apparently there really were no other alternatives presented within the ad hoc committee.

A high-level DND officer declared that no changes were possible or permissible to Canada's NORAD commitment. In a similar vein, the overlap in the Navy's commitments made it impossible to effect savings of the order necessary without having a spill-over effect on other naval commitments which were considered sacrosanct. Ultimately, the only possible source of significant savings was CFE. Reductions to the Army in Canada were out because of the aid of the civil power requirement in the wake of the Oka insurrection and the Army's standing continental defence commitments.

Thus, what seems to have been a predetermined decision to reduce the CFE commitment drove the ad hoc group's brief deliberative process, which was completed prior to Christmas 1990. DND apparently had argued that it could not afford to continue with the CFE commitment at present levels, therefore it would have to eliminate the role. External Affairs countered by stating that the elimination of CFE would undermine Canada's foreign policy and severely diminish Canada's influence

Soviet Western
Group of Forces,
1993
2 Guards
Tank Army
xxxx
GERMANY
Berlin
20 Guards
Combined Arms
Army
xxxx
Warsaw
POLAND
Prague
xxxx
CGF
xxxx
1 CZ
xxxx
4 CZ
Previous
boundry
between
East and West
Germany
CZECHOSLOVAKIA
xxx
CZ
EMD
USSR
HUNGARY
AUSTRIA
Budapest

CENTRAL REGION THREAT ORBAT, 1993

WESTERN GROUP of FORCES:
- 20 Gds Mtr Rifle Div
- 16 Gds Tk Div
- 10 Gds Tk Div
- 47 Gds Tk Div
- 90 Gds Tk Div

CZECH WESTERN
MILITARY DISTRICT

4th CZECH ARMY:
- 15 Mtr Rifle Div
- 9 Tk Div

1st CZECH ARMY:
- 1 Tk Div
- 20 Mtr Rifle Div
- 19 Mtr Rifle Div

CZECH EASTERN
MILITARY DISTRICT:
- 14 Tk Div
- 3 Mtr Rifle Div

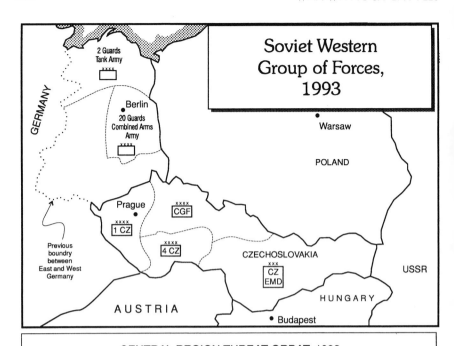

FIGURE 7-3

in Europe. DND then asked what it would take in the form of a Canadian presence in Europe to 'buy' that influence. External Affairs didn't really know, but intimated that a symbolic presence was probably sufficient.

This led to a series of alternative force packages being developed by DND and External Affairs in the process of selecting one that would ensure that Canada could still keep its 'seat at the table'. Defence and foreign policy considerations were thus driven entirely by budgetary constraints. No real consideration was given by DND to other factors. According to a number of participants, it was similar to a game of chicken in which DND argued that it had no control over its own fate and that it had to eliminate the CFE commitment for budgetary reasons. Ironically it was External Affairs which argued that the CFE commitment was vital. In the end, External Affairs gave way first by conceding that a reduced, symbolic commitment would probably be enough. This led to the Stationed Task Force proposal.

NATO's new strategic concept, unveiled in November 1991, recognized that the number and disposition of land forces within ACE would be completely altered before 1994, because of the Soviet withdrawal and the unification of Germany. It also recognized, however, that NATO still had to have the ability to respond within ACE to hostile activity. Part of NATO's response to a threat situation thus would now be met by the newly conceived ACE Rapid Reaction Corps (or ARRC). The theory behind the ARRC's employment was not unlike that of the ACE Mobile Force (Land) except that the scale of response was greater. The ARRC was a Corps level, international headquarters in peacetime; its fighting formations were earmarked brigades and divisions which would come from a number of NATO members. Since the distance between NATO and Russia was now greater because of the collapse of the Warsaw Pact, required NATO reaction time was greatly increased. Planners also believed that forces removed from Germany could be brought back in time to meet any serious crisis in the Central Region should one develop. And if new threats developed in the Southern Region, a more mobile force would be required anyway.

Early options for the draw-down of Canadian Forces Europe left some possibility that a small force could remain in Germany, and there was hope in some circles that this force could become the advanced guard of a Canadian brigade assigned to the ARRC. This unit was referred to in planning as the Stationed Task Force or STF. There were a number of possible organizations drawn up for the STF, including 400, 1200 and 1600 man options. Colonel Bob Meating, the final commander of 4 Brigade before it was disbanded, was involved in STF planning:

> ...NATO was going through its restructuring, thinking about the Rapid Reaction Corps. We said, OK, if I were commander of the ARRC, would I be able to use an organization like this 1200 man [one]? .... a 1200 man force – lean, mean, with a lot of firepower, a lot of combat capability...that can resupply itself, and can fight. It has tanks – two squadrons worth, it's got TOW – [between] 18 and 36, and as it turned out, a [M-109] battery [and three infantry companies]. It was a powerful little battle group....There were people who suggested that we take this thing and tell NATO that we will provide two of them, then you've got a mini-brigade, and maybe if we had a brigadier and a headquarters.....

Colonel Meating and his staff looked for a place to put the STF, and a number of possibilities were investigated. Ironically, the British offered Canada the now empty Soest-area bases!

The STF was, however, not to be. The new Government's mini-budget of 26 February 1992 put paid to the STF plan. This budget not only wiped out the STF, it also accelerated the closure of CFE and the demise of 4 CMB: all Canadian Forces had to be out of Germany by 1994. Moreover, 4 CMB was not to be reconstituted in Canada. Instead, the two infantry battalions, the artillery regiment and the armoured regiment were to be reduced to become Total Force reserve units. The other brigade units such as 4 Service Battalion, 444 Tactical Squadron, 4 Field Ambulance and 4 MP Platoon were to be disbanded. The only unit left in Europe would be a 54 man Canadian Forces Support Unit (Europe), specifically structured to support Canadian representatives at the various NATO headquarters in Europe. CFSU(E) was officially stood up in May 1993 in Geilenkirchen, Germany, near the Dutch border, with Lieutenant Colonel Daniel Bastien, the last SSO Ops of 4 CMB, in command. Problems resulting from the lack of consultation with the German Government and NATO in Brussels over the cancellation of the European

CHAPTER SEVEN

commitments, though interesting and controversial, will have to be left to future historians.

The final close out proceedings brought on by the February 1992 budget picked up momentum as 1992 progressed. The demise of 4 Brigade was not quick; the process took nearly 18 months. 444 Squadron's *Kiowa* helicopters conducted their last flypast on 31 March 1992, and 4 Field Ambulance closed its doors on the centre marg on 24 April. 1 RCHA and 4 Air Defence Regiment were withdrawn from Lahr and Baden by 6 June. 1st Canadian Division HQ (Forward) vacated the attic of building K-1, repatriating to Kingston on 13 June. Personnel from 4 Service Battalion remained in Lahr into 1993, but the battalion itself started closing down in June.

4 MP Platoon, 4 CMB's smallest unit, was disbanded at the end of October. 4 Combat Engineer Regiment returned from Yugoslavia in time to hold its final parade on 24 October. 3 RCR followed suit on 3 December, and moved its colours and a small cadre to CFB Borden to begin its new existence as a 10/90 battalion (that is 10 per cent Regulars, 90 per cent Militia). The Van Doos marched out in April 1993, after parading through Lahr. (3 R22eR in Valcartier at the same time was re-numbered to 1 R22eR in order to perpetuate a regular force lineage in the Regiment's first battalion.) The remaining 8th Canadian Hussars officers and troopers waited until 4 April 1993, then flew to Moncton, New Brunswick to form the first Total Force armoured unit with their Militia brethren.

Many 4 CMB officers and men remained in Lahr and Baden to finalize closeouts and tie up loose ends. This included 4 CMB Headquarters and Signal Squadron which stayed on into 1993 to support the overall closure effort.

There were just enough 8 CH and 3 RCR soldiers left to travel up to Soest on the *Boerdetag* weekend of 16-17 May 1993 to partake in one final farewell celebration. This event was, fittingly, the last hurrah and final march past for Canada's NATO Brigade in Europe, significantly in the very place where it established its professionalism and reputation back in the 1950s. Included in the panoply of parades, receptions, concerts and displays was a moving ceremony held at the Werl cemetery for the soldiers and dependents who had died while serving in northern

Germany with 27 Brigade, 1 CIBG, 2 CIBG, and 4 CIBG. In the weekend's culminating event, the band of The Royal Canadian Regiment, flown over especially for the occasion from CFB Gagetown, together with the pioneers and the Pipes and Drums of 3 RCR, all resplendent in full dress scarlets and white shell jackets led the final parade through the historic streets of Soest. At the same time, the Freedom of the City of Soest, first granted to The RCR in 1964 was exercised one last time. There were many wet eyes as both Canadians and Germans understood the historical significance of the moment – that these Canadian young men marching past were the visible manifestation of a commitment to freedom which for two generations had helped guarantee the security of the West German people and enabled their country to develop into a prosperous, thriving and now re-united democracy. These soldiers, along with their Brigade, were now passing into history, their mission well and truly accomplished. And all that weekend from the Soest Rathaus proudly flew the red and white Maple Leaf flag in honour of all Canadians who had served in Germany for the cause of peace and freedom. It was indeed a weekend to be treasured and long remembered.

Militarily, one of 4 CMB's last activities was to pass on to the Bundeswehr Canadian experiences and lessons learned in peacekeeping. By 1992, the German government was coming under increasing pressure from its allies, the United Nations, and even certain German political circles to provide forces for UN peacekeeping operations. This touched off a highly charged political debate in Germany; could such a deployment of German troops be viewed as a precedent for future military intervention elsewhere on Germany's part? The test case for this was Somalia, and a German brigade prepared to deploy to Mogadishu. The problem for the Germans though, was the lack of any kind of peacekeeping experience on the part of the Bundeswehr, in addition to the considerable public opposition to such ventures.

Headquarters 4 Panzer Grenadier Division in Regensburg, which 4 CMB had worked with regularly and knew intimately, was designated to become a task force headquarters for future possible German UN deployments, commanding units drawn as necessary from elsewhere in the Bundeswehr. Many Canadians serving with 4 CMB had prior peacekeeping experience in Cyprus and now in former Yugoslavia. This and the close relationship between 4 CMB and 4 Panzer Grenadier Division, and the respect the Bundeswehr in general accorded 4 CMB, led to the setting up of over a dozen seminars and presentations on peacekeeping for Bundeswehr officers; two were held in Lahr, the rest in German casernes and headquarters, including at the Ministry of Defence in Bonn. Canadian officers who had served with UNPROFOR and in Somalia, as well as officers from the peacekeeping operations staff in NDHQ were brought in to lecture and present on the Canadian experience in peacekeeping. It hardly need be said that such support and co-operation could not have occurred without the mutual Canadian-German respect that had developed since 1971, and the excellent relationships fostered and maintained by 4 CMB(G)'s hard working liaison officers to 4 Panzer Grenadier Division and II (GE) Korps.

The draw down of 4 CMB and CFE was somewhat surreal in its own way. The facilities in the Kaserne – CANEX, HQ CFE, HQ 4 CMB and others – gradually disappeared. What had been a bustling facility in November 1992 slowly, inexorably, became a ghost town. Equipment which was too expensive to transport home was sold off to the German public as surplus or was destroyed. Interestingly, all of the 10 ton MAN trucks and the *Lynx* recce vehicles were purchased by a Dutch "entrepreneur", for reasons one could only speculate on.

As services and units reduced in size, they moved to the airfield; and, then, according to assigned flight dates, soldiers and their families boarded chartered aircraft for the final trip home. A number of Brigade members, returned by sea, travelling on the *Queen Elizabeth II* ; apparently, it was a considerably more comfortable journey than their predecessors experienced on the *Fairsea* back in 1951. The Kaserne was emptied by July 1993 and the vaunted Black Forest Officers Mess, host to heads of state and the scene of much carousing over the years, closed its doors for the last time to the ballad "The Day CFE Died", a farewell anthem written and performed by the "Bunker Boys" – the crew of officers who manned the CFE HQ wartime command post. A similar dismantling process was occurring at the airfield. By the fall of 1993, visiting the Lahr airfield resembled the opening scene from the movie "Twelve O'Clock High", a movie which starts out with a veteran returning to a deserted airfield in England long after the Second World War. The closeout of 4 CMB was completed by the end of August 1993, far ahead of schedule. It would have been easy to delay the draw–down, to subvert the process bureaucratically, hoping or lobbying for a political reconsideration. The Brigade did not do so, and its professionalism was maintained right to the end.

CONCLUSION

A number of themes should become clear to the reader in this history of Canada's NATO Brigade, the most important being the military viability of the Canadian land commitment to NATO's Central Region. The prevailing view amongst many Canadian academics and security policy experts tends to be one of disdain and a firm belief that 4 CMBG (and its predecessors) was merely a *symbolic* commitment because of its small size relative to other NATO forces in the Central Region, and its limited combat capability relative to its potential adversaries. This attitude developed in the 1970s, carried over into the 1980s and still had adherents up to 4 CMB's final demise in 1993.

This view is not entirely without justification, particularly with regard to the lean years of the 1970s. However, the viability question should be viewed in the larger context, that is, within the full scope of the Brigade's development between 1951 and 1993. It is important then that any assessment of the Brigade's viability also examine the strategic and operational environment in which it operated as well as its tactical role,

CONCLUSION

assigned tasks, equipment, logistics, and sustainability.

The initial commitment of a significant portion of the Canadian Army to NATO's Central Region, as conceived in 1951, rested on the belief that the commitment was *not* an open ended one. The dominant idea governing the deployment of 27 Brigade to Germany was that the stationing of forces there might end sometime in the mid to late 1950s once Western Europe was able to develop adequate defences of its own, capable of deterring Soviet aggression. At the time, Canada had a number of defence engagements including a brigade in Korea and forces committed to the shared defence of North America. These, combined with economic and domestic political factors, limited the size of the Canadian contribution to SACEUR's Integrated Force. Nonetheless, Canada agreed to the immediate commitment of an army division of three brigades on M-Day, with one of the brigades of that division being forward based in Germany in peacetime. A second division was to be raised from the Militia and deployed within 180 days. Plans were developed to move the balance of the first division to Europe, and enough equipment then existed to equip all three of its brigades. Mobilization plans were drawn up to sustain this division and also to form the remainder of the formations and units of a Canadian Corps, which planners envisaged as ultimately being created, similar to what occured in World Wars I and II.

In NATO planning circles it was realized from the beginning that the West did not have sufficient conventional forces in Europe to mount an adequate defence in the event of a full scale Soviet attack. It would be ridiculous, however, to suggest that NATO not try to develop defence contingencies, since defending the Atlantic area was NATO's raison d'être. Trying to do so was not mere symbolism; the considerable effort that was made did send a powerful deterrent message to the other side. The realities of the conventional force imbalance in the Central Region were accepted by NATO planners, and they set about to do the best they could with what they had.

The task confronting NATO, should war have broken out, was to effect some form of coherent delaying action with whatever forces were available until the full resources of the United States, along with Canada, could be mobilized and brought to bear. In this context, 27 Brigade (and later 1 CIBG), as a component of I (BR) Corps, was responsible for conducting a delaying action to the Rhine and then holding on that line, buying the needed time for NATO reinforcements to assemble and arrive. The Brigade was organized and equipped to do this as part of I (BR) Corps. Designed to be infantry heavy, it was well suited for operating in the built up areas of industrial, north-central Germany. Although the Brigade was dependent upon the British for some items, it could and did function independently. Given the length of the I (BR) Corps frontage, any brigade-sized force would have been a valuable asset in the Rhine defence. Despite some deficiencies, this was a viable Canadian commitment.

This situation was not dramatically altered with the development by NATO in 1954 of a limited tactical nuclear capability. The availability of American nuclear delivery systems in support of NORTHAG and I (BR) Corps, however, only increased the probability of a successful allied withdrawal to the Rhine. Nuclear weapons did *not* replace troops; rather they enhanced the capability of the forces that already existed. Thus, conventional forces were still needed.

The realities of the destructive power of the hydrogen bomb had the most significant and lasting impact on the Brigade's viability. It was fully accepted by the Canadian government by 1958 that any global war between the West and the Soviet Union would include the use of thermonuclear weapons, at least in the first phase of the conflict. While NATO believed that sustainability and reinforcement of forces in Europe was necessary for the second phase of such a conflict, the Canadian government did not, and chose to fund only those forces they believed capable of participating in the first phase. Thus, the Militia role was reduced to national survival and urban re-entry operations, and the earmarked equipment for the mobilization forces was given away under the Mutual Defence Assistance Programme. The lack of strategic lift to get or sustain forces overseas compounded the problem. By the mid-1960s, the two other brigade groups for the NATO earmarked division had had their equipment levels reduced to light training scales, leaving 4 CIBG the Army's only fully equipped formation. But it was not sustainable after 30 days of operations, nor was it meant to be.

The equipping and employment of 4 CIBG was, however, taken seriously. By 1960 the mission in the Central Region was no longer tied to

CONCLUSION 493

conducting a fighting withdrawal to the Rhine. Defence of the NATO area as far forward as possible was a political necessity if NATO was to continue to exist at all. As a result, the Brigade developed an impressive anti-tank capability, its infantry battalions being equipped with vehicle mounted recoiless rifles and ATGMs. It also had a full regiment of tanks, and possessed excellent surveillance and reconnaissance capabilities. The addition of the M113 APC in 1964 further enhanced the Brigade's mobility and protection. Throughout the 1960s 4 CMBG remained a significant proportion of I (BR) Corps' fighting strength, even more so when some British units were withdrawn. The Brigade's structure and its ability to operate with relative independence significantly enhanced I (BR) Corps, providing it important flexibility and substantial firepower on its vulnerable right flank.

Because the concept of Forward Defence in the Central Region incorporated the integration of battlefield nuclear and conventional weapons, Canada was asked to provide tactical surface-to-surface missile nuclear delivery units. Thus, with the acquisition of the *Honest Johns*, 4 CIBG became the repository of 25 percent of I (BR) Corps nuclear firepower. The view that nuclear firepower supplemented the conventional effort had also by now swung around so that conventional forces supplemented the nuclear effort.

In this sense, then, prior to 1968 4 CIBG was well equipped to operate within the role that it had been assigned. The role was an important one, not only strategically from a Forward Defence point of view, but from an operational one as well, given the "Belgian Problem" on the right flank. 4 CIBG's capabilities were vital to helping maintain the integrity of the NATO area through the destruction of Warsaw Pact forces within the first phase of a war, and then holding the line until the full effect of strategic nuclear bombardment was felt by the Soviet Union. Given the context of the concept of operations in the Central Region and the realities of nuclear warfighting prevalent at the time, the role and contribution of the Canadian Brigade was both a viable and vital one.

NATO's adoption of Flexible Response in 1967 dictated that conventional and nuclear forces were no longer considered to be intertwined in the intimate way that they had been since 1954. This in turn dictated that stronger and sustainable conventional forces were needed once again.

And there were still the imperatives of Forward Defence. The Canadian government, however, chose not to equip or structure its forces to support the new strategy, and in fact reduced conventional forces and refused to keep pace with technological change.

With the election of the Trudeau government in 1968, and with it the Prime Minister's own particular views of what Canada's role in the world should be, the Brigade was reduced by more than half and consolidated with the air force commitment in southern Germany. This arbitrary act, combined with the decision not to rebuild Canada's conventional forces, had an immediate and severely damaging effect on the viability of the Brigade. It was removed from an especially vital front line area in NORTHAG to a rear holding area in CENTAG. It also lost any intimate connection to a higher formation and the benefits which accrue from such a relationship. In the cut the Brigade also lost many of its special capabilities, most notably its nuclear capability. Weapons systems and specialized kit also were not upgraded. Nor did the Brigade any longer have the numbers of men and resources to conduct a sustained defence for longer than five days. There were no sustainability forces in Canada, nor were there any detailed, realistic plans for such. There was not enough strategic lift to get sustainability forces to Europe in any case.

Prior to this, and despite the reductions in the size of the Canadian Army throughout the 1960s including the decision to adopt man-for-man rotation, the fact was that 4 Brigade was experienced in working within a division and corps context, and was the only formation in the Canadian Army truly capable of engaging in modern mechanized warfare. As such, it properly served Canada's military commitment to the Central Region and contributed substantially to military deterrence. Apart from its operational imperatives, the Brigade also benefitted from being so closely associated with larger allied armies, which afforded Canadian officers important professional contacts and training opportunities. All of this enabled 4 Brigade to hone its skills, training and capabilities to a degree unattainable in Canadian based formations. At the same time, as the Army's operational centrepiece, it drove and influenced all matters of army developments in doctrine, training, organization and equipment. In the words of former Brigade Commander, Major-General Tom de Faye, 4 Brigade was "the cradle of professionalism for the Canadian Army".

CONCLUSION

Despite the lack of viability of Canada's Central Region land commitment resulting from the reduction of 4 CMBG and its move south in 1970, the Brigade did serve as a symbolic presence, and so it was somewhat useful at the higher level of Alliance politics. It is clear, however, that a succession of brigade commanders believed that, at some point in the future, equipment and sustainability problems would be improved to make the commitment a militarily viable one once again. Indeed, they continually worked to this end. Likewise, to maintain the Brigade's professional edge and to remain involved in the planning process in the Central Army Group, Canadian commanders sought a real operational mission, something that 4 CMBG could do within the limits of its capabilities.

This was facilitated by the operational situation in the II (GE) Korps Sector and the threat on the Donau and Nürnberg approaches. II (GE) Korps was stretched thin, and any formation – even a reduced brigade group – would be a useful asset. Thus, the Canadian offer to fill in was quickly taken up. As in the 1960s, 4 CMBG's role here was to conduct a holding action in a vital sector critical to maintaining the integrity of the NATO area. Unlike the 1960s, the idea of destroying Warsaw Pact forces with nuclear weapons was replaced by meeting the threat, at least initially, with strong conventional forces backed up by conventional reinforcement. Anything that NATO could do to buy time in the Central Region so to raise the nuclear threshold and allow such reinforcement to occur, was valuable.

In the 1970s, then, 4 Brigade was capable of handling a one-time-only blocking mission. It was never fully manned or equipped, nor did it have adequate logistics, although some planning was done to fill out critical units if enough warning time was given. Also, much of the equipment it did possess was decrepit or obsolescent. In the final analysis, this can only be seen, at best, as a marginally viable commitment within the operational context of Forward Defence or, at worst, a Hong Kong-like commitment. The Brigade could have made a useful contribution to operations within II (GE) Korps' area of responsibility in the event of war with the Warsaw Pact, but probably only by dying in place in the first battle.

This situation did change significantly in the 1980s. 4 CMBG commanders knew full well what the Brigade's operational deficiencies were and, given the more favourable political climate vis à vis NATO's conventional forces, valiantly attempted to right the balance and stop the decay. A number of equipment programmes, like TOW ATGMs and *Leopard* tanks, combined with a significant increase in personnel strength in 1985-86, went a long way towards revitalizing the Brigade's operational capabilities.

In terms of operational role, the Brigade retained the blocking or counter-penetration role in the II (GE) Korps and VII (US) Corps sectors. New equipment, increased numbers of personnel and improved logistics and sustainment capabilities combined to give the Brigade significantly more staying power than it had in the 1970s. Careful selection of the Brigade's GDP ground on the II (GE) Korps and VII (US) Corps boundary also contributed to staying power. On the negative side, personnel augmentation, casualty replacement and equipment sustainability problems persisted, despite determined efforts to correct them in the mid and late 1980s. Though 4 CMBG never did fully regain the capabilities that it had in the 1960s, the situation was a definite improvement over the 1970s. The diminished threat to NATO's Central Region in 1990, however, ensured that a full recovery would not occur. It may be stated then that the viability of Canada's land force commitment to the Central Region in the 1980s fell somewhere between the pinnacle of the 1960s and the nadir of the 1970s.

In the matter of 4 CMBG's non-participation in the Gulf War (save for the airfield security company and a defence and security platoon for the Canadian Joint Force Headquarters), it is clear that the Army's anticipatory planning for the Gulf (Operation BROADSWORD) does not conclusively demonstrate that Canada's land force commitment to the Central Region was not viable. While BROADSWORD highlighted many of the Brigade's (and the Army's) deficiencies, these were already well known in the early 1980s, but steps to remedy them were in most instances precluded by Canadian political and budgetary policies of the day. (The ill-fated proposals in the 1987 White Paper on Defence are a case in point.) Additionally, the parameters for preparing a mechanized brigade group for operations in the Middle East were quite different from those that would have been required by 4 CMBG to undertake operations in Europe. These included a strategic re-deployment to a different climate and region, a different threat, different terrain, and a significant change in operational role. However, given the required logistic support, the time, the strategic lift, and, more importantly the political will, the Brigade could have been expected to adapt to this new role with few problems. In the context of a protracted land battle it still would not have been sustainable over the long term from a battle casualty point of view, but given a mission commensurate with its equipment capabilities 4 Brigade would probably have given a good account of itself in the initial stages of a conflict. More importantly, 4 CMBG's participation would have obtained for Canada a significant measure of respect and influence vis à vis the other principal coalition members and entitlement to a seat higher up at the table of international decision-making.

All of the preceeding, though important for the historical record, is mainly of academic interest. In more human terms, the Brigade's purpose was to function as part of a larger deterrent system and, in doing so, to prevent a world war that could result not only in the destruction of our democratic way of life, but of civilization itself. Two generations of Canadians – soldiers as well as their dependents – did their duty to ensure the preservation of peace and freedom in Europe and, ultimately at home. We demonstrated by our physical presence in Germany that we were prepared to stand up and confront the evil and powerful totalitarian system that held Eastern Europe in its grip and which threatened our own security and well-being. The fact that this system was inefficient, corrupt, and economically dislocated did not make it any less dangerous or less evil. By committing ourselves to this war without battles, Canadians affirmed that we would do our part to ensure that Soviet communist expansionism would not run unchecked, and that we would not stand idly by and allow the subjugation of Western Europe. Consistent with our history as a nation and our character as a people, we were prepared to stand up and defend our ideals, to the point of war if necessary. The soldiers of Canada's NATO Brigade in Germany were the most comprehensive and visible manifestation of that ideal. It was, in the words of one Canadian officer, "A damn fine engine for peace."

APPENDIX A

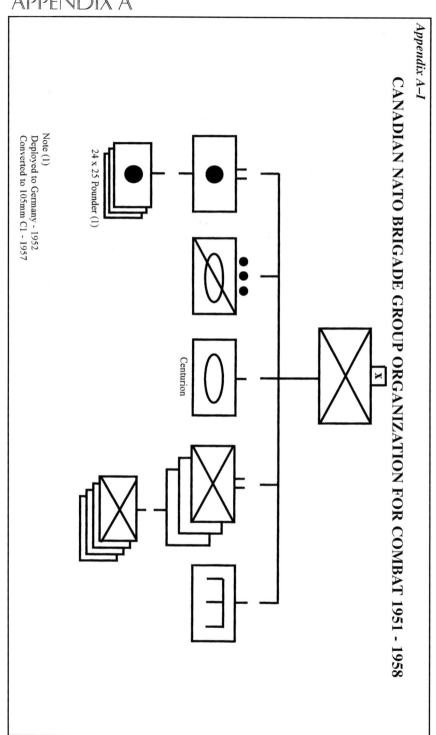

Appendix A–1

CANADIAN NATO BRIGADE GROUP ORGANIZATION FOR COMBAT 1951 - 1958

24 x 25 Pounder (1)

Centurion

Note (1)
Deployed to Germany - 1952
Converted to 105mm C1 - 1957

APPENDIX A

Appendix A–II

CANADIAN NATO BRIGADE GROUP ORGANIZATION FOR COMBAT 1958 - 1968

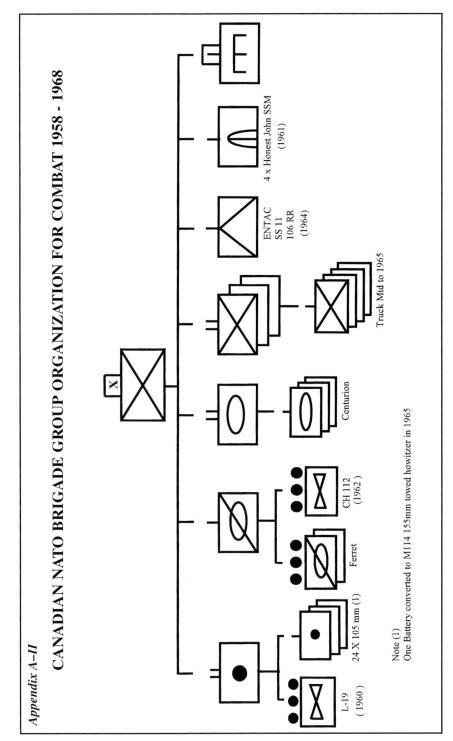

Appendix A–III

CANADIAN NATO BRIGADE GROUP ORGANIZATION FOR COMBAT 1968 - 1970

X
2x Honest John SSM
24 X M1O9 (1)
(155 mm)
L-19
CH 112
Centurion
M 113
(1965)

Note (1)
Converted to M109 in 1969

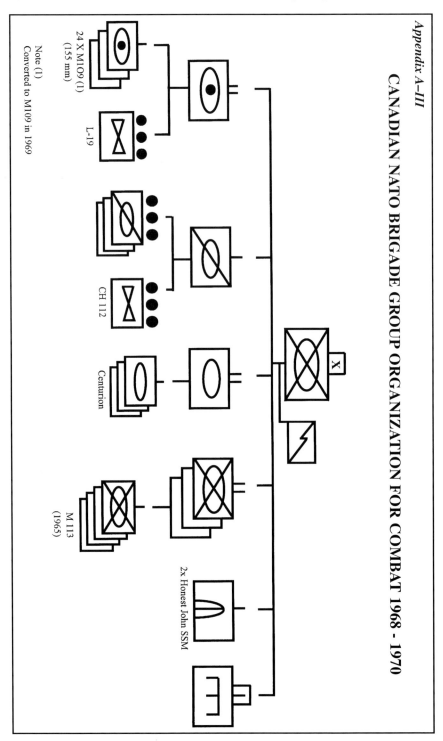

APPENDIX A

Appendix A–IV

CANADIAN NATO BRIGADE GROUP ORGANIZATION FOR COMBAT 1970 - 1979

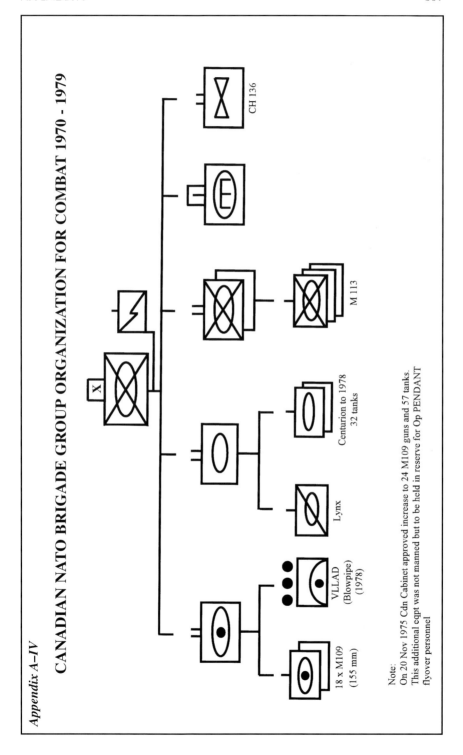

Note:
On 20 Nov 1975 Cdn Cabinet approved increase to 24 M109 guns and 57 tanks. This additional eqpt was not manned but to be held in reserve for Op PENDANT flyover personnel

Appendix A–V

CANADIAN NATO BRIGADE GROUP ORGANIZATION FOR COMBAT 1979- 1985

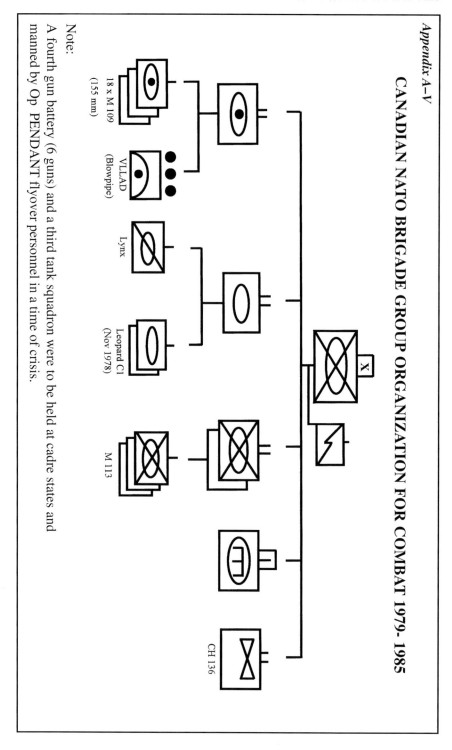

Note:

A fourth gun battery (6 guns) and a third tank squadron were to be held at cadre states and manned by Op PENDANT flyover personnel in a time of crisis.

APPENDIX A 503

Appendix A–VI

CANADIAN NATO BRIGADE GROUP ORGANIZATION FOR COMBAT 1985 - 1991

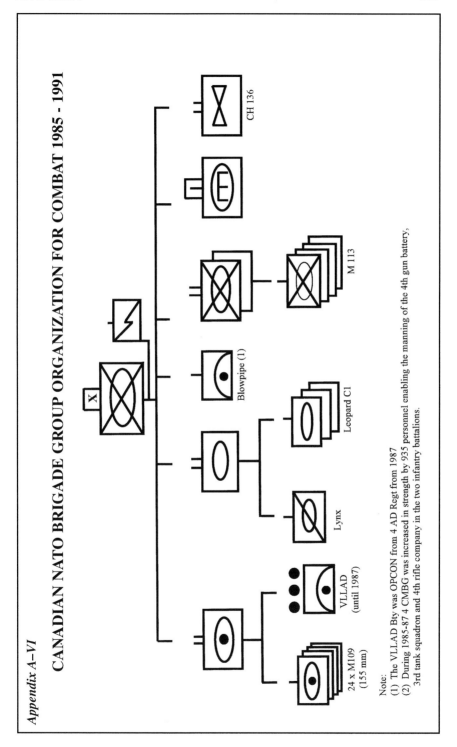

Note:
(1) The VLLAD Bty was OPCON from 4 AD Regt from 1987
(2) During 1985-87 4 CMBG was increased in strength by 935 personnel enabling the manning of the 4th gun battery, 3rd tank squadron and 4th rifle company in the two infantry battalions.

Appendix A-VII

CANADIAN NATO BRIGADE GROUP ORGANIZATION FOR COMBAT 1991 - 1993

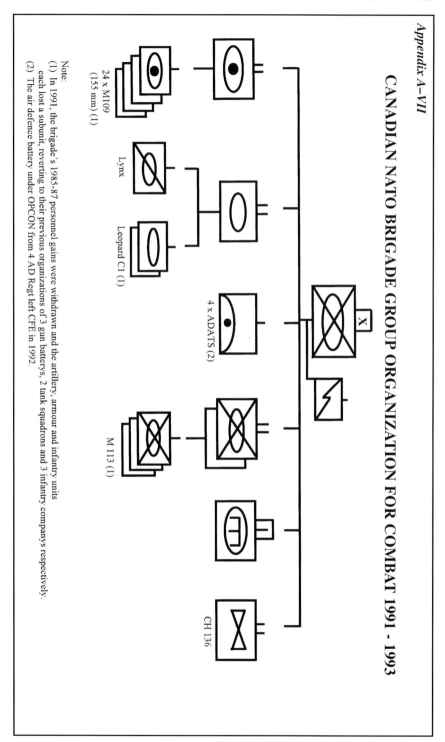

Note:
(1) In 1991, the brigade's 1985-87 personnel gains were withdrawn and the artillery, armour and infantry units each lost a subunit, reverting to their previous organizations of 3 gun battery's, 2 tank squadrons and 3 infantry company's respectively.
(2) The air defence battery under OPCON from 4 AD Regt left CFE in 1992.

APPENDIX B

A Note on Exercises

As this work demonstrates, Canadian soldiers serving in Germany expended a great deal of training time and effort on exercises. Though the exercise narratives in the text are written as though they were battles, it is important to note that live ammunition was not used except on special ranges in clearly delineated training areas. Obviously, the nuclear strikes referred to in Exercise BATTLE ROYAL and Exercise CANADA CUP were only simulated events; the real testing with live nuclear weapons and live troops was conducted in Nevada, in the US and Maralinga, Australia during this time. Prior to the advent of the MILES laser casualty assessment system in the late 1980s, simulated exercise casualties were assessed by elaborate umpire systems. Neutral umpires accompanied each manouevre unit, sometimes down to troop/section level but more commonly at the combat team, squadron, and company level. In encounter battles, umpires conferred between units to assess casualties. The umpires maintained their own communications nets and the 'score' was kept at the higher level umpire control. It was never a perfect system and at times units ignored umpire orders, simulated minefields or 'blown' bridges.

There were many types of exercises. Command Post Exercises (CPXs) and Signals Exercises (SIGEXs) tested command decision making and radio procedures without deploying whole formations into the field. These exercises were 'scripted' and had very little free play. Usually only the headquarters and signals units participated. Tactical Exercises Without Troops (TEWTs) were primarily officer training vehicles analogous to the Prussian "staff ride". TEWTs had no live enemy and no forces were deployed on the ground.

Field training exercises (FTXs) included the wholesale deployment of entire field formations into the field. FTXs could be either scripted, whereby the units were told where to move, when to move and what to do, or they could be free play. Free play FTXs were the most valuable training tool for larger formations due to their realism. Free play allowed units to move as they would under real conditions and allowed for realistic or semi-realistic logistical play. FTXs, depending on their size, were held in training areas if they were small enough or in the German countryside if they were larger exercises.

Finally, and becoming more common by the time of 4 CMBG's demise were Command Field Exercises (CFXs). These were part CPX, part FTX in that command posts and formation/unit headquarters, complete with all their vehicles and equipment deployed to the field, while manoeuvre trips were notional or extremely limited in numbers. In this way commanders and headquarters staff were able to practise operating in field conditions and a measure of exercise realism for them was maintained, while manoeuvre damages normally incurred by deployed units were reduced.

APPENDIX C

BRIGADE COMMANDERS 1951-1993

5 Jun 51 - 5 Dec 52	Brigadier Geoffrey Walsh
5 Dec 52 - 15 Oct 53	Brigadier J.E.C. Pangman
15 Oct 53 - 31 Oct 55	Brigadier W.A.B. Anderson
31 Oct 55 - 14 Nov 57	Brigadier Roger Rowley
14 Nov 57 - 20 Dec 60	Brigadier D.C. Cameron
20 Dec 60 - 25 Aug 62	Brigadier C.B. Ware
25 Aug 62 - 10 Dec 64	Brigadier Michael Dare
10 Dec 64 - 15 Sep 66	Brigadier A.J. Tedlie
15 Sep 66 - 27 Jan 68	Brigadier E.A.C. Amy
27 Jan 68 - 3 Jul 70	Brigadier General J.C. Gardner
3 Jul 70 - 27 Jul 71	Brigadier General W.C. Leonard
27 Jul 71 - 13 Jul 72	Brigadier General J. Chouinard
13 Jul 72 - 1 Jul 74	Brigadier General Patrick Grieve
1 Jul 74 - 19 Jul 76	Brigadier General Charles Belzile
19 Jul 76 - 1 Jul 78	Brigadier General Jack Vance
01 Jul 78 - 1 Jul 80	Brigadier General J.A. Fox
23 Jun 80 - 22 Jun 82	Brigadier General A.G.D. de Chastelain
27 Jun 82 - 26 Jun 84	Brigadier General Richard Evraire
27 Jun 84 - 27 Jun 86	Brigadier General Jack Dangerfield
02 Jul 86 - 01 Jun 87	Brigadier General Pierre Lalonde
07 Sep 87 - 02 Jul 89	Brigadier General Thomas de Faye
03 Jul 89 - 08 Apr 91	Brigadier General J.M.R. Gaudreau
09 Apr 91 - 15 Jul 92	Brigadier General Clive Addy
15 Jul 92 - 23 Jul 93	Colonel Robert G. Meating

BIBLIOGRAPHY

SELECTED BIBLIOGRAPHY

Archives:
Bundesarchiv/Militararchive, Freiburg.
DND Director General, History, Ottawa
MilitarGeschichtlichesForschungsAmt, Freiburg.
National Archives of Canada, Ottawa
National Security Archive, Washington D.C.
Public Record Office, Kew UK
U.S. National Archives and Record Administration Washington D.C.

Periodicals:
Armed Forces Journal International
Armour Bulletin
Canadian Army Journal
Canadian Defence Quarterly
Canadian Military Journal
Counterattack
Der Spiegel
International Defence Review
Jane's Soviet Review
Jane's Intelligence Review
MilitarGeschichte
Military Review
NATO's Fifteen Nations
NATO Handbook
NATO Letter
NATO Review
NATO's Sixteen Nations
Osterreichische Militarische Zeitschrift
RUSI Journal
Sentinel
Soldier Magazine
Strategy and Tactics
Waffen-Arsenal

Newspapers:
Der Kanadier
The Beaver
Beobachter an Der Haar
Werler Anzeiger
Westfalennoch
Westfalenpost Soest

BOOKS AND STUDIES:

Arnold, Lorna. *A Very Special Relationship: UK Atomic Warfare Trials in Australia* London: HMSO 1989.

Bercuson and Granatstein. *War and Peacekeeping: From South Africa to the Gulf, Canada's Limited Wars* Toronto: Key Porter Books, 1991.

Bacevich, A.J. *The Pentomic Era: The U.S. Army Between Korea and Vietnam* Washington: NDU Press, 1988.

Barnard, W.T. *The Queen's Own Rifles of Canada 1860-1960 One Hundred Years of Canada* Don Mills: The Ontario Publishing Co., 1960.

Beckmann, Heinrich Felix. *Schild und Schwert: Die Panzertruppe der Bundeswehr* Friedberg: Podzun-Pallas Verlag, 1989.

Bergot, Erwan and Alain Gandy. *Operations Daguet: Les Francais dans la Guerre du Golfe* Paris: Presses de la Citie, 1991.

Blair, Bruce. *The Logic Of Accidental Nuclear War* Washington: The Brookings Institute, 1993.

Brogan, Patrick. *The Captive Nations: Eastern Europe 1945-1990* New York: Avon Books, 1990.

Burgess, William H. (ed) *Inside Spetsnaz: Soviet Special Operations A Critical Analysis* Novato: Presidio, 1990.

Carlson, Adolf. *Who Will Stand the Nordic Guard?* Kingston: Queen's University Martello Papers, 1991.

Chang and Kornbluh. *The Cuban Missile Crisis 1962* New York: The New Press, 1992.

Cook, Don. *Forging The Alliance* New York: Armor House, 1989.

Crook, E.D. and John Marteinson, *A Pictorial History of 8th Canadian Hussars (Princess Louises)* 8CH Association, Sussex, 1973.

Corriveau, Paul. *Le Royal 22e Regiment – 75 ans d'histoire, 1914-1989* Quebec: La Regie, 1989.

Debay, Yves. *Blitzkrieg in the Gulf: Armor of the 100 Hour War* Concord Publications, 1991.

De jong, Sjouke. *NATO's Reserve Forces* Brassey's Atlantic Commentaries No. 6.

De La Billiere, Peter. *Storm Command: A Personal Account of the Gulf War* London: Harper-Collins, 1992.

Deere, David N.(ed) *Desert Cats: The Canadian Fighter Squadron in the Gulf War* Stoney Creek: Fortress Publications, 1991.

Donnelly, Christopher. *Red Banner: The Soviet Military System in Peace and War* London: Jane's, 1988.

Durniok, Manfred and Peter Schultze. *Berlin: Kriegsende 1945-1991* Berlin: Westkreutz-Verlag, 1992.

Faringdon, Hugh. *Strategic Geography, 2nd ed.* New York: Routledge, 1989.

Flanagan, Stephen J. *NATO's Conventional Defences* Cambridge: Ballinger, 1988.

Foss, Christopher. *Jane's Armoured Personnel Carriers* London: Jane's, 1985.

Fraser, W.B. *Always a Strathcona* Calgary: Comprint publishing, 1976.

Gaffen, Fred. *In The Eye of the Storm: A History of Canadian Peacekeeping* Toronto: Deneau and Wayne, 1987.

Garthoff, Raymond L. *Detente and Confrontation: American-Soviet Relations from Nixon to Reagan* Washington: The Brookings Institute, 1985.

Glenny, Misha. *The Fall of Yugoslavia: The Third Balkan War* New York: Penguin, 1992.

Granatstein and Bothwell, *Pirouette: Pierre Trudeau and Canadian Foreign Policy* Toronto: U of T Press, 1990.

Greenhous, Brereton. *Dragoon: The Centennial History of The Royal Canadian Dragoons* Ottawa: Guild of the RCD's, 1983.

Hackett, Sir John. *The Third World War: August 1985* London; Sidgewick and Jackson, 1978.

Hackett, Sir John. *The Third World War: The Untold Story* New York: Macmillan, 1982.

Halle, Louis. *The Cold War As History (rev ed)* New York: Harper Perrenial, 1991.

Hansen, Chuck. *U.S. Nuclear Weapons; The Secret History* New York: Orion, 1988.

Hellyer, Paul. *Damn The Torpedoes: My Fight To Unify Canada's Armed Forces* Toronto: McClelland and Stewart, 1990.

Hutchison, Paul P. *Canada's Black Watch: The First Hundred Years 1862-1962* Montreal: The RHR of Canada, 1962.

Isby, David C. *Weapons and Tactics of the Soviet Army (rev ed)* London; Jane's, 1988.

Isby, David C. and Charles Kamps Jr. *Armies of NATO's Central Front* London: Jane's, 1985.

Jockel, Joseph T. *Canada and NATO's Northern Flank* Toronto: York University, 1986.

Jordan, Robert S. (ed) *Generals in International Politics: NATO's Supreme Allied Commander Europe* Lexington: the University Press of Kentucky, 1987.

Kissinger, Henry. *Nuclear Weapons and Foreign Policy* Washington: Council on Foreign Relations, 1957.

Laber, Thomas. *Leopard 1 and 2: The Spearheads of the West German Armoured Forces* Hong Kong; Concord Publications, 1990.

Lockwood, Jonathan and Kathleen Lockwood, *The Russian View of U.S. Strategy: Its Past, Its Future* London: Transaction Publishers, 1993.

MacKenzie, Lewis. *Peacekeeper: The Road to Sarajevo* Toronto: Douglas and McIntyre, 1993.

Maclean, Alan.(ed) *Outstanding Support in Peace and War: A History of 4 Field Ambulance* Lahr: Edmund Demer, 1992.

Macksey, Kenneth. *First Clash: The Canadians in World War Three* Toronto: Stoddart, 1985.

Maier, Klaus and Norbert Wiggershaus, (eds) *Das Nordatlantische Bundnis 1949-1956* Munich: R. Oldenbour Verlag, 1993.

Martin, Laurence. *NATO and the Defence of the West* New York: Holt, Rhinehart and Winston, 1985.

Martin, Lawrence. *Pledge of Allegiance: The Americanization of Canada in the Mulroney Years* Toronto: M^cCLelland and Stewart, 1993.

McCandie, Ian (ed) *Forty Years 1953-1993: A Pictoral Overview of the Canadian Forces Stationed at 4 Wing/CFB Baden-Soellingen, West Germany* Ottawa: Esprit de Corps, 1993.

McLin, John B. *Canada's Changing Defence Policy 1957-1963* Baltimore: Johns Hopkins, 1967.

Meisner, Arnold. *Reforger: Return of Forces to Germany* Hong Kong; Concord Publications, 1989.

Micheletti, Eric, and Yves Debay, *Yougoslavie En Flammes: 600 Jours De Guerre Dans Les Balkans* Paris: Histoire & Collections, 1993.

Middlemiss, D.W. and J.J. Sokolsky, *Canadian Defence Decisions and Determinants* Toronto: Harcourt Brace and Jovanovich, 1989.

Morrison, Bob. *Operation Granby: Desert Rats Armour and Transport in the Gulf War* Hong Kong: Concord Publications, 1991.

Morrison, Bob. *Operation Desert Sabre: The Desert Rat's Liberation of Kuwait* Hong Kong: Concord Publications, 1991.

Midgley, John J. *Deadly Illusions: Army Policy for the Nuclear Battlefield* London: Westview Press, 1986.

Nicholson, G.W.L. *The Gunners of Canada Volume II: 1919-1967* Toronto: McClelland and Stewart, 1972.

Nicks, Don. *Lahr Schwarzwald: Canadian Forces Base Lahr 1967-1992* Ottawa: Esprit de Corps, 1993.

Paul, David W. *Czechoslovakia: Profile of a Socialist Republic at the Crossroads of Europe* Boulder: Westview Press, 1981.

Porter, Gerald. *In Retreat: The Canadian Forces in the Trudeau Years* Toronto: Deneau and Greenberg, (n/d)

Rachwald, Arthur R. *In Search of Poland: The Superpower's Response to Solidarity, 1980-1989* Stanford: Hoover Institute Press, 1990.

Rose, Clive. *Campaigns Against Western Defence: NATO's Adversaries and Critics* New York: St Martin's, 1985.

Rotman, Gordon L. *Warsaw Pact Ground Forces* London: Osprey Publishing, 1987.

Rush, Kenneth and others, *Strengthening Deterrence: NATO and the Credibility of Western Defense in the 1980's* Cambridge: Ballinger Publishing, (n/d).

Scheibert, Michael. *The Leopard Family* West Chester: Shieffer Publshing Co., 1989.

Schwartz, David N. *NATO's Nuclear Dilemmas* Washington: Brookings Institution, 1983.

Schwartzkopf, H. Norman with Peter Petre. *It Doesn't Take A Hero* Toronto; Bantam, 1992.

Scott, Harriet Fast and William F. Scott. *The Armed Forces of the USSR (2nd ed)* Boulder: Westview Press, 1981.

Service, G.T. and J.K. Marteinsen, *The Gate: A History of the Fort Garry Horse* [no publishing data]

Sharp, Mitchell. *Which Reminds Me...A Memoir* Toronto: U of T Press, 1994.

Snyder, William P. and James Brown, eds. *Defence Policy in the Reagan Administration* Washington: NDU Press, 1988.

Spiers, Edward M. *Chemical Weaponry: A Continuing Challenge* London: Macmillan, 1989.

Stevens, G.R. *The Royal Canadian Regiment Volume Two 1933-1966* London: London Printing and Lithographing, 1967.

Stevens, G.R. *Princess Patricia's Canadian Light Infantry 1919-1957 Volume Three* Griesbach: Historical Committee of the Regiment, (n/d)

Stewart, Larry. (ed) *Canadian Defence Policy: Selected Documents 1964-1981* Kingston: Queen's, 1981.

Tugwell, Maurice. *Peace With Freedom* Toronto: Key Porter Books, 1988.

Tunbridge, Steven. *The Centurion in Action* New Carrolton,Tx: Squadron Signal publications, 1976.

U.S. News and World Report Staff. *Triumph Without Victory: The Unreported History of the Persian Gulf War* New York: Random House, 1992.

Von Roland G. Foerster et al, *Anfange westdeutscher Sicherheitspolitik 1945-1956 Band 1: Von der Kapitulation bis zum Pleven-plan* Munich: R. Oldenbour Verlag, 1982.

Von Lutz Koellner et al, *Anfange westdeutscher Sicherheitspolitik 1945-1956 Band 2: Die EVG-Phase* Munich: R. Oldenbour Verlag, 1990.

Weiden, Peter. *The Wall: The Inside Story of a Divided Berlin* Toronto: Simon and Shuster, 1989.

Weinberger, Casper. *Fighting for Peace: Seven Critical Years in the Pentagon* New York: Warner Books, 1991.

Wood, Herbert Fairlie. *Strange Battleground: The Official History of the Canadian Army In Korea* Ottawa: Crown Publishers, 1966.

Zaloga, Steven J. *Tank War Central Front: NATO vs. Warsaw Pact* London: Osprey Publishing, 1989.

INDEX

1 Canadian Air Division: 62, 98, 150, 226, 440
1 Canadian Air Group: 269, 278, 381
2 Allied Tactical Air Force: 45, 46
4 Allied Tactical Air Force: 381

A

Active Defense: 317, 318, 324, 327, 364, 379
Addy, Clive, BGen: **437**, 461, 468, 469, 474
Afghanistan: 358, 365, 377
AFNORTH: 277, 278
AirLand Battle doctrine: 327, 379
Alexander, Lord: 49
Allard, Jean Victor, MGen: 171, 172, 242
Allied Command Europe (ACE): 18, 19, 62, 108, 126, 128, 129, 149, 188, 236, 276, 278, 303, 441, 483
    ACE Mobile Force (Land): 149, 188, 276, 483
    ACE Rapid Reaction Corps (ARRC): 483, 484
American Forces Recreation Centre: 222
Amy, E.A.C. (Ned), Brigadier: 194, 210, 220
Anderson, W.A.B., Brigadier: 61
Antwerp: 56, 105, 106, 130, 190
ASSIST, Operation: 460
Atomic Annie: **64**, 72, 92
Atomic Demolition Munition: 143, 205, 206, 209
Atomic Information Agreement: 128
Atomic weapons: 15, 17, 61; See also Nuclear weapons
Australia: 89
Austria: 34, 284, 285, 295, 306, 371, 373, 374, 395, 440

B

Baden / Baden-Soellingen: 240, 241, 242, **260**, 266, 268, 269, 271, 272, 273, 274, 278, 292, 297, 300, 302, 303, 321, 378, 382, 391, 392, 393, 399, 401, 403, 404, 412, 413, 421, 446, 449, 458, 459, 485
Baker, James: 452
BARBET, Operation Plan: 293, 294, 387, 401, 404, 452
Barr, Mike: 310
Bastien, Daniel: 416
Beaver, The: 95, 176, **218**, 223, 237, 271
Belgian Army
    I (Belgian) Corps: 53, 81, 139
    1 Belgian Infantry Division: 90
    4 Belgian Infantry Brigade Group: 46
    16 Belgian Armoured Division: 90, 92
Belgian Problem: 139, 178, 493
Belgium: 16, 19, 45, 52, 56, 88, 105, 106, 139, 154, 361, 413, 416, 465
Belleville: 76, 273
Belzile, Charles, BGen: 293, 313
Bergen-Hohne: **12**, 30, 143, 300, 367
Beria, Laverenti: 69
Berlin: **113**, 147, 149, 158, 170, 196, 200, 223
    Blockade 1948: 15

Contingency Plans (BERCONS): 171, 172, 199, 206, 232
    HALFMOON: 36
Crisis 1948: 16, 17
Crisis 1961: 149, 152, 153, 159, 161, 162, 178, 196
Wall: 159, 162, 357, 440, 447
Black Forest Officers Mess: 242, 487
Blanchard, George: 304
Bobcat: 170, 192
Boerdetag: **438**, 485
Boeselager Cup: 301
Böhmerwald: 285
BOLSTER, Operation: 464
Bonnland: **263**, 300, **347**, 367
Bosnia-Hercegovina: 462, 464, 465, 475, 480
BOXER, Operation Plan: 406, 407, 408
Boy Scouts of Canada: 147
Boynton, Jeff: 459
Britain: See Great Britain
British Army
    Corps
        I (BR) Corps: xxxvii, 34, 39, 41, 53, 61, 81, 83, 85, 86, 87, 89, 90, 102, 109, 135, 137, 139, 140, 141, 142, 150, 152, 156, 164, 172, 173, 177, 178, 189, 190, 192, 203, 205, 206, 208, 209, 211, 212, 234, 236, 240, 280, 291, 299, 364, 410, 491, 492, 493
    Divisions
        I (BR) Armoured Division: 450
        1 (BR) Infantry Division: 206
        2 (BR) Infantry Division: 83, 85, 87, 206, 212
        4 (BR) Infantry Division: 139, 140, 143, 216
        6 (BR) Armoured Division: 46, 83, 90, 274
        7 (BR) Armoured Division: 46, 57, 83, 88
        11 (BR) Armoured Division: 41, 42, 46, 59, 83, 85, 102
    Brigades
        4 Armoured Brigade: 450
        4 Guards Brigade Group: 167, 169
        5 Infantry Brigade Group: 144
        6 Armoured Brigade: 265, 274
        6 Infantry Brigade Group: 206, 212, 229
        7 Armoured Brigade: 450
        11 Infantry Brigade Group: 156, 206
        12 Infantry Brigade Group: 206, 229
        20 Armoured Brigade: 139, 229
        33 Armoured Brigade: 41, 42, 61
        46 Parachute Brigade: 90, 93
        91 Lorried Infantry Brigade: 42, 59
    Units
        14/20 Hussars: 238
        15/19 Hussars: 167
        16/5 Lancers: 238
        3 Regiment Dragoon Guards: 238
        5 Iniskilling Dragoon Guards: 167
        5 Lorried Infantry Battalion: 237
        5 Royal Tank Regiment: 237

7 Para Light Regiment RHA: 212
9 Lancers: 143
25 Field Squadron (RE):   175
44 Para Battalion Group: 45
58 Independent Squadron Royal Engineers: 44
111 Coy RASC: 44
Grenadier Guards: 216
Irish Guards: 169
Queen's Royal Irish Hussars: 216
Scots Guards: 216, 238
Sherwood Foresters: 238
Special Air Service (SAS):   46, 156, 169, 229, 328
The Gordon Highlanders: 238
The Parachute Regiment: 212
British Army of the Rhine (BAOR):   *13*, 26, 29, 30, 33, 34, 37, 41, 42, 44, 45, 51, 53, 54, 55, 85, 86, 98, 102, 103, 107, 109, *113*, 130, 143, 147, 152, 153, 154, 161, 172, 174, 215, 241, 265, 278, 294, 300, 301, 324, 450
British Military Hospital, Iserlohn: 95, 220
BROADSWORD, Operation Plan: 451, 452, 453, 454, 455, 456, 457, 458, 460, 496
Brown, Shaun: 387, 459
Brucker, Philip: 273
Brussels Pact: 16
BUGLE, Operation Plan: 445
Bundeswehr: 109, *114*, *123*, 133, 149, 176, 200, 202, 211, 219, 220, 238, *253*, *256*, 274, 286, 288, 297, 299, 301, 306, 309, 310, 312, 321, 328, *346*, *353*, 367, 369, 370, 374, 378, 390, 393, 396, 417, *433*, 486, 487, 509
  Korps
    I (GE) Korps: 135, 202, 203
    II (GE) Korps: 285, 287, 291, 295, 296, 297, 305, 306, 309, 310, 315, 323, 329, 366, 367, 370, 373, 380, 382, 383, 385, 386, 393, 396, 406, 408, 410, 411, 421, 426, 447, 461, 487, 495, 496
    III (GE) Korps: 202, 284, 285, 364, 382
  Divisions
    1 Mountain Division: 291, 296, 306, 395, 396
    4 Jaeger Division: 291, 296, 306, 315, 366, 383, 385
    4 Panzer Grenadier Division: 366, 367, 406, 408, 410, 412, 417, 424, 426, *433*, 447, 486, 487
    6 Panzer Grenadier Division: 154, 156
    7 Panzer Division: 315
    10 Panzer Division: 291, 296, 297, 315, 317, 366, 367, 395, 396, 411
    12 Panzer Division: 309, 368, 421, 423, 424
  Brigades:
    Airborne Brigade 25:   291, 296, 366, 367, 395
    Home Defence Brigade 18:   315
    Home Defence Brigade 55:   395
    Jaeger Brigade 10:   308
    Jaeger Brigade 11:   308
    Mountain Brigade 23:   306, 308
    Panzer Brigade 3:   176, 317
    Panzer Brigade 12:   296, 317, 367, 406, 408, 410, 411, 417
    Panzer Brigade 24:   395
    Panzer Brigade 28:   366
    Panzer Brigade 29:   312, 326, 328, 395
    Panzer Brigade 30:   313
    Panzer Brigade 35:   309
    Panzer Brigade 36:   317
    Panzer Grenadier Brigade 10:   367, 461
    Panzer Grenadier Brigade 11:   417
    Panzer Grenadier Brigade 19:   211
    Panzer Grenadier Brigade 22:   395
    Panzer Grenadier Brigade 24:   306, 308
    Panzer Grenadier Brigade 29:   395
    Panzer Grenadier Brigade 30:   366, 395
    Panzer Grenadier Brigade 35:   421, 423
  Units
    Airborne Battalion 251:   301
    Airborne Battalion 252:   301
    Airborne Battalion 261:   310
    Mountain Pioneer Battalion 8:   308
    Panzer Battalion 293:   414
    Panzer Grenadier Battalion 102:   416, 418, 419
    Panzer Grenadier Battalion 192:   211
    Panzer Grenadier Battalion 323:   212
    Panzer Regiment 200:   306, 308, 310, 311
    German Territorial Northern Command: 297
    German Territorial Southern Command: 297, 298, 299, 411, 419

C

Cadieux, Leo - Minister of Defence: 235, 273
Cameron, Donald C., Brig: 130, 148
Canada: 6, 14, 15, 16, 17, 18, 19, 20, 21, 22, 23, 24, 25, 27, 30, 33, 45, 50, 53, 54, 55, 56, 61, 62, 73, 74, 75, 83, 87, 95, 96, 101, 104, 105, 106, 108, 109, 115, 125, 128, 129, 130, 137, 140, 141, 142, 145, 147, 148, 149, 152, 153, 154, 158, 159, 160, 163, 164, 165, 167, 171, 172, 187, 188, 189, 191, 192, 194, 208, 209, 210, 211, 213, 214, 215, 216, 223, 228, 234, 235, 236, 239, 241, 242, 243, 266, 276, 277, 278, 280, 292, 293, 294, 311, 320, 321, 322, 330, 355, 360, 369, 382, 398, 432, 439, 441, 442, 443, 444, 445, 447, 448, 450, 451, 452, 454, 455, 457, 460, 465, 467, 468, 470, 480, 481, 483, 484, 491, 493, 494, 497, 508, 509, 510, 511, 512
  Department of External Affairs: 29, 56, 163, 172, 173, 235, 452, 465, 481, 483
  White Paper on Defence
    1964:   187
    1971:   276
    1987:   413, 418, 441, 442, 496
CANADA GOOSE, Contingency Plan: 140
Canadian Army: 14, 17, 20, 21, 24, 28, 29, 41, 53, 56, 62, 74, 75, 96, 101, 104, 105, 109, 130, 132, 140, 141, 153, 166, 178, 187, 188, 189, 192, 234, 492

INDEX

517

Active Force: 73
Militia: xi, 17, 20, 21, 22, 23, 62, 73, 74, 129, 188, 216, 229, 239, 311, *352*, 396, 421, 452, 485, 491, 492
Divisions
   1 Canadian Division: 74, 75, 81, 83, 105, 130, 132, 153, 154, 228, 357, 373, *433*, 439, 440, 442, 443, 445, 446, 447, 451, 452, 456, 461, 467, 485
   2 Canadian Infantry Division: 74, 81, 206, 208
Brigades
   1 Canadian Infantry Brigade Group: 61, 74, 75, 76, 78, 79, 81, 83, 85, 86, 87, 88, 89, 90, 92, 93, 98, 100, 159, 189, 486, 491
   2 Canadian Infantry Brigade Group: *68*, 74, 83, 85, 100, 101, 102, 103, 106, 107, 108, 109, 130, 159, 189, 486

   3 Canadian Infantry Brigade Group: 74, 159, 189
   4 Canadian Infantry Brigade Group: 129, 130, 131, 132, 133, 135, 139, 140, 141, 142, 143, 144, 145, 147, 148, 149, 150, 152, 153, 154, 156, 159, 160, 492
   4 Canadian Mechanized Brigade Group: 210, 225, 226, 227, 228, 229, 231, 232, 238, 239, *250*, *256*, *270*, 274, 288, 304, 305, 309, 323, 327, 330, *336*, *338*, 339, 340, 341, 343, 344, 345, 346, 354, 355, *356*, 357, 365, 389, 391, 432, 433, *438*, 442, 445, 446, 449, 452, 453, 454, 455, 457, 458, 459, 467, 490, 493, 495, 496, 497, 506
     Close-out: 437
     Command and Control: 278, 279
     Creation: 224, 319, 419
     Equipment: 320, 321, 322, 398, 399, 400, 402, 404, 439, 452
     Headquarters and Signal Squadron: 224, *250*, *254*, *262*, 318, 323
     Logistics and Sustainment: 241, 293, 294, 295, 297, 299, 403, 412, 413, 414
     Move South: 264, 265, 266, 268, 269, 270, 271
     Operational Review: 401
     Organization and Structure: 242, 243, 292, 360, 362, 387, 440, 441
     Reductions 1969: 236, 237, 240
     Role: 282, 286, 289, 291, 296, 380, 381, 382, 383, 385, 386, 393, 406, 408, 410, 411, 424, 426, 438, 443, 444, 457, 496
     Training: 300, 301, 306, 308, 310, 311, 312, 313, 314, 315, 317, 324, 326, 328, 329, 361, 363, 364, 366, 367, 368, 369, 370, 371, 395, 396, 415, 416, 417, 418, 420, 423, 424
   5e Groupment Brigade Mécanisée du Canada: 278, 442
   25 Canadian Infantry Brigade: 17, 20, 24, 55, 74
   26 Canadian Infantry Brigade Group: 17, 20

   27 Canadian Infantry Brigade Group: *6*, *11*, *12*, 14, 22, 23, 24, 25, 26, 27, 28, 29, 30, 32, 33, 34, 37, 39, 40, 41, 42, 44, 45, 46, 48, 49, 50, 51, 52, 53, 54, 55, 56, 57, 59, 61, 62, 74, 132, 133, 135, 142, 154, 280, 486
Units / Regiments / Corps (Branches)
   1 Canadian Guards: *113*, *121*, 148, 156, 167
   1 Canadian Highland Battalion: *9*, 22, 23, 32
   1 Canadian Infantry Battalion: *7*, *10*, 12, 22, 23, 29, 30
   1 Canadian Ordnance Unit: 56, 105, 190, 225
   1 Canadian Public Relations Unit: 101, 130
   1 Canadian Rifle Battalion: *9*, *13*, 22, 23, 44, 48, 50
   1 Canadian Signal Regiment: 329, 444, 461
   1 Field Ambulance: 130, 156, 220
   1 Field Dental Unit: 101
   1 Field Detention Barracks: 194, 221, 225
   1 Field Security Section: 101
   1 Field Squadron, RCE: 100
   1 Infantry Division Ordnance Field Park: 101, 194, 224
   1 PPCLI: 100, 159, 194
   1 Provost Company: 101
   1 Queen's Own Rifles: 167
   1 R22eR: 101, *184*, 194, 231, 240, *251*, *254*, *263*, 300, 301, *336*, 361, 363, 410, 411, 416, 419, 423, *430*, *432*, *434*, *436*, 443, 450, 454, 468, 469, 470, *471*, 472, 473, 474, 475, 476, 477, 478, 480, 485
   1 RCHA: 130, 143, 147, 148, 194, 240, 265, 269, 322, *332*, *334*, 361, 396, 399, 400, 423, 444, 485
   1 RCR: 100, *124*, 159, 175, 450
   1 RHC (Black Watch): 22, 23, 74, 75, *122*, 148, 211
   1 SSM Battery: 137, 141, 142, 159, 160, 162, 163, 174, 194, 208, 209, 224, 225, 239, 240
   1 Transport Company, RCASC: 130, 194, 224
   1 Transport Helicopter Platoon: 219
   2 Base Signal Troop, RCCS: 34, 56
   2 Canadian Guards: 130
   2 Electronic Warfare Squadron: 329, 396, 416, 421, 454
   2 Field Regiment, RCA: 265
   2 Field Security Section: 42, 103
   2 Independent Field Squadron, RCE: 75, 76
   2 Line of Communication Postal Unit: 56
   2 Medical Liaison Detachment: 56
   2 PPCLI: *65*, 75, 76, 92, 194, 217, 240, 396, 399, 400, 452, 454, 480
   2 QOR: 130, 148
   2 R22eR: 75, 76, 92, 191, 194
   2 RCHA: 75, 76, 159, 194
   2 RCR: 66, 75, 443, 480
   2 RHC (Black Watch): 194, 211
   2 SSM Battery: 141, 239
   3 Canadian Administration Unit: 56
   3 Canadian Guards: 75
   3 Canadian Support Group (Centre): 414

3 Mechanized Commando: 240, *252*, *255*, *259*, 266, 269, 271, 301, 322
3 R22eR: 130, 159, *180*, 191, 443, 485
3 RCHA: 148, 167, 444
3 RCR: 322, *332*, *333*, *338*, *340*, *341*, *342*, *344*, *345*, *348*, 361, 367, 399, 400, 410, 411, 420, 423, *432*, 443, 449, 454, 459, 468, 469, 485, 486
4 Canadian Medical Support Unit: 224
4 Canadian Motorcycle Group, RCASC: 56
4 CIBG Battle School: 194
4 CMBG Service Battalion: 224, 225
4 Combat Engineer Regiment: 322, 323, *350*, *351*, *353*, 423, *435*, 444, 462, 469, 470, 472, 474, 477, 485
4 Combat Medical Support Unit: 322, 323
4 Field Ambulance: 101, 161, 269, 322, *351*, 389, 399, 413, 419, 423, 444, 460, 461, 484, 485
4 Field Dental Coy: 194
4 Field Engineer Squadron: 322
4 Field Squadron, RCE: 130, 225, 240
4 MP Platoon: 224, 225, 485
4 Provost Platoon: 194, 224
4 RCHA: 100, 239
4 Service Battalion: *261*, *354*, 389, *437*, 423
4 Signals Squadron: 194
5 Field Ambulance: 444
5ᵉ Régiment du génie du Canada: 444
5 Service Battalion: 444
5 Transport Company, RCASC: 101
5ᵉ Régiment d'artillerie légère: 444
6 Combat Engineer Regiment: 444
7 Field Ambulance: 23
8 Canadian Hussars (Princess Louise's):   *113*, *114*, *121*, 132, 148, 156, 165, 167, 174, 175, 194, 239, 268, *348*, 363, 397, 399, 410, 411, 423, 443, 444, 454, 468, 485
9 Field Ambulance: 23
12e Régiment Blindé du Canada: 443, 444, 446
22 Field Engineer Squadron: 469, 480
25 Field Ambulance: 75
27 CIB NCO School: 53
27 Field Ambulance: 22
27 Field Dental Unit: 75
27 Field Detention Barracks: 56
27 Field Security Section: 75
27 Ordnance Company: 75
27 Provost Detachment: 50, 52, 75
27 Public Relations Unit: 75
35 Field Dental Unit: 414
48 Highlanders: 22, 23
54 Transport Company, RCASC: 75
55 Transport Company, RCASC: 22
58 Independent Field Squadron, RCE: 22, 23, 54
78 Field Squadron, RCE: 44
79 Field Ambulance: 23
79 Field Regiment, RCA: 22, 23
127 Air Defence Battery: 321

128 Air Defence Battery: 321
129 Air Defence Battery: 321
195 Infantry Workshop (RCEME):   75
427 Tactical Helicopter Squadron: 421
430 Escadron tactique d'hélioptère: 444
444 Tactical Helicopter Squadron: 318, 323, *334*, 444, 454
Black Watch, Royal Highland Regiment of Canada: 22, 23, *122*, 148, 156, 160, 167, 169, 174, 177, 194, 211, 215, 239
A Squadron, RCD: 100
C Squadron, RCD: 22, 41, 48, 266, 322
Canadian Base Units, Europe: 56, 130, 189, 190, 225
Canadian Guards: 74, 113, 147, 169, 239
Canadian Scottish Regiment: 22, 23
D Squadron, LdSH: 75, 76
Fort Garry Horse: 132, 165, 166, 175, 194, 211, 213, 239, 444
Helicopter Recce Troop, RCAC: 165
HQ 1 CIBG: 74, 76, 90
HQ Canadian Base Units, Europe: 56, 75, 189, 194
J Troop, RCCS: 75
Lord Strathcona's Horse: 74, 92, 130, 159, 194, 213, 221, 223, 231, 268, 444
North Nova Scotia Highlanders: 22, 23
Provost Corps: 100, 130, 221
Queen's Own Rifles: *125*, 194
RCAC Helicopter Recce Troop: 165
Royal Canadian Corps of Signals: *68*, 75
Royal Canadian Dragoons: 33, 74, 130, *251*, *255*, 268, *335*, *339*, 403
Royal Canadian Electrical and Mechanical Engineers: 24, 25, 52, *67*, 75, 130, 145, 165, 194, 224
Royal Canadian Engineers: *115*, 219
Royal Canadian Regiment: 74, 333, 486
Seaforth Highlanders of Canada: 22
Canadian Air-Sea Transportable Brigade Group (CAST):   277, 278, 293, 360, 398, 413, 441, 442
Chiefs of Staff Committee: 19, 150
Electronic Warfare: 313, 329, 457
Mobile Command: 339, 389, 451, 453, 468
Mobile Striking Force: 17, 73, 74
Canadian Army National Force, Europe (CANF(E)):   189, 190, 225, 278
Canadian Army Special Force (CASF):   17, 18
Canadian Army Trophy (CAT):   301, 368
Canadian Broadcasting Corporation: 50, 145, 223
Canadian Canter: 300
Canadian Forces Base Europe: 269
Canadian Forces Europe (CFE):   278, 279, 293, 294, 299, 302, 323, 369, 390, 392, 401, 402, 404, 412, 413, 414, 416, 419, 448, 449, 454, 459, 464, 467, 481, 483, 484, 487
Canadian Forces Exchange System (CANEX):   95, 274, 487
Canadian Forces Network (CFN):   274, 303, 366

INDEX

Canadian Forces Support Unit (Europe):   484
Canadian Land Forces, Europe: 225
Canadian Medical Group (Centre):   414, 444, 454
Carew, P.H.C., LCol: 268
Carew, Tony: 470
Carpathian Military District: 284
Castonguay, LCol: **7**, 30
CAVALIER, Operation: 480
Central Army Group: 53, 81, 90, 135, 140, 150, 171, 196, 199, 203, 227, 241, **250**, **251**, **260**, 264, 278, 280, 282, 284, 285, 286, 287, 288, 289, 291, 294, 295, 296, 297, 298, 299, 300, 301, 302, 304, 305, 306, 309, 314, 322, 323, 329, 364, 368, 369, 370, 371, 373, 378, 380, 381, 382, 383, 385, 386, 387, 390, 406, 411, 412, 415, 420, 426, 427, 440, 442, 443, 445, 447, 494, 495
Central Region: 36, 81, **115**, 149, 154, 164, 170, 171, 178, 195, 199, 200, 228, 234, 236, 244, 276, 277, 278, 287, 288, 293, 297, 317, 326, 327, 328, 329, 357, 359, 360, 373, 378, 379, 380, 381, 389, 390, 490, 491, 492, 493, 494, 495, 496
Charlebois, Trooper: 160
Chemical weapons: 81, 195, 377, 453, 460
Chernobyl: 415
Chouinard, Jacques, BGen: 291, 507
Clark, Gen: 152
Clark, Joe: 359, 452
Claxton, Brooke - Minister of National Defence: 21, 29
Cloutier, Sylvain: 319
Coates, Robert - Minister of National Defence: 398
Coburg Entry: 285
Coderre, Paul, LCol: 323
Collier, Don, CWO: 147
Collins, Mary: **432**
COME AND GO, Operation: 78, 100
Communism: 15, 70, 72, 158, 170, 418, 462
Conference on Security and Cooperation in Europe: 448, 464
Connaught Shield Competition: 86, 156
Conscription Crisis: 17
Contingency Plan VILS RIVER: 408, 410
Conventional Forces in Europe (CFE) Treaty: 448
Coroy, Dick: 221
Cowan, BGen: 364
Cowan, Donna: 220
Croatia: 462, 463, 464, 469, 470, 472, 474
Crowe, D., Col: 209
Cuban Missile Crisis: 121, 122, 162, 164, 166, 170, 174, 178, 198, 200
Cyprus: 188, 276, 292, 293, 401, 462, 464, 479, 486
Czechoslovakia: 15, 34, 70, 107, 196, 202, 282, 284, 364, 365, 380, 382, 408, 412, 439, 440, 448, 465, 512
   Invasion of 1968:   226, 227, 228, 229
Czechoslovakian Peoples Army (CPA):   281, 282, 371, 374, 482

D

DAGGER, Operation: 480
DAGUET, Operation: 450
Dangerfield, Jack: 238, 386, 401, 402, 406, 414, 440, 442
Dare, Mike, Brig: 164, 171, 173, 194, 212, 213
Dauphinee, Wayne: 220, 272
de Chastelain, A.J.G.D., BGen: 364, 451
de Faye, Tom, BGen: 309, 418, 423, 494
De Schmidt, MGen: 211
Defence Structure Review: 319
Denmark: 16, 36, 154, 277, 465
Der Kanadier, Newspaper: 271
Des Laurier, Des, Major: 474
DESERT SHIELD, Operation: 450
Devlin, Peter, Maj: 420, 459
Dextraze, Jacques, Gen: 273, 292, 319, 320
Diefenbaker, John - Prime Minister: 129, 154, 160, 163, 164, 186, 188
Doctrine: 27, 137, 166, 195, 215, 279, 289, 359, 377
DOLOMITE, Operation: **260**, 323, 461
Donau (Danube) Approach: **256**, 285, 295, 371, 373, **374**, 382, 393, 396, 447, 495
Douglas, Ian: 361
Dubcek, Alexander: 226
Dupuy, Pierre: 30

E

East German Army: See National Volkesarmee
Edgecomb, David: 173, 213
Egelseer, Dieter: 419
Eisenhower, Dwight, General: **7**, 19, 27, 30, 36
Emergency Defence Plan (EDP):   139, 140, 161, 166, 170, 171, 172, 200, 202, 203, 205, 206, **207**, 208, 226, 231, 234, 240
European Community Monitoring Mission, Yugoslavia: 464
Evraire, R.J., BGen: 368, 371, 385
Exercises
   ABLE ARCHER: 324, 370
   ACTIVE EDGE: 402
   AUTUMN FORGE: 324, 364
   BADGER: 42
   BATTLE AXE: 103
   BATTLE ROYAL: **64**, 90, 91, 93, 137, 144, 154, 505
   BLAUE DONAU: 329
   BLAUWE DIEMEL: 324
   BLAZING FURY: 156
   BOLD STEP: 412
   BRAVE LION: 398, 412, 441
   BUNTES FAHNLEIN: 417
   CANADA CUP: **119**, **120**, **121**, 166, 167, 168
   CANADIAN CLUB: 310
   CARAVAN GUARD: 446
   CARBINE FORTRESS: **336**, **351**, **352**, **353**, 368, 369
   CARBINE SIGHT: 415
   CARBON EDGE: 328, 415
   CARTE BLANCHE: 133

CERTAIN CHALLENGE: *348*, *349*, 420, 421, 422, 424, 425
CERTAIN CHARGE: 312, 313
CERTAIN FORGE: 308, 309
CERTAIN PLEDGE: 313, 314
CERTAIN RAMPART: *332*, *334*, *335*, *336*, 364, 369
CERTAIN SENTINEL: 360, 361, 363, 415
CERTAIN SHIELD: 311, 329
CERTAIN TREK: 317, 318, 320
CHECK MATE: 215
CLEAN CUT: 310
COLD STEEL: 211
COMMONWEALTH: 57
COMMONWEALTH III: *66*, 88
CONFIDENT ENTERPRISE: 370
CONSTANT ENFORCER: 363
COOL GIN: 324
DONAU DASH: 312
DVINA: 284
ESPERANTO ONE: 210
FLASHBACK: 153
FLAT OUT: 87
FLINKER IGEL: 393, 394, 396, 397, 398, 416
FLY CATCHER: 214
GOPHER III: 41
GORDIAN SHIELD: 324
GRAND REPULSE: 59, 61
GRAND REPULSE I: 60
GROSSE ROCHADE: *253*, *254*, *256*, *257*, *258*, 315, 316, 317, 329
GROSSER BAER: 324
GRUNER LAUBFROSCH: 368
GUTES OMEN: 251, 306, 307, 308, 309, 367
HIGH GEAR: 88
HOLD FAST: 47, 157
HOLDFAST (1952): 45, 46, 49, 51, 57
HOLD FAST (1960): *114*, *125*, 154
HOSTAGE JAUNE: 209
INDIAN SUMMER: 90
IRON MAIDEN: 176
JAVELIN CPX: 102
JAVELIN FIVE: 57, 58
JAVELIN VII: 89
KEEN BLADE: *123*, *124*, 176
KEYSTONE: 228, 229, 230, 232
LARES TEAM: 324, 325, 327
LARGO PASSAGE: 310
LION CAGE: 165
LOWLAND FLING: 212
MAPLE LEAF X: 211
MARSHMALLOW: 237, 238, 239
MORNING STAR: 106
NEW HARPOON VII: 211
NO NAME: 41
POWER PLAY: 312
PRINTEMPS: 211
PUENYARD: 103
QUICK TRAIN: 85, 177, 226, 302
RADIANT SABRE: 416
RAM: 42
RAPID THRUST: 414, 416
RAPIER: 103
RASOIRE SALAIRE: 461
RAUB VOGEL: 312
REBEL SADDLE: 414, 416
RED PATCH: 41
RIGID RUNABOUT: 403
ROB ROY: 216, *218*, 219
ROCHET SABOT: 461
ROCKY MOUNTAIN: 306
ROYAL ALLIANCE: 461
ROYAL SWORD: 418, 419, 446, 447, 458
SABRE: 102
ST. GEORGE: 364
SCHARFE KLINGE: 366, 367, 369
SCHWARZE LOEWE: 227, 228, 306, 366
SHAKEDOWN 2: 87
SILVER DOLLAR: *116*, 166
SNOW FIRE: 143
SNOWBALL: 302, 365, 366, 392, 403
SOLO SABRE: 414
SPEAR POINT: 324, 364
SPEARHEAD II: *11*, 42, 43, 45, 46, 51, 61
SUMAVA: 226
SWIFT THRUST III: 370
TOMAHAWK: 237, 238
TRAMPLE: 57
TRAVAIL: 102
TREBLE CHANCE: *181*, *184*, 212
VANITY FAIR: 144
WAR AXE: 237
EXODUS, Operation: 266

F

Fairsea, MV: *6*, 14, 29, 487
Federal Republic of Germany: 16, 33, 71, 81, 133, 202, 286, 298, 391, 420, 440, 447
Feldmann, Olaf: 393
FIBUA: *13*, *263*, 300, 327, *346*, 367
Fiddler, Bill: 175
Field Ambulance Trophy: 156
"First Clash", book: 339, 389
Flexible Response: 199, 232, 243, 276, 379, 493
Flyover: 210, 213, 226, 229, 311, 312, 321, 322, 352, 361, 389, 396, 400, 421
Follow-On Forces Attack: 359, 379, 380, 381, 410, 441
Forts
  Anne: 76, 194
  Beausejour: 78, 194
  Chambly: 76, 95
  Henry: 76, 95, 194
  Macleod: 76, 194
  Prince of Wales: 76, 194
  Qu' Appelle: 78
  St. Louis: 76, 95, 194
  Victoria: 76, 194
  York: 76, 194

INDEX

Forward Defence: 72, 127, 133, 200, 202, 203, 205, 277, 286, 287, 289, 379, 380, 410, 412, 426, 493, 494, 495
Forward Mobile Support Unit (FMSU): 404, 412, 413, 414, 421
Foulkes, Charles, Gen: 19, 150
Fox, J.A., BGen: 329, 361
France: 15, 16, 19, 52, 70, 81, 98, 107, 128, 148, 160, 171, 175, 232, 241, 286, 300, 359, 361, 416, 450, 460, 465
French Commando Course: 300, 301, 368
FRICTION, Operation: 449
Frye, Leading Seaman: 473
Fulda Gap: 285, 373, 381, 382
Fürth Gap: 285

G

Gale, Sir Richard, Gen: 53, 104
Galvin, General: **349**, 385
Gardner, BGen: 264
Gaudreau, J.M.R., BGen: 442, 445, 446
General Defence Plan (GDP): 291, 292, 297, 299, 304, 357, 364, 368, 369, 373, 382, 383, 385, 404, 406, 408, 410, 414, 415, 417, 445, 496
German Democratic Republic: 37, 39, 69, 70, 79, 137, 158, 171, 172, 196, 202, 205, 206, 209, 227, 356, 379, 439, 447, 481
German Reunification: 202, 374, 447
Germany: See Federal Republic of Germany; German Democratic Republic
Glenny, Misha: 463
GONDOLA Base: 105
GONDOLA, Operation: 56
Goodpaster, Andrew, Gen: 236
Gorbachev, Mikhail: 417, 418, 448
Gottingen Gap: 137, 206, 209
Gouzenko, Igor: 15
Grafenwöhr: 299, 309, 367, 383, 387, 388, 406
GRANBY, Operation: 450
Gravelle, Gordie: 174, 177
Great Britain: 16, 19, 28, 36, 45, 52, 54, 55, 61, 70, 105, 106, 107, 128, 153, 154, 162, 171, 205, 229, 280, 359, 361, 413, 414, 450, 454, 455, 460
Greece: 15, 16, 193
Green, Howard: 163
Green Party: 369
Grieve, Pat, BGen: 289, 310, 311, 312, 319
GRIZZLY, GDP Option: 296, 385
Group of Soviet Forces Germany (GSFG): See Soviet Army
Gulf War: 195, 358, 390, **432**, 448, 449, 450, 452, 453, 456, 457, 458, 460, 496
Guteknecht, René: 238

H

Hackett, Sir John, Gen: xxix, 242, 331
Haig, Alexander, Gen: 390
Hamilton, Barry: 311
Hammelburg: **263**, 300, **346**, **347**, 367

Hannover: **8**, **13**, 29, 30, 33, 37, 39, 41, 42, 49, 50, 52, 54, 55, 75, 76, 95, 100, 144, 154, 205, 217
Harding, Sir John, Gen: 30
Harkness, Douglas - Minister of National Defence: 164
HARMONY, Operation: 465, 467, 468, 469, 470
Hasluck, Isabel: 146
Hasselman, B.R.P.F., LGen: 30
HATLESS, Operation Plan: 414
Hatton, General: 33
Hellyer, Paul - Minister of National Defence: 187, 189
Highway 14: 285, 296, 370, 373, 381, 382, 383, 396, 410, 411
Hill, Ken, Lt: 449
Hintze, Bill: 175
Hof Corridor/Gap: 284, 285, **355**
Hohenfels: 296, 299, 306, 310, 312, 328, **338**, **339**, **340**, 367, 382, 414, 416, 418, **430**, **431**, 446, 461
Holt, David: 122, 132, 310
Honest John: **118**, 137, 140, 141, 142, 143, 172, 178, 205, 208, 209, 239, 493
Hopkinson, Capt: 96
Host Nation Support: **259**, 297, 298, 299, 328, 460
Huggins, John: 32, 40
Hungary: 127, 365
  Uprising, 1956: 70, 108, 126
Hungerford, Bill: 397
Hussein, Saddam: 439, 448, 450, 456, 458, 460
Hydrogen bomb: 69, 106, 492

I

Ignatieff, George: 173
Integrated Lines of Communication (Canada/US): 413, 414, 421, 445, 454
Interoperability: 237, **253**, 300, 304, 305, 309, 313, 314, 328, 330, 364, 367, 368, 396, 417, 419, 421, 423, 424, 426, 454
Iraq: 195, 439, 448, 449, 450, 451, 453, 455, 456, 460
Iserlohn: 98, 133, 146, 147, 148, 221, 222, 223, 225, 226, 264, 266
Italy: 15, 16, 36, 53, 152, 170, **260**, 323, 359
Ivey, Wayne, WO: 390, 472

J

JNA: See Yugoslavian National Army
Joint Exercise Simulation System: 446
Jones, Michel, LCol: 469, 473, 476

K

Kearny, Rick: 397
Kennedy, John F.: 174, 177
Khrushchev, Nikita: 69, 158, 162, 170, 171, 174
King, Mackenzie: 17
Kitching, MGen: 150
Klene, Hans: 175
Korean War: 17, 34

Kroesen, Frederick, Gen: 364, 390
Kuwait: 439, 448, 451, 456

L

Lahr: 175, 240, 242, 243, **250**, **260**, 264, 265, 266, 268, 269, **270**, 271, 272, 273, 274, 278, 291, 292, 294, 297, 299, 300, 302, 303, 306, 311, 319, 321, 327, 363, 378, 382, 390, 392, 393, 398, 400, 401, 403, 412, 413, 414, 421, 440, 443, 444, 446, 453, 458, 459, 460, 465, 467, 468, 470, 476, 480, 485, 487
Lalonde, Pierre, BGen: 403, 404, 406, 416, 418
LANDJUT: 154, 156, 196, 203
Lemnitzer, Lyman L., Gen: 227
Leonard, W.C., BGen: 264, 291
LIVE OAK, Contingency Plan: 171, 200, 206, 232

M

MacDougal, Barbara: 465
MacInnis, Don, Maj: **344**
Mackenzie, Lewis, MGen: 465, 468, 470, 477, 479, 480
Macksey, Kenneth: **339**, 389
Maloney, Mike: 174
Manoeuvre damage: 144, 363, 369, 370, 419, 420, 446
Maple Leaf Services (MLS): 95
Marsh, Sgt: **353**
Marteinson, John: 166, 213
Martin, Jack: 42, 44, 46
Massu, Jacques, Gen: 242
MAYFLOWER, Operation Plan: 292, 366, 387, 401
McBride, Buck, Capt: 323
McCarthy, Joe: 69
Meating, Bob: 266, 269, 484
Middle East: 15, 36, 223, 286, 359, 448, 451, 454
Minister of National Defence: See Cadieux, Leo; Claxton, Brooke; Coates, Robert; Harkness, Douglas; McKnight, Bill; Neilson, Erik; Richardson, James
Mitterand, Francois: 477
Mobile Command: See Canadian Army
Mobile Striking Force: See Canadian Army
Montgomery, Field Marshal: 62
Morillon, M., Gen: 465
Mountain, Bill: 37, 40
Mulroney, Brian - Prime Minister: 399, 441, 448
Münsingen: 300, 367

N

Nagy, Imre: 107
Nambiar, LGen: 465
NASHORN (GDP Option): 296, 385
National Volkesarmee (NVA): 196, 202, 282, **356**, **374**, **375**, **376**, 378
Near, Bob, Maj: 367, **433**
Neilson, Erik: 398

Neilson, Robert: 311
Netherlands, The: 16, 19, 29, 30, 45, 53, 54, 56, 59, 61, 81, 90, 196, 203, 216, 237, 320, 359, 416, 460, 465
Netherlands Army
  1 (NL) Corps: 53, 59, 61, 90, 92, 135, 203
  1 Falsterke Fod Infantry Regiment: 216
  4 (NL) Infantry Division: 59, 90
  101 (NL) Tank Battalion: 216
Nijmegen Marches: 301
Norstad, Lauris, Gen: 149, 198
North Atlantic Treaty Organization (NATO): 14, 16, 27, 28, 36, 492
  Alert System: 173, 303
  Article 5: 16
  Canada-US Regional Planning Group: 16
  Composite Force: 442
  Defence Committee: 18
  Defence planning: 16, 18, 36, 37
  Defence Planning Questionnaire: 360
  Integrated Force: 19, 21, 27, 28, 34, 36, 53, 64, 69, 70, 71, 72, 73, 81, 127, 491
  Medium Term Defence Plan (MTDP): 16, 17, 18, 19
  Military Committee
    MC 100/1: 198
    MC 14: 36, 135, 149, 152, 154, 276, 278, 286, 287
    MC 14/2: 127, 196, 198, 232, 233
    MC 14/3: 199, 232, 233, 234, 236, 237, 239, 243
    MC 48: 71
    MC 70: 128, 140
  Mutual Defence Assistance Programme (MDAP): 129, 188, 193, 492
  North Atlantic Ocean Regional Planning Group: 16
  Nuclear planning: 71
    Athens Guidelines: 198, 209
  Operational planning: 133
  Regional Planning Groups: 16, 17
  Shield Forces: 127
  Short Term Defence Plan: 16, 17
  Sword Forces: 127, 170
  Western Europe Regional Planning Group: 17
Northern Army Group: 53, 59, 61, **64**, 79, 81, 83, 85, 90, 105, 107, 109, 129, 133, 135, 137, 139, 140, 147, 150, 154, 163, 164, 165, 170, 171, 172, 173, 176, 178, 189, 191, 195, 196, 199, 202, 203, 205, 208, 209, 211, 212, 216, 226, 228, 234, 236, 237, 240, 242, 243, 264, 265, 280, 282, 284, 286, 288, 289, 294, 302, 303, 304, 311, 314, 320, 322, 324, 364, 369, 371, 426, 492
Norway: 16, 19, 127, 152, 277, 398, 441, 442
Nuclear weapons: 15, 65, 70, 71, 72, 73, 76, 81, 89, 90, 93, 102, 107, **112**, **115**, 127, 128, 129, 133, 135, 137, 144, 149, 150, 152, 158, 163, 167, 171, 175, 186, 187, 195, 196, 198, 199, 200, 203, 205, 206, 208, 209, 229, 231, 232, 233, 234, 236, 239, 241, 243, 244, 269, 275, 285,

INDEX

286, 287, 289, 358, 378, 379, 380, 381, 392, 492

O

O'Connor, Terry: 312
Oehring, George: 404
Operational Manoeuvre Group (OMG): 377
ORION SPECIAL, Operation: 216, 229, 239
Ostashower, Rick: 387
Otis, Glen, MGen: 361
OTTER (GDP Option): 296

P

Pacholzuk, 'Buck': 175
PANDA, Operation: 22, 24
Pangman, J.E.C., Brig: 53
Pearson, Lester B.: 5, 29, 108, 163, 186, 187, 223, 241, 243
PENDANT, Operation Plan: 292, 293, 294, 360, 387, 400, 401, 404, 420, 421, 445, 452, 454
Pilsen/Highway 14: 285
PLUTO (GDP Option): 385
Poland: 15, 70, 79, 196, 365, 373, 379, 465
  Solidarity trade union movement: 364
Polish Army: 79, 365, 437
Polish Crisis of 1980: **333**, 364
POMCUS: 288, 289, 380, 411
Pope John Paul II: 359
Porter, Gerald: 320
Powell, E.C.: 24
PRINCESS ROYAL I, Operation: 399
PRINCESS ROYAL II, Operation: 399
Prix LeClerc: 86, 156
PROVIDE COMFORT, Operation: 460
PUMA, Tactical Assembly Area: 383
Putlos: 40, 53, 86, 102

Q

R

Radio Canadian Army Europe: 95, 145
Radio Forces Canadien: 274
Radley-Walters, LCol: 156
Ralph, Mike: 480
READINESS, Operation: 459
Reagan, Ronald: 359
REFORGER: 106, 259, 289, 302, 304, 308, 309, 311, 312, 313, 314, 315, 317, 318, 324, 328, 329, 336, 360, 368, 370, 383, 414, 415, 420, 443, 445
Reichardt, Jurgen, MGen: 412, 426, **433**
Reid, Dennis, Cpl: 480
Rettie, I.M.: 11, 34
Richards, Ray, Maj: 362
Richardson, James: 319
Ritchie, Charles: 104

Ritchie, Mike: 86, 266
Rogers, Bernard, Gen: 379
Ross, Richard: 52
Royal Canadian Air Force: 21, 73, 125, 131, 153, 175, 178, 222, 241, 242, 243, 268, 269
Rudneu, Max: 365

S

SACEUR: 7, 19, 20, 21, 28, 29, 34, 53, 54, 59, **64**, 70, 71, 72, 73, 74, 128, 133, 135, 140, 149, 150, 152, 153, 158, 160, 164, 172, 173, 178, 188, 198, 199, 200, 202, 208, 209, 227, 236, 239, 241, 269, 277, 287, 297, 324, 328, **349**, 363, 370, 379, 390, 401, 440, 441, 445, 451, 491
SAFE KEEP, Operation: 161
St Aubin d'Ancey, Ivor: 419
St. Laurent, Louis: 18, 21, 26
Salvation Army: 49, 95, 96, 146, **182**, 274
Sarajevo: **434**, 465, 475, 476, 477, 478, 479, 480
Saudi Arabia: 448, 449, 450, 451, 452, 455
Saunders, W.: 30
Sawchuck, Jeff: 300, 302
Schimpf, Richard, MGen: 109
SCIMITAR, Operation: 449
Seed, Doug - RSM: 397
Seguin, WO: 103
Sennelager: **13**, 40, **65**, 89, 102, 103, 240, 268, 300, **340**
Serbia: 462, 463, 465
SETTER, Tactical Assembly Area: 370, 383, 406, 408, 410, 413, 445
SHAPE: 19, 59, 71, 104, 105, 106, 133, 149, 152, 153, 228, 236, 287, 293, 302, 390, 441
  School, Oberammergau: 71
Shapiro, Lionel: 51
Sharp, Mitchell: 235
Shaver, D.K.: 39
Sim, Corporal: 95
Simonds, Guy, Gen: 18, 20, 21, 24, 28, 29, 32, 39
Slovenia: 462
Smillie, Roy: 161
Snider, Curley: 238
Soest: 46, 54, 57, 61, **68**, 75, 76, 86, 94, 95, 96, 98, 99, 100, 105, 132, 140, 143, 145, 146, 148, 154, 175, 177, 194, 216, 221, 225, 240, 242, 264, 272, 274, **438**, 484, 485
Soltau: 40, 41, 57, **65**, **66**, **68**, 86, 87, 88, 102, 103, 212
Somalia: 486, 487
South Korea: 15
Soviet Army
  1 Guards Mechanized Army: 79
  1 Guards Tank Army: 196, 371
  2 Guards Army: 196
  2 Guards Mechanized Army: 79
  2 Guards Tank Army: 282
  3 Guards Mechanized Army: 85
  3 Shock Army: 79, 85, 196, 209, 371
  4 Guards Mechanized Army: 85

8 Guards Army: 79, 196, 282, 371
8 Guards Combined Arms Army: 371
18 Guards Army: 196
19 Guards Mechanized Division: 87
20 Guards Army: 196
Doctrine: 195, 284, 377
Exercises
    DVINA: 284
    SUMAVA: 226
Group of Soviet Forces Germany (GSFG): 79, 158, 195, 196, 209, 275, 282, 284, 285, 373, 377, 447
Southern Group of Forces: 282, 284, 296
Soviet Military Liaison Mission (SMLM): *349*, *350*, 390, 391
Soviet Occupation Exchange Mission (SOXMIS): 42, 61, 103, 390
Soviet Union: 15, 16, 18, 19, 34, 36, 62, 69, 70, 71, 107, 108, 126, 127, 128, 158, 159, 162, 170, 199, 200, 227, 228, 237, 275, 286, 287, 357, 358, 366, 370, 380, 417, 418, 440, 481, 492, 493
Special Operations Forces: 361
Speidel, Hans / Speidel Proposal: 149, 150, 152
Spetsnaz: 377, 378
SPIRAL, Operation: 462
SPRINGBOK-CORONET, Operation: 399
Stalin, Josef: 15, 69, 79, 238
Stationed Task Force (STF): 483, 484
Stikker, Dirk: 30
Strawbridge, R.L.: 265
Suez Crisis: 70, 107, 108
Supreme Allied Commander, Europe: See SACEUR
Supreme Headquarters, Allied Powers Europe: See SHAPE
SWINTER trials: 389

T

TABLE TOP, Operational Plan: 107, 162
Tappin, Percy: 361
Tedlie, A. James, BGen: 118, 142, *184*, 190, 194, 206, 211, 214
Terrorism: 359, 389, 390, 392, 393, 458, 460
Teutobergerwald: 83, 92, 135, 203
Thatcher, Margaret: 359
Thériault, Gerard, Gen: 385
Thomas, Charles, Adm: 458
Tiffany's: 398
Tito, Josef Broz: 462
Tramble, W.J.: 176
Transport International Routier: 391
TRICAP division: 279
Tromme, Lt Gen: 90
Trudeau, Pierre: 186, 188, 223, 224, 234, 235, 236, 239, 240, 241, 243, 276, 277, 279, 289, 292, 293, 294, 319, 320, 359, 360, 398, 494
Turkey: 15, 16, 127, 170, 174, 277, 449, 460

U

Unification (Canadian Forces): 76, 189, 190, 241, 272, 274, 278, 399, 483
Union of Soviet Socialist Republic: See Soviet Union
United Kingdom: See Great Britain
United Nations: 107, 108, 434, *436*, 439, 440, 448, 464, 465, 486
    Operations: 187, 188, 189
United Nations Emergency Force: 108
United Nations Protection Force (UNPROFOR): *434*, 465, 469, 470, 472, 474, 475, 476, 478, 479, 480, 487
United States: 16, 17, 19, 27, 42, 69, 70, 71, 127, 142, 160, 163, 166, 171, 172, 174, 177, 199, 227, 228, 236, 240, 287, 288, 359, 369, 449, 460, 491
United States Army
    Corps
        V (US) Corps: 284, 285, 314, 324, 329, 370, 418
        VII (US) Corps: 284, 287, 291, 292, 296, 304, 305, 310, 314, 318, 323, 329, 364, 368, 369, 370, 380, 382, 383, 385, 386, 393, 406, 408, 410, 411, 415, 418, 419, 421, 426, 454, 457, 496
    Divisions
        1 (US) Armored Division: 291, 311, 313, 326, 361, 364, 368, 369, 406
        1 (US) Infantry Division: 304, 308, 309, 311, 312, 313, 317, 324, 326, 328, 361, 363, 368, 423, 424, 443
        2 (US) Armored Division: 309, 311
        3 (US) Armored Division: 446
        3 (US) Infantry Division: 292, 312, 317, 328, 364, 368, 419, 423
        4 (US) Infantry Division: 383
        8 (US) Infantry Division: 368, 446
        101 Airborne Division: 324, 326
    Brigades
        3 (US) Infantry Brigade: 292
        3 (US) Mechanized Infantry Brigade: 421
    Nuclear Custodial Detachments: 163, 164, 173, 205, 269
    Units
        2 (US) Armored Cavalry Regiment: 292, 317, 318, 326
        3 (US) Armored Cavalry Regiment: 423
        3/11 Armored Cavalry Regiment: 418
        4/27 MLRS Battalion: 421
        11 Chemical Company: 370, 371
        16 Engineer Battalion: 362
        259 Field Artillery Missile Battalion: 102
        337 Army Security Agency Company: 313
        501 Attack Helicopter Battalion: 418
    Special Forces: 460, 461
United States European Command (USEUCOM): 55, 56, 278

INDEX

V

Vance, Cyrus: 464
Vance, Jack: 86, 215, 326, 328, 329
Vance Plan: 465, 472
Verstl, MGen: 423
VILS RIVER, Contingency Plan: 408, 410
Vimy Ridge: 89
von Rodde, Col: 310

W

Wallmeisters: 298, 411
Walsh, Geoffrey, BGen: 24, 25, 26, 28, 29, 32, 33, 37, 39, 45, 48, 52, 53, 62
Ward, Sir Alfred Dudley, Gen: 109
Ware, C.B., Brig: 148, 160, 162
Warsaw Pact: 70, 85, 107, 108, 127, 128, 149, 195, 198, 206, 226, 236, 243, 244, 286, 289, 299, **333**, 339, **350**, 358, 365, 366, 370, 373, **374**, **375**, 377, 378, 379, 380, 381, 382, 389, 390, 391, 418, 441, 445, 447, 448, 481, 483, 493
Waters, Barbara: 78
Waters, Stan: 78
Wendt, Jack: 30
Werl: 76, 78, 94, 95, 98, 133, 146, 148, 194, 225, 485
West Berlin: 15, 149, 158, 162, 196: See also Berlin
West Germany: See Federal Republic of Germany
Whelan, R.M.: 50
Wilhelmi, Hans Jurgen, BGen: 417
Willi Sanger Brigade: 378
WINTEX: 289, 310, 323
Women's Volunteer Service: 146

X

Y

Yom Kippur War: 286, 289, 322
Yugoslavia: **434**, **436**, 439, 440, 462, 464, 465, 467, 469, 470, 474, 475, 476, 480, 485, 486
Yugoslavian National Army (JNA): 462, 463, 465, 472, 473, 474, 475, 478

Z

Zypchen, Jerry: 131, 145

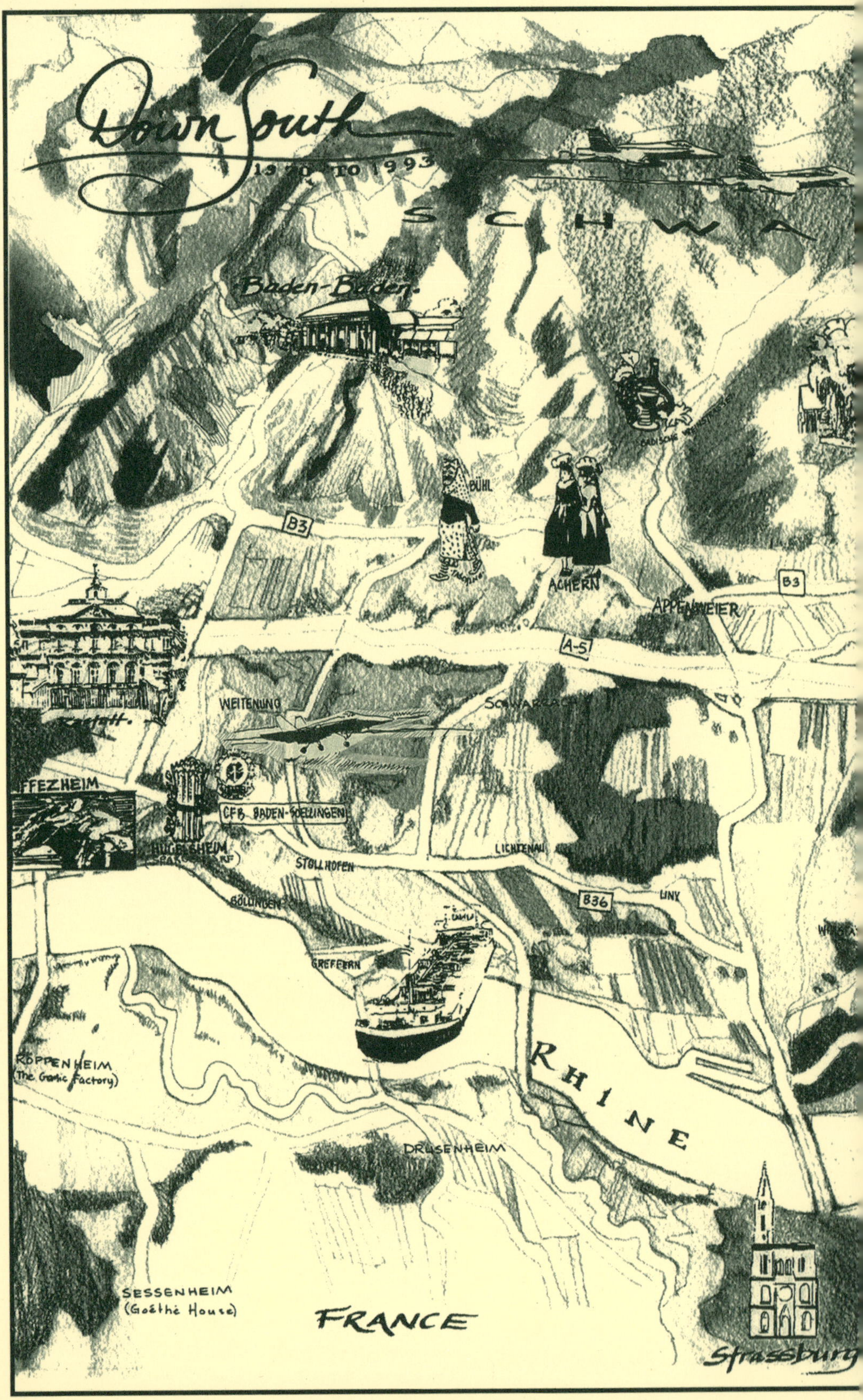
Down South
Baden-Baden
BÜHL
ACHERN
APPENWEIER
B3
A-5
WEITENUNG
SCHWARZACH
CFB BADEN-SOELLINGEN
STOLLHOFEN
LICHTENAU
B36
LINX
GREFFERN
RHINE
ROPPENHEIM
(The Garlic Factory)
DRUSENHEIM
SESSENHEIM
(Goethe House)
FRANCE
Strassburg